FOURTH EDITION

SOFTWARE ENGINEERING

INTERNATIONAL COMPUTER SCIENCE SERIES

Consulting editors   **A D McGettrick** University of Strathclyde
         J van Leeuwen University of Utrecht

SELECTED TITLES IN THE SERIES

FOURTH EDITION

SOFTWARE ENGINEERING

IAN SOMMERVILLE
Lancaster University

Addison-Wesley Publishing Company

Wokingham, England • Reading, Massachusetts • Menlo Park, California • New York
Don Mills, Ontario • Amsterdam • Bonn • Sydney • Singapore • Tokyo • Madrid
San Juan • Milan • Paris • Mexico City • Seoul • Taipei

Cover designed by Designers & Partners of Oxford.
Typeset by Columns Design and Production Services Ltd, Reading.
Printed in the United States of America.

First edition published 1982. Reprinted 1983 and 1984.
Second edition published 1984. Reprinted 1985, 1986, 1987 and 1988.
Third edition published 1989. Reprinted 1989, 1990 (twice) and 1991.
Fourth edition printed 1992. Reprinted 1992.

British Library Cataloguing in Publication Data
A catalogue record for this book is available from the British Library.

Library of Congress Cataloging in Publication Data
Sommerville, Ian.
    Software engineering / Ian Sommerville. — 4th ed.
      p. cm.
    Includes bibliographical references and index.
    ISBN 0–201–56529–3
    1. Software engineering. I. Title.
QA76.758.S657   1992
005.1—dc20   91–42102
                                   CIP

Preface

The explosion of computer applications made possible by low-cost computer hardware means that current demand for software is increasing exponentially. We cannot meet the increased demand simply by increasing the numbers of software engineers. We must apply effective software engineering techniques and technology to tackle this problem.

This book is an introduction to software engineering which takes a broad view of the subject. As in previous editions, my intention is to introduce the reader to a spectrum of state-of-the-art software engineering techniques which can be applied in practical software projects. The book has a pragmatic bias but introduces theory when it is appropriate to do so. In writing the book, I have tried to communicate several of my own views of the subject:

- Software engineering is an engineering discipline concerned with the practical problems of developing large software systems. It is not just programming nor is it computer science. Software engineers must be professionals who use theory from other disciplines and apply this cost-effectively to solve difficult problems.

- Formal methods of software engineering are important but address only a relatively small part of the software engineering problem. Software engineers should be aware of developments in this area but should not overestimate the effect this technology will have on the software development process.

- I do not believe that there is a single solution to the problem of software engineering so I don't preach the benefits of any particular specification or design method or CASE toolset. I see no merit in including a superficial description of a range of methods or tools in a book of this nature.

Software engineering is now taking its place alongside other engineering disciplines such as electrical and mechanical engineering. This book cannot cover everything in the discipline but it can provide a firm foundation for further and deeper study.

Changes from the third edition

The general structure of the third edition of *Software Engineering* has been maintained, with five major parts covering specification, design, implementation issues, validation and management. In this edition, there are several new chapters and some chapters have been radically rewritten to include new material and to improve the quality of explanation.

- The introduction concentrates on software process models.
- There are completely new chapters on real-time systems and software safety.
- Prototyping and software reliability, which were covered in the third edition, are discussed in more detail here as separate chapters.
- All of the chapters on requirements have been extensively revised.
- The chapters discussing tools and environments now take a higher level viewpoint instead of concentrating on specific classes of tool.
- The documentation chapter has been restructured and rewritten.
- Some material on programming and abstract data type implementation has been excluded.
- Chapter reference lists have been omitted and all references are presented in a collected list. Appendix B has been omitted and is now included in the *Instructor's Guide*. These changes have been made to reduce the number of pages (and hence the cost) in this edition.
- Most other chapters have been slightly revised and updated with new references and suggested reading.

As always, some material has had to be omitted through lack of space. There is less material on programming and topics such as legal issues and professional and social responsibilities are not covered. This is not just due to lack of space but also because the book has an international readership and laws differ dramatically from one country to another.

Readership

The book is aimed at students in undergraduate and graduate courses and at software engineers in commerce and industry. It may be used in general software engineering courses or in courses such as advanced programming, software specification, software design or management. Practitioners may find the book useful as general reading and as a means of updating their knowledge on particular topics such as formal specification, object-oriented design, reliability and software development environments. Wherever practicable, the examples in the text have been given a practical bias to reflect the type of applications which software engineers must develop.

I assume that readers have a basic familiarity with programming and modern computer systems. Some examples rely on knowledge of basic data structures such as stacks, lists and queues. The chapters on formal specification assume knowledge of very elementary set theory. No other mathematical background is required.

Ada is used as the example language but the examples are self-contained and an Appendix has been provided giving an overview of the language. Knowledge of Ada is not a prerequisite and the examples should be easily understandable by readers with a knowledge of Pascal, C, Modula-2 or other similar high-level programming language.

Using the book as a course text

I have tried to make this text usable in a variety of software engineering courses. It has been designed either as a stand-alone introductory text or as a core text for more advanced courses on topics such as software specification, reliability and project management. The book is deliberately broad rather than deep. When used in an advanced course, it may be supplemented by the suggested further reading and by some of the papers referenced in each chapter.

The structure of the book roughly follows the conventional life cycle model so includes sections on specifications, design, implementation and verification and validation. However, it would be unusual to find a single software engineering course which included all of the material in the book or which followed it in strictly sequential order. Rather, the instructor may select material in various combinations and, perhaps, supplement this with further reading to create a course of their own design. Some examples are shown in Figure 1 and further possibilities are discussed in the *Instructor's Guide*.

The ACM/IEEE Joint Curriculum Task Force has recently published a set of curricular recommendations for computing courses. Software

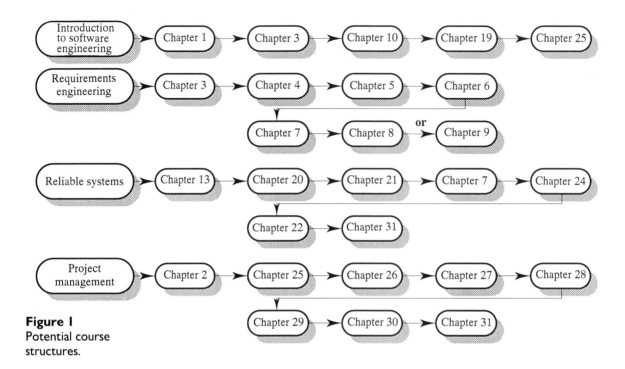

Figure I
Potential course
structures.

engineering occupies an important place in these recommendations. This book covers all suggested material in Units SE2 to SE5 plus material to supplement an introductory programming text which would normally cover Unit SE1. The book also covers all material in the suggested course entitled 'Advanced Software Engineering'.

Each chapter includes a key point summary, suggested further reading and a list of exercises. One exercise (a newspaper delivery system) is included in several chapters so can provide a basis for a continuing project. Chapters are extensively illustrated with diagrams and tables and, where appropriate, program examples are given.

Supplements

The following supplements are available to adoptors of this book, who should contact their nearest Addison-Wesley sales office.

> *Instructor's Guide*, including teaching advice for each chapter, selected solutions to exercises, and suggestions for coursework and project work.

Source Code for all programs is available on either PC or Macintosh disks.

Transparency Masters featuring key points, major figures and program listings are available either on paper or on Macintosh disks.

Acknowledgements

Many friends and colleagues have provided invaluable help and advice in the preparation of all of the editions of this text. Members of the Software Engineering Research Groups at the University of Lancaster and, previously, at the University of Strathclyde provided a stimulating environment and a source for many of the ideas discussed here.

Thanks are due to users who provided comments on earlier editions of the book and to the reviewers of earlier drafts of this edition, including Ronald S. Curtis of the State University of New York at Buffalo, Garry Donnan of the University of Ulster, Anthony Finkelstein of Imperial College, Greg Jones of Utah State University, David Lee of GEC–Marconi Software Systems, David C. Rine of George Mason University, Lee H. Tichenor of Western Illinois University and Laurie Werth of the University of Texas at Austin.

Particular mention must be made of Tom Rodden, Pete Sawyer and John Mariani, who commented on the material, provided examples and slides and generally assisted with the work of the Lancaster group. Particular thanks also go to Ray Welland of the University of Glasgow who again provided very helpful and constructive comments on the book.

Finally, my wife Anne and my daughters Alison and Jane again tolerated several months of fatherless evenings while this book was being written. Thank you, Anne, Ali and Jay, for your support.

Ian Sommerville,
Lancaster, July 1991

Contents

Introduction

■ OBJECTIVES

The objectives of this chapter are to define software engineering, to discuss the distinguishing characteristics of well-engineered software and to introduce the notion of the software process, that is, the activities involved in software production. Software process models are introduced and two of these models, the waterfall model and exploratory programming, are covered here. The final part of the chapter considers the software process from the point of view of project management. Deliverable-based and risk-based process models (Boehm's spiral model) and the relationships between these and the process models introduced in the previous section are discussed.

■ CONTENTS

As the cost of computer hardware decreases, computer systems are being incorporated in more and more products. Millions of personal computer systems are now in use. Some advanced computer applications, such as expert systems, have become economically viable as hardware to support their heavy computation demands can be built at moderate cost. The end result of this proliferation of computer systems into all aspects of life and business is that personal, corporate, national and international economies are increasingly dependent on computers and their software systems. As software costs are the major component of system costs, it is probably not an exaggeration to suggest that the future prosperity of an industrialized economy depends on effective software engineering.

The real costs of software development are immense. Precise, up-to-date figures are difficult to establish, but Boehm (1987) suggested that in 1985 worldwide software costs were in excess of $140 billion. Costs are growing at approximately 12% per year. If this trend continues worldwide annual software costs in 1995 will exceed $435 billion (Figure 1.1). Even small improvements in software productivity can therefore result in a significant reduction in absolute costs.

There are a number of possible definitions of software engineering. Their common factors are that software engineering is concerned with software systems built by teams rather than by individuals, uses engineering principles in the development of these systems and includes both technical and non-technical aspects. As well as having a thorough knowledge of computing techniques, software engineers must be able to communicate orally and in writing. They should be aware of the importance of project management and should appreciate the problems system users may have in interacting with software whose workings they may not understand.

Software does not simply mean the computer programs associated with some application or product. As well as programs, 'software' includes the documentation necessary to install, use, develop and maintain these programs. For large systems, the effort needed to write this documentation is often as great as that required for program development.

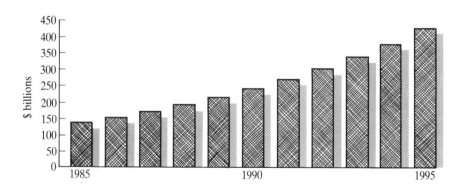

Figure 1.1
Predicted annual
software costs.

The term 'software engineering' was first introduced in the late 1960s at a conference held to discuss what was then called the 'software crisis'. This software crisis resulted directly from the introduction of third generation computer hardware. These machines were orders of magnitude more powerful than second generation machines and their power made hitherto unrealizable applications a feasible proposition. The implementation of these applications required large software systems to be built.

Early experience in building large software systems showed that existing methods of software development were not good enough. Techniques applicable to small systems could not be scaled up. Major projects were sometimes years late, cost much more than originally predicted, were unreliable, difficult to maintain and performed poorly. Software development was in crisis. Hardware costs were tumbling while software costs were rising rapidly. New techniques and methods were needed to control the complexity inherent in large software systems.

Now, more than 20 years later, the 'software crisis' has not been resolved. Although there have been real improvements in software engineering methods and techniques, in tools for system development and in the skills of development staff, the demand for software is increasing faster than improvements in software productivity. Many more people are now involved in software development. Some of the mistakes made by software engineers in the 1970s are still being repeated.

We need even better tools, techniques and methods and, perhaps most importantly, better education and training. Software engineering is still largely labour-intensive with relatively low capital expenditure per software engineer. As new software development environments are introduced, software engineering is becoming capital-intensive. Staff must be better trained and offer greater skills if the most effective use is to be made of this expensive environmental support.

1.1 Well-engineered software

Like all engineering, software engineering is not just about producing products but involves producing products in a cost-effective way. Given unlimited resources, the majority of software problems can probably be solved but the challenge for software engineers is to produce high-quality software with a finite amount of resources and to a predicted schedule.

A general assessment of system quality requires the identification of common attributes which we would expect to find in all well-engineered software. Assuming the software provides the required functionality, there are four key attributes which a well-engineered software system should possess:

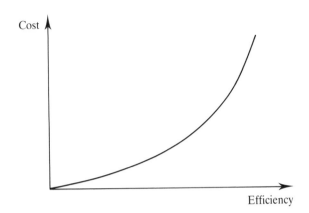

Figure 1.2
Costs versus efficiency.

(1)   The software should be maintainable. As long-lifetime software is subject to regular change, it should be written and documented so that changes can be made without undue costs.

(2)   The software should be reliable. This means that it should perform as expected by users and should not fail more often than is allowed for in its specification.

(3)   The software should be efficient. This does not necessarily mean that the last ounce of performance is squeezed out of the system hardware; maximizing efficiency may make the software more difficult to change. Efficiency means that a system should not make wasteful use of system resources such as memory and processor cycles.

(4)   The software should offer an appropriate user interface. Much software is not used to its full potential because its interface makes it difficult to use. The user interface design must be tailored to the capabilities and background of the system users.

Cost considerations must be taken into account when defining well-engineered software. Maintainability is a key attribute because most costs associated with software products are incurred after the software has been put into use.

Optimizing all of these attributes is difficult as some are exclusive (for example, providing a better user interface may reduce system efficiency) and all are subject to the law of diminishing returns. The relationship between cost and improvements in each of these attributes is not a linear one and small improvements in any of the attributes can be expensive. Figure 1.2 shows how costs may rise exponentially as efficiency improvements are required.

For some kinds of system, such as avionic systems, efficiency is a prime consideration. The software may have to run on a computer where weight and size considerations restrict the power of the hardware which can be used, and the software may have to run in a relatively small memory with little or no backing store. It may be necessary to optimize efficiency at the expense of the other system attributes.

When efficiency is critical, the trade-offs required should be made explicit. Individual software engineers should not have to make decisions on whether maintainability or efficiency should be optimized. Efficiency trade-offs must be clarified in the system requirements. The cost consequences of maximizing efficiency should be made clear to the software procurer.

In this book, methods, strategies, tools and policies which lead to reliable and maintainable software are given most emphasis. Some particularly relevant aspects of user interface design are covered in Chapter 14. Achieving efficiency usually depends on application characteristics so techniques for efficiency improvement are not discussed.

1.2 The software process

The identification of the 'software crisis' in the late 1960s and the notion that software development is an engineering discipline led to the view that the process of software development is like other engineering processes. Thus, a model of the software development process was derived from other engineering activities (Royce, 1970). This was enthusiastically accepted by software project management as it offered a means of making the development process more visible. Because of the cascade from one phase to another, this model is known as the 'waterfall' model (Figure 1.3).

This development model was put into use but it soon became clear that it was only appropriate for some classes of software system. Although

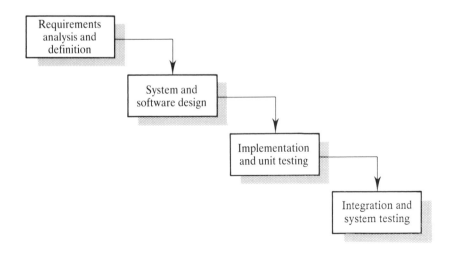

Figure 1.3
The waterfall model of software development.

management found the model useful for planning and reporting, the realities of software development did not accord with the activities identified in the model. The software process (the activities involved in software development and maintenance) is a complex and variable process which cannot readily be described using a simple model.

Detailed software process models are still the subject of research but it is now clear that a number of different general models or paradigms of software development can be identified. The original waterfall model is one of these general models rather than a detailed process model. Some of these development paradigms are:

(1) *The waterfall approach* This views the software process as being made up of a number of stages such as requirements specification, software design, implementation, testing and so on. After each stage is defined it is 'signed-off' and development proceeds to the following stage.

(2) *Exploratory programming* This approach involves developing a working system, as quickly as possible, and then modifying that system until it performs in an adequate way. This approach is usually used in artificial intelligence (AI) systems development where users cannot formulate a detailed requirements specification and where adequacy rather than correctness is the aim of the system designers.

(3) *Prototyping* This approach is similar to exploratory programming in that the first phase of development involves developing a program for user experiment. However, the objective of the development is to establish the system requirements. This is followed by a re-implementation of the software to produce a production-quality system.

(4) *Formal transformation* This approach involves developing a formal specification of the software system and transforming this specification, using correctness-preserving transformations, to a program.

(5) *System assembly from reusable components* This technique assumes that systems are mostly made up of components which already exist. The system development process becomes one of assembly rather than creation.

The first three of these approaches – the waterfall approach, exploratory programming and prototyping – are all currently used for practical systems development. Some systems have been built using correctness-preserving transformations but this is still a relatively untried approach. The reuse-oriented model is still not commercially viable because of the lack of reusable component libraries. In this chapter, the conventional 'waterfall' approach and exploratory programming are covered. The other process models are discussed in Chapter 6 (prototyping), Chapter 7 (formal transformation) and Chapter 16 (reuse).

1.2.1 The 'waterfall' model of the life cycle

There are numerous variations of this process model (sometimes called the software life cycle). All of these can be encompassed in the 'waterfall' model (Figure 1.3) whose stages are:

(1) *Requirements analysis and definition* The system's services, constraints and goals are established by consultation with system users. They are then defined in a manner which is understandable by both users and development staff.

(2) *System and software design* The systems design process partitions the requirements to either hardware or software systems and establishes an overall system architecture. Software design involves representing the software system functions so that they may be transformed into one or more executable programs.

(3) *Implementation and unit testing* During this stage, the software design is realized as a set of programs or program units. Unit testing involves verifying that each unit meets its specification.

(4) *Integration and system testing* The individual program units or programs are integrated and tested as a complete system to ensure that the software requirements have been met. After testing, the software system is delivered to the customer.

(5) *Operation and maintenance* Normally (although not necessarily) this is the longest life cycle phase. The system is installed and put into practical use. Maintenance involves correcting errors which were not discovered in earlier stages of the life cycle, improving the implementation of system units and enhancing the system's services as new requirements are discovered.

It is useful for management to consider the phases of the software life cycle to be distinct (see Section 1.3). In practice, however, the development stages overlap and feed information to each other. During design, problems with requirements are identified; during coding, design problems are found; and so on. The software process is not a simple linear model but involves a sequence of iterations of the development activities (Figure 1.4).

Unfortunately, a model which includes frequent iterations makes it difficult to identify definite management checkpoints to be used for planning and reporting. Therefore, after a small number of iterations, the tendency is to freeze parts of the development, such as the specification, and to continue with the later development stages. Problems are either left for later resolution, ignored or programmed around. This premature freezing of requirements may mean that the system will not do what the user wants. It may also lead to badly structured systems as design problems are circumvented by implementation tricks.

The testing phase of the software process where the complete

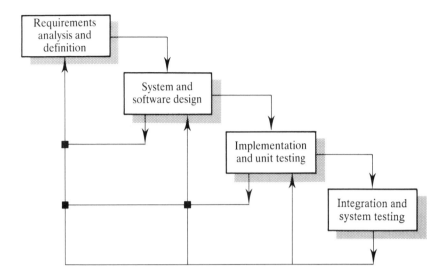

Figure 1.4
Iteration in the
waterfall model.

software system is integrated and exercised, represents the ultimate validation stage in the development cycle. At this stage, the system developer must convince the system buyer that the system meets its requirements. However, verification and validation (V & V) should be part of earlier life cycle stages. During V & V activities, information is fed back to earlier life cycle phases.

Although verification and validation may appear to be synonymous, perhaps the most succinct expression of the difference between them is given by Boehm (1981):

> Verification: 'Are we building the product right?'
> Validation: 'Are we building the right product?'

Verification checks if the product which is under construction meets the requirements definition. Validation checks if the product's functions are what the customer really wants.

During the final life cycle phase (operation and maintenance), information is fed back to previous development phases (Figure 1.5). This final phase is an operational phase where the software is used. Errors and omissions in the original software requirements are discovered, program and design errors come to light and the need for new functionality is identified. Modifications become necessary for the software to remain useful. Making these changes is usually called 'software maintenance'.

Maintenance may involve changes in requirements, design and implementation, and it may highlight the need for further system testing. The development process (or part of it) is repeated during the maintenance phase as software modifications are made.

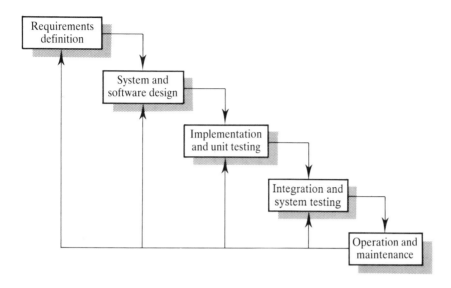

Figure 1.5
The software life cycle.

An aim of software engineering is to reduce overall software costs so the cost distribution across the software process must be known. Unfortunately, for anything apart from the conventional 'waterfall' model, development costs are not broken down. Even for systems developed using a conventional approach, costs vary dramatically depending on the application, the development organization and the development methods. Furthermore, cost information is sometimes commercially sensitive. If available, only a few organizations are willing to publish software costs. It is thus difficult to get an overall picture of development costs throughout the software industry.

Some figures given by Boehm (1975) for different types of software system give an approximate indication of cost distribution during software development (Figure 1.6).

System type	Phase costs %		
	Requirements/design	Implementation	Testing
Command and control systems	46	20	34
Spaceborne systems	34	20	46
Operating systems	33	17	50
Scientific systems	44	26	30
Business systems	44	28	28

Figure 1.6
Life cycle cost distribution.

Boehm (1981) has also suggested somewhat different figures where the implementation costs are higher and design costs are lower. These, however, appear to be based on a life cycle model whose emphasis is different from that of the conventional model. In this alternative model, detailed design is considered to be part of the implementation phase whereas in the model costings in Figure 1.6 detailed design is part of the software design process.

Figure 1.6 shows that software development costs are greatest at the beginning and at the end of the development cycle. Thus a reduction in overall software development costs is best accomplished by more effective requirements assessment, design and life cycle verification and validation.

The need to improve requirements specification and design and to make verification and validation a whole life cycle activity has promoted other approaches to software development where emphasis is placed on requirements (prototyping model) and validation (formal transformation model). The class of systems which are usually developed using exploratory programming are not covered by the above figures and detailed development costs for these systems are unobtainable at present.

Figure 1.6 does not show the costs of software maintenance. Again, there is immense variation from system to system. For most large, long-lifetime software systems maintenance costs normally exceed development costs by factors ranging from 2 to 4. High maintenance costs appear to be independent of the approach used for software development. Boehm (1975) quotes a pathological case where the development cost of an avionics system was $30 per instruction but the maintenance cost was $4000 per instruction. This illustrates how efficiency requirements can lead to very high total life cycle costs.

The waterfall model of the life cycle has been rightly criticized (McCracken and Jackson, 1982; Gladden, 1982) as being nothing like actual software process activities. Part of the problem with the model is that it does not recognize the role of iteration in the software process. Another failing is that it implies that specifications should be frozen at an early stage in the development process. This leads to software systems whose functionality does not match that which is really required by users. Both the exploratory programming model and the prototyping process model try to resolve these difficulties.

1.2.2   Exploratory programming

Exploratory programming is based on the idea of developing an initial implementation, exposing this to user comment and refining this through many stages until an adequate system has been developed (Figure 1.7).

Exploratory programming is a good way to develop systems where it is difficult (or impossible) to establish a detailed system specification. Some might argue that all systems fall into this class but exploratory programming

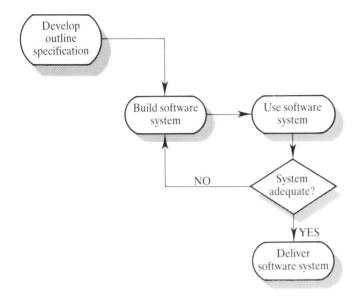

Figure 1.7
Exploratory
programming.

has actually been mostly used for the development of AI systems which attempt to emulate some human capabilities. As we don't understand how humans carry out tasks, setting out a detailed specification for software to imitate humans is impossible.

The key to success in this approach is to use techniques which allow for rapid system iterations. Suggested changes may be incorporated and demonstrated as quickly as possible. This requires a very high level programming language such as LISP or Prolog for software development, and the use of powerful, dedicated hardware systems and integrated software tools to support the system developer.

An important difference between exploratory programming and a specification-based approach to development is in verification and validation. Verification is only meaningful when a program is compared to its specification. If there is no specification, verification is impossible. The notion of a 'correct' program must be discarded. The validation process should demonstrate the adequacy of the program rather than its conformance to a specification.

Adequacy, of course, is not readily measurable and only subjective judgements of a program's adequacy can be made. This does not invalidate its usefulness; human performance cannot be guaranteed to be correct but we are satisfied if performance is adequate for the task in hand.

Exploratory programming has mostly been used to develop AI systems and it has been little used in the development of large, long-lifetime systems. There are three main reasons for this:

(1)   Existing software management structures are set up to deal with a software process model which results in regular deliverables which are used to measure progress. In exploratory programming, it is not cost-effective to produce a great deal of system documentation as the system is changed so regularly.

(2)   Exploratory programming tends to result in systems whose structure is not well-defined. Continual change tends to corrupt the software structure. Maintenance is therefore likely to be difficult and costly, particularly when, as is usual with large systems, the system maintainers are not the original developers.

(3)   It is not clear how the range of skills normally available in software engineering teams can be used effectively for this mode of development. Most available systems developed in this way have been implemented by small teams of highly skilled and motivated individuals.

These difficulties do not mean that exploratory programming should be rejected. There are some classes of system which cannot be developed by setting out specifications then constructing a system according to these specifications, and it is the only reasonable development technique in such cases. One possible approach might be to develop a prototype using exploratory programming and use this as a basis for a system rewritten in a more structured way. However, system maintenance may also need an exploratory approach and it is not clear how this can be supported.

1.3   Management process models

Section 1.2 discussed some generic models of the software process and hinted that management difficulties were the reasons why some of these models are not widely used. Project management is one thing which distinguishes professional software engineering and no process model can be acceptable if it results in an unmanageable process.

Because of the intangible nature of software systems (unlike other engineered systems, management cannot simply look at the work itself to assess progress), effective management relies on adopting a process model which makes the process visible by means of documents, reports and reviews. This has resulted in the general adoption of a 'deliverable-oriented' model where the software process is split into a number of stages and each stage is deemed to be complete when some deliverable document has been produced, reviewed and accepted. The assumption is that the output from one stage acts as the defining input for the following stage of the process.

The waterfall process model is by far the most widely adopted

Activity	Output documents
Requirements analysis	Feasibility study Outline requirements
Requirements definition	Requirements specification
System specification	Functional specification Acceptance test specification Draft user manual
Architectural design	Design architecture specification System test specification
Interface design	Interface specification Integration test specification
Detailed design	Design specification Unit test specification
Coding	Program code
Unit testing	Unit test result report
Module testing	Module test result report
Integration testing	Integration test report Final user manual
System testing	System test report
Acceptance testing	Final system

Figure 1.8
Documents from the
waterfall model.

'deliverable' model and Figure 1.8 shows one possible way of splitting it into stages and the deliverables which should be produced at each stage.

The other process models discussed in Section 1.2 have not been widely used because they are not well-adapted to a document-based process model. Figure 1.9 summarizes their suitability and shows that only the formal transformation model is really suited to this model. However, it has the problem that managers are often non-technical and may not be able to understand the mathematical notations which are essential in this process. Although documents can be produced, process visibility is not improved.

The problems with a document-oriented model are:

(1) Management needs deliverable documents produced at regular intervals to assess project progress. The timing of management requirements may not necessarily correspond with the time required to complete an activity so artificial documents may be produced.

(2) The need to approve documents tends to constrain process iteration as the costs of going back and adapting a completed deliverable are high. If problems are discovered during the process, inelegant

Activity	Output documents
Waterfall model	Well-suited. Designed around documents.
Prototyping	Uneconomic to generate documents during initial phase of fast iteration. Later phases OK if waterfall model followed.
Exploratory programming	Not suitable. Iterations are so rapid that generating documents is very expensive.
Formal transformations	Well-suited. Formal documents are essential for this approach.
Reuse-oriented model	Not suitable. Documents describing the system are likely to constrain reuse.

Figure 1.9
Process model
suitability.

solutions are sometimes adopted to avoid the costs of iteration and the need to change 'final' project documents.

(3)   The notion that the document from one stage should act as the defining input to the next stage is flawed. It suggests that the development process is linear. At any stage of the process, software engineers take into account both earlier stages and future stages. There is no point, for example, in creating a design which will be difficult to implement even if it meets the requirements. A document-based process tends to hide information from developers as all they may have to work on is the documents and this may result in increased software costs.

(4)   The time required to review and approve a document is significant and there is rarely a smooth transition from one phase of the process to the next. In reality, formal procedures are sometimes ignored and a phase started before the previous phase document has been completed.

(5)   Certain problems simply cannot be tackled by creating a detailed specification, then a design, then an implementation, and so on. Blind application of the document-oriented model has meant that very high project costs have been incurred in such projects.

A document-oriented waterfall process model has been adopted as a general standard by many government agencies and large software procurers. Thus,

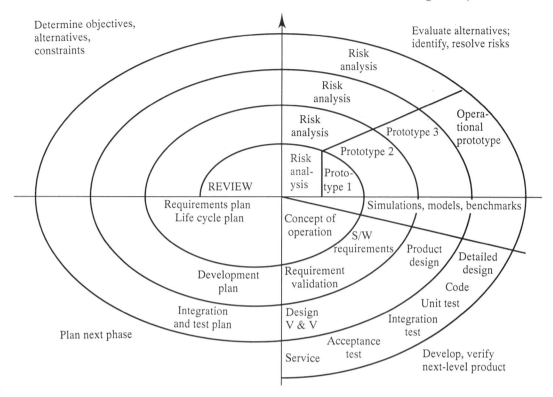

Determine objectives,
alternatives,
constraints

Evaluate alternatives;
identify, resolve risks

Risk
analysis

Risk
analysis

Risk
analysis

Opera-
tional
prototype

Prototype 3

Prototype 2

Risk
anal-
ysis

Proto-
type 1

REVIEW

Requirements plan
Life cycle plan

Concept of
operation

Simulations, models, benchmarks

S/W
requirements

Product
design

Detailed
design

Development
plan

Requirement
validation

Code

Unit test

Integration
and test plan

Design
V & V

Integration
test

Plan next phase

Service

Acceptance
test

Develop, verify
next-level product

Figure 1.10
Boehm's spiral model
(© 1988 IEEE).

it cannot simply be wished away in spite of its difficulties. We need an improved process model for management which can subsume all of the generic models discussed in the previous section and is capable of satisfying the requirements of software procurers. Currently, the best alternative appears to be the 'risk-based' or spiral model described by Boehm (1988).

An outline of the spiral model is shown in Figure 1.10. Its key characteristic is an assessment of management risk items at regular stages in the project and the initiation of actions to counteract these risks. Before each cycle, a risk analysis is initiated and at the end of each cycle, a review procedure assesses whether to move on to the next cycle of the spiral.

Risk is a concept which is difficult to define precisely. A good way to think of a risk in this model is simply something which can go wrong. For example, if the intention is to use a new programming language, a risk is that no suitable compiler is available. Risks are a consequence of inadequate information and are resolved by initiating some actions to discover information which reduces uncertainty. In the above example, the risk would be resolved by a market survey to find out which compilers were available. If no suitable system was discovered, the decision to use a new language would have to be changed.

Objectives	Significantly improve software quality
Constraints	Within a three-year timescale Without large-scale capital investment Without radical change to company standards
Alternatives	Reuse existing certified software Introduce formal specification and verification Invest in testing and validation tools
Risks	No cost effective quality improvement possible Quality improvements may increase costs excessively New methods might cause existing staff to leave
Risk resolution	Literature survey Pilot project Survey of potential reusable components Assessment of available tool support Staff training and motivation seminars
Results	Experience of formal methods is limited. Hard to quantify improvements Limited tool support available for company standard development system Reusable components available but little reuse tool support
Plans	Explore reuse option in more detail Develop prototype reuse support tools Explore component certification scheme
Committment	Fund further 12 month development

Figure 1.11
Quality spiral.

A cycle of the spiral begins by elaborating objectives such as performance, functionality, and so on. Alternative ways of achieving these objectives and the constraints imposed on each of these alternatives are then enumerated. Each alternative is then assessed against each objective. This usually results in the identification of sources of project risk. The next step is to evaluate these risks by activities such as more detailed analysis, prototyping, simulation, and so on.

After risk evaluation, a development model for the system is then chosen. For example, if user interface risks are dominant, an appropriate development model might be evolutionary prototyping; if safety risks are the main consideration, development based on formal transformations may be the most appropriate, and so on. The waterfall model may be the most appropriate development model if the main identified risk is sub-system integration.

There is no need to adopt a single model in each cycle of the spiral or, indeed, for the whole of one software system. The spiral model encompasses

Objectives	Procure software component catalogue
Constraints	Within a year Must support existing component types Total cost less that $100,000
Alternatives	Buy existing information retrieval software Buy a database and develop catalogue using the query language Develop a special purpose catalogue
Risks	May be impossible to procure within constraints Catalogue functionality may be inappropriate
Risk resolution	Develop prototype catalogue to clarify requirements Commission consultants report on existing information retrieval systems Relax time constraints
Results	Information retrieval systems are inflexible Identified requirements cannot be met Prototype developed using DBMS may be enhanced to complete system Special-purpose catalogue development is not cost effective
Plans	Develop catalogue using existing DBMS by enhancing prototype and user interface
Committment	Fund further 12 month development

Figure 1.12
Catalogue spiral.

other process models. Prototyping may be used in one spiral to resolve requirements risk and this may be followed by a conventional waterfall development. Formal transformation may be used for parts of the system with high security requirements and a reuse-oriented approach used for implementing the system user interface.

To use the spiral model, Boehm suggests a standard form which is filled in for each round of the spiral. This may be completed at an abstract level or may be a fairly detailed assessment of a software product development.

To illustrate this approach, consider an organization which has an overall objective of significantly improving the quality of the software it produces. Figure 1.11 shows the standard form setting out the objectives, risks and plans.

Obviously the form is not filled in all at once, but progressively as a spiral proceeds. Clearly Figure 1.11 is at an abstract level but its virtue is that it makes explicit choices and risks and forces managers to consider all possibilities. Exactly the same format can be used at a more detailed level when a particular software system (say a reusable components catalogue) is to be developed. Figure 1.12 shows the form for this system.

The risk assessment for the catalogue can then be developed in more detail, examining, say, the user interface requirements for the catalogue. As Figure 1.12 shows, this risk-driven approach to the software process can accommodate development models such as evolutionary prototyping. By identifying and assessing the risks, the most appropriate development model can be used; indeed different models may be adopted for different parts of the same software system.

Risk assessment and management is a key task of software project management and we return to this subject in Chapter 25.

■ KEY POINTS

- ■ Software engineering involves technical and non-technical issues. As well as knowledge of specification, design and implementation techniques, software engineers must know something about human factors and software management.

- ■ Well-engineered software is software which provides the services required by its users. It should be maintainable, reliable and efficient, and should provide an appropriate user interface.

- ■ The waterfall model of software development suffers from inadequacies but will continue to be widely used because it simplifies management of the software process.

- ■ Exploratory programming is not suited to the development of most large, long-lifetime software systems because it is likely to result in systems which are expensive to maintain.

- ■ Document-driven management process models suffer from the disadvantage that they inhibit process iteration because documents are 'frozen' and then become very expensive to change.

- ■ A risk-oriented spiral model of process management forces the consideration of all alternatives and risks and can accommodate all other models of development.

FURTHER READING

Software Engineering Economics. In spite of the title, this book is a wide-ranging look at many aspects of software engineering by one of the best respected authorities in this field. Early chapters discuss the software life cycle and life cycle costs. (B.W.Boehm, 1981, Prentice-Hall.)

Managing the Software Process. This is a general text on software management which is oriented around the concept of a software process. It is good general background for this chapter. (W. S. Humphrey, 1989, Addison-Wesley.)

New Paradigms for Software Development. This is set of papers on new process models and their application in software development. It is particularly good as background reading as it contains some classic papers on some of these process models. (W.W. Agresti, 1986, IEEE Press.)

'A spiral model of software development and enhancement'. Although this was not the first paper on the spiral model, it is an excellent introduction to this approach and discusses practical experience in using the model to develop a software engineering environment. (B.W. Boehm, *IEEE Computer*, **21** (5), May 1988.)

'No silver bullet: Essence and accidents of software engineering'. This paper does not directly discuss the material in this chapter but as an introductory paper to the problems of software engineering it is very good indeed. (F.P. Brooks, *IEEE Computer*, **20** (4), April 1987.)

EXERCISES

1.1 In this chapter, well-engineered software was defined as possessing four attributes. List these attributes and suggest four further attributes which such software might possess. Under what circumstances might these be more important than those suggested here?

1.2 Suggest reasons why the waterfall model of the software process is not a true reflection of the activities which are involved in software development.

1.3 What is the distinction between verification and validation? Illustrate your answer with examples of each of these activities.

1.4 Explain why programs which are developed using an exploratory programming approach are likely to be difficult to maintain. If you are familiar with LISP, Prolog or some other exploratory programming language, examine such programs and estimate how hard these would be to change.

1.5 Explain how both the waterfall model of the software process and the prototyping model can be accommodated in the spiral process model.

1.6 A university intends to procure an integrated student management system holding all details of registered students including personal information, courses taken and examination marks achieved. The alternative approaches to be adopted are:

(a) Buy a database management system and develop an in-house system based on this database.

(b) Buy a comparable system from another university and modify it to local requirements.

(c) Join a consortium of other universities, establish a common set of requirements and contract a software house to develop a single system for all of the universities in the consortium.

Identify two possible risks in each of these strategies and suggest techniques for risk resolution which would help in deciding which approach to adopt.

Human Factors in Software Engineering

2

■ OBJECTIVES

Knowledge of human factors can provide insights into a number of areas of software engineering. The objectives of this chapter are to describe how human factors influence the software engineering process. Topics discussed include the way in which we process information, individual and group characteristics and ergonomics. The first two sections focus on individual characteristics such as memory organization and our knowledge processing model. The practical impact of these on software engineering is described. Software development is usually a team operation and the following section looks at how group organization and structure affect the development process. Finally, ergonomics in workplace design and the need for effective equipment support for software engineering is discussed.

■ CONTENTS

In an engineering text, it is unusual to find a chapter on human factors. Its inclusion reflects my conviction that an understanding of the people involved in software engineering as system users, specifiers, designers, programmers and managers helps with the technical processes of systems development. This has been reinforced by the fact that much greater attention is now paid to human factors aspects of computer systems, particularly by those involved in user interface design.

Seminal works were produced some years ago (Weinberg, 1971; Shneiderman, 1980), and, since the mid-1980s, there has been an increasing amount of research on human factors and the software process (Curtis *et al.*, 1988; Rosson *et al.*, 1988). Some of this has confirmed the relevance of other psychological research to software engineering but there is still uncertainty in this area. We must be wary of drawing conclusions about software engineering from data collected in unrelated studies.

A study of human factors is important for several reasons:

(1)   To be effective, software managers must understand their staff as individuals and understand how these individuals interact. A better understanding of the relevant psychology helps managers to understand human limits and to tailor software projects so that development staff are not set unrealizable objectives.

(2)   Computer systems are used by people. If the limitations and abilities of these people are not taken into account when designing the system, they will not use it in the best possible way.

(3)   Programmer productivity is a critical cost factor in software engineering. An understanding of human factors can help identify possible ways of increasing productivity.

Human factors research is sometimes criticized by pragmatic technicians as 'common sense' and some of the conclusions which are drawn in psychological studies simply seem to confirm everyday experience. However, common sense is actually the result of much experience and acquired wisdom. It is often worth confirming this experience experimentally and establishing some model to explain it.

2.1 Human diversity

Software development is an individual, creative task. It is comparable with composing music, designing buildings and writing books. Although a software engineer may work as part of a team, the team is only necessary because the required software system is so large that it cannot be produced by one person in a reasonable amount of time. Within the team, the work is partitioned and individuals work on their own, creating part of the system.

Psychologists have identified a number of so-called 'personality traits' such as assertive/humble, trusting/suspicious, and so on, and have developed tests which allow personality classification according to these traits. An individual personality is a dynamic combination of all these traits. Personalities can change depending on individual circumstances, environments, and the personalities of co-workers.

Using a personality test devised for job aptitude, Perry and Cannon (1966) produced a programmer profile by testing existing programmers. If new recruits have personality profiles matching those of experienced programmers, this may imply that they would make suitable programmers. However, their 'ideal' personality profile was obtained by testing programmers already in the profession without reference to their ability, so the sample chosen may not be representative of competent programmers.

Selecting software engineers on the basis of personality is unlikely to be successful for the following reasons:

(1) Personality is dynamic not static. Personalities change in the course of a programming career.

(2) Different personalities may be suited to different aspects of programming such as systems design, testing, and so on. Should personality testing attempt to identify a 'programming personality' or should it be more precise and identify program design personalities, program testing personalities, and so on?

(3) Intelligent programmers filling in personality tests might cheat. Instead of presenting their true personality, they might present the personality which they think the tester wants. This is a natural human reaction to any kind of assessment and just like people presenting a favourable picture of themselves at a job interview. Indeed, the ability to recognize and deliver what is required by a user is an attribute which is desirable in potential software engineers!

There is no real evidence to suggest that programming ability is related to any particular personality trait. Weinberg confirms that it is probably impossible to identify programming personalities but suggests that the absence of certain characteristics may mean that some people are not well suited to software engineering.

An example of such a trait is the ability to withstand a certain amount of stress. The nature of software projects (indeed, any engineering projects) is such that the schedule for the project is imposed on the programmer. Work must be completed by a particular date. As that date approaches, the stress imposed on the software engineer becomes greater. As stress builds up, performance starts to suffer which causes further delays resulting in more stress and the cycle continues to some sort of unsatisfactory conclusion.

Software engineers may also need adaptive ability. The rate of change of both hardware and software technology is extremely rapid and engineers must be able to adapt to these changes. Without adaptive ability, individuals tend to continue with obsolete practices to the detriment of overall performance. This problem is particularly acute if it is combined with a promotion strategy which results in these individuals becoming managers. They stifle innovation and cause frustration among other technical staff. This results in high staff turnover, low morale and general dissatisfaction.

2.2   Knowledge processing

The activity of software development is a cognitive skill and, like all such skills, is subject to the limitations of the human brain. There is great diversity in individual abilities reflecting differences in intelligence, education and experience but all of us seem to be subject to some basic constraints on our thinking. These result from the way in which information is stored and modelled in our brains It is therefore worth looking at our knowledge processing model to identify the effects this might have on software development.

2.2.1   Memory organization

Software systems are abstract entities and engineers must remember their characteristics during the development process. Developers must understand and remember the relationship between a source code listing and the dynamic behaviour of the program and apply this stored knowledge in further program development.

The retention of information in the memory depends on the memory structure. This seems to be hierarchical with three distinct, connected areas (Figure 2.1):

- *A limited capacity, fast-access, short-term memory*   Input from the senses is received here for initial processing. This memory is comparable with registers in a computer; it is used for information processing and not for information storage.

- *A larger capacity, working memory area*   This memory area has a longer access time than short-term memory. It is used for information processing but can retain information for longer periods than short-term memory. It is not used for long-term information retention. By analogy with the computer, this is like the volatile store where information is maintained for the duration of a computation.

- *Long-term memory*   This has a large capacity, relatively slow access

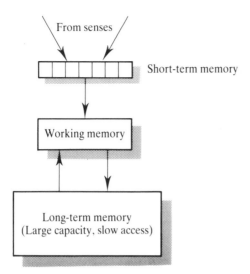

Figure 2.1
Memory organization.

time and unreliable retrieval mechanisms (we forget things!). Long-term memory is used for the 'permanent' storage of information. To continue the analogy, long-term memory is like disk memory on a computer.

Problem information is received in short-term memory and is integrated with existing, relevant information from long-term memory in working memory. The result of this integration forms the basis for problem solutions which may be stored in long-term memory for future use. Of course, the solution may be incorrect which involves future revision of the long-term memory. However, old, incorrect information is not completely discarded but is retained to help avoid repeating the same mistakes.

The limited size of short-term memory constrains our cognitive processes. In a classic experiment, Miller (1957) found that the short-term memory can store about seven quanta of information. A quantum of information is not a fixed number of bits. It may be a telephone number, the function of a procedure or a street name. Miller also describes the process of 'chunking' where information quanta are collected together into chunks.

If a problem involves the input of more information than the short-term memory can handle, there has to be information processing and transfer during the input process. This can result in information being lost and errors arising because this information processing cannot keep up with the memory input.

This is a particular problem when new information is being processed. For example, if we are presented with pictures of common animals, these can be processed quickly because they have been known since childhood.

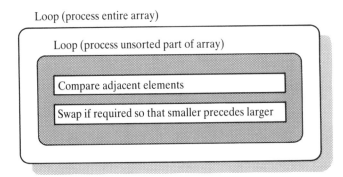

Figure 2.2
Bubblesort chunking.

On the other hand, if we are presented with descriptions of new software components, it takes much longer to work out what these mean.

Shneiderman (1980) conjectures that the information chunking process is used in understanding programs. Program readers abstract the information in the program into chunks which are built into an internal semantic structure representing the program. Programs are not understood on a statement by statement basis unless a statement represents a logical chunk. Figure 2.2 shows how a simple bubblesort program might be 'chunked' by a reader.

Once the internal semantic structure representing the program has been established, this knowledge is transferred to long-term memory and is not usually forgotten. It can be reproduced in different notations without much difficulty.

For example, consider the binary search algorithm where an ordered collection is searched for a particular item. This involves examining the mid-point of the collection and using knowledge of the ordering relationship to check if the key item is in the upper or the lower part of the collection. A programmer who understands this algorithm can produce a version in Pascal, Ada or other programming language. It is obvious that this information is not retained as a program description because, if nothing else, an English language description of the algorithmic model can be produced.

2.2.2 Knowledge modelling

Information enters short-term memory and is processed before being stored in long-term memory. We don't store raw information but store information abstractions which we call 'knowledge'. Although the distinction between information and knowledge is not a rigid one, a possible view is that neural information processing involves the integration of new and

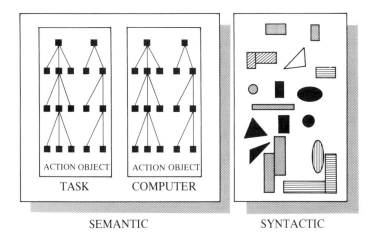

Figure 2.3
Syntactic and semantic knowledge.

existing information to create knowledge.

The knowledge acquired during software development and stored in long-term memory falls into two classes:

(1) *Semantic knowledge* This is the knowledge of concepts such as the operation of an assignment statement, the notion of a linked list and how a hash search technique operates. This knowledge is acquired through experience and learning and is retained in a representation independent fashion.

(2) *Syntactic knowledge* This is detailed representation knowledge such as how to write a procedure declaration in Pascal, what standard functions are available in a programming language, whether an assignment is written using an '=' or a ':=' sign, etc. This knowledge seems to be retained in a form which is much closer to raw, detailed information.

This knowledge organization is illustrated in Figure 2.3, taken from Shneiderman's book (1986) on user interface design.

Semantic knowledge is acquired by experience and through active learning where new information is consciously integrated with existing semantic structures. Syntactic knowledge, on the other hand, seems to be acquired by memorization. New syntactic knowledge is not immediately integrated with existing knowledge but may interfere with it. It can only be arbitrarily added to that knowledge.

The different acquisition modes for syntactic and semantic knowledge explain the typical situation which arises when experienced programmers learn a new programming language. Normally, they have no difficulty with the language concepts such as assignments, loops, conditional statements and so on. The language syntax, however, tends to get mixed-up with the syntax of familiar languages. For example, a Fortran programmer learning Pascal might write the assignment operator as '=' rather than ':=', a Pascal programmer might write 'type x =. . .' rather than 'type x is . . .' when learning Ada, and so on.

When learning to program, beginners must master the semantic concepts implied in the computational model as well as arbitrary syntax. It is difficult for them to distinguish between syntactic and semantic problems and to perform knowledge integration to create the appropriate semantic concepts.

Instructors have successfully understood and processed the semantic information so they may find it hard to explain the semantic concepts in terms novice programmers can understand. The model explains why, for many people, learning to program is a skill which seems to arrive all at once after a period of difficulties. Programming is understood when the semantic and syntactic concepts have been separated and the semantic concepts understood.

Semantic knowledge appears to be stored as knowledge of computing concepts, such as the notion of a writable store, and knowledge of task concepts, such as binary search or radar tracking (Soloway *et al.*, 1982; Card *et al.*, 1983).

Problem solving involves integration of these task and computer concepts. Organizational factors such as the need to complete a solution within budget are also part of the problem solving process. Thus, a user may be expert in the task concepts, a software designer an expert in the computer concepts, and a manager an expert in the organization factors. Software engineering involves integrating all of this expertise.

2.2.3 Practical implications

Pragmatic software engineers are primarily interested in how cognitive processes affect software management, design and development. Devising and writing a program is a problem solving process. The software engineer must understand the problem, work out a solution strategy then translate it into a program. The first stage involves the problem statement entering working memory from short-term memory. It is integrated with existing knowledge from long-term memory and analysed to work out an overall solution. Finally, the general solution is refined into an executable program (Figure 2.4).

The development of the solution (the program) involves building an internal semantic model of the problem and a corresponding model of the solution. When this model has been built, it may be represented in any appropriate syntactic notation. An experienced programmer who under-stands a number of programming languages will have roughly the same degree of difficulty in writing a program, irrespective of the language used.

Programming ability seems to be an ability to take existing computer

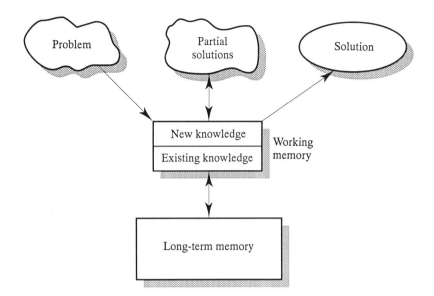

Figure 2.4
Problem solving.

and task knowledge in combination with new task information and integrate this to create new knowledge. The problem-solving process is language-independent and virtuosity with particular languages is no guarantee of programming skills. Language skills are necessary and take time to develop (particularly for complex languages like Ada) but managers should be wary of hiring staff simply on the basis of previous language experience. Studies suggest (Curtis *et al.*, 1988) that application experience is particularly important as understanding task concepts is a time-consuming aspect of software projects.

The translation from solution model to program is more likely to be error-free if the syntactic facilities of the notation match the lowest level semantic structures used. Although these may vary from individual to individual, programming teaching now emphasizes assignments, conditional statements, while loops, type declarations and so on as the lowest level concepts. A programming language should represent these abstractions directly.

Programs written in Ada should therefore contain fewer errors than those written in Fortran or assembly code because low-level semantic concepts can be encoded directly as language statements. Consequently, if the final representation is to be in Ada, the internal semantics need not be developed to such a detailed level of detail as is required for Fortran programs.

Recall that short-term memory capacity is limited, information is encoded in chunks and that semantic and syntactic knowledge is stored. If a program can be read from top to bottom, the abstractions involved in forming chunks can be made sequentially, without reference to other parts of the program. The short-term memory can be devoted to a single section of code. It is not necessary to maintain information about several sections connected by arbitrary goto statements.

For the same reasons, if programmers try to program without the use of goto statements, they are less likely to make programming errors. Short-term memory can be devoted to information relevant to the program section being coded. Information from working memory about other parts of the program which interfere with that section need not be retrieved.

The idea of structured programming, which is programming using only conditionals and while-loops, received a great deal of publicity in the 1970s. This is the best strategy for program control structure design as it does not overload short-term memory. Programs are easier to understand and more likely to be error-free.

Because programming ability is language-independent, it is easy for programmers who know one programming language to learn a new language of the same type. All that need be learnt is a new syntax as the concepts are already understood. However, this is only true if the semantic concepts underlying both of these languages are the same. For example, Fortran programmers have few real difficulties learning Pascal as both languages reflect the underlying Von Neumann machine architecture. However, the same programmers might have difficulty learning Prolog as its underlying model is quite different.

Rather than trying to identify familiar semantic concepts such as assignment statements, loops and conditionals (which don't exist in Prolog), novices are not constrained by fixed ideas when presented with a new programming language. They may find learning the language easier than experienced programmers because they do not try to fit language concepts into an existing, understood model.

When organizing programmer education, it should be borne in mind that experienced programmers and inexperienced programmers have different requirements. Experienced programmers need to know the syntax of a language whereas inexperienced programmers need to be taught concepts such as how an assignment statement works, the notion of a procedure and so on. Language-directed editing systems are useful for novices as they handle syntactic detail, leaving the beginner to concentrate on the semantic concepts. Experienced programmers may have evolved a programming style where syntactic program correctness is not always maintained and may thus find language-directed editors obtrusive.

A language like Ada presents a particular problem. It is based on a Von Neumann model but contains constructs such as packages, tasks and exceptions which may not be familiar to the Fortran or Pascal programmer. Thus, they may learn to write simple Ada programs fairly quickly but will need to spend considerably more time in learning the new features of the language.

2.3   Group working

The popular image of programmers is that they work as individuals peering into a terminal or poring over reams of paper covered with arcane symbols. They might be technology-mad teenagers who are somehow different from their peers and who are most interested in hacking into other computers. Indeed, Cougar and Zawacki (1978) found that data processing professional staff had a comparable self-image and felt that they had a negligible need to work with other people.

In fact, most software engineers work in teams which vary in size from two to several hundred people. In a study undertaken by IBM (McCue, 1978), the proportion of time spent in various activities was as shown in Figure 2.5.

Half of a typical programmer's time is spent interacting with other team members, 30% working alone and 20% in activities such as travel and training. While the public and the self-image may be an individual one, the reality is that most software engineering is a team activity.

An understanding of group dynamics helps software managers and engineers working in a group. Managers are faced with the difficult task of forming groups. They must ensure that the group has the right balance in both technical skills and experience and in terms of personalities. Software engineers working in groups can achieve better results and more harmonious working conditions if they understand how the group members interact and how the group, as a separate entity, takes its place within an organization.

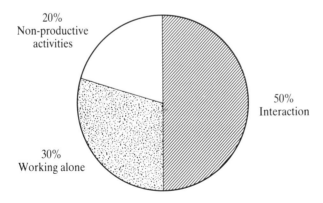

Figure 2.5
Distribution of a software engineer's time.

2.3.1 **Personalities in groups**

Sometimes individuals working in a group work well together and sometimes they clash so dramatically that little or no productive work is possible. This section attempts to describe why personality clashes sometimes occur and why some groups work together very successfully.

Very roughly, individuals in a work situation can be classified into three types:

(1) *Task-oriented* This type is motivated by the work itself. In software engineering, they are technicians who are motivated by the intellectual challenge of software development.

(2) *Self-oriented* This type is principally motivated by personal success. They are interested in software development as a means of achieving their own goals. Attaining these goals may mean that they will move away from technical software development into management.

(3) *Interaction-oriented* This type of individual is motivated by the presence and actions of co-workers. Until recently, there probably weren't many individuals of this type involved in software development because of the apparent lack of human interaction involved in the process. However, as software engineering becomes more user-centred, interaction-oriented individuals may be attracted to software development work.

Each individual's motivation is made up of elements of each class but one type of motivation is usually dominant. However, personalities are not static and individuals can change. For example, technicians who feel they are not being properly rewarded can become self-oriented and put personal interests before technical concerns.

In an experiment by Bass and Dunteman (1963), task-oriented persons described themselves as being self-sufficient, resourceful, aloof, introverted, aggressive, competitive and independent. Interaction-oriented individuals considered themselves to be unaggressive, with low needs for autonomy and achievement, considerate and helpful. They preferred to work in a group rather than alone.

Self-oriented individuals described themselves as disagreeable, dogmatic, aggressive, competitive, introverted and jealous. They preferred to work alone. Men tended to be task-oriented but women were more likely to be interaction-oriented. Whether this is a result of natural tendencies or of role stereotyping is not clear.

When individuals worked in groups composed entirely of members belonging to the same personality class, only the group composed of interaction-oriented persons was successful. Task-oriented and self-oriented group members felt negatively about their groups. There was, perhaps, an oversupply of leaders. The difficulties encountered when individuals of the same personality class worked together suggest that the most successful groups are made up of people from each class with the group leader task-oriented.

Most software engineers are probably task-oriented, motivated primarily by their work. Software development groups, therefore, are likely to be composed of individuals who have their own idea on how the project should be undertaken. This is borne out by regularly reported problems of interface standards being ignored, systems being redesigned as they are coded, unnecessary system embellishments, and so on.

Management must therefore pay attention to group composition. Selecting individuals who have complementary personalities may produce a better working group than a group selected according to technical ability. If a selection based on complementary personalities is impossible (a likely situation, given that most programmers are task-oriented), the tendency of group members to go their own way implies that strict managerial control is needed to stop individual goals transcending organizational and group objectives.

This control is easier to achieve if all group members participate in each stage of the project. Individual initiative is most likely when group members are given instructions without being aware of the part that their task plays in the overall project. For example, say an engineer is given a program design for coding and notices possible design improvements. If these improvements are implemented without understanding the rationale for the original design, they might have adverse implications for other parts of the system. If engineers are involved in the design from the start, they will understand why design decisions have been made. They will identify with these decisions rather than oppose them.

The involvement of all group members at each stage of the project is impossible for large groups. For psychological reasons, therefore, large groups are less likely to be successful than small groups. This is borne out by many project failures and cost overruns where large programming groups were used. Failure was attributed to the lack of effective group communications.

2.3.2 Egoless programming

Egoless programming (Weinberg, 1971) is a style of project group working which considers programs to be the common property and responsibility of the group irrespective of which group member was responsible for their production. The notion is not confined to programs; it may be generalized to include all software including specifications, designs and user documentation.

Weinberg recommends this way of working because it makes program production a group rather than an individual effort. His argument is based on the theory of cognitive dissonance (Festinger, 1957). This theory argues that individuals who hold a set of beliefs or have made a particular decision avoid anything which contradicts those beliefs or that decision. For example, supporters of a political party will normally only attend political speeches made by a member of the same party, although the material presented in the speech is probably familiar. Buyers of a particular make of computer usually read articles which praise that computer. They avoid reading material which suggests that other machines are superior.

Programmers who feel personally responsible for a program tend to defend that program against criticism, even if it has obvious shortcomings. The programmer's ego is tied up with the program itself. If, however, programmers consider their work to be common group property, they are more likely to offer their programs for inspection by other group members, to accept criticism, and to work with the group to improve the program.

Egoless programming is an example of an approach to development where it is accepted that errors will occur but these errors should be trapped as a natural part of the development process. It is an informal form of program inspection (see Chapter 24) or quality review.

As well as improving the quality of programs, documents and designs, egoless programming also improves intra-group communications. It draws the members of a programming group together and encourages uninhibited communications without regard to status, experience or sex. Individual members actively cooperate with other group members throughout the course of the project.

Although egoless programming is to be encouraged, it is best used in combination with more formal inspections and reviews (see Chapters 24 and 31) so that the group goals do not diverge from wider organizational goals.

2.3.3   Group leadership

The performance of group leaders may govern the success or otherwise of a software project. While most programming groups have a titular leader or project manager appointed by higher management, that individual may not be the real leader of the group as far as the technical work of the project is concerned. A more technically capable individual may adopt this role with the appointed leader being responsible for administrative tasks. Technical competence and administrative competence are not necessarily synonymous and the roles of technical leader and administrative leader may be complementary.

The actual leader in a software development group is the member who has most influence on other members. This influence can be a result of technical abilities, individual status or because of a dominant personality. The leadership may change at different stages of a project. Because of expertise or experience at a particular stage, the best qualified group member may command respect and take over leadership for that stage of the project.

If an unwanted leader is imposed, this is likely to introduce tensions into the group. The members will not respect the leader and may reject group loyalty in favour of individual goals. This is a particular problem in a fast-changing field such as software engineering where new members may be more up-to-date and better educated than experienced group leaders.

The implication of this is that competent individuals should not be promoted out of programming. An alternative career structure for technically able individuals should be provided so that they may be properly rewarded yet remain directly involved in software development. Such a structure has been created by IBM and other organizations in chief programmer teams, described in Chapter 25.

2.3.4 Group loyalties

Members of a well-led group are loyal to that group. Group members identify with group goals and with other group members. They attempt to protect the group, as an entity, from outside interference. Group loyalty implies that there is a coherence in decision making and universal acceptance of decisions.

Members think of the group as more important than the individuals in the group. If a strong group feeling exists, membership changes can be accommodated. The group can adapt to changed circumstances, such as a drastic change in software requirements, by providing mutual support and help.

There are, nevertheless, two disadvantages of group loyalty which become obvious when the group is cohesive and tightly knit. These are the resistance of group members to a change in leadership and a loss of overall critical faculties because group loyalty overrides all other considerations.

If the leader of a tightly knit group has to be replaced and the new leader is not a group member, the group members may band together against the new leader. The new leader will not have the same feelings of group loyalty and may attempt to change the overall goals of the group. Group members may spend time resisting the changes with a consequent decrease in productivity. The best way of avoiding this situation is to appoint a new leader from within the group itself.

Another consequence of group loyalty has been termed 'groupthink' by Janis (1972). Groupthink is the state where the critical faculties of the group members are eroded by group loyalties. Consideration of alternatives is replaced by loyalty to group norms and decisions. Any proposal favoured by the majority of the group may be adopted without proper consideration of alternatives. Janis suggests that groupthink is most prevalent under conditions of stress. This stress may arise as deadlines and delivery dates approach when it is particularly important to make reasoned decisions.

Management should make active efforts to avoid groupthink. Formal sessions may be organized where group members are encouraged to criticize decisions. Outside experts may be introduced to review the group's decisions. It should be policy for someone outside the group to be involved in reviews even when other group members might be better qualified as reviewers.

Personnel policies can also be used to avoid groupthink. Some individuals are naturally argumentative, questioning and disrespectful of the status quo. Such people are positive assets in spite of the fact that they may appear to be troublesome. They act as devil's advocate, constantly questioning group decisions and thus forcing other group members to think about and evaluate their activities.

2.3.5 Group interaction

Group members spend a lot of time communicating with other group members. Some of these communications are essential in that they may form part of the activity of egoless programming, they may be collective design meetings or they may be progress reporting sessions. Often, however, the communication takes place because of an organizational meeting culture or is necessary because of poor group organization or inadequate documentation.

Unproductive group communication should be minimized to make the best possible use of time for essential interaction. As well as being time consuming, group communications have to be managed. The more communications a group member is involved in, the more difficult they are to manage. Consequently, when large numbers of interpersonal communications become the norm, errors are more likely to occur.

Effective communication between the members of a software development group is essential if the group is to work efficiently. Factors which affect the effectiveness of intra-group communications include:

- The size of the group.
- The structure of the group.
- The status and personalities of group members.
- The physical work environment of the group.

As the size of a group increases, the number of potential communication links between individual members increases as the square of the group size. The number of potential communication links between members of an n-member group is $n*(n-1)$. If there are two members A and B, there are two links AB and BA. If there are three members A, B and C, there are six links. Even in relatively small groups there are, therefore, many potential communication channels.

Group communications are influenced by the status, personalities and sexes of group members. Higher-status members tend to dominate communications with lower-status members, who may be reluctant to start a conversation. The effect of status on communications can be minimized by active efforts of the higher-status individual to encourage uninhibited communication in the group. However, it is practically impossible to eliminate in hierarchical organizations where the progress of a junior member of staff is dependent on reports by more experienced colleagues.

Group communication and hence group efficiency can be influenced by personality clashes between members. These personality clashes may be a consequence of all members being task-oriented (too many leaders) as discussed previously or may be the result of personal likes, dislikes and prejudices. Such clashes are difficult for management to resolve. People cannot be coerced into liking each other. If group effectiveness is hampered by personality clashes, the best solution is to reorganize the programming group, transferring some members elsewhere.

The sexual composition of groups also affects communications. A study by Marshall and Heslin (1976) showed that both men and women prefer to work in mixed sex groups. The importance of interaction-oriented individuals has already been discussed. As women tend to be more interaction-oriented than men, the female group members may act as interaction controllers within the group.

However, with mixed-sex groups there may be problems with role stereotyping. Some men may be content to see a woman adopt the role of interaction specialist but may be less happy with women adopting an aggressive leadership role. Senior management must recognize these potential difficulties and provide support for women placed in such awkward situations.

Sometimes it is better to organize communications informally rather than formally. Instead of scheduling regular formal meetings, informal get-togethers over coffee or while travelling can sometimes result in useful information exchange.

More formal group communications can be structured as either a star or a network (Figure 2.6). In the star organization, the group is structured so that communications pass through a central coordinator. If A wishes to

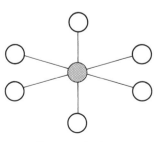

Star organization

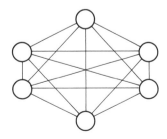

Network organization

Figure 2.6
Group communication patterns.

describe some work to other project members in a project where C is the team leader, A would write a descriptive document and pass this to C, who decides who needs to know about the document and passes it to the appropriate group members.

In the network organization, documents produced by group members are circulated to all other group members. Group size should therefore be small so that an unreasonable reading load is not placed on group members.

Research by Leavitt (1951) and Shaw (1964, 1971) suggests that the second alternative is the more effective. Group members preferred to work in loosely structured groups. Problem solving performance of loosely structured groups was superior to that of centralized groups. Groups where the communication passed through a centralized coordinator were better for simple tasks such as the collection and dissemination of information.

2.4   Ergonomics

The workplace has important effects on the performance of people. Psychological experiments have shown that behaviour is affected by room size, furniture, equipment, temperature, humidity, brightness and quality of light, noise and the degree of privacy available. Group behaviour is affected by architectural organization and telecommunication facilities.

If people are unhappy about their working conditions, staff turnover may be high. More costs must be expended on recruitment and training. Software projects may be delayed because of lack of qualified staff.

There has been little attention paid to tailoring the design of buildings specifically for software development. Most software engineering work takes place in environments designed for other functions, principally business offices. Software development staff often work in large open-plan office areas and only senior management have individual offices.

However, McCue (1978) carried out a study which showed that the open-plan architecture favoured by many organizations was neither popular nor productive. The most important environmental factors identified in that design study were:

(1)   *Privacy*   Programmers require an area where they can concentrate and work without interruption.

(2)   *Outside awareness*   People prefer to work in natural light and with a view of the outside environment.

(3)   *Personalization*   Individuals adopt different working practices and have different opinions on decor. The ability to rearrange the workplace to suit working practices and to personalize that environment is important.

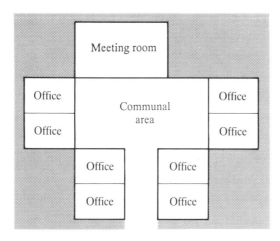

Figure 2.7
Office and meeting room grouping.

Obviously, it is not always possible to custom design buildings for programming. Nevertheless, software management should recognize the importance of providing a pleasant and congenial working environment.

Providing individual offices for software engineering staff makes a significant difference to productivity due to the lower level of disruption than that found in open-plan organizations. In open-plan offices, people are denied privacy and a quiet working environment and are limited in the degree to which they can personalize their workspace.

Group effectiveness and communications are affected by the physical environment. Development groups require areas where all members of the group can get together and discuss their project, both formally and informally. Meeting rooms must be able to accommodate the whole group in privacy; it is unreasonable to expect group meetings to take place in the corner of some larger office.

Individual privacy requirements and group communication requirements seem to be exclusive objectives but the resolution of this problem, described by McCue, is to group individual offices round larger central rooms which can be used for group meetings and discussions (Figure 2.7).

Although individual offices make for better productivity, it is more difficult for informal communications between members of the same or different programming groups to take place. Individuals tend to 'disappear' into their offices and may not communicate much with their co-workers. This is a particular problem for those people who are not gregarious by nature and who are shy about seeking out other people to talk to.

Weinberg suggests that this type of communication is important as it allows problems to be solved and information to be disseminated in an informal but effective way. He cites an anecdotal example of how the removal of a coffee machine to stop programmers 'wasting time' chatting to each other resulted in a dramatic increase in the demand for formal programming assistance. An organization should therefore provide coffee rooms and other informal meeting places as well as formal conference rooms.

2.4.1   Equipment provision

The capital costs of computing equipment are now much less than software engineering personnel costs. Individual productivity is increased significantly in situations where software engineers have direct access to a large amount of computer power, so each engineer should be provided with a personal workstation.

The most effective support system is a network of host computers used for software development which are used to develop systems for different target machines (Figure 2.8). The software for such an environment is discussed in Chapters 17 and 18.

Providing personal computer workstations networked together for equipment support has the following advantages:

- The work of individuals is largely unaffected by the work of others. In timesharing systems, programs such as compilers which have large processing requirements can slow down the system for all other users. With personal systems, users control their own machine.

- Effective networking utilities can be provided to enhance formal and informal group communications. These include electronic notice boards, computer conferencing systems (Hiltz and Turoff, 1979) and electronic mail systems.

As well as local network access, organizations which have a number of geographically separated sites may find it useful to connect all of these sites

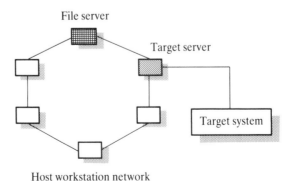

Figure 2.8
Host–target
development.

via a wide area network or may subscribe to public data networking systems.

Effective electronic communication facilities, in conjunction with telephone and facsimile systems, can reduce the number of face to face meetings which are required. Electronic mail allows the rapid interchange of documents so that a document may be circulated, commented on, revised and recirculated all in one day. My experience is that electronic discussions tend to be much more focused than face to face meetings, perhaps because there is less scope for digression. However, they do lack immediacy and, obviously, there is no non-verbal communication as occurs in meetings.

The emerging technology of Computer Support for Cooperative Working (CSCW) (Grief, 1988) addresses the general problem of providing support for group communications. CSCW systems may be either asynchronous, where the systems are essentially developments of electronic message handling systems, or synchronous, where active automation of meetings is supported. Multi-media systems such as the Rapport system (Ahuja *et al.*, 1988) support simultaneous verbal, textual and graphical communications. Products in this area are now becoming available and CSCW appears to offer an opportunity for improving overall group productivity.

■ KEY POINTS

- Software engineers should have some understanding of human factors because their software is used by people. If the software does not take human capabilities and limitations into account it will be found wanting.

- Human memory organization is structured into fast, short-term memory, working memory and long-term memory. Mistakes are minimized when transfers between these memory areas are minimized.

- Knowledge falls into two classes, namely arbitrary syntactic knowledge and deeper semantic knowledge. Semantic knowledge is held in some internal way rather than in a language-oriented way.

- In group working, it is common for leaders who are technically competent to emerge. The titular group leader may simply be responsible for administrative activities.

- Personalities working in groups fall into three classes, namely task-oriented, self-oriented and interaction-oriented.

- Group interaction should be structured so that the number of group communication links is minimized.

- The workplace has important effects on software productivity.

FURTHER READING

The Psychology of Computer Programming.   This is a readable book which uses mainly anecdotal evidence to suggest how programming groups and individual programmers should be managed. (G.M. Weinberg, 1971, Van Nostrand Reinhold.)

Human Factors in Software Engineering.   This is an IEEE tutorial which includes papers on a variety of relevant topics from cognitive models to how human factors aid in debugging. (B. Curtis (ed.), 1985, IEEE Press.)

Working with Computers: Theory versus Outcome.   This book is a collection of papers which are mostly written by cognitive scientists with an interest in software development. (G. van der Veer, T.R. Green, J.-M. Hoc and D.M. Murray (eds), 1988, Academic Press.)

'Groupware: Some issues and experiences'.   This review article surveys groupware (the name given to software supporting collaborative working) and presents a good overview of the field of CSCW in general. (C.A. Ellis, S.J. Gibbs and G.L. Rein, *Comm. ACM*, **34** (1), January 1991.)

EXERCISES

2.1   Consider a number of your fellow software engineers. List the types of different personalities which they appear to exhibit.

2.2   Explain why our immediate recall seems to be limited to about seven items.

2.3   Describe human memory organization and explain how this explains why structured programming is effective.

2.4   What is the difference between syntactic and semantic knowledge? From your own experience, write down a number of instances of each of these types of knowledge.

2.5   What are the different types of orientation which can be observed in group working?

2.6   Why is egoless programming an effective technique?

2.7   Explain what you understand by 'groupthink'. Describe the dangers of this phenomenon and explain how it can be avoided.

2.8 What are the factors affecting group communication? Give four ways in which group communication can be maximized.

2.9 Why are open-plan and communal offices less suitable for software development than individual offices?

2.10 Suggest five ways in which a computer conferencing system can be used in the support of software development.

2.11 Review the available literature on CSCW and write a report suggesting how the technology may be used in a software development environment.

Part One
Software Specification

■ The chapters in this part of the book discuss the various software process activities concerned with specifying what services a software system should provide and the constraints under which that system should operate. Chapters 3 to 5 cover the specification of the software requirements and Chapter 6 discusses prototyping as a means of requirements validation. Chapters 7 to 9 discuss the use of mathematically formal specification techniques and show that these help to reduce the ambiguity in a system specification.

■ CONTENTS

Software Requirements Definition

3

■ OBJECTIVES

This objective of this chapter is to introduce requirements definition, the first stage in producing a software specification. The first section discusses the place of specification in the software process and the problems of producing complete and consistent specifications. The structure of a requirements document is described and data flow techniques are suggested as appropriate means of defining the context in which a system operates. This is followed by a section which shows how structured natural language can be used to express requirements in a way that can readily be understood by non-technical readers. The final section discusses planning for requirements evolution. Evolution is always necessary as users and system procurers discover requirements errors and as new requirements emerge.

■ CONTENTS

The problems which software engineers are called upon to solve are often immensely complex. Understanding the nature of the problem can be very difficult, particularly if the system is new and there is no existing system to serve as a model for the software. The process of establishing the services the system should provide and the constraints under which it must operate is called *requirements capture and analysis*. The result of this analysis is a requirements specification which often constitutes the first formal document produced in the software process.

User needs and user requirements are not the same. An organization may decide that it needs a software system to support its accounting. However, it is unrealistic to present this simple need to a software engineer and expect an acceptable and usable software system to be developed. Rather, information about the problem to be solved must be collected and analysed and a comprehensive problem definition produced. A software solution can then be designed and implemented.

The principal difficulty which arises in establishing large software system requirements is that the problems being tackled are usually 'wicked' problems. Rittel and Webber (1973) define a wicked problem as a problem for which there is no definitive formulation. For example, an extreme example of a wicked problem is the problem of planning for the next San Francisco earthquake! Any formulation (the requirements) of the problem is bound to be inadequate and, during the software process, the developer's understanding of the problem is constantly changing.

There are several reasons why it is virtually impossible to be definitive about a problem specification:

(1)   Large software systems are usually required to improve upon the *status quo* where either no system or an inadequate system is in place. Although difficulties with the current system may be known, it is hard to anticipate what effects the 'improved' system is likely to have on an organization.

(2)   Large systems usually have a diverse user community who have different, and sometimes conflicting, requirements and priorities. The final system requirements are inevitably a compromise.

(3)   The procurers of a system (those who pay for it) and the users of a system are rarely the same people. System procurers impose requirements because of organizational and budgetary constraints. These are likely to conflict with actual user requirements.

Sometimes, system goals and system requirements are confused. The distinction is that a requirement is something that can be tested whereas a goal is a more general characteristic which the system should exhibit. For example, a goal might be that the system should be 'user friendly'. This is not testable as 'friendliness' is a subjective attribute. An associated requirement might be that all user command selection should take place using command menus.

This is an example of different interpretations of what 'requirements definition and specification' actually means. Depending on particular organizations, the system requirements specification can be anything from a broad outline statement in natural language of what services the system should provide to a mathematically formal system specification. The line between requirements and design specification is a tenuous one and the terms may be used to mean the same thing.

Problems arise because of the need to document a system so that it can be understood by potential users and, at the same time, produce a system specification (often called the functional specification) which can act as a basis for a contract between a procurer and a software supplier. Generally, users prefer an abstract system description which is at a higher level than a detailed contractual specification. Furthermore, it is probably impossible to construct a detailed specification without some design activity so further blurring the distinction between requirements and design specification.

Therefore specifications should be produced at several different levels of abstraction with careful correlations made between these levels. Each level is intended for a different class of reader who make decisions about the system procurement and implementation. These levels of specification are:

- *A requirements definition* is a statement, in a natural language, of what user services the system is expected to provide. This should be written so that it is understandable by client and contractor management and by potential system procurers and users.

- *A requirements specification* is a structured document which sets out the system services in more detail. This document (sometimes called a functional specification), should be precise so that it may act as a contract between the system procurer and software developer. It should be written so that it is understandable to technical staff from both procurers and developers. Formal specification techniques may be appropriate for expressing such a specification but this will depend on the background of the system procurer.

- *A software specification* (design specification) is an abstract description of the software which is a basis for its design and implementation. There should be a clear relationship between this document and the requirements specification but the important distinction is that the readers of this are principally software designers rather than users or management. Thus, the use of formal specification techniques, introduced in Chapters 7, 8 and 9, is appropriate in this document.

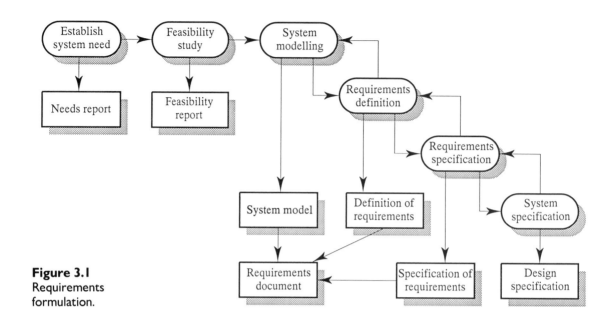

Figure 3.1
Requirements
formulation.

Sometimes, formulating outline requirements for a project is difficult as the application domain is poorly understood. In such cases, it is unrealistic to expect a definitive requirements definition before system development begins and a process model based on system prototyping is more appropriate than the classical waterfall model. A process model based on prototyping for requirements derivation is discussed in Chapter 6.

If a process model is used which does not involve system prototyping, the derivation of requirements involves a number of steps.

(1)   *Feasibility study*   An estimate is made of whether the identified user needs can be satisfied using current software and hardware techno-logies, whether the proposed system will be cost-effective from a business point of view and whether it can be developed given existing budgetary constraints. The techniques involved in carrying out such a study are outside the scope of this text and the reader is referred to a systems analysis text (Davis, 1983; Kendall, 1989) for further discussion of this phase.

(2)   *Requirements capture and analysis*   This is the process of deriving the system requirements through observation of existing systems, discus-sions with potential users and procurers, task analysis, and so on.

(3)   *Requirements definition*   A system model is formulated and used as the basis for an abstract description of the system requirements. This document describes the system from the end-user's point of view.

(4)   *Requirements specification*   A detailed and precise description of the
       system requirements is set out to act as a basis for a contract between
       client and software developer. The creation of this document might be
       carried out in parallel with some high-level design (indeed, this is
       often essential) and the design and requirements activities influence
       each other as they develop. During the creation of this document,
       errors in the requirements definition are inevitably discovered and it
       must be modified accordingly.

The sequence of activities and activity iterations are shown in Figure 3.1
where activities are represented as round-edged rectangles and deliverables
as square boxes.

       Of course, the activities in the requirements process are not simply
carried out in sequence but are iterated. The requirements analysis
continues during definition and specification and new requirements arise
during the process. Thus, the documents are subject to frequent change and
should be placed under the control of a configuration management system
(Chapter 29).

3.1   The software requirements document

The software requirements document defines the system to be built and thus
is the basis of a contract between the system procurer and the system
contractor. Terminology in this area can be confusing as the requirements
definition is sometimes seen as a basis for bidding for a system contract and
the requirements specification (or functional specification) is the basis for
the contract. In essence, the distinction between these is arbitrary and it is
important that the combined definition/specification is structured in such a
way that it may be readily understood and analysed as a whole.

       In principle, the requirements set out in such a document ought to be
complete and consistent. All system functions should be specified and no
requirement should conflict with any other. In practice, this is difficult to
achieve, particularly if the requirements are stated as natural language text.
Errors and omissions will inevitably exist in the document so it should be
structured to be easy to change.

       Heninger (1980) claims that there are six requirements which a
software requirements document must satisfy:

(1)   It should only specify external system behaviour.
(2)   It should specify constraints on the implementation.
(3)   It should be easy to change.
(4)   It should serve as a reference tool for system maintainers.
(5)   It should record forethought about the life cycle of the system.
(6)   It should characterize acceptable responses to undesired events.

The requirements document is a reference tool. It should record forethought about the system life cycle because it will be used by maintenance programmers to find out what the system is supposed to do. The document should have a detailed table of contents, one or more indexes, a glossary of terms used and a definition of the changes anticipated when the requirements were originally formulated.

The requirements document is a combination of requirements definition and requirements specification. The best organization is as a series of chapters with the detailed specification presented as an appendix to the document. A possible structure for a requirements document is:

- *Introduction* This should describe the need for the system and should place the system in context, briefly describing its functions and presenting a rationale for the software. It should describe how the system fits into the overall business or strategic objectives of the organization commissioning the software.

- *The system model* This section should set out the system model, showing the relationships between the system components and the system and its environment. An abstract data model should also be described.

- *System evolution* This section should describe the fundamental assumptions on which the system is based and describe anticipated changes due to hardware evolution, changing user needs, and so on.

- *Functional requirements* The services provided for the user should be described in this section using natural language with cross-references to the more detailed requirements specification.

- *Non-functional requirements* The constraints imposed on the software must operate, and restrictions on the freedom of the designer should be expressed and related to the functional requirements.

- *Glossary* This should define the technical terms used in the document. No assumptions should be made about the experience or expertise of the reader.

It is particularly important in the introduction to present the business objectives of the organization procuring the system and the business rationale for that procurement. It must be clear to those responsible for paying for the system that there is a case for the system procurement.

The appendices to the requirements document should include at least the following information:

- *Functional requirements specification* This is a detailed specification of the system requirements (see Chapter 5) and will probably make up the bulk of the requirements document.

- *Non-functional requirements specification*   This is an amplification of the non-functional requirements definition presented earlier in the document. It should include details such as data representation, specific response times, memory requirements, and so on. Any specific product and process standards which must be followed should be specified.

- *Hardware*   If the system is to be implemented on special hardware, this hardware and its interfaces should be described. If off-the-shelf hardware is to be used, the minimal and optimal configurations for the system should be defined.

- *Database requirements*   The logical organization of the data used by the system and its interrelationships should be described. Data modelling techniques such as entity-relational modelling (covered in Chapter 4) may be used to describe the database requirements.

- *Index*   More than one kind of index to the document may be provided. As well as a normal alphabetic index, there may be an index per chapter, an index of functions, and so on.

The task of developing a software requirements document should not be underestimated. Bell *et al.* (1977) report that the requirements document for a ballistic missile defence system contained over 8000 distinct requirements and support paragraphs and was made up of 2500 pages of text. This is larger than most systems but it illustrates that a great deal of resources have to be dedicated to the production of a requirements document, representing a significant life cycle cost.

The software requirements document is not a design document. It should set out what the system should do without specifying how it should be done. The requirements should be stated so that the design may be validated. If the services, constraints and properties specified in the software requirements document are satisfied by the software design then that design is an acceptable solution to the problem.

3.2   System contexts

Requirements misunderstandings are common because the system procurer, different users and the software developer have different views of the role of the system in its environment. Therefore, an important part of the requirements definition process is to establish a system context where the relationships between the system being specified and other human and computer systems are documented.

Simple block diagrams, supplemented by descriptions of the system entities, are an appropriate starting point for describing system contexts. For

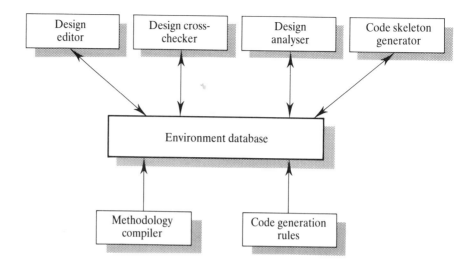

Figure 3.2
The designer's
workbench.

example, Figure 3.2 shows the context in which a design editing system operates. The design editor is one of several CASE tools which make up a designer's workbench. These tools are built around an environment database (sometimes now called a repository) and the tool outputs are stored in that database.

The design editing system is a real system, now marketed as a commercial product, which is part of the ECLIPSE software engineering environment (Bott, 1989). I was involved in defining the requirements for the editor and in part of the overall system design.

The editor is a graphical design editor which incorporates procedures to check that the design being documented conforms to the rules of the method used. The generated design is stored in a database and may be processed by other tools such as skeleton code generators.

The editing system is not method-specific. The notation and rules of any method where a design is a directed graph may be input and a version of

Name	Description
Design editor	An editing system which allows design diagrams to be created, modified, stored in and retrieved from the environment database.
Methodology compiler	A translation system which takes a formal description of a design method and translates it into tables to drive the design editor.
Code generation rules	A set of rules which set out how code may be generated to represent entities in a particular method. These rules drive the code skeleton generator.

Figure 3.3
Design entity
descriptions.

the editor instantiated to support that particular approach (Sommerville *et al.*, 1987; Welland *et al.*, 1990). It is intended to be used as part of a suite of CASE tools (a designer's workbench) which assist the software engineer with design activities.

Descriptive names should be used on system context diagrams but a more detailed description of the diagram entities may also be necessary (Figure 3.3). These descriptions should be maintained in a data dictionary (see Chapter 4) which serves as a central repository for all information about system entities.

Figure 3.2 presents a contextual description which shows the existence of other systems but provides no information about the relationships between these systems and how they might be used in the creation of a design. There are various different types of relationship which may be modelled but data flow relationships (DeMarco, 1978), which show how data is processed by different parts of the system, are often useful. Figure 3.4 is a data flow diagram for the designer's workbench.

Data flow diagrams are discussed in more detail in Chapter 12. They show how data entities are progressively transformed as they are processed by the system. They do not include control information which must be separately specified. Figure 3.4 illustrates how the output from one tool is processed by other tools. Figure 3.2 shows that data transfer between tools is actually via the system database and is not passed directly from tool to tool.

After setting out the context in which the system is to be used, the next step is to produce a system model. This is an activity which continues throughout the whole requirements process; the initial model produced for the requirements definition is abstract and it is developed in more and more detail as the requirements specification proceeds. System modelling is discussed in Chapter 4.

Figure 3.4
Data flow in the designer's workbench.

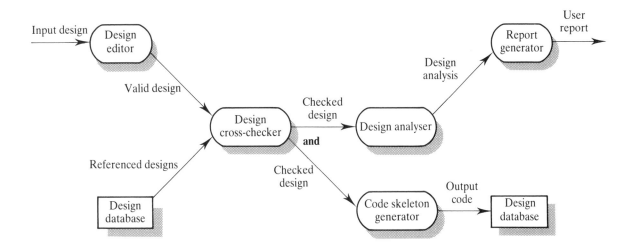

3.3 Requirements definition

A software requirements definition is an abstract description of the services which the system is expected to provide and the constraints under which the system must operate. It should only specify the external behaviour of the system and should not be concerned with design characteristics. It should be written in such a way that it is understandable without knowledge of specialized notations. Requirements fall into two categories:

- *Functional system requirements* These are system services which are expected by the user of the system. In general, the user is uninterested in how these services are implemented so the software engineer should not introduce implementation concepts when describing these requirements.

- *Non-functional requirements* These set out the constraints under which the system must operate and the standards which must be met by the delivered system. For example, a non-functional constraint might be a requirement that all information input should be expressible using the ASCII character set. A standard might be a requirement for the maximum system response time for any user command to be less than 2 seconds.

In principle, the functional requirements of a system should be both complete and consistent. Completeness means that all services required by the user should be specified and consistency means that requirements should not be contradictory. In practice, for large, complex systems, it is practically impossible to achieve requirements consistency and completeness in the initial version of the software requirements document. As problems are discovered during reviews or in later life cycle phases, the requirements document must be corrected.

The requirements definition is usually written using a mixture of natural language, tables and diagrams as it must be understandable by user personnel who do not know specialized notations. Unfortunately, the way in which language is used in requirements definitions is often imprecise and ambiguous. There is sometimes a confusion between expressing concepts and expressing details so that the description contains an unhappy mixture of information presented at different levels of detail.

It is not the intention here to single out any specific document for criticism. Indeed few requirements documents are in the public domain so it is difficult to find documents of this type which may be freely quoted. However, one document which is available is the Stoneman document (Buxton, 1980) which sets out requirements for an Ada programming support environment (APSE). In general, this is not a badly-written document but it does contain some examples of the differing levels of detail

> **4.A.5** The database shall support the generation and control of configuration objects; that is, objects which are themselves groupings of other objects in the database. The configuration control facilities shall allow access to the objects in a version group by the use of an incomplete name.

Figure 3.5
Stoneman requirement
4.A.5.

which can be found in such documents.

For example, requirement 4.A.5 from the Stoneman document is shown in Figure 3.5. This is an example of mixing conceptual and detailed information. The requirement expresses the concept that there should be a configuration control facilities provided as an inherent part of the APSE. However, it also includes the detail that those facilities should allow access to the objects in a version group by use of an incomplete name. This detail would have been better left to a section where the configuration control requirements were specified more fully.

Two major problems may arise when natural language is used for requirements definition:

(1)   Functional requirements, non-functional requirements, system goals and design information are not clearly distinguished.

(2)   Each paragraph may encompass several individual requirements in a single statement.

Some of these problems of requirements definition are illustrated by examples from the requirements definition for the design editing system discussed above. This document was a combined requirements definition and requirements specification which was expressed entirely in natural language. When a requirements definition (for non-technical readers) is combined with a specification (for technicians) there is often confusion between concepts and details. This is evident from the example given.

The user of the design editor may specify that a grid should be displayed so that diagram entities may be accurately positioned (Figure 3.6). The first sentence in this requirement provides three items of information. It states that the editing system should provide a grid and presents a rationale for this. Secondly, it gives detailed information about the grid units (centimetres or inches) and thirdly, it tells how that grid is to be activated by the user. It sets out a conceptual functional requirement, a non-functional requirement concerning an expected standard and a non-functional requirement constraining the grid activation.

The requirement also gives some but not all initialization information. It defines that the grid is initially off but does not define its units when turned on. It provides some detailed information such as the fact that the

Figure 3.6
A requirements definition for an editor grid.

> To assist in the positioning of entities on a diagram, the user may turn on a grid in either centimetres or inches, via an option on the control panel. Initially, the grid is off. The grid may be turned on and off at any time during an editing session and can be toggled between inches and centimetres at any time. A grid option will be provided on the reduce-to-fit view but the number of grid lines shown will be reduced to avoid filling the smaller diagram with grid lines.

user may toggle between units and not other information such as the spacing between grid lines.

Given that a requirements definition is supplemented by a more detailed specification, the definition should concentrate on concepts and refer the reader to the specification for more detailed information. For example, Figure 3.7 might be a simple conceptual grid definition. This definition concentrates on describing the facility required (the grid) and justifying why it is required. This rationale is important. Without it, some facilities may appear arbitrary and their importance may not be understood by engineers developing a more detailed specification or maintaining the system. Notice also the reference to the system specification document where grid details are provided.

It is easy to criticize but much more difficult to write a requirements definition. The first version of a requirements definition is inevitably unstructured as a natural authoring tendency is to include information as it comes to mind. Project management must accept the overhead of reorganizing and restructuring the document so that a more readable and usable definition is provided.

Figure 3.7
An improved definition for an editor grid.

> **2.6. The Grid**
>
> 2.6.1.   The editor shall provide a grid facility where a matrix of horizontal and vertical lines provide a background to the editor window. This grid shall be a passive rather than an active grid. This means that alignment is entirely the responsibility of the user and the system should not attempt to align diagram entities with grid lines.
> *Rationale:*
>   A grid helps the user to create a tidy diagram with well-spaced entities. Although an active grid can be useful, the user is the best person to decide on where entities should be positioned.
>
> 2.6.2.   When used in 'reduce-to-fit' mode, the spacing of grid lines shall be adjusted so that line spacing is increased.
> *Rationale:*
>   If line spacing is not increased, the background will be very cluttered with grid lines.
>
> *Specification*: ECLIPSE/Workstation Tools/DE/FS. Section 2.6.

3.5.1. Adding nodes to a design

3.5.1.1. To add a node, the editor user selects the appropriate node type
from the entity type menu. He or she then moves the mouse so
that the cursor is placed within the drawing area. On entering the
drawing area, the cursor shape changes to a circle.
Rationale:
The editor must know the node type so that it can draw the
correct shape and invoke appropriate checks for that node.
The cursor shape change indicates that the editor is in
'node drawing mode'.

3.5.1.2. The cursor should be moved to the approximate node position
any mouse button pressed and held down. The node
symbol, in a standard size set up by the symbol definer,
should appear surrounding the cursor. The symbol may then be
dragged, keeping the mouse button depressed, to its final position.
Releasing the mouse button fixes the node position and
highlights the node.
Rationale:
The user is the best person to decide where to position a
node on the diagram. This approach gives the user direct control.

3.5.1.3. If the entity type may be represented using variable-sized
symbols, the node highlighting should distinguish this from
fixed-size symbols.

Specification: ECLIPSE/Workstation Tools/DE/FS. Section 3.5.1

Figure 3.8
Node creation
requirements.

Perhaps the most useful approach to writing a readable requirements
definition is to invent a standard format and to ensure that all requirement
definitions adhere to that format. Descriptive paragraphs might be followed
by a rationale and a reference to a more detailed specification as shown in
Figure 3.7. Use should be made of text highlighting facilities such as
emboldening and italicization to add structure to the text and of graphics to
structure the document.

A further example of this format, taken from the design editor, is
shown in Figure 3.8.

3.4   Requirements evolution

Developing software requirements focuses attention on software capabilities,
business objectives and other business systems. As the requirements
definition is developed, a better understanding of users' needs is achieved.
This feeds back and causes the perceived requirements to be changed
(Figure 3.9). Furthermore, the time required to analyse requirements and to
develop a large system may be several years and it must be expected that
requirements changes will be identified in that time. The inevitability of

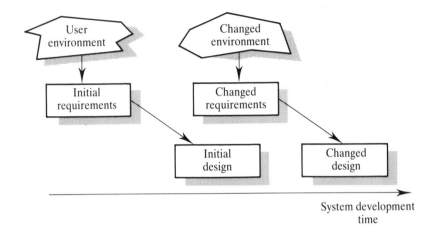

Figure 3.9
Requirements evolution during system development.

change should be recognized and anticipated when producing a requirements document.

The software requirements document should be organized so that changes can be accommodated without extensive rewriting. If changing the document is difficult, changes in the requirements may be directly implemented without recording these changes in the definition. The program and its documentation may get out of step (Figure 3.10) which can cause serious problems during system maintenance.

Although both functional and non-functional requirements are liable to change, non-functional requirements are particularly affected by changes in hardware technology. The development time for a large system may be several years so the power of the hardware available will increase during the development process. Furthermore, the hardware will continue to improve throughout the lifetime of the developed software and the non-functional requirements will be modified while the software is in use.

Hardware improvements while the software is being developed can be anticipated. Hardware dependent non-functional requirements can be specified which assume hardware capability will be available when the software is delivered. However, changes during the project's lifetime should

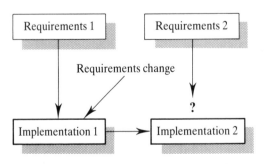

Figure 3.10
Requirements document inconsistency.

not be assumed. The specifier of requirements should avoid, as far as possible, detailed hardware dependencies.

As with programs, changeability in documents is achieved by minimizing external references and making the document sections as modular as possible. Problems are, of course, exacerbated because paper-based documents are used as the means of communication between client and contractor. A requirements document is presented as a book and may not be available in machine-readable form to the system contractor. Changes must be managed using the unwieldy system of change control forms and occasional document updates. It is only immediately after the delivery of a document that all of the requirements are summarized in one place.

The answer to this problem is more extensive use of electronic documentation and documentation tools which support multiple document views and automatic consolidation of change requests and original requirements. However, the diversity of different word and text processing systems still makes document exchange inconvenient. The problem will only be solved when a standard electronic document architecture is established.

■ KEY POINTS

- It is difficult to formulate a definitive specification for large software systems. Thus, it should be assumed that initial system requirements will be both incomplete and inconsistent.

- A requirements definition, a requirements specification and a software specification are all ways of describing specifications at different levels of detail and for different types of reader.

- A requirements definition is intended for use by non-technical staff involved in using and procuring the system. It should be written using natural language, tables and diagrams.

- It is difficult to detect inconsistencies and incompleteness when the specification is written using unstructured natural language. Some structure should always be imposed on the requirements definition.

- Rationale should always be included in a requirements definition.

- Requirements inevitably change. The requirements document should be designed so that it may be easily modified.

FURTHER READING

System and Software Requirements Engineering. This is an excellent volume in the IEEE's tutorial series. Unlike many other tutorials, it does not consist entirely of previously published papers but contains a lot of new material by some of the most established researchers and practitioners in this area. (R.H. Thayer and M. Dorfman (eds), 1990, IEEE Press.)

Comm. ACM, **31** (9), September 1988. This issue of the journal has two papers which are devoted to different aspects of requirements. The paper by Davis is a particularly good summary of different techniques for requirements specification. Davis's book, suggested as further reading in Chapter 5, expands on the material in this paper.

IEEE Trans. Software Engineering, **17** (3), March 1991. This issue has a special section on requirements engineering with papers on a requirements specification language, tools to support requirements development and the problems of specifying requirements for real-time systems.

EXERCISES

3.1 Suggest four other wicked problems in addition to the problem of planning for the next San Francisco earthquake.

3.2 Explain why it is useful to draw a distinction between a requirements definition and a requirements specification.

3.3 You have been given the task of producing guidelines for creating a requirements document which can be readily modified. Write a report setting out standards for the organization of a requirements document which will ensure its maintainability.

3.4 The method of graphical highlighting of requirements is probably only feasible when a document processing system including integrated text and graphics is available. Given that only a text-based system, with multiple fonts and styles, is available, draw up a set of guidelines for presenting requirements definitions in a readable and structured way.

3.5 If you have access to the Stoneman requirements document (or some comparable requirements definition), present a critique of the requirements as expressed in that document.

3.6 Using the structured technique suggested here, write a plausible requirements definition for the following functions:

(a) An unattended petrol (gas) pump system which includes a credit card reader. The customer swipes the card through the reader then specifies the amount of fuel required. The fuel is delivered and the customer's account is debited.

(b) The cash dispensing function in a bank auto-teller machine.

(c) The spell checking and correcting function in a word processor.

3.7 A system is to be procured which holds details of newspaper and magazine deliveries in a small town. As well as recording which households take which newspapers and magazines, this system also includes billing details and details of customer vacations when newspapers are not delivered. For each delivery person, the system prints a daily list of which newspapers and magazines are to be delivered to which households. The system should also be able to produce summary information showing how many copies of each newspaper were sold each day in the week. Bills for each customer are printed at the end of each month and delivered with the first delivery of the following month.

Using the structured method described here, write all or part of a requirements definition for this system. You should use your own knowledge of the application domain to decide on appropriate requirements.

This example is a running example which appears in several other chapters. You may find it useful to tackle related exercises in Chapters 4 and 5 at the same time as this exercise.

System Modelling

4

■ OBJECTIVES

The first stage in establishing a system specification is to formulate a model of the 'real-world' entities which are to be represented in the system. In this chapter, techniques for describing system context are described and viewpoint analysis is introduced. Viewpoint analysis is a method of requirements derivation based on examining the system from several different viewpoints. Graphical model description using the CORE method notation is described. The final part of the chapter covers semantic data modelling using extended entity-relationship diagrams. It is illustrated by examples from the design editing system introduced in Chapter 3.

■ CONTENTS

System modelling was introduced in Chapter 3 where the use of data flow diagrams for showing the system context was described. Abstract system models should be included in the requirements definition but, for more detailed requirements specification, a detailed system model can be used to structure the requirements specification.

System models may be either function-oriented, object-oriented or some combination of both. A functional approach models the system as a set of interacting functions and is typified by the data flow approach described by DeMarco (1978). The system is considered to be a set of functional transforms with data flowing from one to another. An alternative approach, typified by RML (Borgida *et al.*, 1985) models the system as a set of interacting objects where the operations allowed on each object are encapsulated with the object itself. Other object-oriented approaches to modelling are described by Coad and Yourdon (1990) and Rumbaugh *et al.* (1991).

Both of these approaches reflect human ways of system modelling and their proponents sometimes suggest that one approach should be adopted to the exclusion of the other. This is nonsense. Humans are flexible and, when observing systems, regularly switch from an object-oriented to a functional approach and back again. There is no reason why an artificial distinction between function and entity should be drawn.

In this chapter, system modelling techniques are illustrated using the controlled requirements expression (CORE) method of requirements analysis and specification (Mullery, 1979; Potts, 1988). This method was developed for defining aerospace system requirements but is being used increasingly for other classes of large system.

A full description of the method is outside the scope of this chapter but CORE concepts and notation are introduced as required. Other system modelling techniques such as SADT (Schoman and Ross, 1977) and SREM (Alford, 1977) have comparable facilities but are less explicit about the need to consider the system requirements from a variety of different viewpoints. System modelling using state machines for real-time system modelling, is covered in Chapter 13.

4.1   Viewpoint analysis

When formulating a system model, engineers must realize that the sources of information about that system (customers, users, or whatever) do not normally think about or describe the system in a top-down way. For any large system the notion of a single 'top' is illusory and at every decomposition step there are different ways of looking at the system. All of these have a contribution to make to system understanding.

Viewpoint analysis (Finklestein and Fuks, 1989) recognizes this and suggests that a system should be described from a number of different viewpoints. Loosely, a viewpoint is one way of looking at the system so typical viewpoints might be system users, sensors associated with the system, other computer systems connected to the system being analysed, functional processing activities undertaken by the system or non-functional constraints placed on the system.

As a simple example of viewpoint analysis, consider the derivation of requirements for automated teller machines (ATMs) which are now common outside banks. These include an embedded software system to drive the machine hardware and to communicate with the bank's central account database. The system accepts customer requests and produces cash, account information, database updates, and so on. Customers may send standard messages to their own bank branch requesting an account statement or cheque book. Facilities for the customer to initiate an electronic funds transfer may be available. The machines provided by a particular banking company may allow customers of other banks to use a subset (typically cash withdrawal) of their facilities.

The first step in viewpoint analysis is to identify possible viewpoints. A convenient way of expressing the set of viewpoints is to use a viewpoint bubble diagram, which is simply a collection of viewpoint names. Bubble diagrams may be produced in a brainstorming session where users and system developers suggest possible viewpoints.

A viewpoint bubble diagram for the bank auto-teller system is shown in Figure 4.1.

At this stage of the analysis, no attempt should be made to impose a structure on the diagram and any possible way of looking at the system should be written down. Sources of information which may be used in

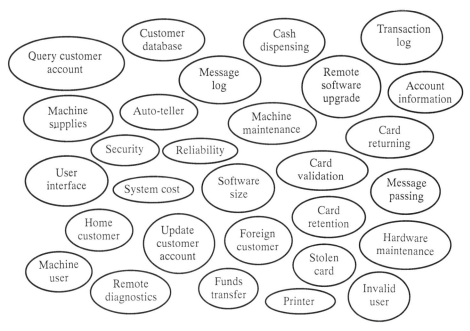

Figure 4.1
Viewpoint bubble diagram.

creating this initial view of the system may be documents setting out the high-level goals of the system, knowledge of software engineers as derived from previous systems, and interviews with bank staff concerned with account management.

It is difficult to be specific about what is and what is not a valid viewpoint. Some points of guidance are:

(1) Viewpoints should not overlap. That is, functions should not span viewpoints and each function should be performed in a single viewpoint.

(2) The source or destination of all system information must be an identified viewpoint.

(3) Non-functional system characteristics (cost, memory requirements, security, and so on) may be considered as separate viewpoints.

(4) Each functional viewpoint should perform some information processing.

There is no such thing as a 'correct' viewpoint bubble diagram and different engineers will construct seemingly quite different diagrams. After analysis and refinement, however, these should converge to comparable views of the system.

The next stage in viewpoint analysis is viewpoint clustering, where related viewpoints are grouped (Figure 4.2).

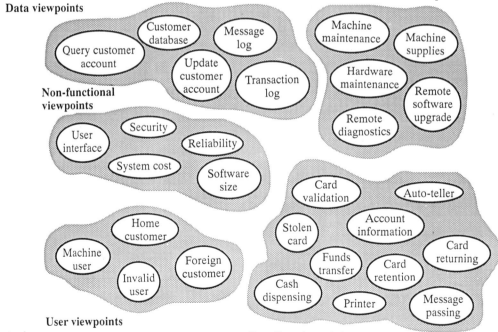

Figure 4.2
Viewpoint clustering.

At this stage, functional and non-functional viewpoints should be identified. Non-functional viewpoints are concerned with constraints such as cost, security and safety imposed on the system. Non-functional requirements specification is covered in Chapter 5.

As well as a cluster of non-functional viewpoints, functional viewpoint clusters have been identified in Figure 4.2. These are concerned with the viewpoints of machine users, the functionality which must be included in the auto-teller system and the viewpoints associated with the central bank database system.

Functional viewpoints fall into two classes:

- Bounding viewpoints are functional viewpoints outside the system but which affect or are affected by the system. An obvious example of this type of viewpoint is the viewpoint of the users of the system.

- Defining viewpoints are part of the system being modelled and are used to define system functionality.

Bounding viewpoints represent the ultimate sources and destinations of all the information used by the system. Defining viewpoints represent localized information processing. Figure 4.3 shows the bounding and defining viewpoints for the auto-teller system. This diagram has been simplified by considering only high-level viewpoints as bounding viewpoints and system functions as defining viewpoints.

The next stage in viewpoint analysis is to impose a structure on the identified viewpoint clusters and represent this in a viewpoint structure diagram. All identified functional viewpoints should appear in the viewpoint structure diagram. As a general rule, no viewpoint should have more than five sub-viewpoints. If necessary, intermediate viewpoints may be introduced and viewpoint names rationalized.

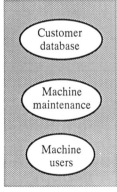

**Bounding
viewpoints**

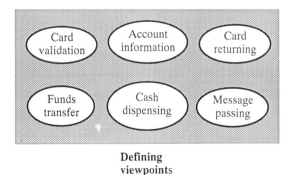

**Defining
viewpoints**

Figure 4.3
Bounding and defining
viewpoints.

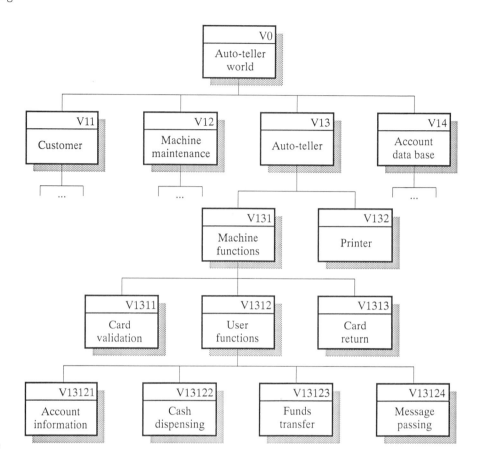

Figure 4.4
Viewpoint structuring.

Part of the viewpoint structure diagram for the auto-teller system is shown in Figure 4.4, which illustrates how a mixed object-oriented and function-oriented approach is appropriate for requirements derivation. At higher viewpoint levels, the viewpoints are objects such as customers, databases, engineers, and so on. As these are decomposed, the viewpoints tend to become functional and are concerned with system actions.

For large systems, there may be tens or hundreds of viewpoints and, in principle, all should be considered during requirements analysis. The identified viewpoints are a way of structuring the system. They may be used to guide the process of requirements elicitation and analysis.

Different viewpoints are likely to place conflicting requirements on a system so it is important to distinguish between direct viewpoints, which impose critical requirements and indirect viewpoints, whose requirements may be less important. Indirect viewpoints of the auto-teller system might be that of remote diagnostic software used to detect machine faults and that of the service engineer who is responsible for repairing the system hardware.

The viewpoint hierarchy is used in the next stage of system modelling which describes the information processing at each viewpoint. However, it is also a useful management tool as it represents the first real breakdown of the system into its components. It can be used as a basis for drawing up initial plans and estimates for the requirements derivation activity.

4.2 Model description

A large part of any requirements definition is made up of contextual descriptions describing its interface to the outside world. These contextual descriptions are abstract system models which lack information about detailed system functionality. A more detailed system model should outline the user services which the system provides. This model description should include:

* Details of the system inputs.
* Details of the system outputs.
* Details of the system data processing.
* Details of control in the system.

DeMarco (1978) suggests that a system model based on a data flow model is easily understood by users. These diagrams are equally useful in systems modelling as they are readily understood by system procurers and users. Data flow diagrams are discussed in Chapter 12.

CORE uses tabular collection diagrams to relate data flows across viewpoints. Action diagrams (sometimes called thread diagrams) are used to describe the processing associated with each viewpoint. Action diagrams are like data flow diagrams but have additional control information. A tabular collection diagram is a five column diagram where the columns describe the information source, the information to be processed, the processing carried out (the action), the generated information and the destination of the information. Both the information source and destination must be other identified system viewpoints.

Figures 4.5 and 4.6 show parts of the tabular collection diagrams for the customer and the auto-teller viewpoints, respectively. In these diagrams, the identified actions are those taken by that viewpoint.

Figure 4.5 shows that, from the customer's viewpoint, the teller machine produces a message asking for the card to be input, and the customer responds by inputting the card. The result of the action is the card which is passed to the ATM. The machine requests a personal identification number (PIN), and the associated customer action is to type in their number. The output is the typed number which is sent to the ATM. Other

CUSTOMER viewpoint

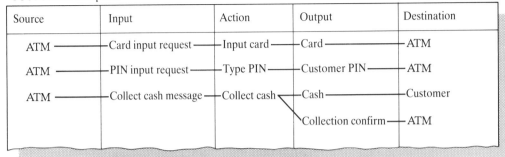

Figure 4.5
Tabular collection
diagram – customer
viewpoint.

possible customer actions should be specified in the same way.

Figure 4.6 shows the tabular collection diagram for the ATM viewpoint. The actions taken are processing actions carried out by the machine. The diagram shows that the 'validate card' action takes a card from the customer and checks if it is a valid card for that type of machine. Possible outputs are the card and an error message (if the card is invalid) or a request for the customer's PIN and a request to the customer database for account information.

If the card is invalid it is returned directly to the customer but the action sends an indicator to the ATM to specify that an appropriate error

Figure 4.6
Tabular collection
diagram – ATM
viewpoint.

ATM viewpoint

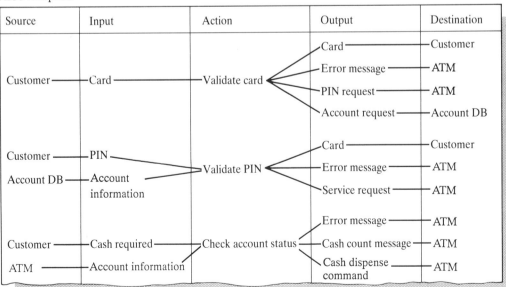

message should be displayed. To keep the example simple, the case where a stolen card is retained by the machine has not been included.

A tabular collection diagram should be produced for each viewpoint. As viewpoints must be the sources or destinations of inputs and outputs, the tabular collection across viewpoints must therefore be consistent. Where an action specifies that it requires a given viewpoint to generate a particular input, the tabular collection diagram for that viewpoint should include an action whose output is the required input and which specifies the correct output destination.

Inconsistencies imply an error or omission in the analysis and are usually obvious because of the tabular form. They can be detected during the review process or by checking tools used to process the diagrams.

The information in a tabular collection diagram provides an abstract view of the processing associated with each viewpoint . The information in the diagram should be supplemented with more detailed information for each of identified entity. In CORE, this more detailed information is called a 'node note' and node notes may describe either data or processing actions. Node notes are initially informal but may be developed in more detail to provide a formal specification of processing actions or data.

Node notes can be used effectively in combination with a data dictionary given that an appropriate CASE tool exists to retrieve the appropriate notes when using a particular tabular collection diagram. Figure 4.7 shows some possible node notes in a data dictionary for the entities referenced in Figure 4.6.

4.2.1   Action diagrams

Tabular collection diagrams are input and output specifications which name the actions involved without specifying associated processing. CORE supplements tabular collection diagrams with *action diagrams* to specify the processing actions associated with a tabular collection diagram. An action diagram should be generated for every action identified, which is a software

Name	Description
Card	A plastic bank identification card with a magnetic stripe which includes account information in the standard international banking format.
PIN	A customer personal identification number which is a sequence of four digits. PIN details must be retrieved from the account database.
Validate PIN	This action involves checking that the number input by the user is the same as the PIN known to the bank. Two retries should be allowed if the PIN is incorrect.

Figure 4.7
Node notes.

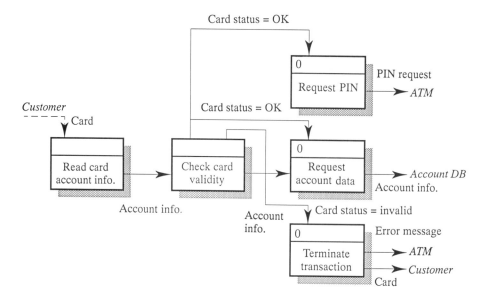

Figure 4.8
Action diagram –
validate card.

system action. For customer actions such as 'input card' it is obviously not necessary to generate an action diagram.

Action diagrams are like data flow diagrams in that they include data flow specifications, which are those arrows entering the left side of a box in the diagram. They also include control information, indicated by an arrow entering or leaving the top of a box; if the control line is a broken line, this means the action is triggered by some event such as a customer entering a card into the machine. Viewpoints which are sources and destinations are shown at the left and at the right side of the diagram, respectively.

The action diagram for validate card is shown in Figure 4.8. The ordering of boxes from left to right is significant and implies sequentiality. Thus, getting account information from the card takes place before account type checking. Where boxes are aligned, this indicates actions which may be (but need not be) carried out in parallel. Boxes annotated with a circle mean a selection from a number of possibilities, boxes annotated with a star (as in 'provide services' in Figure 4.9) mean an iteration. Italicized names show input sources and output destinations.

Therefore, the validate card action involves reading the card account information and checking the account number to see if the card is a type recognized by that machine (card information is standardized). If so, the machine issues a request for the customer's PIN and a request to the remote customer database for account information.

Action diagrams for a single action should be relatively simple but they don't provide a description of the ordering and interleaving of the actions from the different viewpoints. After individual action diagrams have been produced, the next step is to combine them to show how actions are

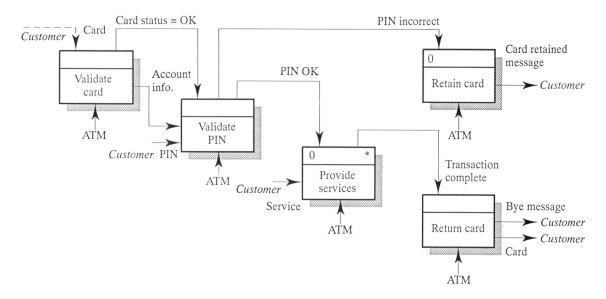

related. Several of these combined action diagrams should be produced, reflecting different system transactions.

Figure 4.9
Action diagram –
service provision.

Figure 4.9 shows a combined action diagram showing the sequence of actions involved in checking the card validity, providing customer services and terminating a transaction. Annotated arrows at the base of a box indicate the viewpoint responsible for that action.

The provision of customer services is shown as an iteration in Figure 4.9. This should be decomposed into an action diagram for each individual service. An action diagram for cash withdrawal is shown in Figure 4.10. A cash withdrawal involves checking that the customer has sufficient funds available, dispensing cash and updating the customer's account.

4.3 Data modelling

Most large software systems make use of a large database of information. In some cases, this database exists independently of the software system, in others it is created for the system being developed. Part of the systems modelling activity is to define the logical form of the data which is manipulated by the system.

A common way of defining the logical form of data is to use a relational model (Codd, 1970; Date, 1990). Using the relational model, the logical data structure is specified as a set of tables, with some tables having common keys. This model allows the relationships between data items to be defined without considering the physical database organization.

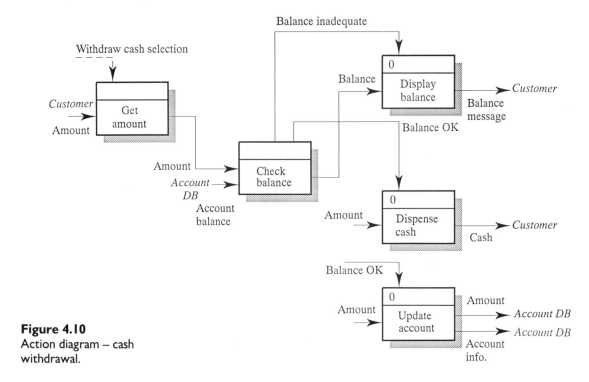

Figure 4.10
Action diagram – cash
withdrawal.

The relational model has been widely used and the advantage of this approach is that the mapping of the model to a commercial relational database management system is straightforward. However, this approach has two main disadvantages. Firstly, data typing is implicit and must be inferred from the relation names. Secondly, logical relations (such as PART-OF, DERIVED-FROM, and so on) between data items are 'second class citizens'. They are represented implicitly rather than explicitly through shared values in a table. The relationships cannot be given attributes.

The lack of typing is a particular problem as systems are increasingly developed using languages like Ada which support a rich type environment. An alternative approach to data modelling with better typing facilities and explicit support of relations allows a more abstract model to be produced. There are a number of possible alternatives which are generically termed semantic data models. These include entity-relation (E-R) modelling (Chen, 1976), SDM (Hammer and McLeod, 1981), and Codd's extension of the relational model, RM/T (1979).

It is not appropriate to describe these semantic data modelling techniques in detail here but, briefly, the E-R model sets out data entities (which, in programming language terms, roughly correspond to record data types) and relations between these entities (which correspond roughly to operations on the entity types). Entities can have attributes (fields of records) as can relations (in programming language terms, private data values). In general, attributes are atomic and are not decomposed although they need not correspond to base types in a programming language.

Types may have subtypes so a special type of relation called an inheritance relation has been introduced to extend the E-R model. Subtypes inherit the attributes of their supertype. Additional private attributes may, of course, be added to the subtype entity. Inheritance is, of course, supported directly in object-oriented programming languages.

The model used here to illustrate this approach is based on an extension of Chen's E-R model as discussed by Hull and King (1987). This involves adding subtyping and supertyping to the basic entity and relation primitives originally defined by Chen.

Semantic data models are invariably described using graphical notations, which is a further advantage over the relational model. These graphical notations are readily understandable by management and users so they can participate in data modelling. The notation used here is set out in Figure 4.11. There are a variety of other notations for describing E-R diagrams, some of which are supported by commercially available CASE tools.

Relations between entities may be 1:1 which means one entity instance participates in a relation with one other entity instance, 1:M which means that an entity instance participates in a relationship with more than one other entity instance or M:N which means that several entity instances

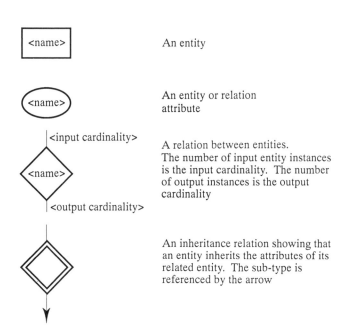

An entity

An entity or relation attribute

A relation between entities. The number of input entity instances is the input cardinality. The number of output instances is the output cardinality

An inheritance relation showing that an entity inherits the attributes of its related entity. The sub-type is referenced by the arrow

Figure 4.11
Notation used in extended E–R models.

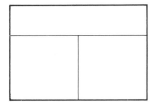

Figure 4.12
An activity symbol.

participate in a relation with several other instances. In this model, M:1 relationships are not supported.

As a simple illustration of data modelling, consider the symbol used in the design editing system shown in Figure 4.12. Symbols representing particular types are composed using built-in primitives such as boxes, ellipses and lines. The editor therefore uses data showing how each composite symbol is made up from simpler symbols. The symbol in Figure 4.12 is built from a box and two lines at particular coordinates with respect to the box.

The model of the data for composite symbols is shown in Figure 4.13.

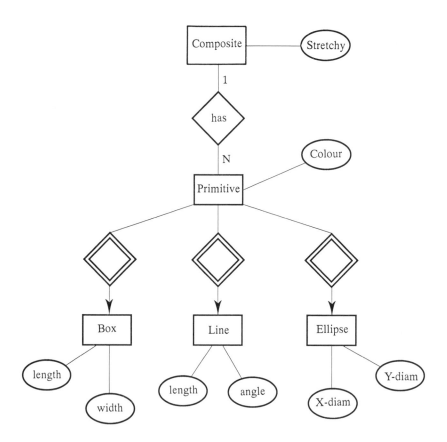

Figure 4.13
Composite symbol model.

This specifies that a composite symbol has a 'stretchy' attribute (which defines whether it is fixed or variable size) and is made up of a number of primitives, each of which has a 'colour' attribute. Primitives may be either boxes, lines or ellipses and each of these subtypes have their own defining attributes.

The design editor is based on the assumption that a design may be represented as a directed graph. The design consists of a set of nodes of different types connected by links representing the relationships between design nodes. There is a screen representation of this graph which is a design diagram and a separate, distinct database representation. The editing system performs a mapping from the database representation to the screen representation every time it draws a diagram.

The information produced by the editor for other tools should include a logical representation of the design graph. Details of the physical screen representation of the design are specific to the editor. Post-processing tools are interested in which entities exist, their logical attributes (such as their name) and their connections. These tools are not interested in information such as the entity coordinates or symbol representations.

The logical organization of this design graph with physical layout information excluded is shown in Figure 4.14. A design is made up of a set of nodes and a set of links. Node and links have name and type attributes and they may have a set of associated labels. Each label has a name and a type and can be either a text label or an icon. A text label has a text attribute and an icon has a bitmap attribute.

On the left of Figure 4.14, a relation 'explodes' is shown which shows that a node can be related to a whole design. Rather than introduce a loop in the model and complicate the layout, the design entity is repeated. To indicate that this is the same entity as the root node in this model, the name is emboldened and the node box is shown with a double line.

Entity-relationship models have been widely used in database design, and Barker (1989) shows that they can be readily implemented using relational databases. The database schemas derived from these models are naturally in third normal form, which is a desirable characteristic of relational schemas. Because of the explicit typing and the recognition of subtypes and supertypes, it is also straightforward to map these models onto object-oriented databases. Although object-oriented database systems are immature, it is likely that they will be widely used in future in application areas such as CAD and software engineering environments.

4.3.1 Data dictionaries

As a system data model is derived, many named entities will be identified which may have to have unique names. Maintaining name uniqueness is

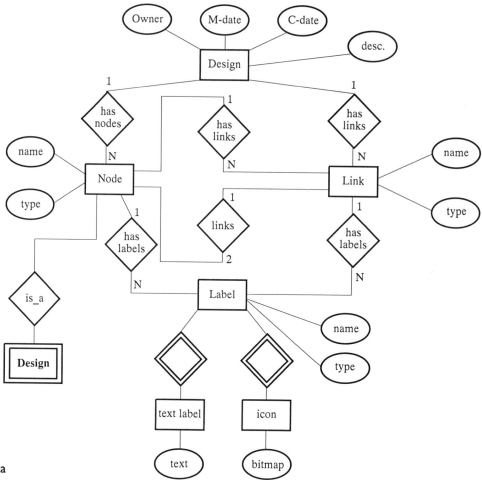

Figure 4.14
Logical editor data
model.

particularly difficult when a number of people are involved in model development and requires automated assistance.

A tool which can be used for name management is a data dictionary. A data dictionary is, simplistically, a list of names used by the system arranged alphabetically. As well as the name, there is normally a description of the named entity and, if the name represents a composite object, there may be a description of the composition. Data dictionaries are valuable in all stages of the software process from initial modelling through to system maintenance.

All system names whether they be names of entities, types, relations, attributes or whatever should be entered in the dictionary. Support software should be available to create, maintain and interrogate the dictionary. This software might be integrated with other tools so that dictionary creation is partially automated.

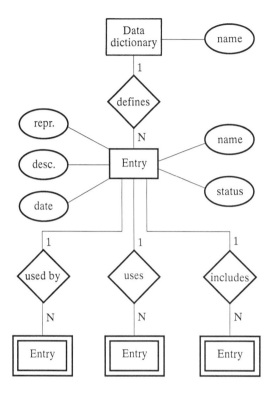

Figure 4.15
Data dictionary model.

A possible logical data model for a data dictionary which is used here and elsewhere in the book is shown in Figure 4.15. This specifies that a data dictionary is made up of a number of entries, each of which has a name, a representation, a description, a creation date and a status (which allows for

Item name	Description	Representation	Date	Status
Item_name	The name of known data items. Used as a key to data dictionary entries.	String	5.10.90	Active
Primitive_set#	An identifier for a set of primitive shapes defining a method symbol.	Integer	8.12.90	Obsolete
Symbol_information	A relation holding a description of a method symbol.	Relation	8.12.90	Active
Top_coord	The coordinate defining the position of the top left-hand corner of a box.	Integer, Integer	8.12.90	Active
Type_name	The name of a basic method type.	String	15.11.90	Active

Figure 4.16
Data dictionary entries.

an entry to become obsolete). Each entry participates in three relations with other entries. These show which entities use that entity, which entities are used by that entity and which entities are included in the entity (for example, operation entities are included in abstract data type entities).

Examples of data dictionary entries are shown in Figure 4.16. The information about the relationships in which each entry participates has been suppressed in Figure 4.16. In an automated data dictionary, this might be made available from a menu associated with each data dictionary entry.

■ KEY POINTS

- A system model presents a description of the real-world entities which are to be represented in the software system. Part of the system model should include a context showing how the system relates to other systems.

- Systems rarely have a single 'top' and the model should be created by considering a number of different viewpoints. Viewpoints can be either functional or non-functional.

- An approach based on data flow is appropriate for modelling the system inputs, processing and outputs. There are a variety of different notations which can be used to express the data flow diagram. A notation from the CORE method is used here.

- It is important to model the data which is imported to the system by other applications and the data which the system exports. An appropriate model is an extended entity-relationship model which shows system entities and attributes and the relationships in which these entities participate. A special type of relationship is used to show how one entity is a subtype of another.

- A data dictionary is an important tool for maintaining information about system entities throughout the lifetime of a project. It is initially populated during system modelling. Entries may be added at any other life cycle stages.

FURTHER READING

Structured Analysis and System Specification. An excellent book covering data flow modelling. Also useful for background reading in software design. (T. DeMarco, 1978, Yourdon Press.)

'Acquisition-environment'. The CORE method is poorly documented but has been successful on a number of aerospace projects. It is mostly documented as internal publications but this book chapter is perhaps the most accessible and reasonably complete description of the method. (G.P. Mullery, in *Distributed Systems: Methods and Tools for Specification*, Paul, M. and Siegert, H.J. (eds), 1985, Springer-Verlag.)

'Semantic database modeling: Survey, applications and research issues'. This is a good survey paper covering the various approaches which have been developed for E-R modelling. (R. Hull and R. King, *ACM Computing Surveys*, **19** (3), 1987.)

EXERCISES

4.1 Modify the viewpoint structure diagram shown in Figure 4.3 to include the viewpoint of a bank employee who is responsible for ensuring that the auto-teller machine is stocked with banknotes.

4.2 Identify the viewpoints which should be considered in implementing the newspaper delivery system introduced in Chapter 3 and produce a system model structured around these viewpoints.

4.3 Construct an action diagram for a bank teller machine which includes a facility allowing a customer to transfer cash from one account to another.

4.4 Expand the 'provide services' box in Figure 4.9 into an action diagram. Use a machine which you know as a basis for deciding what services should be provided.

4.5 A software system is to be developed to automate a library catalogue. This system will contain information about all of the books in a library and will be usable by library staff and by book borrowers and readers. The system should support catalogue browsing, querying, and should provide facilities allowing users to send messages to library staff reserving a book which is on loan. Identify the principal functional viewpoints which must be taken into account in the specification of this system and show their relationships using a viewpoint hierarchy diagram.

4.6 What non-functional viewpoints are likely to be important for the library catalogue system in Exercise 4.5? Give specific reasons why these non-functional viewpoints must be taken into account in this system.

4.7 Using the editor data model shown in Figure 4.14 as a starting point, extend that model to include physical layout information. Nodes may be represented by composite symbols as shown in Figure 4.13 and are displayed at a particular coordinate. Links are made up of a number of line segments which may be solid or dotted lines. Text is displayed in a specified font. The name associated with a node, link or label is positioned relative to the entity.

4.8 Using the model of the data dictionary shown in Figure 4.15, design plausible data dictionary entries for some or all of the names, relations and attributes shown in Figure 4.14 and/or the extended version of the editor model which you have designed in completing exercise 4.6.

4.9 Using an entity-relation approach, describe a possible data model for the newspaper delivery system.

Requirements Specification

■ OBJECTIVES

The principal objective of this chapter is to illustrate how to write a detailed requirements specification. Such a specification is included in most systems as part of the system contract and is the basis for designing system acceptance tests. A detailed specification must include both functional and non-functional requirements and the specification of both of these types of requirement is covered. Functional requirements specification using structured natural language and an Ada-based description language is described, as are metrics for non-functional requirements quantification. The final part of the chapter covers requirements validation and discusses how requirements evolution is inevitable in any useful system.

■ CONTENTS

In this book, I have deliberately separated requirements definition and requirements specification. Requirements definitions are client-oriented specifications and should be written in the client's language. This may require using imprecise notations, natural language and intuitive diagrams. A requirements specification (sometimes called a functional specification) is the basis of the contract for the system; it should not be ambiguous or informal as this may lead to misinterpretation by the client or the system contractor.

Many of the problems of software engineering are difficulties with the requirements specification. It is natural for a system developer to interpret an ambiguous requirement so that its realization is as cheap as possible. Often, however, this is not what the client wants. After a sometimes protracted dispute, new requirements have to be established and changes made to the system. Of course, this delays system delivery and increases costs.

The cost of errors in stating requirements may be very high, particularly if these errors are not discovered until the system is implemented. Boehm (1974) reported that in some large systems up to 95% of the code had to be rewritten to satisfy changed user requirements and that 12% of the faults discovered in a software system over a three year period were due to incorrect system requirements. The majority of program maintenance is not correction of erroneous code. It is required to support changes to system requirements.

The cost of making a system change resulting from a requirements change is much greater than repairing design or coding errors. A requirements change implies that the design and implementation must also be changed and the system testing and validation process repeated. This is more expensive than a program bug fix, for example, which only involves changing and retesting part of the code. The cost of implementing a requirements change, whether it is due to an error or an inconsistency, can be up to one hundred times the cost of fixing an implementation bug.

5.1 Requirements specification notations

A natural language-based notation with accompanying diagrams and tables is appropriate for a requirements definition which must be understood by senior management unfamiliar with specialized notations. However, as the basis of a system contract, a natural language specification is inadequate for the following reasons:

(1) Natural language understanding relies on the specification readers and writers using the same words for the same concept. This can lead to misunderstandings because of the inherent ambiguity of natural

language and because there is no standard computing vocabulary.

(2)   A natural language requirements specification is over-flexible; it allows related requirements to be expressed in completely different ways. The reader has to find related requirements with the consequent likelihood of error and misunderstanding.

(3)   Requirements are not partitioned effectively; the effect of changes can only be determined by examining every requirement rather than a group of related requirements.

It is sometimes suggested that mathematically formal specification languages (covered in Chapters 8 and 9) should be used to express system requirements. These lead to an unambiguous requirements specification, leaving no room for argument between client and contractor about system functionality. Unfortunately, most clients would not understand a formal mathematical specification and would be reluctant to accept it as a system contract.

Hall (1990) suggests that the way to tackle this problem is to develop a formal specification then paraphrase this in a way that is understandable to the user. For some classes of sequential systems, this approach is now technically feasible and, as discussed in Chapter 7, is likely to lead to better specifications and lower development costs. As users become more familiar with the advantages of formal specification and software engineers lose their reluctance to use formal methods, it is likely that more requirements specifications will be based on formal models of the system functionality.

Special-purpose languages have been designed to express software requirements. These include PSL/PSA (Teichrow and Hershey, 1977), SADT (Ross, 1977; Schoman and Ross, 1977) and RSL (Bell et al., 1977; Alford, 1977, 1985). Although each language is intended as a general purpose notation for specifying requirements, these languages were originally designed with different types of application in mind. Other approaches to requirements specification have relied on finite-state machines (discussed in Chapter 13), decision tables (Moret, 1982) and Petri nets (Peterson, 1977). Davis (1988) summarizes and compares these different approaches to requirements specification.

Given that an explicit system model has been created as discussed in Chapter 4, the most appropriate requirements partitioning technique is to use the identified elements of the system model and describe their functionality in more detail. In the CORE method, this is termed adding node notes to the model. These notes may be in the form of mathematical specifications or in any of the notations discussed below.

```
Function:         Check_card_validity

Description:      This operation must ensure that the card input
                  by a user has been issued by a subscribing bank,
                  is in date, contains appropriate account information
                  and includes details of the date and amount of the previous
                  cash withdrawal.

Inputs:           Bank-identifier, Account-number, Expiry-date,
                  Last-transaction-date, Last-transaction
Source:           Input data is read from the card magnetic stripe

Outputs:          Card-status = (OK, invalid)
Destination:      Auto-teller.  The card status is passed to another part
                  of the software.

Requires:         Bank-list, Account-format, Todays-date

Pre-condition:    Card has been input and stripe data read

Post-condition:   Bank-identifier is in Bank-list and
                  Account-number matches Account-format and
                  Expiry-date >= Todays-date and
                  Last-transaction-date <= Todays-date and
                  Card-status = OK
                      or ( if any of these tests fail )
                  Card-status = invalid
Side-effects:     None
```

Figure 5.1
Structured
requirements
specification.

5.1.1 Structured language specifications

Because of the need for understandability, natural language specifications cannot be completely discarded. Many notations have been developed which rely on using natural language in a controlled way using a standard form for requirements specification. They may use control constructs derived from programming languages and use graphical highlighting to structure the requirements specification.

A project which used this approach is described by Heninger (1980). Special purpose forms were designed to describe the input, output and functions of an aircraft software system. The system requirements were specified using these forms. Although the system described by Heninger is a manual one, a form-based approach could obviously be automated.

A form-based approach to requirements specification may be structured around the objects manipulated by the system, the functions performed by the system or the events processed by the system. The form structure will vary depending on the requirements structuring technique used. Functionally-oriented specifications are probably the most common. An example of such a specification, for part of the ATM system, is shown in Figure 5.1.

This specification uses pre- and post-conditions to specify the actions of the function. It is not an operational specification of what the function must do. It uses a number of names (Bank-list, Account-format, and so on) which must, of course, be defined elsewhere in the specification and, if possible, in a data dictionary. This detailed specification does not include any sequencing information – the tests may be carried out in any order. The function sequence is defined in the system model (Figure 4.8).

The form-based approach to specification fits well with formal mathematical specifications. A formal specification can be defined and paraphrased in a set of forms which are understandable as a system contract. Alternatively, a formal specification can be defined from the structured forms as the first stage in the design process and used to refine the requirements specification.

Using formatted specifications removes some of the problems of natural language specification in that the specification is structured but the ambiguity of the description may still be a problem. The other approaches described below go some way towards tackling the problem of specification ambiguity but at the expense, perhaps, of readability.

5.1.2 Requirements specification using a PDL

To counter the inherent ambiguities in natural language specification, it is possible to describe requirements operationally using a program description language (PDL). A PDL is a language derived from a programming language like Ada but it may contain additional, more abstract , constructs to increase its expressive power. The advantage of using a PDL is that it may be checked syntactically and semantically by software tools. Requirements omissions and inconsistencies may be inferred from the results of these checks.

An argument against using a PDL for describing specifications is that it forces the reader to view the specifications in an operational way. The specification is presented as a set of operations on a system model and is hence less abstract than a system description. However, this may be a strength rather than a limitation of this style of requirements specification.

Humans understand abstractions by building models which may be abstract models or may have some other representation. Chemists represent molecules by combinations of coloured balls and wires, architects draw up plans of buildings, and so on. These models are very helpful in understanding the entities in a system and their relationships.

From a user's point of view, specifying the requirements as operations on a system model can make the requirements easier to understand. The dangers are:

(1)   The model will be constrained by the modelling language and not representative of the application domain.

(2)   The model will be seen as a design model rather than a model to help the user understand the system.

```
procedure Check_card_validity ( Bank_identifier : BANK ;
     Bank_list : SET_OF_BANK ; Number : ACCOUNT_NUMBER ;
     Last_transaction_date, Todays_date : DATE ;
     Last_transaction : POSITIVE ; Card_status : in out STATUS ) is
-- Function Is_a_member_of checks if the given Bank identifier is
-- held in the list of participating banks
-- Valid_format  checks the account number to ensure that the
-- initial check digit is correct
begin
  if Expiry_date >= Todays_date and
     Last_transaction_date <= Todays_date and
     Valid_format (Account_number) and
     Is_a_Member_of (Bank_list, Bank_identifier) then
          Card_status := OK ;
     else
          Card_status := Invalid ;
  end if ;
end Check_card_validity ;
```

Figure 5.2
Card validity checking.

Both of these problems can be avoided if the language used is sufficiently abstract; model representation issues can then be ignored.

One of the difficulties of introducing any specialized notation is the high training and start-up costs. These can be reduced when the notation is a derivative of a high-level language like Ada because more teaching material is available and because those involved in the project may have previous language experience. This approach has been described by Mander (1981) and Hill (1983).

Mander compares requirements definition in Ada to definition in notations such as SADT and PSL/PSA. He concludes that Ada is as expressive as these languages as long as extensive use is made of comments to provide additional information to the reader. A similar approach is described by Luckham and Von Henke (1985), who describe a formal specification language based on Ada. In this language, extra information is provided as formal comments. These are introduced by a special comment symbol so that they may be identified for machine processing.

To illustrate the use of an Ada-based PDL for specification, Figure 5.2 shows how the specification of card validity checking (Figure 5.1) may be expressed using a PDL. Ideally, the requirements specification should be produced with the aid of tool support which will ensure the correspondence between the detailed specification and the associated part of the system model.

Ada/PDL descriptions tend to be more concise than corresponding structured language descriptions but are less readable unless staff have experience of Ada programming. The type definition facilities do allow very precise data specifications (see the following section) and there may be situations where it is appropriate to combine structured language and PDL descriptions.

```
procedure Request_PIN (PIN : in out PIN_STRING )
    -- the PIN is represented as a string of 4 characters
    D : CHARACTER ;
begin
    User_request ("Please type your personal number") ;
    for i in 1.. 4 loop
        Get_character _from_keypad (D) ;
        Put_onto_screen ("*") ;
        PIN (i) := D ;
    end loop ;
end Request_PIN ;
```

Figure 5.3
PIN request.

The use of an Ada-based PDL has particular advantages in two situations:

(1)   When an operation is specified as a sequence of simpler actions and the order in which these actions is carried out is important. Descriptions of such sequences in natural language are difficult to read.

(2)   When an object-oriented approach is taken to system modelling and the objects identified in the model have to be specified in more detail.

Figure 5.3, taken from the bank auto-teller system, shows the first of these situations where a sequence of actions is involved. The sequence involves issuing a prompt then reading characters one at a time, and echoing a '*' to show the character has been received.

The auto-teller system is not inherently object-oriented so is not a good source of examples to illustrate this use of an Ada/PDL. Rather,

```
-- The package Node sets out all of the allowed operations on entities
-- of type Node.  These are referenced Node.Delete, Node. Move, etc.
package  Node is
    -- Nodes may be moved around the diagram
    procedure Move ;
    -- Nodes may be deleted. Also deletes associated links
    procedure Delete ;
    -- Nodes may have associated labels giving further information
    -- about the entity they represent.  Name and type are typical labels
    procedure Annotate_with_label ;
    -- Nodes may be adjusted in size
    procedure Resize ;
  -- A new entry for the node in the design database may be made
    procedure Add_to_design ;
    -- The node may be linked to an existing design in the database
    procedure Link_with_database ;
    -- The icon associated with the node may be determined
    procedure Get_icon ;
end Node ;
```

Figure 5.4
The functions
associated with nodes.

Figure 5.4 is taken from the design editing system introduced in Chapter 3. It shows that an object in the system is a node, which represents some design entity. Various operations on that node are defined in the package specification.

The package construct provides a convenient mechanism for grouping operations associated with an object. The operations have been specified as parameterless procedures; at this stage there is no need to define specific inputs and outputs to these procedures. The procedure parameters are specified when the specification is developed in more detail.

Ada is not an ideal notation for requirements specification but when it is necessary to supplement a diagram and natural language based requirements definition with more details and when the client and contractor both have Ada experience, it may be the most cost-effective notation to use. However, its use must be carefully controlled so that the overall system design is not unduly influenced by the requirements specification language.

5.2   Non-functional requirements

Figure 5.5
Types of non-functional requirements.

A non-functional system requirement is a restriction or constraint placed on a system service. This may arise because of user needs, because of budget constraints, because of organizational policies, because of the need for inter-operability with other software or hardware systems or because of external factors such as safety regulations, privacy legislation, and so on. Thus, there are several different types of non-functional requirements (Figure 5.5).

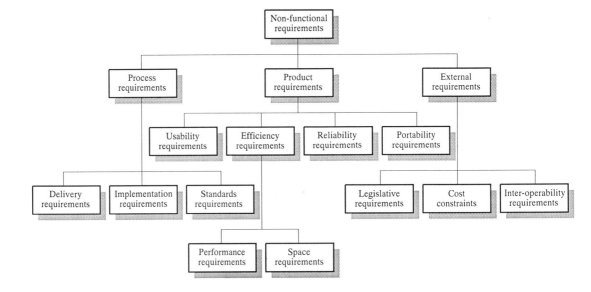

The three principal classes of non-functional requirement are:

(1) *Product requirements*   These are requirements placed on the system under development. Examples include speed and space requirements, reliability requirements, portability requirements and usability requirements. These non-functional requirements may be derived directly from user needs.

(2) *Process requirements*   These are requirements placed on the development process used for system development. Examples include process standards which must be used, implementation requirements such as the programming language or design method used and delivery requirements which set out when the product and its documentation are to be delivered.

(3) *External requirements*   This broad heading covers all requirements which are neither product nor process requirements. These include requirements for inter-operability setting out how the system is to interact with other systems, requirements derived from current legislation, cost requirements which set a budget for product or the group undertaking the development, and so on. It is common for requirements in this class to be left implicit on the understanding that project managers understand the need for them. This often causes problems after development is complete.

Figure 5.6 shows examples of product requirements, process requirements and external requirements.

The product requirement restricts the freedom of APSE designers in their choice of symbols which might be used in the APSE user interface. It says nothing about the functionality of the APSE and clearly identifies a

> 4.C.8 It shall be possible for all necessary communication between the APSE and the user to be expressed in the standard Ada character set.

Product requirement

> 9.3.2 The system development process and deliverable documents shall conform to the process and deliverables set out in DEF-STAN 00-65.

Process requirement

> 7.6.5 The system shall be integrated with the existing company database, specified in DOC-DB-10-90 and shall not require any database schema changes to be made.

External requirement

Figure 5.6
Non-functional
requirements.

Property	Metric
Speed	Processed transactions/second User/Event response time Screen refresh time
Size	K Bytes Number of RAM chips
Ease of use	Training time Number of help frames
Reliability	Mean time to failure Probability of unavailability Rate of failure occurrence Availability
Robustness	Time to restart after failure Percentage of events causing failure Probability of data corruption on failure
Portability	Percentage of target dependent statements Number of target systems

Figure 5.7
Requirements metrics.

system constraint rather than a function. The process requirement specifies that the system must be developed according to a standard process defined as DEF-STAN-0065. The external requirement states that the system must integrate with a database without requiring database changes.

Non-functional requirements define system properties and constraints. Examples of system properties are reliability, response time and store occupancy. Examples of constraints are the capabilities of the I/O devices attached to the system and the data representations used by other systems with which the required system must communicate.

Non-functional requirements must be testable so should be expressed quantitatively using an accepted metric or one devised specially for the system. Figure 5.7 shows possible metrics which may be used.

A very common error in expressing requirements is to express general objectives as system requirements. For example, Figure 5.8 is a typical example of a product 'requirement' concerning system usability. Leaving aside the fact that there might be two requirements expressed in Figure 5.8 (easy to use and tolerant of error), this requirement cannot be tested. The notions of ease of use and error minimization are subjective. Requirements statements of this type are the cause of a great deal of customer dissatisfaction in delivered software systems.

A better expression of this requirement might state it in terms of the time required to learn to make use of the system and the number of errors expected over a given time period (Figure 5.9). This is clearly an imperfect statement of requirement in that ease of use and short training time are not necessarily related. However, it can be tested and this means that it is superior to untestable requirements such as those in Figure 5.8.

> The system should be easy to use by experienced controllers and should be organized in such a way that user errors are minimized.

Figure 5.8
An untestable
non-functional
requirement.

> Experienced controllers should be able to use all of the system functions after a total of two hours training. After this training, the average number of errors made by experienced users should not exceed two per day.

Figure 5.9
A testable
non-functional
requirement.

When expressing non-functional requirements, the level of reliability required of the system should be defined. In many requirement documents, reliability is implicit, leaving opportunities for dispute between client and contractor over whether or not the system is adequately reliable. By expressing an explicit reliability requirement, the client is forced to consider what real reliability the system should exhibit. Reliability quantification is discussed in Chapter 20 and the metrics described should be used to express reliability requirements.

Non-functional requirements often conflict and interact with other system functional requirements. For example, it may be a requirement that the maximum store occupied by a system should be 256K because the entire system has to be fitted into read-only memory (ROM) and installed on a spacecraft. A further requirement might be that the system should be written in Ada but it may be the case that an Ada program providing the required functionality cannot be compiled into less than 256K. Some trade-off must be made either by using some other language, reducing the functionality or by increasing the ROM storage available.

Natural language is the usual means of expressing non-functional requirements as no formal notation is sufficiently expressive. A notable exception to this is in the specification of interface requirements where the software system has to interface with other hardware and software. In this case, a PDL can be used if it includes a means of representation specification.

Say the required system must be integrated with an existing system composed of several processes running on independent processors. The existing system has already established representation standards and the new system must conform to these. For example, processes might communicate their state by exchanging messages with other processes. The following definition states the messages which might be expected by the required system.

```
type STATE is (Halted, Waiting, Ready, Running) ;
for STATE use (Halted => 1, Waiting => 4, Ready => 16,
     Running => 256) ;
```

This declares that Halted is represented by 1, Waiting by 4, Ready by 16, and Running by 256.

Similarly, the required system may be required to communicate with the other processes using a pre-existing message format. Ada type definitions are a particularly suitable means of expressing this interface.

```
type MESSAGE is record
     Sender : SYSTEM_ID ;
     Receiver : SYSTEM_ID ;
     Dispatch_time : DATE ;
     Length : MESSAGE_LENGTH ;
     Terminator : CHARACTER ;
     Message : TEXT ;
end record ;
```

The types used in this structural specification may also be defined.

```
type SYSTEM_ID is range 20_000..30_000 ;
type YEAR_TYPE is range 1980..2080 ;
type DATE is record
     Seconds : NATURAL ;
     Year : YEAR_TYPE ;
end record ;
type MESSAGE_LENGTH is range 0..10_000 ;
type TEXT is array (MESSAGE_LENGTH) of CHARACTER ;
```

Ada's facilities to specify information representation allow the sizes of type representations to be set out. This is accomplished by using the SIZE attribute and specifying the number of bytes entities of that type take up.

```
for SYSTEM_ID'SIZE use 2*BYTE ;
for YEAR_TYPE'SIZE use 2*BYTE ;
for MESSAGE_LENGTH'SIZE use 2*BYTE ;
```

The major problem in analysing non-functional requirements is that functional and non-functional requirements should be differentiated yet individual non-functional requirements may relate to one or more functional requirements. If the non-functional requirements are stated separately from the functional requirements, it is sometimes difficult to see the correspondence between them. If stated with the functional requirements, it may be difficult to separate functional and non-functional considerations.

A tabular summary of system properties, non-functional requirements and the particular requirements definition to which these relate should therefore always be provided as part of a requirements specification.

This fundamental problem arises because requirements participate in many different types of relationship with other requirements. It is not possible to identify explicitly all of these relationships by requirements grouping. This problem can only really be solved when we use electronic document systems supporting multiple document views.

Hypertext systems (Conklin, 1987) allow non-sequential requirements specifications to be developed. However, these will not replace paper documents until they are acceptable as the basis of a legal contract. Rather, we can expect to see requirements 'road-maps' produced using hypertext systems which act as a guide to the reader of a requirements specification.

5.3   Requirements validation

Once a set of system requirements has been established, it must be validated to show that it meets the needs of the system procurer. If this validation is inadequate, errors in the requirements will be propagated to the system design and implementation, and expensive system modifications may be required to correct them.

There are four separate steps involved in validating requirements:

(1)   *The needs of the user should be shown to be valid*   A user may think that a system is needed to perform certain functions but further thought and analysis may identify additional or different functions which are required. Systems have diverse users with different needs and any set of requirements is inevitably a compromise across the user community.

(2)   *The requirements should be shown to be consistent*   Any one requirement should not conflict with any other.

(3)   *The requirements should be shown to be complete*   The definition should include all functions and constraints intended by the system user.

(4)   *The requirements should be shown to be realistic*   There is no point in specifying requirements which are unrealizable. It may be acceptable to anticipate some hardware developments but developments in software technology are much less predictable.

Demonstrating that a set of requirements meets a user's needs is extremely difficult if an abstract approach is adopted. By reading a definition and specification, users must picture the system in operation and imagine how that system would fit into their work. It is difficult for skilled computer professionals to perform this type of abstract analysis; it is almost impossible for system users. As a result, many systems are delivered which do not meet the user's needs and which are simply discarded after delivery. Thus, prototyping (see Chapter 6), where an executable model of the system is

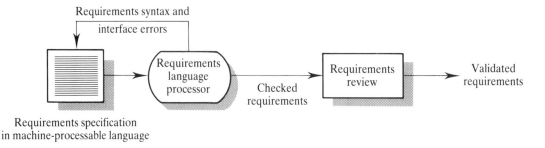

Figure 5.10
Automated checking of
the requirements
specification.

demonstrated to users, is an important requirements validation technique.

Validation should not be seen as a process to be carried out after the requirements document has been completed. Regular requirements reviews involving both users and software engineers are essential while the requirements definition is being formulated. Requirements reviews can be informal or formal. Informal reviews simply involve contractors discussing requirements with clients. It is surprising how often this does not take place and how many problems can be detected by simply talking about the system to users.

In a formal requirements review, the development team should 'walk' the client through the system requirements explaining the implications of each requirement. Conflicts and contradictions should be pointed out. It is then up to the users and system procurer to modify the requirements to resolve these problems and contradictions.

A requirements review is a manual process which involves multiple readers from both client and contractor staff checking the requirements document for anomalies and omissions. The review process may be managed in the same way as design reviews (see Chapter 31) or may be organized on a larger scale with many participants involved in checking different parts of the document.

Requirements reviews are generally successful in detecting many errors in the requirements definition and they are really the only approach which can check the completeness of requirements. However, the consistency of the requirements is best checked using some automated tool and this is only possible when the requirements are expressed in a formal language (Figure 5.10).

Expressing the requirements in an Ada/PDL allows interface inconsistencies to be detected and these are often the most crucial in any large system. If this is supplemented by a precise description of the system expressed using a logic-based notation, behavioural inconsistencies can also be identified using checking tools.

The realism of requirements can be demonstrated, in some cases, by constructing a system simulator. The technique of system simulation is particularly useful to demonstrate that non-functional requirements can be met. One of the tools used in conjunction with the requirements statement language (RSL) is a simulator generator. This tool analyses an RSL definition and automatically generates a system simulator in Pascal. Procedures which simulate each functional definition are provided by the specifier as part of the requirements definition.

However, for complex systems, it can be as expensive and as time-consuming to develop the system simulator as it is to develop the system itself (Davis and Vick, 1977). Furthermore, it may be difficult to change the simulator so that changes in the requirements may be impossible to assess by simulation. As a result, simulation has not been extensively used in validating the requirements of large systems although it can result in a significant reduction in requirements errors.

■ KEY POINTS

- A requirements specification (sometimes called a functional specification) is the basis for the contract for system development.

- Unstructured paragraphs of natural language are inadequate for expressing a clear, understandable and consistent requirements specification.

- An Ada/PDL may be used to present an operational expression of system requirements.

- Detailed requirements specifications should be built around the entities identified in the system model.

- Non-functional requirements tend to be so varied and complex that natural language must be used for their expression.

- Requirements should be expressed in such a way that they are testable.

- Requirements errors are usually more expensive to correct after system delivery than design or implementation errors. Thus, requirements validation is a very important part of the requirements analysis and specification phase.

- Reviews involving both client and contractor are a useful requirements validation technique.

FURTHER READING

The further reading suggested in Chapter 3 is also appropriate for this chapter.

Software Requirements: Analysis and Specification. This relatively new book surveys various techniques for requirements specification and definition and is an excellent general text on software requirements. (A.M. Davis, 1990, Prentice-Hall.)

EXERCISES

5.1 Discuss the problems of using natural language for requirements specification and show, using small examples, how structuring natural language into forms can help avoid some of these difficulties.

5.2 Discover ambiguities or omissions in the following statement of requirements for part of a ticket issuing system.

> A ticket issuing system is intended to automate the sale of rail tickets. Users select their destination, and input a credit card and a personal identification number. The rail ticket is issued and their credit card account charged with its cost. When the user presses the start button, a menu display of potential destinations is activated along with a message to the user to select a destination. Once a destination has been selected, users are requested to input their credit card. Its validity is checked and the user is then requested to input a personal identifier. When the credit transaction has been validated, the ticket is issued.

5.3 Produce a requirements specification of the above system using an Ada-based notation. You may make any reasonable assumptions about the system. Pay particular attention to specifying user errors.

5.4 Write a set of non-functional requirements for the ticket issuing system, setting out its expected reliability and its response time.

5.5 Using an Ada-based notation, write a requirements specification for the newspaper delivery system described in the exercises in Chapter 4. Include both functional and non-functional requirements. Pay particular attention to the fact that people like to have their newspapers delivered whether or not the computer system is operational.

5.6 Discuss the use of Ada representation clauses in the presentation of non-functional requirements. Suggest how Ada representation clauses might be extended in a PDL for requirements specification so that they may be used to describe a greater number of non-functional requirements.

5.7 Who should be involved in a requirements review? Suggest how such a review should be conducted.

5.8 Rewrite the following requirements so that they may be objectively validated. You may make any reasonable assumptions about the requirements.

The software system should provide acceptable performance under maximum load conditions.

The system interface should use a character set as available on a standard terminal.

If the system should fail in operation, there should be minimal loss of data.

The software development process used should ensure that all of the required reviews have been carried out.

Structured programming should be used for program development.

The software must be developed in such a way that it can be used by inexperienced users.

Software Prototyping

6

■ OBJECTIVES

An important technique of requirements validation is rapid prototyping. A prototype software system may be developed from an outline specification. Users experiment with the prototype to refine and improve the specification. This chapter discusses the advantages of prototyping, the activities involved in prototyping and managerial problems which can arise. The role of prototyping in the software process is covered and throw-away prototyping is compared with exploratory programming and incremental development. Some prototyping techniques are briefly discussed, namely executable formal specification languages, very high-level languages, fourth-generation languages and prototyping with reusable components. The final part of the chapter is concerned with user interface prototyping and suggests that user-centred interface design based on prototyping is the most effective way of developing satisfactory user interfaces.

■ CONTENTS

Reviews are a critical part of the requirements validation process but many potential users of a system have difficulty in imagining how the system is used from a requirements specification alone. While a function described in a specification may seem useful and well-defined, the reality of using that function in combination with others may reveal that the user's initial view was incorrect or incomplete.

One way to counter the difficulty which users have in formulating and understanding static specifications is to develop a system prototype and to allow system users to experiment with it. The system requirements are validated because users discover requirements errors or omissions early in the software process.

Software prototyping is quite different from hardware prototyping. When developing hardware systems, it is normal practice to develop a system prototype to validate the system design. An electronic system prototype may be realized and tested using off-the-shelf components before investment is made in expensive, special-purpose integrated circuits to implement the production version of the system. A software prototype is not intended for design validation (its design will often be quite different from the final system developed) but to validate the user requirements.

The benefits of developing a prototype early in the software process are:

(1)   Misunderstandings between software developers and users may be identified as the system functions are demonstrated.

(2)   Missing user services may be detected.

(3)   Difficult-to-use or confusing user services may be identified and refined.

(4)   Software development staff may find incomplete and/or inconsistent requirements as the prototype is developed.

(5)   A working, albeit limited, system is available quickly to demonstrate the feasibility and usefulness of the application to management.

(6)   The prototype serves as a basis for writing the specification for a production quality system.

Although the principal purpose of prototyping is to validate software requirements, Ince and Hekmatpour (1987) point out that a software prototype also has other uses:

(1)   It can be used for training users before the production-quality system has been delivered.

(2)   It can be used during system testing to run 'back-to-back' tests. This means that the same test cases are submitted to both the prototype and to the system being tested. If both systems give the same result, it

probably means that the test case has not detected a fault in the system. If the results are different, this may mean that there is a system fault. Tedious, manual examination of test cases can be reduced using this technique. Back-to-back testing is discussed in Chapter 23.

One way to view prototyping is as a technique of risk reduction. A significant risk in software development is requirements errors and omissions and, as discussed in Chapter 5, the costs of rectifying such errors at later stages in the process can be very high. Experiments have shown (Boehm *et al.*, 1984) that prototyping reduces the number of problems with the requirements specification and the overall development costs may be lower if a prototype is developed.

There are four stages in prototype development:

(1)   Establish prototype objectives.
(2)   Select functions for prototype inclusion and make decisions on what non-functional requirements must be prototyped.
(3)   Develop the prototype.
(4)   Evaluate the prototype system.

The objectives of prototyping should be made explicit before the activity begins. The objective may be to develop a system which is principally concerned with user interface prototyping; it may be to develop a system to validate functional system requirements; it may be to develop a system to demonstrate the feasibility of the application to management and so on. The same prototype cannot meet all objectives. If objectives are left implicit, management or end-users may misunderstand the function of the prototype and fail to gain the full benefit from the prototyping exercise.

The next stage in the process to is decide what to put into and, perhaps more importantly, what to leave out of the prototype system. Software prototyping is expensive if the prototype is implemented using the same tools and to the same standards as the final system. Thus, it may be decided to prototype all system functions but at a reduced level. Alternatively a subset of system functions may be included in the prototype. Normal practice in prototype development is to relax non-functional requirements such as speed and space. Error handling and management may be ignored or may be rudimentary unless the objective of the prototype is to establish a user interface. Standards of reliability and program quality may be reduced.

The final stage of the process is prototype evaluation. Ince and Hekmatpour (1987) suggest that this is the most important stage of prototyping. Provision must be made during this stage for user training and the prototype objectives should be used to derive a plan for evaluation.

Sufficient time must be allowed for users to become comfortable with the system and to settle into a normal pattern of usage and thus discover requirements errors and omissions.

The major technical problems associated with prototyping revolve around the need for rapid software development. However, non-technical problems have meant that rapid prototyping is still not widely used, except in data processing system development. Some of these management problems are:

(1)   Planning, costing and estimating a prototyping project is outside the experience of most software project managers.

(2)   Current procedures for change and configuration management are unsuitable for controlling the rapid change inherent in prototyping. However, if there are no change management procedures, evaluation is difficult because the evaluators are trying to assess a constantly changing system.

(3)   Managers may exert pressure on prototype evaluators to reach swift conclusions about the prototype and these may result in inappropriate requirements.

A common argument against prototyping is that the cost of prototype development represents an unacceptably large fraction of the total system costs. It may be more economic to modify a finished system to meet unperceived needs than to provide an opportunity for the user to understand and refine his needs before the final system is built.

This may be true for some systems but effective prototyping increases software quality and hence can give software developers a competitive edge over their competitors. The experience of the US and the UK automobile industries who failed to invest in quality procedures in the 1960s and 1970s and who lost a great deal of their market share to higher quality Japanese automobiles is a telling illustration of how a 'build it cheap and fix it later' philosophy can be extremely expensive in the long term.

As discussed in Chapter 1, prototyping is a key technique in the spiral process model for risk evaluation. By developing a prototype, uncertainties about the system can be resolved. Short-term additional costs can result in long-term savings as requirements and design decisions are clarified during the prototyping process.

6.1   Prototyping in the software process

The fundamental problem which faces users who are defining a new software system is that it is difficult to assess how it will affect their work.

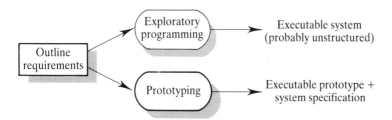

Figure 6.1
Exploratory
programming and
prototyping.

For new systems, particularly if these are large and complex, it is probably impossible to make this assessment before the system is built and put into use.

One way of tackling this difficulty is to use an exploratory approach to systems development. This means presenting the user with a system knowing it to be incomplete and then modifying and augmenting that system as the user's real requirements become apparent. Alternatively, a deliberate decision might be made to build a 'throw-away' prototype as a basis for requirements capture. After evaluation, the prototype is discarded and a production-quality system built.

The distinction between these two approaches is that exploratory programming starts out with a vague understanding of the system requirements and augments the system as new requirements are discovered. There is no such thing as a system specification and, indeed, systems developed by this approach may be unspecifiable (some AI systems cannot be completely specified, for example). By contrast, the prototyping approach is intended to discover the system specification so that the output of the prototype development phase is that specification (Figure 6.1).

A software process model based on an initial prototyping stage is illustrated in Figure 6.2. This approach extends the requirements analysis process with the intention of reducing overall life cycle costs. The prototype is a 'throw-away' prototype whose principal function is to clarify requirements and provide additional information for managers to assess process

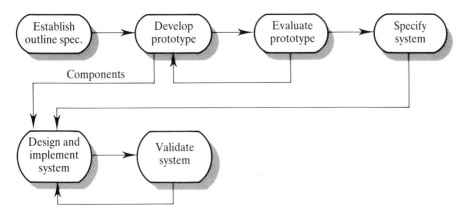

Figure 6.2
Prototyping in the
software process.

risks. After evaluation, the prototype is thrown away and is not used as a basis for further system development.

The process model in Figure 6.2 assumes that the prototype is developed from an outline system specification, delivered for experiment and modified until the client is satisfied with its functionality. At this stage, a conventional software process model is entered, a specification is derived from the prototype and the system re-implemented in a final production version.

Rather than derive a specification from the prototype, it is sometimes suggested that the system specification is the prototype implementation itself. The instruction to the software contractor should simply be 'write a system like this one'. There are several problems with this approach:

(1) Important system features may have been deliberately left out of the prototype to simplify rapid implementation. In fact, it may not be possible to prototype some of the most important parts of the system such as safety-critical features.

(2) An implementation is an inadequate basis for a contract between client and contractor. The ensuing contract will probably have no legal standing.

(3) Non-functional requirements such as those concerning reliability, robustness and safety cannot be adequately expressed in a prototype implementation.

(4) The user may not use the prototype in the same way as an operational system. This may be due to unfamiliarity with the system or may be because of some characteristic of the prototype, For example, if the prototype is slow, users may adjust their way of working and by avoiding some system features, adapt to slow response times. When provided with better response, they may use the system in a different way and utilize functions which have not been evaluated.

When large, long-lifetime systems are to be developed, the prototype should be re-implemented. There are several reasons why this is necessary:

(1) Important system characteristics such as performance, security, robustness and reliability may have been ignored during prototype development so that a rapid implementation could be developed. The nature of the prototype may be such that these cannot be added on to it.

(2) During the prototype development, the prototype will have been changed to reflect user needs and it is likely that these changes will have been made in an uncontrolled way. The only design specification is the prototype code. This an inadequate basis for long-term maintenance.

(3) The changes made during prototype development will probably have degraded the system structure so that subsequent changes because of maintenance requirements become progressively more difficult to make.

An alternative process model which attempts to combine the advantages of exploratory programming with the control required for large-scale development has been reported by Mills *et al.* (1980). This has been termed incremental development (Figure 6.3) and involves developing the requirements and delivering the system in an incremental fashion. Thus, as a part of the system is delivered, the user may experiment with it and provide feedback to later parts of the system. This is a sensible approach but may be limited in applicability because of possible contractual problems.

Incremental development avoids the problems of constant change which characterize exploratory programming. An overall system architecture is established early in the process to act as a framework. System components are incrementally developed and delivered within this framework. Once these have been validated and delivered, neither the framework nor the components are changed unless errors are discovered. User feedback from delivered components, however, can influence the design of components scheduled for later delivery.

Evolutionary development is more manageable than exploratory programming as the normal software process standards are followed. Plans and documentation must be produced for each system increment. It allows some user feedback early in the process and limits system errors as the development team are not concerned with interactions between quite different parts of the software system. Once an increment has been

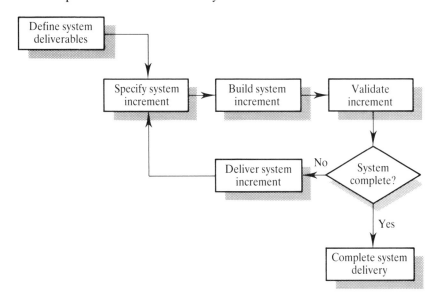

Figure 6.3
Incremental development.

delivered, its interfaces are frozen. Later increments must adapt to these interfaces and can be tested against them.

6.2 Prototyping techniques

System prototyping techniques should allow the rapid development of a prototype system. As staff costs are the principal software cost, rapid development means that prototype costs are minimized. It also means that feedback from users can be obtained early in the overall software process.

There are a number of techniques which have been used for system prototyping. These include:

(1) Executable specification languages.
(2) Very high level languages.
(3) Application-oriented high-level languages (fourth-generation languages).
(4) Composition of reusable components.

Each of these is described below.

6.2.1 Executable specification languages

The formal specification of software systems is the topic of the following three chapters. A formal specification is a mathematical system model which may be executable. This depends on removing generality from the specification (for example, infinite sets cannot be supported) and a number of executable formal specification languages have been developed (Henderson and Minkowitz, 1986; Lee and Sluizer, 1985; Gallimore *et al.*, 1989). Diller (1990) discusses techniques of animating formal specifications written in Z, the specification language covered in Chapter 9.

Examples of formal specifications are presented in Chapters 8 and 9. The advantage of this method of prototype development is that the cost of producing a specification from the prototype is negligible. The code of the prototype is the system specification. However, this is unlikely to be understandable to users so there is still a requirement to derive a descriptive specification from its mathematical equivalent.

There are three problems with this approach to prototype development:

(1) Graphical user interfaces cannot be prototyped using this technique. Although models of a graphical interface can be formally specified (Took, 1986), these cannot be systematically animated using current windowing systems.

(2)   Prototype development may not be particularly rapid. Formal
       specification requires a detailed system analysis and much time may
       be devoted to the detailed modelling of system functions which are
       rejected after prototype evaluation.

(3)   The executable system is usually slow and inefficient. Users may get a
       false impression of the system and compensate for this slowness
       during evaluation. They may not use the system in the same way they
       would use a more efficient version. Users may therefore define a
       different set of requirements from those which would be suggested if a
       faster prototype was available.

The first two problems can be addressed by using functional programming
languages for system development. A functional language is a formal
language which relies on expressing the system as a mathematical function.
Evaluation of that function (which is obviously decomposed into many other
functions) is equivalent to executing a procedural program. Examples of
practical functional languages are Miranda (Turner, 1985) and ML
(Wikstrom, 1988). High quality implementations of both of these languages
are available and both have been used for the development of non-trivial
prototype systems.

     Functional languages might also be classed as very high-level
languages as discussed in the following section. They allow a very concise
expression of the problem to be solved. Because of their mathematical basis,
a functional program can also be viewed as a formal system specification.
However, the execution speed of functional programs on sequential
hardware is typically several orders of magnitude slower than conventional
programs and this limits their utility for prototyping large software systems.

6.2.2 Very high-level languages

Very high-level languages (sometimes misleadingly called fifth-generation
languages) are programming languages with inherent dynamic data structures
and high-level features such as backtracking. The language system includes
many facilities which normally have to be built from more primitive
constructs in languages like Pascal or Ada. Examples of very high-level
languages are LISP (based on list structures), Prolog (based on logic),
Smalltalk (based on objects), APL (based on vectors) and SETL (based on
sets). They are useful prototyping languages because their dynamic features
mean that rapid system development is possible.

     Very high-level dynamic languages are not normally used for large
system development because they need a large run-time support system.
This run-time support increases the storage needs and reduces the execution
speeds of programs written in the language. As performance requirements
can sometimes be ignored in prototype development, however, this is not
necessarily a disadvantage.

Language	Type	Application domain
Smalltalk	Object-oriented	User interfaces
Prolog	Logic	Symbolic processing
LISP	Functional	Symbolic processing
Miranda	Functional	Symbolic processing
SETL	Set-based	Symbolic processing
APL	Mathematical	Scientific systems
4GLs	Database	Business DP
RAPID/USE	Graphical	Business DP
Gist/REFINE	Wide-spectrum	Symbolic processing
LOOPS	Wide-spectrum	As LISP + user interfaces

Figure 6.4
Prototyping languages.

A number of different high-level languages have been used for prototyping. Figure 6.4 summarizes prototype programming languages and suggests the most appropriate application domain where these languages can be applied. However, the domains suggested are not exclusive and the languages may be used for prototyping other classes of application system. This table also includes fourth-generation languages, discussed in the following section.

Gomaa (1983) has reported the successful use of APL as a prototyping language. He describes the advantages of developing a prototype for a process management and information system. Prototype development costs were less than 10% of the total system costs. In the development of the production-quality system, no requirements definition problems were encountered. The project was completed on time and the system was well-received by users.

One of the most powerful prototyping systems for user interfaces (and for other functions) is the Smalltalk system (Goldberg and Robson, 1983). Smalltalk is an object-oriented programming language which is tightly integrated with its environment. This environment includes a graphical user interface as described in Chapter 14. Most system interaction is via menus where selections are made by pointing with the mouse. Smalltalk is an excellent prototyping language for two reasons:

(1)   The object-oriented nature of the language means that systems are resilient to change. Rapid modifications of a Smalltalk system are possible without unforeseen effects on the rest of the system. Indeed, Smalltalk is only suitable for this style of development and is not well suited to a single, monolithic development approach.

(2)   The Smalltalk system and environment is an inherent part of the language. All of the objects defined there are available to the Smalltalk programmer. Thus, a large number of reusable components are available which may be incorporated in the prototype under development.

All the other languages in Figure 6.4 have been used for prototyping and the selection of an appropriate language depends on the application being prototyped. However, an important parameter is the support environment which is available with the language. In this respect, LISP and Smalltalk have far better environments than the alternatives and they have thus been the most widely used prototyping languages.

A class of programming languages which have been proposed as programming languages are the so-called multi-paradigm or wide-spectrum programming languages. Examples of such languages are Gist (Balzer *et al.*, 1982), EPROL (Hekmatpour and Ince, 1988), and LOOPS (Stefik *et al.*, 1986).

A wide-spectrum language is a programming language which combines a number of paradigms. Most languages are based on a single paradigm. Pascal is an imperative language, LISP is based on functions and lists, Prolog is based on facts and logic, and so on. By contrast, a wide-spectrum language is not restricted and may include objects, logic programming, imperative constructs, and so on. Although there has been a good deal of interest in such languages, the practical problems of developing efficient implementations have meant that few commercial language products are available.

Gist and its commercial derivative REFINE (Smith *et al.*, 1985) is perhaps the most developed wide-spectrum language. It is a non-deterministic language in which the user writes a formal, executable, specification of the system to be prototyped. This specification is refined by the user with automated assistance to produce an executable system prototype. Gist incorporates concepts from logic programming, functional programming and imperative programming languages. A LISP implementation of the system is generated by the Gist processor.

As an alternative to using a wide-spectrum language, a mixed-language approach to prototype development may be adopted. Different parts of the system are programmed in different languages and a communication framework established between the parts. Zave (1989) describes this approach to development in the prototyping of a telephone network system. Four different languages were used: Prolog for database prototyping, Awk (Aho *et al.*, 1988)) for billing, CSP (Hoare, 1985) for protocol specification and PAISLey (Zave and Schell, 1986) for performance simulation.

There is never an ideal language for prototyping large systems as different parts of the system are so diverse. The advantage of a mixed-language approach is that the most appropriate language for a logical part of the application can be chosen, thus speeding up prototype development. The disadvantage is that it is may be difficult to establish a communication framework which will allow multiple languages to communicate. The entities used in the different languages are so diverse that it requires a lot of work to write code to translate an entity from one language to another.

6.2.3 Fourth-generation languages

For some classes of application, particularly those in commercial data processing, a prototyping approach may be used instead of the conventional development model as so-called *fourth-generation languages* (4GLs) are used for systems development. There are many such languages and their use speeds up the production of some types of system.

4GLs are successful because there is a great deal of commonality across data processing applications. Many applications are report-generation activities using information in a company database. Thus a typical 4GL is based around a database facility and provides a database query language, a report-generation package and a package to assist with screen layout design (Figure 6.5). Some spreadsheet-type facilities may also be included. A 4GL relies on software reuse where routines to access a database and produce reports are provided and the programmer need only describe how these routines are to be controlled.

The argument put forward by the vendors of these products is that system maintenance is simpler because application development time is rapid. Systems are typically much smaller than the equivalent COBOL programs. Rather than be concerned about structuring the system for maintenance, requirements changes are implemented by a complete system rewrite.

Using 4GLs for data processing systems development is cost-effective in some cases, particularly for relatively small systems. However, the situation at the moment resembles the Tower of Babel with no standardization or uniformity across languages and a potential cost time-bomb as the requirement to maintain all the different 4GLs is demanded by users. Advocates of these languages seem to be unaware of the problems in the real-time systems community of language proliferation which led to the development of Ada as a standard language for defence systems development.

Although they clearly reduce systems development costs, the effect of 4GLs on overall life cycle costs for large DP systems is not yet clear. They

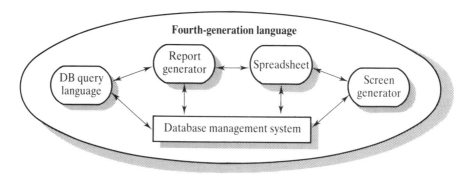

Figure 6.5
Fourth-generation
languages.

are obviously to be recommended for prototyping but the lack of standardization may result in long-term maintenance problems.

4GLs may be used with CASE tools for prototype development. Some CASE toolsets are closely integrated with 4GLs and using such systems has the advantage that documentation is produced at the same time as the prototype system. An early example of such an integrated CASE toolset and 4GL was the RAPID/USE system described by Wasserman *et al.* (1986).

RAPID/USE is built around a relational database, an implementation language called PLAIN which is designed for building interactive information systems and a transition diagram interpreter for prototyping user dialogues. It incorporates comparable facilities to those included in CASE workbenches (see Chapter 18) but has better facilities for user interface prototyping.

6.2.4 Composition of reusable components

Software reuse is discussed, in general, in Chapter 16 and it is clear that the existence of a library of reusable components offers the opportunity of reducing system development times. If these components are sufficiently general and if a mechanism exists to compose these components into systems, prototype systems can be rapidly created (Figure 6.6).

Perhaps the best example of this approach to prototyping is the shell programming language available, in several variants, under UNIX (Bourne, 1978). The UNIX shell is a command language which includes looping and decision constructs. It provides facilities for combining commands which operate on files and strings. The reusable components are other UNIX commands such as '*grep*', '*sort*', '*find*', and so on. The general-purpose nature of UNIX files which are simple character streams, its treatment of I/O devices as files, its pipe facility and the control facilities in the shell programming language combine to make a powerful system for component composition.

However, prototyping using the shell is limited because the granularity of the software components is relatively coarse. This means that the function

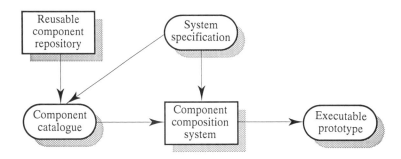

Figure 6.6
Reusable component composition.

of the individual components is often too general-purpose to combine effectively with other components. Furthermore, user interface prototyping using the shell is limited because of the simple I/O model adopted by the UNIX system.

This approach to prototyping can clearly be combined with other approaches using very high-level or fourth-generation languages. Indeed, it can be argued that the success of Smalltalk and LISP as prototyping languages is as much due to their reusable component libraries as to their inbuilt language facilities.

6.3 User interface prototyping

With the advent of graphical user interfaces as typified by the Apple Macintosh, the Windows environment for IBM PCs and compatible machines, and the X-windows system, the effort involved in specifying, designing and implementing a user interface represents a very significant part of application system development costs. As discussed in Chapter 14, it is not acceptable for designers simply to impose their view of an acceptable user interface on users, and the user must take part in the interface design process. This realization has led to an approach to design called user-centred design (Norman and Draper, 1986) which depends on interface prototyping and user involvement throughout the interface design stage.

Design here does not mean, of course, the software design but is rather the 'look and feel' of the user interface. Exploratory programming is used in the process so that an initial interface is produced, it is evaluated with users and new versions are generated until the user is satisfied with the system. After an acceptable interface has been agreed on, it may then be re-implemented although if interface generators are used, this may not be necessary. Interface generators allow interfaces to be specified and a well-structured program is generated from that specification. Thus the iterations inherent in exploratory programming do not degrade the software structure and re-implementation is not required.

Some of the techniques described in Section 6.2 are appropriate for user interface prototyping. Very high-level languages like Smalltalk and LISP have many user interface components as part of the system. These can often be modified to develop the particular application interface required. Fourth-generation language systems usually include screen definition facilities where screen templates can be defined by picking and positioning form fields. Increasingly, comparable facilities are being developed (Harbert *et al.*, 1990) for use with graphical user interfaces.

Other interface generation systems are based around user interface management systems (Myers, 1988) which provide basic user interface functionality such as menu selection, object display, and so on. They are

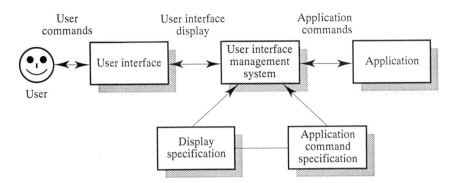

Figure 6.7
User interface
management system.

interposed between the application and the user interface (Figure 6.7) and provide facilities for screen definition and dialogue specification. These facilities may be based on state transition diagrams for command specification (Jacob, 1986) or on formal grammars for dialogue design (Browne, 1986). A survey of tools for user interface design is given by Myers (1989).

From a software engineering point of view, it is important that project managers realize that user interface prototyping is an essential part of the process and, unlike the prototyping of system functionality, it is sometimes acceptable to present an interface prototype as a system specification. Indeed, because of the dynamic nature of user interfaces, paper specifications are not good enough for expressing the user interface requirements.

■ KEY POINTS

- Prototyping is a technique for helping to establish and validate system requirements.

- Prototyping in the software process may involve 'throw-away' prototyping, where a prototype is developed as a basis for a requirements specification, and exploratory programming, where a prototype evolves through a number of versions to the final system.

- Prototyping techniques include the use of executable specification language, the use of very high-level languages, fourth-generation languages and prototype construction from reusable components.

- Fourth-generation languages are effective for prototyping data processing systems. The danger of using these languages for developing production rather than prototype systems is that long-term support for some 4GLs is uncertain.

- For some applications or application fragments such as the user interface, it is essential to use prototyping to derive the requirements as an abstract analysis is unlikely to yield an acceptable result.

■ Management must realize that prototyping is the only effective way to develop a user interface and must not force user interface developers into an unnatural, paper-based process model.

FURTHER READING

Software Prototyping, Formal Methods and VDM.   This is one of the few books on prototyping which is not concerned with the details of data processing systems. The authors' approach to prototyping is based around executable formal specifications but the first few chapters are an excellent general introduction to prototyping. (S. Hekmatpour and D. Ince, 1988, Addison-Wesley.)

IEEE Computer, **22** (5), September 1989.   This is a special issue of the journal devoted to rapid prototyping. Apart from data processing system prototyping, the papers cover a wide area from real-time systems prototyping to user interface development.

IEEE Software, **6** (1), January 1990.   This special issue is concerned with user interfaces in general but it contains several papers devoted to user interface implementation using a prototyping approach.

New Paradigms for Software Development.   This volume in the IEEE tutorial series contains a section devoted to prototyping. (W.W. Agresti, 1986, IEEE Press.)

EXERCISES

6.1   Imagine you are a software engineer who is tasked with investigating the feasibility of prototyping as a standard part of the software development process in your organization. Write a report for your manager discussing the classes of project where prototyping should be used and setting out the expected costs and benefits from using prototyping.

6.2   Explain why, for large systems development, it is recommended that prototypes should be 'throw-away' prototypes.

6.3   What features of languages like Smalltalk and LISP contribute to their support of rapid prototyping?

6.4   Under what circumstances would you recommend that prototyping should be used as a means of validating system requirements?

6.5 There are particular difficulties in prototyping real-time embedded computer systems. Suggest what these might be and think of ways of resolving the difficulties.

6.6 Discuss prototyping using reusable components and explain the problems which arise using this approach (you may find it useful to read Chapter 16). Using examples, explain why the UNIX shell has been very effective as a prototyping system. What are the difficulties of using the shell approach with other types of reusable component?

6.7 A software manager is involved in a project development of a software design support system which is intended to assist with the translation of software requirements to a formal software specification. The system must run on a personal computer but may be developed on another system and ported to that machine. Three possible development strategies are:

(a) Develop a throw-away prototype using a prototyping language such as Smalltalk. Evaluate this prototype then review requirements. Develop the final system using C and X-windows.

(b) Develop the system from the existing requirements using C and X-windows then modify it to adapt to any changed user requirements.

(c) Develop the system using evolutionary prototyping using a prototyping language such as Smalltalk. Modify the system according to the user's requests and deliver the modified prototype.

Comment on the advantages and disadvantages of each of these development strategies.

6.8 Using the UNIX shell, develop a prototype for the data dictionary system whose data model was defined in in Chapter 4. (Hint: use different files for each field in the dictionary.)

6.9 If you have access to a very-high level language (LISP, Prolog, Smalltalk, and so on or a 4GL), develop a prototype for the newspaper delivery system introduced in Exercise 3.7. Use your experience with the prototype to formulate a more definitive set of requirements for such a system.

Formal Specification

■ OBJECTIVES

The objectives of this chapter and the two following chapters are to introduce formal specification techniques, to remove some of the mystique surrounding this subject and to convince software engineers that these techniques can be used in a practical software development process. This chapter sets out the case for formal specifications and discusses their advantages and disadvantages. It shows where they can be used in the software process and suggests that formal specification techniques are now sufficiently mature that they can be used in the specification of sequential systems. A process model based on transformation is briefly discussed. The final part of the chapter is a simple introduction to formal component specification. It introduces the notion of a predicate and shows how a search routine can be specified by means of pre- and post-conditions.

■ CONTENTS

The processes of software specification and design are inextricably intermingled. During the derivation of a detailed system specification, some design activities are necessary both to structure the specification and to establish its feasibility. Specification goes on at a number of different levels from an abstract requirements definition through a contractual requirements specification to a detailed software specification which is sometimes seen as the first stage in the design process.

Historically, detailed software specifications were written using flowcharts or PDL and were not expressed at a level of abstraction which could usefully feed back information to the system requirements specification. However, as implementation languages have become more abstract, the need for this level of specification has almost disappeared. Detailed specifications can now be expressed in an abstract way which can influence the requirements specification. The best way of expressing a detailed specification is to use a formal mathematical notation.

Formal specifications and methods have not been widely used in software development. Many software engineers have been conservative and reluctant to use formal specification because the effort involved in writing a formal specification did not seem to be justified by the advantages of formality. However, development of formal methods has now reached a stage where they can be used in real systems and emerging evidence (Hall, 1990) suggests that using formal techniques both increases system quality and reduces development costs.

Figure 7.1 shows the stages of software specification and its interface with the design process. It also shows the involvement of the client and software contractor at each of these stages.

The involvement of the client decreases and the involvement of the contractor increases as the specification is developed. In the early stages of the process, it is essential that the specification is 'client-oriented'. It should be written so that it is understandable to the client and should make as few assumptions as possible about the software design. However, the final stage of the process, which is the construction of a complete, consistent and precise specification, is principally intended for the software contractor and is a basis for the system implementation.

Figure 7.1
Specification and design.

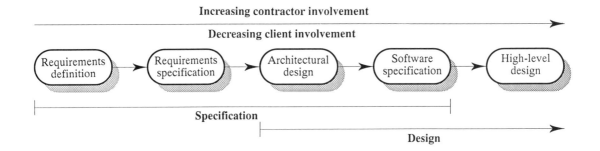

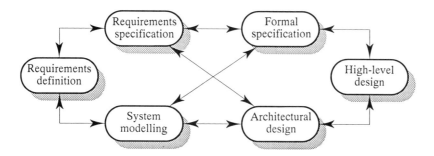

Figure 7.2
Formal specification in
the software process.

The specification stages shown in Figure 7.1 are not independent nor are they necessarily carried out in sequence. Figure 7.2 shows specification and design activities in more detail and illustrates that there is a two-way relation between each stage in the process. Figure 7.2 also shows where formal specifications can be used in the software process.

As a specification is refined, the engineer's understanding of that specification increases. Errors and omissions are detected. These are fed back to allow earlier specifications to be modified. Error detection is the most potent argument for developing a formal specification as requirements errors which remain undetected until later stages of the software process are usually expensive to correct. The production of a formal specification forces a detailed systems analysis which usually reveals errors and inconsistencies in the informal specification.

There have been different approaches taken to formal specification and formal methods in Europe and North America. Work in Europe has focused primarily on formal system specification as a technique of value in its own right and has paid less attention to formal verification. By contrast, North American work has tended to be verification-oriented either at the level of verifying system security or program verification.

As verification is difficult and expensive, there has been relatively little use of formal methods in North American industrial practice (IBM's Cleanroom approach, discussed in Chapter 24, is an exception) and most US practitioners still see formal methods as a topic for research. In Europe, however, there have been a significant number of industrial trials of formal specification. It is likely to be mandated for safety-critical defence systems in the UK and the transfer of this technology into industrial practice is accelerating.

7.1 Formal specification rationale

A formal software specification is a specification expressed in a language whose vocabulary, syntax and semantics are formally defined. The need for a formal semantic definition means that the specification languages cannot be based on natural languages but must be based on mathematics.

There are a number of advantages of using such a formal language for precise specification.

(1) The development of a formal specification provides insights into and an understanding of the software requirements and the software design. This is the best reason for developing a formal specification as it reduces requirements errors and omissions and provides a basis for an elegant software design.

(2) Formal software specifications are mathematical entities and may be analysed using mathematical methods. In particular it may be possible to prove specification consistency and completeness. It may also be possible to prove that an implementation conforms to its specification. Thus, the absence of certain classes of error may be demonstrated. However, program verification is expensive and the ability to reason about the specification itself is probably more significant.

(3) Formal specifications may be automatically processed. Software tools can be built to assist with their development, understanding and debugging. Depending on the formal specification language used, it may be possible to animate a formal specification to provide a prototype system.

Finally, formal specifications may be used as a guide to the tester of a component in identifying appropriate test cases. The use of formal specifications for this purpose is discussed by Hayes (1986).

Research into formal specification techniques was initiated because of interest in formal program verification. However, formal specifications are of value in their own right and it may be worthwhile to develop a formal specification even when there there are no plans to formally verify the developed system. The other advantages of formal specification are sufficient to justify its use in the software process.

Formal specification techniques are not widely used in industrial software development. Indeed, the specification process model in Figure 7.1 is an idealized one. Many organizations commence the design process after the construction of the detailed requirements or functional specification. There are several reasons why formal specification is not widely used:

(1) Software management is inherently conservative and is unwilling to adopt new techniques whose payoff is not obvious. It is hard to demonstrate that the relatively high cost of developing a formal system specification will reduce overall software development costs. Formal specification may increase development costs but should reduce later maintenance costs.

(2)   Most software engineers have not been trained in the techniques required to develop formal software specifications. Developing specifications requires a familiarity with discrete mathematics and logic. Inexperience of these techniques makes specification development appear to be difficult.

(3)   System procurers are unlikely to be familiar with formal specification techniques and may be unwilling to fund development activities which they cannot readily influence.

(4)   Some classes of software system are difficult to specify using existing techniques. In particular, current techniques can't be used for the specification of the interactive components of user interfaces. Some classes of parallel processing system, such as interrupt-driven systems, are difficult to specify.

(5)   There is widespread ignorance of current specification techniques and their applicability. There have probably been several hundred relatively large systems which have been formally specified.

(6)   Most of the effort in specification research has been concerned with the development of notations and techniques. Relatively little effort has been devoted to tool support yet such support is essential if large-scale specifications are to be developed.

(7)   Some members of the computer science community who are active in the development of formal methods misunderstand practical software engineering and suggest that software engineering can be equated with the adoption of formal methods of software development. Understandably, such nonsense makes pragmatic software engineers wary of their proposed solutions.

Hall (1990) refutes some of these arguments against the use of formal methods where he presents 'seven myths of formal methods'. These myths and arguments against them are:

(1)   *Perfect software results from the use of formal methods* This evangelical view is clearly nonsense. A formal specification is a model of the real-world and it may incorporate misunderstandings about the real-world, specification errors and omissions. Its translation into a executable program is limited by the computer hardware, operating system and compilers. However, a formal approach is effective because it makes specification errors easier to detect and provides an unambiguous basis for system design.

(2)   *Formal methods mean program proving* We have already discussed that program proving is just one approach to the use of formal methods.

(3)   *Formal methods are so expensive that their use can only be justified in*

safety-critical systems   Hall suggests that his company's experience has shown that development costs for all classes of system are reduced by the use of formal specifications.

(4)   *Formal methods require a high level of mathematical skill*   This is simply untrue. As we shall see in the following chapters, formal specification uses simple mathematics. Only elementary mathematical skills are required.

(5)   *Formal methods increase development costs*   Hall's experience suggests that this is not the case although the development cost profile is altered, with more costs incurred at the early stages in the software process (Figure 7.3).

(6)   *Clients cannot understand formal specifications*   Hall suggests that specifications can be understood by clients by paraphrasing them in natural language and by specification animation. What he seems to be saying is that the derivation of a formal specification allows a better, easier-to-understand requirements specification to be produced.

(7)   *Formal methods have only been used for trivial system development*   As we have already discussed, this is incorrect. For example, Earl *et al.* (1986) describe the formal specification of a software engineering environment, Morgan and Sufrin (1984) report on the specification of the UNIX filestore, Spivey (1990) discusses the specification of a kernel for a real-time system and Delisle and Garlan (1990) show how an oscilloscope may be formally specified.

Figure 7.3 shows how software process costs are affected by the use of formal specification. When a conventional process is used, validation costs are about 50% of development costs, and implementation and design costs are about twice the costs of specification. With formal specification, specification and implementation costs are comparable and system validation costs are significantly reduced.

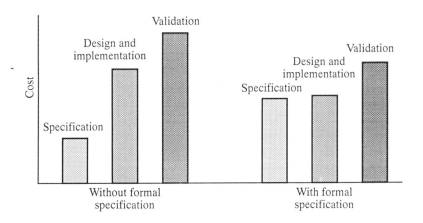

Figure 7.3
Software development costs.

In this book, I discuss the formal specification of sequential systems and do not address the specification of concurrent systems. Concurrent system specification techniques such as CSP (Hoare, 1985) and CCS (Milner, 1980) are not as mature as sequential system specification techniques. They have been used in an industrial context (Zave, 1989) but much less widely than sequential system specification. These concurrent system specification techniques are more difficult to use than sequential specification techniques and I think they require further refinement before they are effectively usable by non-specialists.

7.2   Transformational development

In Chapter 1, a software process based on formal transformations was briefly described. A formal system specification is a prerequisite for this process which involves the transformation of that specification through a series of correctness-preserving steps to a finished program (Figure 7.4).

Each transformation is sufficiently close to the previous description that the effort of verifying the transformation is not excessive. It can therefore be guaranteed, assuming there are no verification errors, that the ultimate developed program is a true implementation of the specification.

The advantage of the transformational approach compared to proving that a program meets its specification is that the distance between each transformation is less than the distance between a specification and a program. Program proofs are very long and impractical for large-scale systems, but a transformational approach made up of a sequence of smaller steps may be more effective. However, the process is not easy. Choosing which transformation to apply is a skilled task and proving the correspondence of transformations is difficult.

Few (if any) large-scale systems have been developed using the transformational model of the software process but it is likely that recent

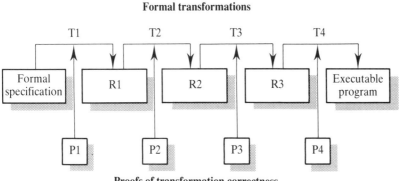

Figure 7.4
Transformational
software development.

developments in formal methods (such as the specification language Z, described in Chapter 9) will make this process a more practical one. Although it is unlikely that a purely transformational approach will ever be adopted for very large systems development, the incorporation of this model into other process models will lead to overall process improvements.

7.3 Developing a simple formal specification

Specification techniques which can be used for non-trivial systems are algebraic specification (Chapter 8) and model-based specification (Chapter 9). However, before going on to consider these techniques, it is instructive to consider the development of a simple example to introduce formality in specifications.

Paradoxically, perhaps, the approach which I use in discussing formal specification is an informal one. This is partly for space reasons as a formal treatment of the subject requires a book to itself. Of equal importance, however, is the fact that readers without a mathematical background are alienated by formality. They tend to reject such material as beyond their abilities. In fact, the practical advantages which result from using formal specification can be achieved without an extensive understanding of the underlying mathematics. An informal approach can illustrate the techniques to readers who are not mathematicians.

Software engineers have been reluctant to make use of formal specification techniques because many of them are intimidated by the specialized notations used. Notations such as VDM (Jones, 1980) and Z (Spivey, 1989) involve the use of specialized symbols invented by the authors of the notation. This leads to precision but involves a significant learning effort before reading or writing specifications.

An alternative approach, used in the Larch specification language (Guttag, *et al.*, 1985) uses a mnemonic notation rather than specialized symbols. This is less alien to many software engineers and has the further advantage that it may be typed using a standard keyboard. I use a mnemonic notation in this chapter and I rely on the reader's intuition to understand it. I also use the excellent device, used in the Z specification language, of using graphics to structure the specification. This improves the readability of a specification and has the additional advantage of encouraging the specifier to develop the specification in an incremental way.

The simplest form of formal specification is where a system is represented as a set of functions with hidden internal state. Each function is specified using pre- and post-conditions. A pre-condition is a specification of the value of the function inputs and a post-condition is a specification of the value of the function's outputs. The difference between them defines how the function transforms its inputs to its outputs.

Pre- and post-conditions are predicates over the inputs and outputs of a function. A predicate is simply a boolean expression which is true or false and whose variables are the parameters of the function being specified.

As well as operators such as =, >=, <=, **not**, **and**, **or**, etc., predicates may also include quantifiers which allow the predicate to be applied to all members of a collection (**for_all**) and to a particular member of a collection (**exists**). These are the universal and existential quantifiers ($\forall$ and $\exists$) used in set theory. The operator **in** is used to select the range over which the quantifier applies. It is analogous to the operator $\in$ used in set theory but, in the simple examples used here, may be applied to arrays as well as sets.

Examples of predicates are shown in Figure 7.5.

The development of a specification of a function using pre- and post-conditions involves a number of stages:

(1) Establish the range of the input parameters over which the function should behave correctly. Specify the input parameter constraints as a predicate.

(2) Specify a predicate defining a condition which must hold on the output of the function if it behaves correctly.

All variables referenced are of type INTEGER

1. The value of variable A is greater than the value of B and the value of variable C is greater than D

$$A > B \text{ and } C > D$$

2. This predicate illustrates the use of the **exists** quantifier. The predicate is true if there are values of i, j and k between M and N such that $i^2 = j^2 + k^2$ Thus, if M is 1 and N is 5, the predicate is true as $3^2 + 4^2 = 5^2$. If M is 7 and N is 11, the predicate is false as there are no values between 7 and 11 which satisfy the condition.

$$\textbf{exists } i, j, k \textbf{ in } M..N: i^2 = j^2 + k^2$$

3. This predicate illustrates the use of the universal quantifier **for_all**. It concerns the values of an array called Squares. It is true if the first ten values in the array take a value which is the square of an integer between 1 and 10.

$$\textbf{for\_all } i \textbf{ in } 1..10, \textbf{exists } j \textbf{ in } 1..10: \text{Squares (i)} = j^2$$

Figure 7.5
Examples of predicates.

(3)   Establish what changes (if any) are made to the function's input parameters and specify these. Of course, a pure mathematical function shouldn't change its inputs but programming languages usually allow function inputs to be modified by passing them by reference.

(4)   Combine these into pre- and post-conditions for the function.

As an example, consider the function Search (Figure 7.6) which accepts an array of integers and an integer key as its parameters. The function returns the array index of the member of the array whose value is equal to that of the key. The original input array is unchanged.

The post-condition must refer to the value returned by the function which does not have its own name. I use the normal convention that the name of the function refers to the value returned by the function.

(1)   If Search is to work properly, one of the array elements must match the key. The pre-condition therefore states that there must exist some element (called i here) whose value matches an element in the array. Assume that the attributes FIRST and LAST (with the same meaning as they have in Ada) refer to the lower and upper bounds of the array.

exists i **in** (X'FIRST..X'LAST) : X (i) = Key

(2)   Search should return the value of the index of the element equal to the key. This can be expressed as a predicate using the function name to refer to the returned value. The notation X" refers to the value of the array X after the function has been evaluated.

X" (Search (X, Key)) = Key

(3)   It is not enough to specify that a particular value of the array matches the key if that can be achieved by modifying the input array. The specifier must also state that the input is unchanged by the function. In many programming languages (like Ada or Pascal) this is achieved by passing the function parameters by value rather than by reference.

X = X"

The function pre-condition states the condition which must hold if the post-condition is to be valid. A specification should also set out the behaviour of

Figure 7.6
The specification of the function Search.

```
function Search (X : in INTEGER_ARRAY ; Key : INTEGER)
        return INTEGER ;

Pre:    exists i in X'FIRST..X'LAST : X(i) = Key
Post:   X" (Search (X, Key)) = Key  and  X = X"
```

```
function Search (X : in INTEGER_ARRAY ; Key : INTEGER)
                    return INTEGER ;

Pre:   exists i in X'FIRST..X'LAST :  X (i) = Key

Post:  X" (Search (X, Key)) = Key and X = X"

Error: Search (X, Key) = X'LAST + 1
```

Figure 7.7
The specification of
Search with error
predicate.

a component if it is presented with unexpected input. How should the function Search behave if there are no array elements which match the input key?

The approach adopted to error specification depends on the number of possible types of error and whether or not the error action depends on the error type. In the case of Search, there is only a single type of error and a single action to be taken. If the pre-condition is not satisfied, an error predicate can be included. This sets out the post-condition which holds in the event of the pre-condition being false (Figure 7.7).

In Figure 7.7, we see that the error is indicated by returning an integer value which is greater than the value of the upper bound of the array. Thus, the user of Search can test the value returned to see if the operation has been successful.

This form of error indication is possible in some cases but is not generally satisfactory. The problem is that the type signature of Search is such that it must evaluate to an integer. In fact, it should really evaluate to a tuple where one value is an integer setting out the key matching the index and the error is an error state indicator which is set true if the pre-condition is satisfied. Furthermore, it is sometimes necessary to have a separate specification for each type of error. The specification of error states is covered in the following chapters, and alternative ways of handling error conditions are illustrated.

■ KEY POINTS

- ■ Formal system specification is complementary to informal specification techniques.

- ■ Formal specifications are precise and unambiguous. They remove areas of doubt in a specification.

- The principal value of using formal specification techniques in the software process is that it forces an analysis of the system requirements at an early stage. Correcting errors at this stage is cheaper than modifying a delivered system.

- Formal specification techniques are now sufficiently mature to be applied in the development of non-trivial systems.

- Formal specification methods rely on the use of predicates which are assertions about the state of a system.

- When writing formal specifications, it is important to specify how the system behaves when presented with erroneous inputs.

FURTHER READING

IEEE Software, **7** (5), September 1990.   This special issue of the journal contains a series of readable, tutorial articles discussing different aspects of formal methods. It is complemented by special issues of *IEEE Computer* and *IEEE Trans. Software Engineering* devoted to this topic. The article by Hall in *IEEE Software* is particularly recommended.

The Specification of Complex Systems.   This is an excellent introduction to formal specification techniques by some of the pioneers of the industrial application of formal specification techniques. As well as being relevant reading for this chapter, it is also very useful reading for the remaining chapters on algebraic and model-based specification techniques. (B. Cohen, W.T. Harwood and M.I. Jackson, 1986, Addison-Wesley.)

New Paradigms for Software Development.   This IEEE tutorial volume has a section on transformational development. (W.W. Agresti, 1986, IEEE Press.)

EXERCISES

7.1 You have been given the task of 'selling' formal specification techniques to a software development organization. Outline how you would go about explaining the advantages of formal specifications and countering the reservations of practising software engineers.

7.2 Write predicates to express the following English language statements.

There exists an array of 100 sensors and associated control valves. Sensors can take the values high and low and the control valves can be in state open or closed. If a sensor reading is high, the state of the control valve is closed.

In an array of integers, there is at least one value in that array which is negative.

In a collection of natural numbers, the lowest number is 20 and the largest number is greater then 250.

Given a collection of processes which have an integer attribute called DELAY and which may be in states running, waiting or stopped, there is no process which is waiting and whose value of DELAY exceeds 2.

7.3 Write pre- and post-conditions for a function which finds the minimum value in an array of integers.

7.4 Write pre- and post-conditions to define a function called Run_process which acts on a process which may be running, waiting or stopped. Run_process takes a process identifier as an example and, if the process is waiting, changes its state to running and modifies the DELAY attribute accordingly.

7.5 Write pre- and post-conditions for a function which sorts an array. You may assume the existence of a predicate called PERM which takes two arrays as its parameters and returns true if one is a permutation of the other.

7.6 Write pre- and post-conditions for a function which creates a 10 element array where, for all elements of the array, the value of the array element is the square of its index.

7.7 Explain why there may be problems in the specification of erroneous conditions when a function returns a single value. Using an example, show how these can be tackled by redefining the function to return a tuple (record).

Algebraic Specification

8

■ OBJECTIVES

The objective of this chapter is to introduce algebraic specification where the operations on an object are specified in terms of their interrelationships. The first part of the chapter illustrates algebraic specification by example. It shows how abstract data types may be specified and how specifications can be built from simpler specification building blocks. As a practical demonstration of the usefulness of this approach, part of the specification of the design editing system introduced in earlier chapters is also described. The examples show how algebraic specification fits with object-oriented design; the natural specification structure is an abstract data type or object class.

■ CONTENTS

Algebraic specification is a technique where an object class or type is specified in terms of the relationships between the operations defined on that type. It was first brought to prominence by Guttag (1977) in the specification of abstract data types but, since then, the technique has been extended into a general-purpose approach to system specification.

The technique is easiest to understand when the objects specified correspond to abstract data types in some programming language and we shall concentrate on this form of specification here. For an example of a broader system specification using this approach, readers are referred to Cohen *et al.*(1986) who specify a document retrieval system.

Various notations for algebraic specification have been developed, including OBJ (Futatsugi *et al.*, 1985) and Larch (Guttag *et al.*, 1985). These are comprehensive notations and space does not permit a description of them here. Rather, a simple notation is used which structures the specification using graphical highlighting (Figure 8.1).

A specification is presented in four parts: an introduction part where the sort of the entity being specified is introduced and the names of any other specifications which are required are set out; an informal description of the operations defined on that sort; a signature part where the names of the operations and the sorts of their parameters are defined; and an axioms part where the relationships between the sort operations are specified. The name part of a specification can include a generic parameter, as explained in Section 8.1.

A sort is like a type in Pascal or Ada. They are not strictly identical as a sort is a set of objects whereas types in Pascal or Ada are rather different. However, sorts are represented as types in the implementation of a specification and it is usually convenient to consider them to be the same thing.

The introduction part of a specification includes an imports part which names the other specifications required by a specification. Importing these specifications makes the defined sorts and their operations available. When names of operations used in an imported specification are the same as names defined in a specification, the name of the imported specification must be used in conjunction with the operation name.

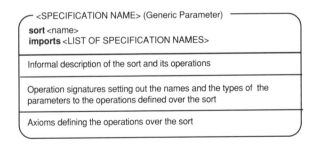

Figure 8.1
The format of an algebraic specification.

For example, say a specification called ZONE (Figure 8.14) defines an operation called Create and imports a specification called COORD (Figure 8.2) where an operation with the same name is defined. Within Zone, the name Create refers to the name of the operation which creates an entity of sort Zone. To refer to the operation which creates entities of sort Coord, a dot notation is used as in Ada packages. Thus COORD.Create refers to the operation Create defined in the specification COORD.

The description part of a specification supplements the formal text with an informal description and the signature part sets out the names of the operations which are defined over the sort, the number and sorts of their parameters and the sort of the result of evaluating the operation. The axioms part defines the operations in terms of their relationships.

The first step in defining an algebraic specification of an abstract data type is to identify a set of required operations. This set must include operations to bring instances of the type into existence, to modify the value of instances and to inspect the instance values and the values of components of the type.

Generally, operations fall into two classes.

(1) *Constructor operations*   Operations which create or modify entities of the sort which is defined in the specification. Typically, these are given names such as Create, Update, Add, etc.

(2) *Inspection operations*   Operations which evaluate attributes of the sort which is defined in the specification. Typically, these are given names which correspond to attribute names or names such as Eval, Get, etc.

Having identified the operations, an informal specification should be written and the operation signatures identified before writing down the formal axioms defining the abstract type. A good rule of thumb for writing an algebraic specification is to establish the constructor operations and write down an axiom for each inspection operation over each constructor. This suggests that if there are m constructor operations and n inspection operations there should be $m*n$ axioms defined.

Sometimes, however, constructor operations are introduced which are actually a combination of simpler constructors. In such cases, it is sometimes possible to reduce this number of axioms required by defining constructors using these primitive constructor operations. This is discussed later in the chapter.

An example of a simple algebraic specification of a sort called Coord, representing a Cartesian coordinate, is shown in Figure 8.2. The operations are create a coordinate, test coordinates for equality and access the X and Y components.

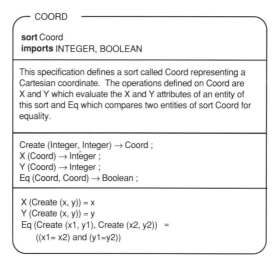

Figure 8.2
The specification of
sort Coord.

The specification of Coord imports specifications called BOOLEAN and INTEGER. These define sorts called Boolean and Integer which have their normal intuitive meaning and operations.

8.1   Structured algebraic specification

When using algebraic specification, normal practice is to define libraries of specifications of simple sorts such as arrays, lists, queues, and so on, and use these to construct more complex specifications. Although it is not always straightforward to use this technique in practical systems (discussed later in this chapter), the basic techniques used for specifying more complex sorts are those illustrated here.

As we shall see, a key technique is to derive specifications in a structured way where simple specifications act as building blocks for more complex specifications. We shall see in this section how to achieve this and how to create a specification lattice as shown in Figure 8.3. Figure 8.3 illustrates how simple basic specifications such as List and Coord are used to build progressively more complex specifications.

To illustrate the general principles of abstract data type specification, consider the specification of an array, a generic abstract data type provided in almost all programming languages. It is an abstract data type (although it is not defined as such in Pascal or Ada) because it has a restricted set of allowed operations. It is a generic type because the elements of an array can usually be of any other type. The specification of a generic array with operations to create the array, discover the lower and upper bounds, find

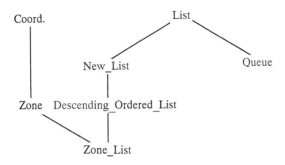

Figure 8.3
Specification building
blocks.

the value of an array element and assign a value to an array element is set
out in Figure 8.4.

The specification is parameterized (in Ada terms, it defines a generic)
in that it defines arrays where the array components may be of any type.
Following the notation used in Cohen *et al.* (1986), the generic parameter is
of type Elem meaning, in essence, any element type. This is set out in the
introductory part of the specification, following the specification name.

As well as the name of a generic parameter, a generic specification
must also include the names of operations on generic parameters which must
be defined. The specification assumes that when the generic parameter type
is instantiated to an actual type, the operation name specified in the generic

```
⎧—— ARRAY ( Elem : [Undefined → Elem] ) ——————⎫
│  sort Array                                              │
│  imports INTEGER                                         │
│                                                          │
│  This specification defines arrays as collections of elements of
│  generic type Elem. Arrays have a lower and upper bound (discovered
│  by the operations First and Last) and individual elements are
│  accessed via their numeric index.
│         The operation Create takes the array bounds as parameters
│  and initializes the values of the array to Undefined. The operation
│  Assign creates a new array where a particular element has been
│  assigned a value and the operation Eval reveals the value of a
│  specified element. Bound checking is specified.
│
│  Create (Integer, Integer) → Array
│  Assign (Array, Integer, Elem) → Array
│  First (Array) → Integer
│  Last (Array) → Integer
│  Eval (Array, Integer) → Elem
│
│  First (Create (x, y)) = x
│  First (Assign (a, n, v)) = First (a)
│  Last (Create (x, y)) = y
│  Last (Assign (a, n, v)) = Last (a)
│  Eval (Create (x, y), n) = Undefined
│  Eval (Assign (a, n, v), m) = if m < First (a) or m > Last (a) then
│                                     Undefined else
│                                          if m = n then v else Eval (a, m)
⎩                                                          ⎭
```

Figure 8.4
The specification of
sort Array.

part will be defined along with other operations for that actual type. The specification of arrays require that an operation called Undefined, which evaluates to Elem, is provided for the generic type. This is a constant operation (it always returns the same value) and it is used to represent the notion that an entity of type Elem has not been given a defined value.

In the specification of Array, the constructor operations are Create which brings an array into existence and Assign which assigns a value to an array element. The access operations are First and Last which return the lower and upper array bounds, and Eval, which is used to determine the value of a particular array element.

The specification shows that the First and Last operations return the bounds of the array as set out in the Create operation, that assigning a value does not change the array size and that the value of an array element is whatever value has been previously assigned to that element. If no value has been assigned, the operation evaluates to Undefined. Thus Create initializes all elements of the array to the value Undefined. The Eval operation checks that the index is within the bounds of the array; if not, it evaluates to Undefined.

An array is an example of a basic specification building block. A further example of a reusable specification building block is shown in Figure 8.5 where a simple list is specified. Lists are commonly used in implementing other data structures and, as we shall see later, the List specification is a component of a number of other specifications.

LIST (Elem : [Undefined → Elem])

sort List
imports INTEGER

This specification defines a list where elements are added at one end and may be removed from the other end. List operations are Create, which brings an empty list into existence, Cons, which creates a new list with an additional member added to the end, Length, which evaluates the list size, Head, which evaluates the front element of the list and Tail, which evaluates to a new list with the head element removed.

Create → List
Cons (List, Elem) → List
Tail (List) → List
Head (List) → Elem
Length (List) → Integer

Head (Create) = Undefined -- Error to evaluate an empty list
Head (Cons (L, v)) = **if** L = Create **then** v **else** Head (L)
Length (Create) = 0
Length (Cons (L, v)) = Length (L) + 1
Tail (Create) = Create
Tail (Cons (L, v)) = **if** L = Create **then** Create **else** Cons (Tail (L), v)

Figure 8.5
The specification of
sort List.

The constructor operations are Create, Cons and Tail, which build lists. The access operations are Head and Length, which are used to discover list attributes. However, the possibility of constructors being represented in terms of other constructors was introduced earlier and we see here the first example of this. The Tail operation can be defined using Cons and Create. There is no need to define axioms over the Tail operation for the Head and Length operations. These would include redundant information which could be derived from other axioms.

Attempting to evaluate the head of an empty list results in an undefined value being returned. The combination of the specifications of Head and Tail show that Head evaluates the front of the list and Tail evaluates to the input list with its head removed. Notice the specification of Head states that the head of a list created using Cons is either the value added to the list (if the initial list is empty) or is the same as the head of the initial list parameter to Cons. Thus, adding an element to a list does not affect its head unless the list is empty.

The definition of the Tail operation is recursive. Recursion is often used in constructing algebraic specifications. It may not be immediately obvious that this specifies that the value resulting from the Tail operation is the list which results from taking the input list and removing its head. However, an example may clarify the operation specification.

Say we have a list [5, 7] where 5 is the front of the list and 7 the end of the list. The operation Cons ([5, 7], 9) should return a list [5, 7, 9] and a Tail operation applied to this should return the list [7, 9]. Consider now the sequence of equations which results from substituting the parameters in the above specification with these values.

Tail ([5, 7, 9]) = Tail (Cons ([5, 7], 9)) =
   Cons (Tail ([5, 7]), 9) = Cons (Tail (Cons ([5], 7)), 9) =
     Cons (Cons (Tail ([5]), 7), 9) =
      Cons (Cons (Tail (Cons ([], 5)), 7), 9) =
       Cons (Cons ([Create], 7), 9) = Cons ([7], 9) = [7, 9]

The systematic rewriting of the axiom for Tail illustrates that it does indeed produce the anticipated result. The axiom for Head can be verified using a similar approach.

The simple model of a list defined in Figure 8.5 has limited functionality but is really intended to be a reusable building block in other specifications. Figure 8.7 shows its use as a component in the definition of a sort New_List which is an enriched version of the sort List. Enrichment is a mechanism which allows specifications to be structured and built out of existing specifications. The sort New_List inherits the operations and axioms defined on List so that these also apply to that sort. They could be included in the specification NEW_LIST with the name List replaced by New_List. When a sort is enriched, new operations in the specification may overwrite operations with the same name in the base sort.

```
Create → New_List
Cons (New_List, Elem) → New_List
Head (New_List) → Elem
Tail (New_List) → New_List
Add (New_List, Elem) → New_List
Member (New_List, Elem) → Boolean
Length (New_List) → Integer
```

Figure 8.6
The operations on sort
New_List.

Enrichment is not the same as importing a specification. When a specification is imported, the sort and its operations defined in the imported specification are made accessible (brought into the scope of in programming language terms) to the specification being defined. They do not become part of that specification.

The operations added in the specification of New_List are an Add operation, which adds an element to the front of the list and a Member operation, which tests if a given value is contained in the list. To complete the specification the access operations Head, Tail and Member must be defined over the new constructor (Add), and Member must be specified over previously defined constructor operations. Figure 8.6 summarizes the operations on New_List.

When a sort is created by enrichment, the names of the generic parameters of the base sort are inherited. The generic parameters in an enriched specification must include the operations from the base sort. The parameterization of NEW_LIST augments the parameters of List with the equality operation '=='. The notation .==. (Elem, Elem) means that '==' is an infix operator with operands of type Elem. It evaluates to true if its operands are equal where the precise notion of equality depends on the sort of the entities to which the operator is applied.

The process of enrichment can be continued. Say there is a requirement to specify an ordered list where the values in the list are held in descending order. Thus, operations to insert a value into the list may place it at the beginning, in the middle or at the end of the list. Assume also that an operation Remove is required which takes an element from the ordered list, maintaining the ordering. The operations on this sort are summarized in Figure 8.8.

The operations do not include the constructor operations Add and Cons, which were defined over the sort New_List. If these operations were included, it could not be guaranteed that the ordering of the list would always be maintained. The enrichment clause therefore incorporates an excluding part which sets out the operations which are not inherited by Descending_Ordered_List.

Figure 8.9 shows a specification for the sort Descending_Ordered_List. Notice that the generic parameter Elem must have an operation .>. (greater

NEW_LIST (Elem : [Undefined → Elem ; .==. → Boolean])
sort New_List **enrich** List
imports INTEGER, BOOLEAN

This specification defines a list which inherits the operations and
properties of the simpler specification of List and which adds new
operations to these.

    The new operations are Add, which adds an element to the
front of the list (cf Cons, which adds to the end) and Member
which, given a value, tests if the list contains an element matching
that value.

Add (New_List, Elem) → New_List
Member (New_List, Elem) → Boolean

Member (Create, v) = FALSE
Member (Add (L, v), v1) = ((v == v1) **or** Member (L, v1))
Member (Cons (L, v), v1) = ((v == v1) **or** Member (L, v1))
Head (Add (L, v)) = v
Tail (Add (L, v)) = L
Length (Add (L, v)) = Length (L) + 1
Add (Create, v) = Cons (Create, v)

Figure 8.7
The specification of
sort New _List.

than) which allows comparisons to be made. The > operator compares two
elements and evaluates to true if its left hand operand is greater than its
right hand operand. Its precise meaning depends on the actual parameter
sort. For integers, the operator should have its usual meaning but, as we
shall see later, ordering may be arbitrary for other sorts.

    The definitions of the Head and Tail operations show the list is
ordered. If a value inserted in the list is greater than the existing list head
then it is the result of the Head operation. Similarly, if the value inserted is
greater than the list head, the Tail operation returns the original list without
the inserted value. Insertion in the correct place is guaranteed because
inserting an element into an empty list makes a new singleton list. The
Remove operation is defined in terms of the Create and Insert constructor
operations. It specifies that a value which is equal to a value previously
inserted into the list may be removed.

    In the above examples, the operations on a sort have been shown as

Create → Descending_Ordered_List
Insert (Descending_Ordered_List, Elem) → Descending_Ordered_List
Remove (Descending_Ordered_List, Elem) → Descending_Ordered_List
Head (Descending_Ordered_List) → Elem
Tail (Descending_Ordered_List) → Descending_Ordered_List
Member (Descending_Ordered_List, Elem) → Boolean
Length (Descending_Ordered_List) → Integer

Figure 8.8
The operations on sort
Descending_Ordered_
List.

DESCENDING_LIST (Elem : [Undefined → Elem ; .==. → Boolean ;
.>. → Boolean])

sort Descending_Ordered_List **enrich** New_List
excluding (Cons, Add)
imports INTEGER, BOOLEAN

This specification defines a list where the elements are arranged in
descending order. It is an enrichment of sort New_List, which means
that it inherits its operations. However, Cons and Add must be
hidden to ensure ordering is not compromised. They are replaced
by a constructor operation, Insert, which inserts an element,
maintaining the list ordering. A new operation, Remove, which
removes a list member matching a parameter is also defined.

Insert (Descending_Ordered_List, Elem) → Descending_Ordered_List
Remove (Descending_Ordered_List, Elem) →
Descending_Ordered_List

Head (Insert (Create, v)) = v
Tail (Insert (Create, v)) = Create
Head (Insert (L, v)) = **if** v > Head (L) **then** v **else** Head (L)
Tail (Insert (L, v)) = **if** v > Head (L) **then** L **else** Insert (Tail (L), v)
Member (Insert (L, v), v1) = (v == v1) **or** Member (L, v1)
Length (Insert (L, v)) = Length (L) + 1
Remove (Create, v) = Create
Remove (Insert (L, v), v1) = **if** v == v1 **then** L **else**
Insert (Remove (L, v1), v)

Figure 8.9
The specification of
sort
Descending_
Ordered_List.

functions which evaluate to a single atomic value. In many cases, this is a
reasonable model of the system which is being specified. However, there are
some classes of operation which, when implemented, involve modifying
more than one entity. For example, the familiar stack pop operation returns
a value from a stack and also removes the top element from the stack.

It is possible to model such operations using multiple simpler
operations which take the top value from the stack and which remove the
top stack element. However, a more natural approach is to define
operations which return a tuple rather than a single value. Rather than
returning a single value, the function has multiple output values. Thus, the
stack pop operation might have the signature:

Pop (Stack) → (Elem, Stack)

Operations which evaluate to a tuple are used in a specification of a queue

Create → Queue
Cons (Queue, Elem) → Queue
Head (Queue) → Elem
Tail (Queue) → Queue
Length (Queue) → Integer
Get (Queue) → (Elem, Queue)

Figure 8.10
The operations on sort
Queue.

```
┌─ QUEUE  ( Elem: [ Undefined → Elem] ) ──────────────────┐
│  sort Queue enrich  List                                │
│  imports INTEGER                                        │
├─────────────────────────────────────────────────────────┤
│  This specification defines a queue which is a first-in, first-out data │
│  structure.  It can therefore be specified as a List where the insert   │
│  operation adds a member to the end of the queue. However, an           │
│  operation called Get is required which evaluates                       │
│  the head of the queue and, at the same time, creates a new             │
│  queue consisting of the tail of the input queue.  Thus, the output     │
│  from this function is specified as a tuple.                            │
├─────────────────────────────────────────────────────────┤
│  Get (Queue) → (Elem, Queue)                            │
├─────────────────────────────────────────────────────────┤
│  Get (Create) = (Undefined, Create)                     │
│  Get (Cons (Q, v)) = (Head (Q), Tail (Cons (Q, v )))    │
└─────────────────────────────────────────────────────────┘
```

Figure 8.11
The specification of a queue.

which can be specified as an enrichment of lists. An operation is added which evaluates to a pair consisting of the first item on the queue and the queue minus its head. The operations on sort Queue are shown in Figure 8.10 and the queue specification in Figure 8.11.

8.2   Error specification

A problem which faces the developer of a specification is how to indicate errors and exceptional conditions. The basic problem is that under normal conditions, the result of an operation may be of sort X, say, but under exceptional conditions, an error should be indicated. The appropriate error indicator may not be of the same sort as the normal result so a type clash occurs.

There are two ways of tackling this problem:

(1)   A special distinguished, constant operation such as Undefined may be defined and, in exceptional cases, an undefined value results. We have already seen examples of this technique.

(2)   The operation may evaluate to a tuple where one component of the tuple indicates whether or not the operation has evaluated successfully.

It is probably more convenient to handle errors in a specification by introducing distinguished undefined values but it is not always easy to implement such values. Thus, even when errors are specified using this technique, the implementation of the operation must usually return a record with one field an error indicator.

```
generic
    -- A private generic type means assignment and equality must be
    -- defined on that type
    type Elem is private ;
package List is
    type T is private ;
    -- Create operation is implicit. Lists created by declaration
    procedure Head (L : T ; V : out Elem ; Err : out ERROR_INDICATOR) ;
    -- Length can't fail so no need for error indicator
    function Length (L : T) return NATURAL ;
    procedure Tail (L : T ; LT : out T ; Err  : out ERROR_INDICATOR ) ;
    -- Cons can't fail so no need for error indicator
    function Cons (L : T ; V : Elem ) return T ;
private
    -- an Ada access type corresponds to a Pascal pointer
    -- the entity referenced by the pointer is defined in the package body
    -- In this case, it would be a record with one field pointing to the next
    -- list element
    type LISTREC ;
    type T is access LISTREC ;
end List ;
```

Figure 8.12
Ada List specification
with error indicators.

It is possible to define the abstract type operations as functions and to define the type the function returns as a record with an error indicator field. This sometimes leads to a proliferation of rather artificial type definitions so an alternative is to define the operations as procedures and to return an error indicator with each procedure. If the operation succeeds, this indicator is set to Success, otherwise it is set to Failure. The calling procedure may then test the value of the error indicator to discover whether or not the operation has been successful.

This is illustrated in Figure 8.12, which is an Ada package specification defining a list. Notice that this is a generic package so that the elements of the list may be of any type, reflecting the genericity of the specification. The type is named T so that when combined with the package name, the readable name List.T results. The Create operation is implicit. Lists are created using the normal language declaration mechanism.

8.3 Design editor specification

The design editor which has been used previously as a source of examples is interfaced to the underlying data store through a portability interface called the abstract data interface (ADI). This was specified algebraically as a set of abstract data types. Figure 8.13 shows that to move the editor to another system, only the ADI need be re-implemented.

The ADI is made up of a number of abstract types such as Node, representing a node on a design, Link, representing a link and Label, representing an annotation to the design. Nodes and labels exist within

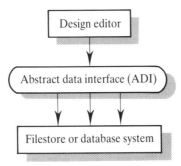

Figure 8.13
The design editor
architecture.

rectangular areas on the design diagram called Zones, where a zone has a position, length and height. To select an entity, the editor user points at it on the design using the mouse and clicks the mouse button. Once an entity is selected, operations such as Translate, Resize and TextEdit are available to the user.

The algebraic specification of the sort Zone is shown in Figure 8.14. Moving an entity is supported directly with a zone operation (Translate) as is changing the entity size (Resize). An Undefined operation is included (evaluating to a zone at the origin with zero length and height) and the Contains operations evaluates to true if a zone includes a given coordinate.

Zone equality and zone ordering operations are defined in Figure 8.14. Zones are equal if they are at the same position and have the same length and height. A zone is greater than another if its X-coordinate is greater or, if the X-coordinates are the same, the zone with the *shortest* height is the greater of the two zones.

This arbitrary definition of zone equality was used in the design editor specification because it simplified the implementation of zone selection. In the original specification, a different (although equally arbitrary) definition of zone ordering was used. When the system was implemented, however, it was found that this caused unacceptable overhead when zones overlapped. When zones are nested (Figure 8.15) the selection operation should select the innermost zone rather than an arbitrary zone containing the coordinate.

The final implementation of selection involved maintaining the list of zones in descending order and searching from the head of the list. The first zone found which contains the coordinate is the most deeply nested zone.

Figure 8.16 shows the specification of Zone_List as an enrichment of Descending_Ordered_List with a Select operation which examines the list from the beginning. Because of the way in which the operation '>' on zones is defined, the zone with the greatest X-coordinate (the most deeply nested) will be discovered first. If zones have a common position but a different size, the zone with the least height will be discovered first.

Figure 8.16 also illustrates how a generic specification (Descending_ Ordered_List) is instantiated to be a list of a specific type. The operator ':='

┌─ ZONE ──┐

sort Zone
imports COORD

───

A zone represents a rectangular area on a picture which has a position
(defined as the position of its top left corner), a height and a length. Zone
operations are Position, Length and Height, which evaluate the zone
position, length and height, respectively, and Translate, Resize and
Contains.
  The Translate operation adjusts the position of a zone by moving it to
the coordinate specified and the Resize operation defines a new zone at
the same position but different dimensions. The Contains operation is
used to test if a zone encloses the specified coordinate and the equality
operation (==) to test if zones are equal. The greater than operation (>) is
arbitrary. The zone with the greater X coordinate is deemed to be the
greatest. If zones have the same position, the zone with the lowest height
(irrespective of length) is the greatest. This definition is helpful in finding
a zone in a collection.

───

Create (Coord, Integer, Integer) → Zone
Position (Zone) → Coord
Length (Zone) → Integer
Height (Zone) → Integer
Translate (Zone, Coord) → Zone
Resize (Zone, Integer, Integer) → Zone
Contains (Zone, Coord) → BOOLEAN
.==. (Zone, Zone) → BOOLEAN
.>. (Zone, Zone) → BOOLEAN
Undefined → Zone

───

Position (Create (C, l, h)) = C
Length (Create (C, l, h)) = l
Height (Create (C, l, h)) = h
Translate (Create (C, l, h), C1) = Create (C1, l, h)
Contains (Create (C, l, h), C1) = X (C1) ≥ X (C) and X (C1) ≤ X (C) + l
                                     and Y (C1) ≤ Y (C) and Y (C1) ≥ Y (C) - h
.==. (Create (C, l, h), Create (C1, l1, h1)) =
                 COORD.Eq (C, C1) and l = l1 and h = h1
.>. (Create (C, l, h), Create (C1, l1, h1)) = (X (C) > X (C1)) or
                                     (X (C) = X (C1) and h < h1)
Undefined = Create (COORD.Create (0, 0), 0, 0)

└──┘

Figure 8.14
The specification of
sort Zone.

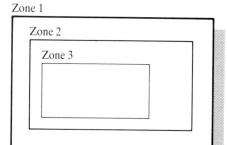

Figure 8.15
Overlapping zones.

```
┌─ ZONE_LIST ( Elem := Zone ) ─────────────────┐
│                                               │
│  sort  Zone_List enrich  Descending_Ordered_ List
│  imports  ZONE                                │
├───────────────────────────────────────────────┤
│  This specification defines a structure which holds a list of zones. It is
│  defined as an enrichment of Ordered_List but has a specific operation
│  called Select which, given a coordinate, finds the first zone in the list
│  which contains that coordinate.              │
├───────────────────────────────────────────────┤
│  Select (Zone_List, Coord) → Zone             │
├───────────────────────────────────────────────┤
│  Select (Create, C) = Undefined               │
│  Select (Insert (ZL, Z), C) = if ZONE.Contains (Head (Insert (ZL, Z)), C)
│           then Head (Insert (ZL, Z)) else Select (Tail (Insert (ZL, Z)), C)
└───────────────────────────────────────────────┘
```

Figure 8.16
The specification of
sort Zone_List.

expresses the binding of the generic parameter Elem (in DESCENDING_LIST) to the specific parameter Zone in the specification ZONE_LIST.

Algebraic specification was a practical technique in the development of the design editing system. Its principal value was in clarifying the design of the system data interface, ensuring that it was orthogonal and consistent. Furthermore, the specification is a maintenance document which provides an unambiguous definition of what the interface ought to do.

The formal specification and the interface implementation were not developed independently. As the system was implemented, problems were fed back to the specification and the specification was changed. This was possible because the specification was not a specification of user requirements but was an abstract design specification. As is the case with most system developments, practical engineering reasons required specification changes to be made. Formal specification will never eliminate such changes. However, the advantage of a formal specification is that it is easier to assess the impact of such changes on the rest of the system.

■ KEY POINTS

- ■ Algebraic specification involves designing the operations on an object and specifying them in terms of their interrelationships.

- ■ An algebraic specification consists of two formal parts: a signature part where the operations and their parameters are set out, and an axioms part where the relationships between these operations are defined. If the specification is built using other specifications these should be indicated and it is good practice to supplement the formal description with an informal explanation of the operations.

■ Enrichment of a sort (type) is the name given to creating a new sort by inheriting the operations and axioms of an existing sort and and adding new operations and axioms to it.

■ Errors in operations can be specified by adding special operations which should evaluate to a distinguished undefined value. These are constant operations which evaluate to the appropriate sort. In the implementation of a specification, the error can be indicated by a function returning an error flag.

■ Algebraic specification is a particularly appropriate technique when data interfaces between software systems must be specified.

FURTHER READING

The Specification of Complex Systems.   This excellent introductory text contains a good chapter discussing algebraic specification. A simple electronic mail system is used as an example and it is compared to the same system described using a model-based approach. (B. Cohen, W.T. Harwood and M.I. Jackson, 1986, Addison-Wesley.)

'Formal specification as a design tool'.   This paper is included in a collection of papers on specification which includes other papers on algebraic specification. I think this paper is particularly useful as it illustrates the practical use of formal specification. (J.V. Guttag and J.J. Horning, in *Software Specification Techniques*, Gehani, N. and McGettrick, A.D. (eds), 1986, Addison-Wesley.)

Abstraction and Specification in Program Development.   This is a general text on systems development with good chapters on algebraic specification. (B. Liskov and J. Guttag, 1986, MIT Press.)

EXERCISES

8.1   Explain how the technique of algebraic specification can be applied to the specification of abstract data types.

8.2   An abstract data type Stack has the following operations:

New: Bring a stack into existence
Push: Add an element to the top of the stack
Top: Evaluate the element on top of the stack
Retract: Remove the top element from the stack and return the modified stack.
Is_empty: True if there are no elements on the stack

Write an algebraic specification of Stack. Make any reasonable assumptions you like about the semantics of the stack operations.

8.3   Modify the example presented in Figure 8.3 (array specification) by adding a new operation called ArrayUpdate which assigns all the values of one array to another array given that the arrays have the same number of elements.

8.4   An abstract data type called Set has a signature defined as follows:

New → Set
Add (Set, Elem) → Set
Size (Set) → Integer
Remove (Set) → Elem
Contains (Set, Elem) → Boolean
Delete (Set, Elem) → Set

Using your intuitive model of sets, explain informally what these operations are likely to do. Write the axioms which formally define your informal English specification.

8.5   Using the equation rewriting approach as used in Example 8.4, verify that the operation Insert ([10, 7, 4], 8) on ordered lists (Figure 8.8) causes the list [10, 8, 7, 4] to be built. (Hint: show that the head of the list is 10 and the tail is [8, 7, 4]).

8.6   Using the same technique with values of your choice, demonstrate the Remove operation in the same specification (Figure 8.8).

8.7   Write a formal algebraic specification of a sort Symbol_table whose operations are informally defined as follows:

Create: Bring a symbol table into existence.
Enter: Enter a symbol and its type into the table. The operation fails if the name is in the table.
Lookup: Return the type associated with a name in the table. The operation fails if the name is not in the table.
Delete: Remove a name, type pair from the table, given a name as a parameter. The operation fails if the name is not in the table.
Replace: Replace the type associated with a given name with the type specified as a parameter. The operation fails if the name is not in the table.

8.8   Discuss how your specification would have to be modified if a block-structured symbol table was required. A block structured symbol table is one used in compiling a language with block structure like

Pascal where declarations in an inner block override the outer block declarations if the same name is used.

8.9 Write a formal algebraic specification of the block-structured symbol table.

8.10 Using an example of your choice, demonstrate that the Lookup operation in the block structured symbol table finds the name in the innermost block in a situation where duplicate names have been entered in the table.

8.11 Write a formal algebraic specification of a binary tree with the following informally defined operations. If you are not familiar with binary trees, you should consult a book on simple data structures before tackling this example.

> Create: Brings a binary tree into existence
> Is_empty: True if the tree is empty
> Left: Evaluates to the left subtree of the tree
> Data: Evaluates to the data held in a tree node
> Right: Evaluates the right subtree of the tree
> Contains: True if the tree contains a value matching its parameter
> Enter: Adds an element to the tree in order so that all of the elements in the left subtree of a tree have data values less than the root value and vice-versa for the right subtree.

(Hint: define a simpler constructor operation called Add which puts an entry into the root of the tree and define Enter in terms of this constructor).

8.12 For all of the abstract data types you have specified, write Ada package specifications defining a package to implement the abstract type. Pay particular attention to error handling.

Model-Based Specification

■ OBJECTIVES

The objective of this chapter is to introduce techniques of model-based specification. Model-based specification is a formal specification technique where the system is modelled using mathematical entities whose properties are well understood, such as sets, relations and sequences. The specification language used, called Z, has recognized the importance of both presentation and specification reuse. Z allows specifications to be highlighted graphically and integrated with other specifications. Z schemas and the use of functions and sequences in modelling systems are covered. The incremental construction of a specification from schema building blocks is discussed. The language and specification technique is illustrated using small examples which could themselves be components of a larger specification.

■ CONTENTS

Model-based specification is a formal method which relies on defining a model of the system using well-understood mathematical entities such as sets and functions. System operations are specified by defining how they affect the overall system model. Using a model-based technique, state changes are straightforward to define and the specification of operations on the state may be grouped with the corresponding state definition. Model-based specification languages are rich in constructs and specifications can be fairly concise.

The earliest model-based specification technique was VDM (Jones, 1980, 1986) which was developed in the late 1970s and refined during the 1980s. In this text, however, model-based specification is illustrated using a notation called Z (pronounced Zed not Zee) which is a specification language developed at the University of Oxford (Hayes, 1987; Spivey, 1989). Z is based on typed set theory because sets are mathematical entities whose semantics are formally defined, but includes a number of constructs which specifically support formal system specification.

Z has been chosen as a basis for discussing model-based specification here because its authors have paid particular attention to the presentational aspects of the specification. Formal specifications can be difficult and tedious to read, especially when they are presented as large mathematical formulae. Understandably, this has inhibited many software engineers from investigating the potential of formal specifications in systems development. Z specifications are normally presented in small, easy to read chunks (called schemas) which are distinguished from associated commentary using graphical highlighting.

Unfortunately, Z relies on an unusual character set and this makes typing a specification difficult on simple text preparation systems. Even where a standard mathematical font is available, Z specifications cannot be typed as the language has its own special characters. Although this problem can be resolved using special-purpose editors, the incompatibility of Z with most word processing systems is a hindrance to its widespread adoption.

As already discussed, the only realistic way to construct a formal specification is to build the specification incrementally. Z is particularly well suited to this approach to formal specification as its schemas allow the specification to be structured. Schema operations such as schema references, schema renaming and schema hiding allow schemas to be manipulated in their own right and provide a powerful tool for system specifiers.

In an introductory chapter like this one, it is only possible to give an overview of how model-based specifications can be developed. One of the difficulties in presenting such an overview is the large amount of notation: a complete description of Z notation would be almost as long as this chapter. Notation is therefore introduced as it is used and a large part of the specification language is not covered. Hayes (1987) describes a number of case studies where Z has been used and gives a summary of Z notation, and Spivey (1989) has written a Z reference manual.

9.1   Z schemas

A specification in Z is presented as a collection of schemas where a schema introduces some specification entities and sets out relationships between them. To be most effective, a formal specification must be supplemented by a good deal of supporting, informal description and the schema presentation has been designed so that it stands out from surrounding text (Figure 9.1).

Figure 9.1 is a specification of a container which can be filled with 'things'. The top line of the schema introduces the schema name and the part between this and the dividing line is called the signature. The signature sets out the names and types of the entities introduced in the schema. Figure 9.1 introduces two entities, namely contents and capacity, which are modelled as natural numbers. A natural number is an integer which is greater than or equal to zero.

The schema predicate (the bottom part of the specification) sets out the relationships between the entities in the signature by defining a predicate over the signature entities. In this case, the predicate states the obvious fact that the contents cannot exceed the capacity of the container.

This specification says nothing about the size of the container or what the container is intended to hold. It merely states that it cannot hold a negative number of things and that its contents are discrete and represented as a natural number.

The specification in Figure 9.1 is a building block which can be used in further specifications and we shall see shortly how this is used. Figure 9.2 shows a specification of a further building block, namely an indicator which might be associated with a container to provide information about its contents.

The signature in Figure 9.2 introduces three entities, namely light, which is modelled by the values off and on, reading, which is modelled as a natural number and danger, which is also modelled as a natural number. The light and the reading would have some physical manifestation in the real system which provides an operator with information about the system. If the reading reaches a dangerously low value, the light should be switched on.

Again, an indicator as specified here is a very general-purpose entity

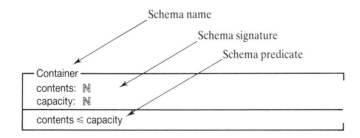

Figure 9.1
A Z schema.

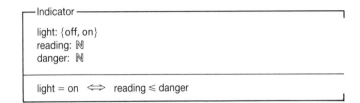

Figure 9.2
The specification of an
indicator.

and we make no attempt to specify, at this stage, what the danger level should be. Thus, the predicate part simply states that if the reading is less than or equal to the danger value, the value of light should be on. The symbol ⇔ means logically equivalent so that so that a low reading is logically equivalent to the light being on.

Given the specification of an indicator and a container, they can be combined (Figure 9.3) to define a hopper which is a type of container. We wish to define a hopper which has a capacity of 5000 'things' and whose light comes on when it is less than 10% full. Notice that again there is no need to specify what is held in the hopper.

The effect of combining specifications is to make a new specification which inherits the signatures and the predicates of the included specifications. Thus, Hopper inherits the signatures of Container and Indicator and their predicates. These are combined with any new signatures and predicates introduced in the specification. In Figure 9.3, three new predicates are introduced.

These predicates are written on separate lines and an implicit 'and' separates the predicates. Thus reading equals contents and capacity equals 5000 and danger equals 50 and the inherited predicates must hold. You can write these on the same line in which case the 'and' symbol (∧) must separate them.

Figure 9.4 shows the expanded specification of Hopper where the signatures and the predicates of Container and Indicator have been explicitly merged. There is some redundancy here in that reading and contents represent the same thing; this results from the use of generalized schema building blocks. Z's schema operations can be used to remove this redundancy but this adds a level of complexity which it is not appropriate to cover here.

```
┌─ Hopper ──────────────────────────────────────────────┐
│                                                        │
│   Container                                            │
│   Indicator                                            │
├────────────────────────────────────────────────────────┤
│   reading = contents                                   │
│   capacity = 5000                                      │
│   danger = 50                                          │
└────────────────────────────────────────────────────────┘
```

Figure 9.3
The specification of a
hopper.

```
┌─Hopper ─────────────────────────────────────────────────────┐
│                                                              │
│  contents: ℕ                                                 │
│  capacity: ℕ                                                 │
│  reading:  ℕ                                                 │
│  danger:   ℕ                                                 │
│  light: {off, on}                                            │
├──────────────────────────────────────────────────────────   │
│  contents ⩽ capacity                                         │
│  light = on⟺reading ⩽ danger                                 │
│  reading = contents                                          │
│  capacity = 5000                                             │
│  danger = 50                                                 │
│                                                              │
└──────────────────────────────────────────────────────────────┘
```

Figure 9.4
The expanded
specification of a
hopper.

Operations can be specified using schemas in a similar way. Figure 9.5 shows the specification of an operation to fill a hopper. The fill operation adds a specified number of entities to the hopper. For the moment, we ignore the problem of trying to add too much to the container.

Two new notions are introduced in Figure 9.5, namely:

- Delta schemas.
- Inputs.

In FillHopper, the name amount is suffixed by a ? character which means that it should be taken as an input to the operation. The ? is part of the name and, by convention, all names whose final character is a ? are inputs. As we shall see in later specifications, names which terminate with a ! symbol are operation outputs.

The predicate for FillHopper specifies that the contents after completion of the operation (referenced as contents′) should equal the sum of the contents before the operation and the amount added to the hopper. The previous predicates which applied to Hopper still apply before and after the operation. By convention, the values of an entity after an operation are referenced by decorating the name of that entity with a quote mark (′). Normally, these decorated names are introduced by using a delta schema (Figure 9.6).

This schema includes both the schema called Hopper and a 'decorated' Hopper schema where the names introduced in Hopper are decorated with a quote mark. Thus, the names contents′, capacity′, light′, danger′ and reading′

```
┌─FillHopper ─────────────────────────────────────────────────┐
│                                                              │
│  Δ Hopper                                                    │
│  amount?: ℕ                                                  │
├──────────────────────────────────────────────────────────   │
│  contents′ = contents + amount?                              │
│                                                              │
└──────────────────────────────────────────────────────────────┘
```

Figure 9.5
The specification of a
hopper filling
operation.

Figure 9.6
A delta schema.

are introduced. The predicates which apply in Hopper also apply in Hopper' and, when the delta schema is used in other schemas, they are also inherited.

The convention in writing Z specifications is to use delta schemas without definition and, when they are encountered by the reader, they indicate that the effect of the operation is to change one or more values. Some operations do not result in a change of value but still find it useful to reference the values before and after the operation. These cases can be catered for by incorporating the schema defined in Figure 9.7.

Figure 9.7 (an Xi schema where Xi is the name of its initial letter) shows a schema which includes the delta schema and a predicate which states explicitly that the values are unchanged. Notice that this predicate uses an explicit 'and' operation between its components.

In the specification of FillHopper given in Figure 9.5, we ignored the possibility of adding too much to the hopper, thus causing it to overflow. Of course, the constraints associated with Hopper exclude the possibility of overflow but give no clue about what should happen if an attempt is made to add too much to the hopper.

A specification should take such errors into account and should define what should happen in the event of an overflow situation. Figure 9.8 shows the specification of an operation called SafeFillHopper which includes a predicate stating that the amount added should be such that the capacity of the hopper should not be exceeded.

To supplement the specification in Figure 9.8, a specification of what happens if an attempt is made to add too much to the hopper must be defined. Let us assume that the effect of trying to overfill a hopper is to abort the fill operation (nothing is added to the hopper) and to print a warning message on an operator's console. This specification is shown in Figure 9.9.

The specification introduces a name r! which refers to an output value. The convention for referencing output values is to postfix them with an

$$
\begin{array}{|l}
\hline
\Xi\ \text{Hopper} \\\\
\Delta\ \text{Hopper} \\
\hline
\text{capacity}' = \text{capacity}\ \wedge\ \ \text{contents}' = \text{contents}\ \wedge \\
\text{reading}' = \text{reading}\ \wedge\ \ \ \ \ \text{light}' = \text{light}\ \wedge\ \ \ \ \ \text{danger}' = \text{danger} \\
\hline
\end{array}
$$

Figure 9.7
An unchanged schema.

```
┌─ SafeFillHopper ─────────────────────────────────────────────────┐
│                                                                   │
│  Δ Hopper                                                         │
│  amount?: ℕ                                                      │
├───────────────────────────────────────────────────────────────────┤
│  contents + amount? ≤ capacity                                   │
│  contents' = contents + amount?                                  │
└───────────────────────────────────────────────────────────────────┘
```

Figure 9.8
The specification of a hopper fill operation avoiding overflow.

exclamation mark (!). The name r! is declared to be a sequence of characters (to hold a message) and, as before, amount? is a natural number.

The predicate associated with OverFillHopper holds when the capacity of the hopper is less than the current contents plus the amount to be added. It also states that the contents are unchanged and that the value r! is 'hopper overflow'. Of course, we could have incorporated an 'unchanged' schema rather than a delta schema but this is simply a question of style.

To complete the specification of hopper filling, SafeFillHopper and OverFillHopper must be combined (Figure 9.10) using a disjunction (or) operator. The effect of this operator is to merge the signatures of the schemas SafeFillHopper and OverFillHopper and to include both predicates, separating them with an 'or' operator (Figure 9.11).

Schemas in Z are a powerful concept and other operators exist to manipulate schemas. The reader will already have inferred that schemas can be used as type names and they can be used to identify sets. An alternative more concise form of schemas is also allowed where schemas are written linearly without graphical highlighting. These are not discussed here but are defined in the Z reference manual (Spivey, 1989).

9.2   Specification using functions

One of the most commonly used techniques in model-based specification is to use functions or mappings in writing specifications. In programming languages, a function is an abstraction over an expression. When provided

```
┌─ OverFillHopper ─────────────────────────────────────────────────┐
│                                                                   │
│  Δ Hopper                                                         │
│  amount?: ℕ                                                      │
│  r!: seq CHAR                                                     │
├───────────────────────────────────────────────────────────────────┤
│  capacity < contents + amount?                                   │
│  contents' = contents                                            │
│  r! = "Hopper overflow"                                          │
└───────────────────────────────────────────────────────────────────┘
```

Figure 9.9
The specification of hopper overfilling.

Figure 9.10
The specification of
hopper filling with
error check.

```
┌─FillHopperOp────────────────────────────────────────────────┐
│                                                              │
│  SafeFillHopper  ∨  OverFillHopper                           │
│                                                              │
└──────────────────────────────────────────────────────────────┘
```

with an input, it computes an output value based on the value of the input. It is possible to think of Z functions or mappings in a comparable way but each function is really a set of pairs. Each pair shows how an output relates to an input. A partial function is a function where not all possible inputs have a defined output. For example, the function SmallSquare below shows the values of the squares of the numbers from 1 to 7.

$$\text{SmallSquare} = \{1 \mapsto 1, 2 \mapsto 4, 3 \mapsto 9, 4 \mapsto 16, 5 \mapsto 25, 6 \mapsto 36, 7 \mapsto 49\}$$

Here we see that 1 is mapped onto 1, 2 to 4, 3 to 9 and so on. Hence, the term *mapping* is sometimes used. In an implementation, of course, an algorithm is used to compute the result from the input but the effect is identical to a mapping.

The domain of a function (written dom f in Z, where f is the function name) is the set of inputs over which the function has a defined result. The range of a function (written rng f in Z) is the set of results which the function can produce. A function is a partial function if its input is a member of some set T but its domain (those inputs which produce a result) is a subset of T. For example, a partial function f may accept any number between 1 and 50 as an input but may only produce a result if the input is a multiple of 7. The domain of f is (7, 14, 21, 28, 35, 42, 49).

If an input i is in the domain of some function f (i $\in$ dom f), the associated result may be specified as f (i), that is, f (i) $\in$ rng f. For example, in the function SmallSquare defined above, SmallSquare (2) = 4,

```
┌─ FillHopperOp ───────────────────────────────────────────────┐
│                                                               │
│  Δ Hopper                                                     │
│  amount?: ℕ                                                   │
│  r!: seq CHAR                                                 │
│                                                               │
├───────────────────────────────────────────────────────────────┤
│  (contents + amount? ≤ capacity                               │
│  contents' = contents + amount?)                             │
│                                                               │
│  ∨                                                            │
│                                                               │
│  (capacity < contents + amount?                              │
│  contents' = contents                                        │
│  r! = "Hopper overflow")                                     │
│                                                               │
└───────────────────────────────────────────────────────────────┘
```

Figure 9.11
Expanded specification
of FillHopperOp.

DataDictionaryEntry ───

ident: NAME
type: {process, data_flow, data_store, user_input, user_output}
description: seq CHAR
───
#description ≤ 2000

Figure 9.12
The format of a data
dictionary entry.

SmallSquare (5) = 25 and so on. The domain and range of square are as
follows:

dom SmallSquare = {1, 2, 3, 4, 5, 6, 7}
rng SmallSquare = {1, 4, 9, 16, 25, 36, 49}

Functions can be used to model data structures. For example, in
Chapter 4 data dictionaries were introduced. A data dictionary holds
information about the names and types of entities used in the system. Data
dictionaries can be useful throughout the system development process but,
for simplicity here, let us assume that the types in the data dictionary are
those used in data flow diagrams. The type and associated description
associated with a data dictionary entry are shown in Figure 9.12.

The type is constrained to be either a process, a data flow, a data
store, a user input or a user output. The description is a sequence of
characters and we have made an arbitrary restriction here, expressed as a
predicate, that this description should be less than 2000 characters in length.
The operator #, applied to sequences or sets, gives the number of members
in the sequence or set.

This schema can be incorporated in a schema describing a data dictionary (Figure 9.13). The schema DataDictionary defines ddict to be a partial
function (indicated by the tagged arrow) from NAME to DataDictionaryEntry.
Given a name, the associated type and description can be discovered. Notice
how the enclosure of the schema name in curly brackets defines a set.

We also have introduced a set called NAME but have not defined this.
The conventions of Z allow a set to be introduced without definition. This is
indicated by writing its name in upper case characters. Names, whose
precise specification is not important at this stage, can be used without
cluttering the specification with extraneous information.

DataDictionary ───

DataDictionaryEntry
ddict: NAME ↦ {DataDictionaryEntry}

Figure 9.13
A data dictionary
specified as a mapping.

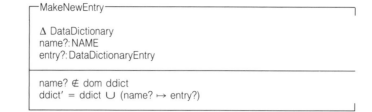

MakeNewEntry

Δ DataDictionary
name?: NAME
entry?: DataDictionaryEntry

name? ∉ dom ddict
ddict' = ddict ∪ (name? ↦ entry?)

Figure 9.14
Adding an entry to the
data dictionary.

Now consider the definition of operations on the data dictionary. Say we wish to define the following operations:

(1)   AddDictionaryEntry   This operation takes a name and a data dictionary entry as parameters. If the name is not in the data dictionary it is added to the dictionary. If the name is in the dictionary and the type in the dictionary and the type in the parameter match, the new entry is added to the data dictionary replacing the previous entry.

(2)   GetDescription   Given a name, this operation evaluates the description associated with that name.

(3)   DeleteEntry   Given a name, the entry associated with that name is deleted from the data dictionary.

For brevity, exceptional situations such as trying to remove a name which does not exist in the dictionary, trying to add a name with a non-matching type and so on are not specified. In a complete specification these would be included using a technique as shown in Figures 9.8 to 9.10.

The specification of AddDictionaryEntry encompasses two possibilities which are described in separate schemas (Figures 9.14 and 9.15).

The signature of the schema named MakeNewEntry shows that the inputs are a name and an associated entry. A delta schema, showing that the dictionary may be modified by the operation, is also included. The predicate part states that if the input name is not a member of the domain of ddict then the name and entry should be considered as a set and the union of this set and ddict should be taken to give the value of ddict after the operation. Set union is a valid operation because a partial function is a set of pairs.

ReplaceEntry

Δ DataDictionary
name?: NAME
entry?: DataDictionaryEntry

name? ∈ dom ddict ∧ ddict (name?).type = entry?.type
ddict' ⊕ {name? ↦ entry?}

Figure 9.15
Replacing a data
dictionary entry.

```
┌─AddDictionaryEntry ─────────────────────────────────────┐
│                                                          │
│   MakeNewEntry   ∨                                       │
│   ReplaceEntry                                           │
│                                                          │
└──────────────────────────────────────────────────┘
```

Figure 9.16
Adding an entry to the
data dictionary.

Figure 9.15 is similar and shows the specification of the operation where the name is already in the data dictionary. The predicate part states that if the name is in the domain of the function and the type associated with entry? and the type in the dictionary referenced by the name are the same, then the function overriding operator ($\oplus$) is used to replace the existing entry with the new entry. The dot notation A.B is used to reference parts of a type. Thus entry?.type refers to the type part of the entry associated with the name.

The function overriding operator is, perhaps, best illustrated with a simpler example. Say we have a function which maps names to telephone numbers.

$$phone = \{Ian \mapsto 3390, Ray \mapsto 3392, Steve \mapsto 3427\}$$

The domain of phone is {Ian, Ray, Steve} and the range is {3390, 3392, 3427}. Now assume we have another function newphone defined as follows.

$$newphone = \{Steve \mapsto 3386, Ron \mapsto 3427\}$$

The operation phone $\oplus$ newphone results in the following function.

$$phone \oplus newphone = \{Ian \mapsto 3390, Ray \mapsto 3392, Steve \mapsto 3386, Ron \mapsto 3427\}$$

Notice that a new mapping for Ron has been added and that the existing mapping for Steve has been modified.

The function overriding operator acts like a set union operator if the name is not in the set. If the name is in the set, the name and its associated value are replaced. A single schema which only uses the function overriding operator cannot be used to define AddDictionaryEntry because of the need to check that the type associated with a name is being replaced by an entry of the same type.

The operation to add a data dictionary entry is specified by a disjunction of the schemas named MakeNewEntry and ReplaceEntry (Figure 9.16).

The operation which retrieves the description associated with a name is a simple one. Its specification is shown in Figure 9.17.

In the schema GetDescription, we see the use of the Xi (unchanged) schema which indicates that the operation does not change the value of the data dictionary. The predicate part specifies that if the name is in the

```
┌─GetDescription ─────────────────────────────────────────┐
│                                                          │
│  Ξ DataDictionary                                        │
│  name?: NAME                                             │
│  desc!: seq CHAR                                         │
├──────────────────────────────────────────────────────── │
│  name? ∈ dom ddict                                       │
│  desc! = ddict (name?). description                      │
└──────────────────────────────────────────────────────── ┘
```

Figure 9.17
Accessing a data
dictionary entry.

dictionary, the description associated with that name is evaluated. Notice how the name ddict is used in the same way as a function name in a programming language with the name acting as a parameter.

The operation to remove an item from the data dictionary makes use of a special operator acting on functions. This is called the domain subtraction operator, which is written $\lhd$. Using the above example of telephone numbers, if Ian is to be removed from the domain of phone, this would be written

$$\{Ian\} \lhd phone$$

The resulting function is:

$$\{Ray \mapsto 3392, Steve \mapsto 3427\}$$

The specification of the remove operation for the data dictionary is shown in Figure 9.18.

The domain subtraction operator removes a member from the domain of a function. The predicate in Figure 9.18 states first that a name must be in the data dictionary before it can be removed. After the application of the domain subtraction operator the name of the identifier to be removed is not a member of the domain of the function. Its related value in the range of the function is thus inaccessible and has been effectively removed.

```
┌─DeleteEntry ────────────────────────────────────────────┐
│                                                          │
│  Δ DataDictionary                                        │
│  name?: NAME                                             │
├──────────────────────────────────────────────────────── │
│  name? ∈ dom ddict                                       │
│  ddict' = {name?} ⊲ ddict                                │
└──────────────────────────────────────────────────────── ┘
```

Figure 9.18
Deleting a data
dictionary entry.

```
┌─SEQUENCE ──────────────────────────────────────────┐
│  s:  ℕ⁺ ↔ ELEM                                      │
│─────────────────────────────────────────────────────│
│  ∃ n:  ℕ⁺ · dom s = 1..n                            │
└─────────────────────────────────────────────────────┘
```

Figure 9.19
Sequence definition.

9.3 Specification using sequences

The above example of a data dictionary specification modelled the data dictionary as a set with no implied ordering on the entries in the dictionary. It is more usual, perhaps, to think of a dictionary as ordered. We have already seen the sequence construct in Z when discussing output messages and this construct can be used in the specification of an ordered dictionary.

Informally, a sequence is a collection where the elements are referenced by their position in the collection. Thus if a sequence is named S, S (1) references the first element in the sequence, S (5) references the fifth element and so on. The specification in Figure 9.19 defines a sequence as a mapping from the positive numbers to entities of type ELEM. If the sequence is of length n, the domain of the mapping is all positive numbers between 1 and n.

To define the data dictionary as a sequence, a slightly different data dictionary entry is specified where the name is included as part of the entry (Figure 9.20).

We can now specify a data dictionary where the entries are held in ascending order (Figure 9.21).

The predicate in Figure 9.21 states that for all integers i and j in the sequence ddict, it is true that if i is less than j then the associated names are related in the same way. We assume here the existence of an ordering over entities which are members of NAME but we do not discuss this here.

The next step in the redefinition of ddict is to redefine the operations on the data dictionary and (presumably) define some operations which make use of the fact that the dictionary is ordered. These will not be covered here.

```
┌─DataDictionaryEntry ────────────────────────────────┐
│  ident: NAME                                         │
│  type: {process, data_flow, data_store, user_input, user_output} │
│  description: seq CHAR                               │
│─────────────────────────────────────────────────────│
│  #description ≤ 2000                                 │
└─────────────────────────────────────────────────────┘
```

Figure 9.20
Revised format for a data dictionary entry.

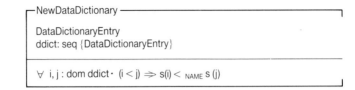

Figure 9.21
Ordered data
dictionary.

This brief introduction to model-based specification has only scratched the surface of the technique and there are many other defined language operations which provide tremendous power to the specifier. It is true that neither Z nor model-based specification in general is yet completely mature and widely usable as a software engineering tool. In particular, the research workers in this area have not yet tackled the problem of structuring specifications at an architectural level. Although Z's schemas are helpful, they are concerned with low-level rather than architectural structuring.

Space does not allow the description of more complex systems here. However, work on the specification of a software engineering environment (Earl *et al*, 1986), on the specification of IBM's CICS system (Johnson, 1987) and on the specification of a real-time kernel (Spivey, 1990) has demonstrated that the technique can be scaled-up to large-scale industrial software systems.

■ KEY POINTS

- ■ Model-based specification relies on building a model of the system using mathematical entities such as sets which have a formal semantics. The principal model-based specification languages are VDM and Z.

- ■ A Z specification is presented as a number of schemas where a schema introduces some typed names and defines predicates over these names. Schemas in Z may be presented using graphical highlighting.

- ■ Schemas are building blocks which may be combined and used in other schemas. The effect of including a schema A in schema B is that schema B inherits the names and predicates of schema A.

- ■ A commonly used technique in Z is to use functions as a means of specifying certain types of data structure. Functions are sets of pairs where the domain of the function is the set of valid inputs and the range the set of associated outputs.

- ■ If ordering is important (sets are unordered), sequences can be used as a specification mechanism. Sequences may be modelled as functions where the domain is the natural numbers greater than zero and the range is the set of entities which may be held in the sequence.

FURTHER READING

There are now many books on Z available which cover the notation and its use. These are broadly similar but the books below are recommended because of their extensive use of case studies.

'Specifying a real-time kernel'.   This is a good introductory paper on Z for readers who are familiar with real-time systems architecture. It includes a summary of Z notation. (J.M. Spivey, *IEEE Software*, **7** (5), September 1990.)

Specification Case Studies.   This book is made up of a number of Z specification examples and although it is not a language tutorial (all of the language is not used in the examples), the examples are well presented and relatively easy to follow. (I. Hayes (ed.), 1987, Prentice-Hall.)

Z: An Introduction to Formal Methods.   This is a good, wide-ranging introduction to Z which contains numerous examples and a Z reference manual. It covers the required mathematical background, the use of Z in formal verification and presents a number of case studies. It also includes a Z reference manual (A. Diller, 1990, John Wiley & Sons.)

EXERCISES

9.1   Explain how the schema combination mechanism which is available in Z is used in constructing complex specifications.

9.2   Modify the specification of a hopper as set out in Figure 9.3 by adding a fill warning light which indicates when the hopper is close to capacity. This should be switched on when the contents is some high percentage of the capacity.

9.3   Write a specification for an operation called Dispense which dispenses a given number of units from a hopper.

9.4   Modify the specification of OverFillHopper (Figure 9.9) so that the effect of the operation is to fill the hopper to capacity and to dump the over-capacity in another container called Overflow.

9.5   What do you understand by the terms domain and range of a function? Explain how functions may be used in defining keyed data structures such as tables.

9.6   Modify the specification of DataDictionaryEntry (Figure 9.12) so that the description of data flows is restricted to 500 characters in length, the description of outputs and inputs to 1000 characters in length and the description of processes and data stores to 1500 characters in length.

9.7 Write a specification for an operation on data dictionaries called ExamineProcesses which discovers the description for all entities in a data dictionary of type process (Hint: use the quantifier $\forall$ in the predicate).

9.8 Modify the specification of the DeleteEntry operation on data dictionaries so that it produces an error report if the entry is not in the data dictionary.

9.9 Using a model-based specification technique, write a specification for the symbol table described in Exercise 8.7.

9.10 Using sequences, write a model-based specification of an array abstract data type. For simplicity, assume that the lower bound of the array is 1.

9.11 Bank teller machines rely on using information on the user's card giving the bank identifier, the account number and the user's personal identifier. They also derive account information from a central database and update that database on completion of a transaction. Using your personal knowledge of the operation of such machines, write Z schemas defining the state of the system, card validation (where the user's identifier is checked) and cash withdrawal.

9.12 Using the informal specification information in Figure 8.14, write a Z specification of Zone.

Part Two
Software Design

The chapters in this part of the book cover different approaches to software design, the specific design requirements of real-time systems and the design of user interfaces. After a general introduction to the design process and design strategies in Chapter 10, Chapters 11 and 12 describe complementary approaches to software design. These are object-oriented design and function-oriented design. Chapter 13 discusses real-time systems design as a collection of cooperating sequential processes. Finally, Chapter 14 addresses the increasingly important area of user interface design, and is specifically concerned with the design of graphical user interfaces.

CONTENTS

Software Design

■ OBJECTIVES

The objective of this chapter is to provide an introduction to the process of software design. The first section in the chapter describes the design process. It emphasizes that design is an iterative process where informal ideas are transformed to a detailed definition of how the system can be implemented. Stages in the process, such as architectural design, interface design and data structure design, are discussed. Object-oriented design and function-oriented design are introduced as the major design strategies. The final section in the chapter introduces the elusive topic of design quality. The principal quality attribute considered here is maintainability and various design characteristics which lead to a maintainable design are discussed.

■ CONTENTS

Design is a creative process which requires experience and some flair on the part of the designer. Design must be practised and learnt by experience and study of existing systems. It cannot be learned from a book. Good design is the key to effective engineering but it is not possible to formalize the design process in any engineering discipline.

Software design involves a number of different stages:

(1)   Study and understand the problem. Without this understanding, effective software design is impossible. The problem should be examined from a number of different angles as these provide different insights into the design requirements.

(2)   Identify gross features of at least one possible solution. It is often useful to identify a number of solutions and to evaluate each of these. The choice of solution depends on the designer's experience (designers tend to choose a familiar, well-understood solution if one exists), the availability of reusable components, and the simplicity of the derived solutions. A good rule of thumb is to choose the simplest solution if all other factors are equal.

(3)   Describe each abstraction used in the solution. Before creating formal documentation, however, the designer may find it necessary to construct an informal design description and debug this by developing it in more detail. Errors and omissions in the high-level design which are discovered during lower-level design may be corrected before the design is documented.

This problem solving process is repeated for each abstraction identified in the initial design and the refinement process continues until a detailed design specification of each abstraction can be prepared. The problem is, of course, when to stop the process of design decomposition. A useful guideline is to stop when a component design can be described on a single sheet of paper.

This chapter is a general introduction to this section on software design. It covers the software design process, design strategies and design quality. Further chapters explore design topics in more detail. Chapter 11 concentrates on object-oriented design and Chapter 12 covers function-oriented design, which is still the most widely used design strategy. Chapter 13 is concerned with the particular problem of real-time systems design and Chapter 14 discusses the design of user interfaces.

10.1   The design process

A general model of a software design is a directed graph. Nodes in this graph represent entities in the design, such as processes, functions or types, and links represent relations between these design entities. The target of the design process is the creation of such a graph without inconsistencies and where all of the relationships between design entities are legal.

Software designers do not arrive at a finished design graph immediately. The design process involves adding formality as a design progresses, with constant backtracking to correct earlier, less formal, designs. The designer starts with a very informal picture of the design and refines it by adding information to make the design more formal (Figure 10.1).

The relationship between design and specification is a close one. Although the process of setting out a requirements specification as the basis of a contract is a separate activity, formalizing that specification may be part of the design process. In practice, the designer iterates between specification and design.

The design process involves describing the system at a number of different levels of abstraction. As a design is decomposed, errors and omissions in earlier stages are discovered. These feed back to allow earlier design stages to be refined. It is common to begin the next stage before a stage is finished simply to get feedback from the refinement process. Figure 10.2 shows design process stages and the design descriptions produced as a result of these activities. These stages are fairly arbitrary but make the design process visible and thus allow it to be managed.

A specification is the output of each design activity. This specification may be an abstract, formal specification which is produced to clarify the requirements or it may be a specification of how part of the system is to be realized. As the design process continues, more and more detail is added to the specification. The ultimate outputs are specifications of algorithms and data structures which are used as a basis for system implementation.

Figure 10.2 suggests that the stages of the design process are sequential. In reality, design process activities go on in parallel with different design products developed to different levels of detail in the course

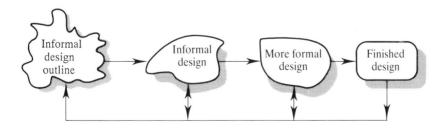

Figure 10.1
The process of design.

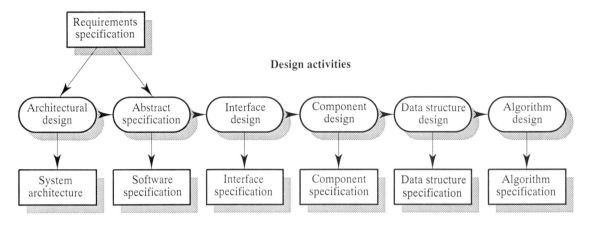

Design activities

Design products

Figure 10.2
Design activities and
design products.

of the design process. However, the activities shown are all essential in the design of large software systems:

(1)   *Architectural design*   The sub-systems making up the overall system and their relationships are identified and documented.

(2)   *Abstract specification*   For each sub-system, an abstract specification of the services it provides and the constraints under which it must operate is produced.

(3)   *Interface design*   For each sub-system, its interface with other sub-systems is designed and documented. This interface specification must be unambiguous as it allows the sub-system to be used without knowledge of the subsystem operation.

(4)   *Component design*   The services provided by a sub-system are partitioned across the components in that sub-system.

(5)   *Data structure design*   The data structures used in the system implementation are designed in detail and specified.

(6)   *Algorithm design*   The algorithms used to provide services are designed in detail and specified.

This process is repeated for each sub-system until the components identified can be mapped directly into programming language components such as packages, procedures or functions.

A widely recommended approach to design is a top-down approach where the problem is recursively partitioned into sub-problems until tractable sub-problems are identified. The general form of the design which usually emerges from such a design process is approximately hierarchical (Figure

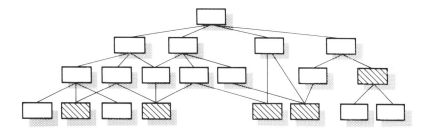

Figure 10.3
Software design
structure.

10.3). Cross-links in the graph emerge at lower levels of the design tree as designers identify possibilities for reuse.

In fact, it is unusual for large systems to be designed in a manner which is strictly top-down. Designers always use their previous design knowledge in the design process. They do not need to decompose all abstractions as they may be aware exactly how one part of the design can be built. They might therefore concentrate on other problematical parts of the design before returning to that part. Indeed, project planning may require difficult parts of the design to be tackled first so that management can make more informed estimates of the system development time.

Top-down design was proposed in conjunction with functional decomposition and it is a valid approach where design components are tightly coupled. However, when an object-oriented approach to design is adopted and many existing objects are available for reuse, top-down design is less useful. The designer uses existing objects as a design framework and builds the design out from them; there is no concept of a single 'top' or of all objects existing in a single object hierarchy.

10.1.1 Design methods

In many organizations, software design is still an *ad hoc* process. Given a set of requirements, usually in natural language, an informal design is prepared. Coding commences and the design is modified as the system is implemented. When the implementation stage is complete, the design has usually changed so much from its initial specification that the original design document is a totally inadequate description of the system.

A more methodical approach to software design is proposed by 'structured methods' which are sets of notations and guidelines about how to create a software design. Some of the most widely used structured methods are surveyed in Birrell and Ould (1985). Examples are structured design (Constantine and Yourdon, 1979), structured systems analysis (Gane and Sarson, 1979), RAPID/USE (Wasserman, 1981), Jackson system development (JSD) (Jackson, 1983) and MASCOT (Simpson, 1986), which is a method used in real-time systems design. There have been a vast number of similar design methods suggested and used in different applications.

Structured methods have been applied successfully in many large projects. They can deliver significant cost reductions because they use standard notations and ensure that designs follow a standard form. The use of structured methods normally involves producing large amounts of diagrammatic design documentation. CASE tools (see Chapter 18) have been developed to support particular methods.

Although there are a large number of methods, they have much in common and usually support some or all of the following views of a system:

(1)   A data flow view where the system is modelled using the data transformations which take place as it is processed. Data flow diagrams are covered in Chapter 12.

(2)   An entity-relation view which is used to describe the logical data structures being used. Entity-relation data specification is covered in Chapter 4.

(3)   A structural view where the system components and their interactions are documented. One approach to providing a structural view is through 'structure charts' as discussed in Chapter 12.

Particular methods supplement these with other system models such as state transition diagrams (see Chapter 13), entity life histories, which show how each entity is transformed as it is processed, and so on. Most methods suggest that a centralized repository for system information (a data dictionary) should be used but this is only really feasible with automated tool support. Because of the variety of methods and the fact that no one method is demonstrably superior to another, I have made a deliberate decision not to cover any particular method in detail in this book.

A mathematical method (such as the method for long division) is a strategy which, if adopted, will always lead to the same result. The term 'structured methods' suggests, therefore, that designers should normally generate similar designs from the same specification.

In practice, the guidance given by the methods is informal so this situation is unlikely. These 'methods' are really standard notations and embodiments of good practice. By following these methods and applying the guidelines, a reasonable design should emerge but designer creativity is still required to decide on the system decomposition and to ensure that the design adequately captures the system specification.

10.1.2 Design description

A software design is a model of a real-world system which has many participating entities and relationships. Different engineers use this design in different ways. It must act as a basis for detailed implementation, it serves as a communication medium between the designers of sub-systems, it provides information to system maintainers about the original intentions of the system designers, and so on. This means that it must be possible to view a design at a number of different levels of abstraction.

There are three types of notation which are widely used for design documentation:

(1) *Graphical notations* These are used to display the relationships between the components making up the design and to relate the design to the real-world system it is modelling. A graphical view of a design is an abstract view and is most useful for giving an overall picture of the system.

(2) *Program description languages* These languages (PDLs) use control and structuring constructs based on programming language constructs but also allow explanatory text and (sometimes) additional types of statement to be used. These allow the intention of the designer to be expressed rather than the details of how the design is to be implemented. The PDL used for design description in this book is described in Appendix A.

(3) *Informal text* Much of the information which is associated with a design cannot be expressed formally. Information about design rationale or non-functional considerations must be expressed using natural language text.

Generally, all of these different notations should be used in describing a system design. The architecture and the logical data design should be described graphically, supplemented by design rationale and further informal or formal descriptive text. The interface design, the detailed data structure design and the algorithm design are best described using a PDL. Descriptive rationale may be included as embedded comments.

10.2 Design strategies

Until relatively recently, most software was developed according to a design strategy which involved decomposing the design into functional components with system state information held in a shared data area. Although Parnas (1972) suggested an alternative strategy in the early 1970s and versions of Smalltalk (Goldberg and Robson, 1983) were in existence in the 1970s, it is only since the mid-1980s that this alternative, object-oriented design, has been widely adopted.

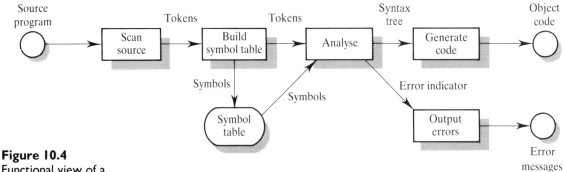

Figure 10.4
Functional view of a compiler.

These two design strategies may be summarized as follows:

(1) *Functional design* The system is designed from a functional view-point, starting with a high-level view and progressively refining this into a more detailed design. The system state is centralized and shared between the functions operating on that state. This strategy is exemplified by structured design (Constantine and Yourdon, 1979) and step-wise refinement (Wirth, 1971, 1976). Methods such as Jackson structured programming (Jackson, 1975) and the Warnier–Orr method (Warnier, 1977) are techniques of functional decomposition where the structure of the data is used to determine the functional structure used to process that data.

(2) *Object-oriented design* The system is viewed as a collection of objects rather than as functions. The system state is decentralized and each object manages its own state information. Objects have a set of attributes defining their state and operations which act on these attributes. Objects are usually members of an object class whose definition defines attributes and operations of class members. These may be inherited from one or more super-classes so that a class definition need merely set out the differences between that class and its super-classes. Conceptually, objects communicate by exchanging messages; in practice, most object communication is achieved by an object calling a procedure associated with another object.
  Object-oriented design is based on the idea of information hiding (Parnas, 1972) and has been described by Meyer (1988) and Booch (1991). JSD (Jackson, 1983) is a design method which falls some-where between function-oriented and object-oriented design.

Top-down functional decomposition has been widely used for both small-scale and large-scale projects in diverse application areas. Object-oriented design is a more recent development which encourages the production of systems composed in independent, interacting components.
  To illustrate the difference between functional and object-oriented

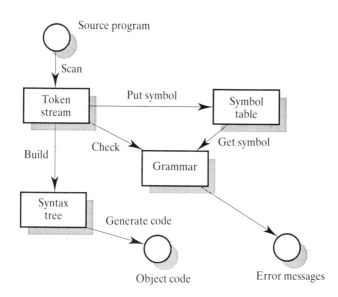

Figure 10.5
Object-oriented view
of a compiler.

approaches to software design, consider the structure of a compiler. It may be viewed as a set of functional transformations with information being passed from one function to another (Figure 10.4).

An alternative, object-oriented view of the same system is shown in Figure 10.5. Here, the objects manipulated by the compiler are central with transformation functions associated with object communications.

Enthusiasts for particular design techniques sometimes suggest that their favourite technique is generally applicable and that other techniques should not be used. In fact, large software systems are such complex entities that different approaches might be used at some stage in the design of different parts of the system. There is no 'best' design strategy for large projects. Functional and object-oriented approaches are complementary rather than opposing techniques and each may be applicable at different stages in the design process. The pragmatic software engineer selects the most appropriate approach for each stage in the design process.

To illustrate this, consider the software systems (Figure 10.6) which might be part of a modern civil aircraft. Some of these might be:

- The navigation system.
- The radar system.
- The external communications system.
- The instrument display system.
- The engine control system.

Our natural high-level view of the overall software system is as a set of

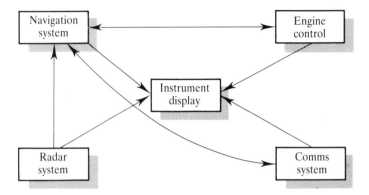

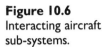

Figure 10.6
Interacting aircraft
sub-systems.

objects (sub-systems) rather than as a set of functions. Thus at abstract design levels, an object-oriented approach is appropriate.

When the system is examined in more detail, its natural description is as a set of interacting functions rather than objects. For example, some of these functions might be:

● Display_Track (radar sub-system).
● Compensate_for_Wind_Speed (navigation sub-system).
● Reduce_Power (engine control sub-system).
● Indicate_Emergency (instrument sub-system).
● Lock_onto_Frequency (communications sub-system).

This functional view may be taken by the requirements definition. This can be converted to an object-oriented view but system validation may be difficult because there is not a simple correspondence between design components and requirements definitions. A single logical function in the requirements definition may be implemented as a sequence of object interactions.

As the system design is further decomposed, an object-oriented view may again become the natural way to view the system. At the detailed design stage, the objects manipulated might be The_engine_status, The_aircraft_position, The_altimeter, The_radio_beacon, and so on. Thus an object-oriented approach to the lower levels of the system design is likely to be effective.

In summary, an object-oriented approach to software design seems to be the most natural at the highest and lowest levels of system design. At these levels, an object-oriented approach leads to the production of independent components which are usually more maintainable than functional components.

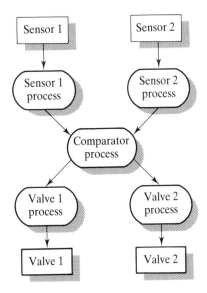

Figure 10.7
Parallel design of a control system.

10.2.1 Concurrent systems design

Many software systems, particularly embedded real-time systems, are structured as a set of parallel communicating processes as shown in Figure 10.7. This is an outline design of a simple control system. Indeed, it is sometimes suggested that this structure of parallel processes is a natural and necessary approach for real-time systems construction.

As discussed in Chapters 11 and 12, both object-oriented and function-oriented designs can be realized as sequential or concurrent programs. Indeed, structuring the design as a set of cooperating processes where each process maintains its own state is a 'half-way house' between these two approaches to design. If no shared memory is used for process communication, the processes hide information in the same way as objects.

Embedded systems must often perform to strict time constraints and, where hardware is relatively slow, only a multiple process/multiple processor approach may be able to provide the necessary performance. However, with fast processors, it may not be necessary to implement embedded systems as parallel processes. A sequential system which uses polling to interrogate and control hardware components may provide adequate performance.

The advantage of avoiding a parallel systems design is that sequential programs are easier to design, implement, verify and test than parallel systems. Time dependencies between processes are hard to formalize, control and verify.

The design process should therefore be considered as a two-stage activity:

(1) Identify the logical design structure, namely the components of a

system and their interrelationships. Either a functional or an object-oriented view may be used.

(2)   Realize this structure in a form which can be executed. This latter stage is sometimes considered detailed design and sometimes programming. I believe that decisions on parallelism should be made at this stage rather than preconceived at earlier stages in the design process.

Parallelism in real-time systems design is covered in Chapter 13. A full discussion of parallelism, including a description of Ada's model of tasking, is given by Sommerville and Morrison (1987).

10.3   Design quality

There is no definitive way of establishing what is meant by a 'good' design. Depending on the application and project requirements, a good design might be a design which allows efficient code to be produced; it might be a minimal design where the implementation is as compact as possible; or it might be the most maintainable design.

This latter criterion is the criterion of 'goodness' used here. A maintainable design can be readily adapted to modify existing functionality and add new functionality. The design should therefore be understandable and changes should be local in effect. The components of the design should be cohesive, which means that all parts of the component should have a close logical relationship. They should be loosely coupled. Coupling is a measure of the independence of components. The looser the coupling, the easier it is to adapt the design.

Some work has been carried out to establish design quality metrics to establish whether or not a design is a 'good' design. These have mostly been developed in conjunction with structured design methods such as Yourdon's structured design. Quality metrics are briefly discussed with a more general description of software metrics in Chapter 31.

Quality characteristics are equally applicable to object-oriented and function-oriented design. Because of the inherent nature of object-oriented designs, it is usually easier to achieve maintainable designs because information is concealed within objects. However, as is discussed in each of the following sections, inheritance in object-oriented systems can compromise design quality. For readers who are unfamiliar with the concept of inheritance, it is discussed briefly in the following chapter.

10.3.1   Cohesion

The cohesion of a component is a measure of how well it fits together. A component should implement a single logical function or should implement a single logical entity. All of the parts of the component should contribute to this implementation. If the component includes parts which are not directly related to its logical function (for example, if it is a grouping of unrelated operations which are executed at the same time) it has a low degree of cohesion.

Constantine and Yourdon (1979) identify seven levels of cohesion in order of increasing strength of cohesion from lowest to highest.

- *Coincidental cohesion*   The parts of a component are not related but simply bundled into a single component.

- *Logical association*   Components which perform similar functions such as input, error handling, etc. are put together in a single component.

- *Temporal cohesion*   All of the components which are activated at a single time, such as start up or shut down, are brought together.

- *Procedural cohesion*   The elements in a component make up a single control sequence.

- *Communicational cohesion*   All of the elements of a component operate on the same input data or produce the same output data.

- *Sequential cohesion*   The output from one element in the component serves as input for some other element.

- *Functional cohesion*   Each part of the component is necessary for the execution of a single function.

These cohesion classes are not strictly defined and Constantine and Yourdon illustrate each by example. It is not always easy to decide under what cohesion category a unit should be classed.

Constantine and Yourdon's method is functional in nature and it is obvious that the most cohesive form of unit is the function. However, a high degree of cohesion is also a feature of object-oriented systems. Indeed, one of the principal advantages of this approach to design is that the objects making up the system are naturally cohesive.

A cohesive object is one where a single entity is represented and all of the operations on that entity are included with the object. For example, an object representing a compiler symbol table is cohesive if all of the functions such as 'Add a symbol', 'Search table', and so on, are included with the symbol table object.

Thus, a further class of cohesion might be defined as follows:

- *Object cohesion*   Each operation provides functionality which allows the attributes of the object to be modified, inspected or used as a basis for service provision.

Cohesion is a desirable characteristic because it means that a unit represents

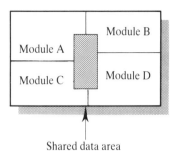

Figure 10.8
Tight coupling.

Shared data area

a single part of the problem solution. If it becomes necessary to change the system, that part exists in a single place and everything to do with it is encapsulated in a single unit. There is no need to modify many components if a change has to be made.

If functionality is provided in an object-oriented system using inheritance from super-classes, the cohesion of the object which inherits attributes and operations is reduced. It is no longer possible to consider that object as a separate unit. All super-classes also have to be inspected if the object's functionality is to be understood completely. System browsers which display object classes and their super-classes assist with this process but understanding a component which inherits attributes from a number of super-classes can be particularly complex.

10.3.2 Coupling

Coupling is related to cohesion. It is an indication of the strength of interconnections between program units. Highly coupled systems have strong interconnections, with program units dependent on each other. Loosely coupled systems are made up of units which are independent or almost independent.

As a general rule, modules are tightly coupled if they make use of shared variables or if they interchange control information. Constantine and Yourdon call this common coupling and control coupling. Loose coupling is achieved by ensuring that, wherever possible, representation information is held within a component and that its data interface with other units is via its parameter list. If shared information is necessary, the sharing should be controlled as in an Ada package. Constantine and Yourdon call this data coupling and stamp coupling. Figures 10.8 and 10.9 illustrate tightly and loosely coupled modules.

Other coupling problems arise when names are bound to values at an early stage in the development of the design. For example, if a program is concerned with tax computations and a tax rate of 30% is encoded as a number in the program, that program is coupled with the tax rate. Changes

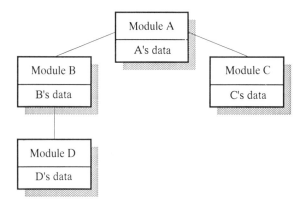

Figure 10.9
Loose coupling.

to the tax rate require changes to the program. If the program reads in the tax rate at run-time, it is easy to accommodate rate changes.

Perhaps the principal advantage of object-oriented design is that the nature of objects leads to the creation of loosely coupled systems. It is fundamental to object-oriented design that the representation of an object is concealed within that object and is not visible to external components. The system does not have a shared state and any object can be replaced by another object with the same interface.

Inheritance in object-oriented systems, however, leads to a different form of coupling. Objects which inherit attributes and operations are coupled to their super-classes. Changes to the super-class must be made carefully as these changes propagate to all of the classes which inherit their characteristics.

10.3.3 Understandability

Changing a design component implies that the person responsible for making the change understands the operation of the component. This understandability is related to a number of component characteristics:

(1) *Cohesion* Can the component be understood without reference to other components?

(2) *Naming* Are the names used in the component meaningful? Meaningful names are names which reflect the names of the real-world entities being modelled by the component.

(3) *Documentation* Is the component documented so that the mapping between the real-world entities and the component is clear? Is the rationale for that mapping documented?

(4) *Complexity* How complex are the algorithms used to implement the component?

We use the term *complexity* here in an informal way. High complexity implies many relationships between different parts of the design component and a complex logical structure which may involve deeply nested if-then-else statements. Complex components are hard to understand so the designer should strive for as simple as possible a component design.

Most work on design quality metrics (Chapter 31) has concentrated on trying to measure the complexity of a component and therefore obtain some measure of the component's understandability. Complexity affects understandability but there are a number of other factors which influence the understandability, such as the data organization and the style in which the design is described. Complexity measures can only provide an indicator to the understandability of a component.

Inheritance in an object-oriented design affects its understandability. If inheritance is used to conceal design details, the design is easier to understand. If, on the other hand, the use of inheritance requires the design reader to look at many different object classes in the inheritance hierarchy, the understandability of the design is reduced.

10.3.4 Adaptability

If a design is to be maintained, it must be readily adaptable. Of course, this implies that its components should be loosely coupled. As well as this, however, adaptability means that the design should be well-documented, the component documentation should be readily understandable and consistent with the implementation, and that the implementation should be written in a readable way.

An adaptable design should have a high level of visibility. There should be a clear relationship between the different levels in the design. It should be possible for a reader of the design to find related representations such as the structure chart representing a transformation on a data flow diagram (Figure 10.10).

It should be easy to incorporate changes made to the design in all design documents. If this is not the case, changes made to a design description may not be included in all related descriptions. The design

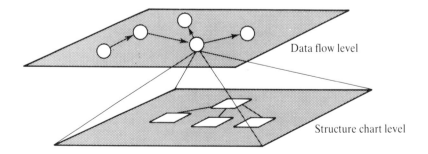

Figure 10.10
Design level visibility.

documentation may become inconsistent. Later changes are more difficult to make (the component is less adaptable) because the modifier cannot rely on the consistency of design documentation.

For optimum adaptability, a component should be self-contained. A component may be loosely coupled in that it only cooperates with other components via message passing. This is not the same as being self-contained as the component may rely on other components, such as system functions or error handling functions. Adaptations to the component may involve changing parts of the component which rely on external functions so the specification of these external functions must also be considered by the modifier.

To be completely self-contained, a component should not use other components which are externally defined. However, this is contrary to good practice which suggests that existing components should be reused. Thus, some balance must be struck between the advantages of reusing components and the loss of component adaptability that this entails.

One of the principal advantages of inheritance in object-oriented systems is that components may be readily adapted. The adaptation mechanism does not rely on modifying the component but on creating a new component which inherits the attributes and operations of the original component. Only those attributes and operations which need be changed are modified. Components which rely on the base component are not affected by the changes made.

This simple adaptability is one reason why object-oriented languages are so effective for rapid prototyping. However, for long lifetime systems, the problem with inheritance is that as more and more changes are made, the inheritance network becomes increasingly complex. Functionality is often replicated at different points in the network and components are harder to understand. Experience of object-oriented programming has shown that the inheritance network must be periodically reviewed and restructured to reduce its complexity and functional duplication. Clearly, this adds to the costs of system change.

■ KEY POINTS

- ■ Design is a creative process. Although methods and guidelines are helpful, judgement and flair on the part of the software engineer are still required to design a software system.

- ■ The main design activities in the software process are architectural design, system specification, interface design, component design, data structure design and algorithm design.

- Functional decomposition involves considering a system as a set of interacting functional units.

- Object-oriented decomposition considers the system as a set of objects where an object is an entity with state and functions to inspect and modify that state.

- A decision on whether a system should be implemented as a single sequential process or as a number of parallel processes is a detailed design decision. The design process should partition the system into logical, interacting units which may be realized as either sequential or parallel components.

- The most important design quality attribute is maintainability. Maximizing cohesion in a component and minimizing the coupling between components is likely to lead to a maintainable design.

- The use of inheritance in object-oriented systems can improve the quality of a design but may make the design more difficult to understand.

FURTHER READING

IEEE Trans. Software Engineering, **12** (2), March 1986. This is a special issue of the journal devoted to design methods. It includes papers on various methods, including object-oriented development, and papers on design documentation and design evaluation.

Object-oriented Design with Applications. This is a full discussion of object-oriented design by one of the pioneers in this field. As well as a good introduction to object-oriented design, it shows how an object-oriented design can be realized in a number of different object-oriented programming languages. (G. Booch, 1991, Benjamin Cummings.)

Software Development with Ada. This book is concerned with software engineering and the use of Ada in building well-engineered systems. A significant part of the book is devoted to a discussion of software design. (I. Sommerville and R. Morrison, 1987, Addison-Wesley.)

EXERCISES

10.1 Describe the main activities in the software design process. Using an entity-relation diagram, show their relationships.

10.2 Explain why sequential software designs are easier to validate than designs which involve parallel processes.

10.3 Discuss the differences between object-oriented and function-oriented design.

10.4 Write down outline object-oriented and function-oriented designs for the following systems:

(a) A cruise control system for a car which maintains a constant speed as set by the driver. The system should adjust the car controls depending on measured road speed.

(b) An automated library catalogue which is queried by users to find which books are available and which books are on loan.

(c) A self-service petrol (gas) pump where the driver sets the pump as required and fills his or her own tank. The amount used is recorded in a booth and the driver may pay by direct credit card debit.

10.5 Using an Ada-based design description language such as that described in Appendix A, describe the design of the following algorithms:

(a) An algorithm to find the maximum, minimum and mean values in an array of integers.

(b) A quicksort algorithm which sorts an array of integers.

(c) A linear search algorithm which searches an array for some key value.

(d) A program which reads a document, identifies each sentence (delimited by a full stop) and prints it on a separate line.

(e) An algorithm which multiplies two matrices.

(f) A program which, given a stream of input with one input item per line, prints this in four columns on a page. The page has a finite width and the size of the input items is not restricted. Take sensible action if the input items are too long for the columns.

(g) A keyword retrieval program which searches a set of records and retrieves those containing a given keyword.

(h) A computerized combination lock which requires the user to input a sequence of five numbers to unlock a door.

10.6 What do you understand by the terms *cohesion*, *coupling* and *adaptability*. Explain why maximizing cohesion and minimizing coupling leads to more maintainable systems.

Object-Oriented Design

■ OBJECTIVES

The objective of this chapter is to describe an approach to software design which is based on objects representing real-world entities. This design strategy maximizes information hiding and usually leads to systems with lower coupling and higher cohesion than the functional approach. The chapter introduces the concepts of objects, object classes and inheritance, and illustrates the object-oriented approach to design using an example of a weather mapping system. The final section in the chapter discusses the difficult problem of object identification, which is the key to successful object-oriented design.

■ CONTENTS

Information hiding is a design strategy where as much information as possible is hidden within design components. The basic premise underlying information hiding is the notion that the binding of logical control and data structures to their implementation should be made as late as possible in the design process. Communication through shared state information (global variables) is minimized, thus increasing the understandability of the design. The design is relatively easy to change as changes to a component should not have unforeseen side-effects on other components.

Object-oriented design is based on information hiding. It differs from the functional approach to design in that it views a software system as a set of interacting objects, with their own private state, rather than as a set of functions (Figure 11.1).

An object-oriented design is based on entities (objects) which have a hidden state and operations on that state. The design is expressed in terms of services requested and provided by interacting objects.

The characteristics of an object-oriented design are:

● Shared data areas are eliminated. Objects communicate by exchanging messages rather than sharing variables. This reduces overall system coupling as there is no possibility of unexpected modifications to shared information.

● Objects are independent entities that may readily be changed because all state and representation information is held within the object itself. No access and hence no deliberate or accidental use of this information by other objects is possible. Changes to the representation may be made without reference to other system objects.

● Objects may be distributed and may execute either sequentially or in parallel. Decisions on parallelism need not be taken at an early stage of the design process.

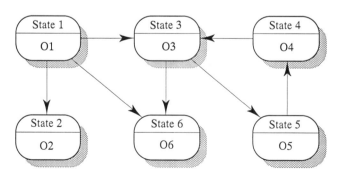

Figure 11.1
The structure of an object-oriented design.

An object-oriented approach to design has the following advantages:

(1) The developed system should be easier to maintain as the objects are independent. They may be understood and modified as stand-alone entities. Changing the implementation of an object or adding services should not affect other system objects.

(2) Objects are appropriate reusable components (because of their independence). Designs can be developed using objects which have been created in previous designs. Reuse is discussed in Chapter 16.

(3) For some classes of system, there is a clear mapping between real-world entities (such as hardware components) and their controlling objects in the system. This improves the understandability of the design.

The disadvantage of object-oriented design is that the identification of appropriate system objects is difficult. Our 'natural' view of many systems is a functional one and adapting to an object-oriented view is sometimes difficult. A particular problem is object identification, which is covered later in this chapter.

Object-oriented design and object-oriented programming are often confused. An object-oriented programming language is a programming language which allows the direct implementation of objects and which provides object classes and inheritance. The language may support run-time binding of operations to objects where several members of a class hierarchy all provide an operation with the same name. The actual operation which is executed is chosen at run-time depending on the types of the operation parameters.

Object-oriented programming languages like Smalltalk are not well-suited to the implementation of embedded systems with stringent performance and memory requirements. This is because of the inherent speed penalty involved in providing run-time binding and the large associated run-time system. To counter this difficulty, languages like C++ (Stroustrup, 1986) and Eiffel (Meyer, 1988) are object-oriented languages with static (compile-time) binding rather than dynamic binding.

Ada is not an object-oriented programming language because it does not support class inheritance. However, it is possible to implement objects in Ada using packages or tasks. Ada can therefore be used to describe object-oriented designs.

Object-oriented design is a *design strategy* and is not dependent on any specific implementation language. Object-oriented programming languages and data encapsulation capabilities (Ada packages or Modula-2 modules) make an object-oriented design simpler to realize. However, an object-oriented design can also be implemented in languages such as Pascal and C which do not have such features. The principle of designing a system as a set of interacting objects is language independent although it is is obviously easier to implement the design if language support for objects is available.

The acceptance of object-oriented design as an effective design strategy has led to the development of object-oriented design methods. The Yourdon method, which was originally based on data flow diagrams and structure charts, has, in its latest version, an object-oriented flavour. This method is based on the work of Coad and Yourdon (1990) on object-oriented analysis and on extensions to the method (Ward and Mellor, 1985) for real-time systems development.

Another object-oriented method which is used in European aerospace systems development is HOOD (Hierarchical Object-Oriented Design). HOOD (HOOD Working Group, 1989) is based on the work by Booch (1986, 1987a) and is specifically intended to support the development of systems written in Ada.

The Jackson design method (JSD) (Jackson, 1983; Cameron, 1986) uses an object-oriented approach in its initial phase but then goes on to realize the design as a set of cooperating sequential processes whose state is exposed to other processes in the system. Although this method has something in common with object-oriented development, claims that it is an object-oriented design method are not true.

Object-oriented methods are still relatively immature and are changing rapidly so are not nearly as widely used as methods based on functional decomposition. They will become more widely used as they mature and as CASE tools to support them become available. For the reasons discussed in Chapter 10, no particular method is used in this chapter.

11.1 Objects, object classes and inheritance

The terms 'object' and 'object-oriented' have become buzzwords and are applied to different types of entity, design methods, systems and programming languages. Anything which is not purely functional might be termed 'object-oriented' and further confusion is sown by the term 'object-based' (Cardelli and Wegner, 1985), which is used to refer to programming languages which support object implementation but not inheritance.

My definition of an object is:

> An object is an entity which has a state (whose representation is hidden) and a defined set of operations which operate on that state. The state is represented as a set of object attributes. The operations associated with the object provide services to other objects (clients) which request these services when some computation is required.

In principle, objects communicate by passing messages to each other and these messages initiate object operations. A message has two parts:

(1)   The name of the service requested by the calling object.

(2)   Copies of information from the calling object which are required to execute the required service and, perhaps, the name of a holder for the results of the service execution.

In some distributed systems, object communications are implemented directly as text messages which objects exchange. The receiving object parses the message, identifies the service and the associated data and carries out the requested service.

More commonly, however, messages are implemented as procedure or function calls. The name of service required corresponds to the name of the object operation providing the service. The copies of information needed to execute the service are variables passed to the procedure or function and the holder for the results of the service execution are values returned by a function or output variables in a procedure's parameter list. Examples of such 'messages' are:

```
-- Call the printing service associated with lists to print the list L1
List.Print (L1)
-- Call the service associated with integer arrays which finds the maximum
-- value of array XX. Return the result in Max_value
IntArray.Max (XX, Max_value)
```

When messages are implemented as procedure calls communication between objects is synchronous. However, messages may also be implemented as calls to entries associated with a concurrent process so communication may be asynchronous. An object-oriented design may be realized as a parallel or as a sequential program.

Objects may be represented graphically using a named round-edged rectangle separated into two sections. The object attributes are listed in the top section. The services provided by the object are set out in the bottom section. Figure 11.2 illustrates this notation using an object which models an electronic mail message.

Listing an attribute in the graphical notation implies the existence of functions to evaluate that attribute (Get) and to assign a value to it (Put). The convention used in this chapter is that each object has operations called Get ‹attribute name› and Put ‹attribute name› where ‹attribute name› is shown as an attribute in the graphical notation.

The notation used in Figure 11.2 is similar to that used by Coad and Yourdon in their book on object-oriented analysis. An alternative notation based on cloud-shaped icons to represent objects and classes is used by Booch (1990). However, regular rather than irregular graphical representa-

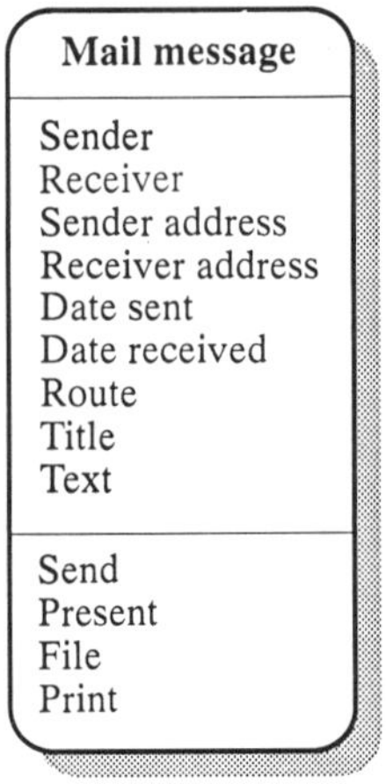

Figure 11.2
A mail message object
class.

tions are easier to draw using personal computer drawing systems or CASE tools.

The attributes of the Mail message object are the identifiers of the sender and receiver, the addresses of the sender and receiver, the date the message was sent, the date it was received, its route from sender to receiver, a message title and the text of the message itself. Operations are Send, Present (display the message on a user's terminal), File and Print.

It is good design practice to hide information so I have deliberately excluded information about how the object attributes are represented. The state representation should not be visible from outside the object. When the object design is developed, the attributes should be accessed and modified through appropriate get and put functions.

Figure 11.3 shows how the object class Mail.MESSAGE may be defined as an Ada abstract data type. Some object-oriented programming languages distinguish between an object class and a type but they can usually be thought of as the same thing.

In the Ada examples in this chapter, object names and associated operation or attribute names are separated by a dot. Objects are defined using the standard language declaration features.

```
-- The with clause specifies the package Mail is used
with Mail ;
-- define an object of type mail message by declaring a
-- variable of the specified abstract data type
Office_memo : Mail.MESSAGE ;
-- print the mail message
Mail.Print (Office_memo, Laser_printer) ;
```

```
package Mail is
   type MESSAGE is private ;
   -- Define operations on the object
   procedure Send (M : MESSAGE; Dest : DESTINATION) ;
   procedure Present (M : MESSAGE; D : DEVICE) ;
   procedure File (M : MESSAGE; File : FILENAME) ;
   procedure Print (M : MESSAGE; D : DEVICE) ;

   -- Sender attribute
   procedure Get_sender (M : MESSAGE; Sender : in out MAIL_USER) ;
   procedure Put_sender (M : in out MESSAGE; Sender : MAIL_USER) ;
   -- Receiver attributes
   procedure Get_receiver  (M : MESSAGE; Receiver : in out MAIL_USER) ;
   procedure Put_receiver  (M : in out MESSAGE; Receiver : MAIL_USER) ;
   -- Similar Get and Put operations should be provided for other attributes
   ...
private
   -- The representation of the attributes is completely concealed by
   -- representing it as an access type. Details are inside the package body
   type MAIL_MESSAGE_RECORD ;
   type MESSAGE is access MAIL_MESSAGE_RECORD ;
end Mail ;
```

Figure 11.3
Part of the detailed
design of a mail
message object class.

Objects which are implemented as instances of abstract data types are passive objects. All state changes are implemented via operations defined in the object interface. Active objects are objects which can change their own state without an explicit call to an interface operation. These are discussed in Section 11.1.2.

11.1.1 Inheritance

One way of looking at object instantiation is to say that objects inherit the attributes and operations of their class. This is taken further in object-oriented languages where object classes are themselves objects. Object classes therefore are members of a super-class and inheritance networks can be established.

Figure 11.4 illustrates inheritance. From a super-class Employee, sub-classes Manager and Programmer may be defined. The attributes of class Employee, which are shared by all employees (such as a name, address, etc.), are inherited by the sub-classes. The sub-classes Manager and Programmer add their own specific attributes which are unique to these jobs.

In the class hierarchy shown in Figure 11.4, project managers are both managers and employees so have attributes inherited from both of these super-classes. Programmers are employees and inherits the attributes defined in class Employee. The class Programmer then adds particular attributes specific to programmers such as the current project and known programming languages.

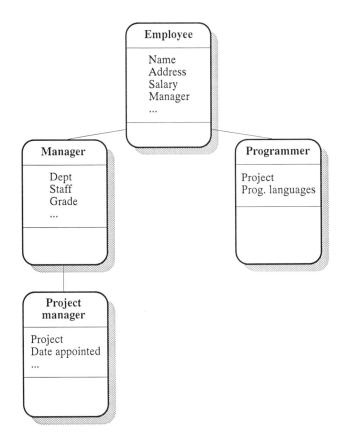

Figure 11.4
A type hierarchy.

An inheritance hierarchy or tree is created when a class can inherit attributes from a single super-class. Multiple inheritance means that attributes can be inherited from more than one super-class. An inheritance network rather than an inheritance tree is created (Figure 11.5).

Figure 11.5 illustrates a situation where a programmer has been appointed as a project manager. The attributes of class Software Project Manager are inherited from both the Manager and the Programmer class. This diagram also illustrates one of the problems of multiple inheritance where the same name is inherited from different super-classes. The usual solution to such name clashes is to allow renaming of attributes and operations as shown in Figure 11.5.

Inheritance is a form of reuse, and reuse through inheritance is discussed in Chapter 16. However, inheritance is not just a convenient mechanism for code sharing. It is also an abstraction technique and provides classification information about system entities. The practical difficulties of inheritance result from the fact that there are many possible theoretical inheritance models. All of these models have some advantages and disadvantages, and no standard semantics for inheritance has yet been agreed.

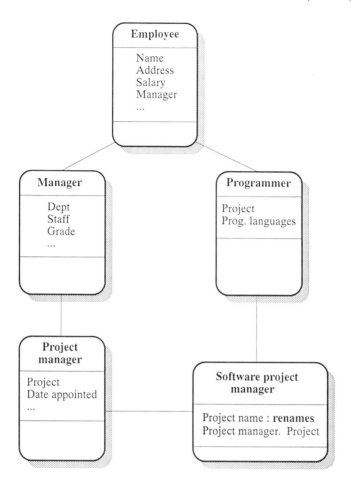

Figure 11.5
A class network.

We now have quite a lot of experience in the use of inheritance in object-oriented programming languages. Inheritance is invaluable in prototyping languages as it permits code reuse and allows rapid changes to be made to an object without side effects which corrupt other parts of the system. However, constructing a consistent inheritance hierarchy is not simple. Good object-oriented programmers regularly review and rewrite their inheritance hierarchy. They remove duplicate attributes which have been introduced on different branches of the hierarchy and they check that attributes and operations are provided at the right level of abstraction.

There are two schools of thought concerning the role of inheritance in object-oriented design. Some designers believe that inheritance is fundamental to object-oriented design and that inheritance hierarchies or networks should always be identified as part of the design process. Other designers believe that inheritance is a useful means of implementing objects but that object classification by defining inheritance networks is not part of object-oriented design.

Inheritance can be a useful abstraction technique to show the relationships between the design types which model the real-world system. However, class inheritance is *not essential* and may sometimes confuse a design because an object class cannot be understood on its own without reference to any super-classes. Without inheritance, all of the operations and attributes of an object class must be explicitly stated, thus reducing the possibility of misunderstandings when reading the design. I therefore prefer to view inheritance as a useful object implementation device rather than fundamental to object-oriented design.

11.1.2 Concurrent objects

Conceptually, an object requests a service from another object by sending a 'service request' message to that object. In practice, this is usually implemented in sequential programming languages as a procedure or function call. However, the model of objects as independent entities exchanging messages allows objects to be implemented as concurrent processes. A detailed discussion of concurrent object-oriented design is given by Agha (1990).

There are two types of concurrent object implementation:

(1) Passive objects where the object is realized as a parallel process with entry points corresponding to the defined object operations. If no calls to the process are available for processing, the object process suspends itself.

(2) Active objects where the state of the object may be changed by internal operations executing within the object itself. The process representing the object continually executes these operations so never suspends itself.

Objects may be implemented as processes in any system which supports some form of concurrency. However, it is obviously simpler in a language which has built-in support for parallelism. In Ada sequential objects are implemented as packages; concurrent objects are implemented as tasks. Ada tasking is described briefly in Appendix A and more fully in Sommerville and Morrison (1987).

Passive objects with concurrent operations are illustrated in Figure 11.6. This shows the specification of a simple counter object. This counter object can be implemented directly as an Ada task with entries associated with the counter operations and the access and constructor functions for the counter attribute (Figure 11.7).

Figure 11.7 defines a single counter rather than a Counter class. Ada also allows task types to be declared which can act as class specifications

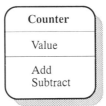

Figure 11.6
A counter object.

(Figure 11.8). Tasks are declared to be of type Concurrent_counter in the same way as any other Ada declaration:

Alpha_counter, Beta_counter : Concurrent_counter ;

The specifications of Counter as a package or as a task are similar with task entries corresponding to the operations defined in the package specification. However, the implementation of an object with concurrent operations is very different (Figure 11.9).

Each **accept** statement handles an entry and has an associated queue of 'calls'. Thus, when an entry is 'called', that call joins the queue associated with the accept statement and is processed (ultimately) by the task according to the code specified between **accept** and **end**. While an **accept** clause is in execution, mutual exclusion is guaranteed. An object wishing to evaluate a counter enters into what is called a *rendezvous* with the Counter task. This simply involves calling the appropriate entry in Counter. For example:

Counter.Get_value (The_value)

This request for service joins the queue of Get_value entries and is eventually processed by the counter task. The Ada **select** construct is used to specify that one outstanding entry should be accepted each time the loop is executed. If there are no pending entries to be processed, the Counter task suspends itself till further processing is required.

The specification and use of parallel and sequential objects is similar. However, the object user must know whether a parallel or sequential object

```
task Counter is
    entry Add (N : NATURAL) ;
    entry Subtract (N : NATURAL) ;
    entry Put_value (N : NATURAL) ;
    entry Get_value (N : out NATURAL) ;
end Counter ;
```

Figure 11.7
Ada task specification
for a counter.

```
task type Concurrent_counter is
    entry Add (N : NATURAL) ;
    entry Subtract (N : NATURAL) ;
    entry Put_value (N : NATURAL) ;
    entry Get_value (N : out NATURAL) ;
end Concurrent_counter ;
```

Figure 11.8
A concurrent counter
task type specification.

implementation is provided because their run-time behaviour may be different. In the sequential implementation, calls on the object operations are executed in sequence; in the task-based implementation this cannot be guaranteed. When there are a number of entries waiting to be accepted, the task may choose any one of them for execution.

Objects such as the Counter object would not, therefore, be defined using concurrent operations in circumstances where the object was frequently evaluated and where it was essential that the value represented the exact counter value based on the preceding sequence of Add and Subtract operations. Rather, it might be used in situations (such as radiation monitoring) where the counter operated as a background activity with other sequential processes going on at the same time. Slight evaluation errors resulting from a timing mismatch in such situations are not significant.

Active objects are used in circumstances where an object updates its own state at specified intervals. The state is evaluated by external objects.

```
task body Counter is
    Value : NATURAL := 0 ;
begin
    loop
        select
            accept Add (N : NATURAL) do
                Value := Value + N ;
            end Add ;
        or
            accept Subtract (N : NATURAL) do
                Value := Value - N ;
            end Subtract ;
        or
            accept Put_value (N : NATURAL) do
                Value := N ;
            end Put_value ;
        or
            accept Get_value (N : out NATURAL) do
                N := Value ;
            end Get_value ;
        end select ;
    end loop ;
end Counter ;
```

Figure 11.9
Task implementation of
a counter object.

```
task type Transponder is
   entry  Give_position (Pos : POSITION ) ;
end Transponder ;

task body Transponder is
   Current_position : POSITION ;
   C1, C2 : Satellite.COORDS ;
   loop
      select
         accept Give_position (Pos : out POSITION) do
            Pos := Current_position ;
         end Give_position ;
      else
         C1 := Satellite1.Position ;
         C2 := Satellite2.Position ;
         Current_position := Navigator.Compute (C1, C2) ;
      end select ;
   end loop ;
end Transponder ;
```

Figure 11.10
An active transponder
object.

Figure 11.10 shows an example of such an object. This represents a transponder on an aircraft which continually keeps track of the aircraft's position using a satellite navigation system. It can respond to messages from air traffic control computers and provides the current aircraft position in response to the service request.

This object is implemented as a task with a continuous loop updating the aircraft's position. When a Give_position entry is accepted, the position (as computed by the previous loop iteration) is returned to the calling task. In this case a conditional **select** statement is used. If there are no entries to be accepted, the task carries out the position computation as specified in the else part of the **select** statement.

11.2   An object-oriented design example

The problem with examples of software design is that they are inevitably artificial. Designs for large software systems involve creating hundreds of pages of documentation yet, in a book, only a few pages are available to convey the essence of the design. Readers must take on trust assertions about the advantages of object-oriented design. It is only when you practise this approach in a real system design that the advantages actually become clear.

A system for creating weather maps is used here as an example of object-oriented design. The requirements for such a weather mapping

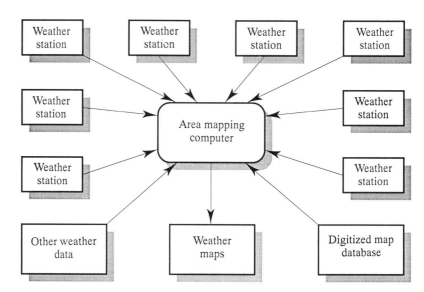

Figure 11.11
Weather mapping
system.

system would take up many pages but an outline design can be developed
from a relatively brief system description:

> A weather data collection system is made up of a number of
> automatic weather stations which collect meteorological data, perform
> some local data processing and periodically send the collected,
> processed information to an area computer for further processing.
> The data which is to be collected is the air temperature, the ground
> temperature, the wind speed and direction, the barometric pressure
> and the amount of rainfall. Weather stations transmit their data to the
> area computer in response to a request from that machine. The area
> computer summarizes the collected data, integrates it with reports
> from other sources and a map database and then generates a set of
> local weather maps.

Figure 11.11 illustrates the structure of this system. In this example, the
principles of object-oriented design are illustrated. Obviously, there is no
room to show the complete design. Rather, the system architecture is
designed, then part of the design (automated data collection) is developed in
more detail.

The first stage in the object-oriented design process is to identify the
entities which are part of the system. From the outline description of the
system, three abstract objects can be identified:

- *Weather station*   A package of software controlled instruments which
  collects data, performs some data processing and transmits this data
  for further processing. There are many different weather stations in
  the system so Weather station should be defined as an object class.

Weather station
Identifier
Weather data
Instrument status
Initialize
Transmit data
Transmit status
Self test
Shutdown

Weather map
Map type
Scale
Area coordinates
Data collection time
Map generation time
Map representation
Print
Transmit
Rescale

Figure 11.12
Attributes and
operations of top-level
objects.

- *Map database* A database of survey information which allows maps of the area to be generated at various scales.
- *Weather map* A representation of the area with superimposed, summarized weather information.

For simplicity, other entities which are part of the system such as additional weather information (perhaps from satellites) are not considered.

Once an initial set of objects has been identified, the state variables or attributes of these objects and the operations associated with the objects should be listed. Figure 11.12 shows the attributes and operations for weather stations and weather maps.

The state of a weather station includes a unique station identifier, a weather data record (which will be considered in more detail later) and an instrument status record. Object attributes may be atomic attributes (for example, the identifier might be an integer) or may themselves be objects. The weather station provides operations to initialize the state, to transmit weather data, to run a self-checking program, to transmit status information and to shut itself down. There is no explicit operation to collect weather information as the weather station functions as an active object. Data collection starts automatically when the system is switched on.

The state information associated with weather map objects includes the type of map such as a rainfall map, a map showing isobars (pressure contours), a map showing temperature distribution, and so on. It also includes the map scale, the area covered by the map, the time the data was collected, the time the map was prepared and the map itself (map representation). The associated operations are operations to print the map, to transmit it to other computers and to rescale the map.

The diagrammatic notation gives an overview of the object structure but little information about the services associated with the object. An Ada/PDL may be used to provide a more detailed design description where packages are used to describe objects or object classes. Figure 11.13 shows the package specification of the Weather_station object class.

```
with Weather_data, Instrument_status, Mapping_computer ;
package Weather_station is
    type T is private ;
    type STATION_IDENTIFIER is STRING (1..6) ;
    procedure Initialize (WS : T) ;
    procedure Transmit_data (Id : STATION_IDENTIFIER ;
                                WR : Weather_data.REC ;
                                Dest : Mapping_computer.ID ) ;
    procedure Transmit_status (Id : STATION_IDENTIFIER ;
                                IS : Instrument_status.REC ;
                                Dest : Mapping_computer.ID ) ;
    procedure Self_test (WS : T) ;
    procedure Shut_down (WS : T) ;

    -- Access and constructor procedures for object attributes
    -- Attribute :  Station identifier
    procedure Put_identifier (WS : in out T ; Id: STATION_IDENTIFIER) ;
    function  Get_identifier (WS : T) return STATION_IDENTIFIER ;
    -- Attribute : Weather data record
    procedure Put_weather_data (WS : in out T ;
                                WR : Weather_data.REC ) ;
    function Get_weather_data (WS : T ) return Weather_data.REC ;
    -- Attribute : Instrument status
    procedure Put_instrument_status (WS : in out T ;
                                IS : Instrument_status.REC ) ;
    function Get_instrument_status (WS : T)
                                return Instrument_status.REC ;
private
    type T is record
        Id : STATION_IDENTIFIER ;
        Weather_data : Weather_data.REC ;
        Instrument_status : Instrument_status.REC ;
    end record ;
end Weather_station ;
```

Figure 11.13
Specification of
weather station object.

The weather station is defined as a package specifying an abstract data type so that many instances of weather station can be created:

Station_1, Station_2, Station_3 : Weather_station.T ;

In Figure 11.13, the objects used by Weather_station objects are specified in the **with** clause preceding the package header. The object attributes are specified in the private part of the package as a record defining the weather station state. Access and constructor functions are provided to evaluate and modify the state components.

The weather station object includes 'hardware' objects which are responsible for managing each of the various instruments associated with a station. In a system which includes a mix of hardware and software, each hardware component should have an associated controlling object.

The term 'hardware' object is not a precise one but in this context I mean an object which interacts directly with a hardware unit. By contrast, a 'software' object is an object which only interacts with other system objects.

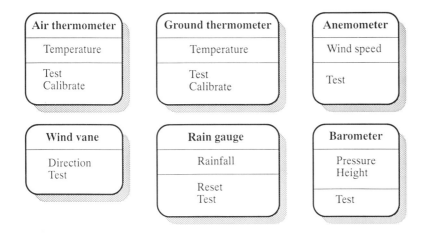

Figure 11.14
Hardware objects.

The 'hardware' objects which can be identified from an analysis of the data collection system description are associated with each of the weather station instruments:

- Air thermometer.
- Ground thermometer.
- Anemometer (measures wind speed).
- Wind vane (measures wind direction).
- Barometer (measures pressure).
- Rain gauge.

Hardware objects are simple objects used to hide details of the hardware in the system. If, for example, the hardware unit provides information by writing into a known memory location, the address of that location is concealed in the hardware object. If the hardware should subsequently be redesigned and a different address used, there is no need to change any of the software which interfaces to the hardware object. When each instrument is considered as an object which conceals hardware details, the instrument design and the software design can go on in parallel. During system validation, the hardware object can be implemented as a simulator with no need to connect it to a real instrument.

Figure 11.14 shows the hardware object attributes and operations. The attributes represent the data collected by the instrument. All objects have a Test operation which runs a self-test program on the instrument. As the rain gauge measures cumulative rainfall, it must also be provided with a Reset operation. The barometer object must have a Height attribute as the barometer pressure reading must be adjusted to compensate for the height of the instrument.

At this stage, the lowest level system objects and high-level objects have been identified. This situation is normal in object-oriented design which is rarely a top-down process. Other objects must now be defined to bridge the gap between the hardware objects and the weather station object itself. For this stage of the design more information about the data to be collected is required. Assume that the requirements are as follows:

In the course of a collection period (typically one hour, four hours maximum), the following data should be collected by the weather station:

- *Air temperature*   Maximum, minimum and average temperature.
- *Ground temperature*   Maximum, minimum and average temperature.
- *Wind speed*   Average speed, maximum gust speed.
- *Wind direction*   Direction every five minutes during collection period.
- *Pressure*   Average barometric pressure.
- *Rainfall*   Cumulative rainfall.

Apart from the rainfall which is a cumulative measurement, other measurements should be made every five minutes.

With this information, the object Weather data can be defined, which gathers and stores this information (Figure 11.15). The attributes of Weather data are themselves objects and their attributes and operations are also shown in Figure 11.15.

In Figure 11.15, Ground temperature data and Air temperature data are instances of the same object class Temperature data (Figure 11.16). The Weather data object acts as a focus for the data collection. At the appropriate intervals, the Weather station object sends Weather data a Make readings message. Weather data then activates lower level objects to evaluate the hardware objects and save the results in the Readings attribute.

The Process data operation in the Weather data object is initiated when a transmission of weather data is required. The Process data operation calls the appropriate operations on lower level objects (Get maximum, Get minimum, etc.). Using the raw weather data which is stored in their attribute called Readings, the lower level objects compute the information required by Process data and return it as a procedure output parameter. For example, the procedure Get average associated with the object Wind speed data might be defined as shown below. The implementation of Get average is completely concealed from Process data.

procedure Get_average (Average_wind_speed : **out** VELOCITY) ;

It would be called from within Process data as follows:

Wind_speed.Get_average (Average_wind_speed)

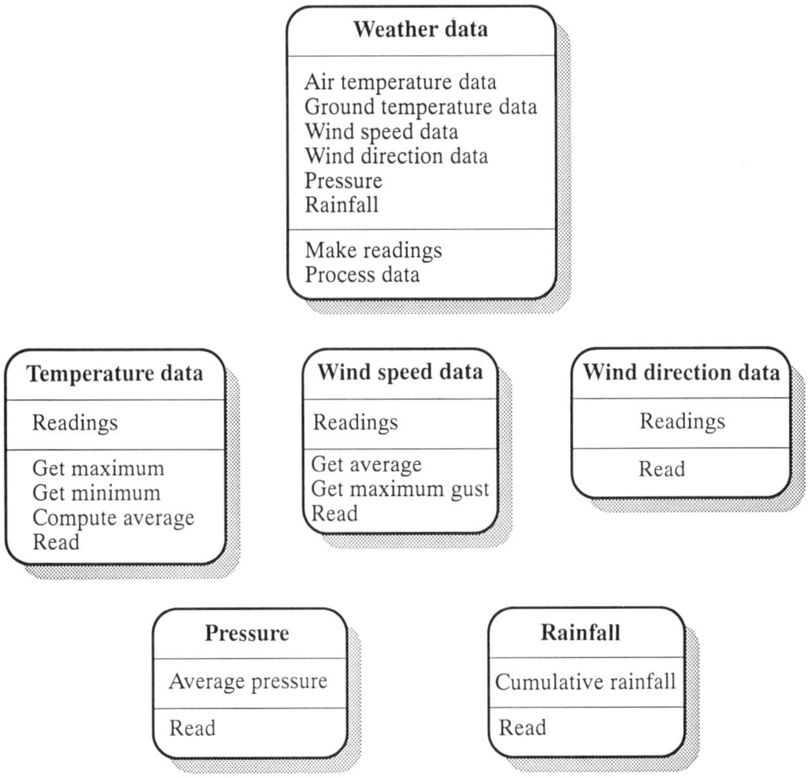

Figure 11.15
Weather data and associated objects.

An alternative implementation for Weather data might have been to bundle all data into a single data block after processing and pass it as a unit to Weather station for transmission. The approach adopted here of having separate attributes was adopted because it is more flexible. If additional processing of the data by the Weather data object is required (data compression, say), it is easy to adapt the object.

Figure 11.16 shows how a class can be defined as a basis for objects which collect temperature data. Ground temperature and air temperature data are similar but the class has to be defined as a generic class with the function used to read the temperature from the appropriate thermometer passed as a generic parameter. This function must be provided by each of the thermometer hardware objects.

The generic package can be instantiated as follows:

```
with Ground_thermometer ;
package Ground_temperature is new Temperature_data
        (Get_temperature = > Ground_thermometer.Get_temperature) ;
```

```
with Global_types ; use Global_types ;
-- The type TEMPERATURE is declared in Global_types package
generic
    with function Get_temperature  return TEMPERATURE ;
package Temperature_data is
    type Readings is private ;
    function Get_average (R : Readings) return TEMPERATURE ;
    function Get_maximum (R : Readings) return TEMPERATURE ;
    function Get_minimum (R : Readings) return TEMPERATURE ;
    procedure Read (R : in out Readings) ;
private
    type Readings_range is range 1..48 ;
    type Readings is  record
        Next : Readings_range ;
        The_readings : array (Readings_range) of TEMPERATURE ;
end  Temperature_data  ;
```

Figure 11.16
Temperature data
object.

Other objects can be identified by considering the attributes and operations defined for each weather station. The operations concerned with the transmission of weather data and instrument status suggest that there should be an object which handles data communications (Communications). The attribute recording instrument status information suggests that the weather station instruments should be packaged in some way under a single object (Instruments). Clearly, as data are collected at regular intervals, there is a need for a clock (Clock). These objects with their attributes and operations are shown in Figure 11.17.

At this stage in the design, it is sometimes useful to document the object structure showing static object/sub-object relationships (Figure 11.18). To simplify the diagram, object attribute and operation details have been hidden.

There are too many objects to show the whole of the hierarchy in a single diagram so the existence of hidden sub-objects is indicated by ellipses (. . .). The star (*) in the Weather station object indicates that there are many instances of this object in the system.

Figure 11.18 describes the static structure of the system but does not show the dynamic structure. It is useful to complement this with a dynamic structure diagram which shows object interactions. Figure 11.19 is part of such a diagram for the weather station object. The arrowed lines indicate

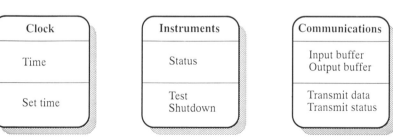

Figure 11.17
Weather station
objects.

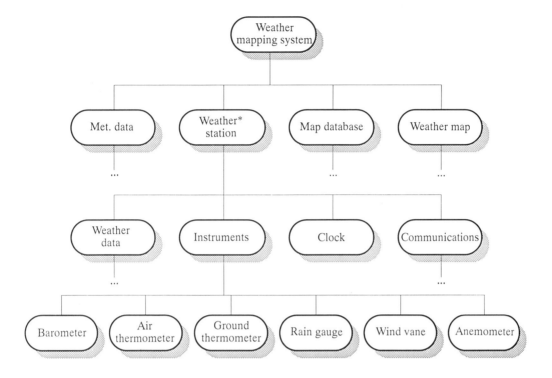

that an object calls on a service provided by another object with the service name indicated as a label on the line.

From Figure 11.19, we can see that the Weather station services are initiated by the Communications object which is an active object which continually monitors the communications line for an incoming command. When an incoming command is recognized, it is then passed to Weather station for execution.

After identifying the object hierarchy and the object interactions, the next step is to develop the design in detail, adding control to the objects. This is a relatively straightforward task which is left as an exercise for the reader.

The principal advantage of an object-oriented approach to design derives from information hiding. The state representation does not influence the design and changing the internal details of one object is unlikely to affect any other system objects. To illustrate the robustness of the object-oriented approach, assume that pollution monitoring capabilities are to be added to each weather station. This involves adding an air quality meter which computes the amount of various pollutants in the atmosphere. The pollution readings are transmitted at the same time as the weather data. The changes required would be as follows:

Figure 11.18
Weather system object hierarchy.

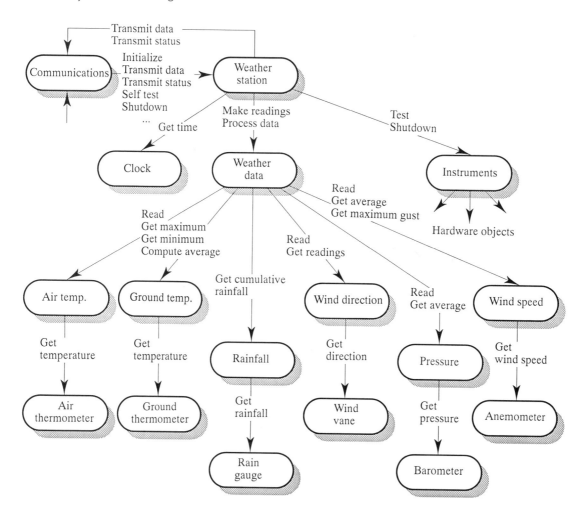

Figure 11.19
Object interactions.

(1) An object Pollution record should be added at the same level as Weather data.

(2) An operation Transmit pollution data should be added to Weather station and the weather station control software modified so that pollution readings are automatically collected when the system is switched on.

(3) An Air quality sub-object to Pollution record should be added at the same level as Pressure, Rainfall, etc.

(4) A hardware object Air quality meter should be added as a sub-object to Air quality.

Notice that, apart from at the highest level of the system (Weather station) no software changes are required and the addition of pollution data collection does not affect weather data collection in any way.

11.3   Object identification

The major problem in object-oriented design is identifying the objects which make up the system, their attributes and associated operations. There is no simple formula which allows such objects to be identified and designers must use their skill and experience in this task.

Of course, this process must start somewhere and an approach suggested by Abbot (1983) can be useful as a starting point in the design process. This approach relies on producing a brief descriptive overview of the system, expressed in natural language, and then identifying relevant nouns (the objects) and verbs (the operations) from this overview. To illustrate this process, consider the following short description of a system which acts as an office information retrieval system (this system is used as a design example in the following chapter).

> The Office Information **Retrieval System** (OIRS) is an automatic file clerk which can *file* **documents** under some name in one or more **indexes**, *retrieve* **documents**, *display* and *maintain* **document indexes**, *archive* **documents** and *destroy* **documents**. The **system** is activated by a *request* from the **user** and always *returns* a message to the **user** indicating the success or failure of the request.

The language analysis approach starts by identifying key nouns (shown emboldened) and verbs (shown italicized) in the system description. However, because of the flexibility of natural language, the description may be made in such a way that the same object is referenced in different ways. The designer should not blindly assume that nouns are always objects and verbs are associated operations.

For example, in the last sentence of the above description, the objects are the retrieval system (simply referenced as the system) and the user. The operations on the system object are retrieval system operations Get user request and Return status message. However, this is only clear after considering the last sentence in detail. The word 'request' is actually used as a noun in that sentence which would imply that it is an object rather than an operation.

It would be possible to include operations called Get user request and Return status message as operations associated with the Retrieval System object. However, to do so would reduce the coherence of that object. Not only would the object be concerned with coordinating and processing requests for service from users, it would also be responsible for managing the physical user interaction which is required.

This illustrates one of the problems of object-oriented design. User interaction is inherently functional rather than object-oriented. Although the input and output of specific objects can be managed using associated

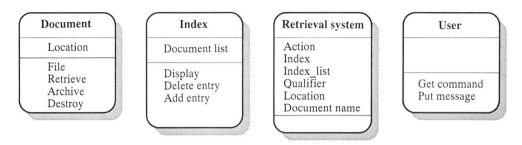

Figure 11.20
Preliminary object
identification.

Input and Output operations these should, as far as possible, be independent of the actual I/O devices which are used.

As we have seen device management can be handled by using 'hardware' objects. A similar approach can be adopted to handle interaction with users by introducing a User object. This is somewhat artificial as it does not have any natural state. Rather, it is a collection of functions for managing user input and output. These functions are activated by other system objects when they need to interact with the user.

From the description of the OIRS, the objects and associated operations shown in Figure 11.20 can be identified. Other state information and services may be added to these as more information becomes available.

The Retrieval System object does not have identified services which can be called upon by other objects. The reason for this is that it is an active object whose main function is the coordination of other objects. It identifies the user input and activates other system objects depending on that input. It does not provide services to other objects although some services within Retrieval System (such as System Shutdown) may be activated by user commands.

We have thus identified some objects and operations but the looseness of natural language can cause problems. For example, what does 'maintain' an index mean? What does 'filing' mean, and so on? It is not enough to rely on normal usage of these terms, a more complete explanation is required to derive the design. We can again turn to the system description for more information.

> When a document is filed, the location of the document, a document name and the indexes under which it should be filed must be specified. Retrieval requests involve the specification of one or more indexes along with the document name. Index examination involves specifying an index name and a qualifier. This qualifier is a condition determining which parts of the index are required for examination.

From this paragraph, we see that the file operation involves specifying indexes. We get the information that index examination requires the specification of the index name and qualifier. There is also the implicit

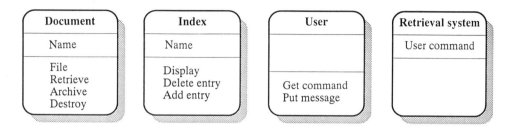

Figure 11.21
Object refinement.

statement that this is specified as part of the user command. Documents have a location and are entered in an index using a specified name. It is not stated whether or not this name must be the same in all indexes or if different names may be used.

Figure 11.21 is a refinement of the objects using the additional information.

The name attribute in Document and Index has been factored out. Document and Index are object classes and the particular instance of these classes has been named. The individual components of a command have been identified in Retrieval System. The design process should continue with further object decompositions and the identification of associated sub-objects.

The problem with using natural language specifications to identify objects, their attributes and their operations is that these descriptions are usually written on the assumption that the reader has a 'common sense' understanding of the application domain. The description leaves out 'obvious' knowledge that the index itself must have a name, that documents have owners, and so on. If designers do not have detailed domain knowledge, it is likely that they will make design errors and leave out important system services.

The initial objects and operations identified from the informal system description can be a starting point for the design but will almost always need to be extended using additional system information. This must be collected in the usual way from requirements documents, from discussions with users and from an analysis of existing, comparable systems.

■ KEY POINTS

■ Object-oriented design is a means of designing with information hiding. Information hiding allows the information representation to be changed without other extensive system modifications.

■ An object is an entity which has a private state with constructor and inspection functions allowing that state to be modified and examined. No other access to the state is allowed. The object provides services (operations using state information) to other objects.

■ Object-oriented design is not the same as object-oriented programming. Object-oriented programming languages support run-time operation binding and inheritance. An object-oriented design can be implemented in any programming language.

■ Objects may be implemented sequentially or concurrently. A concurrent object may be a passive object whose state is only changed through its interface or an active object which can change its own state without outside intervention.

■ When documenting an object-oriented design, it is useful to draw a hierarchy chart showing objects and their sub-objects. It is also useful to draw a 'use' network showing which objects call on the services of which other objects.

■ An approach to deriving an object-oriented design is to consider nouns and verbs in a natural language system description. Nouns represent objects and verbs operations. However, the inherent ambiguity of natural language descriptions means that this should only be considered as a guide to the designer and other domain information must be used for object identification.

FURTHER READING

Software Engineering with Ada, 2nd edn. Booch is perhaps the foremost proponent of object-oriented design with Ada and this book is an excellent tutorial on the use of Ada and object-oriented design. He can be criticized a little because he makes it look so easy but that is a criticism which can be made of many textbooks, including, perhaps, this one. (G. Booch, 1987, Benjamin Cummings.)

Comm. ACM, **33** (9), September 1990. This is a special issue of this journal devoted to object-oriented design and development. There are a number of good articles on the object-oriented approach although as a perceptive letter in a later issue of the journal points out (January 1991), there is no discussion of the applications where object-oriented design is not appropriate.

Object-oriented Design with Applications. This book represents a more general approach by Booch to object-oriented design than the original Ada-oriented approach. This book is much better than other books on object-oriented design because it has much better examples. Booch has attempted to write a book which will also appeal to all object-oriented programmers and the examples are presented in a variety of different programming languages. (G. Booch, 1990, Benjamin Cummings.)

EXERCISES

11.1 Explain why adopting a design approach based on information hiding is likely to lead to a design which may be readily modified.

11.2 Write abstract data type specifications in Ada or in an object-oriented programming language for the following objects:

   (a) A binary tree.
   (b) A compiler symbol table.
   (c) A personal computer printer.
   (d) A library catalogue.
   (e) A telephone.

11.3 Using examples, explain the difference between an object and an object class.

11.4 If you are familiar with Ada, show how the object class which you have specified in Example 11.3 might be implemented as an Ada package or as an Ada task. If you are not familiar with Ada, suggest how the objects might be realized in another programming language.

11.5 Develop the weather station design in detail by writing more detailed descriptions of the design of the identified objects. This may be expressed in Ada or in any object-oriented programming language.

11.6 Develop an object interaction diagram for the office information retrieval system. You can find further information about this system in Chapter 12.

11.7 Using the graphical techniques described in this chapter, develop an object-oriented design for the newspaper delivery system introduced in Exercise 3.7.

11.8 Describe the detailed design of the objects you have identified in the newspaper delivery system using Ada or some other object-oriented programming language.

11.9 Using an object-oriented approach, derive a design for the systems which are outlined below. Make reasonable assumptions about the systems when deriving the design.

    (a) A software components catalogue is intended to hold details of software components which are potentially reusable. A cataloguer may enter components in the catalogue, may delete components from the catalogue and may associate reuse information with a catalogue component. A user of the catalogue may query the catalogue to find a component using keywords associated with the component description. The catalogue user interface should be based on a structured form where the user enters some details of a component and the catalogue fills in the remainder of the form.

    (b) A group diary and time management system is intended to support the timetabling of meetings and appointments across a group of co-workers. When an appointment is to be made which involves a number of people, the system finds a common slot in each of their diaries and arranges the appointment for that time. If no common slots are available, it interacts with the user to rearrange their personal diary to make room for the appointment.

    (c) A petrol (gas) station is to be set up for fully automated operation. A driver inputs his or her credit card into the pump, the card is verified by communication with a credit company computer and a fuel limit established. The driver may then take the fuel required and, on completion of delivery (when the pump hose is returned to its holster), the driver's credit account is debited with the cost of the fuel taken. The credit card is returned after debiting. If the card is invalid, it is returned by the pump with no fuel dispensed.

Function-Oriented Design

12

◼ OBJECTIVES

The objective of this chapter is to present an approach to software design where the basic design component is a function rather than an object. The method used to derive the functional design makes use of data flow diagrams and structure charts. The design process is illustrated using the example of the office information retrieval system introduced in Chapter 11 and shown in more detail here. A sequential design is derived but the final section in the chapter shows that concurrent designs can also be developed from data flow diagrams. This is illustrated with a concurrent design for the office information system.

◼ CONTENTS

Function-oriented design is an approach to software design where the design is decomposed into a set of interacting units which each have a clearly defined function. Functions have local state but shared system state is centralized and accessible by all functions.

Function-oriented design has probably been practised informally since programming began but it was only in the late 1960s and early 1970s that it was brought to prominence. A number of papers and books were published on this notion, the best known of which are probably those by Wirth (1971, 1976). Myers' work on structured design (1975) adopted a functional view of design and this was refined and described in a definitive book by Constantine and Yourdon (1979).

It has been suggested that function-oriented design is obsolete and should be superseded by an object-oriented approach. However, many organizations have developed standards and methods based on functional decomposition and are understandably reluctant to discard these in favour of object-oriented design. Many design methods and associated CASE tools are functionally oriented. An enormous number of systems have been developed using a functional approach. These will have to be maintained for the foreseeable future. Therefore, functional design is, and will continue to be, widely practised.

In this chapter, an approach to function-oriented design which is based on original work by Constantine and Yourdon (structured design) is described. This uses data flow diagrams which describe the logical data processing, structure charts which shown the software structure and PDL descriptions which describe the design in detail. Their data flow notation has been modified to make it more suitable for use with an automated diagramming system and a slightly different form of structure chart which excludes control information is used.

A function-oriented design strategy relies on decomposing the system into a set of interacting functions with a centralized system state shared by these functions (Figure 12.1). Functions may also maintain local state information but only for the duration of their execution.

Function-oriented design conceals the details of an algorithm in a function but system state information is not hidden. This can cause problems

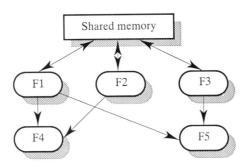

Figure 12.1
A function-oriented
view of design.

```
loop
  loop
    Print_input_message (" Welcome - Please enter your card") ;
    exit when Card_input ;
  end loop ;
  Account_number := Read_card ;
  Get_account_details (PIN, Account_balance, Cash_available) ;
  if Validate_card (PIN) then
    loop
      Print_operation_select_message ;
      case Get_button is
        when Cash_only =>
          Dispense_cash (Cash_available, Amount_dispensed) ;
        when Print_balance =>
          Print_customer_balance (Account_balance) ;
        when Statement =>
          Order_statement (Account_number) ;
        when Cheque_book =>
          Order_cheque_book (Account_number) ;
      end case ;
      Eject_card ;
      Print ("Please take your card or press CONTINUE") ;
      exit when Card_removed ;
    end loop ;
    Update_account_information (Account_number, Amount_dispensed) ;
  else
    Retain_card ;
  end if ;
end loop ;
```

Figure 12.2
ATM system design.

because a function can change the state in a way which other functions do not expect. Changes to a function and the way in which it uses the system state may cause unanticipated interactions with other functions.

A functional approach to design is therefore most successful when the amount of system state information is minimized and information sharing is explicit. Some systems, whose responses depend on a single stimulus or input and which are not affected by input histories are naturally functionally-oriented. A good example of such a system is an ATM system as provided outside banks. Figure 12.2 illustrates a simplified functional design of such a system.

In this design, functions such as Dispense_cash, Get_account_number, Order_statement, Order_chequebook, and so on can be identified which implement system actions. The system state is minimal. Operations are independent and not affected by previous customer requests. In fact, an object-oriented design would not be very different from this (except syntactically) and an object-oriented approach would probably not result in a design which was significantly more maintainable.

12.1 Data flow diagrams

Data flow diagrams show how input data is transformed to output results through a sequence of functional transformations. They are a useful and intuitive way of describing a system and they are understandable without special training. The first stage of function-oriented design should be to develop a system data flow diagram. These diagrams should not normally include control information but should document data transformations.

Data flow diagrams are an integral part of a number of design methods and CASE tools usually support data flow diagram creation. The notations used in different methods are similar and transforming from one notation to another is straightforward. The notation used here has been chosen because it is easy to draw using a personal computer diagram editing system.

The symbols which are used in this notation are as follows:

(1) *Round-edged rectangles*   These represent transformations where an input data flow is transformed to an output. The transformation is annotated with a descriptive name.

(2) *Rectangles*   These represent a data store. Again, they are given a descriptive name.

(3) *Circles*   These represent user interactions with the system. These interactions may provide input or receive output.

(4) *Arrows*   These show the direction of data flow. They are given a name describing the data flowing along that path.

(5) *The keywords 'and', and 'or'*   These have their usual meanings as in boolean expressions. They are used to link data flows when more than one data flow may be input or output from a transformation.

(6) *An arc symbol linking data flows*   This is only used in conjunction with 'and' and 'or' and is used to indicate bracketing. In general, 'and' takes precedence over 'or' but this may be changed by linking the appropriate data flows.

This notation is illustrated in Figure 12.3 which describes the logical design of a report generator system used in conjunction with a design editor. The report generator takes a design and produces a report about each of the entities used in the design. Figure 12.3 shows that the user inputs a design name and the report generator finds all of the names used in that design. The data dictionary is consulted for information about the design entities and a report produced. The information in the report is presented according to whether an entity is a node type or a link type.

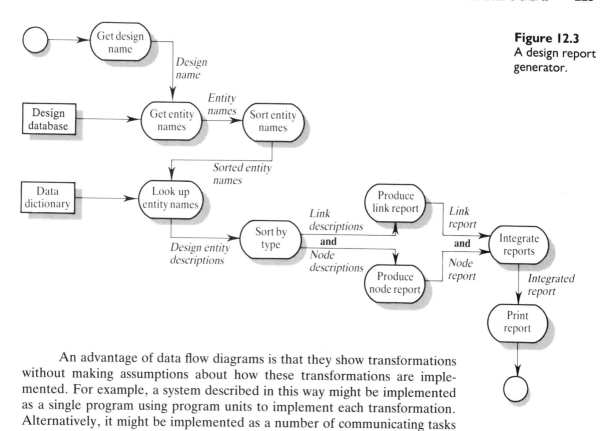

Figure 12.3
A design report
generator.

An advantage of data flow diagrams is that they show transformations without making assumptions about how these transformations are implemented. For example, a system described in this way might be implemented as a single program using program units to implement each transformation. Alternatively, it might be implemented as a number of communicating tasks or, perhaps, the implementation might be an amalgam of these methods.

12.2   Structure charts

Structure charts are a graphical means of showing the hierarchical component structure of a system. They show how elements of a data flow diagram can be realized as a hierarchy of program units. Structure charts can be used as a visual program description with control information defining selection and loops but I believe that control is more clearly documented using a design description language. Structure charts are used here only to display the static organization of a design.

A functional component is represented on a structure chart as a rectangle. The hierarchy is displayed by linking rectangles with lines. Inputs and outputs to a component are indicated by using annotated arrows. An arrow entering a box implies input, one leaving a box implies output. Data stores are shown as round-edged rectangles and user inputs as circles. To

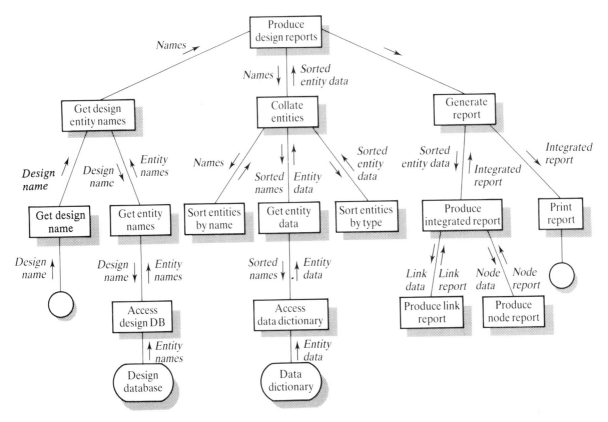

Figure 12.4
A structure chart for
the report generator.

save diagram space, some inputs and outputs are unlabelled. This implies that the label associated with these flows is that of the adjacent data flow.

Given a data flow diagram showing logical transforms, it is usually possible to derive a number of possible structure charts from it. For example, Figures 12.4 and 12.5 show alternative software structures for the design report generator whose flow chart is shown in Figure 12.3.

A problem facing the software engineer is how to derive the 'best' structure chart from a data flow diagram. This is discussed in the following section.

12.2.1 Deriving structure charts

In the previous example of a design report generator, two different structure charts were derived from the system data flow diagram. No comment was made at that stage as to which of these represented the 'best' solution. Although this notion of a 'best' solution is subjective the designer's aim should be to derive a design where program units exhibit a high degree of cohesion and a low degree of coupling.

The identification of loosely coupled, highly cohesive units is

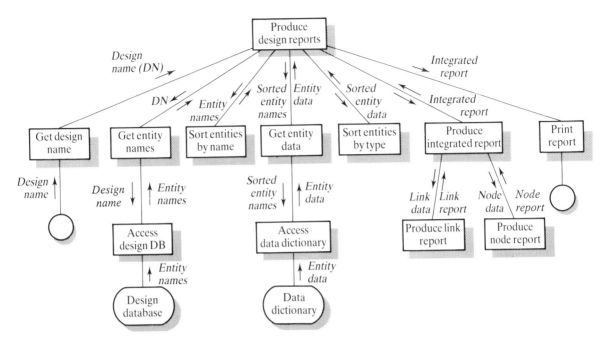

Figure 12.5
An alternative
structure chart for the
report generator.

simplified if units are considered to be principally responsible for dealing with one of four types of data flow.

(1)   *Input*   The program unit is responsible for accepting data from a unit at a lower level in the structure chart and passing that data on to a higher level unit in some modified form. Constantine and Yourdon use the term 'afferent' to describe such units.

(2)   *Output*   The program unit is responsible for accepting data from a higher level unit and passing it to a lower level unit. This is termed 'efferent' by Constantine and Yourdon.

(3)   *Transform*   A program unit accepts data from a higher level unit, transforms that data and passes it back to that unit.

(4)   *Coordinate*   A unit is responsible for controlling and managing other units.

The first step in converting a data flow diagram to a structure chart is to identify the highest level input and output units. These units are those concerned with passing data up and down the hierarchy but are furthest removed from physical input and output. This step does not usually include all transforms and the remaining transforms are termed central transforms.

Identifying the highest level input and output transforms depends on the skill and experience of the system designer. One possible way to approach this task is to trace the inputs until a transform is found whose output is such that its input cannot be deduced from output examination. The previous bubble then represents the highest level input unit. Processes which validate inputs or add information to them are not central transforms; processes which sort input or filter data from it are. A similar criterion is used to establish the highest level output transform.

The first level of the structure chart is produced by representing the input and output units as single boxes and each central transform as a single box. The box at the root of the structure chart is a coordinate unit. This factoring process may then be repeated for the first level units in the structure chart until all bubbles in the data flow diagram are represented in the structure.

In the design report generator data flow diagram (Figure 12.3) the output part of the system are those transforms which are concerned with producing reports for link and node type, report integration and printing. These are all concerned with the formatting and organization of design entity descriptions.

Deciding on which transforms in Figure 12.3 are input transforms is more difficult. Recall the rule of thumb is to examine the transformation and when it is not possible to determine the input from the output, a central transform has been discovered. The sorting of entity names is therefore a central transform. This results in the first level structure chart shown in Figure 12.6. Applying the same process to the sort unit to derive the second level structure results in Figure 12.7. The derivation process is applied a third time to derive the final structure chart as shown previously in Figure 12.4.

Each node in the structure chart of a well-structured design should have between two and seven subordinates. If a node has only a single subordinate, this implies that the unit represented by that node may have a low degree of cohesion. It suggests that the unit is not a single function as

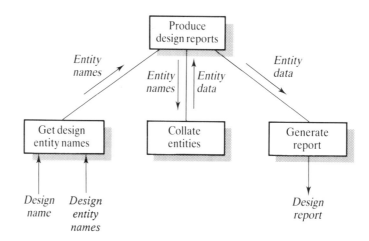

Figure 12.6
Initial design report generator structure.

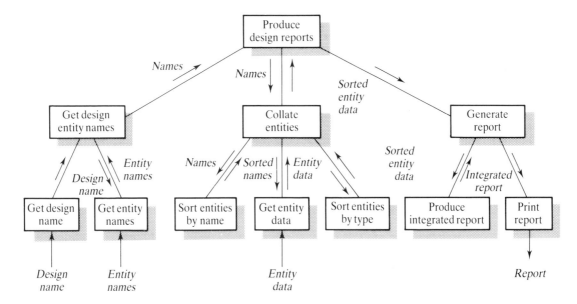

Figure 12.7
Expanded design
report generator
structure chart.

the existence of a single subordinate means that a function has been factored
out. If a node has many subordinates, this implies that the design has been
developed to too low a level at that stage. Design quality metrics based on
structure charts is covered in Chapter 31.

The information available in data flow diagrams is useful in deriving
structure charts but other components may be included in a structure chart
which are not directly concerned with data transformation and which do not
therefore appear on the data flow diagram. For example, components which
are concerned with logging-in and logging-out a user, system initialization
and any other components concerned with system control rather than data
processing may be identified.

Structure chart derivation is therefore a two-stage process. From the
data flow design, an initial structure may be derived and this may be used in
the construction of a design description which includes control information
and which may identify further control functions. Following this design
description, the structure chart may be modified to include additional
control components.

12.3   Data dictionaries

Data dictionaries have already been introduced in Part 1. As well as being
useful in maintaining system specifications, data dictionaries are equally
useful in the design process. Each identified entity in the diagram should
have a data dictionary entry giving information about its type, its function

Entity name	Type	Description
Design name	Data	The name of the design to be processed.
Get design name	Transform	The design on which the report is to be generated is held in the system datebase as a named entity. This transform communicates with the user to get this name.
Get entity names	Transform	Using the design name, this transform finds the database entity holding the design and abstracts the names of design entities from it.
Sorted entity names	Data	The names of design entities in sort order.

Figure 12.8
Part of the design report generator data dictionary.

and, perhaps, a rationale for its inclusion. This is sometimes called a minispec, standing for a short description of the component function.

The data dictionary entry might be a textual description of the component or might be a more detailed description set out in a design description language (described below). Part of the data dictionary for the above system is shown in Figure 12.8.

Data dictionaries are an appropriate way to link descriptive and diagrammatic design descriptions (Figure 12.9). This diagram shows a pop-up window describing the selected transform in the data flow diagram. Some CASE toolsets provide automatic linkage between the data flow diagram and the data dictionary.

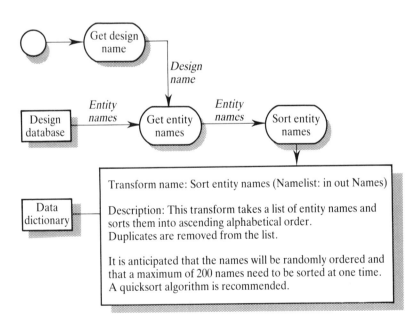

Figure 12.9
Transform information from a data dictionary.

12.4 A design example

The office information retrieval system (OIRS) (introduced in Chapter 11) is an automatic file clerk which can file documents in one or more indexes, retrieve documents, display and maintain document indexes, archive documents and destroy documents. The system is activated by a request from the user's terminal and always returns a message to the user indicating the success or failure of the request.

The interface to this system is a form which has a number of fields (Figure 12.10). Some of these fields are menu fields where the user can choose a particular option. Other fields allow user textual input. Menu items may be selected by pointing with a mouse or by moving a cursor using keyboard commands.

The fields displayed in the form are as follows:

(1)   *The operation field*   Selecting this field causes a menu of allowed operations to be displayed as shown in Figure 12.10.

(2)   *The known indexes field*   Selecting this field causes a menu of existing index names to be displayed. Selecting an item from this list adds it to the current index list.

(3)   *The current indexes field*   Selecting this field displays a list of the current indexes. The current indexes are indexes used in a particular retrieval operation. Thus, if the user issues a save command, the document name is entered in all of the current indexes.

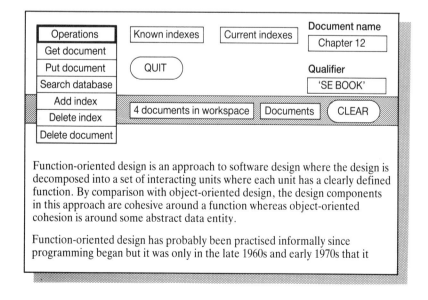

Figure 12.10
The OIRS system interface.

(4)   *The document name field*   This specifies the name of the document which is to be filed or the name of the document which is to be retrieved. If this name is not filled in, the user is prompted for a value.

(5)   *The qualifier field*   This is a pattern which is used in searching. For example, the pattern 'A-K' may be specified with a command to look up the names of documents in the current index lists. The qualifier causes only those names which begin with a letter from A to K to be listed. Alternatively, the qualifier field might contain a keyword such as 'software engineering'. An index search retrieves all documents which contain this keyword.

(6)   *The current workspace*   Documents are retrieved to the current workspace, which may contain several documents. The user may choose a document in the workspace by selecting its name from the workspace menu. Selecting Clear from the workspace menu bar removes the selection from the workspace. Moving the cursor into the workspace causes the system to enter document edit mode.

There are a number of alternative ways of realizing this design. The most appropriate depends on particular parameters such as the I/O devices connected to the system and the programming language to be used. As we shall see, the design may be developed into either a sequential or a parallel system design.

The initial stage of the design of the OIRS should treat the system as a black box and define the inputs and outputs of the system (Figure 12.11). Recall that the arc annotated with 'or' joining the output data flows means that one or the other but not both of these data flows occur.

In the next stage of the design, a data flow transformation is associated with each input and output. These input and output processes might be connected by a transform (Execute Command) converting input to output as shown in Figure 12.12.

The Execute Command transformation can now be considered in isolation. The designer must decide whether this central transform is,

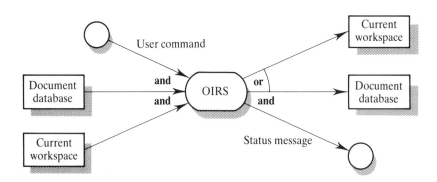

Figure 12.11
Inputs and outputs of
OIRS.

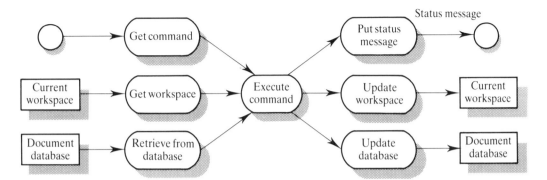

logically, a single transformation or whether it is best implemented as a number of transformations at the same level. Questions that the designer might use to help make the decision are:

Figure 12.12
Initial refinement of the
OIRS design.

- Are the input or output data flows processed independently or are they interdependent? If they are processed independently, this suggests that a central transformation should exist for each independent processing unit.
- Is the central transformation a series of transforms where all of the data processed are passed through the series? If so, each logical processing element in the series should be represented as a single transformation.

Neither of this conditions hold in this case so Execute Command can be implemented as a single transformation. However, it can be decomposed into simpler transformations (Figure 12.13).

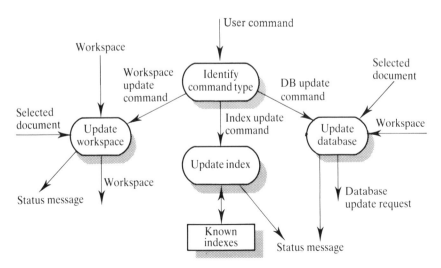

Figure 12.13
A decomposition of
Execute command.

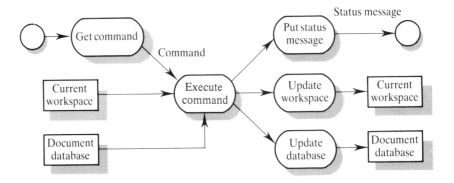

Figure 12.14
Modified OIRS data
flow design.

Figure 12.13 reflects the different types of command. These are commands to update the workspace (Get document, Search database, Clear workspace and the implicit Edit command), commands to update the database (Put document, Delete document) and index commands (Add index, Delete index, Display index lists).

Decomposing Execute Command in this way reveals a possible flaw in the initial design. It shows that the workspace and the database are exclusively accessed from within Execute Command. There is no need for top-level transformations which control access to these entities. These access procedures are subordinate to Execute Command so the top-level description of the design should be modified (Figure 12.14).

The process of design refinement where a design is decomposed, flaws discovered and the higher levels redesigned is a natural part of the design process. Designs do not come about all at once but are the outcome of an iterative refinement process.

For each function in the structure chart, an associated design description should be developed incorporating control information. The level of detail at which this is expressed varies depending on the application and on the final implementation language. The control description should be provided after the structure chart has been completed as a supplement to it. Figure 12.15 is a design description for the top level of the OIRS. Additional functions are included for login and initialization.

At this stage in the design, the software has been described without details of the types of the design components. Thus, the design shown in Figure 12.15 does not include declarations of the entities which are used. However, these names should be entered in a data dictionary along with a description of the entities which they identify. This reduces the chances of mistakenly reusing names and provides design readers with insights into the designer's thinking.

The design process continues by decomposing each of the design components into structure charts or PDL descriptions. As an illustration of this decomposition process, consider the design of Get_command (Figure 12.16). Notice the use of natural language in this description.

```
procedure Office_system is
begin
   User := Login_user ;
   Workspace := Create_user_workspace (User) ;
   -- Get the users own document database using the user id
   DB_id := Open_document_database (User)  ;
   --  get the user's personal index list ;
   Known_indexes := Get_document_indexes (User) ;
   Current_indexes := NULL ;
   -- get/execute command loop
   loop
      Command := Get_command ;
      exit when Command = Quit ;
      Execute_command ( DB_id, Workspace, Command, Status) ;
      if Status = Successful then
         Write_success_message ;
      else
         Write_error_message (Command, Status) ;
      end if ;
   end loop ;
   Close_database (DB_id) ;
   Logout (User) ;
end Office_system ;
```

Figure 12.15
High-level design of the
OIRS system.

```
procedure Get_command is
begin
-- track the cursor until it is over a menu selection or in the workspace
   loop
      Cursor_position := Get_cursor_position ;
      exit when positioned in workspace or
         (positioned over menu and button clicked) ;
      Display_cursor_position ;
   end loop ;
   if In_workspace (Cursor_position) then
      Command := Edit_workspace ;
   elsif In_command_menu  (Cursor_position) then
      Display_command_menu ;
      Command := Get_command_from_menu ;
   elsif In_Known_indexes  (Cursor_position) then
      Command := Display_indexes ;
   elsif In_Current_indexes  (Cursor_position) then
      Command := Display_current_indexes ;
   elsif In_Clear_button then
      Command := Clear_workspace ;
   elsif In_Document_name  (Cursor_position) then
      Command := Edit_document_name ;
   elsif In_Qualifier  (Cursor_position) then
      Command := Edit_qualifier ;
   elsif In_Documents  (Cursor_position) then
      Command := Display_documents ;
   elsif In_Quit_button (Cursor_position) then
      Command := Quit ;
   else
      System_error ;
   end if ;
end Get_command ;
```

Figure 12.16
Command selection.

The OIRS interface is menu-driven and the screen cursor position is used to choose which command to execute. In the design shown in Figure 12.16, the application system itself is responsible for finding out the cursor position, identifying the appropriate command and then calling another component to execute that command. The advantage of this approach is that command execution is localized and independent of the interface. Should the interface be changed so that commands are typed (say), only the Get_command procedure need be changed.

The disadvantage is that additional overhead is incurred by separating command identification and command execution. If a mouse is used for command selection, real-time tracking of the mouse and cursor display is necessary and the computer may include some hardware assistance to speed up this process. It may be necessary to adopt an alternative design strategy where a system procedure is used for mouse tracking. This is supplied with a list of 'action areas' and the names of functions to be called when these areas are entered.

12.5 Concurrent systems design

As with object-oriented design, a function-oriented approach to design does not preclude the realization of that design as a set of parallel communicating processes. Indeed, data flow diagrams explicitly exclude control information so a standard implementation technique for real-time systems is to take a data flow diagram and to implement its transformations as separate processes. This is discussed in the following chapter which covers real-time systems design.

The OIRS system described above may be designed using concurrent processes as shown in Figure 12.17. Command input, command execution, and status reporting, as shown in the data flow diagrams for the system (Figure 12.14), are all implemented as separate tasks. For readers who are unfamiliar with Ada tasking, the notation is described in Appendix A.

The Get_command task continually tracks the mouse and when a command area is selected, initiates the command execution process. Similarly, the command execution process produces status messages which are processed by the output task. Workspace editing is also implemented as a parallel task and the editor is initiated and suspended as the cursor is moved in and out of the workspace window.

This example illustrates the point made in Chapter 10 that design parallelism is often an option available to the designer. Some types of system (typically real-time embedded systems) are usually implemented as collections of parallel processes with a process associated with each system hardware unit. However, problems often have both parallel and sequential design solutions and premature design decisions should be avoided.

```
procedure Office_system is
  task Get_command ;
  task Process_command is
    entry Command_menu ;
    entry Display_indexes ;
    entry Edit_qualifier ;
    -- Additional entries here.  One for each command
  end Process_commands ;
  task Output_message is
    entry  Message_available ;
  end Output_message ;
  task Workspace_editor is
    entry Enter ;
    entry Leave ;
  end Workspace_editor ;

  task body  Get_command is
  begin
    loop
      loop
        Cursor_position := Get_cursor_position ;
        exit when cursor positioned in workspace or
           (cursor positioned over menu and button pressed)
        Display_cursor_position ;
      end loop ;
      if In_workspace (Cursor_position) then
        Workspace_editor.Enter ;
      elsif In_command_menu  (Cursor_position) then
        Process_command.Command_menu ;
      elsif In_Known_indexes  (Cursor_position) then
        Process_command.Display_indexes ;
      elsif In_Current_indexes  (Cursor_position) then

        ...
        Other commands here
        ...
  end Get_command ;

  task body Process_command is
    Command: COMMAND.T ;
    Index: INDEX.T ;
  begin
   Workspace_editor.Leave ;
    loop
      accept Command_menu do
        Display_command_menu ;
        Get_menu_selection (Command) ;
        Execute_menu_command (Command) ;
      end Command_menu ;
      accept Display_indexes do
        Display_current_indexes ;
        Get_index_selection (Index) ;
      end Display_indexes;

      ...
      Other commands here
      ...
    end loop
end Office_system ;
```

Figure 12.17
Concurrent design of
the OIRS system.

■ KEY POINTS

- ■ Function-oriented design is a complementary and not an opposing technique to object-oriented design.

- ■ Data flow diagrams are a means of documenting data flow through a system. They do not include control information such as selections and iterations.

- ■ Structure charts are a way of representing the hierarchical organization of a system. In general, nodes in a structure chart should have more than one and less than seven subordinate nodes.

- ■ Control information in a design is best presented using a design description language which includes selection and looping constructs.

- ■ Data flow diagrams can be implemented directly as a set of cooperating sequential processes. Each transform in the data flow diagram is implemented as a separate process. Alternatively, they can be realized as a number of procedures in a sequential program.

FURTHER READING

IEEE Trans. Software Engineering, **12** (2), March 1986.   This is a special issue of the journal devoted to design methods. Some papers covering the functional approach to design are included.

Structured Design.   A description of the first version of the structured design method. This has been widely and successfully used, particularly in the United States. The book covers all aspects of the method including data flow diagrams, structure charts and data dictionaries. (L.L. Constantine and E. Yourdon, 1979, Prentice-Hall.)

Software Development with Ada.   This is a book about the effective use of Ada and has a number of chapters on software design and on Ada's parallel processing constructs. (I. Sommerville and R. Morrison, 1987, Addison-Wesley.)

EXERCISES

12.1   Using examples, describe how data flow diagrams may be used to document a system design. Explain how these data flow diagrams may be transformed to system structure charts.

12.2   Using a design description language, describe a possible design for the design report generator whose data flow diagram and structure chart are given in Figures 12.3 and 12.7, respectively.

12.3 Modify the design of the report generator so that it becomes an interactive system. The user may give a design entity name and the report generator provides information about that entity. Alternatively, the user may provide a type name and the report generator produces a report about each entity of that type in a design. Document your modified design using data flow diagrams and structure charts.

12.4 The design of a spelling checker is discussed in Appendix A to illustrate design description languages. Document this design using data flow diagrams and structure charts.

12.5 Explain how data dictionaries are used to supplement design information in data flow diagrams and structure charts.

12.6 Develop the data flow diagrams shown in Figure 12.12 so that all transforms are documented with more detailed data flow diagrams.

12.7 Describe the design of Execute Command in the office information retrieval system using a design description language.

12.8 Using data flow diagrams, describe a functionally-oriented design for the newspaper delivery system introduced in Exercise 3.7.

12.9 Transform the data flow design for the newspaper delivery system into a set of structure charts showing the hierarchical design organization.

12.10 Using a design description language or a programming language, describe the detailed design of all or part of the newspaper delivery system.

Real-Time Systems Design

13

■ OBJECTIVES

The objectives of this chapter are to discuss the design of embedded real-time systems and to illustrate some of the particular difficulties of designing and implementing this kind of system. The correctness of a real-time system depends on the results it produces and the time at which these results are produced. After a general overview of embedded systems design, the modelling of real-time systems as finite state machines is described. This is followed by two sections describing characteristic designs for real-time systems. Monitoring and control systems continuously monitor a number of sensors, and control actuators depending on the sensor values. Data acquisition systems collect data from sensors and process that data in some way. To meet their stringent timing requirements, real-time systems are usually implemented as a set of cooperating sequential processes. Both of the characteristic designs are concurrent rather than sequential systems.

■ CONTENTS

As the cost of computer hardware decreases, controlling computers are being embedded in an increasing number of systems. These computers interact directly with hardware devices and their software must be sufficiently responsive to react to events which are being monitored and controlled by the system. Because of the need for the software to respond to 'real-time' events, the controlling software system is called a 'real-time' system.

As can be seen from the following definition, the requirement that the system should react in a timely way is a distinguishing feature of real-time systems:

> A real-time system is a software system where the correct functioning of the system depends on the results produced by the system and the time at which these results are produced. A 'soft' real-time system is a system whose operation is degraded if results are not produced according to the specified timing requirements. A 'hard' real-time system is a system whose operation is incorrect if results are not produced according to the timing specification.

One way of looking at a real-time system is as a stimulus/response system. Given a particular stimulus, the system must produce a corresponding response. The behaviour of a real-time system can be defined by listing stimuli, associated responses and the time at which the response must be produced. In general, the stimuli fall into two classes:

(1)   *Periodic stimuli*   These are stimuli which occur at predictable time intervals. For example, the system may examine a sensor every 50 milliseconds and take action (respond) depending on that sensor value.

(2)   *Aperiodic stimuli*   These are stimuli which occur irregularly. They are usually signalled using the computer's interrupt mechanism. An example of such a stimulus would be an interrupt indicating that an I/O transfer was complete and that data was available in a buffer.

Generally, periodic stimuli in a real-time system are generated from a set of sensors associated with the system. The responses are directed to a set of actuators which operate some hardware unit. Aperiodic stimuli may be generated either by the actuators or by sensors indicating some exceptional condition which must be handled by the system. This general sensor–system–actuator model of an embedded system is illustrated in Figure 13.1.

The need to respond to stimuli which occur at different times means that the architecture of a real-time system must be organized so that control can be transferred to the appropriate program component as soon as a stimulus is received. This is normally achieved by designing the system as a

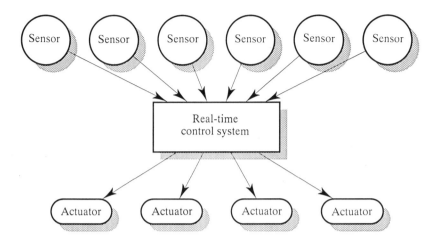

Figure 13.1
A general model of a
real-time system.

set of concurrent, cooperating processes. Part of the real-time system
(sometimes called the real-time executive) is dedicated to managing these
processes.

In general, each class of sensor has an associated process. A process is
also associated with managing each class of actuator and further processes
may be responsible for computational tasks within the system (Figure 13.2).

An alternative architecture would be to associate a single process with
each stimulus/response pair but this can cause difficulties if the timing of the
sensors and the actuators is not the same. The general model shown in
Figure 13.2 allows data to be collected quickly from the sensor (before the
next data item becomes available) but allows for processing and the
associated response to be carried out later.

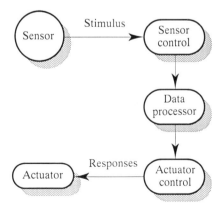

Figure 13.2
Sensor/actuator
processes.

13.1 Systems design

In large-scale embedded systems, one stage of the design process is systems design (Figure 13.3) where functions are partitioned into software and hardware functions. Until relatively recently, the available standard hardware was limited so this constrained what functions were implemented as hardware functions. The role of the software was to coordinate and control the hardware units. It was only economic to develop special-purpose hardware for very large systems or specialized military systems.

The cost of special-purpose integrated circuits has now decreased significantly and the speed of fabrication has increased. For simple circuits, it is now possible to go from an idea to a delivered microchip in a few weeks. The borderline between hardware and software components has blurred. It is becoming increasingly cost-effective to delay decisions about which functions should be implemented in hardware and which functions should be software components.

The advantage of implementing functionality in hardware is that a hardware component delivers much better performance than the equivalent software. System software bottlenecks can be identified and replaced by hardware, thus avoiding expensive software optimization. Providing performance in hardware means that the software design can be structured for adaptability and that performance considerations can take second place.

It is outside the scope of this book to discuss hardware and VLSI design. It is important in the design process to delay hardware/software partitioning until as late as possible. This implies that the system architecture must be made up of stand-alone components which can be implemented in either hardware or software. Fortunately, building a design in this way is exactly the aim of the designer trying to design a maintainable

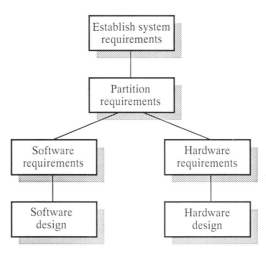

Figure 13.3
The system design process.

system. A good systems design process should result in a system which can be implemented in either hardware or software.

The design process for embedded systems can be expressed as a series of steps:

(1)   Identify the stimuli that the system must process and the associated responses.

(2)   For each stimulus and associated response, identify the timing constraints which apply to both stimulus and response processing.

(3)   Aggregate the stimulus and response processing into a number of concurrent processes. A good general model for the architecture is to associate a process with each class of stimulus and response, as shown in Figure 13.2.

(4)   For each stimulus and response, design algorithms to carry out the required computations. Algorithm designs should be developed at this stage to give an indication of the amount of processing required and the time required to complete that processing.

(5)   Design a scheduling system which will ensure that processes are started at the appropriate time to carry out the required processing within the given time constraints.

(6)   Integrate the system under the control of a real-time executive.

Naturally, this is an iterative process. Once a process architecture has been established and a scheduling policy decided, designers must carry out extensive assessments and simulations to check that the system will meet its timing constraints. In many cases, these simulations will reveal that the system will not perform adequately. The process architecture, the scheduling policy, the executive or all of these may have to be re-designed so that the system meets its timing constraints.

Carrying out a timing assessment of a real-time system is difficult. Because of the unpredictable nature of aperiodic stimuli, the designers must make some assumptions as to the probability of these stimuli occurring (and therefore requiring service) at any particular time. These assumptions may be incorrect and system performance after delivery may not be adequate. General issues of timing validation are covered by Dasarthy (1985).

Because the processes in a real-time system must cooperate, the real-time systems designer must coordinate the communications between processes. Process coordination mechanisms ensure mutual exclusion to shared resources. When one process is modifying a shared resource, other processes should not be able to change that resource. Mechanisms for ensuring mutual exclusion include semaphores (Dijkstra, 1968), monitors (Hoare, 1974) and critical regions (Brinch-Hansen, 1973). I do not cover these mechanisms here as they are well-documented in operating system texts (Silberschaltz *et al.*, 1991).

Because of the importance of timing in real-time systems, good design principles sometimes have to be sacrificed to gain better system performance. For example, an object-oriented approach to design involves hiding data representations and accessing attribute values through operations defined with the object. Inevitably, there is an overhead associated with these operations. In some cases, this overhead may cause an unacceptable delay in the system data processing. I know of anecdotal evidence that, in an aerospace project, object-oriented design was abandoned because of the difficulties of achieving the required system performance.

The language chosen for real-time systems implementation may also influence the design. Ada was originally designed for embedded system implementation and has features such as tasking, exceptions and representation clauses. Its *rendezvous* capability is a good general purpose mechanism for task synchronization but the language is, unfortunately, not suitable for implementing hard real-time systems.

The designers of Ada have made a number of fundamental errors in that there is no way for task deadlines to be explicitly specified, no inbuilt exception if a deadline is not met and a strict first-in, first-out policy for servicing a queue of task entries. Ada's *rendezvous* mechanism is described in Appendix A and, in more detail, by Burns and Wellings (1989) and Sommerville and Morrison (1987). The book by Burns and Wellings is also a good introduction to other real-time programming languages.

Hard real-time systems are still often programmed in assembly language so that tight deadlines can be met. Other languages used include systems level languages such as C, which requires extra run-time support for parallelism.

13.2 State machine modelling

As discussed in the introduction to this chapter, real-time systems have to respond to events occurring at irregular intervals. These events (or stimuli) often cause the system to move to a different state. For this reason, state machine modelling has been widely used as a way of expressing a real-time systems design.

Salter (1976) discusses the use of finite state machines for system modelling and considers a general system model to be a function of three elements – control, function, and data. Intuitively, functions are the information transformers in the system, data are the inputs and outputs of functions and control is the mechanism that activates functions in the desired sequence.

The state machine approach is appropriate for the modelling of real-time systems where a particular input causes a thread of actions to be initiated. Figure 13.4 is an state machine model of a simple microwave oven

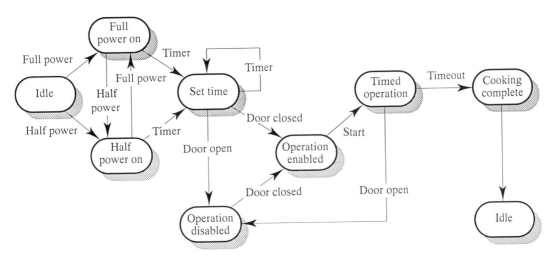

Figure 13.4
State machine model of
a simple microwave
oven.

equipped with buttons to set the power and the timer and to start the system.

The boxes in Figure 13.4 represent system states and the arrowed labels represent stimuli which force a transition from one state to another. The names chosen in the state machine diagram are descriptive and give an indication of operation but it is necessary to provide more detail about both the stimuli and the system states (Figure 13.5).

The problem with the state machine approach is that the number of possible states increases rapidly. Even the microwave oven state model is a relatively complex diagram for such a simple system. It is therefore necessary to adapt the approach for larger systems so that all states need not be included in a single diagram. This may be accomplished by drawing individual thread diagrams which shows how a sequence of actions 'thread' their way through the system. A thread diagram should be produced for every identified combination of messages. Figure 13.6 shows a single message thread from the microwave oven system model.

State machine models are a good, language-independent way of representing the design of a real-time system. For this reason, they are an inherent part of real-time design methods such as that proposed by Ward and Mellor (1985).

13.3 Real-time executives

A real-time executive is responsible for process management and resource allocation in a real-time system. It must start appropriate processes so that stimuli can be processed and must allocate memory and processor resources. A real-time executive is analogous to an operating system in a general-purpose computer.

State	Description
Half power on	The oven power output is set to 300 watts
Full power on	The oven power is set to 600 watts
Set time	The cooking time is set to the user's input value
Operation disabled	Oven operation is disabled for safety. Interior oven light is on
Operation enabled	Oven operation is enabled. Interior oven light is off
Timed operation	Oven in operation cooking for the required time. Interior oven light is on
Cooking complete	Timer has reached zero. Sound audible signal. Oven light is off

Stimulus	Description
Half power	The user has pressed the half power button
Full power	The user has pressed the full power button
Timer	The user has pressed one of the timer buttons
Door open	The oven door is not sealed
Door closed	The oven door is sealed
Start	The user has pressed the start button
Timeout	The timer indicates that the set time has expired

Figure 13.5
Microwave oven
stimulus and state
description.

The components of an executive depend on the size and complexity of the real-time system being developed. Normally, for all except the simplest systems, they will include the following:

(1)   *A real-time clock*   This provides information to schedule processes periodically.

(2)   *An interrupt handler*   This manages aperiodic requests for service.

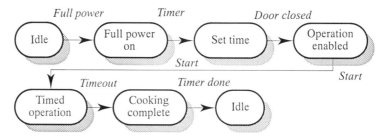

Figure 13.6
A thread diagram for a
microwave oven.

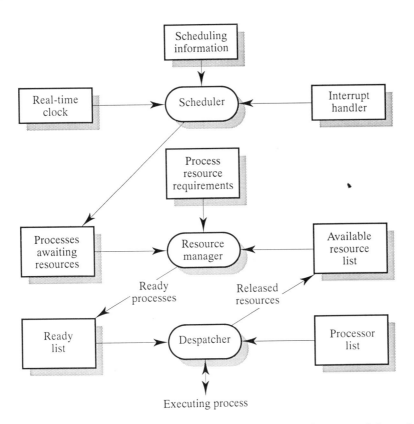

Figure 13.7
Components of a real-time executive.

(3)   *A scheduler* This component is responsible for examining the processes which can be executed and choosing one of these for execution.

(4)   *A resource manager* Given a process which is scheduled for execution, the resource manager allocates appropriate memory and processor resources.

(5)   *A dispatcher* This component is responsible for starting the execution of a process.

These components and their interactions are illustrated in Figure 13.7.

For systems which are required to provide a continuous service with high reliability requirements, the executive might also include the following capabilities:

(1)   *A configuration manager* This is responsible for the dynamic reconfiguration of the system's hardware. Hardware components can be introduced and taken out of service without shutting down the system. Some monitoring and telecommunication systems must be non-stop systems so a dynamic reconfiguration capability is essential.

(2)   *A fault manager* This component is responsible for detecting hardware and software faults and taking appropriate action to recover from these faults. Principles of fault tolerance and recovery are discussed in Chapter 15.

Normally, stimuli which have to be processed by a real-time system have different levels of importance as far as the correct functioning of the system is concerned. For some stimuli, such as those associated with certain exceptional events, it is absolutely essential that their processing should be started immediately and completed within the specified time limits. Other processes may be safely delayed if a more critical process requires service. It is therefore usual to identify at least two levels of priority in a real-time system:

(1)   *Interrupt level* This is the highest priority level which is allocated to processes which require a very fast response. One of these processes will be the real-time clock process.

(2)   *Clock level* This level of priority is allocated to periodic processes.

Within each of these priority levels, different classes of process may be allocated different priorities. For example, there may be several interrupt lines and an interrupt from a very fast device may have to pre-empt processing of an interrupt from a slower device to avoid information loss. The allocation of process priorities so that all processes are serviced in time usually requires extensive analysis and simulation.

There may be a further priority level allocated to background processes which do not need to meet real-time deadlines. These processes are scheduled for execution when processor capacity is available.

13.3.1   Process management

When an interrupt is detected by the executive, this indicates that some service is required. The computer's interrupt mechanism causes control to transfer to a pre-determined memory location and, normally, this location contains an instruction to jump to an interrupt service routine. This service routine should disable further interrupts (to avoid being interrupted itself), discover the cause of the interrupt and initiate (with a high priority) a process which can handle the stimulus causing the interrupt. In some cases of high-speed data acquisition, the interrupt handler will buffer data which the interrupt signalled was available. After this initial processing, interrupts are again enabled and control is returned to the executive.

It is important that the interrupt service routines are simple, short and have very fast execution times. While the interrupt is being serviced, other interrupts are disabled and will be ignored by the system. To make the

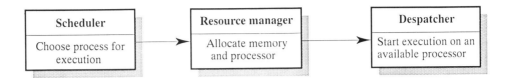

Scheduler	Resource manager	Despatcher
Choose process for execution	Allocate memory and processor	Start execution on an available processor

probability of information loss as low as possible, the time spent in this state must be minimized.

Periodic processes are processes which must be executed at pre-specified time intervals for data acquisition and actuator control. The executive uses its real-time clock to determine when a process is to be executed. In most real-time systems, there will be several classes of periodic process with different periods (the time between process executions), execution times and deadlines (the time by which processing must be complete). The executive must choose the appropriate process for execution at any one time.

The real-time clock is configured to 'tick' periodically where a 'tick' period might typically be a few milliseconds. The clock 'tick' initiates an interrupt level process which will schedule the process manager for periodic processes. The interrupt level process will not normally be completely responsible for managing periodic processes because interrupt processing must be completed as quickly as possible.

The actions taken by the executive for periodic process management are shown in Figure 13.8.

The list of periodic processes is examined by the scheduler and a process which is due to be executed is selected. The choice made depends on the process priority, the periods, the expected execution times and the deadlines of the ready processes. Sometimes, two processes with different deadlines should be executed at the same clock tick. It is acceptable in such cases to delay execution of one of these so long as its deadlines can be met.

There may be other processes which must also be executed and the scheduler must organize the execution of all of these. If *pre-emptive scheduling* is used, the currently executing process may be pre-empted and its execution halted to allow an alternative, higher-priority process to execute.

Information about the process to be executed is passed to the resource manager which allocates memory and, in a multi-processor system, a processor to this process. The process is then placed on the 'ready list' which is a list of processes which are ready for execution.

The dispatcher is invoked whenever a processor becomes available. It scans the ready list to find a process which can be executed on that processor and starts its execution.

Although there are a number of real-time executive products available, the specialized requirements of real-time systems often require

Figure 13.8
Real-time executive actions.

that the executive be designed as part of the system. Space does not allow a fuller discussion of real-time executive design issues and the reader is referred to an overview paper by Baker and Scallon (1986) for more information of this topic.

13.4 Monitoring and control systems

Monitoring and control systems are an important class of real-time system which continuously check sensors and take actions depending on the sensor reading. Monitoring systems are systems which take action when some exceptional sensor value is detected; control systems are systems which continuously control hardware actuators depending on the value of associated sensors. These systems obviously have a great deal in common and differ only in the way in which system actuators are initiated.

Presenting a realistic example of a real-time system design is difficult because the nature of real-time systems is so specialized that a good deal of application domain knowledge is essential if the examples are to be understood. This is particularly true of 'hard' real-time systems which interact with system hardware. The example presented here is therefore, inevitably, artificial but I hope it gives the reader some indications of how to tackle real-time system design.

> An intruder alarm system for a building which is equipped with a number of different types of sensor. These include movement detectors in individual rooms, window sensors on ground floor windows which detect if a window has been broken, and door sensors which detect door opening on corridor doors. There are 50 window sensors, 30 door sensors and 200 movement detectors in the system.

> When a sensor detects the presence of an intruder, the system automatically sets up a call to the local police and, using a voice synthesizer, reports the location of the alarm. It also switches on lights in the rooms around the active sensor and sets off an audible intruder alarm. Multiple sensor alerts may be received by the system and the building lights must be switched on around each sensor. However, calls to the police and the audible alarm are not repeated.

> The sensor system is normally powered by mains power but is equipped with a battery backup which can allow operation for 24 hours after mains power has been lost. Power loss is detected using a separate power circuit monitor which monitors the mains voltage and interrupts the intruder system when a voltage drop is detected. The system is manually switched back to mains power. It is assumed that a separate alarm system is used to notify a power loss.

Stimulus/Response	Timing requirements
Power fail interrupt	The switch to backup power must be completed within a deadline of 50 ms.
Door alarm	Each door alarm should be polled twice per second
Window alarm	Each window alarm should be polled twice per second
Movement detector	Each movement detector should be polled twice per second
Audible alarm	The audible alarm should be switched within 1/2 second of an alarm being raised by a sensor
Lights switch	The lights should be switched on within 1/2 second of an alarm being raised by a sensor
Communications	A call to the police should be started within 2 seconds of an alarm being raised by a sensor
Voice synthesizer	A synthesized message should be available within 8 seconds of an alarm being raised by a sensor

Figure 13.9
Stimulus/response
timing requirements.

This system is a 'soft' real-time system which does not have stringent timing requirements. The events which the sensors detect do not occur at high speed so the sensors need only be polled twice per second. Nevertheless, the design approach discussed in Section 13.2 above can be used for this system although an object-oriented approach would be equally applicable. Obviously, a complete system design cannot be shown in this chapter so only part of the system functionality will be discussed.

The design process starts by identifying the stimuli which the system receives and the associated responses. Stimuli generated by system self-checking procedures will be ignored as will external stimuli which may be generated to test the system or to switch it off in the event of a false alarm. This means there are only two classes of stimulus which must be processed:

(1) *Power failure* This is a stimulus generated by the circuit monitor. The required response is to switch the circuit to backup power by signalling an electronic power switching device.

(2) *Intruder alarm* This is a stimulus generated by one of the system sensors. The response to this stimulus is to compute the room number of the active sensor, set up a call to the police, initiate the voice synthesizer to manage the call, and switch on the audible intruder alarm and the building lights in the area.

The next step in the design process is to consider the timing constraints associated with each stimulus and associated response. These timing constraints are shown in Figure 13.9. In this diagram, the different classes of sensor which can generate an intruder alarm stimulus have been listed as these have different timing requirements.

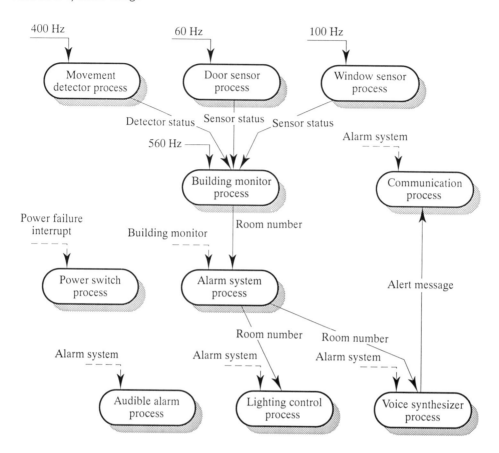

Figure 13.10
Intruder alarm system
process architecture.

Allocation of the system functions to concurrent processes is the next design stage. Recall that there are three different types of sensor which must be polled periodically, an interrupt driven system to handle power failure and switching, a communications system, a voice synthesizer, an audible alarm system system and a light switching system to switch on lights around the sensor. This suggests a system architecture as shown in Figure 13.10.

Annotated arrows joining processes indicate data flows between processes with the annotation indicating the type of data flow. The arrow associated with each process on the top right indicates control. The arrows on a periodic process use solid lines with the minimum number of times a process should be executed per second as an annotation. Each of these processes must be scheduled so that each sensor is serviced within the specified response time. Therefore, the door sensor process is scheduled 60 times per second so that each of the 30 door sensors can be polled twice per second.

Aperiodic processes have dashed lines on the control arrows which are annotated with the event which causes the process to be scheduled. The

```
task Building_monitor is
    entry Initialize ;
    entry Test ;
    entry Monitor ;
end Building_monitor ;

task body Building_monitor is
    type  ROOMS is array (NATURAL range <>) of ROOM_NUMBER ;
    Move_sensor, Window_sensor, Door_sensor : SENSOR ;
    Move_sensor_locations: ROOMS (0..Number-of_move_sensors-1) ;
    Window_sensor_locations: ROOMS (0.. Number_of_window_sensors -1) ;
    Corridor_sensor_locations : ROOMS (0..Number_of_corridor_sensors-1) ;
    Next_move_sensor, Next_window_sensor,
    Next_door_sensor: NATURAL := 0;
begin
  select
      accept Initialize do
            -- code here to read sensor locations from a file and
            -- initialize all location arrays
      end Initialize ;
  or
      accept  Test do
            -- code here to activate a sensor test routine
      end Test ;
  or
      accept Monitor do
          -- the main processing loop
          loop
              -- TIMING:  Each movement sensor  twice/second
              Next_move_sensor :=
                  Next_move_sensor + 1 mod Number_of_move_sensors ;
              -- rendezvous with Movement detector process
              Movement_detector.Interrogate (Move_sensor) ;
              if Move_sensor /= OK then
                  Alarm_system.Initiate (Move_sensor_locations (Next_move_sensor)) ;
              end if ;
              -- TIMING: Each window sensor twice/second
              -- rendevous with Window sensor process
              Next_window_sensor :=
                  Next_window_sensor + 1 mod Number_of_window_sensors ;
              Window_sensor.Interrogate (Window_sensor) ;
              if Window_sensor /= OK then
                  Alarm_system.Initiate (Window_sensor_locations (Next_window_sensor)) ;
              end if ;
              -- TIMING: Each door sensor twice/second
              -- rendevous with Door sensor process
              -- Comparable code here
          end loop ;
      end Monitor ;
end Building_monitor ;
```

Figure 13.11
PDL specification of
Building_monitor
process.

control information on the actuators indicates that these are started by an explicit command from the Alarm system process.

All processes need not receive data from other processes. For example, the process responsible for managing a power failure has no need for data from elsewhere in the system.

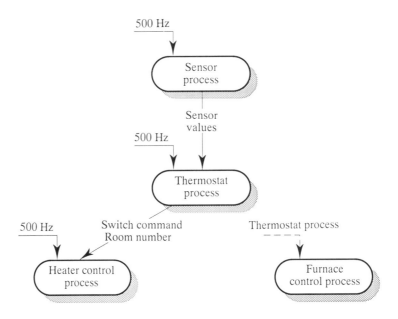

Figure 13.12
A temperature control
system.

Once the system process architecture has been designed, algorithms for stimulus processing and response generation should be designed. As discussed in Section 13.2, this detailed design stage is necessary early in the design process to ensure that the specified timing constraints can be met. If the associated algorithms are complex, it may be necessary to modify the timing constraints. In the intruder alarm system, as in many real-time systems, this algorithm design is a straightforward process and we will skip this stage here.

The final step in the design process is to design a scheduling system which ensures that a process will always be scheduled on a processor to meet its deadlines. In this example, deadlines are not tight so process priorities should be organized so that all sensor polling processes have the same priority but, obviously, the process for handling a power failure should be a higher-priority interrupt level process. The priorities of the processes managing the alarm system should be the same as the sensor processes.

The designs of each of these processes may be expressed in more detail using an Ada-based PDL. Figure 13.11 shows the Ada specification of the Building monitor process which polls the system sensors. If these signal an intruder, the software activates the associated alarm system. It is assumed in this design that the timing requirements (included as comments) can be met. If, in an implementation, it was important that the sensors were interrogated no more often than twice per second, timing code could be included to delay the process as required.

The intruder alarm system is a monitoring system rather than a control system as it does not include actuators which are directly affected by sensor values. As an example of this class of system, consider a building heating control system which monitors temperature sensors in different rooms in the building and switches a heater unit off and on depending on the actual temperature and the temperature set by the room occupant. If more than half the heating units are switched off, the furnace is also switched off until more than half the heaters are switched on. The architecture of this system is shown in Figure 13.12. It is clear that its general form is similar to the intruder monitoring system and further decomposition of the example is left as an exercise for the reader.

13.5   Data acquisition systems

Data acquisition systems are another common class of real-time system. These systems collect data from sensors for subsequent processing and analysis. In real-time systems which involve data acquisition and processing, the execution speeds and periods of the acquisition process and the processing process may be out of step. Sometimes, when significant processing is required, the data acquisition will go faster than the data processing; at other times, when only simple computations need be carried out, the processing will be faster than the data acquisition.

To smooth out these speed differences, most data acquisition systems buffer input data using a circular buffer. The process producing the data (the producer) adds information to this buffer and the process using the data (the consumer) takes information from the buffer (Figure 13.13).

Obviously, mutual exclusion must be implemented to prevent the producer and consumer processes accessing the same element in the buffer at the same time. The system must also ensure that the producer does not try to add information to a full buffer and the consumer does not take

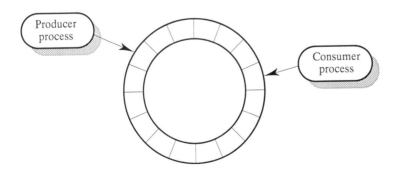

Figure 13.13
A ring buffer for data acquisition.

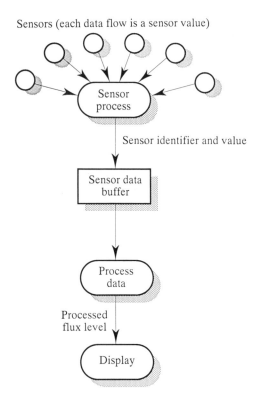

Figure 13.14
Reactor flux
monitoring.

information from an empty buffer. This means that the buffer itself should be implemented as an abstract data type with the buffer operations implemented as parallel processes.

To illustrate this class of system, consider the data flow diagram shown in Figure 13.14. This represents a system which collects data from six sensors monitoring the neutron flux in a nuclear reactor. The sensor data is placed in a buffer from which it is extracted and processed, and the average flux level is displayed on an operator's display.

Each sensor has an associated process which converts the analogue input flux level into a digital signal and passes this, with the sensor identifier, to the buffer (Sensor data). The buffer must also be implemented as a

Figure 13.15
Sensor data buffer task
specification.

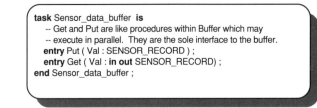

```
task Sensor_data_buffer is
   -- Get and Put are like procedures within Buffer which may
   -- execute in parallel.  They are the sole interface to the buffer.
   entry Put ( Val : SENSOR_RECORD ) ;
   entry Get ( Val : in out SENSOR_RECORD) ;
end Sensor_data_buffer ;
```

```
task body Sensor_data_buffer is
   Size : constant NATURAL := 50000 ;
   type BUFSIZE is range 1..Size ;
   Store : array (BUFSIZE) of SENSOR_RECORD ;
   Entries : NATURAL := 0 ;
   Front, Back : BUFSIZE := 1 ;
begin
   loop
      -- The select construct is called a  conditional entry.
      -- This means that a call  to the Get and Put processes will
      -- only be accepted when one of the conditional expressions
      -- following  is true.
      -- Thus, Put can only execute when  there is space in the buffer,
      -- Get can only take items from the buffer when it is not empty.
      select
         when Entries < Size =>
            accept Put (Val : SENSOR_RECORD) do
               Store (Back) := Val ;
            end Put ;
            Back := Back mod BUFSIZE'LAST + 1 ;
            Entries := Entries + 1 ;
      or
         when Entries > 0 =>
            accept Get (Val : in out SENSOR_RECORD) do
               Val := Store (Front) ;
            end Get ;
            Front := Front mod BUFSIZE'LAST + 1 ;
            Entries := Entries - 1 ;
      end select ;
   end loop ;
end Sensor_data_buffer ;
```

Figure 13.16
Detailed design of
sensor data buffer.

parallel process as this allows synchronization of the sensor processes producing the data and the processing functions which consume the data.

The design of the Sensor data buffer process shown in Figure 13.14 may be described as an abstract data type with concurrent operations. Assume that the information passed to the buffer is of type SENSOR_RECORD. Figure 13.15 shows the specification of the task describing the abstract data type.

The task specification shown in Figure 13.16 describes the buffer interface and shows that Get and Put are the only operations defined on the buffer. The detailed design description (Figure 13.16) shows that the buffer is implemented as a ring buffer with a maximum of 50 000 entries. If the number of entries exceeds 50 000, the processes calling Sensor data buffer must wait until there is buffer space available before making a buffer entry.

■ KEY POINTS

- ■ A real-time system is a software system which must respond to events in real-time. This means that its correctness depends not just on the system's computations but also on the time these computations are produced.

- ■ Systems design includes hardware and software design. It is good design practice to delay partitioning of a design to hardware and software elements until as late as possible in the design process.

- ■ Real-time systems are usually designed as a set of concurrent processes.

- ■ A general model for real-time systems architecture involves associating a process with each class of sensor and actuator device. Other coordination processes may also be required.

- ■ A real-time executive is responsible for process and resource management. It always includes a scheduler which is the component responsible for deciding which process should be scheduled for executing. Scheduling decisions are made using process priorities.

- ■ Monitoring and control systems periodically interrogate a set of sensors and take actions depending on the sensor readings.

- ■ Data acquisition systems are usually organized according to a producer–consumer model. The producer process inputs the data into a buffer where it is consumed by the consumer process. The buffer is also implemented as a process.

FURTHER READING

Introduction to Real-time Software Design. This is an introduction to real-time systems design written from an engineering viewpoint. I find the structure of this book rather artificial but it is one of the few introductory books dedicated to real-time systems. (S.T. Allworth and R.N. Zobel, 1987, Macmillan.)

Hard Real-time Systems. This is an excellent IEEE tutorial volume which covers the problems of implementing hard real-time systems. It contains most of the papers on this topic which are worth reading. However, it does assume that the reader has some familiarity with the subject area, perhaps to the level covered in this chapter. (J.A. Stankovic and K. Ramamritham, 1988, IEEE Press.)

Real-time Systems and their Programming Languages. This is an excellent book on comparative real-time programming languages. Its coverage of real-time systems design, however, is limited. It has good chapters on exception handling and reliability, which are useful background for Chapters 15 and 20. (A. Burns and A. Wellings, 1990, Addison-Wesley.)

EXERCISES

13.1 Using examples, explain why real-time systems usually have to be implemented using concurrent processes.

13.2 Explain why an object-oriented approach to software design where objects are implemented as tasks may result in unacceptable timing delays.

13.3 Draw state machine models of the control software for the following systems:

    (a) An automatic washing machine which has different programs for different types of clothes.

    (b) The software for a compact disc player.

    (c) A telephone answering machine which records incoming messages and displays the number of accepted messages on an LED display. The system should allow the telephone owner to dial in, type a sequence of numbers (identified as tones) and have the recorded messages replayed over the phone.

    (d) A drinks vending machine which can dispense coffee with and without milk and sugar. The user deposits a coin and makes his or her selection by pressing a button on the machine. This causes a cup with powdered coffee to be output. The user places this cup under a tap, presses another button and hot water is dispensed.

13.4 Draw a thread diagram for the action 'dispense coffee with milk' in the above drinks vending machine system.

13.5 Using the real-time system design techniques discussed in this chapter, re-design the weather station data collection system covered in Chapter 11. Discuss the advantages and disadvantages of the design in each case.

13.6 Design a process architecture for an environmental monitoring system which collects data from a set of air quality sensors situated around a city. There are 5000 sensors organized into 100 neighbourhoods. Each sensor must be interrogated four times per second. When more than 30% of the sensors in a particular neighbourhood indicate that the air quality is below an acceptable level, local warning lights are activated. All sensors return the readings to a central computer which generates reports every 15 minutes on the air quality in the city.

13.7 Using an Ada/PDL write task specifications and implementations for the processes identified in Figure 13.6.

13.8 Develop the producer–consumer example discussed in Section 13.5 and describe the design of the producer and consumer processes.

User Interface Design

■ OBJECTIVES

The objective of this chapter is to complete this section on design with a discussion of user interface design. User interface design is becoming increasingly important as computers become more widely used and increasingly complex as graphical interfaces become the norm. After suggesting some general design principles which are applicable for any type of user interface, the major part of the chapter is devoted to a discussion of graphical user interface design. This is followed by a short section covering command line interfaces and a section discussing how user support and guidance should be an inherent part of the interface. The final section briefly describes some techniques for user interface evaluation.

■ CONTENTS

Computer system design encompasses a spectrum of activities from hardware design to user interface design. Electronic engineers have always been responsible for hardware design but software engineers must often take responsibility for the user interface design as well as the design of the software system. Although human factors specialists are becoming increasingly involved in user interface design, their role is usually to advise the software engineer rather than design the interface.

The user interface of a system is often the yardstick by which that system is judged. An interface which is difficult to use will, at best, result in a high level of user errors. At worst, it will cause the software system to be discarded, irrespective of its functionality.

A badly designed interface can cause the user to make potentially catastrophic errors. If information is presented in a confusing or misleading way, the user may misunderstand the meaning of an item of information and initiate a sequence of dangerous actions. Although this chapter cannot cover user interface design in any depth, my intention is to introduce the topic to software engineers in the hope that dangerous design errors can be avoided. For a fuller discussion of user interface design, the reader is referred to texts such as that by Shneiderman (1986) or Preece and Keller (1990).

The emphasis in this chapter is on designing graphical rather than textual interfaces. Increasingly, user terminals include a significant amount of processing power and have a bit-mapped high resolution display supporting multiple text fonts and mixed text and graphics display. Graphical interfaces are rapidly becoming the norm for workstation and personal computer systems.

User interface implementation is not covered. This is an immense subject, requiring knowledge of window systems architecture, toolkits for window systems, language processing and user interface management systems. The reader is referred to books such as that by Young (1990) and articles such as that by Myers (1989) for more information on implementation.

14.1 Design principles

User interface design must take into account the needs, experience and capabilities of the system user. Potential users should be involved in the design process and rapid prototyping should be used to develop the user interface. The prototype should be made available to users and feedback incorporated in the user interface design.

Because of the range of users and applications, guidelines for user interface construction must be general rather than specific. Organizations may have their own interface style and may establish their own guidelines but there are some general principles which are applicable to all user

> (1) The interface should use terms and concepts which are familiar to the anticipated class of user.
> (2) The interface should be appropriately consistent.
> (3) The user should not be surprised by the system.
> (4) The interface should include some mechanism which allows users to recover from their errors.
> (5) The interface should incorporate some form of user guidance.

Figure 14.1
User interface design principles.

interface designs. Of course, many principles can be formulated but I think those shown in Figure 14.1 are the most important.

Users should not be forced to adapt to an interface because it is convenient to implement. The interface should use terms familiar to the user and the objects manipulated by the system should have direct analogues in the user's environment.

For example, if a system is designed for use by secretarial staff, the objects manipulated should be letters, documents, diaries, folders, and so on. The allowed operations might be 'file', 'retrieve', 'index', 'discard', and so on. In practice, these objects may be implemented using different files or database entities but the secretary should not be forced to cope with computing concepts such as workfiles, directories, file identifiers, and so on.

Interface consistency means that system commands and menus should have the same format, parameters should be passed to all commands in the same way, and command punctuation should be similar. Consistent interfaces reduce user learning time. Knowledge learnt in one command or application is applicable in other parts of the system. For example, say system commands accept parameters which may be filenames or which may be flags controlling command operations. If flags have to be distinguished from filenames by some means (such as preceding flags with a '-' character), this should be the convention for every system command.

Interface consistency across sub-systems is also important. Sub-systems should be designed so that commands with similar meanings in different sub-systems are expressed in the same way. It is dangerous for a command, say 'k', to mean 'keep this file' in a system editor and the same command 'k' to mean 'kill this transaction' in an information retrieval system.

This level of consistency is low-level consistency and interface designers should always try to achieve this in a user interface. Consistency at a higher level is also sometimes desirable. For example, it may be appropriate to allow the same operations on all types of system entities. However, Grudin (1989) points out the problems with total consistency in that there are usually several ways of looking at system entities. They cannot all be consistent at the same time.

Users become particularly irritated when a computer system behaves in a way which is unexpected. As a system is used, the user builds a mental model of that system and expects the system to conform to that model. If an action in one context causes a particular type of change, it is reasonable to expect that the same action in a different context will cause a comparable change. If something completely different happens, the user is both surprised and confused. Interface designers must therefore ensure that comparable actions have comparable effects.

Users inevitably make mistakes when using a system. The interface design can minimize these mistakes (e.g. using menus means that typing mistakes are avoided) but mistakes can never be completely eliminated. Therefore, the interface should contain facilities allowing users to recover from their mistakes. These can be of two kinds:

(1)   Confirmation of destructive actions. If a user specifies an action which is potentially destructive, they should be asked to confirm that this is really the intended action before any information is destroyed.

(2)   The inclusion of an undo facility which restores the system to a state before the action occurred. Many levels of undo are useful as users do not always recognize immediately that a mistake has been made. In practice, this is expensive to implement and most systems only allow the last command issued to be 'undone'.

Finally, interfaces should have built-in 'help' facilities. These should be accessible from the user's terminal and should provide different levels of help and advice. These should range from basic information on getting started with the system up to a full description of system facilities and their use. These help facilities should be structured so that users are not overwhelmed with information when they ask for help. Help systems are discussed in more detail in Section 14.4.

These principles emphasize that the interface design process should be *user-centred* (Norman and Draper, 1986). Computer users are trying to solve some problem using the computer yet many existing systems do not take user needs and limitations into account. The designer should always bear in mind that system users have a task to accomplish and the interface should be oriented towards that task.

14.2 Graphical user interfaces

User interfaces which rely on windows, iconic (pictorial) representations of entities, pull-down or pop-up menus and pointing devices are now commonplace on personal computers and workstations. The term 'WIMP interface' (derived from Windows, Icons, Menus and Pointing) was used as

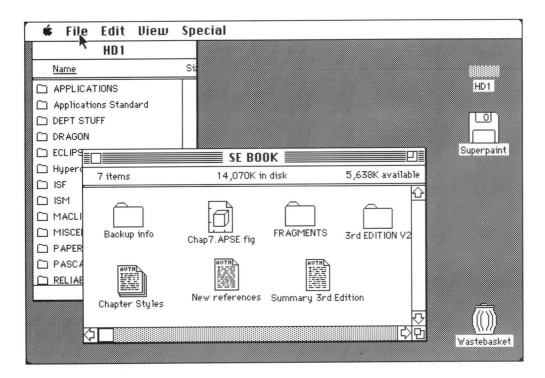

Figure 14.2
The graphical user interface of the Apple Macintosh.

a mnemonic for this type of interface but, because it can be insulting, they are now called *graphical user interfaces* (GUIs). They are characterized by:

(1) Multiple windows allowing different information to be displayed simultaneously on the user's screen.

(2) Iconic information representation. On some systems, icons represent files; on others, icons represent processes.

(3) Command selection via menus rather than a command language.

(4) A pointing device such as a mouse for selecting choices from a menu or indicating items of interest in a window.

(5) Support for graphical as well as textual information display.

An example of this interface style (from the Apple Macintosh interface) is shown in Figure 14.2. Two windows are displayed on the screen with each window showing a collection of documents. In one window these are represented iconically, as are system disks (on the right edge of the screen) and a trashcan. In the other window, only mini-icons are shown and the documents are listed by name.

The advantages of graphical interfaces are:

* They are easy to learn and use. Users with no computing experience can learn to use the interface after a brief training session.
* The user has multiple screens (windows) for system interaction. Switching from one task to another is possible without losing sight of information generated during the first task.
* Fast, full-screen interaction is possible rather than line-oriented interaction required by command interfaces.

Graphical interfaces are more complex than simple textual interfaces so the cost of interface engineering is greater. A significant fraction of the resources devoted to application development must be spent on building the user interface.

Until relatively recently, most vendors offered their own interface management system and these were incompatible with each other. This meant that enormous effort was required to port applications from one machine to another. In many cases, the user interface had to be significantly modified because of different interface conventions.

However, there has now been a welcome move to standardization on the X-window interface (Scheifler and Gettys, 1986) with the Motif (OSF, 1990; Berlage, 1991) interface toolkit. This is now supported by virtually all workstation vendors but, unfortunately, is not yet standard on personal computer systems. Graphical user interface implementations for workstations are now usually based on X-windows.

14.2.1 Direct manipulation

A direct manipulation interface presents users with a model of their information space and they modify their information by direct action. It is not necessary to issue explicit commands to cause information modification.

A familiar example of a direct manipulation interface is provided by many word processors or screen editors. To insert text the cursor is positioned at the appropriate place in the display and text is typed. It appears immediately, showing users the effects of their action. Another example is in graphical user interfaces where the user is presented with a list of filenames. The user selects the filename to be changed then types the new name.

The advantages of direct manipulation are:

* Users feel in control of the computer and are not intimidated by it.
* Typical user learning time is short.
* Users get immediate feedback on their actions so mistakes can be detected and corrected very quickly.

A direct manipulation interface requires a model of the user's information space. The user edits the model, which immediately modifies the underlying information. Interface models are discussed in the next section.

The problems of designing a direct manipulation interface are:

(1)   How can an appropriate model be derived? In some cases, this is straightforward. For example, in the Apple Macintosh, deletion of an entity involves dragging its icon into a trashcan (Figure 14.2). In other applications, it can be difficult to derive an appropriate model as there is no obvious real-world analogue which can be used.

(2)   Given that users have a large information space (normally the case in large systems), how can they navigate around that space and always be aware of their current position? This is comparable to the problems of dealing with multi-level menus covered in Section 14.2.3.

As computer systems are increasingly used by casual and untrained users, direct manipulation interfaces will become more common. This style of interface along with the derivation of appropriate information space models is currently the subject of much research

14.2.2   Interface models

The need for consistency in a user interface was identified as a basic principle of user interface design in the first part of this chapter. One way of helping achieve such consistency is to establish a consistent model or metaphor for user interaction with the computer. The user interface model is analogous to some real-world model familiar to the user.

The best known metaphor is the desktop metaphor (Ellis and Nutt, 1980) where the user's screen represents a desktop and system entities are represented by forms on that desktop. Deleting an entity involves dragging it to a trashcan, reading electronic mail is accomplished by 'opening' a mailbox and documents are stored by dragging them into a filing cabinet. The Apple Macintosh interface (Figure 14.2) has adopted a simplified form of this metaphor.

The desktop metaphor is reasonably intuitive and suitable for some types of system interaction. It suffers from the problem that the system screen size is restricted. Rather than a desktop which is usually a wide expanse, the user has the equivalent of the pull-down tables attached to the back of aircraft seats! There has to be a continual shuffling and rearrangement of windows to make sure the required information is visible.

The desktop metaphor is not suitable for supporting complex system interactions. Other models are based on replicating the control panels of existing systems and providing user interface objects such as buttons, sliders, lights, and so on.

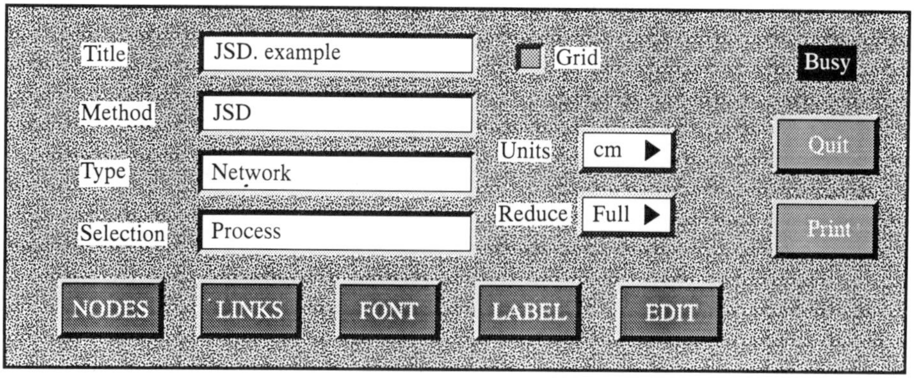

Figure 14.3
Design editor control
panel – Motif style.

Figure 14.3 shows an example of a control panel which was based on that used in the design editing system described in the first part of the book (Welland *et al.*, 1987). This control panel shows the style of the interfaces produced with the Motif toolkit.

There are several different types of entity which may be represented on a control panel:

(1) *Buttons* Picking a button always causes a single action to be initiated. Two buttons, 'Print' and 'Quit', are shown in Figure 14.3.

(2) *Switches* Switches may be set at a number of positions to configure a system or to move a system from one state to another. In Figure 14.3, the switches are named 'Units' (which turns a screen grid on and off) and 'Reduce' (which scales the display).

(3) *Menus* Menus are collections of buttons or switches which may be made visible and selected. They are represented by the dark grey rectangles along the base of the control panel. Picking a menu title causes a pull-down menu to appear.

(4) *Lights* Lights are activated to show some action is taking place. The black rectangle marked 'Busy' in Figure 14.3 is a light.

(5) *Displays* Displays are areas of the panel where graphical or textual information may be displayed. They have a name and a value. In Figure 14.3, displays named 'Title', 'Method', 'Type' and 'Selection' are shown. The user interface designer may control whether or not a display may be edited.

(6) *Sliders* Sliders are input devices used to set a specific input value. The user drags the slider along the scale to set the required value. Sliders are not used in the example in Figure 14.3.

This control panel metaphor has been used to provide a consistent interface to a range of software tools from information retrieval systems to the design editing system discussed above. Although there are overheads in using this approach which slow down some interactions, the interface consistency across tools compensates for this.

14.2.3 Menu systems

In a menu interface, users select one of a number of possibilities and indicate their choice to the machine. Users may type the name or the identifier of the selection; they may point at it with a mouse or some other pointing device; they may use cursor-moving keys to position the cursor over it or, on some types of touch-sensitive terminals, they point at the selection with a finger or a pen.

Menu-based systems have several advantages:

(1)   Users need not know the precise command names. They are always presented with a valid command list and they select from this.

(2)   Typing effort is minimal. This is important for occasional system users who cannot type quickly.

(3)   User errors are trapped by the interface. If an incorrect menu selection is made, the system indicates the selection is invalid and that the user should make another choice.

(4)   Context-dependent help can be provided. With a menu system, it is easy to keep track of the user's context and to link this with a help system.

The problems with menu system design are:

(1)   Actions which involve logical connectives (and/or/not) may be awkward to express using menu choices.

(2)   If there are a large number of possible choices, the menu system must be structured so that the user is not presented with a ridiculously large menu.

(3)   For experienced users, menu systems are sometimes slower to use than a command language.

The major problem with menu interfaces is the need to structure large menus. In some cases there may be tens, hundreds or thousands of possible menu choices. These have to be organized so that they are displayed in reasonably-sized chunks.

There are several solutions to this problem:

(1)   *Scrolling menus*   When a choice is not displayed on a menu, the menu scrolls either automatically or on command from the user to display the next set of choices. This is impractical, of course, if there are thousands of choices.

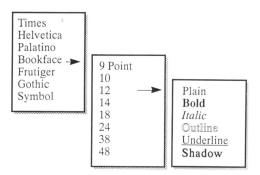

Figure 14.4
Walking menus.

(2)   *Walking menus*   When a menu item is selected, this causes a further menu to be displayed adjacent to it (Figure 14.4). Again, this is feasible if there are tens rather than hundreds of choices presented.

(3)   *Hierarchical menus*   The menus are organized in a hierarchy and selecting a menu item causes the current menu to be replaced by another menu representing its subtree. Walking menus are a form of hierarchical menu which is possible when the tree is shallow. Hierarchical menus can manage very large numbers of choices but present users with navigation problems. They tend to lose track of where they are in the menu hierarchy.

The availability of multiple window systems offers a way round some of the problems of navigating through menu structures. As well as a menu window, another window can display a map of the menu hierarchy. This shows the user's current position in the hierarchy, the path followed to reach that position and other reachable parts of the hierarchy.

As well as being able to find their position in a hierarchy, users should also be able to move around by pointing at the next menu to be displayed. Thus, rather than using the limited movement commands provided with the system menus, large jumps from one part of the hierarchy to another may be made with ease.

14.2.4   Information display

Information presented to a computer system user may be separated into a number of classes:

(1)   Static textual information.

(2)   Dynamic textual information.

(3)   Static numeric information.

(4)   Dynamic numeric information.

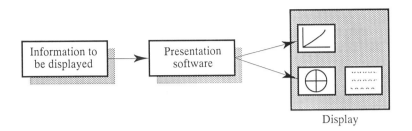

Figure 14.5
Information
presentation.

Static information is information which is initialized at the beginning of a session and does not change its value during that session. Dynamic information is information whose value may change as it is being used. An example of static information is the name of a file which is being edited; the file contents are dynamic information.

It is good design practice to keep the software required for information presentation separate from the information itself (Figure 14.5). This allows the presentation to be changed without having to change the underlying computational system.

In deciding how to present information, the designer must take a number of factors into account:

(1)   Is the user interested in precise information or in the relationships between different data values?

(2)   How quickly do the information values change? Should the change in a value be indicated immediately to the user?

(3)   Must the user take some action in response to a change in information?

(4)   Does the user need to interact with the displayed information via a direct manipulation interface?

Static information may be presented either graphically or as text depending on the application. In general, textual presentation is to be preferred as it takes up less screen space. Static information should be distinguished from dynamic information by using a different presentation style. For example, all static information may be presented in a particular font, may be highlighted using a particular colour or may always have an associated icon.

When precise numeric information is required, the information should be presented as text rather than graphically. However, if the relationships between data are significant but precise data values less important, graphical presentation should usually be used.

For example, consider a system which records and summarizes the sales figures for a company on a monthly basis. These figures may be presented exactly, using alphanumeric text (Figure 14.6).

Usually, managers studying sales figures are more interested in trends or anomalous figures rather than precise values. Graphical presentation of

Jan	Feb	Mar	April	May	June
2842	2851	3164	2789	1273	2835

Figure 14.6
Text display.

this information, as a histogram (Figure 14.7), makes the anomalous figures in March and May immediately obvious.

Dynamically varying numeric information is usually best presented graphically. Constantly changing digital displays become confusing as precise information is difficult to assimilate quickly. The graphical display can be augmented if necessary with a precise digital display which is set by a user command. Some different ways of presenting dynamic numeric information are shown in Figure 14.8.

A further advantage of continuous rather than digital displays are that they give the viewer some sense of relative value. In Figure 14.9, the values of temperature and pressure are approximately the same but the graphical display shows that temperature is close to its maximum value whereas pressure has not reached 25% of its maximum. With only a digital value, the viewer has to be aware of the maximum values and mentally compute the relative state of the reading.

When precise alphanumeric information is presented, graphics can be used as a means of highlighting. Rather than presenting a line of

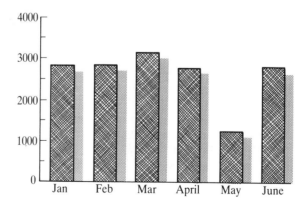

Figure 14.7
Histogram display.

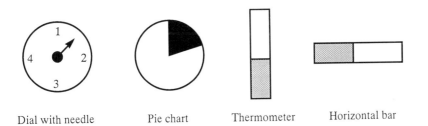

Dial with needle   Pie chart   Thermometer   Horizontal bar

Figure 14.8
Dynamic information display.

information, it might be shown in a box or indicated using an icon (Figure 14.10). The box displaying the message overlays the current screen display and the user's attention is immediately drawn to it.

Graphical highlighting may also be used in the display of text which is dynamically updated. When text is changed, the user's attention may be drawn to the change by some temporarily applied highlighting or colour change. However, if changes occur rapidly, graphical highlighting should not be used as a flashing display may be distracting.

14.2.5 Colour displays

Colour gives the user interface designer an extra dimension which can be exploited in the display of complex information structures. In some systems, such as VLSI layout systems, the system complexity is so high that, without colour, the display would be incomprehensible. In other cases, colour may not be essential but can be used to draw the operator's attention to important events in the underlying software.

Colour is a powerful tool but it is easy to misuse it to produce displays which are error prone and disturbing to the user. The most common mistakes made when using colour are:

- Colour is used to communicate meaning.
- Too many colours are used in the display and/or the colours are used in inconsistent ways.

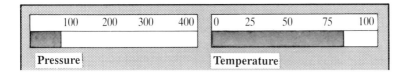

Figure 14.9
Graphical information display showing relative values.

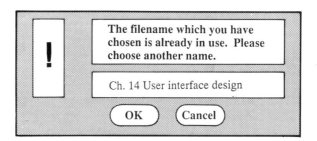

Figure 14.10
Textual highlighting.

There are three problems which can arise if colours are meaningful:

(1) A significant percentage of men are partially colour blind. They may not be able to see a particular colour on the screen.

(2) People's colour perceptions differ so that different individuals see the same colour differently.

(3) There are no standard conventions about the meaning of colours. In some situations (driving) red means danger. In other cases (chemistry) red means hot. Users with different backgrounds may unconsciously interpret the same colour in different ways.

If there are too many colours used in a display or if the colours used are too bright, the display can become confusing. These may disturb the user (in the same way that some abstract paintings cannot be viewed comfortably for a long time) and cause visual fatigue. User confusion is also possible if colours are used inconsistently.

Shneiderman (1986) sets out a number of guidelines for the effective use of colour:

(1) Don't use many colours. No more than four or five separate colours should be used in a window and no more than seven in a system interface.

(2) Use colour coding to support the task which users are trying to perform. If they have to identify anomalous instances, highlight these instances; if similarities are also to be discovered, highlight these using a different colour.

(3) Give users control of the colour coding. They should be able to turn the colour off or change it.

(4) Design for monochrome displays then add colour later. If a display is ineffective in monochrome, colour will only occasionally make it acceptable. Hoadley (1990) has carried out experiments which support this guideline.

(5)   Use colour coding in a consistent way. If one part of a system displays error messages in red (say), all other parts should do likewise. Red should not be used for anything else. If it is, the user may interpret the red display as an error message.

(6)   Be careful about colour pairings. Because of the physiology of the eye, people cannot focus on red and blue simultaneously. Eyestrain is a likely consequence of a red on blue display. Other colour combinations may also be visually disturbing or difficult to read.

(7)   Use colour change to show a change in system status. If a display changes colour, this should mean that a significant event has occurred. Thus, in a fuel gauge, a change of colour may indicate that fuel is running low. Colour highlighting is particularly important in complex displays where hundreds of distinct entities may be displayed.

(8)   Colour displays often have lower resolution than monochrome displays. Sometimes using better graphics is better than using colour.

Colour can improve user interfaces by helping users understand and manage the system complexity. However, there is still much to be learned about the effective use of colour. Given our current knowledge, user interface designers should always err on the side of conservatism when designing colour displays.

14.3   Command interfaces

Command interfaces require the user to type a text command to the system. The command may be a query, the initiation of some sub-system or it may call up a sequence of other commands.

The advantages of command interfaces are:

(1)   They may be implemented using cheap, alphanumeric displays.

(2)   Language processing techniques are well-developed because of the work done on compiler techniques. Creating a command language processor is relatively easy.

(3)   Commands of almost arbitrary complexity can be created by combining individual commands. A powerful feature of the UNIX system is its facility to write command language programs.

(4)   The interface can be made concise with little typing effort on the part of the user.

The disadvantages are:

(1)   Users have to learn a command language which is sometimes very complex. In some cases (such as the UNIX shell language) few users ever learn the complete language.

(2)   Users inevitably make errors in expressing commands. This requires error handling and message generation facilities to be included in the command language processor. In a menu system, users cannot input an incorrect action so the system can always assume its input is correct.

(3)   System interaction is through a keyboard. The interface cannot make full use of pointing devices, like a mouse.

For casual and inexperienced users, command interfaces are not suitable. The time taken to learn the command language is disproportionate to the time spent interacting with the computer. For such users a menu-based interface (or, sometimes, a natural language interface) is the only acceptable interface style.

Experienced, regular computer users sometimes prefer a command-based interface. Command interfaces allow faster interaction with the computer and simplify the input of complex requests. Experienced users may also wish to combine commands into procedures and programs.

In designing a command language interface, there are a number of design decisions which must be made:

(1)   Should it be possible to combine interface commands to create new command procedures? This is a powerful facility in the hands of experienced users but is probably unnecessary for the majority of system users.

(2)   What mnemonics should be chosen for system commands? The designer must try and develop meaningful mnemonics yet retain terseness to minimize the amount of typing required. As users gain experience, they usually prefer a terse interface.

(3)   Should users be allowed to redefine command names to suit their own preferences? The advantage of redefinition is that the command name can be terse for experienced users or expanded for those who are new to the system. Thus 'pc' and 'Compile_with_Pascal' can represent the same operation, namely the initiation of the Pascal compiler. The disadvantage is that wide-scale redefinition means that users no longer share a common language for communicating with the system.

Of course, command language interfaces and menu-based interfaces are not mutually exclusive. Many large software systems must accommodate a wide variety of users, from experienced computer professionals to casual users

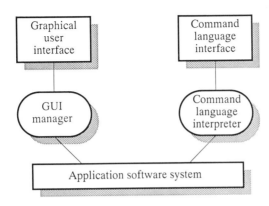

Figure 14.11
Multiple user interfaces.

with no computing background. It is possible, in principle, to attach a number of different user interface processors to a system so that different interface styles may be provided for different classes of user (Figure 14.11).

14.4 User guidance

User interfaces should always provide some form of on-line help system. Help systems are one facet of a general part of user interface design, namely the provision of user guidance which covers three areas:

- The documentation provided with the system.
- The on-line help system.
- The messages produced by the system in response to user actions.

In this chapter, we are concerned with the help system and the system-generated messages. Documentation is covered in Chapter 30.

There is usually an arbitrary distinction made between the provision of help (asked for by the user) and the output of messages (asynchronously produced by the system). Many of the principles which apply to the help system apply equally to the messaging system; some systems (Sommerville *et al.*, 1989) have integrated these into a single system (Figure 14.12).

When designing messages of any type, the following principles should be taken into account.

(1)   Messages should be tailored to the user's context. The user guidance system should be aware of what the user is doing and should alter the output message if it is context-dependent.

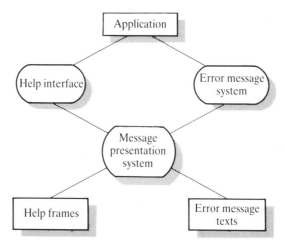

Figure 14.12
Help and message
system.

(2) Messages should be tailored to the user's experience level. As users become familiar with a system they become irritated by long, 'meaningful' messages. However, beginners find it difficult to understand short, terse statements of the problem. The user guidance system should provide both types of message and allow the user to control message verbosity.

(3) Messages should be tailored to the user's skills. This is not the same as the user's experience level. For example, secretarial staff and programming staff may both use an integrated environment. The secretaries may be experienced in computer usage but their skills are different from those of programmers. Different terminology may be appropriate when generating messages.

(4) Messages should be positive rather than negative. They should use the active rather than the passive mode of address. They should never be insulting or try to be funny.

Message design is expensive. Work on the ZOG system (Robertson *et al.*, 1981) which is a network of message frames, showed that each frame (a few sentences) took 10–12 minutes to write. A large system may have thousands of help message frames so the cost of producing these is significant. Shneiderman (1983) suggests that professional editors and copy writers should be used to assist with message design.

14.4.1 Error message design

A user's first impression of a computer system is often produced by the system error messages. Inexperienced users may start work with a terminal, make an initial error and immediately have to understand the resulting error message. This can be difficult enough for skilled software engineers; it is

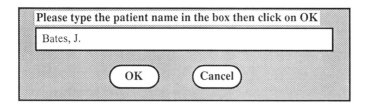

Figure 14.13
Nurse input.

often impossible for inexperienced or casual system users.

Error messages should be polite, concise, consistent and constructive. They must not be abusive and should not have associated noises which might embarrass the user. Wherever possible, the message should suggest how the error might be corrected. If appropriate, the user should be given the option of accessing the on-line help system to find out more about the error situation.

The background and experience of users should be anticipated when designing error messages. For example, say a system user is a nurse in an intensive-care ward in a hospital. Patient monitoring is carried out by a computer system. To view a patient's current state (heart rate, temperature, and so on), the system user selects 'display' from a menu and inputs the patient's name (Figure 14.13).

Say the nurse made an error and the patient's name was Pates rather than Bates as shown in Figure 14.13. A badly-designed (but all too typical) system error message is shown in Figure 14.14.

This message is negative (it accuses the user of making an error), it is not tailored to the user's skill and experience level, it does not take context information into account and makes no suggestion how the situation might be rectified. As well as the negative connotation of user error, this message uses system specific terms (patient-id) rather than terms which are drawn from the user's domain. Figure 14.15 shows a better error message for this situation.

This message is positive, implying that the problem is a system rather than a user problem. The message identifies the problem in the nurse's terms, and offers an easy way to correct the mistake by pressing a single button. The help system is available if required.

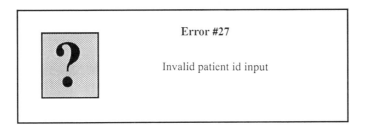

Figure 14.14
A badly designed error message.

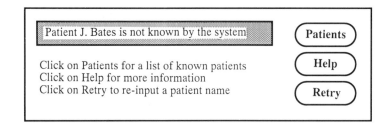

Figure 14.15
A user-oriented error message.

14.4.2 Help system design

When users are presented with an error message they do not understand, they turn to the help system for information on what they should have done. This is an example of *help!* meaning 'help, I'm in trouble'. Another form of help request is *help?* which means 'help, I want information'. Different system facilities and message structures may be needed if both kinds of help are to be properly supported.

Help information should be prepared at the same time as the system user manual but should not simply be a screen listing of a paper manual. The reasons for this are:

• A screen or a single window on a screen is usually smaller and can contain less information than a sheet of paper. Help information should be organized so that users do not have to scroll through pages of information to read a single help frame.

• A screen has dynamic characteristics which can be used to improve information presentation. For example, colour changes can be used to present different types of information.

• People are not as good at reading screens as they are at reading paper-based text.

The actual help text which is created is application-dependent and is best prepared with the help of application specialists.

Help systems should always provide a number of different user entry points (Figure 14.16). These should allow the user to enter the help system at the top of the message hierarchy and browse for information, to enter the help system to get an explanation of an error message and to call on the help system for an explanation of a particular application command.

All comprehensive help systems have a complex network structure where each frame of help information may refer to several other information frames. The structure of this network is usually hierarchical with cross-links. General information is held at the top of the hierarchy, detailed information at the bottom (Figure 14.17).

Problems arise here when users enter a network at a particular point which is not the top (as might happen via an error handling system) and

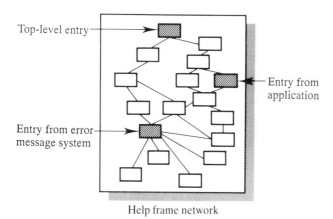

Help frame network

Figure 14.16
Entry points to a help system.

then navigate around the network. Within a short time, they can become hopelessly lost with no idea of the context in which help information is provided. They must abandon the session and start again at some known point in the network.

Multiple windows can help alleviate this situation. Figure 14.18 shows a screen display where there are three help windows.

Window 1 is the help frame, which is relatively short. It is best not to overwhelm the user with information in any one frame. Three buttons are provided in the help frame to request more information, to move onto the next help frame and to call up a list of topics on which help is available.

Window 2 is a 'history' window showing the frames which have been visited. It should be possible to return to these frames by picking an item from this list. Window 3 is a graphical 'map' of the help system network. The current position in this map should be highlighted by using colour, shading or, in this case, by annotation.

Users should be able to move to another frame by selecting it from the frame being read, by selecting a frame in the 'history window' to reread or to retrace their steps or by selecting a node in the network 'map' to move to that node.

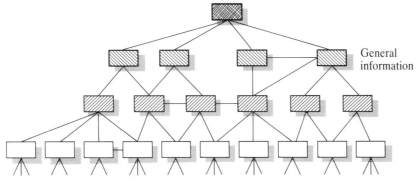

Figure 14.17
Help frame network.

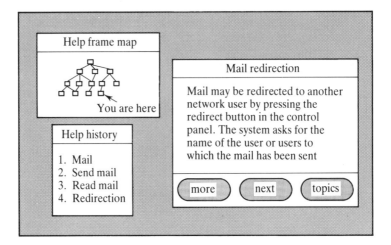

Figure 14.18
Help system windows.

In the above example, movement from one help frame to another is dependent on an explicit user instruction. Developments in hypertext systems (Conklin, 1987) and the relatively low cost of such systems suggest that they will be used more and more for the provision of help information. Hypertext systems are systems where text is structured hierarchically rather than linearly. The hierarchy may be easily traversed by selecting parts of a message or display. Hypertext systems may sometimes be used as the basis of a complete user interface but, like help systems, they suffer from problems of user navigation.

14.5 User interface evaluation

It is easy to be seduced by the attractiveness of the facilities provided on modern bit-mapped workstations and to assume that any interface which uses them must be better than a simple command interface. However, this is not necessarily so. Part of the system quality assurance process should therefore be concerned with user interface evaluation.

Systematic evaluation of a user interface design is an expensive process. It requires the support of cognitive scientists, such as psychologists, and graphical designers. It involves designing and carrying out a statistically significant number of experiments with typical users. A complete evaluation may be economically possible for large and expensive systems development projects. However, it is economically unrealistic for systems developed by small organizations with limited resources.

There are a number of simpler, less expensive techniques of user interface evaluation which can identify particular user interface design deficiencies:

- Questionnaires which collect information about what users thought of the interface.
- Video recording and analysis of typical system use.
- The inclusion in the software of code which collects information about the most heavily used facilities and the most common errors.
- The provision of a 'gripe' button which allows the user to feedback comments about the system to its designers.

Surveying users by using a questionnaire is a relatively cheap way of evaluating an interface. The questions should be precise rather than general. It is no use asking questions like 'Please comment on the usability of the interface' as the responses will probably vary so much that no common trend will emerge. Rather, specific questions such as 'Please rate the understandability of the error messages on a scale from 1 to 5 where one means very clear and 5 means incomprehensible' are more likely to provide useful information to improve the interface.

Users should be asked to rate their own experience and background when filling in the questionnaire. This allows the designer to find out if users from any particular background have problems with the interface.

Relatively low cost video equipment means that it is economically practical to record user sessions and to analyse the session systematically. Ideally, several cameras should be used with user's hand movements, screen display and head and eye movement recorded separately. Unfortunately, because of different scanning rates between the screen and the camera, it is difficult to photograph a screen directly. Direct video output from the display is necessary if stable images are to be produced.

Analysis of recordings allows the designer to find out if the interface requires too much hand movement (a problem with some systems is that users must regularly move their hand from keyboard to mouse) and to see if unnatural eye movements are necessary. An interface which requires many shifts of focus may mean that the user makes more errors and misses parts of the display.

However, analysing video recordings is a time-consuming process. A detailed analysis of a one hour recording is likely to take several hours so that an adequate budget must be assigned for an evaluation over many recording sessions and users.

Instrumenting code to collect usage statistics allows interfaces to be improved in a number of ways. The most common operations can be detected and the interface can be organized so that these are the fastest to select. For example, if pop-up or pull-down menus are used, a good general rule is that the most frequent operations should be at the top of the menu and destructive operations towards the bottom. Code instrumentation also allows error-prone commands to be detected and subsequently modified.

Finally, a means of easy user response can be provided easily by equipping each program with a 'gripe' command which the user can use to pass messages to the tool maintainer. This makes users feel that their views are being considered and provides a means whereby the interface designer (indeed, system designers in general) can gain rapid feedback about individual problems.

■ KEY POINTS

- Interface design should be user-centred. An interface should interact with users in their terms, should be logical and consistent and should include facilities to help users with the system and to recover from their mistakes.

- Graphical user interfaces where the user has multiple windows, menus, iconic object representations and a pointing device are likely to be the most important class of interfaces for future systems.

- Menu systems are good for casual users because they have a low learning overhead. They can be difficult to use when the number of options is very large.

- Graphical information display should be used when it is intended to present trends and approximate values. Digital display should only be used when precision is required.

- Colour must be used very carefully if it is not to confuse an interface.

- User help systems should provide two kinds of help: help! which is 'help, I'm in trouble' and help? which is 'help, I need information'.

- Error messages should not suggest that the user is to blame. They should offer suggestions about how to repair the error and provide a link to a help system.

FURTHER READING

IEEE Software, **6** (1), January 1989. This is a special issue with several good articles on user interface design. The articles are mostly concerned with modern implementation techniques but are aimed at non-specialist readers.

Developing Software for the User Interface.   At the time of writing, I think this is the best available book on user interface design. It concentrates on graphical interfaces and, unlike some books on this subject, covers the engineering problems of building a user interface. (L. Bass and J. Coutaz, 1991, Addison-Wesley.)

Human-Computer Interaction.   This is a selection of papers which cover a variety of user interface topics. These range from cognitive modelling through the use of innovative input devices to user interface design tools. (J. Preece and L. Keller (eds), 1990, Prentice-Hall.)

OSF/Motif Concepts and Programming.   There are now several books on X-windows programming with the Motif toolkit and there is little to choose between them. I recommend this book because it has a good general discussion of concepts as well as details (T. Berlage, 1991, Addison-Wesley.)

EXERCISES

14.1 It was suggested in section 14.1 that the objects manipulated by users should be drawn from their domain rather than a computer domain. Suggest appropriate objects for the following types of user and system.

(a) A warehouse assistant using an automated parts catalogue.
(b) An airline pilot using an aircraft safety monitoring system.
(c) A manager manipulating a financial database.
(d) A policeman using a patrol car control system.

14.2 Using a prototyping approach, design a user interface for the newspaper delivery system introduced in Chapter 3. Assume that the system will be used regularly by people who have no previous computer systems experience.

14.3 Design a menu-based interface suitable for occasional system users for MS-DOS, UNIX or some other command-based system.

14.4 Discuss the advantages of graphical information display and suggest four applications where it would be more appropriate to use graphical rather than digital display of numeric information.

14.5 What are the guidelines which should be followed when using colour in a user interface? Suggest how colour might be used to improve the interface of an application system with which you are familiar.

14.6 Design a user guidance system for the newspaper delivery system introduced in Chapter 3. Pay particular attention to providing different levels of user guidance.

14.7 Consider the error messages produced by MS-DOS, UNIX or some other operating system. Suggest how these might be improved.

14.8 Design a questionnaire to gather information about the user interface of some tool (such as a word processor) with which you are familiar. If possible, distribute this questionnaire to a number of users and try to evaluate the results. What do these tell you about the user interface design?

Part Three
Programming Techniques and Environments

This part of the book covers some advanced programming issues and tool support for the software development process. Chapter 15 describes techniques for reliable systems development including N-version programming, recovery blocks and defensive programming. Chapter 16 addresses the increasingly important topic of software reuse and discusses both development with reuse and development for reuse. Chapters 17 and 18 are concerned with computer-aided software engineering (CASE) and software development environments. Rather than discuss individual CASE tools and environments, these chapters cover the fundamental principles of CASE and describe the various different types of software development environment.

CONTENTS

Programming for Reliability

15

OBJECTIVES

The objective of this chapter is to describe programming techniques which can be used in the development of software with high reliability requirements. Improved reliability results from both fault avoidance and fault tolerance. To reduce the probability of introducing program faults, some potentially error-prone programming language constructs should be avoided. Full use should be made of the data typing facilities of the programming language used. General approaches to fault tolerance are discussed and Ada's exception handling mechanism is illustrated by example. The final part of the chapter covers defensive programming. It shows how errors can be detected and recovery from these errors initiated.

CONTENTS

Programming is a craft. It is dependent on individual skill, attention to detail, and knowledge of how to use available tools in the best way. Most readers of this book will be familiar with good programming practice so this general topic is not covered. Rather, I concentrate on some specific programming techniques which are used in achieving system reliability, portability and component reuse.

The need for reliable systems is increasingly obvious as computer systems become pervasive. The focus of this chapter is how to write reliable programs. Two complementary techniques, namely fault avoidance and fault tolerance, are introduced. Fault avoidance means utilizing development techniques which reduce the probability of introducing faults into a program; fault tolerance is concerned with writing the program so that it will continue to operate in the presence of software faults. General issues concerning the definition and the quantification of reliability are covered in Chapter 20.

15.1   Fault avoidance

All software engineers should aim to produce fault-free software. A development process which is based on fault discovery and elimination rather than on fault avoidance is a poor and outmoded process.

Fault-free software in this context means software which conforms to its specification. Of course, there may be errors in the specification or it may not reflect the real needs of the user so fault-free software does not necessarily mean that the software will always behave as anticipated by the user.

Developing fault-free software is very expensive and, as faults are removed from a program, the cost of finding and removing remaining faults tends to rise exponentially (Figure 15.1). An organization may therefore decide that some residual faults are acceptable. It may be more cost-effective to pay for the consequences of system failure due to these faults rather than discover and remove the faults before system delivery.

Given a fault-free system, it might seem that there is no need for fault tolerance facilities to be included. However, because of the possibility of specification errors, even fault-free systems need fault tolerance facilities for assured reliability.

Fault avoidance and the development of fault-free software rely on:

(1)   The production of a precise (preferably formal) system specification.

(2)   The adoption of an approach to software design which is based on information hiding and encapsulation.

(3)   The extensive use of reviews in the development process (see Chapters 24 and 31) which validate the software system.

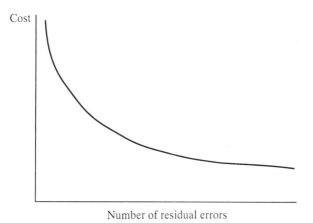

Figure 15.1
Cost of residual error removal.

(4)   The adoption of an organizational quality philosophy where quality is the driver of the software process.

(5)   The careful planning of system testing to expose faults which are not discovered during the review process and to assess system reliability.

It is essential that a high-level programming language with strict typing be used for system development. Achieving fault-free software is virtually impossible if low-level programming languages with limited type checking are used.

15.1.1 Structured programming

Structured programming is a term which was coined in the late 1960s to mean programming without using goto statements, programming using only while loops and if statements as control constructs and designing using a top-down approach. The adoption of structured programming was important because it was the first step away from an undisciplined approach to software development.

Structured programming is important because its disciplined use of control structures forces programmers to think carefully about their program. Hence they are less likely to make mistakes during development. Structured programming means programs can be read sequentially and are therefore easier to understand and inspect. However, avoiding unsafe control statements is only the first step in programming for reliability.

Dijkstra (1968) recognized that the goto statement was an inherently error-prone programming construct. There are several other constructs in programming languages which are also error-prone. Their use is more likely to lead to faults being introduced into a system.

(1) *Floating-point numbers* Floating-point numbers are inherently imprecise and present a particular problem when they are compared because representation imprecision may lead to invalid comparisons. Fixed-point numbers where a number is represented to a given number of decimal places are safer as exact comparisons are possible.

(2) *Pointers* Pointers are low-level constructs which refer directly to areas of the machine memory. They are dangerous because errors in their use can be devastating and because they allow 'aliasing' which means the same entity may be referenced using different names. This makes programs harder to understand. It is often impractical to avoid the use of pointers but their use should normally be confined to abstract data type implementations.

(3) *Parallelism* Parallelism is inherently dangerous because of the difficulties of predicting the subtle effects of timing interactions between parallel processes. Timing problems cannot usually be detected by program inspection and the peculiar combination of circumstances which cause a timing problem may not result during system testing. Parallelism may be unavoidable but its use must be carefully controlled to minimize inter-process dependencies.

(4) *Recursion* Recursion is the situation where a subroutine calls itself or calls another subroutine which then calls the calling subroutine. Its use can result in very concise programs but it can be difficult to follow the logic of recursive programs. Errors in using recursion may result in the allocation of all the system's memory as temporary stack variables are created.

(5) *Interrupts* Interrupts are a means of forcing control to transfer to a section of code irrespective of the code currently executing. The dangers of this are obvious as the interrupt may cause a critical operation to be terminated. Again, their use may be unavoidable but must be minimized.

Of course, all of these constructs and techniques are useful and they need not be completely prohibited (except perhaps in safety-critical systems). However, programmers should use them with great care. Wherever possible, their potentially dangerous effects should be controlled by restricting the constructs to abstract data type implementation.

15.1.2 Data typing

A security principle which is adopted by military organizations is the 'need to know' principle. Only those individuals who need to know a particular piece of information to carry out their duties are given that information. Information which is not directly relevant to their work is withheld.

When programming, an analogous principle should be adopted to control access to system data. Each program component should only be allowed access to data which it needs to implement its function. Access to other data should be denied by using the scope rules of the programming language to conceal its existence.

The advantage of using 'information hiding' is that hidden information cannot be corrupted by program components which are not supposed to use it. The data representation may be changed without changing other components which use it.

The key to effective information hiding is to use the programming language type system to its fullest extent. Although it is possible to implement information hiding in languages like C or Pascal which have limited data typing facilities, it is easier and more secure to use a language such as Ada, Modula-2 or C++ which offers direct support for information hiding.

The type system should also be used to enhance program readability by modelling identified real-world entities using system data types. For every type of entity which exists in the real-world system, there should be a corresponding program type. For example, if a traffic light system is being implemented in Ada, the following declarations might be made:

```
type TrafficLightColor is (red, redamber, amber, green) ;
ColorShowing, NextColor : TrafficLightColor ;
```

The objects ColorShowing and NextColor, which are modelling the traffic light display, may only be assigned the values red, redamber, amber and green.

The above example declares a scalar type, which is the name given to a type where the set of all possible values is known. An alternative means of declaring a scalar type is the range declaration.

```
type POSITIVE is INTEGER range 1..MAXINT ;
```

The type POSITIVE consists of the set of integers between 1 and the maximum integer which may be represented on a particular computer. Declaring the type as a range is a shorthand way of defining the set of values associated with the type.

System entities may take comparatively simple values. For example, if a program is controlling a car dashboard display, there might be a number of entities representing warning conditions such as low oil pressure, doors not closed properly, fuel level dangerously low, and so on. These conditions are either true or false so it makes sense to represent them as boolean values.

```
Low_oil_pressure, Door_open, Fuel_low : BOOLEAN ;
```

In itself, this is a meaningful declaration and the use of descriptive names perhaps makes accidental errors unlikely. However, there is nothing to stop the programmer assigning Low_oil_pressure to Door_open when the oil pressure is low or making any other similar accidental type error.

Although these values may be represented as boolean values (and it makes sense to have boolean operations available), they are distinct types. This has been recognized in Ada where a new type can be derived from an existing type. It inherits the operations of the existing type but each type derived from a common parent is distinct. Derived types representing different lights might be declared as follows:

```
type OIL_STATUS is new BOOLEAN ;
type DOOR_STATUS is new BOOLEAN ;
type FUEL_STATUS is new BOOLEAN ;
```

These derived types inherit the operations defined on their base type (BOOLEAN in this case) but are distinct types. Therefore, when variables are declared of these types, the compiler ensures that the oil pressure (for example) cannot be assigned to the fuel status indicator.

As well as using meaningful type names, the operations which are associated with a type should be packaged with the type declaration to create an abstract data type. The abstract data type hides information about these operations and about the type representation. Operation implementation and the type representation may be changed without changing those parts of the program which use the abstract type.

The abstract data type can be validated as a separate entity from the programs in which it is used as it does not use any external data structures. This leads to improved reliability through reuse as validated abstract data types may be reused in different applications.

An abstract data type is made up of an interface specification and an implementation. The interface specification sets out the type name and the operations which act on that type. It may optionally include a specification of the domain of values of that type but it is better practice to hide such information.

The implementation of the abstract type is distinct from its specification. It defines the type representation and the implementation of operations on the type. If the specification part remains unchanged, the implementation part may be modified without requiring changes to other parts of the program which use the abstract data type.

In Ada, abstract data types are implemented using packages. Ada allows the physical separation of the type specification (the package specification) and the type implementation (the package body) and gives the type specifier control over the visibility of the type representation. The representation may be wholly or partially hidden from other parts of the program. As a general rule, the representation should be completely concealed.

```
package Queue is
   type  T is private ;
   procedure Put (IQ : in out T ;  X : INTEGER) ;
   procedure Remove (IQ : in out T ; X : out INTEGER ) ;
   function Is_empty (IQ :  T ) return BOOLEAN ;
private
   type Q_RANGE is range 0..100 ;
   type Q_VEC is array (1..100) of INTEGER ;
   type T is record
      The_queue : Q_VEC ;
      front, back : Q_RANGE ;
   end record ;
end Queue ;
```

Figure 15.2
A package specification
for an integer queue.

Figure 15.2 is the specification of a simple abstract data type which is a 100-element queue.

This package declares an abstract data type Queue.T and operations Queue.Put, Queue.Remove and Queue.Is_empty. The type T (the name is meaningful when prefixed by the package name to give Queue.T) is specified as a private type. The only operations allowed on that type are assignment, test for equality and the operations defined in the Queue package.

Figure 15.2 defines a fixed-size queue where the elements are integers. However, queues are general data structures and queue operations are usually independent of the type of queue element and the size of the queue. Ada's generic facility can be used to specify this abstract type in a way which is independent of element type and size (Figure 15.3).

Ada generics are a way of creating parameterized, general-purpose templates for packages and subroutines which are inherently reusable. In

```
generic
   type ELEM  is private ;
   type Q_SIZE is range <> ;
package Queue is
   type  T is private ;
   procedure Put (IQ : in out T; X : ELEM ) ;
   procedure Remove (IQ : in out T; X : out ELEM) ;
   function Is_empty (IQ : in  T ) return BOOLEAN ;
private
   type Q_VEC is array  (Q_SIZE) of ELEM ;
   type T is record
      The_queue : Q_VEC ;
      Front : Q_SIZE := Q_SIZE'FIRST ;
      Back : Q_SIZE := Q_SIZE'FIRST ;
   end  record ;
end Queue ;
```

Figure 15.3
An Ada generic
specification of a queue.

Example 15.3, the type of queue element and the size of the queue are generic parameters which are assigned values when the package is instantiated. The queue type is specified as a private type so assignment and equality operations must be defined over the type instantiated to ELEM.

The following instantiations define an integer queue with a maximum of 50 elements and a queue whose elements are lists (defined in another package, we assume) with 200 elements.

```
type IQ_SIZE is range 0..49 ; type LQ_SIZE is range 0..199 ;
package Integer_queue is new Queue (ELEM => INTEGER,
    Q_SIZE => IQ_SIZE) ;
package List_queue is new Queue (ELEM => List.T,
    Q_SIZE => LQ_SIZE) ;
```

Creating a new version of a generic package is a compile-time operation. A generic declares a template for a package and the compile-time instantiation of this generic adds detail to the template. The effect is as if a new package had been declared.

15.2 Fault tolerance

Even if a system is fault-free, fault tolerance facilities must be included if the system is installed in an environment where a very high level of system reliability is required. The reason for this is that 'fault-free' can only mean that the program corresponds to its specification. The specification may contain errors or omissions and may be based on incorrect assumptions about the system's environment.

There are four activities which must be carried out if a system is to be fault tolerant:

(1) *Failure detection*   The system must detect that a particular state combination has resulted or will result in a system failure.

(2) *Damage assessment*   The parts of the system state which have been affected by the failure must be detected.

(3) *Fault recovery*   The system must restore its state to a known 'safe' state. This may be achieved by correcting the damaged state (forward error recovery) or by restoring the system to a known 'safe' state (backward error recovery). Forward error recovery is more complex as it involves embedding knowledge of possible system faults in the software.

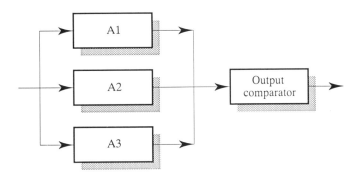

Figure 15.4
Triple-modular
redundancy.

(4)   *Fault repair*   This involves modifying the system so that the fault does
      not recur. In many cases, software failures are transient and due to a
      peculiar combination of system inputs. No repair is necessary as
      normal processing can resume immediately after fault recovery.

When a fault is not a transient fault, fault repair requires either dynamic
system reconfiguration where a replacement component is substituted for
the faulty component without stopping the system or it requires the system
to be halted and a repair initiated.

There has been a need for many years to build fault-tolerant hardware
and the technique which has evolved is based around the notion of triple-
modular redundancy (TMR). The hardware unit is replicated three (or
sometimes more) times and the output from each unit is compared. If one of
the units fails and does not produce the same output as the other units, its
output is ignored and the system functions with two working units (Figure
15.4).

This approach to fault tolerance relies on most hardware failures
being the result of component failures rather than design faults. There is a
low probability of simultaneous component failure in all hardware units. Of
course, they could all have a common design fault and thus all produce the
same (wrong) answer. The probability of this can be reduced by using units
which have a common specification but which are designed and built by
different manufacturers.

There have been two comparable approaches to the provision of
software fault tolerance (Figure 15.5). Both have been derived from
hardware systems architecture where a component (or the whole system) is
replicated.

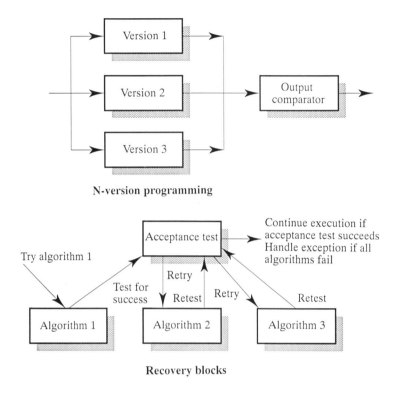

Figure 15.5
Software fault
tolerance.

(1) *N-version programming* The software system is implemented in a number of different versions by different teams and these versions are executed in parallel (Avizienis, 1985). Their outputs are compared using a voting system and inconsistent outputs are rejected. At least three versions of the system should be available.

(2) *Recovery blocks* This is a finer-grain approach to fault tolerance (Randell, 1975) where a program unit contains a test to check for failure and alternative code which allows the system to back-up and repeat the procedure if the test detects a failure. Unlike N-version programming, the different operation implementations are executed in sequence rather than in parallel and the test for a fault is independently derived. A common failure in all units which would be accepted in an N-version system might be detected in a system with recovery blocks. Experiments with this technique have been successful (Anderson *et al.*, 1985).

The provision of software fault tolerance requires the software to be executed under the control of a fault-tolerant controller which will ensure that the steps involved in tolerating a fault are executed. A full discussion is

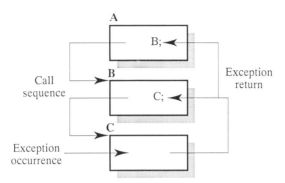

Figure 15.6
Exception return in
nested procedure calls.

beyond the scope of this book. Interested readers should follow up the further reading for more information on fault-tolerant systems architecture.

N-version programming is the most commonly used approach to software fault tolerance. However, a number of experiments have suggested that the assumption that different design teams are unlikely to make the same mistakes, may not be valid (Knight and Leveson, 1986; Brilliant *et al.*, 1990). Furthermore, it does not provide fault tolerance in the presence of specification errors and inconsistencies. To provide such fault tolerance, it must be assumed that the specification may be wrong and defensive programming techniques practised, as discussed in Section 15.4 and in Chapter 21, where safety-critical software is discussed.

15.3 Exception handling

When an error of some kind or an unexpected event occurs during the execution of a program, this is called an exception. Exceptions may be caused by hardware or software errors. When an exception has not been anticipated, control is transferred to a system exception handling mechanism. If an exception has been anticipated, code must be included to detect and handle that exception.

Most programming languages do not include facilities to detect and handle exceptions. The normal decision constructs of the language must be used to detect the exception and control constructs used to transfer control to exception handling code.

This is possible in a monolithic program but when an exception occurs in a sequence of nested procedure calls, there is no convenient and safe mechanism for transmitting it from one procedure to another. Consider a number of nested procedure calls where procedure A calls procedure B which calls procedure C (Figure 15.6). If an exception occurs during the execution of C this may be so serious that execution of B cannot continue. It may also be necessary to transmit the exception to A so that it can take appropriate action.

Exceptions may be signalled using a shared boolean variable which is set to indicate that an exception has occurred. Its value must be checked after each procedure call. In a sequence of nested procedure calls, the same test is repeated several times. Unanticipated exceptions cause transfer to a system exception handler and normally, program termination.

As Ada was designed for implementing embedded, real-time systems an exception handling facility was included in the language. Exception names are declared to be of the special, built-in type **exception**. Drawing attention to an exception is termed *raising* the exception.

Any Ada program unit may have an associated exception handler, which is like a case statement. It states exception names and appropriate actions for each exception. Not every exception raised in a program unit need necessarily be handled by that unit. The exception may be propagated automatically to a higher level unit.

Figure 15.7 illustrates Ada exceptions and exception handling. This program fragment implements a temperature controller on a food freezer. The required temperature may be set between -18 and -40 degrees Centigrade. The control system maintains this temperature by switching a refrigerant pump on and off depending on the value of a temperature

```
with Pump, Temperature_dial, Sensor, Globals, Alarm ;
use Globals ;

procedure Control_freezer is
   Ambient_temperature : FREEZER_TEMP ;
begin
   loop
      Ambient_temperature := Sensor.Get_Temperature ;
      if Ambient_temperature > Temperature_dial.Setting then
         if Pump.Status = Off then
            Pump.Switch (State => On) ;
         end if ;
         if Ambient_temperature > -18.0  then
            raise Freezer_too_hot ;
         end if ;
      elsif Pump.Status = On then
      -- Switch pump off because temperature is low
         Pump.Switch (State => Off) ;
      end if ;
   end loop ;
exception
   when Freezer_too_hot => Alarm.Activate ;
      raise ;
   when others => Alarm_activate ;
      raise Control_problem ;
end Control_freezer ;
```

Figure 15.7
A temperature
controller.

sensor. Food may start to defrost and bacteria become active at temperatures over -18 degrees so the controller incorporates an alarm if it cannot maintain the required temperature. The current temperature is discovered by interrogating an object called Sensor and the required temperature by inspecting an object called Temperature_dial. A pump object responds to signals to switch its state. Assume that the exceptions Freezer_too_hot and Control_problem and the type FREEZER_TEMP are declared in a package called Globals.

The controller tests the temperature and switches the pump as required. If the temperature is too hot, it transfers control to the exception handler which activates an alarm and re-raises the exception. After an exception has been handled, it is usually cleared and normal system execution continues. However, a component may sometimes need to handle the exception then tell other components that an exception has occurred. This is accomplished by re-raising the exception within the exception handler.

It may not make sense to handle the exception within the program unit where that exception is raised. If a component does not have an exception handler, the exception is propagated to the calling program unit until an exception handler is found. If there is no exception handler in the program for that exception, it is finally processed by the system exception handler.

The definition of Ada includes five built-in exceptions. These are:

- CONSTRAINT_ERROR This is raised when an attempt is made to assign an out-of-range value to a state variable. Such an error would result, for example, when an attempt is made to access an array element using an index outside the bounds of the array.

- NUMERIC_ERROR This is raised when some arithmetic operation goes wrong (division by zero, for example).

- PROGRAM_ERROR This is raised when a control structure is violated.

- STORAGE_ERROR This is raised when storage space for dynamically allocated values is exhausted.

- TASKING_ERROR This is raised when there is some failure of inter-task communication.

The Ada run-time system includes a handler for these exceptions and, of course, they may be handled by the application program. Writing a fault-tolerant Ada program requires the developer to include handlers for all of these exceptions if, of course the requisite facility is used. If dynamic storage allocation and tasking are avoided, the STORAGE_ERROR and the TASKING_ERROR exception obviously cannot occur.

Perhaps the principal problem with Ada's exception mechanism is that there is no way, when raising the exception, to signal the cause of the exception to the exception handler. A CONSTRAINT_ERROR can arise from a number of different causes so the exception handler may have to check a large number of possibilities to detect the error and repair the affected state variables.

15.4   Defensive programming

Defensive programming is an approach to program development where the programmer assumes that undetected faults or inconsistencies may exist in programs. Code should be included which checks the system state after modifications and ensures that the state change is consistent. If inconsistencies are detected, the state change is retracted or the state is restored to a known correct state.

Defensive programming is an approach to fault tolerance which can be carried out without a fault-tolerant controller. The techniques used, however, are fundamental to the activities in the fault tolerance process namely fault detection, damage assessment and fault recovery. In practical implementations, fault detection and damage assessment are often combined as they rely on common checks of the system state variables.

15.4.1   Failure detection and damage assessment

In general, a failure results in system state corruption where state variables are assigned invalid values. Typed programming languages (like Ada) allow many such errors to be detected at compile-time. However, compiler checking is obviously limited to static values and some run-time checks cannot be avoided.

One approach to failure detection in Ada programs is to use the exception handling mechanism in combination with range specification. An assignment which results in a variable's value going out of range results in a CONSTRAINT_ERROR exception being raised. This works for some classes of check but has two problems:

(1)   Checks which involve relationships between variables (such as if A is zero then B must be 1) cannot be expressed.

(2)   The exception handler is informed that a CONSTRAINT_ERROR exception has been raised but not where that exception occurred. Further processing may be needed to discover the source of the problem.

```
package Positive_even is
   type NUMB is limited private ;
   procedure  Assign (A : in out NUMB ;  B  : NATURAL ;
                      State_error : in out BOOLEAN) ;
   function Eval (A : NUMB) return NATURAL ;
   function Eq (A, B : NUMB) return BOOLEAN ;
private
   type NUMB is new NATURAL ;
end Positive_even ;
```

Figure 15.8
Even number abstract
type.

An alternative approach is to use state assertions which are logical predicates (see Chapter 7) over the state variables. This predicate is checked immediately before an assignment is made to a referenced state variable and, if an anomalous value for the variable would result from the assignment, an error has occurred. Examples of assertions might be:

A = 1 **and** B = 0 **or** A = 0 **and** B = 1
forall i **in** (1..20) : A (i) ᐳ 0

Some languages allow assertions to be written as part of the program and the compiler generates code to check the assertion. However, where universal and existential quantifiers are allowed, this can cause compilation problems and, in most languages, it is up to the system implementor to include explicit assertion checks with state variables.

Assertion checking is simplified if all assignments to state variables are implemented as operations on abstract data types. The assertion checking code then need only be defined once, in the implementation of the abstract type. Figure 15.8 shows a package which ensures that the value assigned to a variable is always a positive even number.

Within the package body, the function Assign includes an assertion check to ensure that the value to be assigned (Figure 15.9). Note that Ada's strict typing requires the type conversion from NATURAL to NUMB. This assertion checking prohibits the assignment of an incorrect value to a state variable, thus simplifying the problems of damage assessment and fault recovery.

Providing generalized assertion checking takes up space and slows down the system. An alternative approach is to check system state explicitly before critical operations. If the state is found to be invalid, damage assessment and fault recovery procedures are initiated.

Damage assessment is difficult and expensive. It should be minimized by using a fault detection strategy which checks for fault occurrence before

```
procedure  Assign (A : in out NUMB ; B : NATURAL ;
                         State_error : in out BOOLEAN)  is
begin
  if B mod 2 /= 0 then
  State_error := TRUE ;
  else
    State_error := FALSE ;
    A := NUMB (B) ;
end if ;

end Assign ;
```

Figure 15.9
Assertion checking.

finally committing a change of state. If a fault is detected, the state change should be 'undone' to ensure that no damage is caused. However, there may still be a need to initiate a damage assessment to discover whether the individual assignment which violates the assertion is at fault or whether the fault is a consequence of a previous valid but logically incorrect state change.

For example, say that the permitted values of the elements of an array are drawn from the set (1, 2, 4, 8, 16, 32, 64) and that no duplication of values is allowed. An initial assignment to an array element may assign a value of 2 (say) to that element which is a valid assignment but which may be logically incorrect (the value which should have been assigned is, say, 8). A later (correct) assignment of a value of 2 to another element of the same array results in an error being detected by the assertion checking system.

The role of the damage assessment procedures is not to recover from the fault but to assess what parts of the state space have been affected by the fault. This relies on a state space implementation including specific fault signalling capabilities. Figure 15.10 shows how this can be achieved using an abstract data type and including operations Check and Is_damaged in the type specification which set and interrogate a damage indicator.

Other techniques which can be used for fault detection and damage assessment are dependent on specific data types. For example, coding checks can be used when data is exchanged whereby a checksum is associated with numeric data. This checksum is computed by the sender, which applies a function to the data to be exchanged and appends that function value to the data. The receiver applies the same function to the data and compares the checksum values. If these differ, some data corruption has occurred. Fujiwara and Pradhan (1990) discuss coding checks in detail.

When linked data structures are used, redundancy can be included by including backward pointers (that is, for every reference from A to B, there exists a comparable reference from B to A) and by keeping count of the number of elements in the structure. Checking can determine whether or

```
package Checked_array is
   type ELEM is range 1..64 ;
   type INDEX is NATURAL range 1..6 ;
   type T is private ;
   procedure Check (A : in out T) ;
   function Is_damaged (A :  T) return BOOLEAN ;
   function Eval (A : T ; I : INDEX)  return ELEM ;
   -- Assign must check that input is a power of 2 < 128
   function Assign (A : T ;  I : INDEX ;  E :  ELEM)  return T ;
private
   type SHORT_ARRAY is array (INDEX) of ELEM ;
   type T  is record
      A : SHORT_ARRAY ;
      Damaged : BOOLEAN ;
   end record ;
end Checked_array  ;
```

Figure 15.10
Damage assessment in an abstract type specification.

not all pointers have an inverse value and whether or not the stored size and the computed structure size are the same.

When processes must react within a specific time period, a watch-dog timer may be installed. A watch-dog timer is a timer which must be reset by the executing process after its action is complete. If, for some reason, the process fails to terminate, the watch-dog timer is not reset. The system can therefore detect that a problem has arisen.

15.4.2 Fault recovery

Fault recovery is the process of modifying the state space of the system so that the effects of the fault are minimized and the system can continue in operation, perhaps in some degraded form. Forward recovery involves trying to correct the damaged system state. Backward recovery involves restoring the system state to a known 'correct' state.

Forward error recovery is usually application specific, with domain knowledge used to compute possible state corrections. However, there are two general situations where forward error recovery can be successful:

(1) When coded data is corrupted. The use of appropriate coding techniques which add redundancy to the data allows errors to be corrected as well as detected.

(2) When linked structures are corrupted. If forward and backward pointers are included in the data structure, the structure can be recreated if an adequate number of pointers remain uncorrupted. This technique is frequently used for file system and database repair.

```
procedure Sort (X : in out ELEM_ARRAY ) is
  Copy : ELEM_ARRAY ;
begin
  -- Take a copy of the array to be sorted.
  for i in ELEM_ARRAY'RANGE loop
    Copy (i) := X (i) ;
  end loop ;
  -- Code here to sort the array X in ascending order
  -- Now test that the array is actually sorted
  for i in ELEM_ARRAY'FIRST..ELEM_ARRAY'LAST - 1 loop
    if X (i) > X (i + 1) then
      -- a problem has been detected - raise exception
      raise  Sort_error ;
    end if ;
  end loop ;
exception
  -- restore state and indicate to calling procedure
  -- that a problem has arisen
  when Sort_error =>
    for i in ELEM_ARRAY'RANGE loop
      X (i) := Copy (i) ;
    end loop ;
    raise ;
  -- unexpected exception. Restore state and indicate
  -- that the sort has failed
  when Others =>
    for i in ELEM_ARRAY'RANGE loop
      X (i) := Copy (i) ;
    end loop ;
    raise Sort_error;
end Sort ;
```

Figure 15.11
Sort procedure with
backward error
recovery.

Backward error recovery is a simpler technique which involves maintaining details of a safe state and restoring that state after an error has been detected. Most database systems include backward error recovery. When a user initiates a database computation, a *transaction* is initiated, and changes made during that transaction are not immediately incorporated in the database. The database is only updated after the transaction is finished and no problems are detected. If the transaction fails, the database is not updated.

A comparable technique can be used in other classes of system by establishing periodic checkpoints which are copies of a safe system state. When a fault is detected, that safe state can be restored from the latest checkpoint.

Unfortunately, when the system involves cooperating processes, the sequence of process communications can be such that the checkpoints of the processes are out of synchronization and, to recover from a fault, each process has to be rolled back to its starting state. A discussion of this is too long for this chapter and interested readers are referred to Randell (1975) for a solution to this problem.

As an example of how backward recovery can be implemented using Ada's exception mechanism, consider the sort procedure shown in Figure 15.11 which includes code for error detection and backward recovery. It is assumed that the type ELEM_ARRAY and the exception Sort_error are declared outside Sort.

The procedure copies the array before the sort operation. After the sort code has been executed, the procedure checks that the elements are in sorted order. If not, the array is restored to its state before the procedure was called.

■ KEY POINTS

- ■ Reliability in a program can be achieved by avoiding the introduction of faults and by including fault tolerance facilities which allow the system to remain operational after a fault has caused a system failure.

- ■ Some programming language constructs such as goto statements, pointers, recursion and floating-point numbers are inherently error prone and should be avoided if possible.

- ■ The use of data typing facilities for real-world modelling helps to avoid the introduction of software faults.

- ■ N-version programming and recovery blocks are approaches to providing software fault tolerance which rely on redundant code for function execution.

- ■ Ada is one of the few programming languages with a built-in exception handling mechanism. This allows program exceptions to be trapped and processed.

- ■ Defensive programming is a programming technique which involves incorporating checks for faults and fault recovery code in the program.

- ■ Defensive programming is effective on its own without a fault tolerant control system. However, a higher probability of tolerating a fault is provided by combining defensive programming with N-version programming or recovery blocks.

FURTHER READING

IEEE Computer, **23** (7), July 1990.   This is a special issue of the journal devoted to fault-tolerant systems. Most of the articles are concerned with fault-tolerant hardware but software and error recovery are also discussed.

'Software fault tolerance'. This is a good overview of the subject with an excellent comparison of N-version programming and recovery blocks as approaches to software fault tolerance. (M. Moulding, in *Software Reliability Handbook*, Rook, P. (ed.), 1990, Elsevier.)

High-Integrity Software. This is a book of chapters by different authors all on the topic of high-integrity systems development. Moulding's chapter above appears in a revised form and a chapter by Carré discusses unsafe features in Ada and Pascal. (C. Sennett, 1989, Pitman.)

EXERCISES

15.1 Given that pointers are an inherently error-prone construct, design an abstract type to implement binary trees which does not make use of pointers or recursion in its implementation.

15.2 Design an abstract data type called List to implement the list specifications set out in Chapter 8. Produce alternative implementations of this abstract type with and without using pointers.

15.3 Suggest two reasons why it may be the case that the different system versions in an N-version system may all fail in a similar way.

15.4 Describe the exception handling mechanism which is provided in Ada. Consult the literature to discover other approaches to exception handling (start with PL/1) and compare these with Ada's mechanism.

15.5 Using exceptions, write a routine which reads items from a user console and enters them in a table, in alphabetic order, according to their name. The routine should terminate when the user enters an item called STOP. Implement the table as a binary tree object.

15.6 Show, using small examples, how the exception handling facility of Ada can be used in the writing of non-stop systems. (Hint: you must consider the handling of all built in exceptions.)

15.7 Design an abstract data type called Robust_list which implements a linked list and which includes operations to check the list for pointer corruption and list rebuilding if corruption has occurred.

Software Reuse

16

■ OBJECTIVES

The objective of this chapter is to introduce the increasingly important topic of software reuse. Reusing software can significantly reduce software costs and increase software quality. The chapter includes sections which discuss the characteristics of a reusable software component and software development with a library of reusable components. The final section of the chapter is concerned with application system portability, which is really a form of reuse. This section covers standards, which are reducing portability problems, and the need for a system to include a portability interface which is rewritten when the program is moved to another machine.

■ CONTENTS

A characteristic of an engineering discipline is that it is based upon an approach to system design which makes the maximum use of existing components. Design engineers do not specify a design where every component has to be manufactured specially but base their design on components which have been tried and tested in other systems. These components are not necessarily small components such as nuts and bolts but may be major sub-systems such as engines, condensers or turbines.

By contrast, most software production is craft-oriented. There is not a common base of reusable software components which is widely documented and which can be used when developing a software design. As software engineering matures, it is obvious that demands for lower software production and maintenance costs along with increased quality can only be satisfied if more reuse is practised in the construction of new software systems.

The approach to reuse adopted in this chapter is component-oriented. There are several kinds of reusable component:

(1)   *Application systems*   The whole of an application system may be reused. This is a special case which is considered in Section 16.3.

(2)   *Sub-systems*   Major sub-systems of an application may be reused. For example, a pattern-matching system developed as part of a text processing system may be reused in a database management system.

(3)   *Modules or objects*   Components of a system representing a collection of functions may be reused. For example, an Ada package implementing a binary tree may be reused in different applications.

(4)   *Functions*   Software components which implement a single function, such as a mathematical function, may be reused.

Currently, application system reuse is widely practised as software companies implement their systems across a range of machines. Function reuse is also widely practised as use is made of standard libraries of reusable functions such as the UNIX C libraries and mathematical libraries. However, sub-system and module reuse is less common. The problems which inhibit software reuse apply particularly to these types of component.

Component reuse, of course, does not just mean the reuse of code. It is possible to reuse specifications and designs. The potential gains from reusing abstract products, such as specifications, of the development process may be greater than those from reusing code components. Less adaptation may be required for abstract components compared to components which include program-level detail.

An alternative to the component-oriented view of reuse is the generator view. In this approach to reuse, reusable knowledge is captured in a program generator system which can be programmed in a domain-oriented language. The generator program specifies which reusable components are

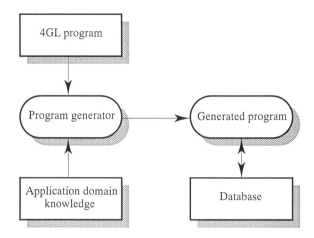

Figure 16.1
Reuse through program generation.

to be used, how they are to be combined and their parameterization. Using this information, an operational software system can be generated.

Although they are not usually classified in this way, the best known program generators are high-level language compilers where the reusable components are fragments of object code corresponding to high-level language constructs. This approach has been developed into fourth-generation languages where the reusable components are at a higher level. Fourth-generation languages are widely used in data processing systems development and embody abstractions from that domain (Figure 16.1).

Broadly, many data processing applications involve abstracting information from a database, performing some relatively simple information processing and then producing reports using that information. This stereotypical structure was recognized and components to carry out these operations devised. On top of these was produced some control language (there is an analogy here with the UNIX shell) which allowed programs to be specified and a complete application to be generated.

This form of reuse is effective but it has not been widely used outside the data processing domain. Stereotypical situations are less obvious in other domains so there seems to be less scope for reuse based on application generators.

In this chapter, I concentrate on three aspects of software reuse:

(1) *Software development for reuse* Software components which are developed as part of an application system are not necessarily immediately reusable. They may need to be generalized to be useful in a wide range of circumstances.

(2) *Software development with reuse*   This is the conventional engineering approach where the development process supports and encourages the reuse of existing components.

(3) *Application system reuse* Many application software systems are available on different computers. Much of the initial implementation is reused when these systems are ported to another machine. The problems here are those of designing the system to minimize and isolate operating system and computer dependencies so that the costs of porting it to another machine/operating system are less than the costs of system redevelopment.

Over the past few years, software reuse has been widely publicized (Tracz, 1988; Biggerstaff and Perlis, 1989) and a number of companies have instigated programmes to investigate how the systematic reuse of software can be incorporated in their development process. In Japan, the leverage which can be gained from reuse has been recognized for a long time (Matsumoto, 1984) and systematic reuse is an integral part of the Japanese 'factory' approach to software development (Cusamano, 1989).

However, in spite of this recognition, there is little available evidence to suggest that systematic reuse at the sub-system level is widely practised outside of Japan. The obstacles to reuse, discussed in the next two sections, still inhibit the widespread introduction of reuse.

16.1 Software development for reuse

Systematic reuse requires a properly catalogued and documented base of reusable components. A common misconception is that these components are available in existing systems and that a component library can be cheaply created by extracting and documenting them.

In fact, components which are created as part of an application system development are unlikely to be immediately reusable. These components are geared towards the requirements of the system in which they are originally included. To be effectively reusable, they have to be generalized to satisfy a wider range of requirements.

Developing generalized components is more expensive than developing components for a specific purpose so increases project costs. As the principal role of project managers is to minimize costs, they are understandably reluctant to invest extra effort in developing components which will bring them no immediate return.

To develop reusable components requires an organizational policy decision to increase short-term costs for long-term gain. The organization rather than individual project managers must make such decisions. Unfortunately, senior managers are often reluctant to cover reuse costs because of the difficulties in quantifying the long-term advantage of a library of reusable components.

To assess the reusability of a component, two questions must be asked:

(1)   How well does the component represent an application domain abstraction?

(2)   Has the component been written so that it is generalized and adaptable?

Answering the first of these questions relies on having a detailed understanding of the application domain for which the component is intended. Although application specialists do have such an understanding, they rarely have the knowledge or time to become involved in reusable component production. There are, therefore, few domains which have been modelled with a view to understanding the way in which they affect reusability.

One domain which has been extensively studied is the domain of abstract data structures (Booch, 1987b). Booch has developed an extensive classification structure for such components and discusses how generalized components can be implemented. Other work in domain analysis in aerospace systems has been reported by McNicol (1986) in the Common Ada Missile Project (CAMP) and by Hutchinson and Hindley (1988) in an analysis of aircraft utility management systems.

The second question concerns the effect language features have on reusability. To give a trivial example of this, a reusable C function which processes arrays should have the array size passed as a parameter to it. The same component, implemented in Ada, should not. Rather, the array size should be discovered in the component using the FIRST and LAST language attributes.

Specification, design and implementation language attributes all affect reusability. However, most work has been done in this area in producing guidelines for Ada reusability (Braun and Goodenough, 1985; Gautier and Wallis, 1990). These guidelines emphasize the need for components to be generalized, self-contained and coherent.

To illustrate the difficulties of producing reusable components and to show what is involved in generalizing a component, let us now look at how to produce a reusable Ada component implementing a linked list abstract data type. Figure 16.2 shows part of the Ada package specification for such a reusable list component.

The list component has been designed following some of the published guidelines for Ada abstract data structures. The applicable guidelines in this case are:

(1)   Implement data structures composed of many elements using generic packages. There is no need to develop a separate package for each element type.

```
with TEXT_IO ;
generic
    type ELEMENT is private ;
package Linked is
    type LIST is limited private ;
    type STATUS is range 1..10 ;
    type ITERATOR is private ;
    procedure Create  (Error_level : out STATUS) ;
    procedure Assign (L1 : in out LIST ; L2 : LIST ;
        Error_level: out Status) ;
    function Equals (L1,  L2 : LIST) return BOOLEAN ;
    procedure Equivalent (L1, L2 : LIST)
                    return BOOLEAN ;

    -- Other procedures and functions here

private
    type LIST_ELEM ;
    type LIST is access LIST_ELEM ;
    type ITERATOR is access LIST_ELEM ;
end Linked  ;
```

Figure 16.2
Linked list component.

(2)   Provide operations to create instances of the abstract type and an assignment procedure.

(3)   Provide a mechanism for operations on the abstract structure to return an indication of whether or not they have been successful. In the examples here, operations return a variable of type STATUS which indicates the type of error (if any) which has occurred.

(4)   Minimize the amount of representation information defined in the package specification. Here, a list is simply represented as a pointer. More detailed representation information is included in the package body.

(5)   Implement operations which can result in an error as procedures and return the error status as well as the operation result. Implement operations which cannot fail as functions.

(6)   Provide an equality operation. In this case, two operations are provided. Equals tests if two lists are the same size and all corresponding members have the same values. Equivalent tests if the references identify exactly the same list.

(7)   Provide an iterator which allows each element in the structure to be visited without affecting the structure itself. This is discussed later.

The operations on an abstract structure should always include access operations to discover characteristics of the structure and to access structure components (Figure 16.3). If the abstract type is a composite type (that is, a collection of elements), functions to provide information about attributes of the composition (such as size) should be provided.

```
function Is_empty (L : LIST) return BOOLEAN ;
function Size_of (L : LIST ) return NATURAL ;
function Contains (E : ELEMENT ;  L : LIST )
        return BOOLEAN ;
procedure Head (L : LIST ; E : in out ELEMENT ;
        Error_level : out STATUS ) ;
procedure Tail (L : LIST;  Outlist : in out LIST ;
        Error_level : out STATUS ) ;
```

Figure 16.3
Access operations.

Access operations do not affect the structure. Constructor operations allow the structure to be updated (Figure 16.4). Operations to add objects to and to delete objects from the collection should always be provided. If the collection is ordered, multiple add and delete functions should be

```
-- Append adds an element to the end of the list
procedure Append ( E : ELEMENT ; Outlist : in out LIST ;
    Error_level : out STATUS ) ;
-- Add adds an element to the front of the list
procedure Add ( E : ELEMENT ; Outlist : in out LIST ;
    Error_level : out STATUS ) ;
-- Add_before adds an element before element value  E
procedure Add_before ( E : ELEMENT ; Outlist : in out LIST ;
    Error_level : out STATUS ) ;
-- Add_after adds an element after element E
procedure Add_after ( E : ELEMENT ; Outlist: in out LIST ;
    Error_level : out STATUS ) ;
-- Replace replaces the element matching E1 with E2
procedure Replace ( E1, E2 : ELEMENT ; Outlist : in out LIST ;
    Error_level : out STATUS ) ;
-- Clear deletes all members of a list
procedure Clear ( Outlist : in out LIST ;
    Error_level  : out STATUS ) ;
-- Prune removes the last element from the list
procedure Prune ( Outlist : in out LIST ;
    Error_level  : out STATUS ) ;
-- Prune_to deletes the list up to and including
-- the element matching E
procedure Prune_to ( E : ELEMENT; Outlist : in out LIST ;
    Error_level : out STATUS ) ;
-- Prune_from deletes list after element matching E
procedure Prune_from( E : ELEMENT; Outlist : in out LIST ;
    Error_level : out STATUS ) ;
-- Remove deletes the element which matches E
procedure Remove ( E : ELEMENT; Outlist : in out LIST ;
    Error_level : out STATUS ) ;
-- Remove_before and Remove_after delete the element before
-- and after E respectively
procedure Remove_before ( E : ELEMENT ; Outlist : in out LIST ;
    Error_level : out STATUS ) ;
procedure Remove_after ( E : ELEMENT ; Outlist : in out LIST ;
    Error_level : out STATUS ) ;
```

Figure 16.4
Constructor
operations.

```
procedure Print_list (L : LIST ; Error_level : out STATUS ) ;
procedure Write_list (F : TEXT_IO.FILE_TYPE ; L : LIST ;
        Error_level : out STATUS ) ;
    procedure Read_list (F : TEXT_IO.FILE_TYPE ;
        Outlist : out LIST ; Error_level : out STATUS )  ;
```

Figure 16.5
I/O procedures.

provided. For a list type, operations should be available to add and delete an element to and from the front and the end of the list.

For lists, a particularly rich set of constructor operations is required if the component is to be practically reusable. It is possible to implement most of these constructor operations using the simple operations Create, Append, Head, Tail and Equals but the implementation is inefficient. Reusers will avoid reusing a component if it does not work efficiently. It is always a difficult decision for the reusable component designer to find an acceptable balance between providing an economic and an efficient set of operations.

A common omission from reusable components is I/O operations because they may not have been needed in the original component development. I/O operations are inefficient to implement without access to the structure of the component so operations to print the structure, to write it to permanent store and to read it from permanent store should be provided (Figure 16.5).

For every possible exception condition which might occur, a test function should be available to check that condition before initiating the operation. For example, if an operation on lists might fail if the list is empty, a function should be provided which allows the user to check if the list has any members. In this example, the Is_empty operation can be used but other types may need special exception checking procedures.

If the abstract type is a composite type, an iterator should be provided which allows each element of the type to be visited (Figure 16.6).

Iterators allow each component of a composite to be visited and evaluated without destroying the structure of the composite. This is useful if every element must be examined to check if it meets some criterion. Again, such operations can be implemented using simpler operations but are

```
procedure Iterator_initialize (L : LIST ; Iter : in out ITERATOR ;
        Error_status : in out STATUS) ;
procedure Go_next (L : LIST ; Iter : in out ITERATOR ;
        Error_status : in out STATUS) ;
procedure Eval (L : List ; Iter : in out ITERATOR ;
        Val : out ELEMENT ;  Error_status : in out STATUS) ;
function At_end (L : LIST ; Iter : ITERATOR) return BOOLEAN ;
```

Figure 16.6
Iterator operations.

inefficient. Iterator operations which should be provided are an operation to initialize it (set it to reference the first structure element), an operation to evaluate the currently referenced element, an operation to check if all elements have been visited and an operation to advance the reference to the next element.

Ideally, once a reusable component has been constructed, it can be used without change. More commonly, however, it will be necessary to adapt the component in some way to take account of the particular requirements for the system being developed. This adaptation may take a number of forms:

(1)   Extra functionality may be added to the component. In this case, the adapted component may be returned to the reusable component library.

(2)   Unneeded functionality may be removed from the component. This may be necessary for efficiency reasons.

(3)   The implementation of some of the component operations may be modified. If this is necessary, it implies that the component is not a truly general abstraction and it should be reviewed to discover why such changes were required.

Because of the need for adaptability, reusable components should be understandable, documented according to a set of organizational standards and portable (see Section 16.3).

16.1.1   Reuse and inheritance

When an object-oriented programming language is used for systems development, the inheritance mechanism in that language can be used to adapt components for reuse. Object-oriented languages, such as Smalltalk, are well-suited for reusable component production because of this adaptive ability and because of the encapsulation provided by the language object/object class mechanism.

When an implementation language supports inheritance, a base object class with minimal functionality can be provided. When additional or different functionality is required, a new version is created taking the base class as a starting point. The functions provided in the base object need not be re-implemented; they are reused in the new implementation.

Multiple inheritance allows several objects to act as base objects and is supported in object-oriented languages such as Eiffel (Meyer, 1988). The characteristics of several different object classes can be combined to make up a new object. For example, say we have an object class CAR which encapsulates information about cars and an object class PERSON which encapsulates information about people. We could use both of these to define

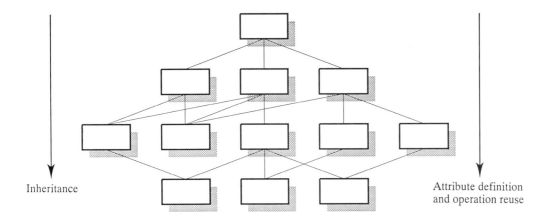

Inheritance

Attribute definition
and operation reuse

Figure 16.7
A class lattice.

a new object class CAR-OWNER which combine the attributes of CAR and PERSON.

When inheritance is supported in a programming language, a class lattice is built-up defining the classes used (Figure 16.7). This lattice shows the super-classes for each class in the system. As more and more classes are reused, the lattice becomes more and more complex.

Inheritance is a useful mechanism for supporting adaptation for reuse and for practically reusing software. However, as classes are reused by implementing sub-classes, the class lattice becomes more complex. It becomes progressively more difficult to understand individual components.

With inheritance, the code of a component is not collected together in one place. Rather, it is spread through the class lattice and the reuser must examine a number of classes before a component can be completely understood. Furthermore, adaptation through inheritance tends to lead to extra unwanted functionality being inherited, which can make components inefficient and bulky. Inheritance is not, therefore, a simple answer to reusability although it can play a part in supporting development for reuse.

16.2 Software development with reuse

Software development with reuse is an approach to development which tries to maximize the reuse of existing software components. An obvious advantage of this approach is that overall development costs should be reduced. Fewer software components need be specified, designed, implemented and validated. However, it is difficult to quantify what the cost reductions might be. In some cases, development costs may not be significantly reduced. The cost of component adaptation might occasionally

Figure 16.8
Development with reuse.

cost as much as the original component development.

Cost reduction is not the only advantage of reuse. Systematic reuse in the development process offers further advantages:

(1)   *System reliability is increased*   It can be argued that only actual operational use adequately tests components. Reused components, which have been exercised in working systems, should be more reliable than new components.

(2)   *Overall risk is reduced*   If a component exists, there is less uncertainty in the costs of reusing that component than in the costs of development. This is an important factor for project management as it reduces the risk in the project cost estimation.

(3)   *Effective use can be made of specialists*   Instead of application specialists joining a project for a short time and often doing the same work with different projects, these specialists can develop reusable components which encapsulate their knowledge.

(4)   *Organizational standards can be embodied in reusable components*   For example, say a number of applications present users with menus. Reusable components providing these menus mean that all applications present the same menu format to users.

(5)   *Software development time can be reduced*   Bringing a system to market as early as possible is often more important than overall development costs. Reusing components speeds up system production because both development and validation time should be reduced.

Currently, the process of development with reuse is usually as shown in Figure 16.8. The engineer developing a system completes a high-level design and specifications of the components of that design. These specifications are used to find components to reuse. This contrasts with the approach adopted in other engineering disciplines where reusability is often the driver of the design. Rather than design, specify then search, engineers should search for reusable components then base their design on these components (Figure 16.9).

In reuse-driven development, the system requirements are modified according to the reusable components available. The design is also based around existing components. Of course, this means that there may have to be requirements compromises and that the design may be less efficient. However, the lower costs of a development and increased system reliability will often compensate for this.

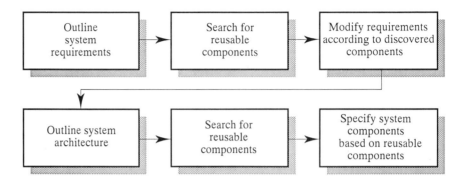

Figure 16.9
Reuse-driven
development.

There are three requirements for software development with reuse:

(1)   It must be possible to find appropriate reusable components.
(2)   The reuser of the components must be able to understand them and must have confidence in their suitability.
(3)   The components must have associated information discussing how they can be reused.

An organization must have a base of properly catalogued and documented reusable components and this is a factor which inhibits systematic software reuse. Development with reuse will not be possible until such a component base is created, but until reuse is demonstrated to be cost-effective, organizations are reluctant to invest in creating a component library.

Other problems hindering development with reuse are:

(1)   CASE toolsets do not support development with reuse. It is difficult or impossible to integrate these tools with a component library system.
(2)   Some software engineers sometimes prefer to rewrite components as they believe that they can improve on the reusable component.
(3)   Our current techniques for classifying, cataloguing and retrieving software components are immature. Engineers must be reasonably confident of finding a component in the library before they will routinely include a component search as part of their normal development process.

These difficulties have meant that development with reuse is the exception rather than the norm in Europe and the Americas. However, there has been a great deal of work in Japan on development with reuse (Matsumoto, 1984) and reuse seems to have now become an integral part of the development process. Particular attention is paid to generalizing components for reuse then ensuring that they are actually reused.

16.3   Application system portability

A special case of software reuse is application system reuse where a whole application system is reused by implementing it across a range of different computers and operating systems. The problem here is not to discover components for reuse or to understand them but to develop the system in such a way that it is portable across different machines.

The rate of change of computer hardware technology is so fast that computers become obsolete long before the programs which execute on them. Techniques for achieving software portability have been widely documented (Brown, 1977; Tanenbaum *et al.*, 1978; Wallis, 1982; Nissen and Wallis, 1985; Mooney, 1990). They include emulating one machine on another using microcode; compiling a program into some abstract machine language then implementing that abstract machine on a variety of computers; and using preprocessors to translate from one dialect of a programming language to another.

The portability of an application is proportional to the amount of work needed to make it work in a new environment. If significantly less work is required than the original development effort, the application is portable.

Mooney (1990) points out that there are two major aspects of program portability:

(1)   *Transportation*   This is the movement of the program's code and associated data from one environment to another.

(2)   *Adaptation*   This is the changes required to the program to make it work in a new environment.

Transportation problems have become less significant as commercial pressures have forced manufacturers to produce systems which read the disks and tapes written by other manufacturer's machines. Widespread networking means that electronic interchange of programs and data can replace physical transportation and this has removed many of the problems of physical device incompatibility.

The environment in which a program operates is made up of the system hardware, operating system, I/O system and language run-time support system. Its operation may depend on any or all of these. When this environment is changed, those dependent parts of the program must be identified and modified to adapt the program to its new environment.

16.3.1   The portability interface

The general approach which should be adopted in building a portable system is to isolate the parts of the system which depend on the external

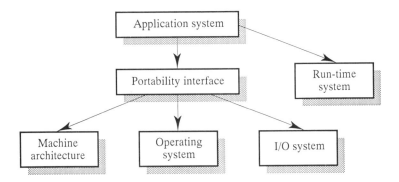

Figure 16.10
A portability interface.

environment in a portability interface (Figure 16.10). All operations which make use of non-portable characteristics should go through this interface.

In Figure 16.10, the interface with the run-time system is distinct from the portability interface. This interface can be implemented through the portability interface but this usually introduces unacceptable inefficiencies. As programming language standards are developed, the problems of run-time system differences are gradually being reduced, so run-time system interfacing is becoming a less serious portability problem.

The portability interface should be designed as a set of abstract data types or objects which encapsulate non-portable features and which hide representation characteristics from the client software. When the system is moved to some other hardware or operating system, only the portability interface need be rewritten.

A portability interface was used in the implementation of the design editing system discussed in earlier chapters. The intention in building this system was to make it possible to store the design representation in either a UNIX file system or in a database. Thus, we had to avoid building representation dependencies into the system.

A logical design representation was specified and implemented as an abstract data interface (ADI). All operations on the design representation took place through this ADI (Figure 16.11). Porting the program to a different underlying database or filestore was accomplished by rewriting the ADI code.

As an illustration of the relative amount of work involved, the ADI is implemented in about 1000 lines of C code whereas the entire system is about 14 000 lines of C. Given that some of the ADI code can be reused, porting the program to another data storage system takes about one-twentieth of the effort required to rewrite the editing system.

Portability problems arise because different machine architectures adopt different conventions for information representation and because different operating systems provide different sets of system calls to accomplish operations such as file system and process management.

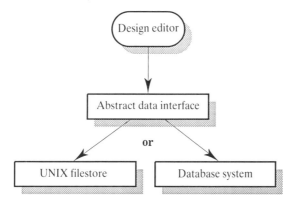

Figure 16.11
The portability
interface of the design
editor.

Machine architecture dependencies arise in programs because the application program must rely on the conventions of information representation adopted by the host machine. Different machines have different word lengths, different character sets and different techniques for representing integer and real numbers.

The length of a computer word directly affects the range of integers available on that machine, the precision of real numbers and the number of characters which may be packed into a single word. It is extremely difficult to program so that implicit dependencies on machine word lengths are avoided.

Say a program is intended to count instances of some occurrence where the maximum number of instances which might arise is 500 000. Assume instance counts are compared. If this program is implemented on a machine with a 32-bit word size, instance counts can be represented as integers and comparisons made directly. If this program is subsequently moved to a 16-bit machine, it will fail because the maximum possible positive integer which can be held in a 16-bit word is 32 767.

Where types depend on machine representations, the type definition and its related operations should be grouped as a self-contained abstract data type where the underlying implementation is hidden (Figure 16.12).

```
package Counter is
    type T is limited private ;
    procedure Inc (Cnt : in out T ) ;
    procedure Dec (Cnt : in out T ) ;
    procedure Copy (Cnt1 : T ; Cnt2 : out T ) ;
    function Cequals (Cnt1, Cnt2 : T ) return BOOLEAN ;
private
    type T  is range  0..500_000 ;
end Counter ;
```

Figure 16.12
A portable counter
package.

```
generic
    Size : NATURAL := 32 ;
package Bit_Manipulation is
    type BITSTRING is private ;
    type BITVAL is (Zero, One) ;
    function Create return BITSTRING ;
    function And (B1, B2 : BITSTRING) return BITSTRING ;
    function Or  (B1, B2 : BITSTRING) return BITSTRING ;
    function Xor (B1, B2 : BITSTRING) return BITSTRING ;
    function Mask (B1, B2 : BITSTRING) return BITSTRING ;
    function Most_significant (B1 : BITSTRING) return BITVAL ;
    function Least_significant (B1 : BITSTRING) return BITVAL ;
    function Setbit (B1 : BITSTRING ; N : NATURAL ; V : BITVAL)
                   return BITSTRING ;
    function Testbit (B1 : BITSTRING ; N : NATURAL)
                   return BITVAL ;
    function NatToBits (N : NATURAL) return BITSTRING ;
    function BitstoNat (B1 : BITSTRING) return NATURAL ;
private
    -- Some appropriate representation
    type BITSTRING is array (0..Size-1) of BOOLEAN ;
end Bit_Manipulation ;
```

Figure 16.13
An abstract data type
BITSTRING.

Only the type name and related operations need be visible outside the package with representation details confined to the package. If the program is ported to another system which uses a different counter representation only the counter package need be changed. None of the uses of counter are affected. In languages such as Pascal, where no module facility is available, the operations on each type should be grouped and delimited by comments.

A related portability problem which is also a machine architecture dependency is that different machines may represent exactly the same information in different ways. For example, a 16-bit machine which uses two's complement notation to represent negative numbers would represent -1 as 1111111111111111; a machine which uses one's complement notation would represent the same number as 1111111111111110.

In some machines, the most significant bit of a number is the leftmost bit and on others it is the rightmost bit. On 16-bit machines where it is the leftmost bit, the number 2 would be represented as 0000000000000010, whereas if the rightmost bit is significant, 2 is represented as 0100000000000000, assuming two's complement representation is used.

These representation considerations do not normally cause problems for high-level language programmers because the representation is concealed by the language. If, however, it is necessary to generate specific bit patterns and the programming language does not allow direct operations on bitstrings, it may be necessary to simulate bitstrings using integers. The representation of integers on a particular machine must be known if bit patterns are to be generated.

Again, this problem can be addressed by defining an abstract data type BITSTRING, along with associated operations (Figure 16.13).

```
package Process_management is
   type PID is private ;
   type STATUS is (READY, RUNNING, WAITING, KILLED)
   function Create return PID ;
   function Kill  (Process : PID) return STATUS ;
   function Get_status  (P : PID) return STATUS ;
   function Wake_up  (P : PID) return STATUS ;
   function Put_to_sleep  (P : PID) return STATUS ;
   procedure Wait  (P : PID ; S : STATUS) ;
private
   type PID is new NATURAL ;
end Process_management ;
```

Figure 16.14
A process management
package.

The other major portability problem which arises in high-level
language programs is operating system dependency. Different machines
support different operating systems. Although common facilities are
provided, this is rarely in a compatible way.

Where a program needs to make use of operating system calls for file
and process management, these should be isolated in one or more packages.
For example, Figure 16.14 shows a package specification for process
management.

Again, the effective use of abstract data types which abstract the
operating system details is the best way of reducing operating system
dependencies.

16.3.2 Standards

Because of the emergence of workable standards and their acceptance by
large segments of the software development community, it is now easier to
produce portable application systems than it was in the 1970s and 1980s. If a
standard is adopted by the implementors of an application system, that
system should be portable, without change, to any other system which
follows that standard. Some of the standards which have been developed
are:

(1) *Programming language standards* Standards for Ada, COBOL,
     Pascal, C and Fortran have been agreed. Programs which follow these
     standards are readily portable to any compiler following the
     standards. However, differences between language translators can still
     introduce portability problems.

(2) *Operating system standards* The widespread use of UNIX as a base
     operating system has meant that work is now underway to produce a
     standard for UNIX (Posix). This is necessary because of subtle
     variations in the different versions of UNIX. MS-DOS has become a
     de facto standard for the current generation of IBM-compatible
     personal computers.

(3) *Networking standards* There is a great deal of international standardization effort going on concerned with networking standards, and the OSI layered model has been adopted although not widely implemented. TCP/IP protocols and Sun's Network File system (NFS) have become *de facto* standards for local area networks running UNIX and some other operating systems. Electronic mail is now widespread and can be used for transferring programs from machine to machine with forthcoming X400 and X500 standards.

(4) *Window system standards* The X-window system (Scheifler and Gettys, 1986) has become accepted as the standard for graphical user interfaces for workstations. The Motif toolkit has been widely adopted on top of X-windows as a standard toolkit (OSF, 1990).

While these standards significantly reduce the problems of moving an application system from one environment to another, there is still a need to think carefully about application system portability and to design the portability interface to minimize portability problems.

■ KEY POINTS

- Software reuse is an important technique of software cost reduction and productivity improvement. However, systematic reuse is still not widely practised.

- Reusable software components do not simply emerge as a by-product of software development. Extra effort must be added to generalize system components to make them reusable.

- Abstract data types and objects are effective encapsulations of reusable components.

- Software development with reuse needs a library of reusable components which can be understood by the reuser. Information on how to reuse the components should also be provided.

- Application system portability is a specialized form of reuse where an entire application system is adapted for reuse on a different computer.

- Portable systems should be implemented so that environment dependent sections are isolated in a portability interface.

- Emerging standards for languages, operating systems, networking and graphical user interfaces mean that portability problems are less significant than in the past.

FURTHER READING

Software Reusability. These two volumes of papers include most of the significant papers in this area to 1988. They include papers covering both the component-oriented and the generator view of reuse. (T.J. Biggerstaff and A.J. Perlis, 1989, Addison-Wesley.)

Software Reuse: Emerging Technology. There is some overlap between this collection of papers and *Software Reusability*. However, most of the papers are different and include some other important papers on reuse which were published too late to appear in the above collection. (W. Tracz, 1989, IEEE Press.)

'Strategies for supporting application portability'. This is an excellent article on portability. Although it focuses on operating system portability it is of general interest. Its discussion of operating system standards is particularly good. (J.D. Mooney, *IEEE Computer*, **23** (11), November 1990.)

EXERCISES

16.1 What are the major technical and non-technical factors which militate against widespread software reuse. From your own experience, do you reuse much software? If not, why not?

16.2 Write a set of guidelines for the Pascal or C programmer when writing functions or procedures which describe how to make these functions or procedures more reusable.

16.3 Using the suggestions set out in the chapter, construct reusable packages for the following abstract data structures:

   (a) A stack.
   (b) A table with keyed access to table elements.
   (c) A binary tree.
   (d) A priority queue.
   (e) An array.
   (f) A character string.

16.4 Suggest a set of software tools which might be provided to support software development with and for reuse.

16.5 Design an experiment which might demonstrate the advantages of software development with reuse. You may assume that you have a component catalogue which is populated with abstract data structure components.

16.6 Implement the newspaper delivery system introduced in Chapter 3 using a language with which you are familiar. Make as much use as possible of existing reusable components and try and create new reusable components when implementing the system. Write a report on the difficulties of reuse which you encountered.

16.7 Explain why the use of a standard high-level language does not guarantee that software will be portable across a range of machines.

16.8 You have been given the task of implementing a calendar and clock which gives time and data information. This has to operate on a range of computers from 8-bit micros to 64-bit special processors. Design and implement an abstract data type to representing the calendar and clock which can be readily ported from machine to machine.

16.9 Design the architecture of a Pascal, Ada or C compiler so that it may be implemented on a range of computers. Identify the key features of the portability interface in your design.

Computer-Aided Software Engineering

17

■ OBJECTIVES

The objectives of this chapter are to introduce the concept of computer-aided software engineering (CASE), to examine how well existing CASE tools provide software process support and to discuss the infrastructure requirements of CASE tools. CASE tools are classified according to the functions they provide and the activities they support. The general problems of tool integration are discussed and three types of integration, namely data integration through the object management system, user interface integration and activity integration, are described. The CAIS and PCTE public tool interface standards are compared in the final section of the chapter.

■ CONTENTS

Historically, the most significant productivity increases in manufacturing or building processes have come about when human skills are augmented by powerful tools. One man and a bulldozer can probably shift more earth in a day than fifty men working with hand tools. Similarly, the productivity of engineering designers is improved when they are supported by CAD systems which take over tedious drawing chores and which check the design to ensure its validity.

Automated tool support for software engineers should lead to corresponding improvements in productivity. Over the past few years, a wide range of tools to support software development have been developed and the term *computer-aided software engineering* (CASE) has come into use as a generic term for the automated support of software engineering.

Many CASE tools are now available. Although these individual software tools are useful, the true power of a CASE toolset can only be realized when these tools are integrated into a common framework or environment. In an integrated environment, tools can access the data produced by other tools so can be designed to act in tandem. Incremental toolsets may also be built where operations common to a number of tools are factored out and provided as a single, shareable tool.

Software tools for prototyping, testing, reliability measurement, program analysis and various management functions are discussed elsewhere in this book. Rather than cover individual tools, this chapter is concerned with identifying classes of tool and with the infrastructure which underlies the environment. The following chapter looks at different classes of environment and discusses the problems of introducing CASE technology.

17.1   CASE tools

There are now several hundred commercially available CASE tools which support different activities in the software process. These can be classified in two, orthogonal ways:

(1)   *Activity-oriented*   Using this approach, the classification scheme is based on process activities such as requirements specification, design, implementation and so on.

(2)   *Function-oriented*   This classification scheme is based on the functionality of the tools rather than the activity which the tools support.

Figure 17.1 illustrates a number of functional tool classes. These are general classes and, obviously, there are other, more specialized, tool classes, such as tools to support software reuse, tools for software re-engineering, and so on.

(1)   Planning and estimation tools
(2)   Text editing tools
(3)   Document preparation tools
(4)   Configuration management tools
(5)   Prototyping tools
(6)   Diagram editing tools
(7)   Data dictionary tools
(8)   User interface management systems
(9)   Method support tools
(10)   Language processing tools
(11)   Program analysis tools
(12)   Interactive debugging systems
(13)   Program transformation tools
(14)   Modelling and simulation tools
(15)   Test data generation tools

Figure 17.1
CASE tool
classification.

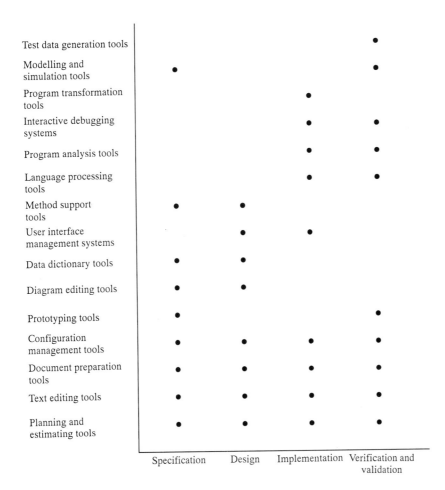

Figure 17.2
Tool support for
process activities.

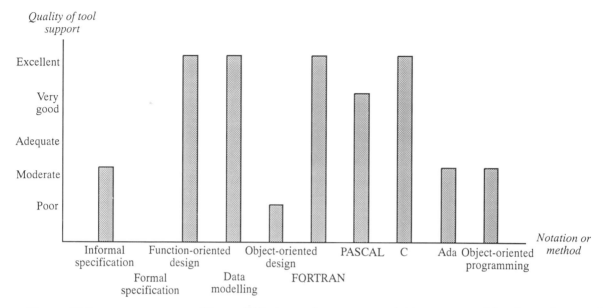

Figure 17.3
Quality of tool support.

Figure 17.2 shows the process activities supported by these classes of CASE tool. Tools for planning and estimating, text editing, document preparation and configuration management may be used throughout the software process.

Apart from these general purpose tools, Figure 17.2 shows that tool support is available for all process activities from specification through to verification and validation. Obviously, these tools are also used in system maintenance. This would appear to suggest that computer-aided software engineering has now matured with good coverage of all process activities.

However, if we now examine in more detail how well specific notations and methods used in the software process are supported, a rather different picture emerges. Figure 17.3 is my subjective estimate (in 1991) of the tool support for specification, design and implementation notations. This picture may change over the lifetime of the book as new tools become available.

From Figure 17.3, it is clear that support for specification, particularly formal specification, is poor. Functional design methods and data modelling are well supported, as are languages like Pascal, Fortran and C. Object-oriented design, however, is not well supported. Tool support for Ada is limited, as is support for object-oriented languages such as C++. In short, modern software engineering is not well supported by CASE tools.

This uneven distribution of tool support is one reason why it is difficult and costly to introduce new languages, methods and techniques in the software development process. The cost and productivity advantages of using techniques such as object-oriented design are at least partially negated by inadequate tool support. Software developers may have invested large capital sums in tooling up for function-oriented design with C or Fortran as the development language. They are understandably reluctant to discard this investment in favour of poorly-supported techniques.

17.2   Tool integration

Individual CASE tools are useful and cost-effective in their own right but more leverage is obtained when CASE tools work together in an integrated way. Integration means that, from the user's perspective, the tools exhibit some measure of uniformity. The degree of uniformity supported in different environments varies considerably. Loosely coupled systems may only provide limited data interchange. In tightly integrated systems, tools may operate on a single, shared representation of the software using a consistent user interface.

The discussion of integration in this section is based around a model of a CASE environment as shown in Figure 17.4.

Tools are hosted on top of an operating system which provides basic file management and process management capabilities. Between the tools and the operating system is a logical object management system. The object management system (OMS) provides facilities to map the logical entities (designs, programs, and so on) being manipulated by the tools onto the underlying storage management system. OMSs vary in complexity from very simple (consisting merely of a directory showing which files are used to store logical objects) to very complex, integrated systems where multiple classes of objects and relationships are supported. In many CASE toolsets, the term object management system is not explicitly used; these systems claim to be integrated around a data dictionary. In fact, the data dictionary is simply a way of viewing an underlying OMS.

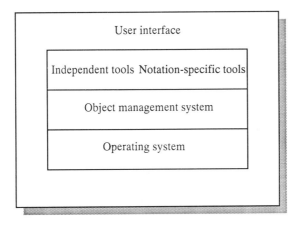

Figure 17.4
CASE environment structure.

Tools which interact with the object management system fall into two classes:

(1) *Independent tools*   These are tools which do not depend on a specific notation or programming language. They include document processors, diagram editors, simulators, and so on. Loose integration between these tools is sometimes supported with limited data interchange capabilities.

(2) *Notation-specific tools*   These are tools which operate on specific notations such as programming languages, design notations, and so on. The notation is often the integration framework for these tools.

All tools, the operating system and the OMS have some form of user interface. As discussed below, user interface integration makes it easier for the user to interact with the different CASE tools as the overhead of learning how to use each tool is reduced.

CASE environments may be either open or closed. In a closed environment, the tools populating the environment are integrated with the environment infrastructure. It is usually impossible to bring in tools developed elsewhere and integrate these in a closed environment. It may also be impossible for users to write new tools if the data representation is not published by the environment vendor.

In contrast, open environments provide facilities to support the introduction of new tools. The representations used in the environment are publicly available. Open environments are often compatible with industry-standard file systems and 'foreign' tools can operate in a private space where they need not convert their representation to that used by the other environment tools.

There are three different types of integration which have to be considered by environment procurers and developers:

(1) *Data integration*   Tools operate using a shared data model.

(2) *User interface integration*   Tools in an environment are integrated around a common user interface.

(3) *Activity integration*   The environment incorporates a model of the software process and uses this model to coordinate tool activation and use.

Data integration depends on tools operating on data whose format is known to the tools. Data can be integrated at several different levels:

(1) *Simple character files*   All tools recognize a single file format. The most general purpose shareable file format is where files are made up of lines of characters.

(2) *Language-oriented notations*   The tools make use of programming or design language information. They are integrated around a data model which represents language syntactic and semantic information.

(3) *Object-management systems*   The tools are integrated around an object management system which includes a public, shared data model describing the data entities and relationships which are manipulable by the tools.

The simplest form of data integration is integration around a shared set of files, as supported by the UNIX system. UNIX has a simple model of files which are unstructured sequences of characters. Any tool can write character files and can read the files produced by other tools. The simple file format allows I/O devices to be treated as files and makes it easy to provide pipes for direct process communication. When processes are connected by a pipe, streams of characters are passed directly from one process to another without the need for intermediate file creation.

Files are physically simple but applications must know the logical structure of a file if they are to use the information produced by another tool. This logical structure is embedded in the program which wrote the file. Cooperating tools must know each other's internal details if they are to be integrated.

This is feasible if a single programmer or programming team is responsible for developing all of the tools in the environment. This was the case in the early versions of UNIX, which was one of the first effective programming environments. However, tools developed in different organizations will rarely have the same logical data representations, with the result that no effective data integration is possible. As new tools are developed, it becomes progressively more difficult to make these compatible with existing system tools.

An alternative approach which is supported in several personal computer language products is integration around a notation used in the software process. A good example of this can be seen in programming language translation and support tools. These tools rely on a syntactic and semantic analysis of the program and are often bundled with the compilation system. Figure 17.5 shows a possible structure for an integrated programming language toolkit.

An integrated, language-oriented toolset might offer the following facilities:

(1) A compiler for language translation. This may have options which allow debugging information to be included and options to optimize the generated code. The compiler produces the program syntax tree and symbol table which are used by the other integrated tools.

(2) Static and dynamic program analysers and an integrated debugging system. These are covered in Chapters 23 and 24.

(3) A structure editing system where language knowledge is embedded in the editor, which assists the user to input syntactically correct programs.

(4) Prettyprinters and cross-referencers which format the program listing and produce a cross-reference list of where program names are declared and used.

Integration based on the programming language is effective in concealing the differences between individual tools and presenting the user with a coherent program development system. However, it is difficult to import tools into this environment because of the complex data integration representation. Although these environments can be effective *programming* environments, they cannot readily be integrated with other support tools such as method-oriented workbenches.

Integration around a database or object management system is the most flexible form of data integration. Object management systems are covered in detail in the next section so will only be introduced here. The essence of this form of integration is a public database schema where a set of data types and relationships is defined. Tools read and write data according to this schema. If a tool wishes to use data produced by another tool, the schema is used to discover the data structure generated by that tool (Figure 17.6).

User interface integration means that the tools in a system use a common metaphor or style and a set of common standards for user interaction. Tools have a similar appearance and users have a reduced learning overhead when a new tool is introduced as some of the interface is already familiar.

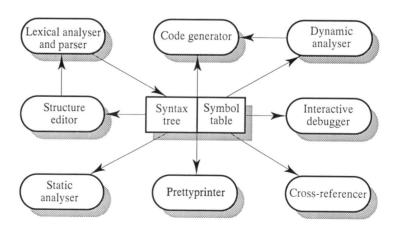

Figure 17.5
Language processing toolkit.

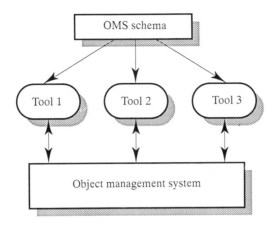

Figure 17.6
Object management via
a schema.

There are three different levels of user interface integration:

(1)   *Windowing system integration*   Tools which are integrated at this level all use the same underlying windowing system and present a common interface for window manipulation commands. Windows have the same appearance and the same commands for window movement, re-sizing, iconification, and so on.

(2)   *Command integration*   Tools which are integrated at this level all use the same form of commands for comparable functions. This means that, if a textual interface is used, the syntax of command lines and parameters is the same for all commands. If a graphical interface using menus and buttons is used, comparable commands should have the same name and occupy the same relative positions in the interface in each application. The same representation is used in all sub-systems for buttons, menus, and so on.

(3)   *Interaction integration*   This applies in systems with a direct manipulation interface where the user interacts directly with a graphical or textual view of an entity. Interaction integration means that the same direct manipulation facilities such as selection, deletion, and so on are provided in all sub-systems. Examples of systems where interaction integration is required are word processing systems and graphical editing systems.

Young *et al.* (1988) describe the user interface system for the Arcadia environment which supports all of these classes of integration.

The best-known example of an integrated user interface is the Apple Macintosh computer, which supports all three of the above integration levels. Applications running on that machine have a common 'look and feel' which is achieved by following a set of guidelines on Macintosh application program interfaces. These guidelines are implemented by a toolbox of user interface functions. Following the user interface guidelines is the simplest way to build a user interface.

Until recently, a barrier to windowing system integration in open environments, where the toolkit is procured from a number of different sources, has been the lack of standards for graphical user interfaces (GUIs). Tools were usually built using a vendor-supplied windowing system and this was incompatible with other systems. However, this situation is now changing rapidly for UNIX workstation tools with the emergence of the X-windows system as a GUI standard and the widespread use of the Motif toolkit for higher level interaction support. Although X-windows is available for personal computers, vendors of these systems have been slower to adopt it and still provide incompatible windowing systems.

Control integration means that application and environment control functions are supported in a uniform way. For example, all applications require some mechanism which allows the user to stop their execution and this should be provided in the same way, via a 'quit' button, for example. If the tools are driven by textual command, commands should have comparable formats and parameter names.

Control integration can be achieved if implementors follow a set of guidelines defining the representations of abstract user interface actions such as selection of a choice from a set of alternatives, toggling a switch, numerical and character information display, and so on. An early example of such guidelines were those defined for the ECLIPSE environment where the user interface was defined in terms of menus, buttons, display panels, toggles and 'lights' (Reid and Welland, 1986; Sommerville *et al.*, 1989).

Most software tools depict the objects which they manipulate as either diagrams or text. Interaction integration means that the mechanisms used to interact with these graphical or textual objects are, wherever possible, consistent and uniform. For example, if text is normally selected by traversing it using cursor control keys, all tools which require text selection should use the same approach.

Providing guidelines for interaction integration is particularly difficult because of the range of interaction possibilities and because of the range of potential textual and graphical object representations. It is relatively straightforward to define possible interactions with unstructured text and untyped graphical objects; it is more difficult when the text or diagram represents structured entities with specialized operations initiated through the screen representation.

Closed environments such as language-oriented environments and method-support environments usually have a reasonable user interface integration. As new tools cannot be introduced by other suppliers it is possible to achieve user interface commonality across applications.

In open environments, user interface integration above the windowing system level is more difficult to achieve. In these environments, tools are

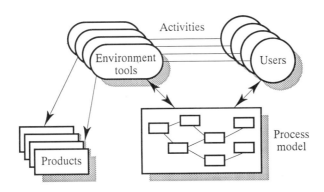

Figure 17.7
Activity integration.

developed at different times by different developers. As the environment evolves and new tools are introduced, it becomes progressively more difficult to maintain user interface uniformity. Although comprehensive guidelines for user interface integration may be provided, the guideline designers cannot anticipate every possible use of the environment. As new facilities, such as the use of sound, are introduced, user interface conventions are invented to support them. Inevitably, uniformity is lost in the process.

Activity integration means that the environment has embedded knowledge about the activities which it supports, their phasing and their constraints. The environment participates actively in the scheduling of these activities and in checking that the required activity sequence is maintained (Figure 17.7).

Activity integration relies on the environment maintaining a model of the software process and then using this model to drive the process activities. A number of prototype environments which incorporate process models have been built (Taylor *et al.*, 1988; Warboys, 1989) but, at the time of writing, I am not aware of any commercial toolkit or environment which incorporates process modelling in a general way.

There are several steps involved in creating a process model:

(1)   Identify the activities involved in the process.
(2)   Identify the deliverables (or process products) of these activities. Steps 1 and 2 may be interchanged.
(3)   Define how activities are coordinated and the dependencies between activities.
(4)   Allocate individual engineers to each activity.
(5)   Specify the tools required to execute an activity.

Many activities are concurrent activities and this must be reflected in the process model. As activities and their coordination are interdependent, the process model should be dynamic and should change as more information regarding process activities is obtained.

Process models are not new. They have always been the basis for project plans, and managers continually refine an informal process model in the course of a project. While managers can easily interpret an informal model, a more formal approach is required if this model is to be interpretable and is to be used to drive the software development process. This has led to the development of languages for process modelling (Ould and Roberts, 1988; Tully, 1988) and what are sometimes called process programs (Osterweil, 1987).

The principal difficulties in building a CASE environment with activity integration are:

(1)   Models of the software process as discussed in Chapter 1 are generic models and rely on human interpretation to instantiate them in any particular set of circumstances. The activities and their implementation is not defined in detail in these process models. Breaking down the process into finer-grain activities is a project specific task. If a model is to be used to integrate activities, there is a significant cost in process programming and validation which adds to the project management costs.

(2)   There is never a single right way to organize a software development and both the project manager and the development engineers change the process 'on the fly' as the system is being developed. Humans can switch between activities relatively quickly if unforeseen circumstances (e.g. a printer failure) arises. Embedding this flexibility in a model is difficult.

(3)   Process models specify the products of the software process and the communications between developers. Although communication speci-fication is possible for well structured tasks such as invoice processing, the coordination patterns in loosely structured, problem-solving tasks, which are normal in software development are difficult to specify.

A further difficulty with activity integration is that engineers and managers may view this as a form of deskilling and may actively resist the introduction of CASE tools and environment with activity integration. The engineers may have evolved their own, informal, undocumented ways to tackle development and may be reluctant to conform to the more rigid strategies imposed by an environment.

17.3 Object management

CASE tools interact with structured entities which represent software. These entities may be specifications, designs, test data, project plans, and so on, and may be depicted in a variety of textual and graphical ways. Entities have associated attributes which identify the entity, its type, creator, date of creation, date of modification, and so on.

The entities in an environment participate in relationships with other entities. These include relationships such as 'calls' between entities, which represent procedures, 'uses' when one entity uses the services of another entity, 'implements' when one entity represents the implementation of a design and so on. There are hundreds of possible relation types which may be identified between the entities in a complex software system.

The function of the OMS in an environment is to manage these entities and their relations with other entities. It must provide facilities for entity and relation definition and classification, for altering the attributes of entities and relations, and for dynamically creating and destroying entity instances. It should have built-in relationship types, particularly those types required to support configuration management.

It is not generally practical to use a commercial database management system directly as an OMS. Commercial database systems are geared towards supporting large volumes of information structured as simple, relatively short records. There are few types of record and large numbers of type instances. Operations are often batch operations which operate on groups of database records. Transactions are usually short (fractions of a second) so locking parts of the database while a transaction is in progress is feasible.

By contrast, software development requires a large number of entity and relation types with, perhaps, only a few instances of each type. The tools in the environment may operate on only a few entities. The data entities may be large items such as programs or designs. Transactions are long as the manipulation of an entity representing a program or a design may take several hours or even days. Locking of large sections of the database is impractical.

One approach to providing an OMS is to build the system on top of a relational database and a filestore. The filestore is used for the storage of bulk information such as program text, test data, and so on, and the database is used to store entity attributes and relations between the environment entities. Figure 17.8 shows an example of this approach where the values of entities A, B, C, and D are maintained in the filestore but the relation in which they participate (CALLS) is maintained in the database.

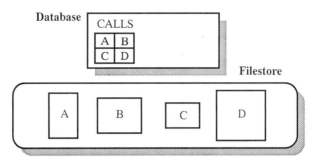

Figure 17.8
OMS implementation using a database and a filestore.

There are two disadvantages to this approach to OMS provision. Firstly, the control of the entities is split between two storage systems. It is possible to alter files without following the path through the database. The database can become inconsistent. Secondly, relational databases are not well suited to the representation of relations between entities. It is possible to implement such relations by maintaining a table of participating entities but using these relationships is generally inefficient.

An alternative approach is to build the OMS using a semantic database, such as those provided by the CAIS and PCTE public tool interfaces (see the next section), or directly using the storage management facilities of the host operating system. The ECLIPSE environment (Bott, 1989) is an example of an environment which has adopted a two-tier approach with a fine-grain object management system implemented on top of an entity-relation database provided by PCTE. Most CASE workbenches or toolkits, however, implement the OMS directly and manage the objects through a data dictionary.

Semantic databases support the entity-relation model of data (Chen, 1976) and allow both entities and relations to be given user defined types and to have associated attributes. Figure 17.9 shows similar information to that in Figure 17.8 but with additional type information.

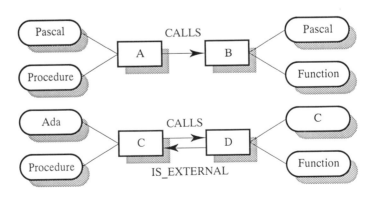

Figure 17.9
OMS implementation using a semantic database.

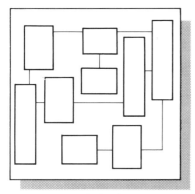

Coarse-grain database

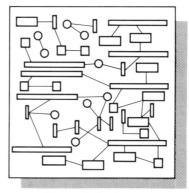

Fine-grain database

Figure 17.10
Fine-grain and coarse-grain databases.

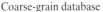

The granularity of an OMS or database is the minimum size of entity which may be efficiently stored and manipulated in the database (Figure 17.10). Coarse-grain systems usually have higher performance but the minimum entity size which may be stored is something like an entire Ada package or a complete design document. Fine grain databases allow smaller entities (such as a single declaration) to be stored but performance is generally poorer.

Object-oriented databases (Won, 1990) are generalizations of OMSs. OMSs provide typed entities which have associated attributes. Object-oriented databases support entities and attributes but also allow methods (operations) to be stored as part of the database. This means that there can be a closer link between activities and the entities manipulated by these activities. As object-oriented database technology matures, it will be exploited in CASE environments (Andrews and Harris, 1987; Hudson and King, 1988).

17.4   Public tool interfaces

A public tool interface (PTI) is a set of interface primitives which can be used by tool and environment builders. The interface defines basic integration facilities such as object management, process management and tool communications. It is usually implemented as a library of routines, akin to operating system calls, which may be accessed by CASE tools. The term 'public tool interface' is used to distinguish these interfaces from proprietary interfaces for tool integration defined by CASE tool vendors.

The initial proposal for a public tool interface was put forward by Buxton (1980) in a document setting out requirements for an Ada support environment. He proposed the notion of an Ada programming support

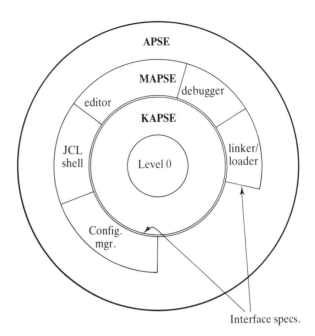

Figure 17.11
The organization of an
APSE.

environment (APSE) which was layered, with the innermost layer called a
kernel-APSE. This kernel-APSE should insulate the environment facilities
from the underlying hardware, operating system and data management
facilities and should provide object management primitives (Figure 17.11).
Other levels in the APSE were the minimal-APSE (MAPSE), which
provided a basic toolset, and the full APSE, which supported a full range of
software engineering tools.

After a number of trial projects, a working party in the US (with
European representatives) was set up to define a kernel-APSE interface
standard and this became known as the CAIS (common APSE interface set)
standard (Oberndorf, 1988). The initial version of this standard (CAIS-1)
lacked support for user-defined typing or support for bit-mapped workstations. The standard has since been developed and a revised version
(CAIS-A) of this standard was accepted in early 1989 (Munck *et al.*, 1988).

At the same time as the US CAIS work, the European Commission
funded a multinational project under the ESPRIT programme to define a
comparable public tool interface. This was called PCTE (portable common
tool environment) and the first version of the PCTE was published in 1984
(Campbell, 1986). By contrast with the CAIS standard which was Ada-
oriented, the PCTE standard was UNIX- and C-oriented and was intended
for general-purpose rather than language-oriented environment support.
The PCTE lacked support for security and access control and a further
project, PCTE+, (Boudier *et al.*, 1988; Tedd, 1989) funded by European
Defense Departments, developed the PCTE to include security capabilities.
Revisions of the PCTE are based on the work done in PCTE+.

	PCTE	CAIS	PCTE+	CAIS-A
Object management	ERA	ERA	ERA	ERA
Typed objects	Yes	No	Yes	Yes
Composite objects	No	No	Yes	Indirectly
Transactions	Yes	No	Yes	Yes
Process management	Yes	Yes	Yes	Yes
Process objects	No	Yes	Yes	Yes
Distribution	Yes	No	Yes	Indirectly
Security and access control	No	Yes	Yes	Yes
Language binding	C/Ada	Ada	C/Ada	Ada
Operating system	UNIX	Not OS dependent	Not OS dependent	Not OS dependent
User interface	Graphical	Text	Graphical (X-windows)	Undefined

Figure 17.12
PCTE and CAIS
comparison.

PCTE+ and CAIS-A have much in common and they differ in detail rather than in substance. Figure 17.12 shows the similarities between these systems and also illustrates how earlier work done in the PCTE and CAIS-1 projects have influenced their successors. The similarities have been recognized in both the US and in Europe. Future development of each of these interfaces will be coordinated and a new standard called PCIS will be developed which will be a progressive evolution from PCTE and CAIS-A suitable for both commercial and military applications.

Object-management in PCTE and CAIS-A is based on an entity-relationship-attribute (ERA) model where objects are represented by database entities, may participate in relationships with other objects and may have inherent attributes. Entities are typed and user-defined subtyping is supported. For example, from a basic type TEXT, it is possible to derive subtypes such as PASCAL-SOURCE-TEXT. This typing allows tools to check that the objects which they manipulate are the correct type, thus reducing the scope for error. To simplify migration to these interfaces, PTIs emulate existing file systems so that file-based tools may be ported to them without change.

To provide data recovery and resilience, transactions are supported where a transaction is an atomic set of actions whose effect on data is either to apply all or none of these actions. This means that if a failure occurs during the transaction, it is possible to restore the database to a consistent state.

Both interfaces also provide facilities for execution management allowing processes to be started, terminated and controlled, facilities for interprocess communication including standard UNIX pipes and signals, message passing and shared memory, and I/O facilities comparable to those provided in UNIX.

Process and OMS distribution is supported in the PCTE. It has been recognized that development environments are likely to be built using a network of workstations and it is possible to distribute executing processes across this network. Thus, a process controlling a number of compilations (say) could set each compilation off in different network workstations. Similarly, data need not all reside in a single system but may be distributed over different nodes in the network. CAIS-A defines process distribution but considers the provision of a distributed OMS an implementation rather than an interface issue.

In the original definition, the PCTE set out a set of user interface primitives for bit-mapped workstation support. CAIS, however, simply supported simple text terminals. However, with the emergence of X-windows as a standard, the developers of both interfaces have recognized that it is unwise to attempt to define different user interface primitives. The definers of both PCTE+ and CAIS-A have therefore paid little attention to user interface definition with the implicit assumption that a standard GUI based on X-windows and one or more toolkits will emerge.

The PCTE has been more generally accepted than the CAIS in terms of the number of systems implemented using the PTIs. This is partly because of European Commission funding and partly because CAIS is perceived as a military rather than a commercial system. Examples of environments which have been built using the PCTE include ECLIPSE (Bott, 1989) and PACT (Thomas, 1989).

■ KEY POINTS

■ Computer-aided software engineering (CASE) is the term for software tool support for the software engineering process.

■ Good tool support exists for functional software design methods, implementation and validation. Tool support for specification and object-oriented design is immature.

- Tool integration can be achieved through data integration allowing tools to share data, user interface integration where a uniform user interface is available and activity integration which is based on a model of the software process.

- Object management systems support data integration by allowing entities to be named, typed and to participate in relationships with each other.

- Current object management systems are mostly based on an entity-relationship-attribute semantic database model.

- PCTE and CAIS are public tool interfaces which define standards for object and process management. They both use an ERA database for object management and their development will be integrated in a future system called PCIS.

FURTHER READING

'Difficulties in integrating multiview environments'.   This is an excellent overview of the problems of environment integration. Its focus is principally on data integration and it compares the different approaches which may be adopted. (S. Meyers, *IEEE Software*, **8** (1), January 1991.)

IEEE Trans. Software Engineering, **14** (6), June 1988.   This is a special issue of the journal which is concerned with architectures for software development environments. Although mostly concerned with research systems, the general problems of environment infrastructure are covered. A good introduction to the CAIS is also provided.

EXERCISES

17.1 Identify entity and relation types which might be used in an OMS supporting a CASE tool for object-oriented design.

17.2 What attributes and relations are required for configuration management support (see Chapter 29).

17.3 Survey the tool availability in your local development environment and produce a table showing what software process activities are supported.

17.4 Write user interface guidelines for menus in a user interface so that applications offer an integrated user interface. These guidelines should cater for the situation where the number of menu items is more than can reasonably be displayed on a single menu.

17.5 Explain why typed OMSs should always include a FILE type of entity.

17.6 Survey the available literature and write a report summarizing the current state of the art in process modelling.

17.7 By analysing your own way of working, design process models for the following activities:

   (a) Discovering and repairing errors in a program using a static analysis tool (see Chapter 24 if you have no experience of such tools).
   (b) Writing a user manual for a program.
   (c) Submitting a set of test input files to a program and checking the results of these tests.

17.8 Describe the difficulties which might arise if you tried to embed these models in an environment and use them to control the process.

17.9 Explain how public tool interfaces can simplify the problems of tool integration.

Software Development Environments

18

■ OBJECTIVES

The objectives of this chapter are to describe the different classes of software development environment (SDE) and to discuss the problems of introducing and using an SDE. Three classes of SDE are discussed, namely programming environments, CASE workbenches and software engineering environments. Programming environments and CASE workbenches are geared towards the support of parts of the software process; software engineering environments are intended to support the entire process from requirements definition through to software maintenance. The final section in the chapter covers the environment life cycle and discusses environment procurement, introduction and use.

■ CONTENTS

The high cost and the difficulties of developing software systems are well known. Accordingly, as the costs of computer hardware have decreased, it has become cost-effective to provide individual software engineers with automated tools to support the software development process. Although it is possible to operate CASE tools in conjunction with application systems, it is generally the case that software development is best supported on a separate system which is called a software development environment (SDE).

An SDE is a collection of software and hardware tools which is explicitly tailored to support the production of software systems in a particular application domain.

This definition makes two important points:

(1)   The software development environment may include hardware tools. For example, microprocessor development systems usually include an in-circuit emulator as an integral part of the environment.

(2)   The software development environment is specific rather than general. It should support the development of a particular class of systems, such as microprocessor systems, artificial intelligence systems, and so on. The environment need not support all types of application systems development.

SDEs usually run on a host computer system (or network) and the software is developed for a separate target computer (Figure 18.1).

There are several reasons why the host–target model is the most appropriate for software development environments:

(1)   In some cases, the application software under development may be for a machine with no software development facilities.

(2)   The target machine may be application-oriented (a vector processor, say) and not well suited to supporting software development environments.

(3)   The target machine may be dedicated to running a particular application (such as a transaction processing system) and this must be given priority over software development.

The disadvantage of a host–target approach to development is that the facilities and components which are available to developers using the environment cannot be incorporated in the delivered application system. If the environment has a graphical editor (say), and this is also an application requirement, this graphical editing system cannot simply be reused. For this reason, interpretative environments, such as Smalltalk and LISP environments, have rejected the host–target development model and deliver the environment as part of the application system. The problems with this approach are discussed in Section 18.1.1.

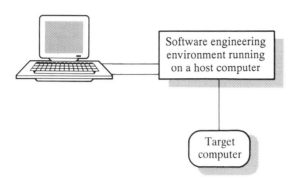

Figure 18.1
Host–target working.

There are many different types of software development environment which are now in use (Figure 18.2). Environments may be classified into three major groups:

(1) *Programming environments* These are environments which are principally intended to support the processes of programming, testing and debugging. Their support for requirements definition, specification and software design is limited.

(2) *CASE workbenches* In contrast to programming environments, these are environments which are principally oriented towards software specification and design. They usually only provide rudimentary programming support (sometimes for 4GLs). They are usually available on personal computers and can, of course, be used in conjunction with a programming environment.

(3) *Software engineering environments* This class of SDE is intended to support the production of large, long-lifetime software systems whose maintenance costs typically exceed development costs and which are produced by a team rather than by individual programmers. They provide support for all development and maintenance activities.

Within each of these broad environment classes, there are various types of environment. These will be discussed in the appropriate section below.

While it is convenient to classify environments as above, in practice the boundaries between the different classes of environment are not clear-cut. As programming environments are populated with tools, their facilities resemble those of software engineering environments. As CASE workbenches mature and are made available on more powerful hardware, they offer increasing support for programming and testing, and so also resemble software engineering environments.

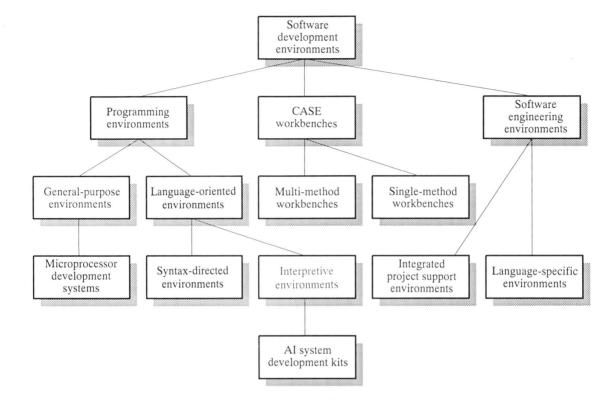

18.1   Programming environments

Environments to support the programming process were the first SDEs. They always include language processing tools and program testing and debugging tools. Because of their maturity, the tools available in programming environments are usually powerful, reliable and robust.

Programming environments can be grouped into different classes as shown in Figure 18.2.

(1)   *General-purpose environments*   These are environments which provide a set of general-purpose software tools for the development of programs in a variety of different languages. Microprocessor development systems, which usually include hardware tools such as in-circuit emulators and cross-compilers, are general-purpose programming environments.

(2)   *Language-oriented environments*   These are environments which are designed to support the development of programs in a single programming language.

The best known general-purpose programming environment is based on UNIX. UNIX is a general-purpose operating system with a comprehensive set of software tools. Since the first versions of the UNIX programming environment (Ivie, 1977; Dolotta *et al.*, 1978), the system has been refined by various vendors. Sophisticated programming environments such as Sun's NSE environment (Courington *et al.*, 1988) are now available.

Because of their evolution from operating systems, general-purpose programming environments are not usually tightly integrated. Tools exchange information via files and, as discussed in Chapter 17, this causes integration problems. Each tool must know the data structures used by cooperating tools and the way in which these data structures are represented in a file.

There may be a variety of tools available in a programming environment. As an illustration of the tools which might populate an environment for developing real-time software on a target microprocessor system, the following tools might be available:

(1) *Host–target communications software* This links the development computer to the computer on which the software is to execute (the target machine).

(2) *Target machine simulators* These allow target machine software to be executed and tested on the host machine.

(3) *Cross-compilers* These are language processing systems which execute on the host machine and generate code for the target machine.

(4) *Testing and debugging tools* These might include test drivers, dynamic and static program analysers and test output analysis programs. Debugging on the host of programs executing on the target should be supported if possible.

(5) *Configuration management tools* These might include version management tools such as SCCS (Rochkind, 1975) and MAKE (Feldman, 1979) which assist with the process of controlling different software versions and building executable systems. Usually, these tools are not closely integrated with other tools in a programming environment.

(6) *Communication tools* These include an electronic mail system and, perhaps, a teleconferencing system.

There is not a rigid dividing line between general-purpose programming environments and software engineering environments (discussed in Section 18.3). Programming environments often include some support for specification, design and management. However, the important distinction between programming environments and software engineering environments is in the degree of integration. Software engineering environments are tightly integrated around an object management system; general-purpose programming environments are usually integrated around a filestore.

18.1.1 Language-oriented environments

Language-oriented environments are an important and widely used class of programming environment. They are intended to support the development of systems in a single programming language. Because of this specialization, knowledge of the language can be embedded in the environment and powerful support facilities can be made available.

There are two classes of language-oriented environment:

(1) *Interpretative environments* These are environments such as the Interlisp environment (Teitleman and Masinter, 1984) or the Smalltalk environment (Goldberg, 1984) where the environment includes a programming language interpreter.

(2) *Structure-oriented environments* These are environments which are based on manipulation of an abstract model of the program structure through a structured editing system.

Interpretative environments are excellent environments for software prototyping. Not only do they provide an expressive, high-level language for system development, they also allow the application software developer to use the facilities of the environment in their application. Typically, interpretative environments provide support for incremental compiling and execution, persistent storage, and system browsers which allow the source code of the environment to be examined (Figure 18.3).

A development of interpretative environments are artificial intelligence (AI) development systems such as ART and KEE which are based on an interpretative environment (typically a LISP environment) and add facilities to simplify the production of AI systems. The added facilities may include truth maintenance systems, object-oriented facilities and mechanisms for knowledge representation and rule application.

However, this class of environment is not well suited to the development of large, long-lifetime systems. The environment and the system are closely integrated so system users must install the environment as well as the application system. This increases the overall cost of the system. Both the environment and the system have to be maintained throughout the lifetime of the application, by which time the environment may be obsolete.

Structure-oriented environments were originally developed for teaching programming (Teitelbaum and Reps, 1981) as they allowed an editing system to be constructed which trapped syntax errors in the program before compilation. Rather than operate on the text of a program, these structured editors operate on an abstract syntax tree decorated with semantic information (Figure 18.4).

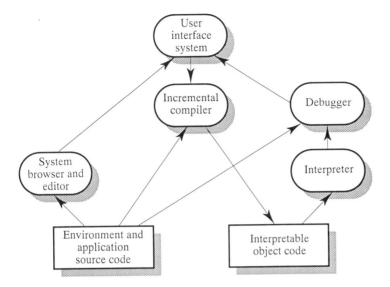

Figure 18.3
A model of a language-oriented environment.

As well as the obvious advantage of incremental program checking as the program is input, structure-oriented environments have the further advantage that different views of a program can be presented. As well as a view of a system as text, the user of the environment may specify that a compressed view of the system should be generated showing only procedure headings (say) and that program control should be illustrated via a graphical view (Figure 18.5).

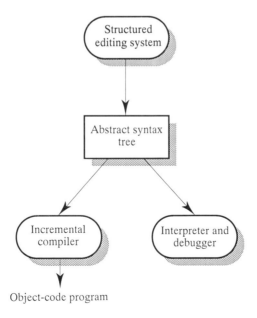

Figure 18.4
A model of a structure-oriented environment.

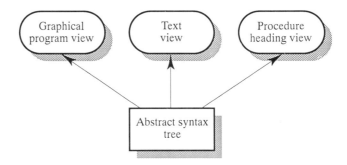

Figure 18.5
Multiple program
views.

Because much of the manipulation of program structures provided in structure-oriented environments is language independent (basically imperative languages all require comparable support), it is possible to produce structure-oriented environment generation systems. Systems such as Mentor (Donzeau-Gouge *et al.*, 1984), Gandalf (Habermann and Notkin, 1986) and the Synthesizer Generator (Reps and Teitelbaum, 1984) are systems which generate a language-oriented environment from a language definition (Figure 18.6).

Interpretative language-oriented environments have been successful commercially as prototyping environments. Structure-oriented environments, however, have mostly been used for program teaching rather than in industrial systems development. However, many of the structured editing ideas from these environments have influenced commercial language systems, such as Turbo Pascal, which provide an editor integrated with a language compiler.

18.2 CASE workbenches

CASE workbench systems are designed to support the analysis and design stages of the software process. These systems are oriented towards the support of graphical notations such as those used in the various design

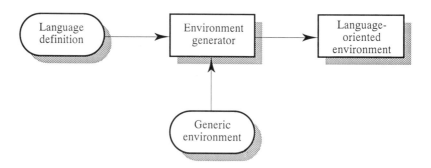

Figure 18.6
Environment
generation.

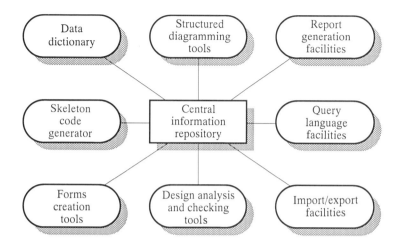

Figure 18.7
CASE workbench
components.

methods. As shown in Figure 18.2, they are either intended for the support of a specific method, such as JSD or the Yourdon method, or support a range of diagram types, encompassing those used in the most common methods.

Typical components of a CASE workbench (Figure 18.7) are:

(1)   A diagram editing system to create data flow diagrams, structure charts, entity-relationship diagrams, and so on. The editor is not just a drafting tool but is aware of the types of entities in the diagram. It captures information about these entities and saves this information in a central repository (sometimes called an encyclopedia). The design editing system discussed in previous chapters is an example of such a tool.

(2)   Design analysis and checking facilities which process the design and report on errors and anomalies. These may be integrated with the editing system so that the user may be informed of errors during diagram creation.

(3)   Query language facilities which allow the user to browse the stored information and examine completed designs.

(4)   Data dictionary facilities which maintain information about named entities used in a system design.

(5)   Report generation facilities which take information from the central store and automatically generate system documentation.

(6)   Form generation tools which allow screen and document formats to be specified.

(7)   Import/export facilities which allow the interchange of information from the central repository with other development tools.

(8)   Some systems support skeleton code generators which generate code or code segments automatically from the design captured in the central store.

CASE workbench systems, like structured methods, have been mostly used in the development of data processing systems but they can also be used in the development of other classes of system. Chikofsky and Rubenstein (1988) suggest that productivity improvements of up to 40% may be achieved with the use of such systems. They also suggest that, as well as these improvements, the quality of the developed systems is higher with fewer errors and inconsistencies and the developed systems are more appropriate to the user's needs.

Current CASE workbench products are first-generation systems; Martin (1988) identified a number of deficiencies which many of them have:

(1)   The workbenches are not integrated with other document preparation tools such as word processors and desktop publishing systems. Import/export facilities are usually confined to ASCII text.

(2)   There is a lack of standardization which makes information interchange across different workbenches difficult or impossible.

(3)   They lack facilities which allow a method to be tailored to a particular application or class of application. For example, it is not usually possible for users to override built-in rules.

(4)   The workbenches have inadequate facilities for creating high-quality documentation. Martin observes that simply producing copies of screens is not good enough and that the requirements for paper documentation are distinct from those for screen documentation.

(5)   The diagraming facilities are slow to use so that even a moderately complex diagram can take several hours to input and arrange. Martin suggests that there is a need for automated diagramming and diagram arrangement given a textual input.

Since Martin's critique of these systems, some of the deficiencies have been addressed by the system vendors. This has been simplified by the fact that CASE workbenches are mostly now available on IBM PC or PC-compatible hardware or on workstation UNIX systems. Some workbenches allow data transfer to and from common applications, such as word processors, available on these systems. Many systems now support high-quality PostScript (Adobe Systems Inc., 1987) output to laser printers.

The lack of data interchange standards makes it difficult or impossible to transfer information in the central repository to other workbench systems. Users may have to maintain obsolete CASE workbenches and their supporting computers for many years in order to support systems developed using them. However, this lack of standards is now being tackled by CASE workbench vendors. At the time of writing, work has started on defining a standard for CASE information.

A serious deficiency of CASE workbenches, from the point of view of large-scale software engineering, is the difficulty of integrating them with configuration management systems. Large software systems are in use for many years and, in that time, are subject to many changes and exist in many versions. Configuration management tools allow individual versions of a system to be retrieved, support system building from components and maintain relationships between components and their documentation.

The user of a CASE workbench is provided with support for parts of the design process but designs are not automatically linked to other products such as source code, test data suites and user documentation. It is not easy to create and track multiple versions of a design nor is there a straightforward way to interface the workbench with external configuration management tools.

The problems of integrating CASE workbenches with a configuration management system are a result of their closed nature and the tight integration around a defined data structure. As a standard for CASE information is developed and published, it will be possible to interface other tools to workbenches. This means that CASE workbenches will become open rather than closed environments. They will evolve into software engineering environments.

18.3   Software engineering environments

Software engineering environments (SEEs) are natural developments of programming environments such as UNIX. An SEE might be defined as follows:

> An SEE is a collection of hardware and software tools which can act in combination in an integrated way. The environment should support all software processes from initial specification through to testing and system delivery. In addition, the environment should support the configuration management of all of the products of the software process.

The key points in this definition are:

(1)   The environment facilities are integrated. We identified three types of integration, namely data integration, interface integration and activity integration, in Chapter 17. Current environments support data integration and interface integration but activity integration is still a research topic.

(2)   All products may be subjected to configuration management. The most expensive activity in managing long-lifetime systems is ensuring that, for all versions of the system, all of the documents associated with a version (specifications, design, code, user documentation, and so on) are complete and consistent. Configuration management is covered in Chapter 29.

(3)   Facilities are available to support all software development activities. Thus, the tools available in an SEE should support specification, design, documentation, programming, testing, debugging, and so on.

Two types of software engineering environment are identified in Figure 18.1. Language-oriented environments are environments for systems development in a single programming language. Examples of such environments are the Cedar environment (Teitleman, 1984) and Rational's Ada environment (Archer and Devlin, 1986). The Rational environment is an instance of an Ada programming support environment (APSE), a concept first suggested by Buxton (1980).

Integrated project support environments (IPSEs) are 'open' environments which may be tailored to support development in a number of different programming languages using different design methods. Examples of IPSEs include ISTAR (Dowson, 1987), ECLIPSE (Bott, 1989) and the Arcadia environment (Taylor *et al.*, 1988).

The advantages of using a software engineering environment to support the development process are:

(1)   All tools are interfaced to an object management system (OMS). The output of any tool can be an input to any other tool. Tool interactions are usually predictable but there are many cases of serendipitous tool combinations. The OMS allows these combinations to occur when required. Recall, one of the problems with CASE workbenches is the problem of exchanging information with other tools.

(2)   The use of an OMS allows fine-grain (small) objects to be recorded, named and subjected to configuration control. This means that the structure of the storage system can reflect the structure of the software system.

(3)   It becomes possible to build more powerful software tools because these tools can make use of the relationships recorded in the OMS.

(4)   The documents produced in the course of a project from feasibility studies to fault reports can be managed by the configuration management tools which are an integral part of the environment. The OMS facilities allow relationships between documents to be recorded so that designs (say) can be linked to their associated code and changes tracked automatically.

(5) If the environment is properly integrated, all of the support tools will have a consistent user interface. Users find it straightforward to learn to use new tools.

(6) Project management has direct access to project information and management tools can use actual data collected during the course of a project.

Given these advantages, the introduction and use of a software engineering environment ought to have a significant effect on total life cycle costs. However, the start-up costs of introducing an SEE are greater than those of introducing a programming environment or a CASE workbench. Programming environments and CASE workbenches have been commercially successful and are widely used; SEE products have been generally less successful although they are used in specialist applications such as aerospace software development.

18.3.1 The environment toolset

The environment toolset should be tailored to an application domain and the development paradigm used in that domain. Although some facilities, such as object management, are required by all classes of system, other tools are domain-specific. It is impractical for all tools for all domains to be provided in an integrated environment.

There are three types of tool found in SEEs, as shown in Figure 18.8.

(1) *Integrated tools*   Tools which have been built or modified by the SEE developers so that they can make intimate use of the facilities provided by the OMS.

(2) *Imported tools*   These are less tightly integrated with the OMS. They communicate with the SEE via the public tools interface (PTI). Such tools may communicate using system objects but will generally not be able to make use of inbuilt information about objects in the same way as integrated tools.

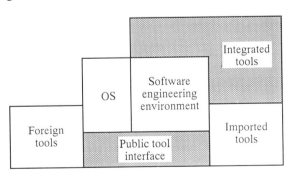

Figure 18.8
Tool integration with a software engineering environment.

(3) *Foreign tools* These are tools which do not integrate with the OMS but which interface directly to the underlying operating system. In order for SEEs to be viable, they must support an upgrade path from existing toolkit machines so that users can continue to use familiar file-based tools when an SEE is introduced. Thus most environments support file-based tools and, in particular, support the tools provided with UNIX.

As well as the tools populating a programming environment as discussed in Section 18.1, most SEEs will provide the following types of tool:

(1) *Method support tools* These are comparable to those incorporated in CASE workbenches and provide graphical editing and checking facilities. As SEEs are particularly suitable for supporting long-lifetime, embedded systems, a real-time method such as MASCOT (Simpson, 1986) or the Ward–Mellor extensions to the Yourdon method (Ward and Mellor, 1985) might be included.

(2) *Document preparation systems* These support the writing of documentation on the same machine as program development. These tools simplify producing and updating the documentation associated with the system under development.

(3) *Project management tools* These software tools allow estimates of the time required for a project and the cost of that project to be made. Furthermore, they may provide facilities for generating management reports on the status of a project at any time.

The term 'project support environment' implies that a range of tools is available to support all of the activities which are involved in the software process. In practice, given our current understanding of that process, it is unlikely that such a range of tools will be available. Although programming tools such as compilers, debuggers and program analysers are well developed, tools to support activities such as requirements analysis, design transformation and program maintenance are still immature and may not be included in an SEE.

18.4 The SDE life cycle

The introduction and use of an SDE requires careful planning. SDEs are expensive and their lifetime is comparable to that of the software developed using the environment. Unless adequate resources are devoted to environment procurement and support, it is unlikely that the benefits of using an

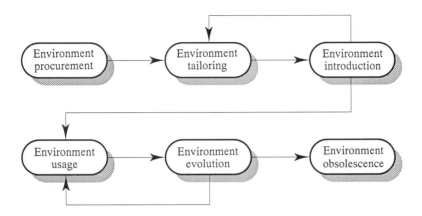

Figure 18.9
The SDE life cycle.

environment will be achieved. If wrong decisions regarding the environment are made, software costs may increase rather than decrease when it is put into use.

There are several stages which can be identified in the use of an environment (Figure 18.9).

The stages of the life cycle are:

(1) *Environment procurement* This involves choosing an appropriate environment for the type of software being developed.

(2) *Environment tailoring* This phase involves adapting an environment to a particular set of organizational requirements.

(3) *Environment introduction* This phase introduces the environment and ensures that software engineers are adequately trained in its use.

(4) *Environment usage* This is the phase where the environment is in everyday use for software development.

(5) *Environment evolution* Evolution is not really a separate phase but is a continuing activity throughout the life of the environment. It involves modifying the hardware or software to adapt the environment to new requirements.

(6) *Environment obsolescence* During this phase the environment is taken out of use. Most of the work involves ensuring that software developed using the environment can still be supported by the organization.

There is obviously feedback from the introduction phase to the tailoring phase as tailoring problems are discovered. There is also a feedback loop between evolution and usage.

Management must adopt a sensitive approach when introducing an SDE in order to convince engineers of its usefulness. The cost advantages of environments are long-term rather than the short-term and immediate cost savings should not be expected. Attempting to introduce an environment without an understanding of the concerns of the software developer may lead to an exodus of the workforce.

18.4.1 Environment procurement

Hundreds of different software development environments are now available. The majority of these are CASE workbenches, most of which seem, superficially at least, to be similar. However, all of the other types of environment discussed above are also available as products.

The factors which must be taken into account when procuring an environment are:

(1) *Existing company standards and methods* The environment should support existing practices rather than introduce new standards and methods which are likely to be resisted by users.

(2) *Existing hardware and future hardware developments* It may be sensible to procure an environment which runs on existing computers. However, if the current hardware is heavily used, there may not be spare capacity for further software systems. Environments have a long lifetime so it is generally unwise to procure a system which does not run on industry-standard computers.

(3) *The class of applications to be developed* Clearly, an environment should be chosen which provides facilities for developing the type of applications required by an organization. There is no point in investing in a CASE workbench intended for commercial systems development if the major systems development activity is in scientific Fortran programs.

(4) *Security* Some classes of system development require that the software and its associated documentation is classified. The environment must provide appropriate security features so that the security manager can specify access permissions in the environment. Most CASE workbenches are not particularly secure.

Another factor is, obviously, the cost of the environment. It has been estimated that an effective environment can offer productivity improvements in the range 40%–100% for large systems but can require capital expenditure up to $15 000 per person. To this must be added the cost of maintaining and evolving the environment. An organization must decide whether the significant capital expenditure involved might result in better savings if invested elsewhere.

18.4.2 Environment tailoring

Environments are general-purpose software systems and they must be adapted to particular organizational requirements. The activities required to customize an environment for a particular organization and application domain are:

(1) *Environment installation* The environment must be installed and tested on the organization's hardware configuration. This may involve changing system-dependent environment parameters.

(2) *Process model definition* The purpose of an environment is to support a particular development process and tailoring an environment depends on an explicit model of the process. It may not be possible to embed this model in the environment but making the model explicit provides a framework for environment tailoring.

(3) *Schema definition*   If the environment is based on a shared OMS, the schema must be defined and validated. This involves identifying all of the entities and relationships which are important in an organization's software development process. Getting the schema right is a key factor in environmental success and this stage is likely to take several months of development.

(4) *Tool population* The environment will obviously include many standard tools but it may be necessary to introduce other tools required for a particular software development process.

(5) *Documentation* As part of the tailoring process, the particular instantiation of the environment must be documented.

The time required for environment tailoring and the costs involved should not be underestimated. Tailoring an environment will always take several months; it may take more than a year before an effective system is available.

18.4.3 Environment introduction and usage

Introducing an environment into an organization inevitably means changing working practices. The full benefit from using the environment will not be gained until it has been in use for some time. There are predictable difficulties which are likely to arise but there will probably also be unanticipated problems. Resources must be available for tackling these problems.

Some of the problems which may arise when an SEE is introduced are:

(1)   *User resistance*   With few exceptions, humans are innately conservative and tend to resist new developments unless they have obvious advantages. Environments have advantages for management as they provide more control over the software process. The advantages for the individual software developer are less obvious. It may be argued that SDEs are prescriptive and constrain the creativity of individual engineers.

(2)   *Lack of training*   Some engineers may feel that new developments are inherently difficult and that they cannot understand some of the environment facilities. This is most likely to be a problem with staff who have little formal training in software engineering. The pace of change in software development has been such that they may just have adapted to working with some new operating system and they may be reluctant to spend time learning another new system.

(3)   *Management resistance*   Some managers may be resistant to introducing an environment into a known development process. Managers are responsible for cost control but the cost advantages of introducing an SDE are unquantifiable. Using an unknown support environment increases the risk associated with a project.

These objections to an environment are valid. However, a properly designed environment should provide tools to assist with the tedious chores which are part of software development (such as redrawing design diagrams, finding associated code and documentation, and so on). Individual engineers should have more time for the creative and fulfilling parts of their job. Environments need not deskill the software engineering process.

Training is the answer to the second objection. An adequate training budget must be available and the move to environment-based development should be incremental. Rather than move all projects at one time, the environment should be introduced in conjunction with existing support systems. As new projects are started, they should make use of environmental support and the costs should be carefully measured. These figures can then be used to convince management of the value of that environment.

After the introductory pilot projects, the environment may be made available to all new projects. Initially, it is probably unwise to demand its use but as experience develops in the practical value of the environment, its use may be made mandatory.

When an environment has been introduced, projects which started before the introduction of the environment will not be supported. Ideally, their support should be migrated to the environment but, because of the volume of data associated with a project, this is usually unrealistic.

18.4.4 Environment evolution

Like all software systems, environments cannot remain static if they are to remain useful. They must be evolved as new requirements become apparent and as new hardware and software platforms become available. The lifetime of an environment is comparable to the lifetime of the systems developed using that environment.

One of the problems of environment evolution is that new and old versions of the environment may not be compatible. This incompatibility may be due to hardware or software changes and it may require several versions of the environment to be concurrently used in an organization. If the incompatibilities are due to hardware changes, this may mean that old hardware has to be maintained to support the software systems.

18.4.5 Environment obsolescence

At some stage in an environment's lifetime, a decision may be made to replace that environment. This may be forced on the organization because of the lack of support provided by the environment vendor or because of other decisions to change hardware and software platforms. Alternatively, it may be decided that other environments offer a more suitable framework for that particular organization and that these should replace the environment which is in use.

Environments should not simply be scrapped and subsequently replaced by some other system. Rather, a transition period, which may be several years, should be planned where the new and the old systems are both in use. During this transition period, software which was developed using the old system and whose maintenance must continue must be moved to the new environment.

The scale of this problem depends on the amount of software to be moved and the facilities offered by the old and new systems. Often, the decision to make an environment obsolete is taken at the same time as the decision to make the software systems it supports obsolete. The environment is therefore redundant and there are no significant costs involved in scrapping the system.

■ KEY POINTS

- Programming environments support program development, testing and debugging. They may be general-purpose environments or may be tailored to support the development of programs in a specific programming language.

■ CASE workbenches are oriented towards the support of the earlier stages of the life cycle and incorporate powerful diagramming and report generation facilities.

■ The principal disadvantage of CASE workbenches is that they are not integrated with other software tools such as programming tools and configuration management systems.

■ A software engineering environment is integrated around an object management system and offers support for all software process activities. All products of the software process may be placed under configuration management.

■ The tool population of an environment depends on the type of development that the environment is intended to support. Given current technology, it is not possible to support all process activities.

■ The environment life cycle has six stages, namely procurement, tailoring, introduction, usage, evolution and obsolescence.

■ Introducing a support environment is expensive. Its benefits are long-term rather than short-term. Some users are wary of environments because they believe that environmental support deskills the activity of software engineering.

FURTHER READING

'Software development environments'. This is a survey article which discusses the different kinds of software engineering environments. In fact, the journal in which it appears is a special issue on environments, and other papers are also valuable as background to this chapter. (S.A. Dart, R.J. Ellison, P.H. Feiler and A.N. Habermann, *IEEE Computer*, **20** (11), 1987.)

IEEE Software, **5** (2), March 1988. This is a special issue of this journal which is concerned with CASE tools. It does not simply discuss current systems but also includes articles on research projects investigating advanced CASE tool facilities.

Software Development Environments and CASE Technology. This book is the proceedings of a European symposium. However, the papers are general rather than specialized and it presents a good description of the state of the art in SDEs. (A. Endres and H. Weber (eds), 1991, Springer-Verlag.)

EXERCISES

18.1 Describe why UNIX is not a software engineering environment according to the definition here.

18.2 Explain the differences between an interpretative environment and a structure-oriented programming environment. Why are interpretative environments mostly used to support programming languages which are not imperative languages?

18.3 If you have access to a CASE workbench, explore its capabilities and list the process activities which it supports.

18.4 Outline the structure of a software engineering environment and describe the role of the components in that structure.

18.5 Suggest tools which should be included in a software engineering environment to support the development of (a) software engineering environments and (b) transaction processing systems.

18.6 Explain why it is important that tools in an environment offer a consistent user interface.

18.7 What support tools might be included in an Ada support environment?

18.8 Explain why the initial costs of introducing a software engineering environment are high.

18.9 Study the literature and draw up an outline of the facilities which might be included in the next generation of project support environments.

Part Four
Software Validation

■ This section is concerned with various aspects of software verification and validation. After a general introduction to this topic in Chapter 19, Chapters 20 and 21 discuss the problems of assessing and quantifying the reliability of a system and assuring the safety of software systems in critical applications. Chapter 22 describes specific techniques for defect testing. Chapter 23 supplements this with a discussion of the various types of software tool which can be used to support the testing process. Finally, Chapter 24 is concerned with static software verification and describes program inspections using formal correctness arguments and cleanroom software development.

■ CONTENTS

Verification and Validation

19

■ OBJECTIVES

The objectives of this chapter are to provide an overview of the processes of verification and validation and to introduce testing as a means of system validation. Testing is a multi-stage process and these stages are discussed in the first part of the chapter. Test planning and scheduling is covered and an outline structure for test plans is suggested. In the final section of the chapter, various testing strategies including top-down testing, bottom-up testing, thread-testing and stress testing are described.

■ CONTENTS

The verification and validation of a software system is a continuing process through each stage of the software process. Verification and validation (V & V) is the generic term for checking processes which ensure that the software meets its requirements and that the requirements meet the needs of the software procurer.

V & V is a whole-life cycle process. It starts with requirements reviews and continues through regular and structured reviews to product testing. The V & V process has two objectives:

(1) The discovery of defects in the system.
(2) The assessment of whether or not the system is usable in an operational situation.

The important difference between verification and validation is succinctly summarized by Boehm (1979):

- Validation: Are we building the right product?
- Verification: Are we building the product right?

Verification involves checking that the program conforms to its specification. Validation involves checking that the program as implemented meets the expectations of the software procurer. Requirements validation techniques, such as prototyping, help in this respect but sometimes flaws and deficiencies in the requirements can only be discovered when the system implementation is complete.

To satisfy the objectives of the V & V process, both static and dynamic techniques of system checking and analysis may be used. Static techniques are concerned with the analysis of the system representations such as the requirements, design and program listing. They are applied at all stages of the process through structured reviews. Dynamic techniques or tests involve exercising an implementation. Dynamic techniques are discussed in this chapter and in Chapter 22. Static verification techniques are covered in Chapter 24. Testing tools are covered in Chapter 23.

Figure 19.1 shows the role of static and dynamic techniques in the software process.

Static techniques include program inspections, analysis and formal verification. Some purists have suggested that these techniques should completely replace dynamic techniques in the V & V process. This is nonsense. Static techniques can only check the correspondence between a program and its specification (verification); they cannot demonstrate that the software is operationally useful.

Although static verification techniques are becoming more widely used, program testing is still the predominant V & V technique. Testing is normally carried out during implementation and also, in a different form,

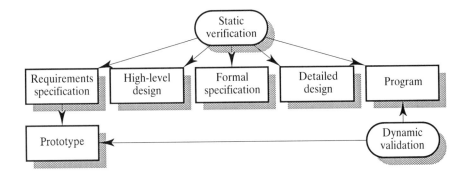

Figure 19.1
Static and dynamic verification and validation.

when implementation is complete. Testing involves exercising the program using data like the real data processed by the program. The existence of program defects or inadequacies is inferred from any output anomalies.

To meet the dual objectives of the V & V process, there are two kinds of testing:

(1)   *Statistical testing*   Tests are designed to reflect the frequency of actual user inputs and after running the tests, an estimate of the operational reliability of the system can be made. This is covered in Chapter 20.

(2)   *Defect testing*   Tests are designed to reveal the presence of defects in the system. Defect testing is the topic of Chapter 22.

Program testing can only demonstrate the presence of defects in a program, it cannot demonstrate that the program is error-free. Undetected defects can still exist even after the most comprehensive testing. Following Myers (1979) therefore, I define a successful defect test as one which reveals the presence of defects in the software being tested.

This differs from the frequently used notion of a successful defect test which is a test displaying no output anomalies. The alternative definition is appealing in some ways (statements such as 'the system has passed all its tests' are seductive) but it can lead to complacency. If the test suite for a program does not detect defects, this simply means that the tests chosen have not exercised the system so that defects are revealed. It does not mean that program defects do not exist.

Defect testing and debugging are sometimes considered to be parts of the same process. In fact, they are quite different. Testing establishes the existence of defects. Debugging is concerned with locating and correcting these defects.

There are various stages in the debugging process (Figure 19.2). Defects in the code must be located and the program must be modified to meet its requirements. Testing must then be repeated to ensure that the change has been carried out correctly.

Figure 19.2
The debugging process.

The debugger must generate hypotheses about the observable behaviour of the program then test these hypotheses in the hope of finding the error in the system. Testing the hypotheses may involve tracing the program code manually or may require new test cases to localize the problem.

It is impossible to present a set of instructions for program debugging. The skilled debugger looks for patterns in the test output where the defect is exhibited and uses knowledge of the defect, the pattern and the programming process to locate the defect. Process knowledge is important. Debuggers know of common programmer errors (such as failing to increment a counter) and match these against the observed patterns.

After a defect in the program has been discovered, it must be corrected. This may involve the redesign of parts of the program and, consequently the whole system may have to be re-tested. Because of the costs associated with re-testing, design reviews and static validation before coding commences are cost-effective defect discovery techniques as they find defects without incurring additional costs.

19.1 The testing process

Except for small computer programs, systems should not be tested as a single, monolithic unit. Large systems are built out of sub-systems, which are built out of modules, which are composed of procedures and functions. The testing process should therefore proceed in stages where testing is carried out incrementally in conjunction with system implementation.

The testing process may consist of five stages (Figure 19.3):

(1) *Unit testing* Individual components are tested to ensure that they operate correctly. Unit testing treats each component as a stand-alone entity which does not need other components during the testing process.

(2) *Module testing* A module is a collection of dependent components such as an object or some looser collection of procedures and functions. A module encapsulates related components so can be tested without other system modules.

(3) *Sub-system testing* This phase involves testing collections of modules which have been integrated into sub-systems. Sub-systems may be independently designed and implemented, and the most common

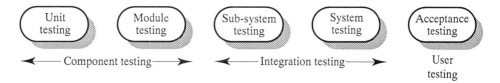

Figure 19.3
Stages of testing.

problems which arise in large software systems are sub-system interface mismatches. The sub-system test process should concentrate on the detection of interface errors by rigorously exercising these interfaces.

(4)   *System testing*   The sub-systems are integrated to make up the entire system. The testing process is concerned with finding errors which normally result from unanticipated interactions between sub-systems and components. It is also concerned with validating that the system meets its functional and non-functional requirements.

(5)   *Acceptance testing*   This is the final stage in the testing process before the system is accepted for operational use. It involves testing the system with data supplied by the system procurer rather than simulated data developed as part of the testing process. Acceptance testing often reveals errors and omissions in the system requirements definition. The requirements may not reflect the actual facilities and performance required by the user and testing may demonstrate that the system does not exhibit the anticipated performance and functionality.

Acceptance testing is sometimes called *alpha testing*. For bespoke systems (systems developed specially for a single client), the alpha testing process continues until the system developer and the system procurer reach agreement that the delivered system is an acceptable representation of the system requirements.

When a system is to be marketed as a software product, a testing process called *beta testing* is often used. Beta testing involves delivering a system to a number of potential customers who agree to use that system and to report problems to the system developers. This exposes the product to real use and detects errors which may not have been anticipated by the system builders. After this feedback, the system is modified and either released for further beta testing or for general sale.

In general, the sequence of testing activities is component testing, integration testing then acceptance testing. However, as defects are discovered at any one stage, they require program modifications to correct them and this may require other stages in the testing process to be repeated (Figure 19.4). Errors in program components, say, may come to light at a later stage of the testing process. The process is therefore an iterative one

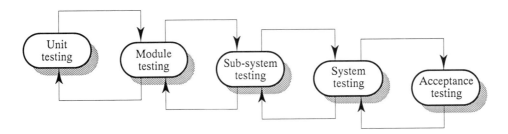

with information being fed back from later stages to earlier parts of the process.

Repairing program defects may introduce new defects so testing should be repeated after the system is modified. This is sometimes called *regression testing*. In principle, all tests should be repeated after every defect repair; in practice this is too expensive. As part of the test plan, dependencies between parts of the system should be identified and a subset of the entire test data set should be used to check that the repair of a component has not corrupted other parts of the system.

19.2 Test planning

System testing is expensive. For some large systems such as real-time systems with complex timing constraints, testing may consume about half of the overall development costs. Thus, careful planning is necessary to get the most out of testing and to control testing costs.

Test planning is concerned with setting out standards for the testing process rather than describing product tests. The major components of a test plan are shown in Figure 19.5.

The test plan should include significant amounts of contingency so that slippages in design and implementation can be accommodated and staff allocated to testing can be deployed in other activities. A good description of test plans and their relation to more general quality plans is given in Frewin and Hatton (1986).

Test plans are not just management documents. They are also intended for software engineers involved in designing and carrying out system tests. They allow technical staff to get an overall picture of the system tests and to place their own work in this context. Test plans provide information to staff responsible for ensuring that appropriate hardware and software resources are available to the testing team.

Like other plans, the test plan is not a static document. It should be revised regularly as testing is an activity which is dependent on implementa-

The testing process
A description of the major phases of the testing process. These might be as
described earlier in this chapter.

Requirements traceability
Users are most interested in the system meeting its requirements and testing
should be planned so that all requirements are individually tested.

Tested items
The products of the software process which are to be tested should be specified

Testing schedule
An overall testing schedule and resource allocation for this schedule. This,
obviously, is linked to the more general project development schedule.

Test recording procedures
It is not enough simply to run tests. The results of the tests must be systematically
recorded. It must be possible to audit the testing process to check that it has been
carried out correctly.

Hardware and software requirements
This section should set out software tools required and estimated hardware
utilization.

Constraints
Constraints affecting the testing process such as staff shortages should be
anticipated in this section.

Figure 19.5
Test plan contents.

tion being complete. If only a single part of a system is incomplete, the
system testing process cannot begin.

The preparation of the test plan should begin when the system
requirements are formulated and it should be developed in detail as the
software is designed. Figure 19.6 shows the relationships between test plans
and the software process.

Figure 19.6
Test plan components.

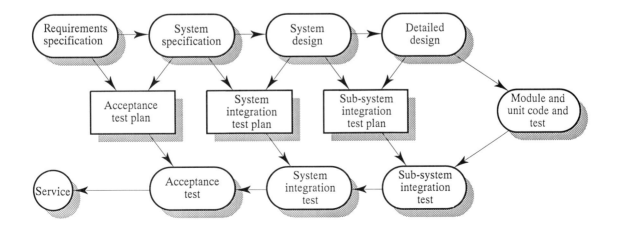

Unit testing and module testing may be the responsibility of the programmers developing the component. Programmers make up their own test data and incrementally test the code as it is developed. This is an economically sensible approach as the programmer knows the component best and is most able to generate test data. Unit testing is part of the implementation process and it is expected that a component conforming to its specification will be delivered as part of that process.

As it is a natural human trait for individuals to feel an affinity with objects they have constructed, programmers responsible for system implementation may feel that testing threatens their creations. Psychologically, programmers do not usually want to 'destroy' their work. Consciously or subconsciously, tests may be selected which will not demonstrate the presence of system defects.

If unit testing is left to the component implementor, it should be subject to some monitoring procedure to ensure that the components have been properly tested. Some of the components should be re-tested by an independent tester using a different set of test cases. If independent testing and programmer testing come to the same conclusions, it may be assumed that the programmer's testing methods are adequate.

Later stages of testing involve integrating work from a number of programmers and must be planned in advance. They should be undertaken by an independent team of testers. Module and sub-system testing should be planned as the design of the sub-system is formulated. Integration tests should be developed in conjunction with the system design. Acceptance tests should be designed with the program specification and may be written into the contract for the system development.

19.3   Testing strategies

There are various testing strategies which can be adopted. Each strategy has its own advantages and disadvantages and is discussed in a separate section below. Large systems are usually tested using a mixture of testing strategies. Different techniques may be used for different parts of the system and at different stages in the testing process. The techniques adopted should depend on the organization, the application and the engineers working on a project.

Testing strategies include:

(1)   Top-down testing.
(2)   Bottom-up testing.
(3)   Thread testing.
(4)   Stress testing.

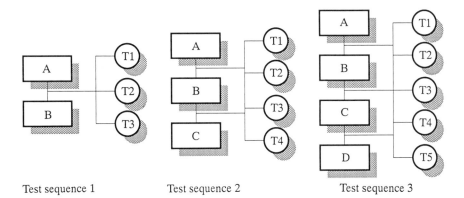

Test sequence 1   Test sequence 2   Test sequence 3

Figure 19.7
Incremental testing.

Whatever testing strategy is adopted, it is always sensible to adopt an incremental approach to sub-system and system testing (Figure 19.7). Rather than take all modules, combine them then start testing, the system should be built in increments. Each increment should be tested before the next increment is added to the system.

In the example shown in Figure 19.7, tests T1, T2 and T3 are first run on the system composed of Module A and Module B. Module C is integrated and the tests repeated with test T4 added. Finally, module D is integrated and tested. As new modules are added, new tests may have to be added to the test set.

The process should continue until all modules have been integrated into a complete system. When a module is introduced at some stage in this process, tests, which were previously unsuccessful, may now detect defects. These defects are probably due to the introduction of the new module. The source of the problem is localized, thus simplifying defect location and repair.

19.3.1 Top-down testing

Top-down testing involves starting at the sub-system level with modules represented by stubs. Stubs are simple components which have the same interface as the module. After sub-system testing is complete, each module is tested in the same way. The functions are represented by stubs. Finally, the program components are replaced by the actual code and this is tested (Figure 19.8).

Top-down testing should be used with top-down program development so that a module is tested as soon as it is coded. Coding and testing are a single activity with no separate component or module testing phase.

If top-down testing is used, unnoticed design errors may be detected at an early stage in the testing process. As these errors are usually structural errors, early detection means that they can be corrected without undue costs. Early error detection means that extensive redesign and re-implementation may be avoided.

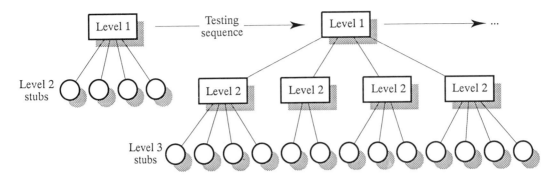

Figure 19.8
Top-down testing.

Top-down testing has the further advantage that a limited, working system is available at an early stage in the development. This is an important psychological boost to those involved in the system development, and it demonstrates the feasibility of the system to management. Validation, as distinct from verification, can begin early in the testing process as a demonstrable system can be made available to users.

Strict top-down testing is difficult to implement because of the requirement that program stubs, simulating lower levels of the system, must be produced. The mechanism for implementing these program stubs involves either producing a very simplified version of the component required, returning some random value of the correct type or interacting with the tester who inputs an appropriate value or simulates the action of the component.

If the component is a complex one, it may be impractical to produce a program stub which simulates it accurately. Consider a function which relies on the conversion of an array of objects into a linked list. Computing its result involves internal program objects, the pointers linking elements in the list. It is unrealistic to generate a random list and return that object. The list components must correspond to the array elements. It is equally unrealistic for the programmer to input the created list as this requires knowledge of the internal pointer representation. Therefore, the routine to perform the conversion from array to list must exist before top-down testing is possible.

Another disadvantage of top-down testing is that test output may be difficult to observe. In many systems, the higher levels of that system do not generate output but, to test these levels, they must be forced to do so. The tester must create an artificial environment to generate the test results.

19.3.2 Bottom-up testing

Bottom-up testing is the converse of top-down testing. It involves testing the modules at the lower levels in the hierarchy, and then working up the hierarchy of modules until the final module is tested (Figure 19.9). The advantages of bottom-up testing are the disadvantages of top-down testing and vice versa.

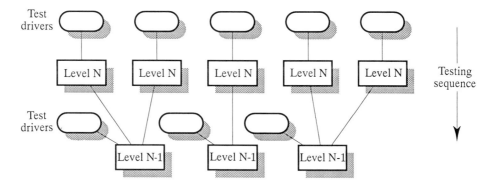

Figure 19.9
Bottom-up testing.

When using bottom-up testing, test drivers must be written to exercise the lower level components. These test drivers simulate the components' environment and are valuable components in their own right. If the components being tested are reusable components, the test drivers should be distributed along with them so that potential reusers can experiment with the components.

If top-down development is combined with bottom-up testing, all parts of the system must be implemented before testing can begin. Architectural faults will not be discovered until much of the system has been tested. Correction of these faults might involve the re-writing and consequent retesting of lower level modules in the system.

Because of this problem, bottom-up testing was criticized by the proponents of top-down development in the 1970s. However, a strict top-down development process including testing is an impractical approach, particularly if existing software components are to be reused. Bottom-up testing of critical, low-level system components is always necessary.

19.3.3 Thread testing

Real-time systems are usually made up of a number of cooperating processes and may be interrupt driven. An external event, such as an input from a sensor, causes control to be transferred from the currently executing process to the process which handles that event.

Real-time systems are difficult to test because of the subtle, time-dependent interactions between the processes in the system. Time dependent defects may only cause system failures when the processes are each in a particular state.

Consider the real-time system made up of five processes shown in Figure 19.10. These processes interact with each other and some of them collect inputs from their environment and generate outputs to that environment. These inputs may be from sensors, keyboards or from some other computer system. Similarly, outputs may be to control lines, other computers or user terminals.

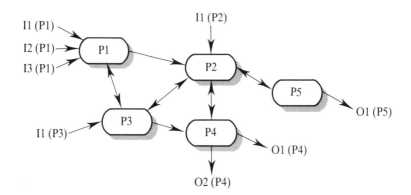

Figure 19.10
Real-time process
interactions.

The first stage in the testing process is to test each process individually. In the system model shown in Figure 19.10, therefore, P1, P2, P3, P4 and P5 should first be tested in isolation and debugged until each process appears to meet its specification. Top-down and bottom-up strategies may be used.

Thread testing is a testing strategy which follows individual process testing. The processing of each external event 'threads' its way through the system processes. Thread testing involves identifying and executing each possible processing 'thread'. Of course, complete thread testing may be impossible because of the number of possible input and output combinations. In such cases, the most commonly exercised threads should be identified and selected for testing.

A possible thread is shown in Figure 19.11 where an input is transformed by a number of processes in turn to produce an output.

After each thread has been tested with a single event, the processing of multiple events of the same class may be tested without events of any other class. For example, a multi-user system, might first be tested using a single terminal then multiple terminal testing gradually introduced. In the above model, this type of testing might involve processing all inputs in multiple-input processes. Figure 19.12 illustrates an example of this process where three inputs to the same process are used as test data.

After the system's reaction to each class of event has been tested, it can then be tested for its reactions to more than one class of simultaneous event. At this stage, new event tests should be introduced gradually so that system errors can be localized. In the above model, this might be tested as shown in Figure 19.13.

Figure 19.11
Single thread testing.

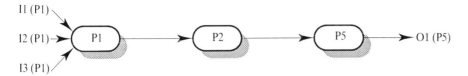

Figure 19.12
Multiple input thread
testing.

19.3.4   Stress testing

Some classes of system are designed to handle a specified load. For example, a bank transaction processing system may be designed to process up to 100 transactions per second; an operating system may be designed to handle up to 200 separate terminals. Tests have to be designed to ensure that the system can process its intended load. This usually involves planning a series of tests where the load is steadily increased.

Stress testing continues these tests beyond the maximum design load of the system. The loading is steadily increased until the system fails. This type of testing has a dual function:

(1)   It tests the failure behaviour of the system. Circumstances may arise through an unexpected combination of events where the load placed on the system exceeds the maximum anticipated load. In these circumstances, it is important that system failure should be 'soft' rather than 'hard'. Stress testing checks that overloading the system does not cause unacceptable loss of data or user service.

(2)   It stresses the system and may cause defects to come to light which would not normally manifest themselves. Although it can be argued that these defects are unlikely to cause system failures in normal usage, there may be unusual combinations of normal circumstances which the stress testing replicates.

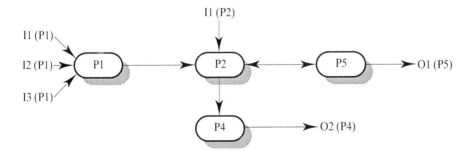

Figure 19.13
Multiple thread testing.

Stress testing is particularly relevant to distributed systems based on a network of processors. These systems often exhibit severe degradation when they are heavily loaded as the network becomes swamped with operating system calls.

■ KEY POINTS

- ■ Verification and validation are not the same thing. Verification is intended to show that a program meets its specification. Validation is intended to show that the program does what the user wants it to do.

- ■ Testing has a dual function; it is used to establish the presence of defects in a program and it is used to estimate whether or not the program is operationally usable.

- ■ Testing can only demonstrate the presence of errors. It cannot prove their absence.

- ■ The testing process involves unit testing, module testing, sub-system testing, integration testing and acceptance testing.

- ■ Testing should be scheduled as part of the project planning process. Adequate resources must be made available for testing.

- ■ Testing strategies which may be adopted include top-down testing, bottom-up testing, thread testing of real-time systems and stress testing.

FURTHER READING

The Art of Software Testing. This is now a relatively old book on the subject but it includes good advice on testing which has not become out-of-date. It is also appropriate reading for the other chapters in this section. (G.J. Myers, 1979, John Wiley & Sons.)

IEEE Software, **6** (3), May 1989. This special issue has several articles concerned with verification and validation. These present a good overview of the topic and its relevance in the software process. Both testing and static verification techniques are covered in separate articles.

Comm. ACM, **31** (6), June 1988. This special issue includes several papers on testing. The introduction by Hamlet and the paper by Gelperin and Hetzel are good background reading for the material in this chapter.

EXERCISES

19.1 Discuss the differences between verification and validation and explain why validation is a particularly difficult process.

19.2 Suggest alternative models of the testing process which might be used when a system is (a) to be built from reusable components and (b) to be built as a support tool and not part of a software product.

19.3 What is the distinction between alpha and beta testing? Explain why these forms of testing are particularly valuable.

19.4 Using a program which you have written, devise top-down and bottom-up testing strategies for it.

19.5 Draw up a testing schedule and estimate the resources required to implement that schedule for the newspaper delivery system described in Exercise 3.7.

19.6 Explain how you would go about stress testing the newspaper delivery system described in Exercise 3.7.

19.7 Describe four classes of system encountered in everyday life which might be subjected to stress testing.

19.8 Write a report for non-technical management explaining the problems of verifying and validating real-time systems.

Software Reliability

20

■ OBJECTIVES

The objectives of this chapter are to define, both qualitatively and quantitatively, what software reliability means and to discuss techniques for assessing the reliability of a software system. After a general, qualitative discussion on the nature of reliability, a number of reliability metrics are introduced. The use of these metrics in quantitative reliability specification is illustrated. Reliability achievement is assessed using statistical testing, which relies on test data conforming to the expected software usage. Finally, reliability growth models are discussed. These are used to predict when a required level of reliability will be reached.

■ CONTENTS

As computer applications become more diverse and pervade almost every area of everyday life, it is increasingly apparent that the most important dynamic characteristic of software is its reliability. Informally, the reliability of a software system is a measure of how well it provides the services expected of it by its users but a useful formal definition of reliability is much harder to express. Software reliability metrics such as 'mean time between failures' may be used but they do not take into account the subjective nature of software failures; the informal intuitive meaning is often more appropriate and useful.

Users do not consider all services to be of equal importance and a system might be viewed as unreliable if it ever failed to provide some critical service. For example, say a system was used to control braking on an aircraft but failed to work under a single set of very rare conditions. If the aircraft crashed because these failure conditions occurred, pilots of similar aircraft would (reasonably) regard the software as unreliable.

On the other hand, say a comparable software system provided some visual indication of its actions to the pilot. Assume this failed once per month in a predictable way without the main system function being affected and other indicators showed that the controlled system was working normally. In spite of frequent failure, pilots would not consider that software as unreliable as the system which caused the catastrophic failure.

Reliability is a dynamic system characteristic which is a function of the number of software failures. A software *failure* is an execution event where the software behaves in an unexpected way. This is not the same as a software *fault*, which is a static program characteristic. Software faults cause software failures when the faulty code is executed with a particular set of inputs. Faults do not always manifest themselves as failures so the reliability depends on how the software is used. It is not possible to produce a single, universal statement of the software reliability.

Software faults are not just program defects. Unexpected behaviour can occur in circumstances where the software conforms to its requirements but the requirements themselves are incomplete. Omissions in software documentation can also lead to unexpected behaviour although the software may not contain defects.

There is a complex relationship between observed system reliability and the number of latent software faults. Mills *et al.* (1987) point out that not all software faults have an equal probability of manifestation. Removing software faults from parts of the system which are rarely used makes little difference to the perceived reliability. Their work suggested that, for the products studied, removing 60% of product defects would lead to only a 3% improvement in reliability.

This is illustrated in Figure 20.1, derived from Littlewood (1990), which shows a software system as a mapping of an input to an output set. A program has many possible inputs (for simplicity, combinations and sequences of inputs are considered as a single input). The program responds

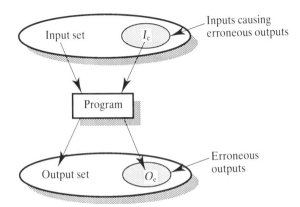

Figure 20.1
A system as an input/output mapping.

to these inputs by producing an output or a set of outputs. Some of these inputs (shown in the shaded ellipse in Figure 20.1) cause system failures where erroneous outputs are generated by the program. The product reliability is related to the probability that, in a particular execution of the program, the input to the system will be a member of the set of inputs which causes an erroneous output.

It is probable that there will be a small number of members of I_e which are much more likely to be selected than others. The reliability of the program is therefore related to that probability rather than the mean probability of selecting an erroneous input. In a study of errors in IBM software products, Adams (1984) noted that many defects in the products were only likely to result in failures after hundreds or thousands of months of usage.

Reliability depends on how the software is used so it cannot be specified absolutely. Each user uses a program in different ways so faults which affect the reliability of the system for one user may never manifest themselves under a different mode of working (Figure 20.2). Reliability can only be accurately specified if the normal software operational profile (see Section 20.3) is also specified.

As reliability is related to the probability of an error occurring in operational use, a program may contain known faults but may still be seen as reliable by its users. They may use the system in such a way that they never select an erroneous input; the program always appears to be reliable. Furthermore, experienced users may 'work around' known software faults and deliberately avoid using features which they know to be faulty. Repairing the faults in these features may make no practical difference to the reliability as perceived by these users.

For example, the word processor used to write this book has an automatic hyphenation capability. This facility is used when text columns are short and any faults might manifest themselves when users produce multi-column documents. I never use hyphenation so, from my viewpoint,

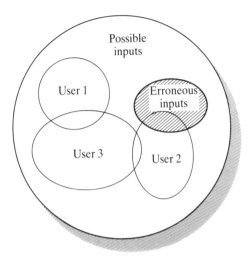

Figure 20.2
Software usage
patterns.

faults in the hyphenation code do not affect the reliability of the word processor.

In Figure 20.2, the set of erroneous inputs corresponding to the shaded ellipse in Figure 20.1 is shaded. The set of inputs produced by User 2 intersects with this erroneous input set so, for some inputs from User 2, the system will fail. User 1 and User 3, however, never choose inputs from the erroneous set so will always see the system as completely reliable.

If software is to be very reliable, it must include extra, often redundant, code to perform the necessary checking as discussed in Chapter 15. This reduces the program execution speed and increases the amount of store required by the program. It can dramatically increase development costs. Figure 20.3 shows the relationship between costs and incremental improvements in reliability.

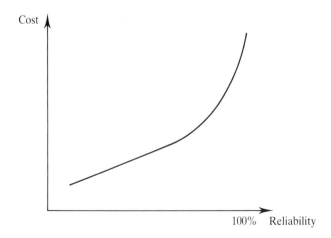

Figure 20.3
Costs versus reliability.

Increasing the reliability of a program usually slows it down. However, reliability should normally take precedence over efficiency for the following reasons:

(1)   Computers are now cheap and fast so there is little need to maximize equipment usage. Paradoxically, however, faster equipment leads to increasing expectations on the part of the user so efficiency considerations cannot be completely ignored.

(2)   Unreliable software is liable to be avoided by users. If a company attains a reputation for unreliability because of a single unreliable product, this is likely to affect future sales of all of that company's products.

(3)   For some applications, such as a reactor control system or an aircraft navigation system, the cost of system failure is orders of magnitude greater than the cost of the control system. There are an increasing number of systems coming into use where the human and economic costs of a catastrophic system failure are unacceptable.

(4)   It is usually possible to tune an inefficient system because most execution time is spent in small program sections. An unreliable system is more difficult to improve as unreliability tends to be distributed throughout the system.

(5)   Inefficiency is predictable. Programs take a long time to execute. Unreliability is much worse. Software which is unreliable can have hidden errors which can violate system and user data without warning and which do not immediately manifest themselves. For example, a fault in a CAD program used to design aircraft might not be discovered until several planes have crashed.

(6)   Unreliable systems often result in information being lost. Data is expensive and may be worth much more than the computer system on which it is processed. A great deal of effort and money is spent duplicating valuable data to guard against unreliability.

Product reliability is difficult to quantify and it can be difficult and expensive to check if the system meets the required standards. Because of this, some organizations place constraints on the process of software development on the assumption that adherence to process standards (such as testing standards) will naturally lead to systems whose reliability is acceptable. Process reliability is discussed in Chapter 31, which covers quality assurance.

A well-managed, standardized process assists with the production of reliable software. The danger is that adherence to standards may become more important than objective assessments of the software product. There is no quantitative relationship between product and process reliability. Conforming to a particular process does not allow any product reliability judgements to be made. A good process is essential if reliable software is to be developed but it does not guarantee product reliability.

It might appear that the use of formal methods for system development will necessarily lead to more reliable systems. There is no doubt that a formal system specification is less likely to contain anomalies which must be resolved by the system designer. However, there is no guarantee that the specification defines a system which meets the user's needs and provides a high level of perceived reliability. Indeed, it may be the case that the opaqueness of formal notations makes it more difficult for users to establish whether or not a system meets their needs.

A reliable system must conform to its specification and, if a formal specification has been produced, the system may be proved to meet that specification. Such a proof increases confidence in the system's correctness (although proofs can contain errors). However, you should not assume that a system which has been proved to be correct will necessarily be reliable. Proving a program correct depends on making assumptions about that program's environment. If the major cause of unreliability is environmental rather than inherent in the program, the perceived reliability of the system may not be improved.

20.1 Reliability metrics

Software reliability metrics have, by and large, evolved from hardware reliability metrics. However, hardware metrics cannot be used without modification because of the differing nature of software and hardware failures. A hardware component failure tends to be permanent. The component stops working until repair is effected. Thus, there is an obvious relationship between system availability and the mean time between hardware component failures.

By contrast, software component failures are transient. They are only exhibited for some inputs so the system can continue in operation in the presence of these failures. This distinction has meant that commonly used hardware reliability metrics such as mean time to failure are less useful for quantifying software systems reliability. It is not simple to relate system availability to system failure because it depends on factors such as restart time, the degree (if any) of data corruption caused by the software fault and so on.

Some of the metrics which have been used to assess software reliability are:

(1)   *Probability of failure on demand*   This is a measure of the likelihood that the system will behave in an unexpected way when some demand is made on it. It is most relevant for safety-critical systems and 'non-

stop' systems whose continuous operation is critical. In these systems, a measure of failure occurrence is less important that the chance that the system will not perform as expected.

(2) *Rate of failure occurrence (ROCOF)* This is a measure of the frequency of occurrence with which unexpected behaviour is likely to be observed. For example, if the ROCOF is 2/100 this indicates that 2 failures are likely to occur in each 100 operational time units. Appropriate time units are discussed shortly. This is, possibly, the most generally useful reliability metric.

(3) *Mean time to failure (MTTF)* This is a measure of the time between observed failures. This metric is a direct analogue of a comparable metric used in hardware reliability assessment where it reflects the lifetime of system components. In software systems, components do not wear out and, after a single failure, usually remain operational. Therefore, mean time to failure is only useful in software reliability assessment when the system is stable and no changes are being made to it. In this case, it provides an indication of how long the system will remain operational before a failure occurs.

(4) *Availability* This is a measure of how likely the system is to be available for use. For example, an availability of 998/1000 means that in every 1000 time units, the system is likely to be available for 998 of these. This measure is most appropriate for systems like telecommunication systems, where the repair or restart time is significant and the loss of service during that time is important.

No single metric is universally appropriate and the particular metric used should depend on the application domain and the expected usage of the system. For large systems, it may be appropriate to use different reliability metrics for different parts of the system.

Time is a factor in all of these metrics and appropriate time units should be chosen. Time units may be calendar time, processor time or may be some discrete unit such as number of transactions. This depends on the application and on the time as perceived by system users. For systems which are in continuous use, it may be appropriate to use calendar time. For systems which are used periodically but which are idle for much of the time (for example, a bank auto-teller system), the number of transactions is a more appropriate time unit.

Reliability metrics are all based around the probability of a system failure but take no account of the consequences of such a failure. Some faults, particularly those which are transient and whose consequences are not serious, are of little practical importance in the operational use of the software. For example, say a software system averaged several temperature readings taken at one minute intervals. The loss of some of this data is unlikely to have any significant effect on the average value computed.

Other types of failure may be catastrophic and might cause complete system failure with loss of life, property or valuable data. These are not equivalent to transient, inconsequential failures yet current techniques of reliability quantification would not distinguish between them. A possible way of tackling this problem using failure classification is described in the following section.

20.2   Software reliability specification

In most system specifications, reliability requirements are expressed in an informal, qualitative, untestable way. Furthermore, most specifications are incomplete and do not describe what should happen when every possible error condition arises. A lack of perceived reliability may not be due to system faults but may be a result of misunderstandings between the specifier and the designer. We now have a sufficient understanding of software reliability to improve this situation.

The required level of reliability should always be set out in the software requirements specification and the software test plan should include an operational profile of the software to assess its reliability. Depending on the type of system, one or more of the metrics discussed in the previous section should be used for reliability specification and statistical testing techniques used to measure the reliability of the system.

Unfortunately, many requirements analysts have little knowledge of reliability theory and state reliability requirements in subjective, irrelevant or unmeasurable ways. For example, statements such as 'The software shall be as reliable as possible' are meaningless. Quasi-quantitative statements such as 'The software shall exhibit no more than N faults/1000 lines' are equally irrelevant. Not only is it impossible to measure the number of faults/1000 lines of code (how can you tell when all have been discovered), the statement means nothing in terms of the dynamic behaviour of the system. As we have already discussed, reliable operation in the presence of faults is quite possible.

The types of failure which can occur are system specific and, as previously discussed, the consequences of a system failure depend on the nature of that failure. When establishing a reliability specification, the specifier should identify different types of failure and consider whether these should be treated differently in the specification. Examples of different types of failure are shown in Figure 20.4. Obviously combinations of these can occur such as a failure which is transient, recoverable and corrupting.

Failure class	Description
Transient	Occurs only with certain inputs
Permanent	Occurs with all inputs
Recoverable	System can recover without operator intervention
Unrecoverable	Operator intervention is needed to recover from failure
Non-corrupting	Failure does not corrupt data
Corrupting	Failure corrupts system data

Figure 20.4
Failure classification.

The steps involved in setting out a reliability specification are as follows:

(1) For each identified sub-system, analyse the consequences of possible system failures. Most large systems are composed of several sub-systems and it is unlikely that these will all have the same reliability requirements.

(2) From the system failure analysis, partition failures into appropriate classes. A reasonable starting point is to use the failure types shown in Figure 20.4.

(3) For each failure class identified, set out the reliability requirement using the appropriate reliability metric. It may be necessary to use different metrics for different sub-systems.

As an example of a reliability specification, consider the bank auto-teller system which has been described elsewhere in the book. Figure 20.5 shows some possible failure classes and a possible reliability specification for that system. This is quite a small system so it is not appropriate to identify sub-systems with separate reliability requirements.

Figure 20.5
Examples of reliability specification.

Failure class	Example	Reliability
Permanent	No card magnetic stripe data can be read	1 in 100 000 transactions
Transient, non-corrupting	Failure to read magnetic stripe data on a particular card	1 in 10 000 transactions
Transient, corrupting	Cards issued from foreign banks cause database corruption	1 in 20 000 000 transactions
Unrecoverable, non-corrupting	Failure of software which initiates card return	1 in 30 000 transactions
Recoverable, corrupting	Loss of users input	1 in 50 000 transactions
Recoverable, non-corrupting	Loss of magnetic stripe data	1 in 5 000 transactions

The reliability requirements in Figure 20.5 are my arbitrary estimates of what the system reliability should be. The absolute values are not particularly important but are based on a total of about 100 000 transactions per day with 5% of these being transactions from 'foreign' banks. The relative values are important. Corrupting faults should be very rare indeed. Thus, only 1 permanent failure but 10 transient failures per day are acceptable. The fault which causes unrecoverable database corruption should not occur more than once every 4000 days.

Specifiers must be careful not to specify untestable reliability requirements. Say, for example, a system was intended for use in a safety-critical application so it should never fail over the total life-time of the system. Assume that 1000 copies of the system are to be installed and the system is 'executed' 1000 times per second. The projected lifetime of the system is 10 years.

This means that the total estimated number of system executions is approximately 3×10^{14}. There is no point whatsoever in specifying that the probability of a failure in demand should be $1/10^{15}$ (allowing some safety factor, say) as there is no practical way in which this reliability can be validated in the developed software system.

Unfortunately, software engineers often have to work with imperfect specifications and cannot evade responsibility for producing reliable systems. As well as meeting the agreed specifications, a program should never produce 'incorrect' output irrespective of the input (no output is usually better than incorrect output), should never allow itself to be corrupted, should take meaningful and useful actions in unexpected situations and it should only fail completely when further progress is impossible. Failure should not affect other components of the system. Development techniques, such as defensive programming (discussed in Chapter 15) should be applied to produce reliable systems.

20.3   Statistical testing

The principal objective of statistical testing is to determine the reliability of the software rather than to discover software faults. The steps involved in the statistical testing process are:

(1)   Determine the operational profile of the software. The operational profile is the probable pattern of usage of the software and its determination involves discovering the different classes of input to the program and estimating their probability.

(2)   Select or generate a set of test data corresponding to the operational profile.

(3)   Apply these test cases to the program, recording the amount of execution time between each observed system failure. It may not be appropriate to use raw execution time; as discussed in the previous section, the time units chosen should be appropriate for the reliability metric used.

(4)   After a statistically significant number of failures have been observed, the software reliability can then be computed.

Statistical testing is usually combined with reliability growth modelling (discussed in the following section) so that predictions concerning the final system reliability and when that will be achieved can be made. The reliability of the system should improve in the course of the testing process as failures are discovered and the underlying fault causing the failure is repaired.

    This conceptually attractive approach to reliability estimation is not easy to apply in practice. The principal difficulties which arise are due to the uncertainties in determining the operational profile of the software, the high costs of generating a large enough data set for statistical testing and the problems of achieving statistically significant results when very high reliability requirements are placed on the software.

    The operational profile of the software reflects how it will be used in practice. It consists of a specification of classes of input and the probability of their occurrence. When a new software system replaces an existing manual or automated system, the determination of the probable pattern of usage of the new software is reasonably straightforward. It should roughly correspond to the existing pattern of usage with some allowance made for the new functionality which is (presumably) included in the new software. An operational profile can be specified with reasonable confidence.

    However, when a software system is new and innovative it is more difficult to anticipate how it will be used. The system developers and procurers may have their own model of how they would like the system to be used but computer users often make use of systems in ways which are not anticipated by their developers. The problem is further compounded by the fact that the operational profile may change as the system is used. Systems are used by a range of users with different expectations, backgrounds and experience. When the abilities and confidence of users change as they gain experience with the system, they may use it in more sophisticated ways.

    Statistical testing, as the name implies, relies on utilizing a large test data set to exercise the software and is based on the assumption that only a small percentage of the test inputs is likely to cause a system failure. By far the best way to create a large data set is to use some form of test data generator which can be set up to generate random inputs automatically. However, as discussed in Chapter 23, it is difficult to automate the production of test data for some classes of system, particularly interactive

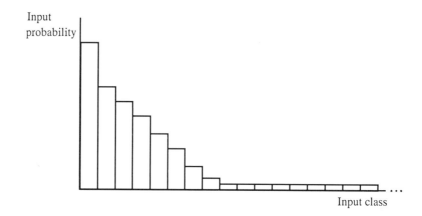

Figure 20.6
A typical operational profile.

systems. Data sets for these systems have to be generated manually with correspondingly high costs.

Typically, the operational profile is such that the inputs which have the highest probability of being generated fall into a small number of classes but there are an extremely large number of classes where there is a very low but finite probability that an input in that class will be generated (Figure 20.6).

While it may be straightforward to generate tests taken from the most common inputs, it is important that a statistically significant percentage of the unlikely inputs are included in the test set. Creating these may be difficult. This is particularly true if a test data generator is used as it may have to be specially modified to create these rare but valid inputs.

When the software has a very high reliability requirement this implies that very few inputs in the test data set should cause a system failure. Thus, the test data set has to be extremely large and the elapsed time required to generate a statistically significant number of failures (and hence estimate the system reliability) may be so long that it is quite impractical to carry out the tests.

In safety-critical systems, the operational profile cannot be complete as a safety criterion is that the software must be safe when exercised in a completely unexpected way. Safety critical systems must include features which cause them to fail-safe in the presence of unanticipated, occasional, life-threatening, exceptional situations. By their very nature, such situations are uncommon and unanticipated. This problem is discussed in the following chapter.

There is anecdotal evidence which suggests that statistical testing is as effective as defect testing in discovering system failures. This does not mean, of course, that defect testing should be abandoned. Defect testing, where a relatively small number of test cases are developed with the aim of discovering software faults, should be seen as a precursor to statistical testing. Techniques of defect testing are discussed in Chapter 22.

20.4 Reliability growth modelling

A reliability growth model is a mathematical model of software reliability which can be used to predict when (or if) a particular level of reliability is likely to be attained. The model provides a means of assessing whether or not the software quality is improving with time. It allows the software testers or quality assurance team to decide when the software is likely to be of adequate quality for release. Reliability growth modelling must be carried out in conjunction with statistical testing. As testing reveals software faults, these are repaired and the software reliability grows.

Reliability growth models are used during the quality assurance process when a software product has been delivered for quality assessment. During quality assurance, faults are discovered and repair requests submitted. As these repairs are made, the reliability of the software should (but need not) increase. Reliability will not necessarily increase after a fault has been repaired. The repair may introduce new faults whose probability of occurrence might be higher than the occurrence probability of the fault which has been repaired.

The simplest reliability growth model is a step function model where the reliability increases by a constant increment each time a fault repair is effected. Such a model was first discussed by Jelinski and Moranda (1972) and its form is illustrated in Figure 20.7.

There are two problems with this model. It assumes that software repairs are always correct and never increase the number of faults present in the software. This is not always true. Secondly, it assumes that all faults contribute equally to reliability and that each fault repair contributes the same amount of reliability growth. However, not all faults are equally probable. Repairing faults which are more likely to occur contributes more to reliability growth than repairing faults which only manifest themselves very occasionally.

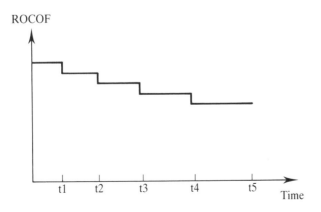

Figure 20.7
Equal-step function model of reliability growth.

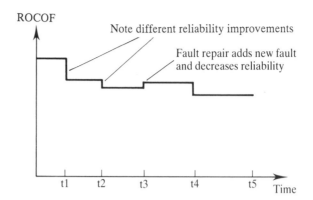

Figure 20.8
Random-step function
model of reliability
growth.

Other models, such as that described by Littlewood and Verrall (1973) take these problems into account by introducing a random element into the reliability growth improvement effected by a software repair. Thus, each repair does not result in an equal amount of reliability improvement but varies depending on the random perturbation (Figure 20.8).

Littlewood and Verrall's model allows for negative reliability growth when a software repair introduces further errors. It also models the fact that as faults are repaired, the average improvement in reliability per repair decreases. The most probable faults are likely to be discovered early in the testing process. Repairing these contributes most to reliability growth.

Littlewood (1990) points out that there is no universally applicable reliability growth model. All of the models can be useful in different circumstances. He recommends that reliability growth predictions should be based on fitting observed data to several growth models. Whichever model exhibits the best fit should then be used to predict the reliability for that system.

To use a reliability growth model, the software is tested statistically and the reliability metric chosen is plotted against execution time. The target system reliability is indicated on the graph. Given that the target reliability has not been reached when the model is being used, the next step is to fit the observed failure data to one of the known reliability models (Figure 20.9).

Once the best curve-fit has been achieved, the model can then be extrapolated to suggest when the required reliability will be reached. Given that there is a known relationship between system execution time and calendar time, the system testers can then estimate when system testing can finish. Alternatively, the reliability growth model may show that the required level of reliability is never likely to be reached. The reliability growth of the software may be so small that it will not reach the required value in the projected lifetime of the system. Either the reliability requirements have to be modified or the software has to be rewritten to eliminate large numbers of inherent faults.

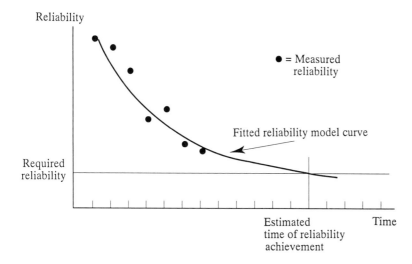

Figure 20.9
Reliability prediction.

A proper discussion on reliability growth models requires an understanding of statistical theory and is outside the scope of this book. A paper by Abdel-Ghaly *et al.* (1986) compares the various reliability growth models which have been developed and Littlewood (1990) describes and compares eight different reliability growth models. Experience with the use of reliability growth models is described by Ehrlich *et al.* (1990).

■ KEY POINTS

- ■ The most important dynamic characteristic of a software system is its reliability. The reason for this is that the costs of system failure often exceed the costs of developing the software system.

- ■ The reliability of a software system is not a simple measure which can be associated with the system. It depends on the pattern of usage of that system. It is quite possible for a system to contain faults yet be seen as reliable.

- ■ There are a number of ways of quantifying reliability. The particular metric chosen depends on the individual system and application domain. The reliability required should be set out in the system requirements specification.

- ■ Reliability specifications are often imperfect but software engineers are still responsible for producing reliable systems. Programs should not produce incorrect output, should not corrupt themselves or other programs and should take meaningful actions in unexpected situations.

- Statistical testing is used to estimate software reliability. It relies on testing the system with a test data set which reflects the operational profile of the software. The test data may be generated automatically.

- Reliability growth models are a means of assessing the change in reliability as a product is developed. They should not assume that reliability always increases with changes to the system.

FURTHER READING

Software Reliability Handbook.   In spite of its title this book has a much broader scope than simply reliability issues. It also has excellent sections on metrics and quality assurance. (P. Rook (ed.), 1990, Elsevier.)

'Quantifying software validation: When to stop testing'.   This is an excellent article which introduces the notions of statistical testing and reliability growth and shows how these can be used in test planning. It provides details of actual experiences with statistical testing. (J.D. Musa and A. Frank Ackerman, *IEEE Software*, **6** (3), May 1989.)

Software Reliability: Measurement, Prediction, Application.   This book is a detailed description of reliability modelling from both a practical and a theoretical standpoint. It explores in depth the ideas introduced in the above paper (J.D. Musa, A. Iannino and K. Okumoto, 1987, McGraw-Hill.)

EXERCISES

20.1   Suggest six reasons why software reliability is important? Using an example, explain the difficulties of describing what software reliability means.

20.2   Why is it inappropriate to use reliability metrics which were developed for hardware systems in estimating software systems reliability. Illustrate your answer with an example.

20.3   Assess the reliability of some software system which you use regularly by keeping a log of system failures and observed faults. Write a user's handbook which describes how to make effective use of the system in the presence of these faults.

20.4 Suggest appropriate reliability metrics for the following classes of software system. Give reasons for your choice of metric. Suggest also, approximate acceptable values for the system reliability.

(a) A system which monitors patients in a hospital intensive care unit.

(b) A word processor.

(c) An automated vending machine control system.

(d) A system to control braking in a car.

(e) A system to control a refrigeration unit.

(f) A management report generator.

20.5 You are responsible for writing the specification for a software system which controls a network of EPOS (electronic point of sale) terminals in a supermarket. The system accepts bar code information from a terminal, queries a product database and returns the item name and its price to the terminal for display. The system must be continually available during the supermarket's opening hours.

Giving reasons for your choice, select appropriate reliability metrics for specifying the reliability of such a system and write a plausible reliability specification taking into account the fact that some faults are more serious than others. You should consider three classes of fault, namely faults which result in data corruption, faults which result in the system being unavailable for service and faults which cause incorrect information to be transmitted to the EPOS terminal. It may be necessary to use different metrics for different fault classes.

20.6 Describe how you would go about validating the reliability specification you have defined in Exercise 20.5. Your answer should include a description of any validation tools which might be used. You may find it useful to read Chapter 23 before attempting this exercise.

20.7 Using the literature as background information, write a report for management (who have no previous experience in this area) on the use of reliability growth models.

20.6 Describe how you would go about validating the reliability specification you have defined in Exercise 20.5. Your answer should include a description of any validation tools which might be used. You may find it useful to read Chapter 23 before attempting this exercise.

20.7 Using the literature as background information, write a report for management (who have no previous experience in this area) on the use of reliability growth models.

Software Safety

21

■ OBJECTIVES

There are two main objectives of this chapter: firstly, to describe the problems which arise when software is used as an inherent part of a system whose malfunction can threaten human life, and secondly, to illustrate approaches to software development which can be used to improve our confidence that system malfunctions will not be safety-critical. A safety-critical system life cycle is introduced and safety specification identified as the key to effective safety achievement. Hazard analysis using fault trees is discussed. Safety assurance via a certified safety process and via product assurance techniques such as safety proofs are covered. Throughout the chapter, a control system for a personal insulin pump for diabetics is used as a source of examples.

■ CONTENTS

There are now many systems where failure or malfunctioning of the system software can pose a threat to human life. Examples of such *safety-critical systems* are control and monitoring systems in aircraft, process control systems in chemical and pharmaceutical plants and automobile control systems.

It is a useful shorthand to use the term 'safety-critical software' to refer to software in systems whose malfunction can be dangerous. Obviously, however, software on its own does not pose a threat to anyone. Hardware failure of some kind is the ultimate result of software malfunction. Thus, when considering safety-critical issues, it is important to take a systems viewpoint and consider the interactions of hardware, software and humans who make up the complete system.

Techniques for system safety analysis and assurance which have been derived for electro-mechanical hardware systems are inadequate for software-controlled systems. This is partly due to the greater inherent complexity of software and partly due to the fact that overall system complexity has increased because flexible software control is possible. An example of such complexity is found in advanced military aircraft which are aerodynamically unstable. They require continual software-controlled adjustment of their flight surfaces to ensure that they do not crash.

Safety-critical software falls into two classes:

(1) *Primary safety-critical software* This is software embedded in a hardware system used to control or monitor some other process. Malfunctioning of such software can result directly in human injury or environmental damage.

(2) *Secondary safety-critical software* This is software which can indirectly result in injury. Examples of such systems are computer-aided engineering design systems whose malfunctioning might result in a design fault in the object being designed. This fault may pose a threat to humans if the designed system malfunctions. Other examples of such systems are medical databases holding details of drugs administered to patients. Errors in this system might result in an incorrect drug dosage being administered.

It is very hard to say when a system has secondary safety-critical characteristics. For example, an automobile manufacturer may maintain a database holding details of car owners so that models can be recalled if a design fault has to be rectified. Say this system malfunctions, some owners are not notified, the design fault occurs and causes an accident. Should a safety analysis be made of the database system? There is no definitive answer to such questions so, in this chapter, the discussion will be confined to primary safety-critical software.

A specialized vocabulary has evolved to discuss safety-critical systems and it is important to understand the specific terms used. As defined by Leveson (1985), one of the most authoritative safety-critical systems researchers, these are:

(1) *Mishap (or accident)*   An unplanned event or event sequence which results in human death or injury. In some cases it may be more generally defined as also covering damage to property or the environment.

(2) *Hazard*   A condition with the potential for causing or contributing to a mishap.

(3) *Damage*   A measure of the loss resulting from a mishap.

(4) *Hazard severity*   An assessment of the worst possible damage which could result from a particular hazard.

(5) *Hazard probability*   The probability of the events occurring which create a hazard.

(6) *Risk*   This is a complex concept which is related to the hazard severity, the hazard probability and the probability that the hazard will result in a mishap. Essentially, it is a measure of the probability that the system will behave in a way which threatens humans. The objective of all safety systems is to minimize risk.

An assumption which underlies work in system safety is that the number of faults which can result in hazards is significantly less than the total number of faults which may exist in the system. Safety achievement can concentrate on these faults with hazard potential. If it can be demonstrated that these faults cannot occur or, if they occur, the associated hazard will not result in a mishap, then the system is safe.

Software reliability is closely related to software safety and the concepts are often confused. Of course, it is essential that a safety-critical system should be fault-free (that is, in conformance with its specification) and it may incorporate fault-tolerant characteristics. However, even when this has been achieved, the system may not be safe. The software may malfunction and cause system behaviour which results in an accident.

Apart from the fact that we can never be 100% certain that a system is fault-free and fault-tolerant, there are several other reasons why safety and reliability should not be equated:

(1) The software specification may be incomplete in that it does not describe the required behaviour of the software in certain situations. Fault-free software only means software as specified. A high percentage of system malfunctions (Boehm *et al.*, 1975; Endres, 1975) are the result of specification rather than design errors.

(2) Hardware malfunctions may cause the system to behave in an unpredictable way and may present the software with an unanticipated environment. For example, when components are close to failure they may behave erratically and generate signals which cannot be handled by the software.

(3) The operator of the system may generate inputs which are not individually incorrect but which, in particular situations can lead to a system malfunction. An anecdotal example of this is where an aircraft mechanic instructed the utility management software on an airplane to raise the undercarriage. The plane was on the ground at the time; unfortunately, the software carried out the mechanic's instruction.

All of these possibilities can arise at the same time. An analysis of serious accidents (Perrow, 1984) suggested that they were almost all due to a combination of malfunctions rather than single failures. The unanticipated combination led to interactions which resulted in system failure. Perrow also suggests that it is impossible to anticipate all possible combinations of system malfunction and that accidents are an inevitable part of using complex systems. Software tends to increase system complexity so using software control *may* increase the probability of system accident.

However, there are advantages of using software in safety-critical applications. The system can monitor a wider range of conditions than electro-mechanical systems; it can be adapted relatively easily; it involves the use of computers which have very high inherent reliability and which are physically small and lightweight; it can provide sophisticated safety interlocks and can support control strategies which reduce the amount of time people need to spend in hazardous environments.

Thus, software control and monitoring can potentially increase the safety of systems. Even when there are doubts over the 'safeness' of the software, overall system safety may be improved even when potentially hazardous software failures can occasionally occur. It is a social and political decision as to whether the benefits which are gained from software control and monitoring outweigh the increased risk which may ensue.

21.1 An insulin delivery system

Understanding safety-critical control and monitoring systems obviously requires an understanding of the underlying system being controlled. It is difficult to find an example for discussion which does not require specialized application-domain knowledge. The example used in this chapter is an insulin delivery system for the control of diabetes. I hope that most readers will have general knowledge of this condition and its treatment.

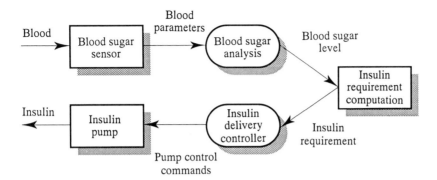

Figure 21.1
An insulin delivery system.

Diabetes is a relatively common condition (affecting about 1% of the population) where the body is unable to produce sufficient quantities of a hormone called insulin. Insulin metabolizes glucose (sugar) in the blood. The conventional treatment of diabetes involves regular injections of manufactured insulin.

The problem with this treatment is that the level of insulin in the blood does not depend on the blood glucose level but is a function of the time when the insulin injection was taken. This can lead to very low levels of blood sugar (if there is too much insulin) or very high levels of blood sugar (if there is too little insulin). Low blood sugar is, in the short term, a more serious condition as it can result in temporary brain malfunctioning and, ultimately, unconsciousness and death. In the long term, continual high levels of blood sugar can lead to eye damage, kidney damage and heart problems.

Current advances in developing miniaturized sensors have meant that it is now possible to develop insulin delivery systems which regularly monitor blood sugar levels and deliver an appropriate dose of insulin. Insulin delivery systems already exist for the treatment of hospital patients and it is predicted that in the relatively near future, it will be possible for many diabetics to use such systems.

An insulin delivery system might work by using a micro-sensor embedded in the patient to measure some blood parameter which is proportional to the sugar level. This is then sent to the pump controller. This controller computes the sugar level, judges how much insulin is required and sends signals to a miniaturized pump to deliver the insulin via a permanently attached needle. Insulin delivery systems are likely to be software controlled. A data-flow model of such a system is shown in Figure 21.1.

21.2 Safety specification

Safe operation is the required characteristic of a safety-related software system. This requires that particular attention should be paid during the specification of a system to potential hazards which might arise. Each hazard should be assessed for the risk it poses and the specification may either describe how the software should behave to minimize the risk or might require that the hazard should never arise. It then becomes the responsibility of the safety assurance process to demonstrate that the safety specification has been met. The process of safety specification and assurance is sometimes called the 'safety-life cycle' (IEE, 1989) and is illustrated in Figure 21.2. A

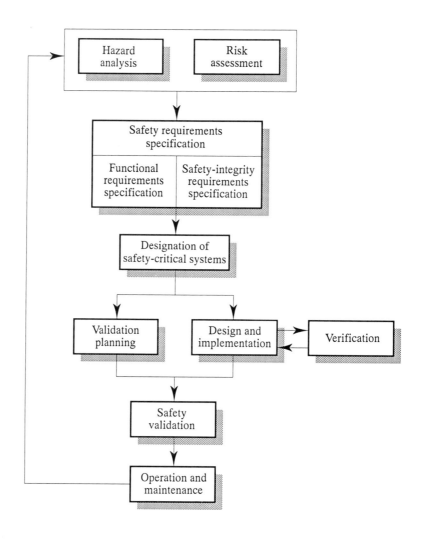

Figure 21.2
The safety life cycle.

comparable process model is likely to be adopted in a forthcoming international standard for safety-critical systems.

The first stages of the life cycle involve assessing the potential system hazards and estimating the risk they pose. This is followed by a safety requirements specification which is concerned with identifying safety-critical functions (functional requirements specification) and the safety integrity level for each of these functions. The designation of safety critical systems involves assigning explicit responsibility for safety to individual engineers. A 'normal' process model is then followed with particular attention paid to the validation of the system. Part of that validation should be an explicit safety validation activity.

Of course, it is possible that potential hazards might not be foreseen by the specifier and part of the specification should be concerned with how the software behaves should an unforeseen condition arise. Exception handling mechanisms, as discussed in Chapter 15, can be used to handle unforeseen errors.

Safety specification is the first step in the process of safety assurance. It should be integrated with other steps in that process as discussed in Section 21.3.1.

21.2.1 Hazard analysis

Hazard analysis is an essential precursor to safety specification, and involves analysing the system and discovering potentially dangerous states. Hazard analysis should be undertaken by systems engineers in conjunction with domain experts and professional safety advisers. For large systems, hazard analysis is usually structured into a number of phases (Leveson, 1986):

(1)   *Preliminary hazard analysis*   This activity is undertaken early in the specification phase. The principal hazards which can arise are identified and the risk of each hazard is assessed.

(2)   *Sub-system hazard analysis*   This is a more detailed hazard analysis which is carried out for each safety-critical sub-system.

(3)   *System hazard analysis*   This analysis is concerned with hazards which arise through sub-system interaction involving interface errors and incompatibilities, simultaneous failure of several sub-systems, and so on.

(4)   *Software hazard analysis*   This analysis is explicitly concerned with discovering software-related hazards in the system or sub-system. It may be undertaken as part of sub-system or system hazard analysis.

(5)   *Operational hazard analysis*   This is a study of the hazards which might arise as a result of the use of the system. In safety-critical software systems, it is concerned with user interface analysis and possible related operator errors.

Identified hazard	Hazard probability	Hazard severity	Estimated risk
Insulin overdose	Medium	High	High
Insulin underdose	High	Low	Low
Power failure	High	Low	Low
Machine breaks off in patient	Low	High	Medium
Machine causes infection	Medium	Medium	Medium
Electrical interference	Low	High	Medium
Allergic reaction	Low	Low	Low

Figure 21.3
Risk analysis of identified hazards.

These analyses identify hazards and associate a risk with each hazard. This involves estimating the probability that the hazard will arise, estimating the probability that the hazard will cause a mishap and estimating the likely severity of that mishap. Engineering judgement is the only way of making such risk assessments.

The insulin delivery system discussed in Section 21.1 is a relatively small system. There is no need for as structured a hazard analysis as discussed above. Rather, hazards can be identified as follows:

(1)   Insulin overdose.

(2)   Insulin underdose.

(3)   Power failure due to exhausted battery.

(4)   Parts of machine break off in patient's body.

(5)   Infection caused by introduction of machine.

(6)   Machine interferes electrically with other medical equipment such as a heart pacemaker.

(7)   Allergic reaction to the materials or insulin used in the machine.

Figure 21.3 shows a risk analysis of these identified hazards. As I am not a physician, the estimates in that table are for illustration only. Notice that an insulin overdose is potentially more serious than an insulin underdose in the short term. Hazards 3–7 are not software related and will not be discussed further here.

21.2.2   Fault tree analysis

For each identified hazard, a detailed analysis should be carried out to discover the conditions which might cause that hazard. There are various techniques which have been proposed as possible approaches to such analyses. These include reviews and checklists, and more formal techniques such as Petri net analysis (Peterson, 1981), formal logic (Jahanian and Mok, 1986) and fault tree analysis (Leveson and Harvey, 1983).

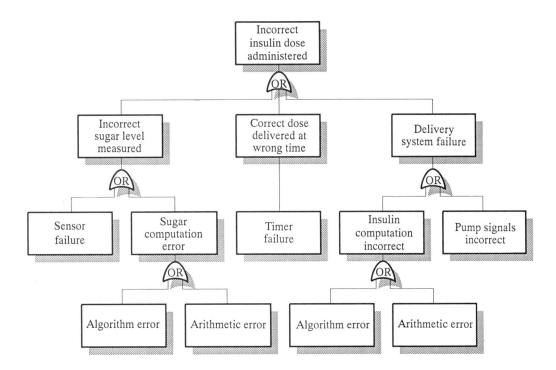

Figure 21.4
Fault tree for insulin
delivery system.

Fault tree analysis is, perhaps, the most widely used of these techniques. It involves identifying the undesired event and working backwards from that event to discover the possible causes of the hazard. The hazard is at the root of the tree and the leaves of the tree represent potential causes of the hazard which must be explicitly addressed in the safety specification.

Figure 21.4 is the fault tree which can be identified for the possible software-related hazards in the insulin delivery system. Insulin underdose and insulin overdose really represent a single hazard, namely incorrect insulin dose administered, and a single fault tree can be drawn. Of course, when specifying how the software should react to hazards, whether or not the hazard is an insulin underdose or overdose must be taken into account.

The fault tree in Figure 21.4 is incomplete. Only potential software faults have been fully decomposed. Hardware faults such as low battery power causing a sensor failure are not shown. At this level, further analysis is not possible but as a design and implementation is developed, further fault tree development should be carried out. Leveson and Harvey (1983) and Leveson (1985) show how fault trees can be developed at the individual programming language statement level.

The potential causes of a hazard can be identified from the fault tree and the system specification then formulated so that the cause cannot occur or the risk associated with the hazard is minimized. This may involve defining a 'safe state' (which may not be an operational state) and specifying that in the event of a potential hazard, this safe state should be entered.

In an insulin delivery system, a 'safe state' is a shut down state where no insulin is injected. Over a short period this will not pose a threat to the diabetic's health. If the potential software problems identified in Figure 21.4 are considered, the following 'solutions' might be developed:

(1) *Arithmetic error* This arises when some arithmetic computation causes a representation failure. The specification must identify all possible arithmetic errors which may occur (these depend on the algorithm used) and must set out the action to be taken for each of these errors if they arise. A safe action is to shut down the delivery system and activate a warning alarm.

In order that exceptions may be handled, the specification might set out that software development must be in Ada with an appropriate exception handler to handle the NUMERIC_ERROR exception which may arise. However, the physical size of a delivery system is restricted and all software must fit into ROM. Using Ada means that a substantial run-time system must be present and this may not be acceptable because of the need to keep the device size as small as possible. If another language is used, each possible exception must be individually handled.

(2) *Algorithmic error* This is a more difficult situation as no definite anomalous situation can be detected. It might be detected by comparing the required insulin dose computed with the previously delivered dose and imposing some arbitrary threshold so that very large doses of insulin are never delivered. At the same time, the system may keep track of the dose sequence and after a certain number of above-average doses have been delivered, a warning is issued and further dosage limited. If the diabetic's condition genuinely requires unusually large doses of insulin, it probably means that medical intervention is necessary. A warning is appropriate even if no error has occurred.

The fault tree is also used to identify potential hardware problems and may provide insights into requirements for software to detect and, perhaps, correct these problems. For example, insulin doses are not administered at a very high frequency (no more than 2 or 3 times per hour, perhaps) so there is a great deal of available processor capacity in the system to run diagnostic and self-checking programs. Hardware errors such as sensor, pump or timer errors can be discovered and warnings issued before they have a serious effect on the patient.

21.3   Safety assurance

General design principles for safety-critical software revolve around information hiding and protection and software simplicity. Those parts of the system which are safety-critical should be isolated from other parts of the system. This may be achieved through the use of data and control abstraction or may be achieved using physical separation. The safety-critical software may execute on a separate computer with minimal communication links to other parts of the system.

Safety-critical software should be as simple as possible. Potentially error-prone language features such as those discussed in Chapter 15 should be avoided and may be disallowed by standards for safety-critical systems development. Subsets of languages such as Pascal and Ada have been devised for safety-critical application. These subsets have excluded language features which are not properly defined and features which are inherently unsafe (such as real numbers, pointers, and so on.)

It is arguable whether or not fault-tolerant techniques should be adopted. One view is that they increase complexity, so making the software harder to validate. Furthermore, Knight and Leveson (1986) and Brilliant *et al.* (1990) have demonstrated that the arguments for reliability through diversity (N-version programming) are not always valid. When developing software from the same specification, different teams made the same mistakes. Software redundancy did not give the theoretically predicted increase in system reliability.

This does not mean that N-version programming is useless as it may well reduce the absolute number of failures in the system. It means that the increased confidence in the system reliability offered by N-version programming may be less than claimed by some developers of safety-critical systems.

Parnas *et al.* (1990) suggest that safety can best be assured by minimizing and isolating safety-critical code components and by using the simplest possible techniques for writing safety-critical code sections. This means avoiding the use of the inherently dangerous program constructs discussed in Chapter 15 and avoiding multiplication and division as these are most likely to lead to arithmetic errors. They also suggest that validation should be based on a combination of thorough testing, reviews based on mathematical specifications and a certified development process.

21.3.1   Process assurance

As shown in Figure 21.2, a life cycle model for safety-critical systems development requires explicit attention to be paid to safety during the software process. It cannot be assumed that safety will automatically result from a good development process. Specific safety assurance activities must be included in the process. These include:

(1) The creation of a hazard logging and monitoring system which traces hazards from preliminary hazard analysis through to testing and system validation.

(2) The appointment of project safety engineers who have explicit responsibility for the safety aspects of the system.

(3) The extensive use of safety reviews throughout the development process.

(4) The creation of a safety certification system whereby safety-critical components are formally certified for their assessed safety.

(5) The use of a very detailed configuration management system which is used to track all safety-related documentation and keep it in step with the associated technical documentation.

The central safety document is the hazard log where hazards identified during the specification process are documented. This hazard log is then used at each stage of the software development process to assess how that development stage has taken the hazards into account. A simplified example of a hazard log entry for the insulin delivery system is shown in Figure 21.5.

Points to note in Figure 21.5 are the explicit identification of individuals who have safety responsibility. It is important to appoint a project safety engineer who should not be involved in the system development. The responsibility of this engineer is to ensure that appropriate safety checks have been made and documented. The system procurer may require an independent safety assessor to be appointed from an outside organization. He or she reports directly to the client on safety matters.

System engineers who are concerned with safety generally have to be certified engineers. In the UK, for example, this means that they have to have been accepted as a member of one of the engineering institutes (civil, electrical, mechanical, and so on) and have to be chartered engineers. Inexperienced, poorly qualified engineers may not take responsibility for safety. While this does not currently apply to software engineers, it is likely that future standards for safety-critical software development will require that project safety engineers must be formally certified as having undergone appropriate training.

Parnas *et al.* (1990) comment on the importance of the review process in safety-critical systems development. They suggest five classes of review which should be mandatory for safety-critical systems:

(1) Review for correct intended function.

(2) Review for maintainable, understandable structure.

```
Hazard Log. Page 4: Printed  21.12.90

System: Insulin Delivery System          File:  Insulin System/Safety/HLog
Safety Engineer:  James Brown            Log version: 1.3
────────────────────────────────────────────────────────────────────────
Identified Hazard:  Insulin overdose delivered to patient

Identified by:   Jane Williams

Criticality Class:  1

Identified Risk:  High

Fault tree identified:  YES     Date: 10.11.90     Location:  Hazard Log, Page 5

Fault tree creator:   Jane Williams and Bill Smith

Fault tree checked:  YES     Date:  20.11.90     Checker:  James Brown

System design safety requirements:

1.   Incorporate self-testing software for sensor system, clock and delivery
system.  This should be executed at least once per minute and should cause an
audible warning to be emitted if a fault is discovered.  If a fault is discovered, no
further insulin deliveries should be made until the system has been reset.

2.   Incorporate a patient override facility so that the patient may modify the dose
to be delivered by manual intervention.   However, a limit should be set on the
dose administered by the patient. This limit should be set by medical staff when
the system is installed.

3.   ...
```

Figure 21.5
A simplified hazard log
page.

(3)   Review to verify that the algorithm and data structure design are consistent with the specified behaviour.

(4)   Review the code for consistency with the algorithm and data structure design.

(5)   Review the adequacy of the system test cases.

They also suggest that informal documentation and verification is not acceptable for safety-critical systems development and that formal mathematical specifications and verification arguments are required.

Currently an international process standard for safety-critical systems is under development and it is likely that this standard will be the basis for process standards required by particular system procurers such as the Department of Defense, and so on.

21.3.2 Product safety assurance

Product safety assurance is part of an effective safety process and, as discussed in the previous section, is based on testing and reviews. The testing of safety critical systems has much in common with the testing of any other systems with high reliability requirements. Thus, the techniques discussed in Chapters 20, 22 and 24 should be applied. However, because of the ultra-low failure rates required in many safety-critical systems, it is unlikely that statistical testing can provide a quantitative estimate of the system reliability because of the unrealistically large number of tests required. Engineering judgement must be used to assess the safety of the product.

Static analysis techniques based on the use of automatic static analysers are useful in detecting potential faults in a system. Their use is mandated by some safety process standards. These techniques and some currently available tools are discussed in Chapter 24.

Safety proofs

Proofs of program correctness have been postulated as a key validation technique for over 20 years but these have been little used in real systems. The practical problems of constructing a correctness proof (discussed in Chapter 24) are so great that few organizations have considered them to be cost-effective. However, for some critical safety-related applications and for security-related systems, correctness proofs are a valuable aid in increasing confidence in the system. Moser and Melliar-Smith (1990) describe how such a proof was developed during the verification of a safety-critical operating system for flight-control.

While it may not be cost-effective to develop correctness proofs for most systems, it is sometimes possible to develop a weaker proof, namely a safety proof, which demonstrates that the program meets its safety

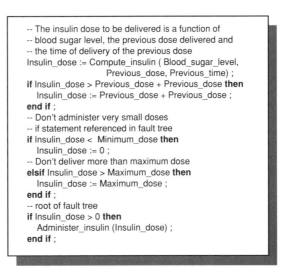

```
-- The insulin dose to be delivered is a function of
-- blood sugar level, the previous dose delivered and
-- the time of delivery of the previous dose
Insulin_dose := Compute_insulin ( Blood_sugar_level,
                    Previous_dose, Previous_time) ;
if Insulin_dose > Previous_dose + Previous_dose then
    Insulin_dose := Previous_dose + Previous_dose ;
end if ;
-- Don't administer very small doses
-- if statement referenced in fault tree
if Insulin_dose < Minimum_dose then
    Insulin_dose := 0 ;
-- Don't deliver more than maximum dose
elsif Insulin_dose > Maximum_dose then
    Insulin_dose := Maximum_dose ;
end if ;
-- root of fault tree
if Insulin_dose > 0 then
    Administer_insulin (Insulin_dose) ;
end if ;
```

Figure 21.6
Insulin delivery code.

obligations. It is not necessary to prove that the program meets its specification; it is only necessary to prove that program execution cannot result in an unsafe state.

A useful technique in developing safety proofs is to use proof by contradiction. This means assuming that the unsafe state (identified by the hazard analysis) can be reached then demonstrating that this is a contradiction. As an example, consider the (hypothetical) code in Figure 21.6 which might be part of the implementation of the insulin delivery system. Some comments have been added to this code to relate it to the fault tree shown in Figure 21.7.

Developing a safety proof of this code involves demonstrating that the dose of insulin administered is never greater than some maximum level which is established for each individual diabetic. Therefore, it is not necessary to prove that the system delivers the 'correct' dose, merely that it never delivers an overdose.

An informal proof of safety is shown in Figure 21.7. The unsafe state is assumed and the demonstration of safety works backwards from the

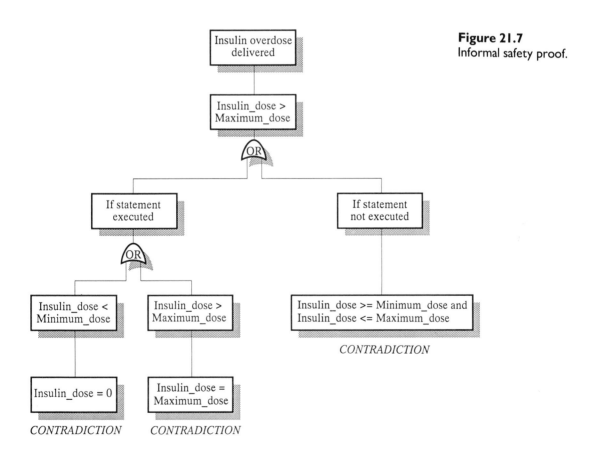

Figure 21.7
Informal safety proof.

```
procedure Administer_insulin (Insulin_dose : DOSE)
   Insulin_increments : NATURAL ;
begin
   --* assert  Insulin_dose <= Maximum_dose
   Insulin_increments := Compute_requirement (Insulin_dose) ;
   --* assert Insulin_increments <= Maximum_increments
   for i in range 1..Insulin_increments loop
      Generate_pump_signal ;
      --* assert i <= Maximum_increments ;
   end loop ;
end Administer_insulin ;
```

Figure 21.8
Insulin administration.

insulin delivery statement. Once it has been demonstrated that all paths lead
to a contradiction, there is no need for further analysis. The system is safe
inasmuch as it cannot compute an insulin overdose to be delivered. Of
course, the delivery system may be faulty but this has to be addressed
elsewhere in the safety assurance process.

The safety proof assumes that an insulin overdose has been delivered,
that is, that the Administer_insulin procedure has been called with a
parameter greater than the allowed maximum value. It then traces how that
parameter must have been computed either in the preceding **if** statement or
in the statement before it. If the **if** statement is not executed, this means that
the insulin dose is either less than the minimum dose (safe) or less than the
maximum dose (safe). If the **if** statement is executed the dose is either set to
zero (safe) or is set equal to the maximum dose (safe). All paths therefore
lead to a safe state.

Safety assertions

The use of assertions in defensive programming was discussed in Chapter 15
and a similar technique can be used in safety-critical systems. The assertions
are derived from the system safety requirements rather than the specification. They are intended to assure safe behaviour rather than behaviour
which conforms to the specification.

Assertions can be particularly valuable to assure the safety of
communications between components of the system. For example, in the
insulin delivery system, the dose of insulin administered involves generating
signals to the insulin pump to deliver a specified number of insulin
increments (Figure 21.8). The number of insulin increments associated with
the allowed maximum insulin dose can be pre-computed and included as an
assertion in the system.

Assertions may be included as formal comments in the program.
Using a pre-processor, these comments can be identified and code generated
to check the assertions at run-time.

■ KEY POINTS

■ Software is increasingly used in safety-critical control and monitoring systems. Existing hardware safety assurance techniques have to be modified to cope with software systems.

■ The use of software control can increase system safety by improving the number of control variables which can be monitored and by increasing the sophistication of safety interlocks.

■ Hazard analysis is a key activity in the safety specification process. It involves identifying hazardous conditions which can compromise system safety. Fault tree analysis is a technique which can be used in the hazard analysis process.

■ Safety assurance relies on an effective, certified process which includes specific product safety assurance mechanisms.

■ Safety assurance should be the responsibility of named individuals who are external to the software development team.

■ Safety proofs are an effective product safety assurance technique. They are usually simpler than proving that a program meets its specification as they must only show that an identified hazardous condition can never occur.

FURTHER READING

'Software safety: why, what and how'. This is a good introductory survey of software safety issues and Leveson cites a number of examples of safety-critical systems where the system safety has been compromised by software faults. It is a comprehensive overview of system safety and covers many aspects of safety-critical systems (such as human factors) which I have not had space to discuss. It is probably the best starting point for readers interested in this topic. (N.G. Leveson, *ACM Computing Surveys*, **18** (2), 1986.)

'Evaluation of safety-critical software'.   This paper discusses the problems of safety assurance and suggests that approaches based on mathematical specification and verification are essential. (D.L. Parnas, J. van Schouwen, and P.K. Shu, *Comm. ACM*, **33** (6), 1990.)

Developing Safety Systems. This is general book on safety-critical systems engineering which is particularly concerned with the use of Ada for safety-critical systems development. It also discusses relevant safety standards. (I.C. Pyle, 1991, Prentice-Hall.)

EXERCISES

21.1 Identify six consumer products which may contain, or which may contain in future, safety-critical software systems.

21.2 For the insulin delivery system example, write a possible *safe* implementation of a procedure which computes the Blood_sugar_level given a parameter BP, which is some blood characteristic. A function Compute_sugar should be used to derive the sugar level associated with BP. Your function should take into account the previously measured blood sugar levels and likely blood sugar levels which can occur.

21.3 Develop a safety proof of your function which demonstrates that it cannot compute an artificially low level (and thus cause excessive insulin to be administered).

21.4 A system model of a microwave oven is discussed in Chapter 13. As far as is possible, develop a hazard analysis for this system with associated fault trees. The principal hazard is clearly microwave leakage but over-heating should also be taken into account.

21.5 For a programming language which you use regularly, identify language constructs which should be avoided if safety-critical systems are to be developed in that language.

21.6 Using the further reading suggested here as a starting point, write a report discussing how safety should be considered in designing the user interface of a system.

Defect Testing

22

■ OBJECTIVES

The objective of this chapter is to describe an approach to software testing which is explicitly aimed at discovering program defects rather than assessing program reliability. A number of techniques of deriving program test cases which are likely to be effective in highlighting possible defects are discussed. These include functional or black-box testing with equivalence partitioning, where the program specification is used to derive test cases, and structural or 'white-box' testing. In this approach, the tester can make use of the code being tested to help guide test case selection. Residual defect estimation using error seeding is also briefly covered.

■ CONTENTS

The testing of a program has two objectives. Firstly, it is intended to show that the system meets its specification; secondly, it is intended to exercise the system in such a way that latent defects are exposed. These objectives are distinct. Validation testing requires the system to perform correctly using given acceptance test cases, whereas a successful defect test is a test which causes the system to go wrong and hence expose a defect.

These different types of testing are carried out at different phases of the testing process. Final system testing and acceptance testing should be concerned with validation. Earlier phases in the testing process, namely component and module testing and sub-system testing, should be oriented towards the discovery of defects in the program. A successful test is therefore a test which discovers a problem in the system.

In principle, testing of a program for defects should be exhaustive. Every statement in the program should be exercised and every possible path combination through the program should be executed at least once. In practice, this is impossible in a program which contains loops as the number of possible path combinations is astronomical.

A subset of the possible set of test cases must be used. This subset might be selected using the guidelines discussed here and should be supplemented by other tests generated using knowledge of the program, its application domain and its users. Petschenik (1985) suggests that test cases should be selected using the following heuristics:

(1)   'Testing a system's capabilities is more important than testing its components.' Users are interested in getting a job done and test cases should be chosen to identify aspects of the system which will stop them doing their job. Although errors, such as screen corruption, are irritating, they are less disruptive than errors which cause loss of data or program termination.

(2)   'Testing old capabilities is more important than testing new capabilities.' If a program is a revision of an existing system, users expect existing features to keep working. They are less concerned by failure of new capabilities which they may not use.

(3)   'Testing typical situations is more important than testing boundary value cases.' It is more important that a system works under normal usage conditions than under occasional conditions which only arise with extreme data values. This does not mean that boundary value testing (discussed below) is unimportant. It simply means that if it is necessary to restrict the number of test cases, it may be advisable to concentrate on typical input values.

Test cases and test data are not the same thing. Test data are the inputs which have been devised to test the system; test cases are input and output specifications plus a statement of the function under test. It is sometimes

```
generic
    type ELEM is private ;
    type ELEM_INDEX is range <> ;
    type ELEM_ARRAY is  array (ELEM_INDEX) of ELEM ;
    with function "<" (A, B: ELEM) return BOOLEAN is <> ;
    procedure Binary_search (Key : ELEM ; T : ELEM_ARRAY ;
            Found : in out BOOLEAN ;  L : in out ELEM_INDEX) ;


Pre-condition
    T'LAST - T'FIRST > 0  and Ordered (T) and T'FIRST >= 0


Post-condition
    ( Found and T (L) = Key)
or
    ( not Found and
        not (exists i, T'FIRST >= i <= T'LAST, T (i) = Key ))
```

Figure 22.1
Specification of binary
search procedure.

possible to generate test data automatically. It is impossible to generate test cases as the generator would have to have the same functions as the program being tested. Tests may be developed in parallel with the design and implementation by an engineer who is not involved in the design. These tests are available for immediate application when the implementation is complete.

This chapter is concerned with functional or black-box testing, where the tests are derived from the program specification, and structural or white-box testing where the tests are derived using knowledge of the program's implementation. Basili and Selby (1987) conducted an experiment comparing these approaches to testing and comparing them with program reviewing. The results of this experiment showed that, with professional programmers, static code reviewing found more faults and had a higher rate of fault detection than either testing technique. Functional testing discovered more faults than structural testing but the fault detection rate was similar.

A single, small example program is used throughout this chapter. This is unavoidably artificial but a practical testing example would be unmanageably large. The component to be tested is the well known, binary search routine which searches an array of elements and returns the array index of the element matching the input key. The specification of this routine, using pre- and post-conditions, is shown in Figure 22.1.

The post-conditions state that the variable Found is true and Index marks the array element matching the key, or that Found is false and there is no element of the array which matches the key. The pre-conditions specify that the array should be ordered, should have at least one element and its lower bound should be less than or equal to its upper bound. The code of this routine is shown in Figure 22.7.

22.1   Functional testing

Functional testing is an approach to testing where the specification of the component being tested is used to derive test cases. The component is a 'black box' whose behaviour can only be determined by studying its inputs and the related outputs. Figure 22.2 illustrates the model of a component which is assumed in functional testing. Notice this model of a component is the same as that used for reliability testing, discussed in Chapter 20.

The key problem for the tester whose aim is to discover defects is to select inputs which have a high probability of being members of the set I_e. Effective selection is dependent on the skill and experience of the tester but there are some structured approaches which can be used to guide the selection of test data.

22.1.1   Equivalence partitioning

Equivalence partitioning is a technique for determining which classes of input data have common properties. A program should behave in a comparable way for all members of an equivalence partition. Figure 22.3 shows how there are both input and output equivalence partitions; correct and incorrect inputs also form partitions.

The equivalence partitions may be identified by using the program specification or user documentation and by the tester using experience to predict which classes of input value are likely to detect errors. For example, if an input specification states that the range of some input values must be a 5-digit integer, that is, between 10 000 and 99 999, equivalence partitions might be those values less than 10 000, values between 10 000 and 99 999 and values greater than 99 999. Similarly, if four to eight values are to be input, equivalence partitions are less than four, between four and eight and more than eight.

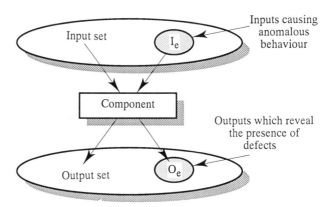

Figure 22.2
Black-box testing.

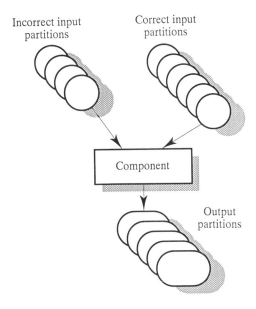

Figure 22.3
Equivalence
partitioning.

Input values which generate outputs in each output partition should also be chosen as tests. Say a program is designed to produce between three and six outputs, with each output lying in the range 1000–2500. Test input should be selected which produces three values at 1000, three values at 2500, six values at 1000 and six values at 2500. Furthermore, as far as is possible, input should be selected so that erroneous output values result if that input was processed as correct input. This input should attempt to force the program to produce less than three values, more than six values, values less than 1000 and values greater than 2500.

The specification of the binary search routine allows some equivalence partitions to be identified:

(1)   Inputs which conform to the pre-conditions.
(2)   Inputs where the pre-condition is false.
(3)   Inputs where the key element is a member of the array.
(4)   Inputs where the key element is not a member of the array.

Obviously, 1 and 2 may be combined with 3 and 4 in any combination, suggesting four equivalence partitions:

(1)   Inputs conforming to pre-conditions where the key element is in the array.
(2)   Inputs conforming to pre-conditions where the key element is not in the array.

(3)   Inputs which do not conform to pre-conditions where the key element is in the array.

(4)   Inputs which do not conform to pre-conditions where the key element is not in the array.

It may not be necessary to distinguish between cases 3 and 4. If the pre-conditions do not hold, the routine may return some error indicator. In the specification shown in Figure 22.1, nothing is said about how the component should behave if the pre-conditions do not hold, so in this example this state will not be considered. In a practical component, of course, the component's behaviour in this situation must be specified.

In some cases, the equivalence partitions are obvious or can be derived directly from the specifications. In others, the tester's experience must be used. In this case, we know that the input array should be ordered. Sometimes, ordered collections behave differently if they have an even or an odd number of members. It is also a good general principle to always test components which use arrays with single-value arrays as these may have to be treated as a special case in the implementation. Thus, three equivalence partitions can be identified:

(1)   The input array has a single value.

(2)   The input array has an even number of values.

(3)   The input array has an odd number of values, greater than 1.

In each of these cases, tests should be devised where the key element is or is not in the array.

There now remains the problem of deciding which members of the test arrays should match the keys. Again a heuristic is used. When a programmer has made a mistake in an algorithm, this is often because of a misunderstanding of its behaviour at the boundaries of its input domain. Thus, inputs at the edges of the equivalence partitions should be chosen. Myers (1979) calls this approach to test selection *boundary value analysis*.

Boundary value analysis of the identified equivalence partitions for the binary search routine suggests the following partitions:

(1)   Inputs where the key element is the first element in the array.

(2)   Inputs where the key element is the last element in the array.

Obviously, a test should also be constructed where the key element is neither the first nor the last element in the array. Combining all of these leads to the equivalence partitions shown in Figure 22.4.

A set of possible test cases based on these partitions is shown in Figure 22.5. If the key element is not in the array, the value of L is undefined ('??').

```
(1)    Array size of 1, element in array.
(2)    Array size of 1, element not in array.
(3)    Even array size, element 1st element in array.
(4)    Even array size, element last element in array.
(5)    Even array size, element not in array.
(6)    Even array size, element in array, not first or last.
(7)    Odd array size, element 1st element in array.
(8)    Odd array size, element last element in array.
(9)    Odd array size, element not in array.
(10)   Odd array size, element in array, not first or last.
```

Figure 22.4
Equivalence partitions
for binary search.

The set of input values used to test Binary_search is not exhaustive. The routine may fail if the input array happens to be 1, 2, 3, 4 but the tester cannot be expected to guess this from the specification. It is reasonable to surmise that if the test fails to detect defects when one member of a class is processed, no other members of that class will identify defects. Of course, defects may still exist because all equivalence partitions have not been identified and because errors may have been made in equivalence partition identification or in the preparation of the test data.

Given that the tester knows that the component is to be written in Ada, there is no need to design tests to check how the routine behaves with incorrectly typed input. The Ada compiler will catch all such errors. If the routine was to be written in assembly language or in a low-level language like C, there may be a need for further tests to check type compatibility of formal and actual parameters.

```
(1)    Input : T = 17 ;  Key = 17
       Output : Found = true ;  L= 1
(2)    Input : T = 17 ;  Key = 0
       Output : Found = false ;  L= ??
(3)    Input : T = 17, 18, 21, 23, 29, 33 ;  Key = 17
       Output : Found = true ;  L= 1
(4)    Input : T = 17, 18, 21, 23, 29, 33 ;  Key = 33
       Output : Found = true ;  L= 6
(5)    Input : T = 17, 18, 21, 23, 29, 33 ;  Key = 25
       Output : Found = false ;  L= ??
(6)    Input : T = 17, 18, 21, 23, 29, 33 ;  Key = 23
       Output : Found = true ; L= 4
(7)    Input : T = 17, 18, 21, 23, 29, 33, 38 ;  Key = 17
       Output : Found = true ;  L= 1
(8)    Input : T = 17, 18, 21, 23, 29, 33, 38 ;  Key = 38
       Output : Found = true ;  L= 7
(9)    Input : T = 17, 18, 21, 23, 29, 33, 38 ;  Key = 25
       Output : Found = false ;  L= ??
(10)   Input : T = 17, 18, 21, 23, 29, 33; Key = 23
       Output : Found = true ;  L = 4
```

Figure 22.5
Test cases for binary
search routines.

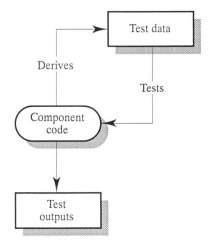

Figure 22.6
White-box testing.

The tests do not check for corruption of data outside the component. It does not make sense for black-box tests to check such corruption. Examination of the code, if the component is written in a structured high-level language, will reveal such problems. Only if pointers (Ada access variables) are used, is such corruption likely.

The technique of equivalence partitioning is a useful one for selecting instances of each possible input for test. However, even when a program operates successfully for individual test inputs, combinations of these inputs may detect program errors. Equivalence partitioning provides no help in selecting these combinations. Experienced testers, however, usually develop their own set of heuristics to select combinations likely to cause program failure.

One approach which can be used is called *cause–effect analysis*. This involves examining the output and analysing it to see if combinations of input partitions always cause outputs in the same output partition to be produced. The different output effects are examined and the causes of these effects used as test cases.

22.2 Structural testing

A complementary approach to testing is sometimes called structural, 'white-box' or 'glass-box' testing (Figure 22.6). The name contrasts with 'black-box' testing because the tester can analyse the code and use knowledge about it and the structure of a component to derive the test data. The advantage of structural testing is that test cases can be derived systematically and test

```
procedure Binary_search (Key : ELEM ; T : ELEM_ARRAY ;
            Found : in out BOOLEAN ; L : in out ELEM_INDEX )
is
    -- Assume that T'FIRST and T'LAST are both
    -- greater than or equal to zero and T'LAST >= T'FIRST
    Bott : ELEM_INDEX := T'FIRST ;
    Top : ELEM_INDEX := T'LAST ;
    Mid : ELEM_INDEX ;
begin
    L := (T'FIRST + T'LAST ) mod 2 ;
    Found := T( L ) = Key ;
    while Bott <= Top and not Found loop
        Mid := (Top + Bott) mod 2 ;
        if T( Mid ) = Key then
            Found := true ;
            L := Mid ;
        elsif T( Mid ) < Key then
            Bott :=  Mid + 1 ;
        else
            Top :=  Mid - 1;
        end if ;
    end loop ;
end Binary_search ;
```

Figure 22.7
Binary search
procedure.

coverage measured. The quality assurance mechanisms which are set up to control testing can quantify what level of testing is required and what has been carried out. The binary search routine is used again as an example. The Ada code for this routine is shown in Figure 22.7.

The equivalence partitions identified in black-box testing can be refined by examining the operation of the component being tested. Binary searching involves splitting the search space into three parts (Figure 22.8). Test cases where the key lies at the boundaries of each of these partitions should be chosen.

The test cases shown in Figure 22.5 test some but not all of the equivalence partition boundaries. Further cases (Figure 22.9) can be added to the test set. These are elements which are adjacent to the mid-point of the array.

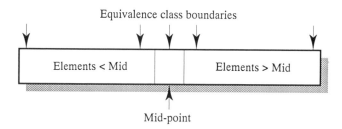

Figure 22.8
Binary search
equivalence classes.

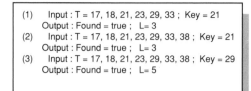

(1) Input : T = 17, 18, 21, 23, 29, 33 ; Key = 21
     Output : Found = true ; L= 3
(2) Input : T = 17, 18, 21, 23, 29, 33, 38 ; Key = 21
     Output : Found = true ; L= 3
(3) Input : T = 17, 18, 21, 23, 29, 33, 38 ; Key = 29
     Output : Found = true ; L= 5

Figure 22.9
Additional test cases
for binary search.

22.2.1 Path testing

Path testing is a white-box testing strategy which exercises every independent execution path through the component. This ensures that all statements in the program are executed at least once and that conditional statements are tested for both true and false cases.

Exhaustive path testing involves testing all possible combinations of all paths through the program. For any components apart from very trivial ones without loops, this is an impossible objective. Although all statements in the program are executed, defects which manifest themselves when particular path combinations arise may still be present.

The starting point for path testing is to derive a program flow graph which makes all paths through the program explicit. A flow graph consists of nodes representing decisions and edges showing flow of control. The flow graph representation for if-then-else, while-do and case statements is shown in Figure 22.10.

If goto statements are not used, it is a straightforward manual or automatic process to derive the flow graph for any program by substituting the above representations for program statements. Sequential statements (assignments, procedure calls and I/O statements) can be ignored in the flow graph construction. An independent program path is one which traverses at least one new edge in the flow graph. In program terms, this means exercising one or more new conditions. The flow graph for binary search procedure is showin in Figure 22.11.

Figure 22.10
Flow graph
representations.

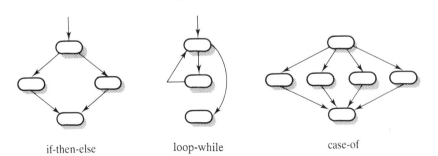

if-then-else   loop-while   case-of

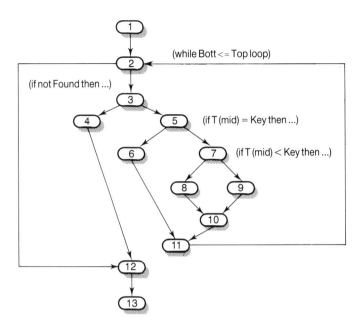

Figure 22.11
Flow graph for a binary
search procedure.

In Figure 22.11, the compound condition in the while statement has
been simplified into a simple while and an if statement:

```
while Bott <= Top loop
    if Found then
        exit
    else
        . . .
```

The reason for this simplification is that flow graphs are intended to show all
program decisions and a compound logical expression is shorthand for two
conditions.

An independent path through a flow graph is a path which includes an
edge which is not included in any other paths. The independent paths
through the binary search flow graph are:

1, 2, 3, 4, 12, 13
1, 2, 3, 5, 6, 11, 2, 12, 13
1, 2, 3, 5, 7, 8, 10, 11, 2, 12, 13
1, 2, 3, 5, 7, 9, 10, 11, 2, 12, 13

This analysis reveals that the test cases which have been derived so far are
appropriate for testing all independent paths through the routine.

Figure 22.12
Control- and
data-driven programs.

```
case A is
   when "One" => i := 1 ;
   when "Two" => i := 2 ;
   when "Three" => i := 3 ;
   when "Four" => i := 4 ;
   when "Five" => i := 5 ;
end case ;
```

```
Strings : array (1..4) of STRING :=
   ("One", "Two", "Three", "Four", "Five") ;
i := 1 ;
loop
   exit when Strings (i) = A ;
   i := i + 1 ;
end loop ;
```

The number of independent paths in a program can be discovered by computing the cyclomatic complexity (McCabe, 1976) from the program flow graph. The number of tests required to test all conditions is equal to the cyclomatic complexity.

The cyclomatic complexity (CC) of a graph (G) (any graph, not just a program flow graph) may be computed according to the following formula:

$$CC (G) = Number (edges) - Number (nodes) + 1$$

For programs without goto statements the cyclomatic complexity is equal to the number of conditions in the program. Compound conditions with N simple predicates are counted as N conditions. Thus, if there are six if-statements and a while loop, with all conditional expressions simple, the cyclomatic complexity is 7. If a conditional expression is a compound expression with an **and** and an **or**, the cyclomatic complexity is 9. The cyclomatic complexity of the binary search routine shown in Figure 22.7 is 4.

Knowing the number of tests required does not necessarily make it easier for the tester to derive test cases. An initial set of test data is proposed and then refined using the experience and judgement of the tester. A testing tool such as a dynamic program analyser (see Chapter 23) can indicate which parts of the program have been executed and its output used to guide the tester in selecting further test cases.

Path testing, based on cyclomatic complexity, is useful but testers must not be seduced into thinking that such testing is adequate. Testing metrics can be dangerous as they may give an impression that the program has been thoroughly tested whereas all that can be said is that some percentage (perhaps 100%) of the independent paths in a program have been executed. It is difficult to relate this to testing adequacy.

A problem with independent path testing is that the cyclomatic complexity is a measure of the program's control complexity. The data complexity is not taken into account. The program fragments in Figure 22.12 are equivalent in function but have different cyclomatic complexities.

These examples use different ways of representing a table. Complete testing requires that A should take all of the values 'One', 'Two', 'Three', 'Four', 'Five'. However, code fragment (a) has a cyclomatic complexity of 5 and fragment (b) a cyclomatic complexity of 1. This implies that the exhaustive testing of fragment (b) requires only a single test case. Of course, both fragments should be tested in exactly the same way.

It is generally true that the number of paths through a program is proportional to its size. Thus, as modules are integrated into systems, it becomes unfeasible to use structural testing techniques. These techniques are most appropriate at the unit testing and module testing stages of the testing process.

22.3 Residual defect estimation

We have already seen, in Chapter 20, that the reliability of a program is not necessarily directly proportional to the number of residual defects in that program. Program validation should continue until some acceptable level of reliability is attained. However, to assist with the test planning process, there are sometimes circumstances where it is useful to estimate how good the testing process is at discovering defects.

One approach which can be used for defect estimation is to use error seeding. Error seeding involves deliberately introducing defects into the program then measuring the effectiveness of program testing in discovering these defects.

Assume that N defects are introduced into a program and the testing process discovers M defects where X of the defects discovered are those introduced into the program. Thus, the proportion of discovered defects is X/N. By simple arithmetic, it can be deduced that the initial number of program defects is:

$$(M - X) \times N/X.$$

Given that M $-$ X defects have been discovered, the number of remaining defects is:

$$(M - X) \times (N/X - 1).$$

Such a metric must be used with care. It is based on the assumption that the types and proportions of defects introduced are the same as the defects in the component and that introducing defects does not interfere in any way with existing defects. This is impossible to verify and defect estimates based on this method are unlikely to be particularly accurate.

A related approach is called mutation testing (DeMillo *et al.,* 1978) which is predicated on the assumption that most program defects are minor defects. Mutation testing involves making small changes (mutations) to the program and running the mutated program using the same test set as the program being tested. If the test set is adequate, it should distinguish between all program mutations.

The problems with mutation testing are firstly the basic assumption that defects are usually caused by minor program errors and, secondly, that there is a vast number of potential program mutations which can be generated. Again, defect estimation based on this approach is unlikely to be particularly accurate.

■ KEY POINTS

- It is more important to test those parts of the system which are commonly used rather than those parts which are only rarely exercised.

- Even simple programs require many test cases if they are to be thoroughly tested.

- Equivalence partitioning is a way of deriving test cases. It depends on finding partitions in the input and output data sets and exercising the program with at least one value from these partitions. Often, the value which is most likely to lead to a successful test is a value at the boundary of a partition.

- Functional testing does not need access to source code. Structural testing uses source code information to derive test cases.

- Structural testing relies on analysing a program to determine paths through it and using this analysis to assist with the selection of test cases. It has the advantage that a test coverage metric can be produced but this is unreliable because it is only based on program control flow.

- Residual defects may be estimated by error seeding but the accuracy of this approach has not been demonstrated.

FURTHER READING

The Art of Software Testing. Contains excellent material on black-box testing, equivalence partitioning and boundary value analysis as well as much wisdom on testing. Its coverage of structural testing is limited. (G.J. Myers, 1979, John Wiley & Sons.)

Functional Program Testing and Analysis. This is a detailed study of the theoretical and practical basis of functional testing. Howden goes into the techniques in very much greater depth than that covered here. (W.E. Howden, 1987, McGraw-Hill.)

Comm. ACM, **31** (6), June 1988. This special issue of the journal contains a number of papers on software testing concerned with functional testing, the testing process and test coverage.

EXERCISES

22.1 Discuss the differences between functional and structural testing and suggest how they can be used together in the defect testing process.

22.2 Identify equivalence partitions for the Ordered list, Queue and Zone components whose algebraic specification is given in Chapter 8.

22.3 What peculiar testing problems can arise when numerical routines designed to handle very large and very small numbers are being tested?

22.4 Derive a set of test cases for the following components:

  (a) A keyed table where entries are made and retrieved using some alphabetic key.
  (b) A sort routine which sorts arrays of integers.
  (c) A routine which takes a line of text as input and counts the number of non-blank characters in that line.
  (d) A routine which takes a line of text as inputs where lines may have leading blank characters. The output from the routine is the text with leading blank characters stripped from the line.
  (e) A routine which examines a line of text and replaces sequences of blank characters with a single blank character.
  (f) An abstract data type called STRING which provides operations on character strings. These include concatenation, length (to give the length of a string) and substring selection.

22.5 Program the above routines using a language of your choice and, for each routine, derive the cyclomatic complexity.

22.6 By examining the code of the routines which you have written, derive further test cases in addition to those you have already considered. Has the code analysis revealed omissions in your initial set of test cases?

22.7 Experiment with producing mutations of one of the routines which you have written and check if your test cases distinguish between these mutations and the original routine.

22.8 Derive a set of test cases which could be used in the validation of the newspaper delivery system described in Exercise 3.7.

22.9 Select some of the routines in the newspaper delivery system and derive their cyclomatic complexity. Use this information to re-design, if necessary, the test cases you have produced for the newspaper delivery system.

Testing and Debugging Tools

23

■ OBJECTIVES

Testing and debugging tools are now widely available and play an important role in testing high-level language programs. The objective of this chapter is to describe some of these tools and their use in the testing and debugging process. Testing tools support the processes of test data generation and testing management. They allow program execution to be analysed and estimates of testing coverage produced. Simulators may be used to replace hardware and software which interact with the program being tested. Debugging environments which allow program execution to be monitored and controlled are briefly described in the final section of the chapter.

■ CONTENTS

Testing is an expensive and laborious phase of the software process. As a result, testing and debugging tools were among the first software tools to be developed. These tools now offer a range of facilities and their use significantly reduces the cost of the testing and debugging process.

The support tools used in the testing process make up a testing environment, as shown in Figure 23.1.

The model of testing suggested in Figure 23.1 involves instrumenting the source code of a program to be tested with extra statements to gather information about how often statements in the program have been executed, variables accessed, and so on. Execution takes place under the control of a test monitor which dynamically collects execution information. This execution profile is passed to a report generator which produces a report on the program's execution behaviour. The program under test may interact

Figure 23.1
Testing environment.

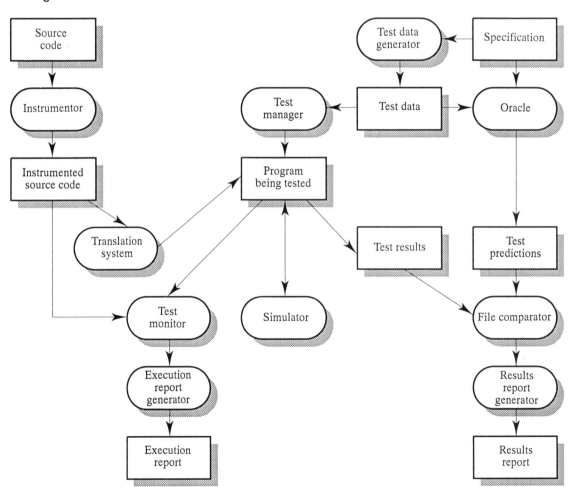

with a simulator taking the place of other hardware, software or system users.

On the right side of the diagram, a test data generator is shown being used in conjunction with an 'oracle'. An oracle is a program which, given a specification, can predict the results of the system test. The actual results and the predicted results are compared and a report on their differences produced. Testing takes place under the control of a test manager which synchronizes the tests and ensures that the program being tested is presented with the appropriate test data.

Many testing and debugging tools are programming language dependent. For example, a dynamic analyser depends on a compiler instrumenting a program. Normally, the more mature a language system, the better are the available testing and debugging tools. Unfortunately this means that when a new language is introduced, it takes some years before good support tools become available. Thus, we now have good testing and debugging tools for Pascal and C, but most Ada compilers do not have as good testing and debugging support.

23.1 Dynamic analysers

Dynamic analysers are programs used to provide information on how often each statement in a program has been executed. Although almost 20 years old, the paper by Satterthwaite (1972) is still, perhaps, the best general description of such systems. Dynamic analysers have two logical components:

(1) *An instrumentation part* This adds instrumentation statements to a program either while it is being compiled or before compilation. When the program is run, these statements gather and collate information on how often each program statement is executed.

(2) *A monitoring and display part* This collects the information provided by the instrumentation statements and prints an execution report. Typically, this is a program listing where each statement is annotated with the number of times it has been executed.

In Figure 23.1, these components are shown separately. However, it is more usual for them to be integrated with the language compiler as language knowledge is necessary for system instrumentation. Normally, dynamic analysis can be switched on and off with a compiler directive.

To instrument a program, all decision statements and loops must be identified and instrumentation code placed at the beginning of each loop and decision. A sequence of statements without loops or decisions need only have a single instrumentation section at the beginning of the sequence.

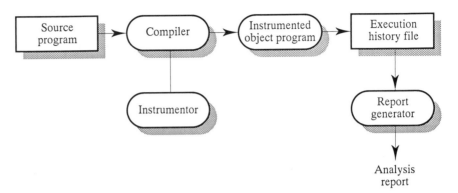

Figure 23.2
Dynamic analysis.

Alternatively, this instrumentation phase may be implemented as a preprocessor which adds high-level language statements to the program which collect information about the program execution. The program is then compiled by the standard compiler with execution information written to a separate file. Execution is normally controlled by a testing monitor which creates a 'history' file recording details of the program's execution behaviour (Figure 23.2).

This history file may then be input to the flow display program which summarizes the history information and collates it with the statements in the original program. Figure 23.3 is an example of a typical flow summary. It was generated using the Pascal execution flow summarizer available under the Berkeley UNIX system.

Dynamic analysers reformat the program and number the reformatted statements. Each statement or statement sequence has an associated number showing how many times that sequence has been executed. In Figure 23.3, you can see that statement 15 has been executed 700 times and each branch of the if-then-else statement has been executed 350 times.

The two principal uses of dynamic analysers are:

(1) *Test coverage assessment* A testing objective may be to ensure that all program statements are executed at least once. Using the reports from a dynamic analyser, program segments which have not been executed can be discovered. Further test cases can be devised to ensure that these segments are executed.

(2) *Program optimization* Programs spend most of their time in a few tight loops and the best way to optimize the program is to optimize these loops. The flow summarizer helps the engineer discover the most frequently executed loops.

Dynamic analysers are useful tools but rely on all of the program source code being instrumented. This is not always possible if pre-compiled program components from a library are used. Such components are not

```
Berkeley Pascal PXP -- Version 2.12 (5/11/83)
Mon  Oct  19 15:30 1987 pascflow.p
Profiled Mon Oct  19 15:38 1987
     1       1.---|program primes(input, output);
  {Prints all prime numbers between 3 and MAXPRIME.
  Uses Sieve of Eratosthenes method }
     6       |const
     6       |   MAXPRIME = 700;
     8       |type
     8       |   boolvec = array [1..MAXPRIME] of boolean;
    10       |var
    10       |   primes: boolvec;
    11       |   i, j, k: 1..MAXPRIME;
    13       |begin
    14       |   for i := 1 to MAXPRIME do
    15     700.---|   if odd(i) then
    16       350.---|   primes[i] := false
    16     350.---|   else
    18       350.---|   primes[i] := true;
    19       |   i := 3;
    20       |   k := trunc(sqrt(MAXPRIME));
    21       |   while i <= k do begin
    23       8.---|   j := i + i;
    23       |     while j <= MAXPRIME do begin
    26       688.---|   primes[j] := true;
    27       |     j := j + i
    27       |   end;
    29       |   i := i + 2;
    30       |   while primes[i] and (i <= k) do
    31       4.---|   i := i + 2
    31       |   end;
    33       |   i := 3;
    34       |   while i <= MAXPRIME do begin
    36     349.---|   if not primes[i] then
    37       123.---|   writeln(i, ' is prime');
    38       |   i := i + 2
    38       |   end
    38       |end.
```

Figure 23.3
A Pascal dynamic
analysis.

normally instrumented so their execution behaviour cannot be monitored. If a program includes library components, the dynamic analyser may not work properly and it may not be possible to abstract information about the program flow.

Another difficulty which sometimes inhibits the use of dynamic analysers is that the inclusion of code to collect program information affects the timing of that program. In real-time systems, timing is often critical and the timing overhead incurred by dynamic data collection is unacceptable. Real-time systems are among the most difficult to test and it is unfortunate that one of the most useful testing tools sometimes cannot be used.

23.2   **Test data generators and oracles**

Test data generators are programs which automatically generate a large number of test inputs for some system. They are particularly useful when the performance of a system in a practical environment must be tested. For example, the testing of a database management system may start by using small databases. That testing is initially designed to detect program errors resulting in incorrect output being produced. Small scale testing does not actually reflect the actual environment where the program is to be used. Given the specification of a database, a test data generator can generate large amounts of data so that the performance of the system may be tested in a realistic environment.

Given a specification of the syntax of the test input, the test data generator generates a large number of syntactically correct inputs. Maurer (1990) describes how context-free grammars may be used as a basis for test data generation and the use of the test data generator in testing VLSI designs. As well as being used in performance testing, this automatically generated test data is also used for statistical testing. In these tests, the distribution of the inputs is not random but depends on the predicted operational profile of the software.

Test data generators do not, of course, relieve the burden of output analysis. However, if the syntax of the output can also be formally specified, a syntax checker can be written to detect syntactically incorrect outputs. Incorrect outputs may be a result of defects in the program under test.

Testing of the syntax analysis phase of a compiler is a situation where automatically processed test input and output may be used. The output from syntax analysis for a correct program may be simply the input program. If an incorrect program is presented, the output also includes error indicators. A test data generator should accept a specification of the language syntax and from that generate correct and incorrect programs.

The output from the compiler can be checked automatically (Figure 23.4) to ensure that error messages are not generated for correct programs and, conversely, error messages are generated for incorrect programs. Of course, the error messages must still be checked manually to make sure that they are appropriate.

In Figure 23.4, the language generator generates correct and incorrect programs and informs the message filter whether a program is correct or incorrect. The message filter analyses the compiler output and highlights those correct programs which cause error messages to be generated and vice versa.

An 'oracle' is a program which, given a set of test data, can predict what the output of the program test ought to be if there are no defects in the part of the system tested by that data. Of course, a completely general-purpose oracle is unrealizable as it would be equivalent to a completely

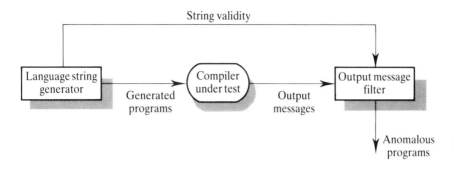

Figure 23.4
Test data generation.

correct program. In general, oracles can only be semi-automated with human assistance required for test result prediction.

If a system prototype is available it can act as a test oracle. Tests are submitted simultaneously to the prototype and to the system under test. The results are compared and differences brought to the tester's attention. Of course, the problem may be that the prototype is defective but this technique can reduce the amount of laborious human checking of test output.

A similar technique can be used when testing fault-tolerant systems where multiple versions of the system have been created from the same specification. To ensure these versions are consistent, they should be 'back-to-back' tested (Figure 23.5).

If there are differences in the outputs generated by different versions, this indicates that further investigation is required.

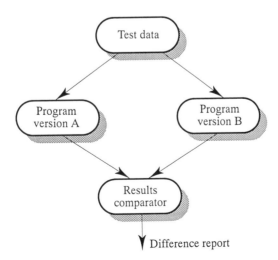

Figure 23.5
Back-to-back testing.

23.3 File comparators

A file comparator is a general-purpose software tool which reports differences between files. As testing involves the tedious examination of large volumes of test output, testers can easily miss anomalous output. If the checking and comparison process can be automated, human errors of this type are reduced.

Automated comparison involves preparing a file containing the output expected from a program if no errors are detected. The tests are then executed and the actual output directed to some other file. The files are then compared automatically and differences highlighted. If the expected output from the program and the actual output are the same, the tests failed to detect any errors.

File comparators are particularly useful when many tests are submitted to a program at once. Generally, only some will succeed and a file comparison program can detect successful tests and bring them to the attention of the tester. Where an automated or a semi-automated oracle is used, it is essential that a comparator tool is used to compare test outputs with predictions.

File comparators may also be used to check that procedures and functions do not have unwanted side effects which affect global program variables. A global dump may be taken before and after exercising a function. These dumps are then automatically compared. Global variable dumping cannot be automated using an external tool but must be implemented using a specially written procedure.

Those globals which have been changed are then highlighted by the file comparison program. This is illustrated in Figure 23.7 which shows the output produced by the UNIX file comparator 'diff' after comparing dumps of globals used in a Pascal program. Figure 23.6 shows the input files. These are the same except for the change in value of Y from 17 to 18 and the change in name from 'J Smith' to 'F Jones'.

File comparators may be completely general-purpose, comparing any two files character by character for equality. Alternatively, comparators can be constructed for a specific application and information about the structure of the test output built into the program.

General-purpose comparators are most useful when the expected output from a program can be compared with other program-generated data. This arises in regression testing where a modified program is tested to

```
X : integer = 20              X : integer = 20
Y : integer = 17              Y : integer = 18
Z : integer = 34              Z : integer = 34
name : chararray = 'J Smith'  name : chararray = 'F Jones'
```

Figure 23.6
Files to be compared.

```
diff Fig23.6a Fig23.6b
2c2
< Y : integer = 17
---
> Y : integer = 18
4c4
< name : chararray = 'J Smith'
---
> name : chararray = 'F Jones'
```

Figure 23.7
UNIX diff program
output.

ensure that the changes have not affected existing program functions. This is comparable to back-to-back testing (Figure 23.5).

The steps involved in regression testing are:

(1)   Prepare a general-purpose set of test cases.

(2)   Exercise the existing program version with these test cases and save the results in one or more files.

(3)   Make program modifications.

(4)   Exercise the modified program with the existing set of test cases and save the results in one or more files.

(5)   Automatically compare the files produced by the modified and unmodified program versions.

If the modifications have been made correctly, the file comparison should show the output files to be identical. It may be that the modifications were intended to affect existing functions in which case some of the output will clearly be different. However, it should be possible to predict which files have changed and use the file comparator to check that the changes are as predicted.

General-purpose comparison programs are less useful when the expected output file is manually input. A trivial input error such as the input of an extra blank which does not affect the meaning will cause a character by character file comparison to fail. In such cases, it is necessary to build special-purpose file comparison programs which have some embedded knowledge of the syntax of the outputs which they are comparing. Thus, spurious separators can be ignored by the program and the comparison made correctly.

23.4   Simulators

A simulator is a program which imitates the actions of some other program, hardware device, or class of devices. They are used to simulate hardware facilities in situations where the hardware is unavailable or where it is

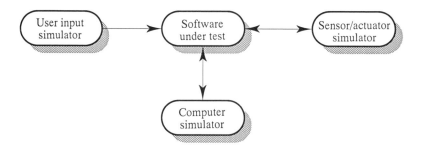

Figure 23.8
Simulators in system testing.

possible that faulty software could damage the interfaced hardware system (Figure 23.8).

Using a simulator means that software faults cannot cause hardware damage. Furthermore, the simulator can be instrumented to gather information about the combined hardware/software system, the software's execution behaviour and how it interacts with the hardware. The main disadvantage is that simulators are much slower than the hardware they are imitating. It is not possible to test functions which are dependent on the hardware timing.

In some cases, simulation is the only way to mimic the events which a real-time system must process. For example, if a program is used for controlling a nuclear reactor that program must obviously be able to deal with failure of the reactor cooling system. This should be signalled by sensor inputs indicating a rise in temperature, a drop in pressure, and so on. This cannot be tested operationally so these sensor inputs must be simulated. The reactions of the reactor control program to these inputs may then be observed.

Simulators are widely used in real-time system testing both to simulate hardware and external events which the system must process. Using a simulator, a sequence of events can be repeated exactly. Consider a situation where a system is accepting input from many sensors and a system failure occurs (Figure 23.9).

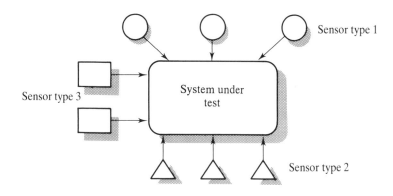

Figure 23.9
A real-time system with multiple input types.

Figure 23.10
Script-driven simulation in program testing.

Each sensor presents different information and the failure may be due to particular information combinations being processed simultaneously or may be due to some historical event sequence which has caused corruption of information. If the system is tested using real sensors interfaced to a changing environment it is impossible to reproduce the exact information and timing from each sensor. If a simulator is used, this can be driven by a prepared script. The exact sequence of inputs and their timings is repeatable (Figure 23.10).

Simulators allow systems to be tested under load. If a system must support a number of terminals with some average response time, a terminal simulator can be set up to imitate these terminals. The simulator can then measure the system response using different combinations of input. System testers can check if the software meets its performance requirements.

When imitating terminal inputs, the relatively slow simulator speed is not usually a problem as humans inputting information usually work more slowly than a simulator. Thus, in this case, the actual timings of the system can be observed.

Running the terminal simulator and the program under test on different computers ensures that timings are not affected by interactions between the simulator and the program under test. If the machines are connected by a high-speed local area network, the communication time between the systems need not perturb the simulator timings.

23.5   Debugging environments

The debugging process involves locating and repairing program defects. Because of subtle interactions within a program, the location of a defect may not be obvious from test output. The engineer responsible for repairing the defect must study the program's execution behaviour to find its source.

Many compilation systems now have an associated source language debugging environment where the control and data flow of the program is monitored. The execution is under the control of an engineer who may interact with it and examine data values at any time (Figure 23.11).

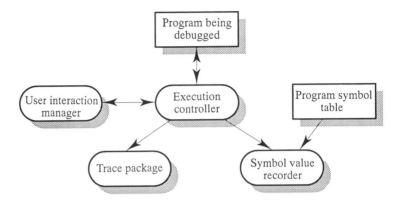

Figure 23.11
A debugging
environment.

An interactive debugging environment has three principal components:

(1)   An execution controller, which allows the engineer to set program breakpoints and allows 'single-stepping' through the program. Single-stepping means a single statement is executed then control immediately returned to the engineer. Breakpoints mark positions in the source code where execution should temporarily halt while the engineer uses the debugging system to examine variable values and control flow information.

(2)   A trace package, which records the control flow of the program. An engineer can examine this trace to discover errors in control which have been made.

(3)   A symbol value recording package, which maintains information about the system variable values. Variable histories may be recorded by this package. The variable values may be discovered using the variable names defined in the program.

Interactive debuggers such as dbxtool (described below), used in a multi-window environment where the program and the debugging tool displays are both visible, have radically changed the debugging process. Before the advent of such systems, programmers may have used a debugger to find out about the dynamic execution sequence but had to view a listing of the program text. Edits had to be marked on this and entered later, the program re-executed and the debugger again used to view the output. Now, the whole debug–edit–compile–execute cycle has been speeded up. Programmer productivity is markedly improved when interactive debugging systems are available.

The C debugging environment dbxtool is available on Sun workstations. The screen window used by dbxtool is shown in Figure 23.12. The display in Figure 23.12 is split into a number of sub-windows. The top

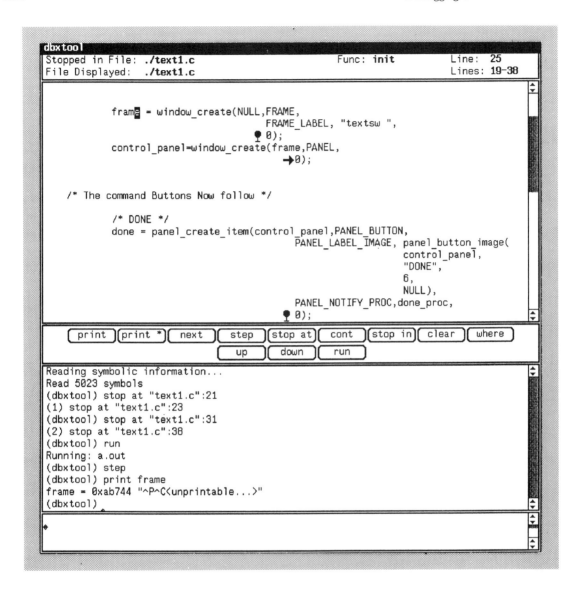

```
dbxtool
Stopped in File:  ./text1.c                    Func: init          Line:  25
File Displayed:   ./text1.c                                        Lines: 19-38

            fram█ = window_create(NULL,FRAME,
                               FRAME_LABEL, "textsw ",
                         ♀ 0);
            control_panel=window_create(frame,PANEL,
                              ➜0);


    /* The command Buttons Now follow */

         /* DONE */
         done = panel_create_item(control_panel,PANEL_BUTTON,
                           PANEL_LABEL_IMAGE, panel_button_image(
                                        control_panel,
                                        "DONE",
                                        6,
                                        NULL),
                       PANEL_NOTIFY_PROC,done_proc,
                         ♀ 0);
```

```
[ print ][ print * ][ next ][ step ][ stop at ][ cont ][ stop in ][ clear ][ where ]
              [ up ][ down ][ run ]
```

```
Reading symbolic information...
Read 5023 symbols
(dbxtool) stop at "text1.c":21
(1) stop at "text1.c":23
(dbxtool) stop at "text1.c":31
(2) stop at "text1.c":38
(dbxtool) run
Running: a.out
(dbxtool) step
(dbxtool) print frame
frame = 0xab744 "^P^C<unprintable...>"
(dbxtool)
```

Figure 23.12
Dbxtool display.

window, under the title bar, provides information about the file in which the displayed program is stored (text1.c), the function where execution has stopped (init), the line where execution has stopped (25) and the numbers of the lines which are on display.

The largest window in the display is the program display window. Several lines of the program are shown, with the arrow indicating the current execution point.

The menu window below the program display provides a number of buttons. Picking one of these buttons causes a debugger command to be executed. Users may single-step through their programs, set breakpoints, execute the program and so on. Other commands may be initiated by typing them in the interaction window, which acts like a character terminal.

The most sophisticated debugging environments include interpreters which give the user complete control over program execution. These environments build a 'history' file recording all program state changes during program execution. They provide facilities for interrogating this history file. Users can watch control and data flow in their program as each statement executes. Defective statements then be detected. At any stage, variable values may be discovered and execution can even be reversed.

The Cornell Program Synthesizer (Teitelbaum and Reps, 1981) is an example of interactive execution/debugging environment. Program execution is controlled by an interpreter. As particular statements in the program are executed, they are picked out by the cursor on the user's terminal. Users may 'single-step' their program executing statements one by one until a previously observed error manifests itself. Should the user overshoot the erroneous statement, the system provides a 'reverse gear' facility. This allows the execution of the program to be undone. Users can therefore quickly converge on the statement which is defective.

■ KEY POINTS

- The use of testing tools reduces the costs of program verification and validation.

- Dynamic analysers instrument the program then output a listing of the program statements along with a count of how often these have been executed. This can be used to identify parts of the program for optimization (those loops which are executed most) and for identifying program sections which have not been executed. Test cases can then be derived to exercise these sections.

- Test data generators, oracles and file comparators may be used together to automate the analysis of test results.

- Regression testing involves checking that changes to a program have not introduced new defects to operational program components. Comparator programs are the principal tools used in regression testing.

- Simulators are essential in the testing of real-time systems. They may simulate unavailable hardware or they may be used in conjunction with a prepared script to simulate terminal or device inputs to a system. Timing behaviour is always predictable.

■ Debugging environments allow the programmer to interact with the program as it is executing and examine program information such as the program's flow of control and variable values.

FURTHER READING

Software Testing and Evaluation.   This is one of the few publications which devotes a significant amount of space to testing tools. Its catalogue is rather outdated but the general description of tools is still valid. An extremely comprehensive bibliography is included. (R.A. DeMillo, W.M. McCracken, R.J. Martin and J.F. Passafiume, 1987, Benjamin Cummings.)

EXERCISES

23.1   Describe how a dynamic analyser can be used in the structural testing of a program.

23.2   Apart from a compiler, describe situations where a test data generator which generates sentences in a formal language might be used in system testing.

23.3   What are the difficulties of using a dynamic analyser when developing large software systems which are built from independently compiled routines?

23.4   Explain why regression testing is necessary and how it can be automated using testing tools.

23.5   Write a program which will take a list of files of test data and submit these to another program for execution. Record the outputs in separate files. Make changes in the program being tested then carry out regression testing using a file comparator.

23.6   Give examples of hardware simulators that might be required when testing real-time systems.

23.7   Explain why system tests based on simulators are not always reliable.

23.8   Suggest other software tools which might be useful in assisting program testing. Consider specific application domains when making your suggestions.

Static Verification

24

■ OBJECTIVES

Static verification is a verification process based on source code examination and analysis. Execution is not required. The objectives of this chapter are to discuss informal and formal static verification techniques, to describe static verification tools and to introduce a development process called cleanroom development, which is based around static system verification. The first section of the chapter covers program inspection, which is a systematic defect check of a program. This is followed by a discussion of mathematically-based verification. Static analysis tools which discover program anomalies are described and the final part of the chapter discusses the cleanroom development process which relies heavily on static verification.

■ CONTENTS

Testing is a dynamic verification and validation technique. The main problem with defect testing, particularly in its early stages, is that each test run tends to discover one or only a few faults. A fault can cause system data corruption so it is sometimes difficult to tell if output anomalies are a result of a new fault or simply a side effect of a fault which has already been discovered. Systematic program testing therefore requires a large number of test runs to be made, which contributes to the high cost of the process.

Static verification techniques do not require the program to be executed. Rather, they involve examining the source code of a program (or a design) and detecting faults before execution. Each error can be considered in isolation. Error interactions are not significant and an entire component can be validated in a single session.

Static verification is effective in finding errors in programs. Fagan (1986) reports that, typically, 60% of the errors in a program can be detected using systematic program inspections. Mills *et al.* (1987) suggest that more formal static validation using mathematical verification can detect more than 90% of the errors in a program.

As an indication of the costs of informal verification, Fagan suggests that about 100 lines of code can be inspected per hour and that this requires about another hour's preparation. Given that four people may be involved in a program inspection, the cost of inspecting 100 lines of code is roughly equivalent to the cost of one person working for one day.

Static verification is usually cost-effective. Defects can be found more quickly and at a lower cost that by defect testing techniques. Furthermore, the process of static verification can also be concerned with other quality attributes (see Chapter 31) such as compliance with standards, portability and maintainability. Even if static verification does not reduce the costs per defect discovered, the overall costs of achieving a required level of software quality will usually be lower if static techniques are used.

However, static and dynamic techniques are not in opposition. Dynamic testing will always be required for performance analysis, user interface validation and to check that the software requirements are what the user really wants. Effective combination of static validation and testing is necessary to achieve high quality software.

24.1 Program inspections

Reviews, as part of the quality assurance process, are discussed in Chapter 31. There are three principal types of review, concerned with management decision making, design strategy and with software verification. This latter type of review, which is discussed in this chapter, is sometimes called a *program inspection* (Fagan, 1976; 1986).

The term 'program inspection' is used here but the techniques used may be applied to any of the outputs of the software process. Requirements specifications, detailed design definitions, data structure designs, test plans and user documentation can all be systematically inspected.

The key difference between inspections and other types of review is that inspections are targeted at defect discovery. Defects may either be logical errors, anomalies in the code which might indicate an erroneous condition or non-compliance with organizational or project standards.

Inspections do not have an explicit educational function nor are they part of the design process where strategy decisions are made. To conduct an inspection effectively, there are a number of conditions which must hold:

(1) A precise specification of the code to be inspected must be available. It is impossible to inspect a component at the level of detail required to detect defects without a complete specification.

(2) The members of the inspection team must be familiar with the organizational standards.

(3) An up-to-date, syntactically correct version of the code must be available. There is no point in inspecting code which is 'almost complete' even if delay causes schedule disruption.

(4) A checklist of likely errors should be available to assist with the inspection process. This should be established initially by discussion with experienced staff and should be refined as more experience is gained of the inspection process.

(5) Management must be prepared to accept that static verification will 'front-load' project costs. There should be a consequent reduction in testing costs.

(6) Project management must consider inspections as part of the verification process and not as personnel appraisals. Inspection results should not be used in an individual's career reviews.

The process of inspection is a formal one carried out by a small team of at least four people. Team members sytematically analyse the code and point out possible defects. The roles in the team are:

- *Author* The programmer or designer responsible for producing the component or components to be inspected.
- *Reader* The reader presents the code to the team during the inspection process.
- *Tester* The tester reviews the code from a testing point of view.

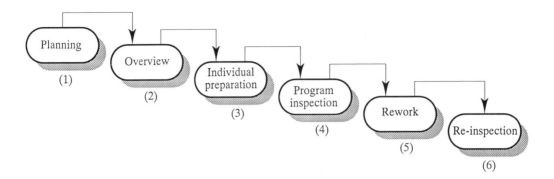

Figure 24.1
Inspection process
stages.

- *Chairman or moderator* The chairman is responsible for conducting the inspection and motivating the other participants. Ideally, the chairman should not be directly involved in the development of the product being inspected although it is sometimes impractical, in small organizations, to bring in people from outside the project.

Fagan suggests that there should be six stages in the inspection process (Figure 24.1) and that it is unwise to leave any of them out.

The planning stage involves selecting an inspection team, organizing a meeting room and ensuring that the material to be inspected and its specifications are complete. The overview stage is concerned with presenting a general description of the material to be inspected to the inspection team. This is followed by a period of individual preparation where each inspection team member studies the code and its specification.

The inspection itself should be relatively short (no more than two hours) and should be exclusively concerned with identifying product defects, anomalies and non-compliance with standards. The inspection team should not suggest how these defects should be corrected nor recommend changes to other components.

Following inspection, the program is modified by its author to correct the identified problems. Re-inspection is then necessary as new defects may be introduced during the rework. However, it may not be necessary to repeat the entire inspection process. The inspection chairman may simply check that the changes have been made correctly.

The amount of code which can be inspected in a given time varies depending on the experience of the inspection team, the programming language and the application domain. Fagan provides approximate figures as follows:

(1)   About 500 source code statements per hour can be considered during the overview stage.

(2)   During individual preparation, about 125 source code statements per hour can be examined.

> (1) Are all program variables initialized before their values are used?
> (2) Have all constants been named?
> (3) For each conditional statement, is the condition correct?
> (4) Is each loop certain to terminate?
> (5) When arrays are processed, should the lower bound be 0, 1, or
>   something else?
>   Should the upper bound be equal to the size of the array or Size -1?
> (6) If character strings are used, is a delimiter explicitly assigned?
> (7) If dynamic storage is used, has space been allocated correctly?
> (8) Do all function and procedure calls have the correct number of
>   parameters?
> (9) Do formal and actual parameter types match? This is not a problem
>   if a strongly typed language is used.
> (10) If a linked structure is being modified, have all links been correctly
>   re-assigned?
> (11) Are compound statements correctly bracketed?
> (12) Have all possible error conditions been taken into account?
> (13) If the component is concerned with checking keyword input, have all
>   keywords been checked?

Figure 24.2
Inspection checks.

(3)   From 90 to 125 statements per hour can be inspected.

Fagan suggests that the maximum time spent on an inspection should be about two hours as the efficiency of the defect detection process falls off after that time. Inspection should therefore be a frequent process, carried out on relatively small software components, during program development.

The inspection process may be driven using a checklist of common programmer mistakes. This checklist will vary, depending on the checking provided by the language compiler. For example, an Ada compiler checks that functions have the correct number of parameters, a C compiler does not. Examples of checks which might be made during the inspection process are shown in Figure 24.2.

24.2 Mathematically-based verification

Formal program verification involves proving, using mathematical arguments, that a program is consistent with its specification. Research on program proving has been going on for more than 20 years. This is built on the work of McCarthy (1962), and a number of other authors such as Floyd (1967), Hoare (1969) and Dijkstra (1976). McGettrick (1982) is a good text for practical programmers interested in formal verification. He uses Ada as the example programming language.

Two pre-conditions must hold before mathematically-based formal verification is possible:

(1) The semantics of the programming language must be formally defined.

(2) The program must be formally specified in a notation which is consistent with the mathematical verification techniques used.

Although there has been some work done in formal language definition, the semantics of most languages are not formally defined. This means that, for most programs, it is not possible to prove them in the strict mathematical sense.

However, less formal logical arguments based on mathematics can be used to increase confidence that a program conforms to its specification. These arguments must demonstrate two things:

(1) That the program code is logically consistent with the program specification.

(2) That the program will always terminate.

It might be imagined that the more rigorous the mathematical demonstration of correctness, the lower the probability of error in the program. This is not necessarily the case. A reasonable assumption is that the number of errors in a symbolic text is proportional to the number of symbols in that text. Thus, the larger a program (or a proof), the more errors it will contain. Informal arguments are much shorter than formal proofs so are less likely to contain errors.

There are a number of different techniques for demonstrating program correctness and the approach illustrated here is an axiomatic one. Linger *et al.*, (1979) describe a slightly different function-based approach which has reportedly been used with some success within IBM.

The basis of the axiomatic approach is as follows. Assume that there are a number of points in a program where assertions can be made about program variables and their relationships. Assertions A_1, A_2, . . ., A_n are associated with points P_1, P_2, . . ., P_n in the program. A_1 (the pre-condition) must be an assertion about the input of the program and A_n (the post-condition) an assertion about the program output. As discussed in Chapter 7, the pre-condition and the post-condition, along with the signature of the component being verified, make up its formal specification.

To prove that the program between points P_i and P_{i+1} is correct, the verifier must show that the statements separating these points cause assertion A_1 to be transformed to assertion A_{i+1}. If it is shown that A_1 leads to A_2, A_2 to A_3 and so on until all statements have been considered, the combination of these 'proofs' shows that assertion A_1 leads to A_n and that

```
generic
    type ELEM is private ;
    type ELEM_INDEX is range <> ;
    type ELEM_ARRAY is array (ELEM_INDEX) of ELEM ;
    with function "<" (A, B: ELEM) return BOOLEAN is <> ;
procedure Binary_search (Key : ELEM ; T : ELEM_ARRAY ;
            Found : in out BOOLEAN ;  L : in out ELEM_INDEX) ;

Pre-condition
    T'LAST - T'FIRST > 0  and Ordered (T) and T'FIRST >= 0

Post-condition
    ( Found and T (L) = Key)
or
    ( not Found and
        not (exists i, T'FIRST >= i <= T'LAST, T (i) = Key ))
```

Figure 24.3
The specification of a binary search procedure.

the program is partially correct. Complete correctness can be demonstrated if it can be proved that the program will always terminate.

In this chapter, I do not present a mathematically formal correctness proof. I do not think such proofs will ever be cost-effective in the software verification and validation process. Rather, a correctness argument based on the specification will be demonstrated. Comparable arguments are the basis of the static verification process which has been successfully used in the 'cleanroom' approach to software development (discussed later in this chapter).

The example used is, again, the binary search routine. Its specification is shown in Figure 24.3.

The function specification includes the function signature (its parameters and their types) and pre- and post-conditions. The pre-condition is a predicate which must be true for the function to execute correctly and the post-condition is a predicate which holds after function execution. The value returned by the function is referenced in the post-condition by using the function name.

A mnemonic notation is used in this chapter. The existential quantifier (∃) is replaced by a mnemonic **exists**. The universal quantifier (∀) is replaced by the mnemonic **for_all**. The membership operator (∈) is replaced by the keyword **in** which may be applied to arrays as well as to sets.

Slices of an array may be specified, as in Ada, by writing their upper and lower bounds. For example, A (3..6) specifies the part of the array which includes elements indexed from 3 to 6 inclusive. Pre-conditions and post-conditions are distinguished by appropriate keywords and names may be given to predicates using a **define** declaration.

The binary search routine code, annotated with assertions, is shown in Figure 24.4.

The precondition states that the upper bound of the array is greater than the lower bound, that the array T is ordered and that the lower and the

Figure 24.4
Annotated binary
search routine.

```
procedure Binary_search (Key : ELEM ; T : ELEM_ARRAY ;
  Found : in out BOOLEAN ; L: in out ELEM_INDEX ) is
--| Pre : T'LAST - T'FIRST > 0  and Ordered (T) and T'FIRST >= 0
Bott : ELEM_INDEX := T'FIRST ;
Top : ELEM_INDEX := T'LAST  ;
Mid : ELEM_INDEX ;
begin
  L := ( T'FIRST + T'LAST ) mod 2 ;
  Found := T( L ) = Key ;
  -- loop invariant
  --|1. Found and T(L) = Key or
  --|  not Found and not Key in
  --|   T(T'FIRST..Bott-1, Top+1..T'LAST)
  while Bott <= Top and not Found loop
    Mid := (Top + Bott) mod 2 ;
    if T( Mid ) = Key  then
        Found := true ;
        L := Mid ;
      --| 2.  Key = T(Mid) and Found
    elsif T( Mid ) < Key then
          --| 3.not Key  in T(T'FIRST..Mid)
        Bott :=  Mid + 1 ;
      --| 4. not  Key  in T(T'FIRST..Bott-1)
     else
          --| 5. not  Key in T( Mid..T'LAST )
        Top :=  Mid - 1 ;
      --| 6. not  Key in T(Top+1..T'LAST)
    end if ;
  end loop ;
--| Post: Found and T (L) = Key or (  not Found
--| and not (exists i, T'FIRST >= i <= T'LAST, T (i) = Key ))
end Binary_search ;
```

upper bound of the array are both non-negative. Figure 24.5 shows the definition of the predicate Ordered.

The post-condition states that either the boolean variable Found is set true and the value of L indexes an element of the array T equal to Key, or that Found is false and there is no value in the array T which is equal to Key. This condition is stated by writing down that there does not exist a value i which is a valid array index such that T(i) is equal to Key. Both a boolean and an integer result are returned as the value of L is undefined if Found is false.

Recall that the earlier discussion of specification required changes to input parameters to be specified. As this routine is written in Ada and the

```
--| define Ordered (T : ELEM_ARRAY) is
--|   for_all i, T'FIRST >= i <= T'LAST-1,
--|      T (i) <= T (i + 1)
```

Figure 24.5
Ordered specification
function.

language rules state that parameters passed by value cannot be modified, this is unnecessary. We also ignore the circumstances where the procedure is presented with input which does not match the precondition. The keyword **in** used in the assertions in Example 24.4 means array membership. Thus, A **in** B means that at least one of the elements of array B has a value equal to the value of A.

The logical argument demonstrating the correctness of the binary search routine first shows that the routine will terminate then describes how the pre-condition and the routine code leads to the binary search post-condition.

Termination argument

(1)   The program contains a single while loop which terminates when Found becomes true or when Bott becomes greater than Top.

(2)   If an element equal to the key exists, Found is explicitly set true.

(3)   The condition Bott <= Top means that (Top − Bott) >= 0 for the loop to execute. If it can be shown that (Top − Bott) < 0, loop termination is guaranteed.

    If an element matching Key is not found during an execution of the loop, either the statement Bott := Mid + 1 of the statement Top := Mid − 1 must be executed. We know from the meaning of the mod operation that the value of Mid is less than Top and greater than or equal to Bott. The effect of assignments to Top or Bott is to reduce (Top − Bott). Eventually (Top − Bott) must become negative.

(4)   Therefore the loop and thus the program must terminate.

Correctness argument

To demonstrate that this design is correct, it must be shown that the final assertion follows from the initial assertion and the program code.

(1)   Assertion 1 is the loop invariant which specifies either that a value matching Key does not lie in the portion of the array already examined or the value at the mid-point of the array matches Key. This is true on the first entry to the loop. None of the array has been examined so a value matching Key cannot lie in the examined portion of the array.

(2)   Assertion 2 follows because of successful test, Key = Mid.

(3)   Assertion 3 follows from the fact that T is ordered and T(Mid) < Key. All values between T'FIRST and Mid must therefore be less than Key.

(4)   Assertion 4 follows by substituting Bott − 1 for Mid.

(5)   Assertion 5 follows using a similar argument to 3 for values greater than Key. All values between Mid and T'LAST must be greater than Key.

(6)   Assertion 6 follows from 5 by substituting Top − 1 for Mid.

(7)   At the end of a loop execution, it follows from the loop invariant that T(L) = Key and Found is true or, alternatively, Found is false and there is no value in the part of the table searched so far that equals Key. On termination Bott is greater than Top so the expression T(T'FIRST..Bott − 1, Top + 1..T'LAST) includes the entire array. There is no value in T = Key.

(8)   Therefore, the binary search program is correct.

Authors such as Macro and Buxton (1986) do not consider program proving to be a cost-effective software engineering technique. On the other hand, reports of work at IBM's Federal System's division (Mills *et al.*, 1987) describe the successful use of verification techniques in the development of large programming systems. They suggest that the effort to develop informal demonstrations of correctness is less than the effort required to verify a program by testing.

Mathematically-based verification techniques may increase our confidence in the program's correctness and may reduce the costs of defect testing. For certain classes of safety-critical or highly secure systems, they are probably the only effective way of achieving a sufficient level of confidence that the program meets its specification. However, mathematically-based verification is only a part of the overall V & V process and must be complemented with effective system testing. Ultimately, the reliability of a program can only be assessed by dynamic methods.

24.2.1 Verification tools

Mathematically formal verification of correctness of a program is an attractive concept but because of the amount of work involved it is not a cost-effective validation technique for large software systems. However, some efforts have been made to develop software tools to reduce this effort. An excellent summary of these systems is given by Lindsay (1988). Completely automated program verifiers have not yet been developed but the current theorem provers can provide assistance in developing a proof and can help check proofs which have been developed.

The SPADE suite of verification and validation tools (Carré, 1989) allows users to annotate programs in a restricted 'safe' subset of Ada or Pascal with program proofs. These tools also provide extensive static analysis capabilities as discussed in the following section.

The SPADE toolset supports an interactive proof checker to assist with the development of these proofs. This is one of the few commercially available tools which supports the verification process. Experience with this system is still limited and the technology used has not yet spread beyond the relatively limited safety-critical systems marketplace.

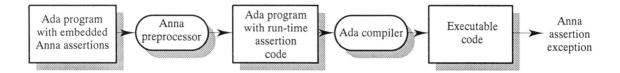

Other tool developments in this area (Luckham and Von Henke, 1985) have introduced the interesting idea of self-checking code where a verification tool is integrated with program execution. Programmers write verification information using a notation called Anna (Annotated Ada) and include this as formal program comments. During execution, this is automatically checked (Figure 24.6). If the verification tool signals a potential inconsistency, program execution may be suspended or some other exception handling mechanism activated.

Figure 24.6
Annotated Ada
self-checking programs.

24.3 Static program analysers

Static program analysers are software tools which scan the source text of a program and detect possible faults and anomalies. They do not require the program to be executed. They may be used as part of the verification process to complement the error detection facilities provided by the language compiler.

The intention of automatic static analysis is to draw the verifier's attention to anomalies in the program such as variables which are used without initialization, variables which are unused, and so on. While these are not necessarily erroneous conditions, it is probable that many of these anomalies are a result of errors of commission or omission. Some of the checks which can be detected by static analysis are shown in Figure 24.7.

Unreachable code
Unconditional branches into loops
Undeclared variables
Variables used before initialization
Variables declared and never used
Variables written twice with no intervening
assignment
Parameter type mismatches
Parameter number mismatches
Uncalled functions and procedures
Non-usage of function results
Possible array bound violations
Misuse of pointers

Figure 24.7
Static analysis checks.

There are a number of stages of static analysis:

(1)   *Control flow analysis*   This stage identifies and highlights loops with multiple exit or entry points and unreachable code. Unreachable code is code which is surrounded by unconditional goto statements and which is not referenced elsewhere in the program. If goto statements are avoided, unreachable code cannot be written.

(2)   *Data use analysis*   This stage is concerned with examining how variables in the program are used. It detects variables which are used without previous initialization, variables which are written twice without an intervening assignment and variables which are declared but never used. Data use analysis can also detect ineffective tests where the test condition always has the same value.

(3)   *Interface analysis*   This analysis checks the consistency of routine and procedure declarations and their use. It is unnecessary if a strongly typed language like Ada is used for implementation but can detect type errors in weakly typed languages like Fortran and C. Interface analysis can also detect functions and procedures which are declared and never called or function results which are never used.

(4)   *Information flow analysis*   This phase of the analysis identifies all input variables on which output variables depend. While it does not detect anomalies, the derivation of the values used in the program are explicitly listed. Erroneous derivations should therefore be easier to detect during a code inspection or review. Information flow analysis can also show the conditions on which a variable's value depends.

(5)   *Path analysis*   This phase of semantic analysis identifies all possible paths through the program and sets out the statements executed as part of that path. It essentially unravels the program's control and allows each possible predicate to be analysed individually.

Information flow analysis and path analysis generate an immense amount of information. This information is really another way of viewing the program and does not highlight anomalous conditions. Because of the large amount of information generated, static analysis is therefore often restricted to those phases which can explicitly detect program anomalies.

Early static analysers such as DAVE (Osterweil and Fosdick, 1976), AUDIT (Culpepper, 1975) and FACES (Ramamoorthy and Ho, 1975) were developed for use with Fortran programs. They check subroutine interfaces to ensure that the number and types of subroutines parameters are consistent with the routine declaration, locate COMMON block errors and flag error-prone practices such as branching into a DO-loop. Fortran-based static analysers are particularly useful because Fortran compilers do not do much program checking and the language leaves much scope for misuse.

```
138% more lint_ex.c
#include <stdio.h>
printarray (Anarray)
      int Anarray ;
{
      printf("%d",Anarray) ;
}
main ()
{
      int Anarray[5] ; int i ;  char c ;
      printarray (Anarray, i, c) ;
      printarray (Anarray) ;
}
139% cc lint_ex.c
140% lint lint_ex.c
lint_ex.c(10) : warning : c may be used before set
lint_ex.c(10) : warning : i may be used before set
printarray: variable # of args. lint_ex.c(4)  ::  lint_ex.c(10)
printarray, arg. 1 used inconsistently  lint_ex.c(4)  ::  lint_ex.c(10)
printarray, arg. 1 used inconsistently  lint_ex.c(4)  ::  lint_ex.c(11)
printf returns value which is always ignored
```

Figure 24.8
LINT static analysis.

A static analyser for C programs, called LINT, is distributed as part of the UNIX system. LINT provides static checking equivalent to that provided by the compiler in a strongly-typed language such as Ada. The reliability advantages of a strictly typed language are combined with the efficient code generation of a systems implementation language. However, many C programmers don't always use LINT to check their programs before execution and hence spend time in unnecessary debugging.

An example of the output produced by LINT is shown in Figure 24.8. This is a transcript of a UNIX terminal session where commands are shown in italics. The first command lists the (nonsensical) program. It defines a function with one parameter called printarray then causes this function to be called with three parameters. Variables i and c are declared but never assigned values. The value returned by the function is never used.

The line numbered 139 shows the C compilation of this program with no errors reported by the C compiler. This is followed by a call of the LINT static analyser which detects and reports program errors.

The static analyser shows that the scalar variables c and i have been used but not initialized and that printarray has been called with a different number of arguments than are declared. It also identifies the inconsistent use of the first argument in printarray and the fact that the function value is never used.

Static analysers are useful tools which can take over some of the error checking functions of the program inspection process. However, they should not be considered as a substitute for inspections as there are a significant number of error types which they cannot detect. For example, they can detect uninitialized variables but they cannot detect initializations which are incorrect. They can detect (in a language like C) functions which have the wrong numbers and types of arguments but they cannot detect situations where an incorrect argument of the correct type has been correctly passed to a function.

24.4 Cleanroom software development

Cleanroom software development (Mills *et al.*, 1987; Cobb and Mills, 1990) is a software development philosophy which is based on static verification techniques. A model of the process adopted is shown in Figure 24.9. The cleanroom process is named by analogy with semiconductor fabrication units, where defects are avoided by manufacturing in an ultra-clean atmosphere.

The cleanroom approach to software development is based on the notion that defects in software should be avoided rather than detected and repaired. It relies on static verification techniques during development to ensure that fault-free software is developed. Instead of unit and module testing, software components are formally specified and mathematically verified as they are developed. The process forces specification development and stability and then verifies the developed software against that specification without executing the software.

There are four characteristics of cleanroom software development.

(1) *Incremental development* The software is partitioned into increments which are developed separately using the cleanroom process.

(2) *Formal specification* The software to be developed is formally specified. Mills (1988) discusses the specification technique used which is based on formally defining how the system responds to stimuli.

(3) *Static verification* The developed software is statically verified using mathematically-based correctness arguments. There is no unit or module testing.

Figure 24.9 Cleanroom software engineering.

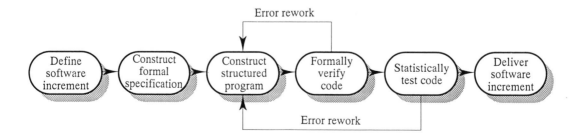

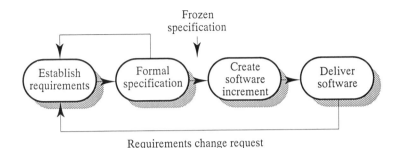

Figure 24.10
Incremental
development.

(4)   *Statistical testing*   The integrated software increment is tested statistically to determine its reliability.

Incremental development (Figure 24.10) involves producing and delivering the software in parts which are made available for user assessment. An increment can be executed by user commands and is a useful, albeit limited, system in its own right. Users can then feed back reports of the system and propose changes that are required. Incremental development is important because it minimizes the disruption to the development process caused by customer-requested requirements changes.

When a specification is specified as a single unit, customer requirements changes (which are inevitable) disrupt the specification and development process. The specification and design must be continually reworked. With incremental development, the specification for the increment is frozen although change requests for the rest of the system are accepted. The software increment is delivered on completion and customers may experiment with it and request changes to be supported in the next release of the increment.

There are three teams involved in the cleanroom process:

(1)   *The specification team*   This group is responsible for developing and maintaining the system specification. Both customer-oriented specifications (requirements definition) and internal, mathematical specifications are produced by this team.

(2)   *The development team*   This team has the responsibility of developing and verifying the software. The software is not executed or even compiled during the development process. A structured, formal approach to verification based on inspection of code supplemented with correctness arguments is used.

(3)   *The certification team*   This team is responsible for developing a set of statistical tests to exercise the software after it has been developed. These tests are based on the formal specification so this process can be carried out in parallel with software development. The individual

software modules are integrated and tested and reliability estimated. If errors are discovered, the software is returned to the development team for rework.

The first stage of testing is an integration test of the complete system (or a major increment of it) and statistical techniques are used during testing to assess reliability. A model of expected usage patterns of the product is created and used to drive the testing process. Reliability growth models, as discussed in Chapter 20, are used to determine when the system has been tested adequately.

The cleanroom approach is reportedly no more expensive than conventional development and testing but it results in software with very few errors. Cobb and Mills (1990) discuss several successful cleanroom development projects which have a uniformly low error rate. The overall development cost was no greater than with other development techniques.

Selby *et al.* (1987), in an independent comparative assessment of cleanroom development (using students as developers), reported that most teams could successfully use the cleanroom method and that the products developed using the cleanroom process were of higher quality than those developed using 'traditional' techniques. More of the cleanroom teams met the development schedule. The developed source code had more comments and a simpler structure.

The cleanroom approach is an interesting experiment in software development which suggests that the use of static verification is cost-effective. Defects are discovered before execution and are not introduced into the developed software. Overall development costs are not increased because less effort is required to test and repair the developed software.

Like most experiments in software engineering, there are many dependent variables such as specification development, formal verification and the skill and experience of the staff involved. The overall process seems to work well when practised by skilled and committed engineers. However, reports of the success of this approach in industry have mostly come from its developers. Their commitment is clearly a factor in making the process work and it is not yet clear whether the technology can be transferred to an environment where the staff are less skilled and less committed to cleanroom development.

■ KEY POINTS

■ Static verification techniques involve examination and analysis of the program source code to detect errors. They complement program testing.

- Program inspections are effective in finding program errors. Program code is systematically checked by a small team. The aim of an inspection is to locate faults and the inspection process is often driven by a fault checklist.

- Mathematical program verification involves producing a mathematically rigorous argument that a program conforms to its specification. The misleading term 'proof of correctness' is sometimes used for this process.

- Verification is accomplished by setting out program pre- and post-conditions and demonstrating that the application of the program statements leads invariably from the pre-conditions to the post-conditions. It also involves showing that the program terminates.

- Static analysers are software tools which process a program source code looking for anomalies such as unused code sections and uninitialized variables.

- Cleanroom software development is an approach to software development which relies on static techniques for program verification and statistical testing for system reliability certification. It has reportedly been successful in producing systems with a small number of residual defects resulting in few software failures.

FURTHER READING

'Advances in software inspections'. An article by the inventor of program inspections which describes the excellent results the inspection process has achieved. (M.E. Fagan, *IEEE Trans. Software Engineering*, **12** (7), July 1986.)

'Using inspections to investigate program correctness'. This article discusses how a mathematically-based but not completely formal inspection process is effective in discovering program errors. (R.N. Britcher, *IEEE Computer*, **21** (11), November 1988.

'Cleanroom software engineering'. This article describes the development technique used in IBM's Federal Systems division, which is based on program correctness arguments and statistical quality checks. (H.D. Mills, M. Dyer, and R. Linger, *IEEE Software*, **4** (5), September 1987.)

'Engineering software under statistical quality control'. This is a good supplement to the 1987 article by Mills and others discussed above. It provides more information about the cleanroom process and more evidence of its effectiveness. (R.H. Cobb and H.D. Mills, *IEEE Software*, **7** (6), November 1990.)

EXERCISES

24.1 The technique of program inspections was derived in a large organization which had a plentiful supply of potential inspectors. Suggest how the method might be revised for use in a small programming group with no outside assistance.

24.2 Using your knowledge of Pascal, C or some other programming language, derive a checklist of common errors (not syntax errors) which could not be detected by a compiler but which might be detected in a program inspection.

24.3 Write a set of routines to implement an abstract data type called SYMBOL_TABLE which could be used as part of a compilation system. Organize a program inspection of your routines and keep a careful account of the errors discovered. Test the routines using a black-box approach and compare errors which are revealed by testing with those discovered by inspection.

24.4 The specification of a routine called Max_value which finds the largest element in an array is shown in Figure 24.11. Code this routine and demonstrate the correctness of your implementation using logical correctness arguments. The specification function Initialized verifies that all elements of the array have been assigned an initial value.

24.5 Modify the routine in Example 24.11 (Max_value) so that it sums the elements of the array and returns the value of that sum. Modify the correctness arguments accordingly.

24.6 Formally specify, implement and produce correctness arguments for the following routines:

(a) A linear search routine.
(b) A routine which sorts an array of integers using bubblesort.

Figure 24.11
Max_value
specification.

```
generic
    type ELEM is private ;   type ELEM_INDEX is range <> ;
    type ELEM_ARRAY is array (ELEM_INDEX) of ELEM ;
    with function ">" (A, B: ELEM) return BOOLEAN is <> ;
function Max_value (X : ELEM_ARRAY) return ELEM ;
-- FIRST and LAST are predefined attributes giving the lower and
-- the upper bounds of the array respectively
--| Pre : X'LAST - X'FIRST >= 0 and
--|       for_all i in {X'FIRST..X'LAST}, Initialized (X(i))
--| Post :   for_all i in {X'FIRST..X'LAST}, Max_value (X) >= X (i) and
--|          exists j in {X'FIRST..X'LAST}, Max_value (X) = X (j)
```

(c) A routine which finds the greatest common divisor of two integers.

(d) A routine which inserts an element into an ordered list.

24.7 If you have access to a UNIX system, process some C source code using the LINT static analyser. Modify the code so that the anomalies revealed by LINT are removed.

24.8 Produce a list of conditions which could be detected by a static analyser for Pascal or Ada.

24.9 Read the published papers on cleanroom development and produce a management report highlighting the advantages and disadvantages of adopting this approach to software development.

Part Five
Software Management

■ The final part of this book is concerned with software project management. Chapter 25 is a general introduction to software management and discusses various management tasks. Chapters 26 and 27 cover the related activities of project planning and scheduling and software cost estimation. Option analysis, the use of bar charts and activity charts and algorithmic cost modelling are major topics in these chapters. Chapter 28 discusses software maintenance management, which is concerned with planning and implementing system change. Chapter 29 discusses configuration management, which is the activity of controlling system change. Chapter 30 discusses the documentation of a software system and, finally, Chapter 31 describes various aspects of software quality assurance.

■ CONTENTS

Software Management

25

■ OBJECTIVES

The objectives of this chapter are to introduce the tasks involved in software management and to set the scene for the remainder of the chapters in this section. The introduction emphasizes the importance of management and the first section sets out typical management activities. This is followed by a discussion of management structures and programming team organizations. Programmer productivity and the difficulties of defining what productivity means are covered in the final section in this chapter.

■ CONTENTS

The failure of many large software projects in the 1960s and early 1970s highlighted the problems of software management. These projects did not fail because the project managers or programmers working on the project were incompetent. These large, challenging projects attracted people of above average ability. The fault lay in the management techniques used. Management techniques derived from small-scale projects were inadequate for large systems development. The delivered software was late, unreliable, cost several times the original estimates and often exhibited poor performance characteristics (Brooks, 1975).

Software managers are responsible for planning project development, overseeing the work and ensuring that it is carried out to the required standards, on time and within budget. Good management cannot guarantee project success but bad management or inadequate management support will probably result in software which is delivered late, exceeds cost estimates and is expensive to maintain.

Software project management is different from other types of engineering project management in a number of ways:

(1) *The product is intangible*   The manager of a shipbuilding project or of a civil engineering project can see the product being developed. If a schedule slips the effect on the product is visible. Parts of the structure are obviously unfinished. Software is intangible. It cannot be seen or touched. The project manager is dependent on documentation to review the progress of the project.

(2) *We do not have a clear understanding of the software process*   In engineering disciplines with a long history, the stages of development are well understood and predictable. In software engineering this is not the case. Models, such as the waterfall model of the software life cycle, are simplified process representations.

(3) *Large software systems are often 'one-off' projects*   They are distinct from previous projects. Historical experience is of limited value in predicting how these projects should be managed.

Because of these problems, it is not surprising that software projects are often late, over-budget and behind schedule. Each large software system development is a new and technically innovative project and many engineering projects (such as new transport systems, bridges, and so on) which are innovative often also have schedule problems. Given the difficulties involved, it is perhaps remarkable that so many software projects are delivered on time and to budget!

25.1   Management activities

It is impossible to write a standard job description for a software manager. The job varies tremendously depending on the organization and on the software product being developed. However, most managers take responsibility at some stage for some or all of the following activities:

- Proposal writing.
- Project costing.
- Project planning and scheduling.
- Project monitoring and reviews.
- Personnel selection and evaluation.
- Report writing and presentations.

The first stage in a software project may involve writing a proposal to carry out that project. This applies whether or not the project is to be commissioned by some client, is specified by some other part of an organization or is an internal development. The proposal sets out an outline of the project work, cost and schedule estimates and a justification of why the project contract should be awarded to a particular organization or team.

Proposal writing is a critical task as the prosperity of many software organizations depends on having a sufficient number of proposals accepted and contracts awarded. There can be no set guidelines for this task and proposal writing is a skill which is acquired by experience. It is really part of an overall marketing activity and is outside the scope of this book. Aron (1983) includes a discussion of proposal writing which is recommended to interested readers.

Project planning and scheduling and project costing are key management activities and are covered in Chapters 26 and 27.

Project monitoring is a continuing project activity. The manager must keep track of the progress of the project and compare actual and planned progress and costs. Although most organizations have formal mechanisms for monitoring, a skilled manager can often form a clear picture of what is going on by informal discussion with project staff.

Informal monitoring activities can often be used to predict potential project problems as they may reveal difficulties as they occur. For example, daily discussions with project staff might reveal a particular problem in finding some software fault. Rather than waiting for a schedule slippage to be reported, the software manager might assign some expert to the problem or might decide that it should be programmed around.

In the course of a project, it is normal to have a number of formal project management reviews. They are concerned with reviewing overall progress and technical development of the project and considering the project's status against the aims of the organization commissioning the project.

The development time for a large software project may be many years and, during that time, organizational objectives are likely to change. The changes may mean that the software is no longer required or that the original project requirements are inappropriate. Management may decide to stop software development or to change the project to accommodate the changes to the organization's objectives.

The manager of a project usually has the responsibility of selecting personnel to work on that project. The ideal is to have available, skilled staff who have the appropriate experience to carry out the project. In the majority of cases, this will be unattainable. The reasons for this are:

(1)   The overall project budget may preclude the use of highly paid staff. Less experienced, less well-paid staff may have to be utilized.

(2)   Staff with the appropriate experience may simply not be available either within an organization or externally. There is still an international shortage of skilled software engineers which is likely to continue until at least the end of the twentieth century. It may be impossible to recruit new staff to the project. Within an organization, the most appropriate staff may be required for work on other projects.

(3)   Long-term organizational goals for staff development and training may require staff without experience to gain that experience on the project.

The software manager must work within these constraints when selecting project staff. At least one project member should have experience of developing a comparable system to that proposed. Without this experience, many simple mistakes are likely to be made. It is also important that appropriate provision is made for training during the course of the project.

Although all members of a project team are likely to have some responsibility for producing documentation, the project manager is principally responsible for reporting on the project to both the client and contractor organizations. Project managers must be able to write concise, coherent documents which abstract the salient features from more detailed project reports. Furthermore, they must be able to present this information during progress reviews. Again, detailed discussion of this reporting is outside the scope of this book.

25.2 Software management structures

Traditional management structure is hierarchical with individuals at each level in the hierarchy reporting to the level above. Typically, a manager might be responsible for 12–25 subordinates. Software management structures are also hierarchical but software managers should handle fewer direct subordinates because of the complexity of the software projects being managed.

In a large organization undertaking a number of simultaneous software development projects, the software management structure might be as shown in Figure 25.1.

There should be an overall director or vice-president in charge of software development. A number of programme managers should report to that director. Each programme manager is responsible for a particular area of development such as business systems development, avionics systems development, CASE tool development, and so on. Each development project has its own project manager reporting to the programme manager. Within each project, there may be a number of team leaders responsible for managing individual sub-projects.

Figure 25.1 shows the quality assurance function as distinct from individual project management. Quality assurance should have its own quality manager, and a number of quality teams will report to that manager. These teams work in conjunction with individual projects but to maintain their independence, do not report to the individual project manager. Quality assurance is discussed in Chapter 31.

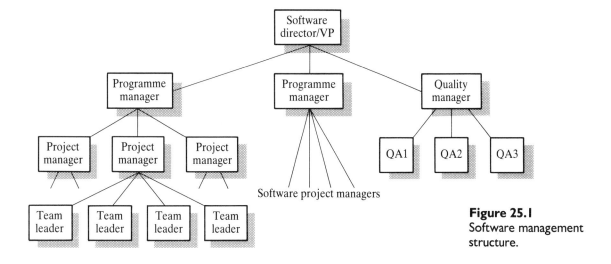

Figure 25.1
Software management structure.

25.2.1 Programming team organizations

Software projects should not be tackled by a single large team of software engineers. As discussed in Chapter 2, large teams mean that the time spent in communication amongst team members is greater than the time spent programming. Furthermore, it is usually impossible to partition a software system into a large number of independent units. If a large programming team is used, program units are often arbitrary and have complex interfaces. Consequently, the probability of interface error is high and additional verification and validation costs are incurred.

Programming team sizes should be relatively small. When small teams are used, communication problems are reduced. The whole team can get round a table for a meeting and can meet in each other's offices. Complex communication structures need not be set up. Unless the circumstances are exceptional, a team should not have more than eight members.

If a project is so big that it cannot be tackled by a single team in the time available, multiple teams must be used. They should work independently with each team tackling a significant part of the project in an autonomous way. The system architecture should be designed so that the interface between the sub-systems developed by the independent teams is simple and well defined.

As well as minimizing communication problems, small programming teams have a number of other benefits:

(1)   *A team quality standard can be developed* Because this standard is established by consensus, it is more likely to be observed than external standards imposed on the team.

(2)   *Team members work closely together* The team can learn from each other. Inhibitions caused by ignorance are minimized as mutual learning is encouraged.

(3)   *Egoless programming can be practised* Programs are regarded as team property rather than personal property.

(4)   *Team members can get to know each other's work* Continuity can be maintained should a team member leave.

Small programming teams are usually organized in an informal way. Although a titular team leader exists, he or she carries out the same tasks as other team members. A technical leader may emerge who effectively controls software production.

In an informal team, the work to be carried out is discussed by the team as a whole and tasks allocated according to ability and experience. High-level system design is carried out by senior team members but low-level design is the responsibility of the member allocated a particular task.

Informal teams can be very successful, particularly where the majority of team members are experienced and competent. The team functions as a democratic team, making decisions by consensus. Psychologically, this improves team spirit with a resultant increase in cohesiveness and performance. If a team is composed mostly of inexperienced or incompetent members, informality can be a hindrance. No definite authority exists to direct the work, causing a lack of coordination between team members and, possibly, eventual project failure.

A problem which sometimes arises is a lack of experienced team members. Teams are often composed of relatively inexperienced engineers. In some software development organizations, technically skilled staff reach a career plateau fairly rapidly. To progress further, they must take on managerial responsibilities which require different abilities from their technical skills. Skilled software engineers do not necessarily make the best software managers. Promotion of these people to managerial status often means that useful technical skills are lost.

To utilize the skills of experienced and competent programmers, these individuals should be given responsibility and rewards commensurate with what they would receive in a management position. To avoid a loss of technical skills to a project, some organizations have developed parallel technical and managerial career structures of equal worth. As an engineer's career develops, he or she may specialize in either technical or managerial activities and may move between them without loss of status or salary.

25.2.2 Chief programmer teams

An alternative programming team organization to the informal democratic team was suggested by Baker (1972) and also described, in a slightly different form, by Brooks (1975) and Aron (1974). The development of this approach was motivated by a number of considerations:

(1) Projects tended to be staffed by relatively inexperienced people as discussed above.

(2) Much programming work is clerical, involving the management of a large amount of information.

(3) Multi-way communications are time-consuming and hence reduce programmer productivity.

The chief programmer team is based on utilizing experienced and talented staff as chief programmers, providing clerical support for these programmers using both human and computer-based procedures, and funnelling all communications through one or two individuals (Figure 25.2).

The chief programmer team has been compared to a medical team responsible for surgery. The leader and principal technical expert in this team is the surgeon. He or she is helped by skilled, specialized staff members such as an anaesthetist, chief nurse, and so on.

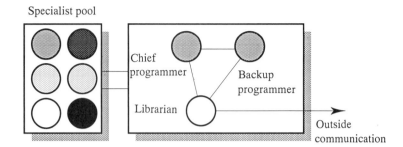

Figure 25.2
A chief programmer
team.

The nucleus of a chief programmer team consists of the following members:

(1)   A chief programmer who is experienced and highly qualified. Chief programmers take full responsibility for the design, programming, testing and installation of the system.

(2)   A skilled and experienced backup programmer who is the chief programmer's deputy. The backup programmer's main function is to provide support by keeping track of what the chief programmer is doing and developing test cases to verify his or her work.

(3)   A librarian whose role is to assume all the clerical functions associated with a project. The librarian is assisted by an automated library system.

Depending on the size and type of the application, other experts might be added temporarily or permanently to a team. These might include:

(1)   A project administrator who relieves the chief programmer of administrative tasks.

(2)   A toolsmith who is responsible for producing software tools to support the project.

(3)   A documentation editor who takes the project documentation written by the chief programmer and backup programmer and prepares it for publication.

(4)   A language/system expert who is familiar with the idiosyncrasies of the programming language and system which is being used and whose role is to advise the chief programmer on how to make use of these facilities.

(5)   A tester whose task is to develop objective test cases to validate the work of the chief programmer.

(6)   One or more support programmers who code from a design specified
        by the chief programmer. These support programmers are necessary
        in large projects where there is too much detailed programming for
        the chief programmer and backup programmer alone.

The main objective of using a chief programmer team is to improve
productivity. Measurements by Baker (1972) and Walston and Felix (1977)
suggest that a chief programmer team is approximately twice as productive
as teams which are not organized in this way. However, this improvement
may not be a result of the team organization. Chief programmers may
simply be better programmers who would be more productive in any team
organization.

Shneiderman (1980) points out that there may be psychological
problems in introducing chief programmer teams. These derive from the
position of the chief programmer, who is the kingpin of the project. If the
project is successful, he or she takes the credit for the success. Other team
members may feel that they have no definite function and be resentful of the
chief programmer's status.

Another problem is that the success of the project is dependent on
one or two individuals working closely together. If they should fall ill at the
same time (very common in winter) or if both leave, the project may have to
be abandoned. No one else in the team or the organization may be able to
take over their role and maintain the project schedule.

Other political problems in using chief programmer teams are
described by Yourdon (1979). In large organizations it may be impossible to
fit the chief programmer team into the existing organizational structure and
adequately reward the chief programmer. The introduction of chief
programmer teams may mean reorganizing existing staff and this might be
resisted. It may be impossible to attract suitably qualified chief programmers
to work in certain application areas.

25.3 Programmer productivity

The estimation of programmer productivity is important for two reasons.
Firstly, without some estimate of productivity, reliable project scheduling is
impossible. Productivity measurement provides data which allow estimates
to be made and cost models to be tuned. Secondly, the benefits of using
improved software engineering techniques and tools can be demonstrated to
senior management by showing that their use results in improved
productivity over the whole of the software life cycle.

Because software is intangible, it is not possible to measure
productivity directly. Productivity in a manufacturing system can be
measured by counting the number of units output and dividing this by the

number of hours input to the work. In software systems, what we really want to estimate is the cost of deriving a particular system with given functionality. This is only indirectly related to some tangible measure such as the system size.

It is not straightforward to derive a formula which allows the measurement of function production per hour although Albrecht and Gaffney (1983) have suggested the use of 'function points' (discussed in Chapter 27) as a means of productivity measurement. Productivity metrics are only a subjective and relative guide to overall productivity. They must be supplemented by human judgement and intuition to estimate the real process productivity.

Productivity cannot be measured over the whole of the system life cycle so productivity over the software development stage is measured. If poor quality software is produced quickly, the developers of that software may appear to be more productive than those programmers who produce reliable and easy to maintain systems.

Productivity units which are expressed in volume/time take no account of the quality of the finished system. They imply that more always means better and take no account of the fact that apparently higher development productivity may ultimately involve increased system maintenance costs.

Several different units have been used as measures of programmer productivity:

- Lines of source code written per programmer-month.
- Object instructions produced per programmer-month.
- Pages of documentation written per programmer-month.
- Test cases written and executed per programmer-month.

The most commonly used measure of productivity is lines of source code per programmer-month. This is computed by taking the total number of lines of source code which are delivered and dividing that number by the total time in programmer-months required to complete the project. This time includes analysis and design time, coding time, testing time and documentation time. Coding only takes up a relatively small part of the total development time (Figure 25.3).

Jones (1978) points out that there are several problems with this productivity metric. The most fundamental of these is determining exactly what is meant by a line of code. Programs are made up of declarations, executable statements and commentary, and may also include macro instructions which expand to several lines of code. Some counting techniques consider executable statements only, some executable statements and data declarations. Some count each non-blank line in the program, irrespective of what is on that line. Because of these different conventions,

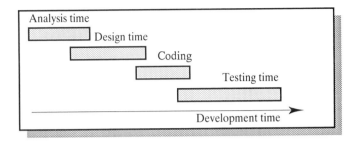

Figure 25.3
System development
time.

published measures of programmer productivity cannot readily be compared.

Another problem which arises when languages such as Pascal are used is how source lines containing more than a single statement should be treated. If such lines are treated as a single line, this implies that higher productivity can apparently be achieved by the judicious use of new lines! However, as long as a consistent line counting technique is used, it doesn't really matter which approach is adopted.

A more serious consequence of using lines of code/month as a productivity measure is the apparent productivity advantages which it indicates when assembly code is used. The problem also occurs, to a lesser extent, when programs in different high-level languages are compared. If lines of code per month are used as a raw productivity measure, it appears that the low-level language programmer is more productive than the high level language programmer for comparable systems. The more expressive the programming language, the lower the apparent productivity.

This paradox results from the fact that all tasks associated with the programming process (design, documentation, testing and so on) are subsumed under the coding task in spite of the fact that the coding time normally represents much less than half the time needed to complete a project (Figure 25.4). The measure places undue emphasis on coding and considers other stages of the life cycle less important. Analysis, design and documentation time are language-independent and low-level language programs have more lines of code than high-level language programs. Dividing code produced by development time gives a biased result.

For example, consider a system which might be coded in 5000 lines of assembly code or 1500 lines of high-level language code. The development time for the various phases is shown in Figure 25.5.

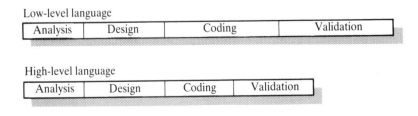

Figure 25.4
Development times
with high-level and
low-level languages.

	Analysis	Design	Coding	Testing	Documentation
Assembly code	3 weeks	5 weeks	8 weeks	10 weeks	2 weeks
High-level language	3 weeks	5 weeks	4 weeks	6 weeks	2 weeks

	Size	Effort	Productivity		
Assembly code	5000 lines	28 weeks	714		
High-level language	1500 lines	20 weeks	300		

Figure 25.5
System development
time.

The assembler programmer has a productivity of 714 lines/month and the high-level language programmer less than half of this, 300 lines/month. Yet the development costs for the high-level language system are lower and it is produced in less time. Because of this paradox, individual productivity standards for each programming language are required and productivity comparisons between projects coded in different languages should not be made.

To avoid some of the problems associated with using lines of code per month as a productivity measure, an alternative method uses the number of object instructions generated per programmer-month. This unit is more objective than lines of code as there is no difficulty in defining what is meant by an object instruction. However, there are also disadvantages in using this measure of productivity:

(1) It is difficult to estimate the source code/object code expansion ratio with most compilers. This means that object code/month is not useful for productivity estimation before code is actually produced.

(2) The amount of object code generated by a compiler is dependent on high-level language programming style. A programmer who takes care over coding and produces tight code is apparently less productive than a programmer who codes in such a way that large object programs are generated.

Other measurements which have been used, such as pages of documentation per programmer-month, also suffer from disadvantages. If productivity is measured by volume of documentation produced, this penalizes writers who take time to express themselves clearly and concisely.

Because of the difficulties in establishing a unit of productivity measurement and because of the variety of factors which influence productivity, it is difficult to give a figure which can be taken as the average productivity of a programmer. For large, complex embedded systems, productivity may be as low as 30 lines/programmer-month whereas for straightforward business application systems which are well understood, it may be as high as 600 lines/month. These figures are approximately independent of the programming language used. It always pays to use as high-level a language as possible for software projects.

25.3.1 Factors affecting programmer productivity

A study by Sackman *et al.* (1968) showed that individual productivity differences can be very large. The best programmers may be ten times more productive than the worst. This aptitude factor is likely to be dominant in individual productivity comparisons. Accordingly, the factors discussed below are only relevant to programming teams which are made up of programmers who have a range of abilities.

Walston and Felix (1977) carried out a productivity survey to identify productivity improvements which result from using methodologies such as top-down development, structured programming, and so on. They collected data from over 60 projects ranging from small commercial DP programs to large complex process control systems. They selected 68 variables for analysis and identified 29 of these as correlating significantly with productivity. These variables included characteristics of the system being developed, the experience of the developers, hardware constraints, the use of new system development technology, program design constraints and the quantity of documentation required.

The most important single factor affecting productivity was the complexity of the user interface. Projects with a low interface complexity showed a productivity of 500 lines/programmer-month whereas high complexity interfaces were produced at 124 lines/programmer-month.

Other significant factors were the extent of user participation in requirements definition and the experience of the programming team. Where the user did not participate in requirements definition, productivity was measured at 491 lines/programmer-month but where there was significant user participation this dropped to 205 lines/month. Teams with a good deal of experience produced at a rate of 410 lines/programmer-month whereas inexperienced teams produced 132 lines/month.

The effects on productivity of user interface complexity and team experience are intuitively obvious although Walston and Felix's study was useful for showing their significance. It might also be expected that if the user had little to do with requirements definition, productivity would be higher although, in such cases, the finished product may not meet the user's needs.

Design and programming methodologies such as structured programming, design and code reviews and top-down development had a positive influence on productivity although this was not as great as the factors previously discussed. However, productivity improvements resulting from the use of these techniques must be seen as a bonus. Their principal function is to improve the reliability and maintainability of software.

Another factor which obviously affects productivity is the amount of time that a software engineer actually spends working on software development. Ignoring holidays and illness, each member of a software development team spends time training, attending meetings and dealing with administrative tasks. If a project involves new techniques, training will be required, if the project involves more than one geographical location, travel time between locations is involved and the larger the programming group, the more time must be spent communicating. McCue (1978) found that 20%–30% of an engineer's time might be spent on 'non-productive' activities.

■ KEY POINTS

- Good software project management is essential if software engineering projects are to be developed on schedule and within budget.

- Software management is different from other engineering management because software is intangible, because we don't understand the software process and because many projects are novel and innovative.

- A software manager has diverse roles but the most significant activities are project planning, estimating and scheduling.

- Various development team organizations have been adopted. Democratic teams work well with experienced and competent staff. Chief programmer teams try to make best use of a scarce resource, namely, programming skills.

- The dominant factor in programmer productivity is the aptitude of the individual programmer.

- Inter-language comparisons using lines of code produced per month should not be made.

- Existing measures of programming productivity do not take the quality of the finished product into account.

FURTHER READING

The problems of software management have been unchanged since the 1960s so reading on this subject does not date in the same way as technical literature. Some of the best books are over ten years old and are still relevant. Other management books are suggested in the later chapters in this section.

IEE/BCS Software Engineering J. **1** (1), January 1986. This is a special issue of a journal devoted to software engineering topics. The first issue includes several papers on the management of software projects. The paper by Rook is particularly recommended.

The Mythical Man Month. An interesting and readable account of management problems which arose during the development of one of the first very large software projects, the IBM OS/360 operating system. The author was manager of this development and distilled much wisdom from the experience. (F.P. Brooks, 1975, Addison-Wesley.)

The Program Development Process: Part 2 – The Programming Team. Another text on software management from an author whose experience is at IBM. This is a very practical book. It is not as entertaining as Brook's book but it is an equally valuable complement to this chapter. (J.D. Aron, 1983, Addison-Wesley.)

Principles of Software Engineering Management. This is an idiosyncratic account of software management but it contains good sense and is written in an easy-to-read way. (T. Gilb, 1988, Addison-Wesley.)

EXERCISES

25.1 Using reported instances of project problems in the literature, list management difficulties which occurred in these failed programming projects. (Start with Brooks's book as suggested in Further Reading.)

25.2 Given the list of management activities in Section 25.2, explain why the best programmers do not always make the best software managers.

25.3 Using the information on human factors given in Chapter 2, carry out an analysis of democratic and chief programmer team organizations. Suggest problems that might arise in each of these organizations.

25.4 Describe metrics which have been used to measure programmer productivity. Suggest other metrics which might be used, taking into account that a software engineer is also involved in specification and design activities.

25.5 From your own experience, list those factors which have most effect on your own programming productivity. Suggest how your productivity might be improved.

25.6 Explain why the productivity of programmers working on embedded systems is usually very much lower than that of programmers developing business information systems.

Project Planning and Scheduling

26

■ OBJECTIVES

The objective of this chapter is to describe the important management responsibilities of project planning and scheduling. These activities often take up most managerial effort on a large software project. After an introduction setting out the steps involved in the planning process, the choice of appropriate project milestones is discussed. This is followed by a description of option analysis where it is suggested that the best managerial strategy is to choose project options which minimize risk. Finally, project scheduling is discussed and graphical representations (activity graphs and bar charts) for planning and scheduling are described.

■ CONTENTS

Effective management of a software project depends on thoroughly planning the progress of the project, anticipating problems which might arise and preparing tentative solutions to those problems in advance. A plan, drawn up at the start of a project, should be used as the driver for the project. This initial plan is not static but must be modified as the project progresses and better information becomes available.

The pseudo-code set out in Figure 26.1 is a description of the project planning process. It shows that planning is an iterative process which is only complete when the project itself is complete.

The planning process starts with an assessment of the constraints (required delivery date, staff available, overall budget, and so on) affecting the project. This is carried out in conjunction with an estimation of project parameters such as its structure, size and distribution of functions. The progress milestones and deliverables are then defined.

The process then enters a loop. A schedule for the project is drawn up and the activities defined in the schedule are initiated or given permission to continue. After some time (usually about 2–3 weeks), progress is reviewed and discrepancies noted. Because initial estimates of project parameters are tentative, the plan will always need to be modified.

As more information becomes available, the project manager revises the assumptions about the project and assesses how these affect the schedule. If their effect is to delay the project, it may be necessary to re-negotiate the project constraints and deliverables with the project customer. If this re-negotiation is unsuccessful and does not allow the schedule to be met, it may then be necessary to initiate a project technical review. The objective of this review is to determine whether some alternative approach is viable which falls within the project constraints and meets the schedule.

Of course, the wise project manager does not assume that all will go well. Problems of some description nearly always arise in the course of a

Figure 26.1
The project planning process.

```
Define constraints under which the project must be carried out
Make initial assessments of the project parameters
Define project milestones and deliverables
while project has not been completed or cancelled loop
    Draw up project schedule
    initiate activities according to schedule
    delay ( for a while )
    review project progress
    revise estimates of project parameters
    apply revisions to project schedule
    re-negotiate project constraints and deliverables
    if (problems arise) then
        initiate technical review and possible revision
    end if
end loop
```

project and the initial assumptions and scheduling should be conservative. There should be sufficient contingency built into the plan so that the project constraints and milestones need not be re-negotiated every time round the planning loop.

The software development plan is only one of the plans which must be drawn up for a project. Other plans which may be required are:

- A validation plan.
- A configuration management plan.
- A staff training and development plan.
- A maintenance plan.

Validation, configuration management and maintenance are discussed in other chapters. Staff training is outside the scope of this book, and a training plan is not discussed.

It will be assumed here that the project manager is responsible for planning from requirements definition to the delivery of the completed system. The planning involved in assessing the need for a software system, the feasibility of producing that system, and the assignment of priority to the system production process will not be discussed. For a discussion of these topics, the reader is referred to Pressman (1987).

26.1 Project milestones

Effective management is reliant on information. As software is intangible, this information can only be provided as documents describing the work which has been carried out. Without this information, control of the project is lost and cost estimates and schedules cannot be updated.

When planning a project, a series of *milestones* should be established where a milestone is an end-point of a software process activity. At each milestone, a formal progress report should be presented to management. These milestones must represent the end of a distinct stage in the project. Indefinite milestones, where it is impossible to decide unequivocally if the milestone has been reached, are useless for project management.

A good milestone is characterized by finished documentation, for example, 'High-level design complete' or 'Test plan formulated'. Milestones should not be indefinite. A poor milestone, for example, is 'Coding 80% complete'. There is no objective way of telling if coding is 80% complete.

To establish milestones, the software process which is being followed for a particular project must be broken down into appropriately sized activities and an output associated with each of these activities. For example, Figure 26.2 shows activities involved in requirements specification

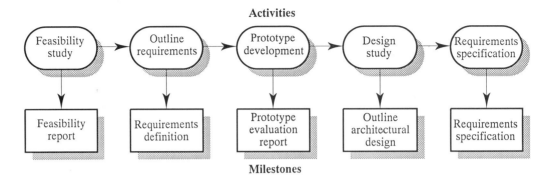

Activities

Feasibility study → Outline requirements → Prototype development → Design study → Requirements specification

Feasibility report | Requirements definition | Prototype evaluation report | Outline architectural design | Requirements specification

Milestones

Figure 26.2
Requirements
milestones.

when prototyping is used as a means of requirements analysis. Major milestones for each activity are shown. Depending on the project size, subsidiary milestones for each of these may also be defined.

Milestones need not be established for every project activity. An approximate rule of thumb is that milestones should be scheduled at intervals of 2–3 weeks although this can vary by up to 100% depending on the software process followed.

A good reason for the widespread adoption of the 'waterfall' model of the software process is that it allows for the straightforward definition of milestones throughout the course of a project. Alternative approaches, such as exploratory programming, are such that milestone definition is a more difficult and a less certain process. Consequently, in spite of its known deficiencies, some variant of the 'waterfall' model will probably continue to be the process model used in most large software projects.

26.2 Option analysis

When formulating a software project plan, the project manager is usually presented with a set of goals which must be achieved (essential goals) and goals which are desirable but not essential. Some of the goals may be mutually opposing. For example, one goal might be to minimize project costs, another to maximize system reliability. In general, increased reliability can only be achieved by increasing costs so some balance point where acceptable cost and reliability levels are achieved must be discovered.

Unfortunately, goals are often left implicit rather than defined at the start of a project. Consequently, the project team does not know what they are trying to achieve and why particular management decisions have been made.

The first stage of the planning process should be the definition of relevant organizational and project-specific goals. Project-specific goals

Option	Cost £ million	Schedule (months)	Reliability	Reuse (%)	Portability (%)	Efficiency
A	1.2	33	5	40	90	0.35
B	0.8	30	9	40	75	0.75
C	1.75	36	13	30	30	1

Figure 26.3
Project options.

might be high maintainability, low cost, high reliability, and so on. Organizational goals might be the production of reusable components, the development and support of particular areas of expertise (because these may lead to future contracts), and the career development of particular members of staff.

Usually, a set of options can be derived which, partially or completely, achieve the project goals. The different options available to the project manager can be scored against the project goals. This scoring is usually relative rather than absolute; options are ranked against a notional 'best' option. The scoring system should also take goal weighting into account. Weighting may be either positive or negative so that the benefit or cost from a particular option may be reduced or increased. For example, high reliability might be paramount and must be achieved irrespective of the other goals. It should therefore be given a higher weighting than staff development, for example.

Say there are three optional approaches to product development. The goals and the scoring of each of the options is shown in Figure 26.3. For simplicity, weighting has not been included. Some of the scores have been expressed as percentages. For example, reuse is the percentage of system components which might be reused and efficiency is expressed as a percentage of the most efficient option. Other scores are absolute, such as the cost and the reliability, which can be quantified as rate of occurrence of failures (see Chapter 20).

Given this analysis, how can the project manager then decide which option should be chosen. One possible approach is to use *polar graphs*, which are derived from techniques used in computer performance evaluation (Ferrari, 1978). Boehm (1981) shows how they can also be used in making multivariate comparisons and in evaluating software project options.

A polar graph is a graph with a number of radial axes. Each axis corresponds to one of the goals which are to be achieved. The particular options are plotted on the appropriate axis. The option which offers the best overall payoff is the one which encloses the greatest area. The polar graph for the options shown in Figure 26.3 is illustrated in Figure 26.4.

The most desirable attainments should be plotted at the extremes of the radii and the least desirable at the origins. For example, in Figure 26.4, reliability is measured as a rate of fault occurrence so the lower this value the better. Thus, the lowest value is at the extreme end of the radius and the

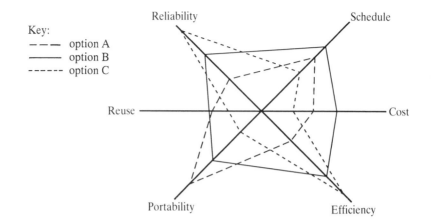

Figure 26.4
A polar graph of project options.

highest in the centre. By contrast, efficiency (expressed as a percentage of the most efficient), is represented so that the highest value is at the end of the axis and the lowest at the origin. Thus, the 'best' overall option is the one which includes the greatest area in the polar graph (Option B in Figure 26.4).

These polar graphs are a guide to project management and should not be interpreted completely literally. One of the options may score best on the polar graph but might conflict with a critical organizational or project objective. For example, the organization may anticipate other projects in the same application area so may select the option which provides the highest number of reusable components so as to save development costs in later projects.

Boehm (1981) describes an option analysis technique called the payoff matrix where the maximum benefit and penalty of each possible strategy is tabulated. For example, say two possible strategies of project implementation are proposed and the maximum and minimum costs of each strategy estimated. The possibilities are shown in Figure 26.5. The payoff is the difference between the maximum and the minimum costs.

Faced with these possibilities, which option should a project manager select? Clearly, if all goes well, Option A leads to the lowest cost project but if things do not go well, it is the most expensive option to chose. Boehm identifies three decision making strategies which can be used.

Option	Maximum cost ($)	Minimum cost ($)	Payoff ($)
A	100,000	40,000	60,000
B	70,000	55,000	15,000

Figure 26.5
Option costs.

The *maximin* strategy is a conservative strategy which aims at the minimization of losses. It is assumed that the maximum rather than the minimum project cost is more likely so the payoff will be negative. The project with the lowest payoff is chosen. In the above example, the minimum loss is $15,000 so Option B would be selected. An alternative strategy is an optimistic strategy (*maximax*) which selects the option that offers the greatest gains (positive payoff). The maximax strategy assumes that the project cost is more likely to be the minimum cost. In this example, a maximax strategy would select Option A.

Neither of these strategies take the relative magnitudes of the gains or losses into account. So if the potential gains in Option A were just slightly larger than the gains from Option B but the losses were, say, ten times larger, the maximax strategy would select that option whereas the majority of project managers would select the safer alternative option.

These approaches do not take *risk* into account where risk can be expressed as a probability that the estimated value will not be exceeded. The sum of the probabilities of each possible outcome should equal 1. In situations of complete uncertainty, the probability of each outcome is equal. In a binary situation, shown in Figure 26.5, the probability associated with each possible situation should therefore be 0.5.

If each possible outcome in Figure 26.5 is equally likely, the probable cost from each option can be computed as follows:

Option A: Probable cost $= (0.5 \times \$100,000) + (0.5 \times \$40,000)$
$= \$70,000.$
Option B: Probable cost $= (0.5 \times \$70,000) + (0.5 \times \$55,000)$
$= \$62,500.$

On the basis of these figures, Option B should be selected as the most acceptable option.

In reality we rarely have to deal with situations of complete uncertainty. If managers are completely uncertain about estimates, they should carry out some analyses (prototyping, simulation or whatever) to reduce that uncertainty. Thus, it should be possible to assign subjective probability estimates to each potential outcome and to use these estimates in option analysis.

For example, say the probability of Option A achieving its minimum cost estimate is 65% and the probability of it reaching its maximum estimate is 35%. Option B has a minimum cost probability of 70% and a maximum cost probability of 30%. Redoing the computation shows that option B should again be selected as the best option.

Option A: Probable cost $= (0.65 \times \$40,000) + (0.35 \times \$100,000)$
$= \$61,000.$
Option B: Probable cost $= (0.70 \times \$55,000) + (0.30 \times \$70,000)$
$= \$59,500.$

Of course, this simplistic analysis is merely a guide to decision making rather than an automated decision making technique. However, it does illustrate the role of risk estimation, which is a critical part of project management.

When project management decisions are made, each decision should have an associated risk estimate. Informally, the risk associated with a decision is the probability that the decision will not have adverse consequences. Notice that it is not a measure of the probability of the correctness of a decision. A decision may be incorrect but may not have adverse effects (it could be an overestimate say) and the risk associated with such a decision is low. Good project managers try to minimize risk even if this means that, on some occasions, costs are not minimized.

Say one way of tackling the project depends on hiring a specific expert whereas an alternative option allows the project to be tackled with existing staff. The first option may be cheaper but has higher risk. If a specialist cannot be found, the project may be cancelled. The second option may cost more but the risk of failure is lower. A wise project manager would accept the higher costs and not face the uncertainties of staff recruitment. Success is always cheaper than project failure!

26.3   Project scheduling

Project scheduling is one of the most difficult tasks of software management. Typically, projects break new ground. Unless the project being scheduled is similar to a previous project, previous estimates are not a good basis for new project scheduling. Different projects use different programming languages and methodologies, which complicates the task of schedule estimation.

If the project is technically advanced, initial estimates will almost certainly be optimistic in spite of endeavours to consider all eventualities. In this respect, software scheduling is no different from scheduling any other type of large advanced project. New aircraft, bridges and even cars are frequently late because of unanticipated problems. Schedules, therefore, must be continually updated as better progress information becomes available.

Project scheduling involves separating the total work involved in a project into separate tasks and assessing when these tasks will be completed. Usually, some of these tasks are carried out in parallel. Project schedulers must coordinate these parallel tasks and organize the work so that the workforce is used optimally. They must avoid a situation where the whole project is delayed because a critical task is unfinished.

In estimating schedules, managers should not assume that every stage of the project will be problem-free. Individuals working on a project may fall ill or may leave, hardware may break down and essential support software or hardware may be late in delivery. If the project is new and

Task	Duration (days)	Dependencies
T1	8	
T2	15	
T3	15	T1
T4	10	
T5	10	T2, T4
T6	5	T1, T2
T7	20	T1
T8	25	T4
T9	15	T3, T6
T10	15	T5, T7
T11	7	T9
T12	10	T11

Figure 26.6
Task durations and
dependencies.

technically advanced, certain parts of it may turn out to be more difficult and take longer than originally anticipated. A rule of thumb in estimating is to estimate as if nothing will go wrong, increase that estimate to cover anticipated problems and then add a contingency factor to cover unanticipated problems. This extra contingency factor depends on the type of project, the process parameters (deadline, standards, and so on) and the quality and experience of the software engineers working on the project.

As a rough guide for the scheduler, requirements analysis and design normally takes twice as long as coding. So too does validation. To estimate the total time required for the project, the system size may be estimated and divided by the expected programmer productivity to give the number of programmer-months required to complete the project. Techniques used in estimation are discussed in the following chapter.

The output from the scheduling process is usually a set of charts showing the work breakdown, tasks dependencies and staff allocations. These charts are discussed in the following section. Manual preparation of these charts is a time-consuming chore but various tools are now available which automate the task of chart production. Using such tools allows the manager to experiment with different schedules.

26.3.1 Bar charts and activity networks

Bar charts and activity networks are graphical notations which are used in project scheduling. Bar charts illustrate who is responsible for each part of the project and when that part is scheduled to begin and end. Activity networks show the different activities making up a project, their projected durations and inter-dependencies.

As an illustration of these notations, consider the set of activities shown in Figure 26.6. This table shows various subtasks, their duration, and the task inter-dependencies.

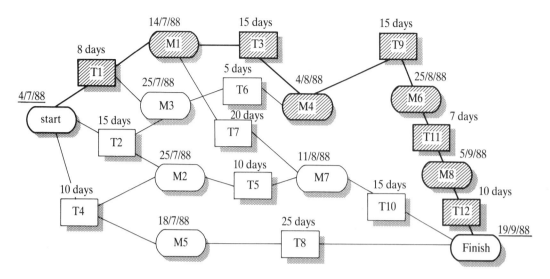

Figure 26.7
An activity network.

From Figure 26.6, we can see that Task T3 is dependent on Task T1. This means that T1 must be completed before T3 starts. For example, T1 might be the preparation of a software design and T3, the implementation of that design. Before implementation begins, the design should be complete.

In practice, of course, the times estimated for each task in Figure 26.6 will include some contingency to cope with unforeseen delays. Estimating errors and unexpected delays are a fact of life for project management and some slippage should always be allowed for in project estimates.

Given dependency and estimated duration of tasks, several different graphical representations of the project schedule can be generated. One example is an activity network which shows task dependencies (Figure 26.7). It shows which activities can be carried out in parallel and which must be executed in sequence because of a dependency on an earlier activity. Dates in this diagram are written in British style where the day precedes the month.

It is not useful to subdivide tasks into units which take less than a week or two to execute. Finer subdivision means that a disproportionate amount of time must be spent on estimating and chart revision. It is also useful to set a maximum amount of time for any task on the chart of about 10–12 weeks.

Rectangular nodes in Figure 26.7 represent tasks and the task duration is shown alongside each node. Rounded nodes represent the culmination of activities or project milestones. These are annotated with the expected completion date of the dependent activities.

Before progress can be made from one milestone to another, all paths leading to it must be complete. For example, Task T9, shown in Figure 26.7, cannot be started until both T3 and T6 are complete and Milestone M4 has been reached.

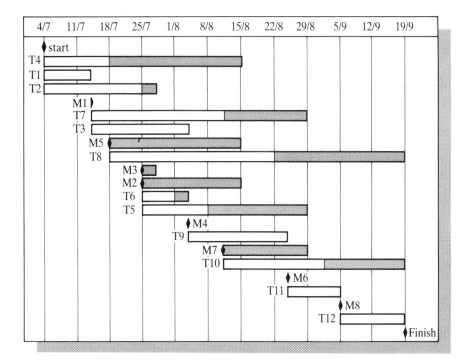

Figure 26.8
Activity bar chart.

The duration of the project can be estimated by considering the longest path in the activity graph (the critical path). In Figure 26.7 the critical path is represented by shaded boxes. The critical path is the series of activities on which the overall schedule of the project depends. Any slippage in the completion of any critical activity causes project delays. Delays in activities which do not lie on the critical path, however, need not cause an overall schedule slippage. For example, a delay in T8 in Figure 26.7 would probably have no effect on the project completion date. From the bar chart shown in Figure 26.8, we can see that T8 could be delayed by up to 4 weeks without affecting the schedule.

PERT charts are a more sophisticated form of activity chart where, instead of making a single estimate for each task, pessimistic, likely, and optimistic estimates are made. There is therefore not one but many potential critical paths, depending on the permutation of estimates for each task. This makes critical path analysis very complex and it must be carried out automatically.

As well as using activity graphs for estimating, management should use these charts when allocating project work. They can often provide insights into task dependencies which are not intuitively obvious. In some cases, it may be possible to modify the system design so that the critical path is shortened. The project schedule may be shortened because of the reduced amount of time spent waiting for activities to finish.

Task	Programmer
T1	Jane
T2	Anne
T3	Jane
T4	Fred
T5	Mary
T6	Anne
T7	Jim
T8	Fred
T9	Jane
T10	Anne
T11	Fred
T12	Fred

Figure 26.9
Staff/task allocations.

Now that personal computers are widely used, it is normal practice for automated tools to be used in activity network generation and maintenance. Figure 26.7 was created with a project management tool and, given an initial starting date and the task durations, the dates for completion of all tasks were computed automatically. Furthermore, other representations of the schedule can be computed with little effort.

Figure 26.8 shows a bar chart (or Gantt chart) illustrating a project calendar and how tasks start and finish at various dates.

Some of the tasks in Figure 26.8 are followed by a shaded bar. This indicates that there is some flexibility in the completion date of these tasks. If a task is not completed on time, the critical path will not be affected until the end of the period marked by the shaded bar. Tasks which lie on the critical path have no margin of error.

As well as considering schedules, project managers must also consider resource allocation and, in particular, the allocation of staff to project tasks. Figure 26.9 suggests an allocation of programmers to the tasks illustrated in Figure 26.7.

Staff allocations can also be processed by project management support tools and a bar chart generated which shows the time periods when staff are employed on the project (Figure 26.10).

Not all staff need be occupied at all times on the project. During intervening periods they may be on holiday, working on other projects, attending training courses or engaged in some other activity.

Large organizations usually employ a number of specialists and these specialists work on a project as required. This can cause scheduling problems. If one project is delayed while a specialist is working on it, this may have a knock-on effect and other projects may also be delayed because that specialist is not available.

Inevitably, initial project schedules will be incorrect and, as a project develops, estimates should be compared with actual elapsed time. This comparison can be used as a basis for revising the schedule for later parts of

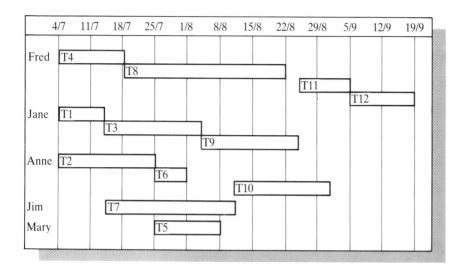

the project. When actual figures are known, it is also important to review the activity chart and perhaps re-partition the later project tasks in order to reduce the length of the critical path.

Figure 26.10
Staff allocation chart.

■ KEY POINTS

- ■ Effective management of a software project depends on good planning and problem anticipation.

- ■ Planning and estimating are iterative processes which continue throughout the course of a project. As more information becomes available, plans and schedules must be revised.

- ■ A project milestone is a predictable state where some formal report of progress may be presented to management. Milestones should occur regularly throughout the course of a software project.

- ■ Managers should carry out some kind of option analysis when deciding on how best to organize a project. The risk of each option should be considered and a management strategy which minimizes risk should be adopted. Techniques such as polar graphs may be useful in this analysis.

- ■ Project scheduling involves the creation of activity charts showing the interrelationships of project activities and bar charts. These are best prepared using software tools, which are now widely available on personal computers.

FURTHER READING

Software Engineering Economics. This is a good general text on software management which has excellent chapters on risk analysis. (B.W. Boehm, 1981, Prentice-Hall.)

Software Engineering Concepts. This is a general software engineering text which has a particularly good chapter on project planning. (R.E. Fairley, 1985, McGraw Hill.)

Managing the Software Process. Chapter 6 in this book is a good description of project planning in general although it is not particularly detailed. (W.S. Humphries, 1989, Addison-Wesley.)

EXERCISES

26.1 Explain why the process of project planning is an iterative one and why a plan must be continually reviewed during the course of a software project.

26.2 Draw up a project plan showing the major milestones and the development schedule for the newspaper delivery system project introduced in Exercise 3.7.

26.3 Describe the contingencies which you have allowed for in drawing up the project plans in Example 26.2.

26.4 If you have access to a project management package, draw up activity charts and bar charts for your project plans devised in Example 26.2. (You can try this without automated tools but it's long and tedious!)

Option	Cost (£)	Efficiency	Tool cost (£)	Schedule (years)	Staff utilization (%)	Risk
A	750,000	0.8	25,000	2	85	0.75
B	850,000	1	50,000	1.3	70	0.6
C	700,000	0.6	50,000	2	100	0.9

Figure 26.11
Alternative project options.

Task	Duration (days)	Dependencies
T1	10	
T2	15	T1
T3	10	T1, T2
T4	20	
T5	10	
T6	15	T3, T4
T7	20	T3
T8	35	T7
T9	15	T3, T6
T10	5	T5, T9
T11	10	T9
T12	20	T10
T13	35	T3, T4
T14	10	T8, T9
T15	20	T9, T14
T16	10	T15

Figure 26.12
Task durations and dependencies.

26.5 Draw up alternative project plans which will allow the newspaper delivery system project to be completed in 70% of your original development schedule. What assumptions have you had to make? Estimate the risk associated with the different options and present an option analysis as discussed in Section 26.2.

26.6 Show how polar graphs may be used for option analysis using the project estimates shown in Figure 26.11.

26.7 Figure 26.12 sets out a number of tasks, durations and dependencies. Draw up activity charts and bar charts for these tasks.

26.8 Figure 26.12 gives task durations for software project tasks. Assume that a serious, unanticipated setback occurs and instead of taking 10 days, task T5 takes 40 days. Revise the activity chart accordingly, highlighting the new critical path. Draw up new bar charts showing how the project might be organized. (Use a project management tool if you have access to one.)

Software Cost Estimation

OBJECTIVES

The objectives of this chapter are to discuss the general difficulties of software cost estimation and to illustrate an algorithmic approach to software cost estimation. Different estimation techniques are discussed and it is suggested that use of more than one technique is the most effective way of reducing cost estimation uncertainties. The advantages and problems of algorithmic cost modelling are covered and the method is illustrated using the COCOMO model. The final section of the chapter shows that, in spite of inherent uncertainties, algorithmic modelling can be an effective tool for providing project information and hence managing risk.

CONTENTS

Software project managers are responsible for controlling project budgets. To do so, they must be able to make estimates of how much a software development or part of that development is going to cost. This estimation activity is carried out in tandem with project scheduling.

The principal components of project costs are:

- Hardware costs.
- Travel and training costs.
- Effort costs (the costs of paying software engineers).

The dominant cost is the effort cost, although travel and training costs can make up a substantial and controllable budget item. However, the discussion here will concentrate on the cost of effort in a project . This is the most difficult to estimate and control, and has the most significant effect on overall costs.

The relationship between the project cost and the price ultimately charged to the software procurer is not a simple one. Software costing should be carried out objectively with the aim of accurately predicting the cost to the contractor of developing the software. Software pricing must take into account broader organizational, economic, political and business considerations. The price is not usually simply the cost plus profit as the organization may choose to accept part of the costs as a means of furthering its wider goals.

Software cost estimation is a continuing activity which starts at the proposal stage and continues throughout the lifetime of a project. Projects normally have a budget, and continual cost estimation is necessary to ensure that spending is in line with the budget.

Boehm (1981) discusses seven different techniques of software cost estimation:

(1)   *Algorithmic cost modelling* A model is developed using historical cost information which relates some software metric (usually its size) to the project cost. An estimate is made of that metric and the model predicts the effort required.

(2)   *Expert judgement* One or more experts on the software development techniques to be used and on the application domain are consulted. They each estimate the project cost and the final cost estimate is arrived at by consensus.

(3)   *Estimation by analogy* This technique is applicable when other projects in the same application domain have been completed. The cost of a new project is estimated by analogy with these completed projects. Myers (1989) gives a very clear description of this approach.

(4)   *Parkinson's Law*   Parkinson's Law states that work expands to fill the time available. In software costing, this means that the cost is determined by available resources rather than by objective assessment. If the software has to be delivered in 12 months and 5 people are available, the effort required is estimated to be 60 person-months.

(5)   *Pricing to win*   The software cost is estimated to be whatever the customer has available to spend on the project. The estimated effort depends on the customer's budget and not on the software functionality.

(6)   *Top-down estimation*   A cost estimate is established by considering the overall functionality of the product and how that functionality is provided by interacting sub-functions. Cost estimates are made on the basis of the logical function rather than the components implementing that function.

(7)   *Bottom-up estimation*   The cost of each component is estimated. All these costs are added to produce a final cost estimate.

Each technique has advantages and disadvantages. The most important point made by Boehm is that no one technique is better or worse than any other technique. For large projects, several cost estimation techniques should be used in parallel and their results compared. If these predict radically different costs, this implies that not enough costing information is available. More information should be sought and the costing process repeated. The process should continue until the estimates converge.

An assumption which seems to underlie all of the published cost models is that a firm set of requirements has been drawn up and costing is carried out using these requirements as a basis. Although this is an appropriate model of some projects (particularly military projects which have funded a separate requirements phase), the costs of many projects must be estimated using only an outline of the work which is to be done.

This can be justifiably criticized as an unscientific approach but it may be cost-effective from a business point of view. Requirements capture and definition is expensive and the cost may not be justified if the project does not gain funding approval.

Although the notion of pricing to win may seem amoral, the reality of product development is that this is a common approach to costing. A project cost is agreed on the basis of an outline proposal. Negotiations then take place between client and customer to establish the detailed project specification. This specification is constrained by the agreed cost and the buyer and seller must agree on what is acceptable system functionality. The fixed factor in many projects is not the project requirements but the cost. The requirements may be changed so that the cost is not exceeded.

Software costing is often simply a matter of experience or political judgement and these skills cannot be explained in a book of this nature.

Thus, in the remainder of this chapter, I concentrate on one specific costing technique, namely algorithmic cost modelling. This technique is objective but it is not necessarily more accurate than other approaches to cost estimation.

27.1 Algorithmic cost modelling

The most scientific, although not necessarily the most accurate, approach to software costing and scheduling is to use an algorithmic costing model. Such a model can be built by analysing the costs and attributes of completed projects. A mathematical formula or formulae can be established linking costs with one or more metrics such as project size, number of programmers, and so on. Kitchenham (1990b) describes thirteen different models which have been developed from empirical observations.

Several algorithmic models have been used for software costing. These are compared by Mohanty (1981) and Boehm (1981). Mohanty exercised a number of these models with the same hypothetical project data. This was a system with about 36K executable instructions, mostly mathematical software but with elements of interactive working and real-time command and control and with an assumed labour cost of $50,000 per year. He received cost estimates from different models ranging from $362,000 to $2,766,667 for the same input data.

This vast discrepancy in these figures does not, in itself, discredit algorithmic cost modelling but illustrates that the parameters associated with each model are highly organization-dependent. Because of different measurement techniques for quantities such as lines of code, the number of days in a person-month, and so on, it is impossible to establish a single costing model applicable across a wide range of organizations and projects.

Kemerer (1987) compared four different cost models using business data processing applications. One of these was the COCOMO model discussed here. He compared this with Putnam's model (1978) and with other models which were not based on lines of source code as an input parameter. Again, very wide variations in the predicted costs were found from 230 person-months to 3857 person-months for the same project. Kemerer used a historical database for cost estimation and found that the costs predicted by uncalibrated models could vary by several hundred per cent from the actual project costs. However, after calibration, the model prediction errors were reduced.

The basic difficulty with algorithmic cost modelling is that it relies on the quantification of some attribute of the finished software product. Cost estimation is probably most critical early in the software process long before the product is completed so the manager must estimate the appropriate attribute value for input to the costing model. Unfortunately, this estimate must usually be made with inadequate information and is therefore often inaccurate. Furthermore, the degree of inaccuracy is unknown so the probable error in the estimate is uncertain.

The most commonly used metric for cost estimation is the number of lines of source code in the finished system. Size estimation may involve estimation by analogy with other projects, estimation by ranking the sizes of system components and using a known reference component to estimate the component size or may simply be a question of engineering judgement. Application domain knowledge may be used to provide a reasonable size estimate. However, many projects break new ground and estimating their size is difficult.

Code size estimates are inherently uncertain because there are many factors which influence code size. For example, code size depends on hardware and software choices. The use of a commercial database management system might mean that database code need not be written. The use of a language such as Ada might mean that more lines of code are necessary then if Fortran (say) were used. However, these lines provide redundant information and checking, and Ada programmers are likely to be more productive than Fortran programmers. Hardware and software selection is often an integral part of a project and the selected choices may not be known to project managers when making initial size estimates.

An alternative to using code size as the estimated product attribute was proposed by Albrecht (1979) and refined by Albrecht and Gaffney (1983). Albrecht proposed the use of 'function-points', which are related to the functionality of the software rather than to its size.

Function points are computed by counting the following software characteristics:

- External inputs and outputs.
- User interactions.
- External interfaces.
- Files used by the system.

Each of these is then individually assessed for complexity and given a weighting value which varies from 3 (for simple external inputs) to 15 (for complex internal files).

The function point count is computed by multiplying each raw count by the estimated weight and summing all values. This 'unadjusted' function point count is then further modified by considering the overall complexity of the project according to a range of factors such as the degree of distributed processing, the amount of reuse, the performance, and so on. The unadjusted function point count is multiplied by the project complexity factors to produce a final function point count.

Symons (1988) points out problems with this approach to estimation. In particular, the assessment of the complexity factors leads to wide variations in estimates depending on the judgement of the estimator. Function points are heavily biased towards a data processing environment and Kemerer (1987) found them a useful effort predictor for such applications in his comparative model study. However, it is not clear how well this approach translates into other application domains which are less dominated by input and output processing.

Function point counts can be used in conjunction with lines of code estimation techniques. The number of function points is used to estimate the final code size. Based on historical data analysis, the average number of lines of code in a particular language required to implement a function point can be estimated (AVC). The estimated code size for a new application is computed as follows:

Code size = AVC × Number of function points

The advantage of this approach is that the number of function points can often be estimated from the requirements specification so an early code size prediction can be made.

Users of algorithmic models for project costing must be wary of the figures they produce. It is only in situations where the product is well understood, where the model has been calibrated for the organization using it, where it is similar to previous products and where language and hardware choices are pre-defined that the margin of error in the model estimate is likely to be small.

This warning is not really contradicted by reports of successful usage of algorithmic models. Project cost estimates are often self-fulfilling as the estimate is used to define the project budget and the product is adjusted so that the budget figure is realized. I know of no controlled experiments with cost modelling systems where the model outputs were not used to bias the experiment. A controlled experiment would not reveal the cost estimate to the project manager and then would compare actual with estimated costs.

Although the margin of error in initial cost estimates produced by these models is likely to be high, this does not mean that this approach to cost estimation is useless. It may provide more accurate results during the development of a project when a better estimate of product size may be made. Furthermore, as we shall see in a later section, algorithmic cost estimates provide a decision making aid to project managers, allowing alternative means of tackling a project to be compared.

27.2 The COCOMO model

A well documented software costing model, whose parameters can be tailored to particular modes of working, is the COCOMO model described by Boehm (1981). I concentrate on the COCOMO model here to give the reader an overview of algorithmic cost estimation. The further reading associated with this chapter includes a description of other algorithmic models.

The COCOMO model exists in basic (simple), intermediate and detailed forms but a full description of all of these is outside the scope of this book. Rather, an overview of the basic and intermediate COCOMO models is presented to introduce algorithmic cost modelling. The model assumes that the software requirements are relatively stable and that the project will be well managed by both the customer and the software developer.

The basic COCOMO model gives an order of magnitude estimation of software costs. It only uses the estimated size of the software project and the type of software being developed. There are versions of the estimation formula for three classes of software project:

(1) *Organic mode projects* These are projects where relatively small teams are working in a familiar environment developing well understood applications. Communications overhead is low, team members know what they are doing and they can quickly get on with the job.

(2) *Semi-detached mode projects* This mode represents an intermediate stage between organic mode projects and embedded mode projects described below. In semi-detached mode projects, the project team may be made up of experienced and inexperienced staff. Team members may have limited experience of related systems and may be unfamiliar with some (but not all) aspects of the system being developed.

(3) *Embedded mode projects* Embedded mode projects are concerned with developing software which is part of a strongly coupled complex of hardware, software, regulations and operational procedures. Requirements modifications to get round software problems are usually impractical and validation costs are high. Because of the diverse nature of embedded mode projects, it is unusual for project team members to have much experience in the application being developed.

The formulae to compute costs for these types of project or, more precisely, the effort required for software development all have the same form, namely:

$$\text{Effort} = A \ (\text{KDSI})^b$$

KDSI is the number of thousands of delivered source instructions (DSIs). A and b are constants which vary depending on the type of project. The equation suggests that cost is an exponential function of size although the value of b is usually close to 1.

Boehm's interpretation of a DSI is any line of source text irrespective of the actual number of instructions on that line. Therefore, if there are two or more statements on a line this counts as a single DSI and if a statement is spread over five lines this counts as five DSIs. Comments are excluded. Undelivered support software, whose development may take up a significant fraction of the project's resources, is not included when counting lines of code.

The values which should be assigned to these constants in any particular situation should be determined by analysis of historical project data. Using data from other organizations is likely to increase the margin of model error because of different inherent assumptions and working practices. From an analysis of his organization's data, Boehm reports the following formulae for the different classes of project:

Organic mode: $\quad$ PM $= 2.4 \ (\text{KDSI})^{1.05}$
Semi-detached mode: PM $= 3 \ (\text{KDSI})^{1.12}$
Embedded mode: $\quad$ PM $= 3.6 \ (\text{KDSI})^{1.20}$

Figure 27.1 shows the estimated effort for a range of project sizes.

The result of the estimate is PM, the number of person-months required to complete the project. In the version of the COCOMO model described by Boehm, a person-month is defined as consisting of 152 hours of working time. This figure takes into account the average monthly time off for holidays, training and sick leave.

These effort curves, particularly for smaller systems, are almost straight lines. It can be argued that the margin of error in the estimates is likely to be such that a linear estimating function may produce equally valid estimates, particularly as the basic COCOMO model only provides an approximate 'ball-park' figure.

The basic COCOMO model also suggests equations to estimate the development schedule of a project. This is the time required to complete the project given that sufficient personnel resources are available. The development schedule equations for the different modes of the project are:

Organic mode: $\quad$ TDEV $= 2.5 \ (\text{PM})^{0.38}$
Semi-detached mode: TDEV $= 2.5 \ (\text{PM})^{0.35}$
Embedded mode: $\quad$ TDEV $= 2.5 \ (\text{PM})^{0.32}$

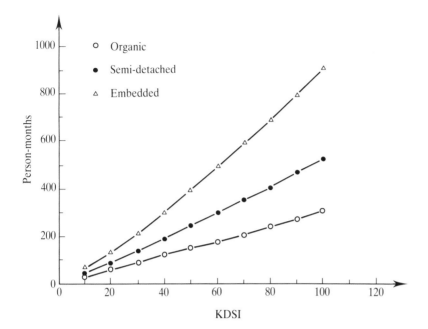

Figure 27.1
COCOMO effort
estimates.

The development schedule for different sizes of semi-detached mode projects is shown in Figure 27.2. The shapes of the curve for different project modes are similar. The differences between the exponents in the above development schedule equations may not be significant.

To illustrate the basic COCOMO model, assume that an organic mode software project has an estimated size of 32 000 delivered source instructions. From the effort equation, the number of person-months required for this project is:

$$PM = 2.4 \ (32)^{1.05} = 91 \ \text{p.m.}$$

From the schedule equation, the time required to complete the project is:

$$TDEV = 2.5 \ (91)^{0.38} = 14 \ \text{months}$$

The number of people employed on the project over its development time is not uniform so dividing the effort required by the development schedule does not give a meaningful figure of the number of people required for the project team. Putnam (1978) suggests that the optimal staff build-up on a project should follow a Rayleigh curve. Depending on the rate of staff build-up, there are several possible Rayleigh curves (Figure 27.3).

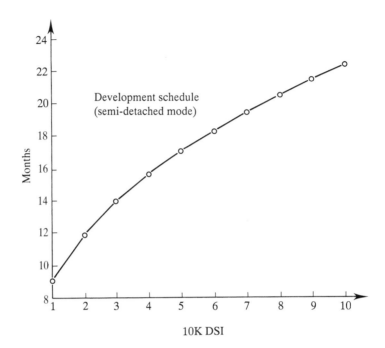

Figure 27.2
COCOMO
development schedule,
semi-detached mode.

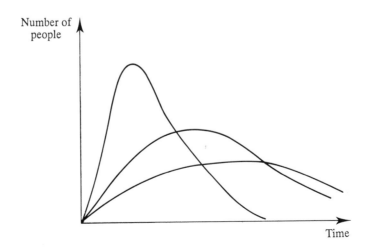

Figure 27.3
Rayleigh manpower
curves.

Only a small number of people are needed at the beginning of a project to carry out planning and specification. As the project progresses and more detailed work is required, the number of staff builds up to a peak. After implementation and unit testing is complete, the number of staff required starts to fall until it reaches one or two when the product is delivered.

Londeix (1987) discusses Rayleigh curves and project staffing in some detail. Experience has shown that a very rapid build-up of project staff correlates with project schedule slippage so it is recommended that project managers should not try to add too many staff to a project early in the project's lifetime.

Consider now a large embedded mode software project consisting of about 128 000 delivered source instructions. The basic COCOMO equations give results as follows:

$$PM = 3.6 \ (128)^{1.20} = 1216 \text{ p.m.}$$
$$TDEV = 2.5 \ (1216)^{0.32} = 24 \text{ months}$$

The basic COCOMO model is intended to give an order of magnitude estimate of the effort required to complete a software project. The model uses an implicit productivity estimate which was presumably derived from existing project data. In the case of organic mode projects, the productivity is 352 DSI/p.m. which is about 16 instructions per person day. The effort required for the embedded system implies a productivity of 105 DSI/p.m. which is about four instructions per person-day. These figures roughly correspond to productivity estimates from other sources.

An interesting implication of the COCOMO model is that the time required to complete the project is a function of the total effort required for the project and not a function of the number of software engineers working on the project. This confirms the notion that adding more people to a project which is behind schedule is unlikely to help that schedule to be regained. Myers (1989) discusses the problems of schedule acceleration and suggests that projects are likely to run into significant problems if they try to develop software without allowing sufficient calendar time.

27.2.1 The intermediate COCOMO model

The basic COCOMO model is a starting point for project estimation but there are many factors apart from project size and type which affect the effort involved in a project. The intermediate COCOMO model takes some of these factors into account.

The intermediate model takes the basic COCOMO effort and schedule computations as its starting point. A series of multipliers are then applied to the basic COCOMO figures which take into account factors such as required product reliability, database size, execution and storage constraints, personnel attributes and the use of software tools. Boehm describes fifteen factors which may be taken into consideration. These are divided into four classes, namely product attributes, computer attributes, personnel attributes and project attributes.

Product attributes are concerned with required characteristics of the software product being developed. They are rated on a scale from very low through nominal to very high. Low values imply a multiplier less than 1, a nominal value means a multiplier of 1 and a high value means a multiplier greater than 1.

(1)   *Reliability*   Low reliability means a software failure would result in only slight inconvenience; nominal means a failure would result in moderate recoverable losses; very high means failure involves risk to human life.

(2)   *Database size*   A low value for this attribute means the size of the database (in bytes) is less than 10 times the number of DSIs; nominal means the database size is between 10 and 100 times the system size; very high means the database is more than 1000 times larger than the program.

(3)   *Product complexity*   Low complexity code uses simple I/O operations, simple data structures and 'straight line' code. Nominal complexity implies some I/O processing, multi-file input/output, the use of library routines and some inter-module communication. Very high complexity means the use of re-entrant or recursive code, complex file handling, parallel processing, complex data management, and so on.

Computer attributes are constraints imposed on the software by the hardware platform. Examples of these constraints are limited memory size or processor speed. These affect software productivity because effort must be expended to tailor the software to meet the hardware limitations.

(1)   *Execution time constraints*   A nominal rating means that less than 50% of available execution time is used and an extra high rating means that 95% of available time must be used.

(2)   *Storage constraint*   A nominal value means that less than half the available store is used and an extra-high rating means that 95% of the available store is used.

(3)   *Virtual machine volatility*   The virtual machine is the combination of hardware and software on which the software product is built. A low rating for this factor means that it is only changed occasionally (once/year), a nominal rating implies major changes every six months and a very high rating suggests that the virtual machine changes very frequently.

(4)   *Computer turnround time*   This is rated from low, which implies interactive systems development, to very high, which means that turnround time is more than 12 hours. Most systems development now takes place using timesharing systems or workstation networks so that this attribute is now probably irrelevant except when specialized test rigs are being used for embedded systems development.

There are five personnel attributes taken into consideration which reflect the experience and capabilities of development staff working on the project. These attributes are analyst capability, application experience, virtual machine experience, programmer capability and programming language experience. These are all rated from very low, which means little or no experience, through nominal, which means at least one year's experience, to very high, which means more than three years' experience.

The project attributes are concerned with the use of software tools, the project development schedule and the use of modern programming practices. Boehm defines modern programming practices as practices such as top-down design, design and code reviews, structured programming, program support libraries, and so on. It was decided to classify these under a single heading rather than attempt to assess the effect of each factor in isolation.

When the COCOMO model was originally formulated, the use of structured programming was limited as were available software tools. Now, tool use is widespread and the use of structured techniques is normal practice, so the originally identified attributes are perhaps now less significant. The schedule attribute, however, is obviously still important. It is a measure of how well the required development schedule fits the nominal schedule estimated using the COCOMO model. Either an accelerated or an extended schedule requirement will give positive values to this multiplier.

In previous editions of this book, the values originally published by Boehm were reproduced but changes in development practice mean that these original values are now obsolete. However, the general multiplier classes, namely product, computer, personnel and project, are still appropriate and should be used as a basis for determining appropriate multiplier values. To use the multipliers effectively, historical project data must be analysed and appropriate values computed.

Figure 27.4 shows an example of how these multipliers affect effort estimates. The figures are rather contrived but they show how radically the multipliers can affect the total effort required.

The basic and intermediate COCOMO models suffer from the disadvantage that they consider the software product as a single entity and apply multipliers to it as a whole. In fact, most large systems are made up of sub-systems which are not homogeneous. Some may be considered to be organic mode systems, some embedded mode, for some the reliability requirements may be high, for others, low and so on.

System type	Embedded
System size	128 000DSI
Basic COCOMO estimate	1216 p.m.

Reliability required	Very high, Multiplier = 1.4
Complexity	Very high, Multiplier = 1.3
Memory limitation	High, Multiplier = 1.2
Tool use	Low, Multiplier = 1.1
Schedule	Accelerated, Multiplier = 1.23

Intermediate COCOMO estimate = 3593 p.m.

Reliability required	Very low, Multiplier = 0.75
Complexity	Very low, Multiplier = 0.7
Memory limitation	None, Multiplier = 1
Tool use	High, Multiplier = 0.9
Schedule	Normal, Multiplier = 1

Intermediate COCOMO estimate = 575 p.m.

Figure 27.4
The effect of multipliers on effort estimates.

The complete COCOMO model takes this into account and estimates the total system costs as the sum of sub-system costs with each sub-system estimated separately. This approach reduces the margin of error in the final cost estimate but a full discussion is outside the scope of this text. Interested readers should turn to Boehm's book for a complete description of the model.

27.2.2 Model tuning

To use an estimation model such as COCOMO effectively, it must be tuned to reflect local circumstances. Boehm discusses how the model may be re-calibrated by comparing actual costs to predicted costs and by using a least squares approximation to fit estimated to measured costs. This allows the constant factor and the scale factor in the basic COCOMO model to be re-computed.

For example, Figure 27.5 shows the predicted project costs and a set of measured project costs.

These figures are graphed in Figure 27.6. The least squares technique is a statistical technique which allows the best-fit line to the measured values to be discovered and the constant value in the COCOMO equation to be re-calibrated. Graphical software usually includes curve-fitting capabilities and can be used in model re-calibration.

The exponent value can be calculated in a similar way but probably requires more data, particularly for large projects, for a valid calibration to be made. As we have seen, this value is normally close to 1. It is possible to compute new exponent values but the difference between the new value and

Size	Predicted effort	Measured effort
14	57.65	65.72
17	71.65	82.40
26	115.32	131.46
40	186.82	249.10
55	266.89	304.25
60	294.21	323.63
64	316.26	302.55
97	503.86	571.04

Figure 27.5
Predicted and
measured software
costs.

the values suggested in the previous section is probably not significant.

The list of attributes proposed by Boehm is neither exhaustive nor exclusive. Some other organization might use a different set of attributes as cost multipliers. For example, the availability of a library of software components, the use of an integrated software engineering environment or the availability of personal workstations might all be taken into account.

Depending on particular modes of working within an organization, it may be possible to eliminate or combine intermediate COCOMO attributes or to add new attributes which are of particular importance. For example, the personnel attributes might be combined into a single attribute, interactive working may be the only development mode and the use of a

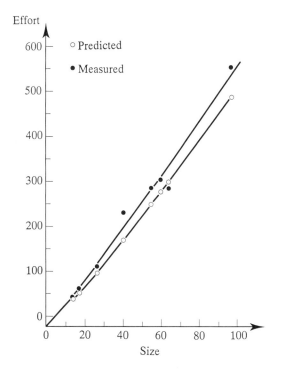

Figure 27.6
Predicted and
measured cost curves.

standard development system such as UNIX may mean that a standard toolset is always available. New attributes which might be added include the effect of working with classified data and its associated security and privacy considerations, and an attribute reflecting the type of application being developed.

Values for multipliers may be computed by estimating the product costs without using a particular multiplier, measuring the actual costs then finding the best multiplier value which fits estimated to measured data. The difficulty, of course, in adjusting the multipliers is that they are not independent variables. Few organizations have time for controlled experiments which allow the values to be calibrated.

For example, say an organization decides to invest in a software engineering environment, thus affecting the tools attribute, the virtual machine volatility attribute and the turnround attribute. Calibrating the model accurately would require each attribute to be considered in isolation and the new system might have to be degraded to isolate the different attributes. It is unrealistic to expect any organization which has invested in support to reduce the effectiveness of that support to calibrate a costing model.

27.3   Algorithmic cost models in project planning

The problem with the COCOMO model and other algorithmic models for absolute project cost estimation is that the scope for error is high. It is very difficult to estimate product size; the amount of support software required for different products may vary dramatically; products don't just fall into three classes; the multiplier values are average rather than specific and so on. Furthermore, it is equally difficult to estimate the margin of error so we cannot readily ascribe a confidence factor to the project estimates.

However, given that errors are fairly constant, algorithmic cost models can be used for computing relative project costs where the model parameters are varied and the cost differences observed. Thus, the technique provides some quantitative basis for management on how to tackle a particular project. It allows a reasoned consideration of how resources are best used. This is valuable for reducing risk, even if the actual cost estimates produced by the model are inaccurate.

The widespread availability of spreadsheets means that the project manager using an algorithmic cost model can model different ways of tackling a project and then decide on the most appropriate strategy. This is particularly important where there must be hardware/software cost trade-offs and where there may be a need to recruit new staff with specific project skills.

Effort	RELY	TIME	STORE	TOOLS	EXP	Hardware cost ($)	Software cost ($)	System cost ($)	Comments
45	1.22	1.1	1.1	0.85	1	100,000	451,717	551,717	Standard development environment
45	1.22	1.1	0.85	0.85	1	110,000	349,504	459,054	Add memory, some hardware change
45	1.22	0.9	0.85	1.1	1.2	135,000	443,504	578,504	Change processor, hardware redesign
45	1.22	0.9	0.85	0.75	1	185,000	251,991	436,991	Buy new development system
45	1.22	0.9	0.85	1.1	0.9	135,000	332,628	467,628	Hire staff with hardware experience
45	1.22	1.1	1.1	0.85	0.8	100,000	361,374	461,374	Use more experienced staff
45	1.22	0.9	0.85	1.1	1.1	135,000	406,545	541,545	More hardware, less experienced staff

Figure 27.7
Management options.

Consider a situation where an embedded system is to be developed for an experiment which is to be launched into space. Such experiments are subject to stringent weight limits so the number of chips has to be minimized. Furthermore, they have to be highly reliable so typical reliability and computer attributes are greater than 1 and increase the effort required for product development.

Let us assume that the basic COCOMO model predicts an effort of 45 p.m. to develop an embedded software system for this application. The software contractor has a standard development system which includes tool support for a particular microprocessor and which allows hardware using that processor and standard memory chips to be designed and built quickly. The contractor's normal preference is to make use of that processor for this experiment but the software requirements are such that this imposes tight execution time and space constraints.

Figure 27.7 shows a number of ways of tackling this project. Attribute values are hypothetical (but realistic) and hardware costs have been estimated. Average costs of $8000 per month for each software engineer have been assumed. The relevant multipliers are the required reliability (RELY), storage and execution time constraints (TIME and STOR), software tool use (TOOL) and development team experience (EXP).

The top line in Figure 27.7 shows that the estimated cost of building the system using the standard development environment with an average project team is $551 717, of which approximately 80% of the costs are software costs. This is the baseline value for option comparison.

Line 2 shows an option where higher capacity memory chips are used in the system (4 Mbit rather than 1 Mbit chips, say) which allows the available memory to be expanded without increasing the overall chip count. This necessitates some hardware redesign resulting in an increase of $10 000 in hardware costs. However, reducing the STORE multiplier allows a reduction of about $100 000 in software costs which more than compensates for the increased hardware cost.

Line 3 shows the costs for another option which might seem potentially attractive, namely replacing the processor with a faster microprocessor as well as increasing the memory requirements. More hardware redesign, costing an extra $35 000 may be required. However,

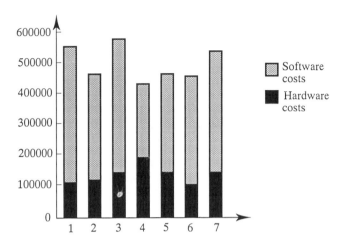

Figure 27.8
Hardware/software
cost comparisons.

there may not be a development system available for that microprocessor and staff experience with the system may be limited. Thus, the overall costs of this option are actually higher than the baseline costs.

Line 4 shows the same hardware changes but a development system for the new microprocessor is purchased at a cost of $50 000. Good tools become available and the staff inexperience is reduced because there is some commonality between this system and the existing system. The overall cost falls significantly in spite of the increased hardware costs. The model demonstrates that an investment of $50 000 can pay for itself in a single project and the organization still has the asset of the development system for future projects.

Other lines in the spreadsheet show other possibilities and allow the trade-offs between hardware costs, software costs and the use of experienced staff to be quantified. Given these figures, the project manager can make an informed choice as to what might be the most appropriate project option. Figure 27.8 shows a graphical comparison of the various options.

It does not follow that the lowest cost option is necessarily always the best choice. For example, there may be experienced staff available who would otherwise have been unused (thus constituting an extra organizational cost) and, from an organizational point of view, using these staff may be a better approach than investing in new hardware.

The use of a spreadsheet allows the effects of errors in the basic effort computation to be explored. Figure 27.9 shows how overall system costs change when it is assumed that there is an error of 30% either way in required effort.

The three histograms in Figure 27.9 represent costs when the software effort estimate is 30 person-months, 45 person-months and 60 person-months respectively. Hardware costs become less important as software

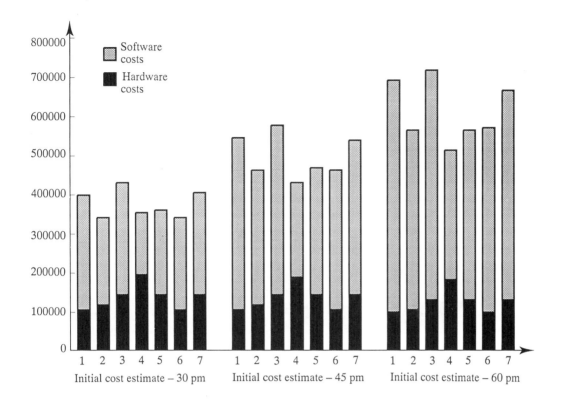

Figure 27.9
Graphical comparison
of cost estimates.

costs increase and more important as they decrease. The wise project manager will always choose a low-risk strategy. This graph suggests that such a strategy involves investing in a development system. As costs increase, the saving from this option increases. Although not the cheapest option for the lowest software costs, this option means that organizational cost of effort underestimates is minimized.

■ KEY POINTS

- There are various techniques of software cost estimation. In preparing an estimate, several of these should be used. If the estimates diverge widely, this reveals that inadequate estimating information is available.

- The reality of estimation is that estimates are often priced to gain a contract and the functionality of the system is adjusted to meet the estimate.

- Algorithmic cost modelling suffers from the fundamental difficulty that it relies on attributes of the finished product to make the cost estimate. At early stages of the project, these attributes are difficult to estimate accurately.

- The COCOMO costing model is a well developed model which takes project, product, hardware and personnel attributes into account when formulating a cost estimate. It also includes a means of estimating development schedules.

- To be useful, the COCOMO model has to be tuned to the needs of a user organization using historical project data. Unfortunately, such historical data is not always available.

- Algorithmic cost models are valuable to management as they support quantitative option analysis. They allow the cost of various options to be computed and, even with errors, the options can be compared on an objective basis.

FURTHER READING

'Allow plenty of time for large-scale software'. This is a good introduction to cost estimation. Myers makes the point that it is important to allow plenty of calendar time for projects and not to try and compress the project schedule. (W. Myers, *IEEE Software*, **6** (4), July 1989.)

Software Engineering Economics. This is the definitive book on cost estimation and it covers a range of techniques. It has a complete and thorough discussion of the COCOMO model, which was invented by Boehm and his collaborators. The one slight criticism of it is that it is dated in places and does not reflect trends such as workstation usage. (B.W. Boehm, 1981, Prentice-Hall.)

Cost Estimation for Software Development. This is a good complement to Boehm's book. It provides a more concise summary of cost estimation problems and techniques and concentrates on Putnam's cost estimation model rather than the COCOMO model. (B. Londeix, 1987, Addison-Wesley.)

Software Reliability Handbook. As well as having a chapter on algorithmic cost modelling which is unusual in that it is written by users rather than model developers, this book has a useful appendix which compares a number of different cost models. (P. Rook (ed.), 1990, Elsevier.)

EXERCISES

27.1 Make an estimate of the costs of developing the newspaper delivery system introduced in Exercise 3.7. Use more than one estimating method and compare the results. Given that different people make estimates, compare the different results and account for their discrepancies.

27.2 If you decide to implement the newspaper delivery system, use the COCOMO model after implementation to predict the cost and development schedule. Compare this with the original estimates and with the actual development schedule.

27.3 Write an interactive program in Pascal, C or some other programming language which implements the basic and intermediate COCOMO models and allows users to experiment with various parameter values.

27.4 Implement the COCOMO model using a spreadsheet such as Microsoft Excel or Lotus 1-2-3.

27.5 Using the basic COCOMO model, estimate the costs of the following projects:

    (a) A semi-detached mode project delivering 50 000 lines of code.
    (b) An embedded mode project delivering 25 000 lines of code.
    (c) An embedded mode project delivering 300 000 lines of code.
    (d) An organic mode project delivering 80 000 lines of code.

27.6 Using the examples from Exercise 27.5, illustrate how project multipliers such as support tool availability affect the costs of a project.

27.7 Some very large software projects involve the writing of millions of lines of code. Suggest how useful the cost estimation models are likely to be for such systems. Why might the assumptions on which they are based be invalid for very large software systems?

27.8 Cost estimates are inherently risky, irrespective of the estimation technique used. Suggest four ways in which the inherent risk in a cost estimate can be reduced.

Software Maintenance

28

OBJECTIVES

The objective of this chapter is to discuss software maintenance from a managerial point of view. After introducing different types of software maintenance, program evolution dynamics is discussed. Program evolution dynamics is concerned with the processes of change affecting software systems. Maintenance costs, which are usually higher than development costs, are the topic of the following two sections. Some maintenance metrics are described and the final section in the chapter covers software re-engineering. This involves re-structuring existing software systems to make them easier to maintain.

CONTENTS

Historically, the term 'maintenance' has been applied to the process of modifying a program after it has been delivered and is in use. These modifications may involve simple changes to correct coding errors, more extensive changes to correct design errors or drastic rewrites to correct specification errors or to accommodate new requirements.

This chapter has been deliberately included in the management section of the book as most of the material covered is managerial rather than technical. It is mostly concerned with planning and implementing the process of change. It is complemented by Chapter 29 (Configuration Management), which discusses the management of change.

It is impossible to produce systems of any size which do not need to be maintained. Over the lifetime of a system, its original requirements will be modified to reflect changing needs, the system's environment will change and errors, undiscovered during system validation, may emerge. Because maintenance is unavoidable, systems should be designed and implemented so that maintenance problems are minimized.

Software maintenance falls into three categories:

- Perfective maintenance.
- Adaptive maintenance.
- Corrective maintenance.

Perfective maintenance means changes which improve the system in some way without changing its functionality. Adaptive maintenance is maintenance which is required because of changes in the environment of the program. Corrective maintenance is the correction of previously undiscovered system errors. A survey by Lientz and Swanson (1980) discovered that about 65% of maintenance was perfective, 18% adaptive and 17% corrective (Figure 28.1).

Coding errors are usually relatively cheap to correct; design errors are more expensive as they may involve the rewriting of several program components. Requirements errors are the most expensive to repair because of the redesign which is usually involved.

Lientz and Swanson found that large organizations devoted at least 50% of their total programming effort to maintaining existing systems. McKee (1984) suggests a broadly comparable distribution of maintenance effort across the types of maintenance but suggests that the amount of effort spent on maintenance is between 65% and 75% of total available effort.

Figure 28.2 shows a model of the maintenance process, adapted from Arthur (1988), which recognizes these different classes of maintenance.

The maintenance process is triggered by a set of change requests from system users or management. The costs and impact of these changes is assessed and, assuming it is decided to accept the proposed changes, a new release of the system is planned. This release will usually involve elements

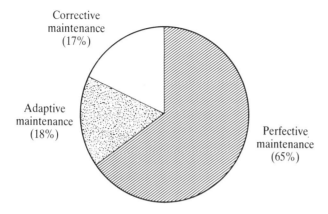

Figure 28.1
Maintenance effort
distribution.

of adaptive, corrective and perfective maintenance. The changes are implemented and validated and a new version of the system is released. The process then iterates with a new set of changes proposed for the new release.

Maintenance is an iteration of the development process and comparable standards and procedures should be applied. New requirements must be formulated and validated, components of the system must be redesigned and implemented and part or all of the system must be tested.

It is a characteristic of any change that the original program structure is corrupted by the change. The greater the corruption, the less understandable the program becomes and the more difficult it is to change. The maintenance engineer should try to minimize effects on the program structure. This can be achieved by applying the principles of information hiding during both development and maintenance. Effective information hiding results in a program structure which is robust and less liable to degradation during the maintenance process.

Figure 28.2
A maintenance process
model.

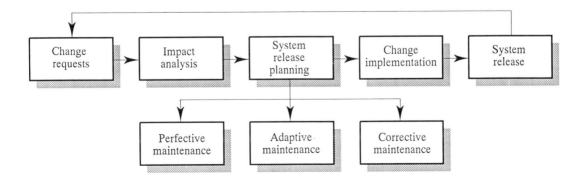

Maintenance has a poor image among software engineers. It is seen as a less skilled process than program development and, in many organizations, maintenance is allocated to inexperienced staff. This negative image means that maintenance costs are probably increased because staff allocated to the task are less skilled and experienced than those involved in system design.

Boehm (1983) suggests several steps that can be taken to improve maintenance staff motivation:

(1)   Couple software objectives to organizational goals.

(2)   Couple software maintenance rewards to organizational performance.

(3)   Integrate software maintenance personnel into operational teams.

(4)   Create a discretionary perfective maintenance budget which allows the maintenance team to decide when to re-engineer parts of the software.

(5)   Involve maintenance staff early in the software process during standards preparation, reviews and test preparation.

Management must demonstrate to engineers that maintenance is of equal value and is as challenging as original software development. The best designers and programmers should be challenged and motivated by system maintenance and it should be rewarded in the same way as system development.

28.1   Program evolution dynamics

Program evolution dynamics is the study of system change and the majority of work in this area has been carried out by Lehman and Belady (1985). The result of their studies has been a set of 'laws' (Lehman's laws) concerning system change which they claim are invariant and widely applicable.

Lehman's laws are one of the few examples in software engineering of theories which have been derived from observations. It is normal practice in other sciences to base theories on observations, but objective observations in software engineering are difficult and expensive to make.

Lehman and Belady examined the growth and evolution of a number of large software systems and the proposed laws were derived from these measurements. The 'laws' (hypotheses, really) are shown in Figure 28.3.

The first law states that system maintenance is an inevitable process. Fault repair is only part of the maintenance activity. System requirements will always change so that a system must evolve if it is to remain useful. Thus, as discussed in Chapter 1, an essential attribute of a well-engineered system is maintainability. Techniques such as object-oriented design and information hiding contribute directly to system maintainability.

(1) The law of continuing change
A program that is used in a real-world environment necessarily must change or become progressively less useful in that environment.

(2) The law of increasing complexity
As an evolving program changes, its structure tends to become more complex. Extra resources must be devoted to preserving and simplifying the structure.

(3) The law of large program evolution
Program evolution is a self-regulating process. System attributes such as size, time between releases, and the number of reported errors are approximately invariant for each system release.

(4) The law of organizational stability
Over a program's lifetime, its rate of development is approximately constant and independent of the resources devoted to system development.

(5) The law of conservation of familiarity
Over the lifetime of a system, the incremental system change in each release is approximately constant.

Figure 28.3
Lehman's laws.

The second law states that, as a system is changed, its structure is degraded. Additional costs, over and above those of implementing the change, must be accepted if the structural degradation is to be reversed. The maintenance process might include explicit restructuring activities aimed at improving the adaptability of the system.

The third law is, perhaps, the most interesting and the most contentious of Lehman's laws. It suggests that large systems have a dynamic of their own that is established at an early stage in the development process. This determines the gross trends of the system maintenance process and limits the number of possible system changes. Maintenance management cannot do whatever it wants as far as changing the system is concerned. Lehman and Belady suggest that this law is a result of fundamental structural and organizational factors.

As changes are made to a system, these changes introduce new system faults which then require more changes to correct them. Once a system exceeds some minimal size it acts in the same way as an inertial mass. It inhibits major change because these changes are expensive to make and result in a system whose reliability is degraded. The number of changes which may be implemented at any one time is limited.

Furthermore, large systems are inevitably produced by large organizations. These organizations have their own internal bureaucracies which slow down the process of change and which determine the budget allocated to a particular system. Major system changes require organizational decision making and changes to the project budget.

Such decisions take time to make and, during that time, other, higher priory system changes may be proposed. It may be necessary to shelve the changes to a later date when the the change approval process must be re-initiated. Thus, the rate of change of the system is partially governed by the organization's decision making processes.

Lehman's fourth law suggests that most large programming projects work in what he terms a 'saturated' state. That is, a change to resources or staffing has imperceptible effects on the long-term evolution of the system. Of course, this is also suggested by the third law which suggests that program evolution is largely independent of management decisions. This law confirms that large software development teams are unproductive as the communication overheads dominate the work of the team.

Lehman's fifth law is concerned with the change increments in each system release and is discussed in the following chapter on configuration management.

Lehman's laws are really hypotheses and it is unfortunate that more work has not been carried out to validate them. They seem sensible, and maintenance management should not attempt to circumvent them but should use them as a basis for planning the maintenance process. It may be that business considerations require them to be ignored at any one time (say it is necessary to make several major system changes). In itself, this is not impossible but management should realize the likely consequences for future system change and the high costs involved if such changes are proposed.

28.2 Maintenance costs

Maintenance costs are difficult to estimate. Evidence from existing systems suggests that maintenance costs are, by far, the greatest cost incurred in developing and using a system. In general, these costs were dramatically underestimated when the system was designed and implemented.

Maintenance costs vary widely from one application domain to another. On average, they seem to be between two and four times development costs for large embedded software systems. For business application systems, a study by Guimaraes (1983) showed that maintenance costs were broadly comparable with system development costs.

It is usually cost-effective to invest time and effort when designing and implementing a system to reduce maintenance costs. Increasing development costs will result in an overall decrease in system costs if the percentage saving in maintenance costs is comparable with the percentage development cost increase.

Figure 28.4 shows how overall lifetime costs can decrease as more effort is expended during system development to produce a maintainable system. In this diagram, it is assumed that maintenance costs are four times development costs and that a percentage increase in development costs

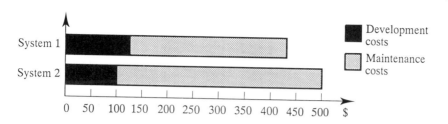

Figure 28.4
Development and
maintenance costs.

results in the corresponding decrease in maintenance costs. Assume Systems 1 and 2 are comparable. The development costs of System 1 were $110 000 (10% more than System 2) but the total life cycle costs were $450 000 (10% less than System 3).

Maintenance costs are difficult to estimate. The difficulties arise because these costs are related to a number of product, process and organizational factors (Figure 28.5).

Some of the factors which are unrelated to the engineering techniques used for software development are:

(1)   *The application being supported*   If the application is clearly defined and well understood, the system requirements are likely to be complete. Relatively little adaptive maintenance is necessary. If the application is completely new, it is likely that the initial requirements will be modified frequently, as users gain experience with the system.

(2)   *Staff stability*   Maintenance costs are reduced if system developers are responsible for maintaining their own programs. There is no need for other engineers to spend time understanding the system. In practice, it is very unusual for developers to maintain a program throughout its useful life.

(3)   *The lifetime of the program*   The useful life of a program depends on its application. Programs become obsolete when the application becomes obsolete or when their original hardware is replaced and conversion costs exceed rewriting costs. The older a program, the more it has been maintained and the more degraded its structure. Maintenance costs usually rise with program age.

Non-technical factors	Technical factors
Application domain Staff stability Program age External environment Hardware stability	Module independence Programming language Programming style Program validation Documentation

Figure 28.5
Maintenance cost
factors.

(4)   *The dependence of the program on its external environment*   If a program is dependent on its external environment it must be modified as that environment changes. For example, changes in a taxation system might require payroll, accounting and stock control programs to be modified.

(5)   *Hardware stability*   If a program is designed for a particular hardware configuration which does not change during the program's lifetime, no maintenance due to hardware changes will be required. However, this situation is rare. Programs must often be modified to use new hardware which replaces obsolete equipment.

Maintenance costs are also governed by the approaches adopted to system development:

(1)   *Module independence*   It should be possible to modify one component of a system without affecting other system components.

(2)   *Programming language*   Programs written in a high-level programming language are usually easier to understand (and hence maintain) than programs written in a low-level language.

(3)   *Programming style*   The way in which a program is written contributes to its understandability and hence the ease with which it can be modified.

(4)   *Program validation and testing*   Generally, the more time and effort spent on design validation and program testing, the fewer errors in the program. Consequently, corrective maintenance costs are minimized.

(5)   *The quality of program documentation*   If a program is supported by clear, complete yet concise documentation, the task of understanding the program can be relatively straightforward. Program maintenance costs tend to be less for well documented systems than for systems supplied with poor or incomplete documentation.

(6)   *The configuration management techniques used*   One of the most significant costs of maintenance is keeping track of all system documents and ensuring that these are kept consistent. Effective configuration management can help control this cost.

As systems age, maintenance costs more. Old systems may be written in programming languages which are no longer used for new development or may have been developed using design methods which have been supplanted by newer techniques. Special provision may have to be made to train staff members to maintain these programs.

This problem is becoming more severe as newer languages like Ada and C++ take over from older languages such as Fortran and as object-oriented development replaces function-oriented development. As discussed in Chapter 12, object-oriented design will not replace functional approaches for many years because of the immense amount of software developed using these functional design techniques. This software will have to be maintained well into the twenty-first century.

28.3   Maintenance cost estimation

Many factors affect maintenance costs so there is no single technique of maintenance cost estimation which has general applicability. Cost estimates can only be made using cost data from past projects and even then are only likely to be accurate when previous cost information was collected for the same type of system. If this information is available, maintenance cost estimation based on algorithmic techniques may be used to assist with maintenance decision making.

Using data gathered from 63 projects in a number of application areas, Boehm (1981) established a formula for estimating maintenance costs. This is part of the COCOMO software cost estimation model, discussed in Chapter 27.

Boehm's maintenance cost estimation is calculated in terms of a quantity called the annual change traffic (ACT) which he defines as follows:

> The fraction of a software product's source instructions which undergo change during a (typical) year either through addition or modification

Boehm's estimation method for maintenance costs uses the ACT and the estimated or actual development effort in person-months to derive the annual effort required for software maintenance. This is computed as follows:

$$AME := ACT \times SDT$$

AME and SDT are the annual maintenance effort and the software development time and the units of each are person-months (p.m.). Notice that this is a simple linear relationship. Figure 28.6 shows the computed maintenance costs for systems of various sizes assuming ACTs of 10%, 20% and 30%.

Say a software project required 236 person-months of development effort and it was estimated that 15% of the code would be modified in a typical year. The basic maintenance effort estimate is:

$$AME := 0.15 \times 236 = 35.4 \text{ p.m.}$$

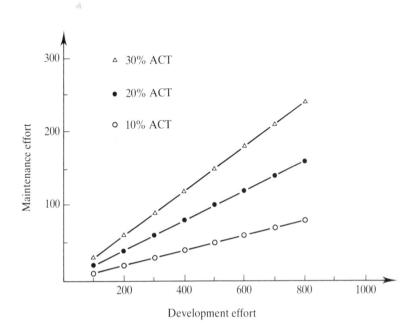

Figure 28.6
Maintenance costs.

This formula gives a rough approximation of maintenance costs and is a basis for computing a more precise figure based on the attribute multipliers, as discussed in Chapter 27. These take into account process, project, product and personnel factors. The maintenance cost estimate may be refined by judging the importance of each factor affecting the cost and selecting the appropriate cost multiplier. The basic maintenance cost is then multiplied by each multiplier to give the revised cost estimate.

For example, say in the above system the factors having most affect on maintenance costs were reliability (RELY), which had to be very high, the availability of support staff with language and applications experience (AEXP and LEXP), which was also high, and the use of modern programming practices for system development (very high). These might have multipliers as follows:

RELY   1.10
AEXP   0.91
LEXP   0.95
MODP   0.72

By applying these multipliers to the initial cost estimate, a more precise figure may be computed:

$$\text{AME} := 35.4 \times 1.10 \times 0.91 \times 0.95 \times 0.72 = 24.2 \text{ p.m.}$$

The reduction in estimated costs has come about partly because experienced staff are available for maintenance work but mostly because modern programming practices had been used during software development. As an illustration of their importance, if modern programming practices are not used and other factors are unchanged the development cost is increased to 53.53 p.m. The maintenance cost estimate is also much larger:

$$\text{AME} := 53.53 \times 1.10 \times 0.91 \times 0.95 \times 1.40 = 71.26 \text{ p.m.}$$

Structured development techniques are not yet universal and their use only became widespread in the 1980s. Much of the maintenance effort in an organization is devoted to old systems which have not been developed using these techniques. This is at least part of the reason for high maintenance costs.

Usually, different parts of the system will have different ACTs so a more precise figure can be derived by estimating initial development effort and annual change traffic for each software component. The total maintenance effort is then the sum of these individual component efforts.

A problem with algorithmic maintenance cost estimation is that it is difficult to allow for the fact that the software structure degrades as the software ages. Using the original development time as a key factor in maintenance cost estimation introduces inaccuracies as the software loses its resemblance to the original system.

The cost estimation model used by Boehm estimated maintenance costs which fitted reasonably well with measured actual costs in his company. Boehm does not claim that his organization is necessarily typical and the estimation model may not work so well in other organizations or for other types of work. It may also be the case that the predicted maintenance cost affected the actual cost if it was used to set maintenance budgets. Again, it is clear that algorithmic cost modelling can only be reasonably accurate if the model is calibrated to an organization's own software development practices.

As with development cost estimation, algorithmic cost modelling is most useful as a means of option analysis. It should not be expected to predict costs accurately. A cost estimation model which takes into account factors such as programmer experience, hardware constraints, software complexity, and so on, allows decisions about maintenance to be made on a rational rather than an intuitive basis.

For example, say in the above example system that management decided that money might be saved by using less experienced staff for software maintenance. Assume that inexperienced staff cost $7500 per month compared to $9500 for more experienced software engineers. Figure 28.7 shows how these different approaches to maintenance may be compared. The initial estimate is computed by taking the basic maintenance cost and adjusting it using the RELY and MODP multipliers.

Experience	Initial estimate	Monthly salary ($)	Experience factor	Maintenance cost ($)
Inexperienced	28.04	7,500	1.21	254,245
Mixed	28.04	8,500	1.03	245,057
Experienced	28.04	9,500	0.86	230,259

Figure 28.7
Maintenance cost
comparison.

Therefore, in this example, maintenance costs are reduced by using more experienced engineers in spite of the fact that their unit cost is significantly higher.

As in development cost estimation, algorithmic cost models are useful because they allow relative rather than absolute costs to be assessed. It may be impossible to predict the annual change traffic of a system to any degree of accuracy but the inaccuracy is reflected in all computations. Although the absolute cost figure may be out of step with reality, the information allows management to make reasoned decisions about how best to allocate resources to the maintenance process.

28.4   Measuring program maintainability

Managers hate surprises, especially if these result in unexpectedly high costs. If the maintainability of a component can be assessed, the likely costs of maintenance can be estimated. A maintainability metric can help management make an informed decision on whether a component should be maintained or completely rewritten to reduce future maintenance costs.

Maintainability metrics do not measure the cost of making a particular change to a system nor do they predict whether or not a particular component will have to be maintained. Rather, they are based on the assumption that the maintainability of a program is related to its complexity. The metrics measure some aspects of the program complexity. It is suggested that high complexity values correlate with difficulties in maintaining a system component.

McCabe (1976) devised a measure of program complexity using graph-theoretic techniques. His theory maintains that program complexity is not dependent on size but on the decision structure of the program. The program flow graph and the cyclomatic complexity can be derived as discussed in Chapter 22. McCabe argues that components with a high cyclomatic complexity are likely to require more maintenance than components with a low metric value.

Halstead (1977) suggests that the complexity of a program can be measured by considering the number of unique operators, the number of unique operands, the total frequency of operators and the total frequency of operands in a program. Using these parameters, Halstead has devised metrics allowing program size, programming effort and program 'intelligence count' to be computed.

Both of these techniques may have some validity. Both suffer from the same disadvantage, that they do not take into account the data structures used in the program, the program comments or the use of meaningful variable names. Shepherd *et al.* (1979) have conducted experiments using both techniques. Their results were inconclusive. Hamer and Frewin (1981) have evaluated Halstead's metrics and are dubious of their validity.

Rather than use a single metric, Kafura and Reddy (1987) use a spectrum of seven metrics to assess the complexity of a system. These include Halstead's effort metric, McCabe's complexity metric, the code size, and other metrics which take into account the way in which a component uses its data. Their experiments showed a high correlation between the values of the metrics produced and the perceived maintainability as assessed by human maintainers.

They suggest that it is not the absolute values of the metrics that are important but rather their relative values. If some components have a much higher value than most others, their experiments suggested that these would cause particular problems in maintenance and may well contain a higher proportion of system faults. For example, say the average complexity value for system components was X but three components had complexity ratings much greater than X. The design of these components should be assessed to see if it might be simplified to facilitate future component modifications.

The problem, of course, is that maintainability is related to many factors, as discussed earlier. Complexity is one of these and the metrics suggested above assume it is the dominant one. We do not know if this is actually the case so it is difficult to say whether or not these maintainability metrics are generally useful for predicting maintenance costs.

28.5   Software re-engineering

One of the reasons why maintenance costs are so high is that the structure of the systems which have to be modified may be non-existent or, perhaps, not obvious to the program reader. The reason for this may be that the system is geriatric and was developed without the use of information hiding. Alternatively, continuing maintenance may have corrupted the original structure so much that it is no longer discernible.

There comes a stage in the life of a program where the cost of making incremental changes to a system is so high that it must either be scrapped and rewritten or it must be completely or partially restructured. Restructuring involves examining the existing system and rewriting parts of it to improve its overall structure. Restructuring may be particularly useful when changes are confined to part of the system. Only this part need be restructured. Other parts need not be changed or re-validated.

If a program is written in a high-level language, it is possible to restructure that program automatically although this may require a lot of computer time. Bohm and Jacopini (1966) demonstrated that any program may be rewritten in terms of simple if-then-else conditionals and while loops and that unconditional goto statements were not required. This theorem is the basis for program restructuring.

The process starts by constructing a program flow graph (discussed in Chapter 21). This is relatively simple for structured programs (those without gotos) but is more complex when goto statements are included. Once this graph has been constructed, simplification and transformation techniques are applied. Ultimately, a program which uses only while loops and simple conditional statements can be generated.

This reduces the complexity of a program and should make the system easier to maintain. However, it only affects the program control structure and is of no help in improving the structure of abstractions used to represent the system. Nor can it improve systems which are difficult to maintain because of high coupling caused by the use of shared global tables.

An alternative approach which can be applied to both assembly language and high-level language programs is described by Britcher and Craig (1986). They took a large software system, written in assembly language, discovered its structure and documented the structure using functional and data abstractions.

The system worked on obsolete hardware and had to be re-hosted on modern computers. It was not, however, necessary to change all of the program so it was cost effective to use resources to make the volatile parts of the system more maintainable. The cost of restructuring was less than the cost of a complete system rewrite because some parts of the program were unchanged.

Many parts of the system were not well structured and the effort really involved the imposition of structure onto the program. For example, shared data areas were reconstructed as data abstractions and control structures were all rebuilt as simple conditionals or loops. The outcome of the work was a well-documented system whose life was considerably extended by the restructuring process.

A combination of automatic and manual system restructuring may be the best approach to software re-engineering. The control structure can be improved automatically, thus making the system easier to understand. The abstraction and data structures of the program may then be discovered, documented and improved using a manual approach.

Arthur (1988) suggests that a systematic approach should be used to identify those components which could benefit most from restructuring. For

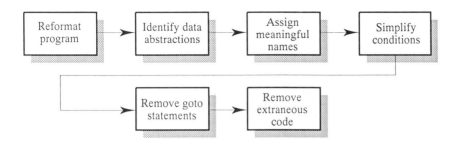

Figure 28.8
Program
re-engineering.

example, the following types of components may be selected for re-engineering:

(1)   Components which exhibit the highest failure rate.
(2)   Components which have had the highest annual change traffic.
(3)   Components with the highest measured complexity.
(4)   Components which do not meet current company standards.

Arthur also suggests that restructuring should be an iterative procedure. One class of structural problem should be dealt with at a time and an intermediate program produced. Figure 28.8 shows how this systematic restructuring may be tackled.

The first stage in re-engineering is to format the program to display the structure. Prettyprinters which lay out the program neatly may be used for this reformatting. The data abstractions used in the program should be identified and meaningful names assigned to all variables and constants.

The logic used in conditional statements should then be examined and simplified wherever possible. For example, not logic, where actions are taken when conditions are not true, is usually confusing. These should be replaced by conditions which test for truth. Complex nested conditionals may be replaced by a simpler conditional statement cascade or by case statements.

Simplifying conditions will remove some goto statements and, wherever possible, all other such statements should be eliminated by replacing them with loops and conditional statements. This will probably result in extraneous code, which can then be eliminated.

Decisions on whether to restructure or rewrite a program can only be made on a case-by-case basis. Some of the factors which must be taken into account are:

(1)   Is a significant proportion of the system stable and not subject to frequent change? If so, this suggests restructuring rather than rewriting as it is only really necessary to restructure that part of the program which is to be changed.

(2) Does the program rely on obsolete support software such as compilers, and so on? If so, this suggests it should be rewritten in a modern language as the future availability of the support software cannot be guaranteed.

(3) Are tools available to support the restructuring process? If not, manual restructuring is the only option.

System re-engineering is likely to become increasingly important. The rate of change of hardware development means that many embedded software systems which are still in use must be changed as the hardware on which they execute cannot be supported. Many systems developed in the early 1970s fall into this category and structured development techniques were only occasionally used at that time. If the life of these systems is to be extended, it is probably essential to carry out some software re-engineering.

■ KEY POINTS

- There are three identifiable types of software maintenance. These are perfective maintenance, which is system improvement; adaptive maintenance, which is system evolution; and corrective maintenance, which is system repair.

- The cost of software maintenance usually exceeds the cost of software development. Typically, maintenance costs are a factor of 2 to 4 higher than development costs for large systems.

- There appear to be a number of invariant relationships (Lehman's laws) which affect the evolution of a software system. These have been derived from empirical observations and show that maintenance costs are inevitable. They also provide guidelines on how to manage the maintenance process.

- Several technical and non-technical factors affect maintenance costs. These include application factors, environmental factors, personnel factors, programming language factors and documentation.

- An algorithmic approach can be used for maintenance cost estimation but its accuracy is limited. However, it can be useful as an aid to management decision making.

- We do not have reliable metrics to measure the maintainability of a program. Complexity metrics, however, can give some hints as to components which may incur high maintenance costs.

- System re-engineering involves systematically restructuring parts of the system which are costly to maintain. It is cost-effective when changes are mostly confined to an identifiable segment of a system.

FURTHER READING

IEEE Software, **7** (1), January 1990. This is a special issue devoted to software maintenance and re-engineering. The papers on re-engineering are a particularly good supplement to the material here.

Program Evolution. Processes of Software Change. This is an edited collection of papers from these authors which charts their thoughts on software evolution from its inception in the early 1970s to the mid-1980s. It is an interesting text although it would have been improved with a little more linking text from the editors. (M.M. Lehman and L. Belady, 1985, Academic Press.)

Software Evolution. This is a very readable book on the maintenance process which contains much practical advice on how to tackle the maintenance problem. (L.J. Arthur, 1988, John Wiley & Sons.)

Software Maintenance and Computers. This is a collection of papers from the IEEE tutorial series and probably contains most papers on maintenance, published up to 1987, that are worth reading. (D.H. Longstreet (ed.), 1990, IEEE Press.)

EXERCISES

28.1 Describe the technical and non-technical factors which affect system maintenance costs. Explain, how, as a software manager, you would attempt to minimize maintenance costs in projects which you are managing.

28.2 Given that the annual change traffic in a system is 14% per year and the initial development cost was $245 000, compute an estimate for the annual system maintenance cost. Given that the lifetime of the system is 12 years, what is the total cost of that software system?

28.3 Explain the difficulties which are involved in measuring program maintainability. Describe why the notion of relating maintainability to complexity is too simplistic.

28.4 Explain the rationale underlying Lehman's laws. Under what circumstances might the laws break down?

28.5 Go back to a program which you wrote some time ago and write documentation describing the structure of that program. Keep a log of the difficulties encountered in understanding the program.

28.6 Explain why the structuring facilities offered by programming languages such as Ada are likely to lead to more maintainable programs. Suggest features of Ada which might cause future maintenance problems.

28.7 Go back to programs which you wrote some time ago and attempt to improve them by applying the restructuring techniques discussed in Section 28.5. Of course, if you engineered your programs properly in the first place, you will find that no restructuring is necessary!

Configuration Management

■ OBJECTIVES

The objective of this chapter is to describe configuration management, an activity which is critical to the management and maintenance of large software systems. The introduction defines configuration management as the management of system change. Major configuration management activities, namely configuration planning, change control and management, system building, and version and release management are discussed. Problems in these areas are highlighted. The final part of the chapter covers CASE tools which partially automate the configuration management process.

■ CONTENTS

Configuration management (CM) is concerned with the development of procedures and standards for managing an evolving software system product. In essence, it is concerned with how to control change, how to manage systems which have been subject to change and how to release these changed systems to customers.

CM is closely allied to the quality assurance process and, in some organizations, the same manager may share quality assurance and CM responsibilities. Both activities are post-development activities. Software is released by the developers first to quality assurance and, once certified, is passed on to the CM team who take control of that software.

CM is necessary because software systems, particularly large ones, have a long lifetime. During that lifetime, they are subjected to frequent change. Furthermore, responsibility for change is a team activity. It is exceptional for it to be the responsibility of the original software developer. CM is intended to ensure that the changes to the software are made in such a way that overall costs are minimized and, most importantly, that minimum disruption is caused to existing system users.

It is inevitable that a useful software system will exist in a number of versions for different computers, for different operating systems, incorporating client-specific functions and so on (Figure 29.1). Configuration managers are responsible for keeping track of the differences between software versions and for ensuring that new versions are derived in a controlled way. They may also be responsible for ensuring that these new versions are released to the correct customers at the appropriate time.

Uncontrolled change quickly leads to chaos. Software versions are created by applying changes to existing software, so perhaps the most critical role of the CM team is change control. Change control involves change impact assessment and costing, and deciding if and when the changes should be implemented. Once changes have been made, the CM team is also usually responsible for rebuilding the software system from its components.

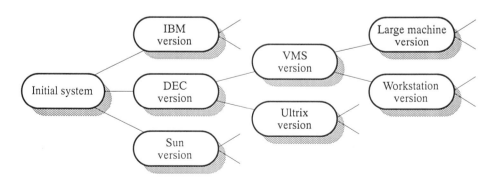

Figure 29.1
System families.

CM relies on an organization establishing a set of standards and publishing these in a CM handbook. An example of such a standard is IEEE standard 828-1983, which is a standard for CM plans. Military software procurers normally insist that their own standards and procedures are used.

Software companies may develop their own in-house standards based on these external standards. The material in these standards documents is too detailed to cover here. As with all standards, the important thing is to have some standard which is consistently applied rather than simply rely on an informal process.

There are various activities which can be considered under the general heading of CM. In this chapter, four CM activities, namely, configuration management planning, change control, system building, and version and release management, are described.

29.1 Configuration management planning

CM is concerned with the management of software systems after they have been developed, but successful CM relies on planning, which should take place before and during the software development. CM planning is not an activity which is carried out in isolation. It is an integral part of the overall project planning process and relates to almost all other activities in that process.

In the course of developing a large software system, literally thousands of documents are produced. Many of these are technical working documents which present a snapshot of ideas for further development. Such documents are subject to frequent and regular change. Others are inter-office memos, minutes of group meetings, outline plans and proposals, and so on. Although these documents may be of interest to a project historian, they are not critical for future maintenance of the system.

All of the documents which may be necessary for future system maintenance must be placed under configuration control. A key task of the CM planning process is to decide exactly which items (or classes of item) are to be controlled. Project plans, specifications, designs, programs and test data suites are called formal documents.

Having established what documents are to be managed, the CM planning process must then define the following:

- A document naming scheme.
- The relationships between formal documents.
- The person responsible for checking formal documents.
- The person responsible for delivering each formal document to CM.

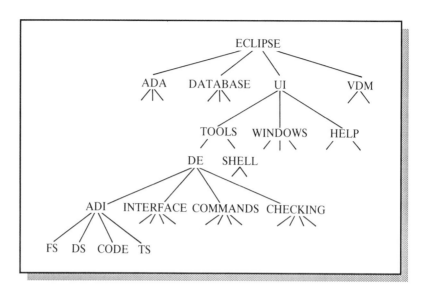

Figure 29.2
Documentation
hierarchy.

The document naming scheme must assign a unique name to all documents under configuration control. Related documents such as specifications and designs should have related names. This can be accomplished using a hierarchical naming scheme where examples of names might be:

> ECLIPSE/UI/TOOLS/DE/ADI/FS
> ECLIPSE/UI/TOOLS/DE/ADI/CODE

These names have a number of components – the project (ECLIPSE), the sub-project (UI), the part of the sub-project (TOOLS), the particular tool being developed (DE, abbreviation of design editor), the part of the tool which is documented (ADI, abstract data interface) and the type of document (FS or CODE, functional specification or program source).

Defining the relationships between formal documents means drawing up the document hierarchy which is embodied in the naming scheme. For example, the above names suggest a hierarchy as shown in Figure 29.2.

The leaves of the documentation hierarchy are the formal project documents. Figure 29.2 shows that four formal documents are required for each managed entity. These are a functional specification (FS), a design specification (DS), the code of the component and a test specification (TS).

The description of this hierarchy is a critical project document as it allows document names to be generated and documents to be located. Thus it should itself be placed under configuration control and should not be changed in an arbitrary way.

The CM plan should define the engineers responsible for document quality control and document delivery. The person responsible for document delivery need not be the same as the person responsible for producing the document. To simplify interfaces, it is usually convenient to make project managers or team leaders responsible for all of the documents produced by their team.

Another aspect of CM planning is the definition of a database schema to record configuration information. The configuration database is used to record all relevant information relating to configurations and is used as a project management tool after the software has been delivered. As well as defining the schema, procedures for recording and retrieving project information must also be defined.

A configuration database must be able to provide answers to a variety of queries about system configurations. Typical queries might be:

(1) Which customers have taken delivery of a particular version of the system?

(2) What hardware and operating system configuration is required to run a given system version?

(3) How many versions of a system have been created and what were their creation dates?

(4) What versions of a system might be affected if a particular component is changed?

(5) How many change requests are outstanding on a particular version?

(6) How many reported faults exist in a particular version?

Some CM databases, particularly for old systems, are still paper rather than computer databases. The range of queries which can be supported with such paper databases is more limited than is possible with computerized systems. Given the existence of low-cost hardware and database management systems, there is no justification for continuing with paper-based systems for new developments. Although it is desirable to have a CM database as part of an integrated development environment, current commercial databases can be used if no tailored system is available.

The CM planning process also involves drawing up procedures for change control, system building and version management. These are discussed later in this chapter.

29.2 Change control

We have already discussed how the necessity for change is inherent in software systems. Irrespective of improvements in the software process, there will always be a need to apply changes to existing software systems.

Change control procedures ensure that the changes to a system are made in a controlled way so that their effect on the system can be predicted.

```
Request change by completing a change request form
Analyse change request
if change is valid then
    Assess how change might be implemented
    Assess change cost
    Submit request to change control board
    if change is accepted then
        repeat
            make changes to software
            submit changed software for quality approval
        until software quality is adequate
        create new system version
    else
        reject change request
else
    reject change request
```

Figure 29.3
The change request
procedure.

Of course, during a system development it may be counter-productive to impose rigid change control but the change control process should come into effect when the software (or associated documentation) is delivered to configuration management. Items accepted for change control are usually called a *baseline*. The pseudo-code, shown in Figure 29.3, defines the change control process.

The first stage in the procedure is to complete a change request form (CRF). This is a formal document where the requester sets out the change required to the system. As well as recording the change required, this form records the recommendations regarding the change, and the estimated costs of the change, the dates when the change was requested, approved, implemented and validated. It may also include a part where the maintenance engineer outlines how the change is to be implemented.

Defining the CRF is part of the CM planning process although for many contracts, forms conforming to some client standard must be used. The information provided in the CRF is the basis of much of the information which is recorded in the CM database. An example of a CRF is shown in Figure 29.4.

Once a CRF has been submitted, it is analysed to ensure that the change is a valid one. Sometimes users of a system submit change requests setting out apparent system errors and the fault is not with the system but in the way in which it has been used. It is also common for different users to request similar changes. If the analysis process discovers that a change request is invalid, duplicated or has already been considered, the change is rejected.

For valid changes, the next stage of the process is change assessment and costing. The impact of the change must be determined and a means of implementing that change discovered. The cost of making the change and possibly changing other system components to accommodate the change is

```
┌────────────────────────────────────────────────────────────┐
│                    CHANGE REQUEST FORM                       │
│                                                              │
│   Project:                                                   │
│                                                              │
│   Change requester:            Date:                         │
│                                                              │
│   Requested change:                                          │
│                                                              │
│   Change analyser:             Date of analysis:             │
│                                                              │
│   Components affected:                                       │
│                                                              │
│   Associated components:                                     │
│                                                              │
│   Change assessment:                                         │
│                                                              │
│   Change priority:                                           │
│                                                              │
│   Change implementation:                                     │
│                                                              │
│   Estimated change costs:                                    │
│                                                              │
│   Date submitted to CCB:       Date of CCB decision:         │
│                                                              │
│   CCB decision:                                              │
│                                                              │
│   Change implementor:          Date of implementation:       │
│                                                              │
│   Date submitted to QA:        QA decision:                  │
│                                                              │
│   Date submitted to CM:                                      │
│                                                              │
│   Comments:                                                  │
│                                                              │
└────────────────────────────────────────────────────────────┘
```

Figure 29.4
A change request form.

then estimated and recorded on the CRF. This assessment process is much simplified if a configuration database is available where all component interrelationships are recorded.

Some classes of change do not require further assessment. For example, change requests which point out typographical errors in documents, which have no other impact on the system and which may be implemented very cheaply, may be immediately accepted and put into effect. Part of the CM planning process is to decide which classes of change fall into this category.

The majority of changes, however, should be submitted to a change control board which decides whether or not the change is to be accepted. The change control board considers the impact of the change from a strategic and organizational rather than a technical point of view and decides whether or not the change is economically justified.

The only exception to this is where a fault which can cause a serious system failure is reported. In such situations, an 'emergency repair' may be

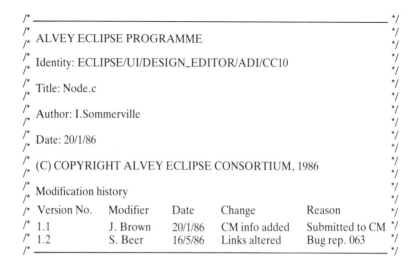

Figure 29.5
A component header comment.

```
/* _____ */
/*                                                              */
/* ALVEY ECLIPSE PROGRAMME                                      */
/*                                                              */
/* Identity: ECLIPSE/UI/DESIGN_EDITOR/ADI/CC10                  */
/*                                                              */
/* Title: Node.c                                                */
/*                                                              */
/* Author: I.Sommerville                                        */
/*                                                              */
/* Date: 20/1/86                                                */
/*                                                              */
/* (C) COPYRIGHT ALVEY ECLIPSE CONSORTIUM, 1986                 */
/*                                                              */
/* Modification history                                         */
/*                                                              */
/* Version No.   Modifier   Date      Change          Reason          */
/* 1.1           J. Brown   20/1/86   CM info added   Submitted to CM */
/* 1.2           S. Beer    16/5/86   Links altered   Bug rep. 063    */
/* _____ */
```

undertaken without formal approval. Such repairs are often distributed as system 'patches', which are object code modifications. Proliferations of patches cause enormous problems for system maintenance and, in general, their use should be kept to an absolute minimum.

The change control board should be independent of the project and should be able to consider the change from a broad organizational perspective. Formally structured change control boards, which include senior client and contractor staff, are a requirement of military projects. For other projects, the make-up of the change control board depends on the project and the organization. It may simply consist of a single reviewer.

If the change is approved by the change control board, it may then be applied to the software. The revised software is re-validated to check that the change has been properly made and has not adversely affected other parts of the system. The changed software is handed over to the CM team and is incorporated in a new version of the system.

As software components are changed, it is important that a record of all of the changes which were made to each component is maintained. This is sometimes called the derivation history of a component. One way to maintain such a record is in a standardized comment prologue kept at the beginning of the component. An example of a standardized comment prologue incorporating change information is shown in Figure 29.5. If a standard prologue style is adopted, tools may be written to process the derivation histories and produce reports about component changes.

29.3 System building

System building is the process of combining the components of a system into a program which executes on a particular target configuration. This may involve compilation of some components and a linking process which puts the object code together to make an executable system. For large systems, the system building process may take several days so is an expensive part of the CM process.

System building requires particular care when a host–target approach to development is used. The system is built on a host machine but executes on a separate target machine. The first sign of build problems may be when the target system simply does not start. Problem diagnosis is difficult in such situations and the build team may have to redo most of the system build to correct the fault.

The factors which the system building team must consider are:

(1)   Have all the components which make up a system been included in the build instructions?

(2)   Has the appropriate version of each required component been included in the build instructions?

(3)   Are all required data files available?

(4)   If data files are referenced within a component is the name used the same as the name of the data file on the target machine?

(5)   Is the appropriate version of the compiler and other required tools available? Current versions of software tools may be incompatible with the older versions used to develop the system.

When component source code exists in multiple versions, it is sometimes unclear which version of the source has been used to derive an object code component. This is a particular problem in environments where component names do not include version identification.

This problem can be tackled using a software tool which examines the modification and creation dates of source and object code and only recreates the object code from the source when the source has been modified after the creation of the available object code component. MAKE, discussed later, is an example of such a tool which is used in UNIX systems.

The fundamental problems in system building arise because the build process usually requires that build instructions are specified in terms of physical storage components (typically files but perhaps database entities). These are fairly large objects and each file may include several logical software components. There is rarely a one-to-one mapping between physical storage organizations and logical software structure.

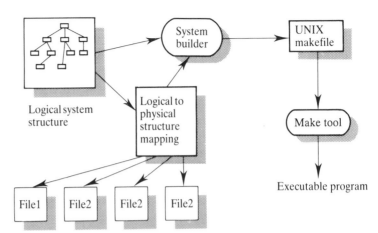

Figure 29.6
System building from a
logical structure
description.

One way to tackle this problem is to use a system modelling language (DeRemer and Kron, 1976; Sommerville and Thomson, 1989) to describe the software structure and to use this description to create the system build instructions (Figure 29.6).

The structural description is simply a specification of the static relationships of the software components and, as such, is a valuable document for software maintenance. The name mapping system relates logical components to their physical storage entity, and the system build instruction generator takes component type information and transformation rules and generates a set of instructions to build the system.

This approach simplifies the process because the build team need not be involved with generating the low-level build instructions. Given that different system versions have the same logical structure, each version is specified by a different mapping from logical to physical components.

29.4 Version and release management

Version and release management involves drawing up an identification scheme for different versions of a system, ensuring that the scheme is applied when new system versions are created and planning when new releases of a system should be distributed to customers.

A system *version* is an instance of a system which differs, in some way, from other instances. It may include new functionality or may operate on a different hardware configuration. A system *release* is a version which is distributed to customers. As an approximate rule of thumb, each system release should offer significantly different functionality from the previous release. There may be multiple versions of the same release tailored, for example, to different operating configurations. Some versions may be created for internal development and may never be released.

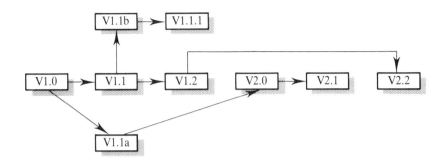

Figure 29.7
Version derivation
structure.

29.4.1 Version naming

Identifying versions of a system appears to be straightforward. The first version of a system is simply called 1.0, subsequent versions are 1.1, 1.2 and so on. At some stage, it is decided to create version 2.0 and the process starts again at version 2.1, 2.2, and so on. The base version (1.0, 2.0, and so on) is a system release. The scheme is a linear one based on the assumption that system versions are created in sequence. Version management tools such as SCCS (Rochkind, 1975) support this approach to version identification.

This scheme has an attractive simplicity but it has associated problems:

(1) When should a new release rather than a new version be created?

(2) If a number of versions are created from a single parent, how should they be numbered? For example, say a system is intended to run on a number of different computer architectures and these are all derived from a single base release numbered 1.0. Should the versions be numbered 1.1, 1.2, and so on, implying sequential derivation?

(3) If many versions of a system are created and distributed to different customers, should the version naming scheme include some customer identifier? Each customer or system user may have a unique version of the system.

These identification problems arise because the naming scheme implies a linear derivation of versions whereas the actual logical derivation structure is a network structure such as that shown in Figure 29.7.

In Figure 29.7, Version 1.0 has spawned two versions 1.1 and 1.1a. Version 1.1 has also spawned two versions, namely 1.2 and 1.1b. Version 2.0 is not derived from 1.2 but from 1.1a. Version 2.2 is not a direct descendant of version 2 as it is derived from version 1.2.

New versions of the system may have new functionality or performance or may repair system faults. It is also possible to derive system versions which are functionally equivalent but which are tailored for different hardware or software configurations. These are sometimes termed system variants. Each of these may also act as a base for further development so may have its own set of associated versions and variants.

An alternative to a numeric naming structure is to use a hierarchical naming scheme in conjunction with symbolic naming. For example, rather than refer to version 1.1.2, a particular instance of a system might be referred to as V1/VAX_VMS/Vaxstation, implying that this was a version for a DEC VAX computer running the VMS operating system and configured for a Vaxstation. This has some advantages over the linear scheme but, again, it does not truly represent the derivation structure.

Because of the needs of different projects, it is not possible to derive a universally suitable version naming scheme. Often, however, the CM team must work with the scheme forced upon them by whatever version management tools are used. In these cases, the configuration database must include information describing the characteristics and derivation of each system version.

29.4.2 Version and release creation

One of the responsibilities of the configuration manager, taken in consultation with product and project management, is to decide when new versions and releases of the system should be created. Different criteria are used for deciding whether or not to create a version and a release. Creating a system release involves expensive system validation and documentation changes. Creating a new version is usually cheaper as it may be created for the purposes of internal development or may involve less expensive validation if the changes to the system are minimal.

New system versions should always be created by the CM team even when they not intended for external release. It is only possible for the CM database to be assuredly consistent if version control is centralized within the project. System developers should not normally change the CM database.

Over the lifetime of a system, changes are likely to be proposed on a fairly regular basis. Corrective changes are intended to fix faults, perfective changes are intended to improve the non-functional behaviour of the system or to improve its maintainability, and adaptive changes are intended to change the system functionality. The configuration manager must decide how often the components affected by these changes should be rebuilt into a new version or release of the system.

Sometimes, this decision is forced on management. A particularly serious fault may be discovered in a released system and customers must be provided with a fix for that error. Although object code patching is

Figure 29.8
System release
strategy.

sometimes possible, this is an error-prone approach to problem repair. A
better approach is to create a new system version (or interim release) which
incorporates the changes required.

The problem posed by change is that changing a system may
introduce new faults or bring other existing faults to light. If a release
incorporates a large number of changes, it is likely that there will be a
correspondingly large number of new faults. System reliability may be
impaired. The need for future fault repair changes will be intensified.

We have already looked at Lehman's laws in Chapter 28, and
Lehman's fifth law, the law of conservation of familiarity, suggests that over
the lifetime of a system, the incremental system change in each release is
approximately constant.

This law was proposed by observing changes to large systems which
showed that if a large number of changes were made in one release of the
system it had to be followed fairly quickly by another release which was
exclusively concerned with fault repair. Over the lifetime of a system, this
was a self-regulating process which tended to a constant number of changes
per system release. The change metric used was the number of system
modules modified in each release.

This law suggests that it is unwise to change too much of a system's
functionality at once otherwise an excessive number of faults may be
introduced. An appropriate change strategy is to interleave fault repair
releases of a system and releases which change the system's behaviour or
functionality (Figure 29.8).

If some system changes are concerned with fault repair and others
with changing the system behaviour, mixing these change types could cause
problems. The faults reported apply to a given version of the system code
and if that code is changed to amend its behaviour, it is expensive to check if
the faults still apply. All serious faults (faults which cause system
corruption) should be repaired before functional or behavioural changes are
applied.

Release management is complicated by the fact that customers may
not actually want a new release of the system. A system user may be happy
with an existing system version and may consider the cost of changing to a
new version unwarranted. Eventually, however, as the system's functionality
is enhanced, it is likely that the customer will decide to change.

This causes CM problems because new releases of the system cannot
depend on the existence of previous releases. Say release 1 of a system is
distributed and put into use. Release 2 follows which requires the
installation of new data files but some customers do not need the facilities of

release 2 so remain with release 1. Release 3 requires the data files installed in release 2 and has no new data files of its own. However, it cannot be assumed that these files have already been installed in all sites where release 3 is to be installed. These data files must also be distributed and installed with release 3 of the system.

29.5 Configuration management tools

Major problems which exist with any large software system are keeping track of the development and maintenance of program modules, determining the interdependence of modules and ensuring that the common code in different versions of a system is consistent. This is an immense information management problem which is best tackled with tool support.

Two principal CM functions have been automated. These are the tracking of different versions of source code components and building a system from its component parts. This latter chore involves both specifying what components make up a system and deciding on how these are to be processed to make up an executable system.

MAKE (Feldman, 1979) and SCCS (Rochkind, 1975) are described here as examples of configuration management tools. SCCS keeps track of system modifications and different system versions. MAKE is a tool for system building which ensures the consistency of source code and its corresponding object code. Other configuration management systems have been described by Tichy (1982), by Lampson and Schmidt (1983), who discuss the problems of system building in a distributed environment, and by Leblang and Chase (1987).

29.5.1 SCCS

SCCS (source code control system) was originally developed for IBM 370 hardware but is now distributed with UNIX. The aim of SCCS is to allow different versions of the system to be maintained without unnecessary code duplication. SCCS controls system updates by ensuring that a system component cannot be updated by more than one programmer at any one time. It also records when updates were made, what source lines were changed and who was responsible for the change.

SCCS is principally a system for storing and recording changes to system modules. Each time a module is changed, that change is recorded and stored in what is termed a delta. Subsequent changes are also recorded as deltas. To produce the latest version of a system, SCCS applies the deltas in turn to the original module until all deltas have been processed (Figure 29.9).

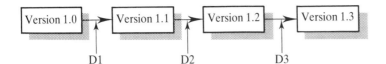

Figure 29.9
Deltas in SCCS.

Users of SCCS can specify that the system should be generated up to any point in the delta chain, allowing systems at different stages of development to be produced. As deltas are date stamped and owner stamped, the user of SCCS can specify that a system version at any particular date should be created and can also generate management reports on system development.

A system may be frozen at any point in the chain to create a new release. When a module is added to SCCS initially, it is deemed to be release 1.0. Subsequent deltas create versions 1.1, 1.2, 1.3, and so on. At some stage, the programmer may wish to freeze his system, for testing say, although further system development, including the addition of more deltas, may be continuing in parallel. Freezing a system involves specifying the set of deltas to be applied to the previous system release (Figure 29.10).

To obtain any particular version of the system, the SCCS user requests that it should be created. The deltas to create that version are applied. Releases can be developed in parallel. Release 1 can be modified after development of release 2 is in progress by adding new level 1 deltas. In the example shown in Figure 29.10, D1.4 is added to release 1 after release 2 has been created.

29.5.2 MAKE

MAKE is a system building tool which maintains the correspondence between source code and object code versions of a system. It automatically re-compiles source code which has been modified after the creation date of

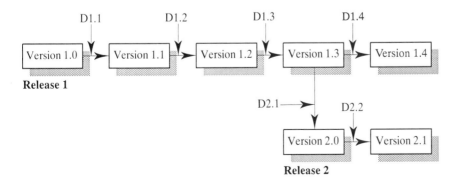

Figure 29.10
Freezing a system using SCCS.

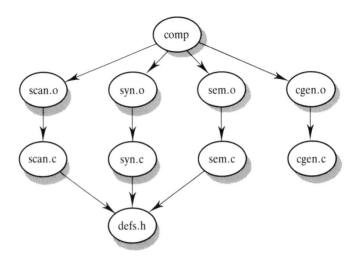

Figure 29.11
Component
dependency graph.

the associated object code. The user must describe the system structure in terms of the files where components are stored.

Sometimes, changing one file also necessitates changing some other file or group of files. MAKE provides a mechanism for specifying file dependencies. Using built-in information and user-specified commands, MAKE can cause the object code of a system to be recreated when a change is made to part of the system source code. For example, say an object code file x.o depends on the source code files x.c and d.c. The file d.c is changed in some way. MAKE uses file update attributes to detect the change and recreates x.o by recompiling x.c and d.c. Manual recompilation after an editing session is unnecessary.

Consider a situation where a program called comp is created out of object modules scan.o, syn.o, sem.o, and cgen.o. For each object module, there exists a source code module called scan.c, syn.c, sem.c, and cgen.c. A file of declarations called defs.h is shared by scan.c, syn.c, and sem.c (Figure 29.11). MAKE represents this dependency graph textually and includes commands which are invoked to build the system. Modifications can be made to any of scan.c, syn.c and sem.c without requiring other files to be recompiled but if defs.c is changed, all other files must be recompiled.

There are two major problems with MAKE as a system building utility:

(1)   It is difficult to write and to understand makefiles for even moderately large systems as the dependency graph quickly becomes complicated. This is particularly true when the order of compilation is important, as it is in Ada. Some Ada systems provide makefile generators which process Ada component dependencies and automatically create a makefile. Unfortunately, makefile generators don't help makefile readers.

(2)   MAKE assumes that a system is structured as a set of files. Systems are actually structured as a set of language abstractions (procedures, functions, packages, and so on). MAKE relies on the programmer to maintain the correspondence between files and the abstractions stored in these files.

Both MAKE and SCCS are relatively old systems which were designed for use with timesharing machines. They are oriented towards a file-based environment where the entities being managed are files of source code. More recent, network-oriented tools which extend the basic UNIX CM tools are Sun's NSE environment (Courington *et al.*, 1988) and Hewlett Packard's DSEE (Leblang and Chase, 1987). Like MAKE and SCCS, these systems support version management and system building but they include a number of innovative features:

(1)   They allows different versions of a system to be built in parallel by different users.

(2)   They support the parallel compilation of system components by distributing build command sequences to idle nodes on the workstation network. Components may be compiled simultaneously, reducing the time required for system building.

(3)   They provide mechanisms to describe system versions and to tie together all of the objects (code, designs, documents, specifications) associated with a system version.

Apart from offering improved performance, the important distinction between these CM tools and stand-alone systems such as SCCS and MAKE is the level of integration which they offer. They recognize that activities involved in configuration management are interlinked and dependent on each other. Mechanisms are provided to describe these dependencies and to track them automatically.

■ KEY POINTS

- Configuration management is the management of system change. When a system is maintained, the role of the CM team is to ensure that changes are incorporated in a controlled way.

- In a large project, a formal document naming scheme should be established and used as a basis for managing the project documents.

- The CM team should be supported by a configuration database which records information about system changes and change requests which are outstanding. Projects should have some formal means of requesting system changes.

- System building is the process of assembling system components into an executable program to run on some target computer system. Problems can arise in this process because the physical storage organization of the components does not match the logical system structure.

- When setting up a configuration management scheme, a consistent scheme of version identification should be established.

- System releases should be phased so that a release which provides new system functionality is followed by a release to repair errors.

- Some tools are available to assist with the process of configuration management. The best known of these is the version management tool SCCS and the system building tool MAKE.

FURTHER READING

Software Configuration Management. Configuration management is not a well-documented area of software engineering, partly because it has not attracted a great deal of academic interest. This is one of the few available books and although it is sometimes annoyingly informal, it contains much wisdom. (W.A. Babich, 1986, Addison-Wesley.)

'Parallel software configuration management in a network environment'. This paper is a clear description of a second generation configuration management tool which is now relatively widely used. (D.B. Leblang and R.P. Chase, *IEEE Software*, **4** (6), November 1987.)

EXERCISES

29.1 Design an appropriate formal document naming scheme for the newspaper delivery system described in Exercise 3.7.

29.2 Using the entity-relational approach to data modelling (described in Chapter 4), design a model of a configuration database recording information about system components, versions, releases and changes.

29.3 Using a data flow diagram, describe a change control procedure which might be used in a large organization concerned with developing software for external clients. Changes may be suggested either from external or internal sources.

29.4 Describe the difficulties which can be encountered in system building. What are the particular problems which can arise when a system is built on a host computer for some target machine?

29.5 With reference to system building, explain why it may sometimes be necessary to maintain obsolete computer systems on which large software systems were developed.

29.6 A common problem with system building occurs when physical file names are incorporated in system code and the file structure implied in these names differs from that of the target machine. Write a set of programmer's guidelines which help avoid this and other system building problems which you can think of.

29.7 What do you understand by Lehman's fifth law and how does it relate to configuration management?

29.8 Describe three difficulties with the simple model of system building adopted by the MAKE utility.

29.9 If you can experiment with a network configuration management system such as Sun's NSE, write a short report outlining the ways in which it is superior to stand-alone tools such as SCCS and MAKE.

Documentation

30

■ OBJECTIVES

The objectives of this chapter are to describe the documentation which must be produced during the software process, to give some hints on effective document writing and to describe tools used in the documentation process. Documentation may be either product or process documentation. Product documentation includes both user and system documents. High quality documents are increasingly important and factors affecting document quality include documentation standards, a document quality assurance process and effective writing style. In the final part of the chapter, tools used in the document preparation process are described, including word processors, desktop publishing systems and document management systems.

■ CONTENTS

All large software systems, irrespective of application, have a prodigious amount of associated documentation. Even for moderately sized systems, the documentation will fill several filing cabinets. For large systems, it may fill several rooms. A high proportion of software process costs is incurred in producing this documentation. Management should therefore pay as much attention to documentation and its associated costs as to the development of the software itself.

The documents associated with a software system have a number of requirements:

(1) They should act as a communication medium between members of the development team.

(2) They should be a system information repository to be used by maintenance engineers.

(3) They should provide information for management to help them plan, budget and schedule the software development process.

(4) Some of the documents should tell users how to use and administer the system.

Satisfying these requirements requires different types of document from informal working documents through to professionally produced user manuals. Software engineers are responsible for producing most of this documentation although professional technical writers may assist with the final polishing of externally released information.

30.1 Document classification

The documentation associated with a system falls into two classes:

(1) *Process documentation* These documents record the process of development and maintenance. Plans, schedules, process quality documents and organizational and project standards are process documentation.

(2) *Product documentation* This documentation describes the product which is being developed. System documentation describes the product from the point of view of the engineers developing and maintaining the system; user documentation provides a product description oriented towards system users.

Process documentation is produced so that the development of the system can be managed. Product documentation is used after the system is operational but is also essential for management of the system development.

The creation of a document, such as a system specification, may represent an important milestone in the software development process.

30.1.1 Process documentation

Effective management requires the process being managed to be visible. Because software is intangible and the software process involves apparently similar cognitive tasks rather than obviously different physical tasks, the only way this visibility can be achieved is through the use of process documentation.

Process documentation falls into a number of categories:

(1) *Plans, estimates and schedules* These are documents produced by managers which are used to predict and to control the software process.

(2) *Reports* These are documents which report how resources were used during the process of development.

(3) *Standards* These are documents which set out how the process is to be implemented. They may be developed from organizational, national or international standards and expressed in great detail.

(4) *Working papers* These are often the principal technical communication documents in a project. They record the ideas and thoughts of the engineers working on the project, are interim versions of product documentation, describe implementation strategies and set out problems which have been identified. They often, implicitly, record the rationale for design decisions.

(5) *Memos and electronic mail messages* These record the details of everyday communications between managers and development engineers.

The major characteristic of process documentation is that most of it becomes outdated. Plans may be drawn up on a weekly, fortnightly or monthly basis. Progress will normally be reported weekly. Memos record thoughts, ideas and intentions which change.

Although of interest to software historians, most of this information is of little real use after it has gone out of date and there is not normally a need to preserve it after the system has been delivered. Of course, there are some exceptions to this.

For example, test schedules are of value during software evolution as they act as a basis for re-planning the validation of system changes. Design rationale should be kept for maintenance engineers but this is usually not implicitly recorded and is difficult to find among the many working papers produced in the course of a project.

30.1.2 Product documentation

Product documentation is concerned with describing the delivered software product. Unlike most process documentation, it has a long life. It must evolve in step with the product which it describes. Product documentation includes user documentation which tells users how to use the software product, and system documentation, which is principally intended for maintenance engineers.

User documentation

Users of a system are not all the same. The producer of documentation must structure it to cater for different user tasks and different levels of expertise and experience. It is particularly important to distinguish between end-users and system administrators:

(1) End-users use the software to assist with some task. This may be flying an aircraft, managing insurance policies, writing a book, and so on. They want to know how the software can help them. They are not interested in computer or administration details.

(2) System administrators are responsible for managing the software used by end-users. This may involve acting as an operator if the system is a large mainframe system, as a network manager if the system involves a network of workstations or as a technical guru who fixes end-users software problems and who liaises between users and the software supplier.

To cater for these different classes of user and different levels of user expertise, there are at least five documents (or perhaps chapters in a single document) which should be delivered with the software system (Figure 30.1).

The *functional description* of the system outlines the system requirements and briefly describes the services provided. This document should provide an overview of the system. Users should be able to read this document with an introductory manual and decide if the system is what they need.

The *introductory manual* should present an informal introduction to the system, describing its 'normal' usage. It should describe how to get started and how end-users might make use of the common system facilities. It should be liberally illustrated with examples. Inevitably beginners, whatever their background and experience, will make mistakes. Easily discovered information on how to recover from these mistakes and restart useful work should be an integral part of this document.

The *system reference manual* should describe the system facilities and their usage, should provide a complete listing of error messages and should

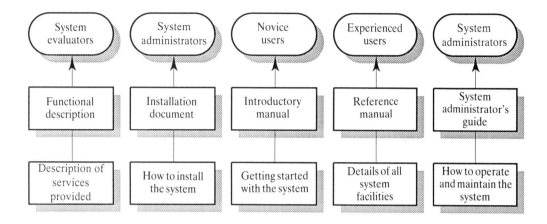

Figure 30.1
User documentation.

describe how to recover from detected errors. It should be complete. Formal descriptive techniques may be used. The style of the reference manual should not be unnecessarily pedantic and turgid, but completeness is more important than readability.

The *system installation document* is intended for system administrators. It should provide details of how to install the system in a particular environment. It should contain a description of the machine-readable media on which the system is supplied, the files making up the system and the minimal hardware configuration required. The permanent files which must be established, how to start the system and the configuration-dependent files which must be changed to tailor the system to a particular host system should also be described.

A more general *system administrator's manual* should be provided. This should describe the messages generated when the system interacts with other systems and how to react to these messages. If system hardware is involved, it might also explain the operator's task in maintaining that hardware. For example, it might describe how to clear faults in the system console, how to connect new peripherals, and so on.

As well as manuals, other, easy-to-use documentation might be provided. A quick reference card listing available system facilities and how to use them is particularly convenient for experienced system users. On-line help systems, which contain brief information about the system, are another facility which saves the user spending time in consultation of manuals. Help systems are discussed in Chapter 14.

System documentation

System documentation includes all of the documents describing the implementation of the system from the requirements specification to the final acceptance test plan. Documents describing the design, implementation and testing of a system are essential if the program is to be understood and maintained. Like user documentation, it is important that system documentation is structured, with overviews leading the reader into more formal and detailed descriptions of each aspect of the system.

The documents making up the system documentation should include:

(1) The requirements document and an associated rationale.

(2) A document describing the system architecture.

(3) For each program in the system, a description of the architecture of that program.

(4) For each component, a specification and design description.

(5) Program source code listings. These should be commented appropriately where the comments should explain complex sections of code and provide a rationale for the coding method used. If meaningful names are used and gotos are avoided, much of the code should be self-documenting without the need for additional comments.

(6) Validation documents describing how each program is validated and how the validation information relates to the requirements.

(7) A system maintenance guide which describes known problems with the system, describes which parts of the system are hardware- and software-dependent and how evolution of the system has been taken into account in its design.

A common system maintenance problem is ensuring that all representations are kept in step when the system is changed. To help with this, the relationships and dependencies between documents and parts of documents should be recorded in a configuration management database.

Unfortunately, documentation maintenance is often neglected. Documentation may become out of step with its associated software, causing problems for both users and maintainers of the system. The natural tendency is to meet a deadline by modifying code with the intention of modifying other documents later.

Often, pressure of work means that this modification is continually set aside until finding what is to be changed becomes very difficult indeed. The best solution to this problem is to support document maintenance with software tools which record document relationships, remind software engineers when changes to one document affect another and record possible inconsistencies in the documentation. Such a system is described by Garg and Scacchi (1990).

30.2 Document quality

Unfortunately, much computer system documentation is badly written, difficult to understand, out-of-date or incomplete. Although the situation is improving, many organizations still do not pay enough attention to producing system documents which are well-written pieces of technical prose.

Document quality is as important as program quality. Without information on how to use a system or how to understand it, the utility of that system is degraded. Achieving document quality requires management commitment to document design, standards, and quality assurance processes. Producing good documents is neither easy nor cheap and the process is at least as difficult as producing good programs.

30.2.1 Document structure

The structure of a document is obviously principally determined by its contents. It is not appropriate to discuss detailed structures here and the reader is referred to Bell and Evans (1989) for an outline of possible structures of different document classes.

However, although I shall not cover detailed document structures, some general structuring principles are generally applicable.

(1)   All documents, however short, should have a cover page which identifies the project, the document, the author, the date of production, the type of document, configuration management and quality assurance information, the intended recipients of the document, and the confidentiality class of the document. It should also include information for document retrieval (an abstract or keywords) and a copyright notice. Figure 30.2 is an example of a possible front cover format.

(2)   Documents which are more than a few pages long should be divided into chapters with each chapter structured into sections and sub-sections. A contents page should be produced listing these chapters, sections and sub-sections. A consistent numbering scheme for chapters, sections and sub-sections should be defined and chapters should be individually page numbered (the page number should be *chapter-page*). This simplifies document change as individual chapters may be replaced without reprinting the whole document.

```
┌─────────────────────────────────────────────────┐
│                                                 │
│        Collaborative Support for Systems Design │
│                                                 │
│                  ACTIVE DISPLAYS                 │
│                                                 │
│                                                 │
│   Title:   Active Displays                      │
│                                                 │
│   Project: MRC 842317                           │
│                                                 │
│   Document identifier:  CSSD/CS/WD/17           │
│                                                 │
│   Document type: Technical working paper        │
│                                                 │
│   Version: 1.2          Date: 20th December 1990│
│                                                 │
│   Author: Ian Sommerville                       │
│                                                 │
│   Inspected: N/A.        Approved:  N/A         │
│                                                 │
│   Submitted to CM:          CM Identifier:      │
│                                                 │
│   Distribution:  Project list                   │
│                                                 │
│   Confidentiality:  Commercial                  │
│                                                 │
│   Keywords:  User interface, display update, agents │
│                                                 │
│            © Lancaster University 1990          │
│                                                 │
└─────────────────────────────────────────────────┘
```

Figure 30.2
A document front
cover.

(3)   If a document contains a lot of detailed, reference information it should have an index. A comprehensive index allows information to be discovered easily and can make a badly written document usable. Without an index, reference documents are virtually useless.

(4)   If a document is intended for a wide spectrum of readers who may have differing vocabularies, a glossary should be provided which defines the technical terms and acronyms used in the document.

Document structures are often defined in advance and set out in documentation standards. This has the advantage of consistency although it can cause problems. Standards may not be appropriate in all cases and an unnatural structure may have to be used if standards are thoughtlessly imposed.

30.2.2   Documentation standards

Documentation standards act as a basis for document quality assurance. Documents produced according to appropriate standards have a consistent appearance, structure and quality. As with other types of standards (discussed in the following chapter), document standards fall into a number of classes:

(1) *Process standards*   These standards define the process which should be followed for high quality document production.

(2) *Product standards*   These are standards which govern the documents themselves.

(3) *Interchange standards*   It is increasingly important to exchange copies of documents via electronic mail and to store documents in databases. Interchange standards ensure that all electronic copies of documents are compatible.

Process standards

Process standards define the approach to be taken in producing documents. This generally means defining the software tools which should be used for document production and defining the quality assurance procedures which ensure that documents are of a high quality.

Document process quality assurance standards must be flexible and must be able to cope with all types of document. In some cases, where documents are simply working papers or memos, no explicit quality checking is required. However, where documents are formal documents, that is, when their evolution is to be controlled by configuration management procedures, a formal quality process should be adopted. Figure 30.3 illustrates one possible process.

Figure 30.3
The document
production process.

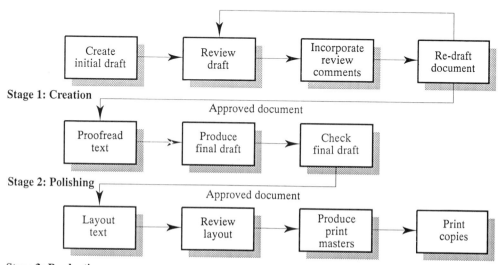

Stage 1: Creation

Stage 2: Polishing

Stage 3: Production

Drafting, checking, revising and re-drafting is an iterative process which should be continued until a document of acceptable quality is produced. The acceptable quality level will depend on the document type and the potential readers of the document.

Product standards

Product standards apply to all documents produced in the course of the software development. Documents should have a consistent appearance and, documents of the same class should have a consistent structure. Document standards are project-specific but should be based on more general organizational standards.

Examples of product standards which should be developed are:

(1) *Document identification standards*   As large projects typically produce thousands of documents, each document must be uniquely identified. For formal documents, this identifier may be the formal identifier defined by the configuration manager. For informal documents, the style of the document identifier should be defined by the project manager.

(2) *Document structure standards*   As discussed in the previous section, there is an appropriate structure for each class of document produced during a software project. Structure standards should define this organization. They should also specify the conventions used for page numbering, page header and footer information, and section and sub-section numbering.

(3) *Document presentation standards*   Document presentation standards define a 'house style' for documents and they contribute significantly to document consistency. They include the definition of fonts and styles used in the document, the use of logos and company names, the use of colour to highlight document structure, and so on.

(4) *Document update standards*   As a document is changed to reflect changes in the system, a consistent way of indicating these changes should be used. These might include the use of different colours of cover to indicate a new document version and the use of change bars to indicate modified or deleted paragraphs.

Document standards should apply to all project documents and to the initial drafts of user documentation. In many cases, however, user documentation has to be presented in a form appropriate to the user rather than the project and it should be recast into that form during the production process.

Interchange standards

Document interchange standards are increasingly important as electronic rather than paper copies of documents are passed from one engineer to another during the development process. Assuming that the use of standard tools is mandated in the process standards, interchange standards define the conventions for using these tools. The use of interchange standards allows documents to be transferred electronically and recreated in their original form.

Examples of interchange standards include the use of an agreed standard macro set if a text formatting system is used for document production or the use of a standard style sheet if a word processor is used. Interchange standards may also limit the fonts and text styles used because of differing printer and display capabilities.

30.2.3 Writing style

Standards and quality assessment are essential if good documentation is to be produced but document quality is fundamentally dependent on the writer's ability to construct clear and concise technical prose. In short, good documentation requires good writing.

Writing documents well is not easy, nor is it a single stage process. Written work must be written, read, criticized and then rewritten until a satisfactory document is produced. Technical writing is a craft rather than a science but some broad guidelines about how to write well are:

(1) *Use active rather than passive tenses* It is better to say 'You should see a flashing cursor at the top left of the screen' rather than 'A flashing cursor should appear at the top left of the screen'.

(2) *Use grammatically correct constructs and correct spelling* To boldly go on splitting infinitives (like this) and to misspell words (like mispell) irritates many readers and reduces the credibility of the writer in their eyes. Unfortunately, English spelling is not standardized and both British and American readers are sometimes irrational in their dislike of alternative spellings.

(3) *Do not use long sentences which present several different facts* It is better to use a number of shorter sentences. Each sentence can then be assimilated on its own. The reader does not need to maintain several pieces of information at one time to understand the complete sentence.

(4) *Keep paragraphs short* As a general rule, no paragraph should be made up of more than seven sentences. Our capacity for holding immediate information is limited. In short paragraphs, all of the concepts in the paragraph can be maintained in short-term memory (see Chapter 2).

(5) *Don't be verbose* If you can say something in five words do so. A lengthy description is not necessarily more profound. Quality is more important than quantity.

(6) *Be precise and define the terms which you use* Computing terminology is fluid and many terms have more than one meaning. If you use terms like *module* or *process* make sure that your definition is clear. Collect definitions in a glossary.

(7) *If a description is complex, repeat yourself* It is often a good idea to present two or more differently phrased descriptions of the same thing. If readers fail to completely understand one description, they may benefit from having the same thing said in a different way.

(8) *Make use of headings and sub-headings* These break up a chapter into parts which may be read separately. Always ensure that a consistent numbering convention is used.

(9) *Itemize facts wherever possible* It is usually clearer to present facts in a list rather than in a sentence. Use textual highlighting (italics or underlining) for emphasis.

(10) *Do not refer to information by reference number alone* Give the reference number and remind the reader what that reference covered. For example, rather than say 'In Section 1.3 . . .' you should say 'In Section 1.3, which described management process models, . . .'

Documents should be inspected in the same way as programs. During a document inspection, the text is criticized, omissions pointed out and suggestions made on how to improve the document. In this latter respect, it differs from a code inspection, which is an error finding rather than an error correction mechanism.

As well as personal criticism, you can also use style checkers, which are software tools which find ungrammatical or clumsy uses of words. These tools also identify long sentences and paragraphs and the use of the passive rather than the active voice. Style checkers are discussed in the following section.

30.3 Document preparation

Document preparation is becoming increasingly automated. Software tools may be used at all stages of the process from initial document creation through checking and proofreading to final document production. The development of *de facto* document interchange standards, based on common word processors, has meant that it is now much easier to transfer documents between tools for processing.

Figure 30.3 showed the document preparation process as being split into three stages, namely document creation, polishing and production. Tools to support each of these stages are:

(1)   *Document creation*   Word processors and text formatters, table and equation processors, drawing and art packages.

(2)   *Document polishing*   Spelling checkers, style checkers.

(3)   *Document production*   Desktop publishing packages, artwork packages, type styling programs.

As well as these tools to support the document production process, configuration management systems, information retrieval systems and hypertext systems can be used to support document maintenance, retrieval and management.

The documentation tool which is most used is the editing system which supports document generation and modification. A general purpose text editor may be used or a word processing package may be preferred.

Modern word processing systems are screen-based and combine text editing and formatting. The image of the document on the user's terminal is, more or less, the same as the final form of the printed document. Finished layout is immediately obvious. Errors can be corrected and layout improved before printing the document. However, programmers who already use an editor for program preparation may be reluctant to learn how to use another type of editor and may prefer to use a separate editor and text formatting system.

Text formatting systems such as TROFF or Latex interpret a layout program specified by the document writer. Layout commands (often chosen from a standard, definable command set) are interspersed with the text of the document. The text formatter processes these commands and the associated text and lays the document out according to the programmer's instructions.

Text formatting systems can look ahead at the text to be laid out so can make better layout decisions than word processing systems whose working context is more restricted. Because the commands are really a programming language, programmers often prefer them to word processors but other, non-technical users usually find them more difficult to use.

The major disadvantage of text processors, once their programming has been mastered, is that they do not provide an immediate display of the output they produce. The user must process the text (this may take several minutes) then display the output using a preview package. If an error is discovered, it cannot be fixed immediately. The original source must be modified and the preview process repeated. Thus, although they can result in higher quality documents, most users find text formatters more inconvenient than word processors.

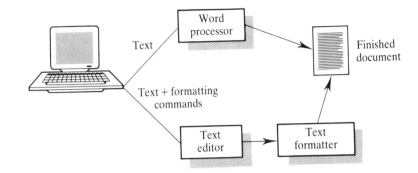

Figure 30.4
Word processing and
text formatting
systems.

Document preparation using word processing systems and formatting systems is illustrated in Figure 30.4.

Documents do not just contain text. They include diagrams, tables and equations, and automated support is now available for their creation. Although some word processing systems now include drawing facilities, separate programs for table processing, diagram production and equation layout usually offer more facilities and are easier to use than word processors. Document interchange standards allow the outputs of these systems to be incorporated in word processed documents.

Early versions of table, equation and diagram processors were usually based around a programming model. The user set out a textual specification of what was required along with the data to be processed. This was interpreted and a set of formatting commands generated. However, easier-to-use interactive tools for these tasks are now available on personal computers.

The document polishing stage is concerned with reviewing and improving the text of a document to make it more readable. This involves finding and removing spelling, punctuation and grammatical errors, detecting clumsy phrases and removing redundancy in the text. Figure 30.5 shows tools which can assist this polishing process.

Figure 30.5
Document checkers.

A spelling checker should be designed so that it may use both a standard system dictionary, and a user's private dictionary. The standard

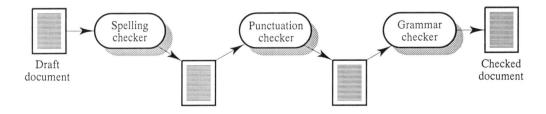

dictionary will not usually contain technical terms or proper names. These should be added to the user's dictionary as they are discovered. Many word processing systems now include an integrated spelling checker which supports interactive correction of misspelled words.

Punctuation checkers and grammar checkers were probably first developed as part of the UNIX Writer's Workbench (Cherry and MacDonald, 1983). They process the document text using grammar and punctuation rules and point out constructs which are probably user errors. These tools find errors such as unbalanced parentheses and quotes, repeated words, incorrect use of plurals and so on. As well as the UNIX tools, punctuation and grammar checkers are widely available for use in conjunction with word processing packages.

A further class of checker, not shown in Figure 30.5, is a style improver which detects commonly used phrases (such as 'in order to', 'at this moment in time', and so on) and clichés and suggests alternatives to them. These programs are simplistic in their approach and I don't find them useful.

The final stage of document production was, until relatively recently, almost entirely a manual process. However, desktop publishing (DTP) systems and graphics systems which support scanning and processing photographs and artwork are now widely available on personal computers. These have revolutionized document production. DTP systems partially automate the layout of text and graphics. They have taken over many of the functions of traditional printworkers.

The advantage of using a DTP is that the cost of producing high quality documents is reduced because some of the steps in the production process are eliminated (Figure 30.6). Even documents which are produced

Figure 30.6
Desktop publishing and conventional production.

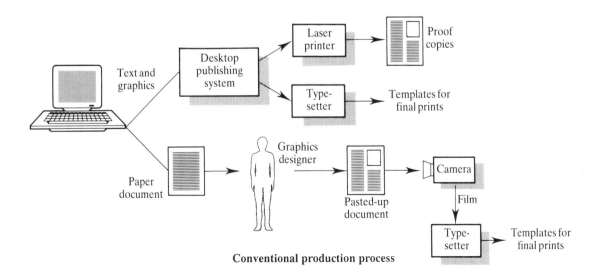

Conventional production process

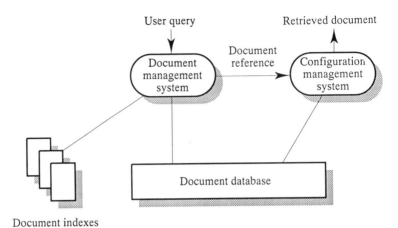

Figure 30.7
Document
management.

in small numbers can be produced to a high standard. The disadvantage of using DTP systems is that they do not automate the skills of the graphic designer. Their seductive ease-of-use means that they are accessible to unskilled, inexperienced users who produce unattractive and badly designed documents.

An enormous number of documents are produced in the course of a project so document management software is almost essential to manage the storage and retrieval of these documents. Document management software (Figure 30.7), which should be integrated with a configuration management system, allows related documents to be linked, may support the compression and decompression of document text and provides indexing and information retrieval facilities so that documents can be found.

The document management system can maintain indexes of supplied document keywords and can create indexes from the text of the documents. Users can retrieve documents using their title, identifier, keywords or using a text string contained in the document.

Document management systems can be constructed using standard databases, configuration management tools and system files. These are loosely integrated systems and they require discipline on the part of system users who must follow the appropriate procedures to ensure that documents are properly stored and indexed. Garg and Scacchi (1990) describe a system based on hypertext technology (Conklin, 1987) which is tightly integrated. This system provides a framework for integrating all of the tools used in the document production process and it is an indicator of future developments in this area.

■ KEY POINTS

■ Documents associated with a software system are used for communication between developers, as information for maintenance engineers, as management information sources and as user guides.

■ Documentation may be either process documentation or product documentation. Product documentation may be either system documentation or user documentation.

■ Document quality depends on structuring a document appropriately, on defining and maintaining standards for document preparation and production, on the appropriate use of graphics and on good technical writing.

■ Document quality is dependent on good technical writing. The best way to produce comprehensible documents is to keep them as simple as possible.

■ Tools to support documentation include preparation tools such as word processors and drawing programs, polishing tools such as spelling and style checkers and production tools such as desktop publishing systems.

■ Documentation should be managed using an automated system which allows documents to be retrieved by title, author, reference or keywords.

FURTHER READING

Mastering Documentation. This book is a practical guide to computer system documentation which is based around a set of document masters. These describe document structures for documents which are produced during the software process. The book is boring to read but a useful reference text. (P. Bell and C. Evans, 1989, John Wiley & Sons.)

Software Validation, Verification, Testing and Documentation. This book, which is a collection of US National Bureau of Standards reports, includes two extensive sections which discuss documentation requirements for US government contracts. (S.J. Andriole (ed.), 1986, Petrocelli Books.)

EXERCISES

30.1 Write a user manual for the implementation of the newspaper delivery system described in Exercise 3.7 and the following chapters.

30.2 Explain why providing hard copies of help frame text does not lead to good user documents.

30.3 Under what circumstances would you suggest using professional technical authors to prepare documentation.

30.4 Assume you are an instructor who requires students to submit documentation for their term projects. Write a standard defining the structure of the documentation required.

30.5 Suggest five further style guidelines in addition to those set out in Section 30.2.3.

30.6 Using the style guidelines as a basis, write a critique of one or more chapters of this book. Identify the major style problems which you discover and write to me about them.

30.7 You have been given the task of creating a toolset for supporting document production. Suggest what components would be included in such a toolset and investigate the literature to see what documentation tools are available. What checking tasks cannot be readily supported with current software tools?

30.8 If you have access to a simple hypertext system such as Hypercard, build a document management system which allows documents to be retrieved by author, title or keyword.

Software Quality Assurance

■ OBJECTIVES

The objective of this chapter is to describe the essentials of software quality assurance. Software quality assurance is concerned with ensuring that software products are of a high quality and this involves both product and process assessment. After a short discussion of process quality assurance, standards and their role in quality assurance are discussed. This is followed by a description of the quality review process, which is an inherent part of quality assurance. The final part of the chapter is concerned with software metrics. After a general introduction, a number of software quality metrics are described.

■ CONTENTS

Software quality assurance (QA) is closely related to the verification and validation activities carried out at each stage of the software life cycle. Indeed, in some organizations there is no distinction made between these activities. However, QA and verification and validation processes should be distinct activities. QA is a management function and verification and validation are technical software development processes.

Within an organization, QA should be carried out by an independent software quality assurance team who report directly to management above the project manager level. The QA team should not be associated with any particular development group but should be responsible for QA across the organization (see Figure 25.1).

A further important distinction is that verification and validation are concerned with fault detection. QA has a broader remit. Rather than software faults, QA is concerned with software reliability as well as other attributes such as maintainability, portability, readability, and so on.

An important role of the QA team is to provide support for 'whole-life cycle' quality. Quality should be engineered into the software product and quality should be the driver of the software process. Quality is not an attribute which can be added to a product and, at all stages of development, achieving high quality results should be the goal. The function of QA should be to support quality achievement, not to judge and criticize the development team.

Bersoff (1984) provides a good working definition of QA:

> Quality assurance consists of those procedures, techniques and tools applied by professionals to ensure that a product meets or exceeds pre-specified standards during a product's development cycle; and without specific prescribed standards, quality assurance entails ensuring that a product meets or exceeds a minimal industrial and/or commercially acceptable level of excellence.

The problem which arises in developing software standards for quality assurance and which makes the assessment of the level of excellence of a software product difficult is the elusive nature of software quality. Boehm *et al.* (1978) suggest that quality criteria include, but are not limited to, the attributes shown in Figure 31.1.

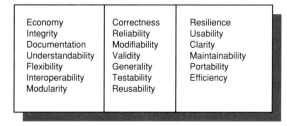

Figure 31.1
Software quality attributes.

Economy	Correctness	Resilience
Integrity	Reliability	Usability
Documentation	Modifiability	Clarity
Understandability	Validity	Maintainability
Flexibility	Generality	Portability
Interoperability	Testability	Efficiency
Modularity	Reusability	

Buckley and Poston (1984) point out that some of these quality criteria may have no relevance for a particular product. For example, it may be possible to transfer a system from a microcomputer to a large mainframe (portability) but this may not be sensible or desirable.

Quality planning should begin at an early stage in the software process. A quality plan should set out the desired product qualities and should define how these are to be assessed. A common error made in QA is the assumption that there is a common understanding of what 'high quality' software actually means. No such common understanding exists. Sometimes different software engineers work to ensure that particular, but different, product attributes are optimized.

The quality plan should clearly set out which quality attributes are most significant for the product being developed. It may be that efficiency is paramount and other factors have to be sacrificed to achieve this. If this is set out in the plan, the engineers working on the development can cooperate to achieve this. The plan should also define the quality assessment process; there is little point in trying to attain some quality if there is no standard way of assessing whether that quality is present in the product.

The quality plan should set out which standards are appropriate to the product and to the process and (if necessary) define the plan for developing these standards. Although the plan may not actually include details of particular standards, it should reference these and quality management should ensure that the standards documents are generally available. Humphrey (1989) and Frewin (1990) discuss structures for quality plans.

31.1 Process quality assurance

An underlying assumption of QA is that the quality of the software process directly affects the quality of delivered software products. The difficulty of assessing product quality has meant that a great deal of emphasis is placed on ensuring the quality of the software process. It is (reasonably) assumed that a well planned, managed process is more likely to lead to high quality products.

This assumption is derived from manufacturing systems where product quality is intimately related to the production process. Indeed, in automated mass production systems once an acceptable level of process quality has been attained, product quality follows. This approach to QA is illustrated in Figure 31.2.

This approach works in manufacturing because the process is relatively easy to standardize and monitor. For software systems, where processes have not been standardized, process and product quality cannot be directly equated. It is reasonable to assume that such a relationship exists but it cannot be assumed that a high quality process will always

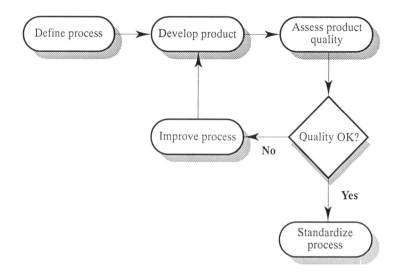

Figure 31.2
Process-based quality
assurance.

automatically lead to a high-quality product. External factors, such as the novelty of an application or commercial pressure for an early product release, might mean that product quality is impaired irrespective of the process used.

However, process quality is clearly important and part of the QA function is ensuring the quality of the process. This involves:

(1) Defining process standards such as how reviews should be conducted, when reviews should be held, and so on.

(2) Monitoring the development process to ensure that the standards are being followed.

(3) Reporting the software process to project management and to the buyer of the software.

Humphrey *et al.* (1991) describe a process assessment procedure which was derived at the Software Engineering Institute.

Unfortunately, process QA sometimes disrupts the development of the software. An artificial development process is imposed because a restricted process model has been defined by quality management to simplify process QA. For example, process QA standards may specify that specification must be complete and approved before implementation can begin. However, some systems may require prototyping which involves implementation. The QA team may suggest that this prototyping should not be carried out because its quality cannot be monitored. In such situations, senior management must intervene to ensure that the QA process supports rather than hinders product development.

31.2 Software standards

One of the most important roles of the QA team is the development of product and process standards. Product standards define characteristics which all product components should exhibit; process standards define how the software process should be conducted. An example of a product standard is a review form which defines the information to be collected during a review. An example of a process standard is a procedural definition of how design reviews should be conducted.

Standards are important for a number of reasons:

(1)   They provide an encapsulation of best, or at least most appropriate, practice. This knowledge is often only acquired after a great deal of trial and error. Building it into a standard avoids the repetition of past mistakes. The standard should capture some wisdom which is of value to an organization.

(2)   They provide a framework around which the QA process may be implemented. Given that standards encapsulate best practice, QA becomes the activity of ensuring that standards have been properly followed.

(3)   They assist in continuity where work carried out by one person is taken up and continued by another. Standards ensure that all engineers within an organization adopt the same practices so that the learning effort when starting new work is reduced.

The development of software engineering project standards is a difficult and time consuming process. National and international bodies such as the US DoD, ANSI, BSI, NATO and the IEEE have been active in the production of standards but these are usually of a general rather than a specific nature. Bodies such as NATO and other defence organizations may require that their own standards are followed in software contracts.

National and international standards have been developed covering software engineering terminology, notations such as charting symbols, procedures for deriving software requirements, quality assurance procedures, programming languages such as Pascal and Ada, ways of using languages such as Ada and software verification and validation.

QA teams who are developing standards should base organizational standards on national and international standards. Using these standards as a base, the QA team should draw up a standards 'handbook' which defines those standards which are appropriate for their organization. Examples of standards which might be included in such a handbook are shown in Figure 31.3.

The need to adhere to standards is often resented by software engineers. They see standards as bureaucratic and irrelevant to the technical

Product standards	Process standards
Design review form Document naming standard Procedure header format Ada programming standard Project plan format Change request form	Design review conduct Submission of documents to CM Version release process Project plan approval process Change control process Test recording process

Figure 31.3
Product and process
standards.

activity of software development. Although they usually agree about the value of standards in general, engineers often find good reasons why standards are not appropriate to their particular project.

Product standards such as standards setting out program formats, design documentation and document structures are often tedious to follow and to check. Unfortunately, these standards are sometimes written by staff who are remote from the software development process and who are not aware of modern practices. Thus, the standards may appear to be out of date and unworkable.

To avoid these problems, the QA organization must be adequately resourced and must take the following steps:

(1)   Involve software engineers in the development of product standards. They should understand the motivation behind the standard development and be committed to these standards. The standards document should not simply state a standard to be followed but should include a rationale of why particular standardization decisions have been made.

(2)   Review and modify standards regularly to reflect changing technologies. Once standards are developed they tend to be enshrined in a company standards handbook and there is often a reluctance to change them. A standards handbook is essential but it should be a dynamic rather than a static document.

(3)   Where standards set out clerical procedures such as document formatting, software tools should be provided to support these standards. Clerical standards are the cause of many complaints because of the tedious work involved in implementing them. If tool support is available, the effort involved in development to the standards is minimal.

Process standards may cause difficulties if an impractical process is imposed on the development team. There are many different approaches to software production and it is probably the case that each large project is developed according to a unique process. Furthermore, much of this process is implicit and badly understood and we have not discovered how to express it in a formal way.

Sometimes process standards are simply guidelines which must be sympathetically interpreted by individual project managers. There is no point in prescribing a particular way of working if that mode of working is inappropriate for a project or project team. Each project manager must have the authority to modify process standards according to individual circumstances. However, standards which relate to product quality and the post-delivery process should only be changed after careful consideration.

To avoid the difficulties and resentment that inappropriate standards may have, the project manager and the QA team should decide, at the beginning of a project, which of the standards in the handbook should be used without change, which should be modified and which should be ignored. It may also be the case that new standards have to be created in response to a particular project requirement (for example, standards for formal specifications if these have not been used in previous projects) and these must be allowed to evolve in the course of the project.

31.3 Quality reviews

A review is a quality assurance mechanism which involves a group of people examining part or all of a software system or its associated documentation with the aim of finding system problems. The conclusions of the review are formally recorded and passed to the author or whoever is responsible for correcting the discovered problems. Reviews are not limited to specifications, designs or code. Documents such as test plans, configuration management procedures, process standards and user manuals should all be reviewed.

There are several types of review:

(1) *Design or program inspections*   These are intended to detect detailed errors in the design or code and check whether standards have been followed. It is common practice for the review process to be driven by a checklist of possible errors (see Chapter 24).

(2) *Management reviews*   This type of review is intended to provide information for management about the overall progress of the software project. This type of review is both a process and a product review and is concerned with costs, plans and schedules. Management reviews are important project checkpoints where decisions about the further development of the project or even product viability are made.

(3) *Quality reviews*   The work of an individual or of a team is reviewed by a panel made up of project members and technical management. This type of review is distinct from a design or code inspection in that the system may not be described (or even developed) in detail. The review process is intended to carry out a technical analysis of product

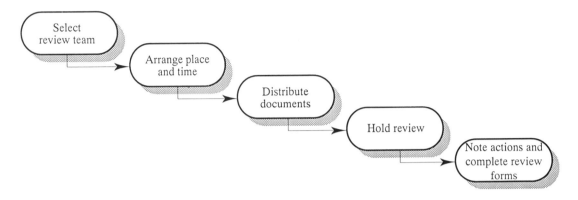

Figure 31.4
The review process.

components or documentation to find faults or mismatches between the specification and the design, code or documentation. It may also be concerned with broader quality issues such as adherence to standards and other quality attributes as set out in the quality plan.

A quality review need not involve a detailed study of individual system components. It may be more concerned with the validation of component interactions and with determining whether a component or document meets the user's requirements. The remit of the review team is to detect errors and inconsistencies and point them out to the designer or document author. The stages involved in a review are illustrated in Figure 31.4.

The review team should include project members who can make an effective contribution but, at the same time, it should not be too large. For example, if a sub-system design is being reviewed, designers of related sub-systems should be included in the review team. They may bring important insights into sub-system interfaces which could be missed if the sub-system is considered in isolation.

There are two ways to approach review team selection. A small team of three or four people may be selected as principal reviewers. They are responsible for checking and reviewing the document being reviewed. The remainder of the team may be composed of others who feels that they have a contribution to make. These other team members may not be involved in reviewing the whole document but may concentrate on those parts which affect their work. During the review, any team member may comment at any time.

An alternative strategy is to restrict the formal review team to principal reviewers. However, the review documentation should be more widely circulated and written comments invited from other project members. During the review, the review chairman is responsible for ensuring that all written comments are considered by the review team.

The next stage in the process is to distribute the document to be reviewed and any related documents. These must be distributed well in advance of the review to allow reviewers time to read and understand the documentation. Although this delay can disrupt the development process, reviewing is ineffective if the review team are not given time to understand the review material.

The technical review itself should be relatively short (two hours at most) and involves the document author 'walking through' the document with the review team. A member of the review team should be appointed chairman and they are responsible for organizing the review. Another should be responsible for recording all decisions made during the review. At least one review team member (often the chairman) should be a senior designer who can take the responsibility for making significant technical decisions.

Depending on the organization, the type of document being reviewed and the individuals concerned, this may mean presenting an overview on a blackboard or may involve a more formal presentation using prepared slides. During this process, the team should note problems and inconsistencies.

On completion of the review, the actions are noted and forms recording the comments and actions are signed by the designer and the review chairman. These are then filed as part of the formal project documentation. If only minor problems are discovered, a further review may be unnecessary. The chairman is responsible for ensuring that the required changes are made. If major changes are necessary, it is normal practice to schedule a further review.

In the course of the review, all of the comments made should be considered along with any other written submissions to the review team. Some of the comments may be incorrect and can be disregarded. The others should be classed under one of three categories:

(1) *No action*   The review discovered some kind of anomaly but it was decided that this was not critical and the cost of rectifying the problem was unjustified.

(2) *Refer for repair*   The review detected a fault and it is the responsibility of the designer or document originator to correct the fault.

(3) *Reconsider overall design*   The design impacts other parts of the system in such a way that changes must be made. However, it may not be cost-effective make these changes. Rather, a decision might be made to change other system components. The review chairman will normally set up a meeting between the engineers involved to reconsider the problem.

Some of the errors discovered in a review may be errors in the software specifications and requirements definition. Requirements errors must be reported to the software contractor and the impact of changing the requirements or the specification must be evaluated. The requirements may be changed. However, if the change involves large-scale modification of the system design, it may be most cost-effective to live with the fault and instruct the design team to design around rather than correct that error.

As well as being part of the QA process, reviews may be used as part of the project management process. Project management usually requires that designs be 'signed off', which means that approval must be given to the design before further work can go ahead. Normally, this approval is given after the review. This is not the same as certifying the design to be fault-free. The review chairman may approve a design for further development before all problems have been repaired if the problems detected do not seriously affect further development.

Finally, reviews are valuable for training purposes. They offer an opportunity for designers to explain their design to other project engineers. Newcomers to the project or designers who must interface with the system being designed may attend the review as observers as it offers an excellent opportunity to learn about the system design.

31.4   Software metrics

It has been suggested that the distinction between a craft and an engineering discipline is that craftsmen use qualitative methods whereas engineering is based on quantitative techniques. There has been much research into the usefulness of various software metrics and many claims made about the efficacy of particular metrics. However, few metrics have been unequivocally demonstrated to be usefully predictive or related to product attributes which might be quantified as part of the QA process.

A software metric is any measurement which relates to a software system, process or related documentation. Examples are measures of the size of a product in lines of code, the Fog index (Gunning, 1962) of a product manual, the number of reported faults in a delivered software product and the number of person-days required to develop a system component.

Metrics fall into two classes (Figure 31.5). Control metrics are those used by management to control the software process. Examples of these metrics are effort expended, elapsed time and disk usage. Estimates and measurements of these metrics can be used in the refinement of the project planning process.

Predictor metrics are measurements of a product attribute which can be used to predict an associated product quality. For example, it has been suggested that the readability of a product manual may be predicted by estimating its Fog index or the ease of maintenance of a software component may be predicted by measuring its cyclomatic complexity (McCabe, 1976).

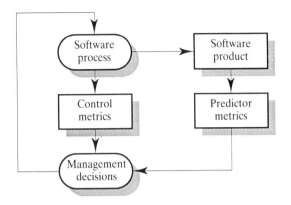

Figure 31.5
Predictor and control metrics.

Whether or not valid quality predictions can be made from such measurements is open to question. Fundamentally, we cannot measure directly what we really want to measure and we have to assume that a relationship exists between what we can measure and what we want to know.

Kitchenham (1990a) articulates the three assumptions on which predictor metrics are based:

(1)   We can accurately measure some property of the software.
(2)   A relationship exists between what we can measure and what we would like to know about the product's behavioural attributes.
(3)   This relationship is understood, has been validated and can be expressed in terms of a formula or model.

She points out that this critical third assumption is often ignored. For example, McCabe's complexity measure is claimed to be useful in predicting the maintainability of a component. Maintainability is said to be related to overall component complexity which is said to be a function of the cyclomatic complexity. However, we cannot actually measure *overall* component complexity as there are a great many attributes which contribute to this, only one of which may be cyclomatic complexity.

In order for metric values to be statistically valid, it is necessary to have a reasonable quantity of data. In circumstances where product data has not been collected during development and management is unwilling to accept high data collection costs, there is no point in trying to evaluate any software metric with small and perhaps atypical data sets.

Kitchenham suggests that data collection is unlikely to be successful unless it is automated and integrated into the development process (Figure 31.6). Data which cannot be automatically collected should be collected during development and should not be based on recollections of past events.

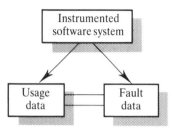

Figure 31.6
Automated data
collection.

Little time should elapse between data collection and data analysis. Finally, product data should be maintained as an organizational resource and historical records of all projects should be maintained even when data has not been used during a particular project.

Once an appropriate data set is available, model evaluation involves identifying the functional form of the model (linear, exponential, and so on), identifying the parameters which are to be included in the model and calibrating these using existing data. Such model development, if it is to be trusted, requires significant experience in statistical techniques and a professional statistician should be involved in the process.

31.4.1 Quality metrics

To find out if any particular metric is a useful predictor of product quality, quality management must evaluate that metric in a systematic way. Firstly, there must be a well-understood and quantifiable relationship between the measurement and the product quality of interest. Secondly, a model must be formulated which allows the quality prediction to be made.

In Chapter 10, attributes such as low coupling and high cohesion were suggested as characteristics of 'good' product designs. Because of the importance of maintainability a 'good' design is one which is understandable and can be changed to meet new requirements. Adaptability is a difficult attribute to measure and empirical evidence relating coupling and coherence to adaptability is difficult to collect.

However, these characteristics probably influence the adaptability of a design. If a design component does not interact with other components, there is no need to be concerned with the affect of changes to the original component. If a component has a single function or role, the component need only be adapted if that role changes.

Thus, it would seem reasonable to measure the cohesion and coupling of a component. Low coupling and high cohesion should suggest adaptability. We require some way of quantifying these attributes, preferably automatically, so that we can decide whether or not a particular design is a 'good' one. Unfortunately, it is not possible to measure cohesion directly. We can only measure other design attributes and hope that these relate to the cohesion of a component. Coupling can be measured if the design is captured using appropriately instrumented CASE tools.

Certain types of design complexity can be measured. The cyclomatic complexity of a program can be measured and it has been suggested that low values of this metric correlate with understandable programs or designs.

The computation of cyclomatic complexity is discussed in Chapter 21. As a measure of overall component complexity it suffers from two drawbacks:

(1) It measures the decision complexity of a program as determined by the predicates in loops and conditional statements. If a program is data-driven, it can have a very low value for the cyclomatic complexity yet still be complex and hard to understand.

(2) The same weight is placed on nested and non-nested loops. However, deeply nested conditional structures are harder to understand than non-nested conditionals.

Oviedo (1980) has developed a metric which takes data references into account. He suggests that the complexity of a component can be estimated using the following formula:

$$C = aE + bN$$

E is the number of edges in the flow graph and N is the number of references to data entities which are not declared in the component. Although this appears to get over some of the problems of measuring complexity, this metric has not been properly validated.

Constantine and Yourdon (1979) suggest that the coupling of a design can be quantified by measuring the fan-in and fan-out of design components in a structure chart. The fan-in value for a component is the number of lines entering the component's box on the structure chart. It is equivalent to the number of other components which call that component. The fan-out value is the number of lines leaving a box on the structure chart. These can be computed automatically if the design is captured using a graphical editing tool.

A high fan-in value suggests that coupling is high because it is a measure of module dependencies. A high fan-out value suggests that the complexity of the calling component may be high because of the complexity of control logic required to coordinate the subordinate components.

Henry and Kafura (1981) identified another form of fan-in/fan-out which is informational fan-in/fan-out. Informational fan-in/fan-out is a count of the number of local data flows from a component plus the number of global data structures the component updates. The data flow count includes updated procedure parameters and procedures called from within a module.

Informational fan-in/fan-out subsumes structural fan-in/fan-out (which is related to procedure calls) discussed above.

Using informational fan-in and fan-out, Henry and Kafura suggest that the complexity of a component can be computed according to the following formula:

Complexity = Length × (Fan-in × Fan-out)^2

Length is any measure of length such as lines of code or McCabe's cyclomatic complexity.

Henry and Kafura validated their metric using the UNIX system and suggested that the measured complexity of a component allowed potentially faulty system components to be identified. They found that high values of this metric were often measured in components which, historically, had caused a disproportionate number of system problems.

The advantage of this metric compared to structural fan-in/fan-out is that it takes into account data-driven programs. As discussed in Chapter 22, where cyclomatic complexity was explained, programs which make extensive use of tables may have a simple control structure yet the program and its tables may interact in a complex way. Structural fan-in/fan-out would not recognize this complexity as it is simply concerned with procedure calls. Informational fan-in/fan-out does measure this type of complexity as it uses data access as a parameter.

The principal disadvantage of informational fan-in/fan-out is that it can give complexity values of zero if a procedure has no external interactions. Components at the lowest level may not call other components but may interact with hardware and be very complex. Similarly, components which interact with users have no fan-in but may also involve complex manipulations.

The definition of informational fan-in and fan-out is also ambiguous. For example, if a record structure is passed as a parameter and several components of that record are accessed, how does that contribute to the fan-in? Should each modified field be considered as a separate data flow or should any number of field changes simply be recorded as a record update?

Henry and Kafura's metric has been the subject of a number of independent studies (Kitchenham *et al.*, 1990; Shepherd, 1990). These studies checked if this metric was a better predictor of subjective complexity that other simpler metrics such as size and number of branches, and assessed if the structural complexity of a design was a useful predictor of development time. These studies concluded that size and number of branches were equally valuable in predicting complexity. Fan-out on its own appeared to be a better complexity predictor than informational fan-in/fan-out. They also concluded that the informational fan-in/fan-out of a design appeared to be a useful predictor of the effort required for implementation.

Finally, it is appropriate to mention perhaps the best known metrics, namely Halstead's 'software science' metrics (Halstead, 1977). These have been widely publicized but independent studies have demonstrated that they are based on very shaky foundations (Hamer and Frewin, 1981). Kitchenham (1990a) concludes:

> There does not appear to be any sound evidence that the complex Software Science formulae are valid or provide good measures of the product attributes they are meant to characterize.

Metrics clearly have a role to play in the QA process. Unfortunately we do not yet know enough about software metrics to arrive at any general conclusions of what that role should be. Measurements are seductive and it is easy to fall into the trap of accepting figures which appear to confirm prejudices and beliefs. Individual experimentation is essential if metrics are to be useful. QA must be applied to suggested metrics as well as the software process and products!

■ KEY POINTS

- Software quality is more than verification and validation. It encompasses software attributes such as maintainability, reliability, portability, and so on. Some quality attributes are subjective and difficult to assess.

- Quality assurance is concerned with checking both product and process quality.

- A software quality plan should explicitly identify quality attributes which are most significant for a particular project and should set out how these attributes can be judged.

- Software standards are important to quality assurance as they represent an identification of 'best practice'. If standards can be developed, quality assurance is the activity of checking that the process and the product conform to these standards.

- Reviews are the principal means of carrying out quality assurance. They should involve all engineers concerned with a product and its related systems.

- Making a quantitative assessment of a design is an attractive notion but existing metrics have serious disadvantages. The state of the art is such that reliable quantitative assessments cannot yet be made.

FURTHER READING

Software Reliability Handbook.   In spite of its title this book has a much broader scope than simply reliability issues. It also has excellent sections on metrics and quality assurance. (P. Rook, (ed.), 1990, Elsevier.)

IEEE Software, **4** (5), September 1987.   This is a special issue of the journal containing a number of papers on quality assurance. It is also relevant reading for the previous chapter on software maintenance.

IEEE Software, **7** (2), March 1990.   This is a special issue on metrics which contains a number of tutorial articles on the subject. Some of the articles are easy to read but the general tone is rather evangelical. The authors try to sell metrics to the reader rather than assess them objectively.

IEE/BCS Software Engineering Journal, **5** (1), January 1990.   Again, a special issue on metrics. I found the papers more convincing than those in the special issue of *IEEE Software* as there was more independent empirical analysis and less conviction that metrics were obviously valuable.

EXERCISES

31.1 Given that you have been assigned the role of a quality manager, write a quality plan which would be appropriate for a QA team assessing the quality of real-time systems products embedded in software used by the general public.

31.2 Explain why assuring the quality of the software process should lead to high quality software products. Discuss also, the difficulties with this system of QA.

31.3 Suggest standards for the following documents and activities:

(a) A software requirements specification.
(b) A software design expressed using data-flow diagrams.
(c) A program inspection.
(d) The quality assurance process.

31.4 What are the stages involved in the review of a software design?

31.5 Design an electronic form which may be used to record review comments and which could be used to electronically mail comments to reviewers.

31.6 Assume you work for an organization which develops database products for microcomputer systems. This organization is interested in quantifying its software development. Write a report suggesting appropriate metrics and suggest how these can be collected.

31.7 Explain why design quality metrics do not allow a reliable estimate of design quality to be made.

31.8 Consult the literature and find other design quality metrics which have been suggested apart from those discussed here. Consider these metrics in detail and assess whether they are likely to be of real value.

Design Description Using Ada

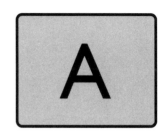

■ OBJECTIVES

This appendix introduces the main features of Ada for readers who are not already familiar with the language. It is clearly impossible to describe all of Ada in a short appendix and no attempt to do so is made here. The differences between Pascal and Ada are described and the reader is given pointers to other parts of the text where specific Ada constructs are discussed. A section is included showing how Ada packages may be used for abstract data type specification and implementation. Ada's support for parallel programming is then briefly described. The appendix concludes with an example showing how Ada can be used to specify the detailed design of a system.

■ CONTENTS

Ada is a programming language which was sponsored by the US Department of Defense for the building of real-time embedded computer systems. The need for such a language arose because of the vast number of languages used for implementing such systems with the associated cost and expense of language support.

Ada embodies much programming language research which was carried out in the 1970s and it is now a mandatory standard in the US, in the UK and elsewhere in the world for implementing military systems. Ada is widely used for large-scale software engineering for a range of system types from real-time systems to transaction processing systems.

The design requirement of Ada was that it should support as much compile-time checking as possible so that program errors could be detected by the language compiler rather than at run-time. This is a laudable aim but it requires the programmer to provide a lot of information which the compiler can use for checking. Sometimes, it forces detailed decisions to be made and this is not desirable when the language is used for describing abstract designs. Thus, when used as a PDL, it is sometimes sensible to relax some of Ada's rules. For example, when used for *design* description, names may be used without pre-declaration and natural language text may be substituted for language clauses.

A.1 Ada and Pascal

Pascal was a 'base-language' for Ada and many of the ideas embodied in Ada were first introduced in Pascal. However, Ada has additional constructs to support information hiding, exception handling and parallelism.

The similarities between Ada and Pascal are:

- Types are defined in a similar way although Ada uses a slightly different syntax which should be obvious to readers who know Pascal. Ada does not require declarations to be made in any particular order so typed constants are allowed. It includes a sub-typing mechanism which means that array sizes need not be bound into the type declaration (thus permitting more general array operations) and a derived type mechanism which is a means of supporting a limited form of inheritance. Variables are declared as in Pascal but there is no need to precede the variable name with the reserved word **var**. Pointers in Ada are called access types. Ada declarations are shown in Figure A.1.
- Control structures (selection and loops) are similar although, again, a slightly different syntax is used in Ada. Perhaps the most obvious difference is that control structures are all delimited by an end statement. A further difference is the introduction of an exit

```
-- scalar type declarations
type COLOUR is (red, orange, yellow, green, blue, indigo, violet) ;
type SMALL_INT is range 0..255 ;
-- array declaration
type INT_ARRAY is array (1..10) of INTEGER ;
-- array declaration without fixed bounds
type TEXT is array (NATURAL range <>) of CHARACTER ;
-- record declaration with pointer component
--- use a forward declaration of the pointer reference type to allow it to
-- be used  in the pointer declaration
type ELEM  ;
type LISTP is access ELEM ;
type ELEM  is record
   Val :  INTEGER ;
   Next :  LISTP ;
end record ;
-- Some variable declarations
Rainbow : COLOUR ;
Char_value : SMALL_INT ;
First_10 : INT_ARRAY  ;
```

Figure A.1
Ada declarations.

statement which allows exit from a loop at any point. Pascal only
supports exit from the beginning (while loop) and at the end (repeat
loop) of loops. Again, readers familiar with Pascal will have no
difficulty in understanding Ada's control constructs. Ada control
statements are shown in Figure A.2.

- A program may be structured into functions and procedures. Instead
of referring to parameter passing by reference as **var** parameters, Ada
parameters which are passed by reference are called **out** parameters.

```
-- An Ada if statement
if A = B and X = Y then
   Some_action ;
else
   Some_other_action ;
end if ;
-- An Ada for loop
for J  in (1..10) loop
   Do_something (J) ;
end loop ;
-- An Ada while loop
while J < 20 loop
   Do_something (J) ;
   J := J + Some_function (J) ;
end loop ;
-- An Ada case statement
case Sensor is
   when Red => Do_danger ;
   when Amber => Do_warning ;
   when Green => Do_safe ;
end case ;
```

Figure A.2
Ada control
statements.

Again a slightly different syntax is used for function and procedure declaration but this should be obvious to Pascal programmers. Examples of procedure and function declarations are given in the discussion of Ada packages (Section A.2).

A.1.1 Additional features in Ada

Ada has much in common with Pascal and many Ada programs are easily understood by those who have Pascal knowledge. However, Ada includes several new features which may be unfamiliar to Pascal programmers. Some of these are:

- *Packages* These are an information hiding construct which allows a group of declarations to be encapsulated and given a name. Packages are discussed in Chapters 15 and 16 and in Section A.2.

- *Tasks* These are sections of code which can operate in parallel rather than sequentially. Tasks are described in Chapters 11, 12 and 13 and in Section A.3.

- *Exceptions* Exceptions are a mechanism for handling error situations or unusual events in an Ada program. Exceptions are particularly useful in real-time systems which must continue in operation in the presence of system faults. Exceptions are discussed in Chapter 15.

- *Representation clauses* Representation clauses are a way of providing machine specific information while still staying within the Ada language. They are discussed briefly in Chapter 5.

- *Independent compilation* Components of an Ada program may be compiled separately.

- *Generics* Generics are a means of parameterizing entities such as packages and procedures so that they can operate on any type. To ensure strict type checking, the generic must be instantiated at compile-time; the programmer specifies the actual type of the generic component. Generics are discussed in Chapter 16 and in Section A.2.

A.2 Ada packages

Ada packages are a means of implementing information hiding. They allow a set of declarations (of constants, variables, procedures, functions, other packages, and so on) to be grouped together and named. They provide facilities which give the programmer control over which of these names can be used outside the package and which are purely internal. They allow the specification of an abstraction to be separated from its implementation.

An Ada package is made up of two parts:

- A package specification which sets out the declarations made in the package which are accessible from outside the package. The package specification is textually separate from the package body in the program and may be compiled independently of the package body.
- A package body which sets out the implementation of the abstraction defined in the package specification. The package body includes the code of procedures and functions declared in the package specification. It may include additional declarations which are inaccessible from outside the package.

Within a package, a type may be declared to be a *private* or a *limited private* type. This means that the type name may be used outside the package but its representation is private to the package within which it is declared. For both kinds of private type declaration, only the procedures and functions declared within the same package may operate on that type. However, if a type is simply a private type, it is assumed that equality and assignment operations have been defined and the standard Ada operators may be used. When a type is a limited private type, standard Ada operators for equality and assignment may not be used. If equality and assignment operations are required, they must be declared as functions within the package specification.

Ada packages are not executable components but collect together other executable components such as procedures and functions. To access an executable object such as a function within a package, the package name and the function name must both be specified, separated by a dot (see later). Packages are illustrated in Figure A.3 which is a specification of a generic package describing a sequence. Comments are used within this package for additional explanation.

During system design, it is often only necessary to construct a package specification. The specification defines the package interface and this can be used by other components without knowledge of the package body. The package body sets out the implementation of the package operations. The body of the package Sequence is not shown here.

The sequence package shown in Figure A.3 is a generic package. Generics are based on the fact that the operation of many algorithms is independent of the type manipulated by the algorithm. For example, given an ordering exists over the type being sorted, the sort operation is type independent. Exactly the same sorting algorithm may be used to sort numbers, strings or any other ordered type. Similarly most data structures which are collections of elements (arrays, lists, and so on) have the same operations which are independent of the element type. Using generics, it is possible to specify a general algorithm then instantiate that with a particular type before use.

```
generic
    -- ANY_TYPE is the formal type name. The package is
    -- instantiated with an actual type before the package is used.
    type ANY_TYPE is private ;
    -- A generic size parameter defines the length of the sequence.
    -- If not instantiated its default value is 100.
    Max : NATURAL := 100 ;
package Sequence is
    -- Declaring a type as private means that its representation is
    -- completely concealed within the package. It may not be
    -- accessed by any external agent.
    type T is private ;
    --Create brings a sequence into existence
    function Create (Seq : T) return T ;
    -- Add adds an item to the end of the sequence
    function Add (Val : ANY_TYPE ; Seq : T) return T ;
    -- Get returns an item referenced by a notional sequence pointer
    function Get (Seq : T) return ANY_TYPE ;
    -- Next moves a notional sequence pointer to refer to the
    -- next item in the sequence. AtEnd is true if the pointer
    -- position refers to the last sequence item, true otherwise
    procedure Next (Seq : in out T ; AtEnd : in out BOOLEAN ) ;
    --Reset sets the notional sequence pointer to refer to the
    --beginning of the sequence
    procedure Reset (Seq : in out T) ;
    --IsEmpty determines if the sequence has any members
    function IsEmpty (Seq : T) return BOOLEAN ;
    -- Length returns the number of sequence members
    function Length (Seq : T) return NATURAL ;
    -- Catenate puts two sequences together
    function Catenate (Seq1, Seq2 : T) return T ;
private
    -- Ada requires that the sequence representation is specified
    -- so that the compiler knows how much space to allocate
    type SEQ_ARRAY is array (1..Max ) of ANY_TYPE ;
    type T is record
        Pointer : NATURAL ;
        Values : SEQ_ARRAY ;
    end record ;
end Sequence ;
```

Figure A.3
An Ada package
specification.

```
-- Create a sequence of integers, maximum length 100 elements
-- There is no need to specify a value for Max. Default is used
package Integer_seq is new Sequence (ANY_TYPE => INTEGER) ;
-- Create a sequence of COORD with a maximum size of 500 elements
package Coord_seq is new Sequence (ANY_TYPE => COORD ;
    Max => 500) ;
-- Create a sequence of TAGS with a maximum length of 300
package Tag_sequence is new Sequence (ANY_TYPE => TAG,
    Max => 300) ;
```

Figure A.4
Generic instantiation.

```
with Integer_seq, Coord_seq, Tag_sequence ;
First_100_primes : Integer_seq.T ;
Zig_zag_line : Coord_seq.T ;
Labels, New_labels : Tag_sequence.T ;
```

Figure A.5
Abstract type
declaration.

Generic instantiation is a compile-time and not a run-time operation. A generic is a template and the programmer must create the actual package or routine from the generic. Figure A.4 shows the package Sequence being instantiated with types INTEGER, COORD and TAG.

Once a generic has been instantiated, it is, of course, possible to declare variables representing abstract sequences (Figure A.5).

Figure A.5 illustrates the declaration of abstract types and also, the use of Ada's with clause. Ada's information hiding strategy means that information is concealed unless it is explicitly made visible. A package is made visible by using a with clause. Thus, in Figure A.5, the with clause makes the packages Integer_seq, Coord_seq and Tag_sequence visible. Therefore, the names declared in these sequences may be used in those parts of the program where the package is visible. Figure A.6 shows how names within a package are accessed. A dot notation (similar to record access) is used with the package name preceding the name of the entity within the package.

It is possible to combine the with clause with a use clause which allows names declared within a package to be used without preceding them with the package name. This is not particularly good style and is not recommended.

A.3   Parallel programming

As Ada was designed as an implementation language for real-time systems, it includes built-in language features to support the development of systems made up of communicating parallel processes. In Ada terminology, a process is called a *task*. Comprehensive facilities are provided in the

```
First_100_primes := Integer_seq.Create ;
Zig_zag_line := Coord_seq.Add (Next_point, Zig_zag_line) ;
Labels := Tag_sequence.Catenate (Labels, New_labels) ;
```

Figure A.6
Accessing package
elements.

```
task Thermocouple is
    entry Get_temperature (T : in out TEMPERATURE) ;
    entry  Calibrate (T : TEMPERATURE) ;
    entry Disconnect ;
end Thermocouple ;

task Controller is
    entry Initialize ;
    entry Control ;
    entry  Shutdown ;
end Controller ;
```

Figure A.7
Task declarations.

language to support tasks and their communications. This section does not attempt to cover all of these but simply introduces the basic tasking model used in Ada.

A.3.1 Tasks

Tasks are program units which can execute in parallel. They may interact with other tasks in what is called a *rendezvous*. They may be controlled by a run-time clock. The management of tasks is the responsibility of the run-time system delivered with the Ada language compiler. User action is not required to start a task. They must be declared within a procedure body and become ready to run when that procedure is called. Thus, if the tasks are declared as part of the main program procedure, they become active when the program starts execution.

Tasks are declared in a manner which is similar to procedures using a task declaration as shown in Figure A.7.

Figure A.7 shows two tasks Thermocouple and Controller. These tasks interact through a rendezvous. During a rendezvous, one task calls on the services provided by another task and waits for that task to complete service provision before continuing execution.

The services provided by a task are called task entries and are listed in the task declaration as shown in Figure A.7. The Thermocouple task can return the temperature, can be calibrated and can disconnect the thermocouple from the system. The Controller task can be initialized, can control the system and can be shut down. Task entry specifications are similar to procedure declarations and, as shown in Figure A.7, may have associated formal parameters which behave in the same way as procedure formal parameters.

Task bodies define the implementation of the task. Figure A.8 shows the task bodies for the Thermocouple and the Controller tasks. The code associated with each entry is set out in an accept statement in the body of the task. If execution of a task reaches an accept statement and there are no

```
task body Thermocouple is
  begin
    accept Get_temperature (T: in out TEMPERATURE) do
       -- code here to interrogate the hardware
     end Get_temperature ;
    accept  Calibrate (T : TEMPERATURE)  do
       -- code here to calibrate the thermocouple
     end Calibrate ;
    accept Disconnect  do
       -- code to implement a hardware shutdown
     end Disconnect ;
end Thermocouple ;

task body Controller is
   Working_temp: TEMPERATURE ;
   -- Other declarations as required
begin
   accept Initialize do
      -- code to initialize system
      -- calibrate the thermocouple
      Thermocouple.Calibrate (T => 20) ;
    end Initialize ;
   accept Control do
      -- code for system control
      Thermocouple.Get-Temperature (Working_temp) ;
      -- take some action here depending on temperature
      -- measured by the thermocouple
    end Control ;
   accept Shutdown do
      -- code to shutdown the entire system
      -- Thermocouple.Disconnect ;
    end Shutdown ;
end Controller ;
```

Figure A.8
Task implementations.

outstanding calls for service waiting to be processed, the task is suspended until a call is made to that entry.

When a service which is provided by a task is required by another task, the entry is called in a way which is similar to a procedure call. This is shown in Figure A.8 where Controller calls the entries in Thermocouple. When, for example, the call Thermocouple.Get_temperature is made, the execution of Controller is suspended until that call has been processed by Thermocouple. Once Thermocouple reaches the end of the code associated with the Get_temperature entry, execution of Controller is resumed.

Each entry in a task has an associated queue of calls made on that entry and processes these calls in a strict first-in/first-out order. There is no way for the calling task to influence when the call for service will be processed nor to specify that processing must be completed within a given number of milliseconds. This is one reason why Ada is not suitable for the development of hard real-time systems whose operation is critically dependent on timely execution.

```
task body Data_collector is
begin
  select
    -- if data is available for processing, process it
    -- otherwise execute the else part of the select statement
    accept Put_data ( Sensor_in : SENSOR_VALUE) do
       Process_data (Sensor_in) ;
     end Put_data ;
  else
    -- execute Self_test rather than wait for data
    Self_test ;
  end select ;
end  Data_collector ;
```

Figure A.9
Conditional acceptance
of an entry.

A.3.2 The select statement

In the examples in the previous section, a simple model of task interaction was demonstrated where tasks called other tasks then waited for the results of that call before continuing execution. In practice, a more complex interaction model is often required with the interaction between tasks dependent on other program conditions. Ada's select statement is a construct which supports conditional task interaction.

When a task reaches an accept statement which has no outstanding entries, the task is suspended until an entry is available for processing. In many situations, however, the behaviour required is to process an entry if available but, if it is not available, to carry out some other processing. This is implemented by a select statement as illustrated in Figure A.9. A task accepts an entry which involves some data acquisition. If no data is available for processing, a self-checking routine is executed.

As well as conditional acceptance of an entry, a select statement may also be used to program conditional entries. In a conditional entry, the calling task will only enter a rendezvous with the called task if the called task is waiting and ready to provide the service. The code fragment in Figure A.10 illustrates this situation. If a sensor has data available, that data is used. Otherwise, the data value is computed from previous data values.

```
select
    -- if a sensor has data available, get the data value
    Window_sensor. Get_value (Val) ;
else
    -- No data available, default to average of previous values
    Val := Average (Previous_values) ;
end select ;
```

Figure A.10
A conditional entry.

```
loop
    select
        -- if a sensor has data available, get the data value
        Window_sensor. Get_value (Val) ;
    else
        -- No data available, wait 1/4 second and try again
        delay 0.25 ;
    end select ;
end loop ;
```

Figure A.11
A delayed entry.

In many cases, there are timing mismatches between tasks which are interacting. In the normal rendezvous mechanism, if one task has to wait for another, it remains active during the waiting period. The processor cannot be switched to other tasks. The select statement, used in conjunction with the delay statement, allows one task to suspend itself for a specified time while waiting for a rendezvous. While suspended, the processor may service other tasks. Figure A.11 illustrates this situation using a modification of the code fragment shown in Figure A.10. In Figure A.11, if no sensor value is available, the task suspends itself for a quarter of a second before trying again.

This brief introduction to concurrent programming in Ada has only covered part of the available tasking model. For more information, one of the books in the suggested further reading should be consulted.

A.4   A design example

Generally, a design is refined through a number of levels of abstraction from a high-level statement of the operation to a detailed design whose representation is close to the programming language. For example, Figure A.12 shows the design of a program intended to detect misspelled words in a document.

```
procedure Spellcheck is
begin
    Unique_words := Get_all_unique_words_in_document ;
    Unknown_words := Lookup_the (Dictionary => English_dictionary,
                        Wordlist => Unique_words) ;
    Display (Unknown_words) ;
    Create_new_dictionary (Based_on => Unknown_words) ;

end Spellcheck ;
```

Figure A.12
The high-level design of
a spelling checker.

```
procedure Spellcheck is
begin
   --* split document into words
   Word := The first word in the document ;
   loop
      Unique_words := Add Word to unique word list in
                         order, eliminating duplicates ;
      exit when the entire document has been processed ;
      Word := Get_next_word_from_document ;
   end loop ;
   --* look up words in dictionary
   Word := The first word in Unique_words ;
   loop
      if Word is not in the dictionary then
         Unknown_words := Add_the_word (Unknown_words,
                            Word) ;
      end if ;
      Word := Get_next_word_in (Unique_words) ;
      exit when all  words in Unique_words have been checked ;
   end loop ;
   --* display unknown words
   while all Unknown_words have not been checked  loop
      Display ( Word = The next unknown word ) ;
      if user marks word  as correctly spelled then
         Good_words := Add_the_Word (Good_words, Word) ;
      end if ;
   end loop ;
   --* create a new dictionary
   Dictionary := Merge (Dictionary, Good_words) ;
end  Spellcheck ;
```

Figure A.13
Detailed design of a
spelling checker.

Notice how named parameter association is used, where the formal parameter name is specified along with the actual parameter name, to help with readability. Thus, in the call of Lookup_the, the formal parameter is called Dictionary and the actual parameter is English_dictionary. The conjunction of the function name and the formal parameter name gives the readable name Lookup_the (Dictionary => English_dictionary).

This very high-level design description may be refined in more detail as shown in Figure A.13. When expressing a design, it is acceptable and sometimes convenient to use natural language text rather than program statements. Of course, this means that part of the design description cannot be checked by a compiler. Nevertheless, the use of natural language may contribute significantly to the readability of the design.

Sequences, as described earlier in this Appendix, are used in Figure A.14 which describes the final part of the spelling checker, namely the merging of the dictionary and the properly spelled words from the document which do not appear in the dictionary.

Notice that this example starts with a statement of the type of entity which is arranged in the sequence. Ada supports the notion of generic sequences instantiated for particular types directly. This means that a

```
package Word_sequence is new Sequence (Seqtype => WORD) ;

Dictionary, Good_words: Word_sequence.T ;

with Word_sequence ;
procedure Merge( In_seq1, In_seq2 : Word_sequence.T ;
    Out_seq : out WORDSEQ) is
    X, Y : WORD ;
begin
    -- If one of the sequences is empty, the output is
    - simply the other sequence
    if Word_sequence.Length (In_seq1) = 0 then
        Out_seq := In_seq1 ;
    elsif Word_sequence.Length (In_seq2) = 0 then
        Out_seq := In_seq2 ;
    else
        X := Word_sequence.Next (In_seq1) ;
        Y := Word_sequence.Next (In_seq2) ;
    end if ;
    -- execute till one sequence exhausted
    while Word_sequence.Length (In_seq1) > 0 and
        Word_sequence.Length (In_seq2) > 0 loop
        if X < Y then
            --select from 1st sequence
            Out_seq := Word_sequence.Add (Out_seq, X)  ;
            X := Word_sequence.Next (In_seq1) ;
        else    -- select from 2nd sequence
            Out_seq := Word_sequence.Add (Out_seq, X)  ;
            Y := Word_sequence.Next (In_seq2) ;
        end if ;
    end loop ;
    -- assign remainder of non exhausted sequence
    if Word_sequence.Length (In_seq1) = 0 then
        Out_seq := Word_sequence.Catenate (Out_seq, In_seq1) ;
    else
        Out_seq := Word_sequence.Catenate (Out_seq, In_seq2) ;
    end if ;
end Merge ;
```

Figure A.14
Dictionary merging.

generalized template for a sequence can be defined with a formal type for sequence members. The new statement in the package definition above defines a particular instance of the sequence for the type WORD.

FURTHER READING

There are a multiplicity of introductory Ada texts which, in general cover more or less the same ground. My recommendations are as follows but I have not looked at all available texts.

Software Engineering with Ada 2nd edn., G. Booch, 1987, Benjamin Cummings.

Programming in Ada 3rd edn., J.G.P. Barnes, 1989, Addison-Wesley.

Ada: Language and Methodology, D. Watt, B. Wichmann and W. Finlay, 1987, Prentice-Hall.

The following texts are not Ada primers but are intended for readers who have some language experience.

Software Development with Ada, I. Sommerville and R. Morrison, 1987, Addison-Wesley.

Software Components with Ada, G. Booch, 1987, Benjamin Cummings.

Collected References

Abbott R. (1983). Program design by informal English descriptions. *Comm. ACM*, **26** (11), 882–94

Abdel–Ghaly A.A., Chan P.Y. and Littlewood B. (1986). Evaluation of competing software reliability predictions. *IEEE Trans. Software Engineering*, **12** (9), 950–67

Adams E.N. (1984). Optimizing preventative service of software products. *IBM J. R. & D.*, **28** (1), 2–14

Adobe Systems Inc. (1987). *POSTSCRIPT Language: Tutorial and Cookbook*. Reading MA: Addison-Wesley

Agha G. (1990). Concurrent object-oriented programming. *Comm. ACM*, **33** (9), 125–40

Aho A.V., Kernighan B.W. and Weinberger P.J. (1988). *The Awk Programming Language*. Englewood Cliffs NJ: Prentice-Hall

Ahuja S.R., Ensor J.R. and Horn D.N. (1988). The Rapport multi-media conferencing system. In *Proc. COIS88, Conf. Office Information Systems*, Palo Alto CA

Albrecht A.J. (1979). Measuring application development productivity. In *Proc. SHARE/GUIDE IBM Application Development Symposium*, 83–92

Albrecht A.J. and Gaffney J.E. (1983). Software function, lines of code and development effort prediction: a software science validation. *IEEE Trans. Software Engineering*, **9** (6), 639–47

Alford M.W. (1977). A requirements engineering methodology for real time processing requirements. *IEEE Trans. Software Engineering*, **3** (1), 60–9

Alford M.W. (1985). SREM at the age of eight: the distributed computing design system. *IEEE Computer*, **18** (4), 36–46

Anderson T., Barrett P.A., Halliwell D.N. and Moulding M.R. (1985). Software fault tolerance: an evaluation. *IEEE Trans. Software Engineering*, **11** (12), 1502–10

Andrews T. and Harris C. (1987). Combining language and database advances in an object-oriented development environment. In *Proc. OOPSLA87*, Orlando FL, 430–40

Archer J.E. and Devlin M.T. (1986). Rational's experience using Ada for very large systems. In *Proc. 1st Int. Conf. on Ada Applications for the NASA Space Station*, 2.5.1–2.4.12

Aron J.D. (1974). *The Program Development Process*. Reading MA: Addison-Wesley

Aron J.D. (1983). *The Program Development Process: Part 2 – The Programming Team*. Reading MA: Addison-Wesley

Arthur L.J. (1988). *Software Evolution*. New York: John Wiley & Sons

Avizienis A. (1985). The N–version approach to fault-tolerant software. *IEEE Trans. Software Engineering*, **11** (12), 1491–501

Baker F.T. (1972). Chief programmer team management of production programming. *IBM Systems J.*, **11** (1), 56–73

Baker T.P. and Scallon G.M. (1986). An architecture for real–time software systems. *IEEE Software*, **3** (3), 50–8

Balzer R.M., Goldman N.M. and Wile D.S. (1982). Operational specification as the basis for rapid prototyping. *ACM Software Engineering Notes*, **7** (5), 3–16

Barker R. (1989). *CASE* Method: Entity Relationship Modelling*. Wokingham: Addison-Wesley

Basili V.R. and Selby R.W. (1987). Comparing the effectiveness of software testing strategies. *IEEE Trans. Software Engineering*, **13** (12), 1278–96

Bass B.M. and Dunteman G. (1963). Behaviour in groups as a function of self, interaction and task orientation. *J. Abnorm. Soc. Psychol.*, **66** (4), 19–28

Bell P. and Evans C. (1989). *Mastering Documentation*. New York: John Wiley & Sons

Bell T.E., Bixler D.C. and Dyer M.E. (1977). An extendable approach to computer aided software requirements engineering. *IEEE Trans. Software Engineering*, **3** (1), 49–60

Berlage T. (1991). *OSF/Motif Concepts and Programming*. Wokingham: Addison-Wesley

Bersoff E.H. (1984). Elements of software configuration management. *IEEE Trans. Software Engineering*, **10** (1), 79–87

Biggerstaff T.J. and Perlis A.J. (1989). *Software Reusability* Vols 1 & 2. Reading MA: Addison-Wesley

Birrell N.D. and Ould M.A. (1985). *A Practical Handbook for Software Development*. Cambridge: Cambridge University Press

Boehm B.W. (1974). Some steps towards formal and automated aids to software requirements analysis and design. In *IFIP 74*, Amsterdam: North-Holland

Boehm B.W. (1975). The high cost of software. In *Practical Strategies for Developing Large Software Systems* (Horowitz E., ed.). Reading MA: Addison-Wesley

Boehm B.W. (1979). Software engineering: R & D trends and defense needs. In *Research Directions in Software Technology* (Wegner P., ed.). Cambridge MA: MIT Press

Boehm B.W. (1981). *Software Engineering Economics*. Englewood Cliffs NJ: Prentice-Hall

Boehm B.W. (1983). The economics of software maintenance. *Proc. Software Maintenance Workshop*, Washington DC, 9–37

Boehm B.W. (1987). Improving software productivity. *IEEE Computer*, **20** (9), 43–58

Boehm B.W. (1988). A spiral model of software development and enhancement. *IEEE Computer*, **21** (5), 61–72

Boehm B.W., Brown J.R., Kaspar H., Lipow M., Macleod G. and Merrit M. (1978). *Characteristics of Software Quality*, TRW Series of Software Technology, Amsterdam: North-Holland

Boehm B.W., Gray T.E. and Seewaldt T. (1984). Prototyping versus specifying: a multi–project experiment. *IEEE Trans. Software Engineering*, **10** (3), 290–303

Boehm B.W., McClean R.L. and Urfig D.B. (1975). Some experience with automated aids to the design of large-scale reliable software. *IEEE Trans. Software Engineering*, **1** (1), 125–33

Bohm C. and Jacopini G. (1966). Flow diagrams, Turing machines and languages with only two formation rules. *Comm. ACM*, **9** (5), 366–71

Booch G. (1986). Object–oriented development. *IEEE Trans. Software Engineering*, **12** (2), 211–21

Booch G. (1987a). *Software Engineering with Ada* 2nd edn. Menlo Park CA: Benjamin Cummings

Booch G. (1987b). *Software Components with Ada: Structures Tools and Subsystems*. Menlo Park CA: Benjamin Cummings

Booch G. (1991). *Object–oriented Design with Applications*. Menlo Park CA: Benjamin Cummings

Borgida A., Greenspan S. and Mylopoulos J. (1985). Knowledge representation as a basis for requirements specification. *IEEE Computer*, **18** (4), 82–101

Bott M.F. (1989). *The ECLIPSE Integrated Project Support Environment*. Stevenage: Peter Perigrinus

Boudier G., Gallo F., Minot R. and Thomas I. (1988). An overview of PCTE and PCTE+. *SIGSOFT Software Engineering Notes*, **13** (5), 248–57

Bourne S.R. (1978). The UNIX Shell. *Bell Systems Tech. J.*, **57** (6), 1971–90

Braun C.L. and Goodenough J.B. (1985). *Ada Reusability Guide-lines*. Softech Report 3285–2–208/2, USAF

Brilliant S.S., Knight J.C. and Leveson N.G. (1990). Analysis of faults in an N–version software experiment. *IEEE Trans. Software Engineering*, **16** (2), 238–47

Brinch–Hansen P. (1973). *Operating System Principles*. Englewood Cliffs NJ: Prentice-Hall

Britcher R.N. and Craig J.J. (1986). Using modern design practices to upgrade aging software systems. *IEEE Software*, **3** (3), 16–26

Brooks F.P. (1975). *The Mythical Man Month*. Reading MA: Addison-Wesley

Brown P.J. (ed.) (1977). *Software Portability*. Cambridge: Cambridge University Press

Browne D.P. (1986). The formal specification of adaptive user interfaces using command language grammar. *Proc. CHI'86*, Boston MA, 256–60

Buckley F.J. and Poston R. (1984). Software quality assurance. *IEEE Trans. Software Engineering*, **10** (1), 36–41

Burns A. and Wellings A. (1989). *Real–time Systems and their Programming Languages*. Wokingham: Addison-Wesley

Buxton J. (1980). *Requirements for Ada Programming Support Environments: Stoneman*. US Department of Defense, Washington DC

Cameron J.R. (1986). An overview of JSD. *IEEE Trans. Software Engineering*, **12** (2), 222–40

Campbell I. (1986). PCTE proposal for a public common tool interface. In *Software Engineering Environments* (Sommerville I., ed.) pp. 57–72. Stevenage: Peter Perigrinus

Card S., Moran T.P. and Newell A. (1983). *The Psychology of Human–Computer Interaction*. Hillsdale NJ: Lawrence Erlbaum Associates

Cardelli L. and Wegner P. (1985). On understanding types, data abstraction and polymorphism. *ACM Computing Surveys*, **17** (4), 471–522

Carré B. (1989). Program analysis and verification. In *High–Integrity Software* (Sennett C., ed.). London: Pitman

Chen P. (1976). The entity relationship model – towards a unified view of data. *ACM Trans. Database Systems*, **1** (1), 9–36

Cherry L. and MacDonald N.H. (1983). The UNIX Writers Workbench Software. *BYTE*, **8** (10), 241–52

Chikofsky E.J. and Rubenstein B.L. (1988). CASE: reliability engineering for information systems. *IEEE Software*, **5** (2), 11–17

Coad P. and Yourdon E. (1990). *Object-oriented Analysis*. Englewood Cliffs NJ: Prentice-Hall

Cobb R.H. and Mills H.D. (1990). Engineering software under statistical quality control. *IEEE Software*, **7** (6), 44–54

Codd E.F. (1970). A relational model of data for large shared data banks. *Comm. ACM*, **13**, 377–387

Codd E.F. (1979). Extending the database relational model to capture more meaning. *ACM Trans. Database Systems*, **4** (4), 397–434

Cohen B., Harwood W.T. and Jackson M.I. (1986). *The Specification of Complex Systems*. Wokingham: Addison-Wesley

Conklin J. (1987). Hypertext: an introduction and survey. *IEEE Software*, **20** (9), 17–42

Constantine L.L. & Yourdon E. (1979). *Structured Design*. Englewood Cliffs NJ: Prentice-Hall

Cougar J.D. and Zawacki R.A. (1978). What motivates DP professionals? *Datamation*, **24** (9), 27–30

Courington W., Feiber J. and Honda M. (1988). NSE highlights. *Sun Technology*, Winter 1988, 49–53

Culpepper L.M. (1975). A system for reliable engineering software. *IEEE Trans. Software Engineering*, **1** (2), 174–8

Curtis B., Krasner H. and Iscoe N. (1988). A field study of the software design process for large systems. *Comm. ACM*, **31** (11), 1268–87

Cusamano M. (1989). The software factory: a historical interpretation. *IEEE Software*, **6** (2), 23–30

Dasarthy B. (1985). Timing constraints for real-time systems: constructs for expressing them, methods of validating them. *IEEE Trans. Software Engineering*, **11** (1), 80–6

Date, C.J. (1990). *An Introduction to Database Systems*, 5th edn. Reading MA: Addison-Wesley

Davis A.M. (1988). A comparison of techniques for the specification of external system behaviour. *Comm. ACM*, **31** (9), 1098–115

Davis C.G. & Vick C.R. (1977). The software development system. *IEEE Trans. Software Engineering*, **3** (1), 69–84

Davis W.S. (1983). *Systems Analysis and Design*. Reading MA: Addison-Wesley

Delisle N. and Garlan D. (1990). A formal specification of an oscilloscope. *IEEE Software*, **7** (5), 29–36

DeMarco T. (1978). *Structured Analysis and System Specification*. New York: Yourdon Press

DeMillo R.A., Lipton R.J. and Sayward F.G. (1978). Hints on test data selection: help for the practising programmer. *IEEE Computer*, **9** (4), 34–41

DeRemer F. and Kron H.H. (1976). Programming in the large versus programming in the small. *IEEE Trans. Software Engineering*, **2** (2), 80–6

Dijkstra E.W. (1968a). Cooperating sequential processes. In *Programming Languages* (Genuys F., ed.). London: Academic Press

Dijkstra E.W. (1968b). Goto statement considered harmful. *Comm. ACM*, **11** (3), 147–8

Dijkstra E.W. (1976). *A Discipline of Programming*. Englewood Cliffs NJ: Prentice-Hall

Diller A. (1990). *Z: An Introduction to Formal Methods*. New York: John Wiley & Sons

Dolotta T.A., Haight R.C. and Mashey J.R. (1978). The programmers workbench. *Bell Systems Tech. J.*, **57** (6), 2177–200

Donzeau-Gouge V., Huet G. and Kahn G. (1984). Programming environments based on structured editors: the MENTOR experience. In *Interactive Programming Environments* (Barstow D.R., Shrobe H.E. and Sandewall E., eds.). New York: McGraw-Hill

Dowson M. (1987). Integrated project support with ISTAR. *IEEE Software*, **4** (6), 6–15

Earl A.N., Whittington R.P., Hitchcock P. and Hall A. (1986). Specifying a semantic model for use in an integrated project support environment. In *Software Engineering Environments* (Sommerville I., ed). London: Peter Perigrinus

Ehrlich W.K., Lee S.K. and Molisani R.H. (1990). Applying reliability measurement: a case study. *IEEE Software*, **7** (2), 56–64

Ellis C.A. and Nutt G.J. (1980). Office information systems and computer science. *ACM Computing Surveys*, **12** (1), 27–60

Endres A. (1975). An analysis of errors and their causes in system programs. *IEEE Trans. Software Engineering*, **1** (2), 140–9

Fagan M.E. (1976). Design and code inspections to reduce errors in program development. *IBM Systems J.*, **15** (3), 182–211

Fagan M.E. (1986). Advances in software inspections. *IEEE Trans. Software Engineering*, **12** (7), 744–51

Feldman S.I. (1979). MAKE – a program for maintaining computer programs. *Software – Practice and Experience*, **9**, 255–65

Ferrari D. (1978). *Computer Systems Performance Evaluation*. Englewood Cliffs NJ: Prentice-Hall

Festinger L.A. (1957). *A Theory of Cognitive Dissonance*. Evanston, Illinois: Row Peterson

Finkelstein A. and Fuks S. (1989). Multi-party specification. In *Proc. 5th Int. Workshop on Software Specification and Design*, Pittsburgh PA, 185–95

Floyd R.W. (1967). Assigning meanings to programs. In *Proc. Symposium Applied Maths*, 19–32

Frewin G.D. (1990). Procuring and maintaining reliable software. In *Software Reliability Handbook* (Rook P., ed.). London: Elsevier

Frewin G.D. and Hatton B.J. (1986). Quality management – procedures and practises. *IEE/BCS Software Engineering J.*, **1** (1), 29–38

Fujiwara E. and Pradhan D.K. (1990). Error-control coding in computers. *IEEE Computer*, **23** (7), 63–72

Futatsugi K., Goguen J.A., Jouannaud J.P. and Meseguer J. (1985). Principles of OBJ2. In *Proc. 12th ACM Sym. on Principles of Programming Languages*, New Orleans, 52–66

Gallimore R.M., Coleman D. and Stavridou V. (1989). UMIST OBJ: a language for executable program specifications. *Comp. J.*, **32** (5), 413–21

Gane C. and Sarson T. (1979). *Structured Systems Analysis*. Englewood Cliffs NJ: Prentice-Hall

Garg P.K. and Scacchi W. (1990). A hypertext system to maintain software life-cycle documents. *IEEE Software*, **7** (3), 90–8

Gautier R.J. and Wallis P.J.L. (eds.) (1990). *Software Reuse with Ada*, Stevenage: Peter Perigrinus

Gladden G.R. (1982). Stop the life cycle – I want to get off. *ACM Software Engineering Notes*, **7** (2), 35–9

Goldberg A. (1984) *Smalltalk-80: The Interactive Programming Environment*. Reading MA: Addison-Wesley

Goldberg A. and Robson D. (1983). *Smalltalk-80. The Language and its Implementation*. Reading MA: Addison-Wesley

Gomaa H. (1983). The impact of rapid prototyping on specifying user requirements. *ACM Software Engineering Notes*, **8** (2), 17–28

Grief I. (ed.) (1988). *Computer Supported Cooperative Work: A Book of Readings*. San Mateo CA: Morgan Kaufmann

Grudin J. (1989). The case against user interface consistency. *Comm. ACM*, **32** (10), 1164–73

Guimaraes T. (1983). Managing application program maintenance expenditures. *Comm. ACM*, **26** (10), 739–46

Gunning R. (1962). *Techniques of Clear Writing*. New York: McGraw-Hill

Guttag J. (1977). Abstract data types and the development of data structures. *Comm. ACM*, **20** (6), 396–405

Guttag J.V., Horning J.J. and Wing J.M. (1985). The Larch family of specification languages. *IEEE Software*, **2** (5), 24–36

Habermann A.N. and Notkin D. (1986). Gandalf: software development environments. *IEEE Trans. Software Engineering*, **12** (12), 1117–27

Hall A. (1990). Seven myths of formal methods. *IEEE Software*, **7** (5), 11–20

Halstead M.H. (1977). *Elements of Software Science*. Amsterdam: North-Holland

Hamer P.G. and Frewin G.D. (1981). M.H. Halstead's software science – a critical examination. In *Proc. 6th Int. Conf. on Software Engineering*, 197–206

Hammer M. and McLeod D. (1981). Database descriptions with SDM: a semantic database model. *ACM Trans. Database Systems*, **6** (3), 351–86

Harbert A., Lively W. and Sheppard S. (1990). A graphical specification system for user interface design. *IEEE Software*, **7** (4), 12–20

Hayes I. (ed.) (1987). *Specification Case Studies*. London: Prentice-Hall

Hayes I.J. (1986). Specification directed module testing. *IEEE Trans. Software Engineering*, **12** (1), 124–33

Hekmatpour S. and Ince D. (1988). *Software Prototyping, Formal Methods and VDM*. Wokingham: Addison-Wesley

Henderson P. and Minkowitz C. (1986). The me too method of software design. *ICL Tech. J.*, **5** (1), 64–95

Heninger K.L. (1980). Specifying software requirements for complex systems. New techniques and their applications. *IEEE Trans. Software Engineering*, **6** (1), 2–13

Henry S. and Kafura D. (1981). Software structure metrics based on information flow. *IEEE Trans. Software Engineering*, **7** (5), 510–18

Hill A. (1983). Towards an Ada-based specification and design language. *ADA UK News*, **4** (4), 16–34

Hiltz S.R. and Turoff M. (1979). *The Network Nation*. Reading MA: Addison-Wesley

Hoadley E. (1990). Investigating the effects of color. *Comm. ACM*, **33** (2), 120–25

Hoare C.A.R. (1969). An axiomatic basis for computer programming. *Comm. ACM*, **12** (10), 576–83

Hoare C.A.R. (1974). Monitors: an operating system structuring concept. *Comm. ACM*, **21** (8), 666–777

Hoare C.A.R. (1985). *Communicating Sequential Processes*. London: Prentice-Hall

Hood Working Group (1989). *HOOD Reference Manual*. European Space Agency Document WME/89–173/JB

Hudson S.E. and King R. (1988). The Cactis project: database support for software environments. *IEEE Trans. Software Engineering*, **14** (6), 709–19

Hull R. and King R. (1987). Semantic database modeling: survey, applications and research issues. *ACM Computing Surveys*, **19** (3), 201–60

Humphrey W.S. (1989). *Managing the Software Process*. Reading MA: Addison-Wesley

Humphrey W.S., Snyder T. and Willis R. (1991). Software process improvement at Hughes aircraft. *IEEE Software*, **8** (4), 11–23

Hutchison J.W. and Hindley P.G. (1988). A preliminary study of large-scale software re-use. *IEE/BCS Software Engineering J.*, **3** (5), 208–12

IEE (1989). *Software in Safety-Related Systems*, Joint BCS/IEE Report, London, Institute of Electrical Engineers

Ince D.C. and Hekmatpour S. (1987). Software prototyping – progress and prospects. *Information and Software Technology*, **29** (1), 8–14

Ivie E.L. (1977). The programmers workbench – a machine for software development. *Comm. ACM*, **20** (10), 746–53

Jackson M.A. (1975). *Principles of Program Design*. London: Academic Press

Jackson M.A. (1983). *System Development*. London: Prentice-Hall

Jacob R. (1986). A specification language for direct-manipulation user interfaces. *ACM Trans. Graphics*, **5** (4), 318–44

Jahanian F. and Mok A.K. (1986). Safety analysis of timing properties in real-time systems. *IEEE Trans. Software Engineering*, **12** (9), 890–904

Janis I.L. (1972). *Victims of Groupthink. A Psychological Study of Foreign Policy Decisions and Fiascos*. Boston: Houghton Mifflin

Jelinski Z. and Moranda P.B. (1972). Software reliability research. In *Statistical Computer Performance Evaluation* (Frieberger W., ed.). New York: Academic Press

Johnson P. (1987). Using Z to specify CICS. In *Proc. SEAS Anniversary Meeting*, Edinburgh, 303–33

Jones C.B. (1980). *Software Development – A Rigorous Approach*. London: Prentice-Hall

Jones C.B. (1986). *Systematic Software Development Using VDM*. London: Prentice-Hall

Jones T.C. (1978). Measuring programming quality and productivity. *IBM Systems J.*, **17** (1), 39–63

Kafura D. and Reddy G.R. (1987) The use of software complexity metrics in software maintenance. *IEEE Trans. Software Engineering*, **13** (3), 335–43

Kemerer C. (1987). An empirical validation of software cost estimation models. *Comm. ACM*, **30** (5), 416–29

Kendall P.A. (1989). *Systems Analysis and Design*, Dubuque IA: Wm. C. Brown

Kitchenham B. (1990a). Software metrics. In *Software Reliability Handbook* (Rook P., ed.). London: Elsevier

Kitchenham B. (1990b). Software development cost models. In *Software Reliability Handbook* (Rook P., ed.). London: Elsevier

Kitchenham B.A., Pickard L.M. and Linkman S.J. (1990). An evaluation of some design metrics. *IEE/BCS Software Engineering J.*, **5** (1), 50–8

Knight J.C. and Leveson N.G. (1986). An experimental evaluation of the assumption of independence in multi-version programming. *IEEE Trans. Software Engineering*, **12** (1), 96–109

Lampson B.W. and Schmidt E.E. (1983) Organising software in a distributed environment. *ACM Sigplan Notices*, **18** (6), 1–13

Leavitt H.J. (1951). Some effects of certain communication patterns on group performance. *J. Abnorm. Soc. Psychol.*, **46** (1), 38–50

Leblang D.B. and Chase R.P. (1987). Parallel software configuration management in a network environment. *IEEE Software*, **4** (6), 28–35

Lee S. and Sluizer S. (1985). On using executable specifications for high-level prototyping. *Proc. 3rd Int. Workshop on Software Specification and Design*, 130–4

Lehman M.M. and Belady L. (1985). *Program Evolution. Processes of Software Change*. London: Academic Press

Leveson N.G. (1985). Software safety. In *Resilient Computing Systems*. London: Collins

Leveson N.G. (1986). Software safety: why, what and how? *ACM Computing Surveys*, **18**, (2), 125–63

Leveson N.G. and Harvey P.R. (1983). Analysing software safety. *IEEE Trans. Software Engineering*, **9** (5), 569–79

Lientz B.P. and Swanson E.B. (1980). *Software Maintenance Management*. Reading MA: Addison-Wesley

Lindsay P.A. (1988). A survey of mechanical support for formal reasoning. *IEE/BCS Software Engineering J.*, **3** (1), 3–27

Linger R.C., Mills H.D. and Witt B.I. (1979). *Structured Programming – Theory and Practice*. Reading MA: Addison-Wesley

Littlewood B. (1990). Software reliability growth models. In *Software Reliability Handbook* (Rook P., ed.). London: Elsevier

Littlewood B. and Verrall J.L. (1973). A Bayesian reliability growth model for computer software. *Applied Statistics*, **22**, 332–46

Londeix B. (1987). *Cost Estimation for Software Development*. Wokingham: Addison-Wesley

Looney M. (1985). *CORE – A Debrief Report*. Manchester: NCC Publications

Luckham D. and Von Henke F.W. (1985). An overview of Anna, a specification language for Ada. *IEEE Software*, **2** (2), 9–23

Macro A. and Buxton J. (1986). *The Craft of Software Engineering*. Wokingham: Addison-Wesley

Mander K.C. (1981). An Ada view of specification and design. *Technical Report 44*, Department of Computer Science, University of York, York, UK

Marshall J.E. and Heslin R. (1976). Boys and girls together. Sexual composition and the effect of density on group size and cohesiveness. *J. Personality Soc. Psychol.*, **36**

Martin C.F. (1988). Second-generation CASE tools: a challenge to vendors. *IEEE Software*, **5** (2), 46–9

Matsumoto Y. (1984). Some experience in promoting reusable software: presentation in higher abstract levels. *IEEE Trans. Software Engineering*, **10** (5), 502–12

Maurer P.M. (1990). Generating test data with enhanced context-free grammars. *IEEE Software*, **7** (4), 50–5

McCabe T.J. (1976). A complexity measure. *IEEE Trans. Software Engineering*, **2** (4), 308–20

McCarthy J. (1962). Towards a mathematical science of computation. In *IFIP 62*, pp. 21–8. Amsterdam: North-Holland

McCracken D.D. and Jackson M.A. (1982). Life cycle concept considered harmful. *ACM Software Engineering Notes*, **7** (2), 28–32

McCue G.M. (1978). IBM's Santa Teresa Laboratory – architectural design for program development. *IBM Systems J.*, **17** (1), 4–25

McGettrick A.D. (1982). *Program Verification Using Ada*. Cambridge: Cambridge University Press

McKee J.R. (1984). Maintenance as a function of design. In *Proc. 1984 AFIPS National Computer Conf.*, 187–93

McNicol D. (1986). CAMP: Common Ada Missile Package. In *Proc. National Conf. on Reusability and Maintainability*, Tysons Corner VA

Meyer B. (1988). *Object–oriented Software Construction*. Englewood Cliffs NJ: Prentice-Hall

Miller G.A. (1957). The magical number 7 plus or minus two: some limits on our capacity for processing information. *Psychol. Rev.*, **63**, 81–97

Mills H.D. (1988). Stepwise refinement and verification in box-structured systems. *IEEE Computer*, **21** (6), 23–37

Mills H.D., Dyer M. and Linger R. (1987). Cleanroom software engineering. *IEEE Software*, **4** (5), 19–25

Mills H.D., O'Neill D., Linger R.C., Dyer M. and Quinnan R.E. (1980). The management of software engineering. *IBM Sys. J.*, **24** (2), 414–77

Milner A.J.R.G. (1980) *A Calculus of Communicating Systems*. Heidelberg: Springer-Verlag

Mohanty S.N., (1981). Software cost estimation: present and future. *Software – Practice and Experience*, **11** (2), 103–21

Mooney J.D. (1990). Strategies for supporting application system portability. *IEEE Computer*, **23** (11), 59–70

Moret B. (1982). Decision trees and diagrams. *ACM Computer Surveys*, **14** (4), 593–623

Morgan C. and Sufrin B. (1984). Specification of the UNIX filing system. *IEEE Trans. Software Engineering*, **10** (2), 128–42

Moser L.E. and Melliar-Smith P.M. (1990). Formal verification of safety-critical systems. *Software – Practice and Experience*, **20** (8), 799–821

Mullery G. (1979). CORE – a method for controlled requirements specification. In *Proc. 4th Int. Conf. on Software Engineering*, Munich

Munck R., Oberndorf P., Ploedereder E. and Thall R. (1988). An overview of DOD-STD-1838A (proposed), the common APSE interface set, revision A. *SIGSOFT Software Engineering Notes*, **13** (5), 235–47

Myers B. (1988). *Creating User Interfaces by Demonstration*. New York: Academic Press

Myers B. (1989). User-interface tools: introduction and survey. *IEEE Software*, **6** (1), 15–23

Myers G.J. (1975). *Reliable Software through Composite Design*. New York: Petrocelli/Charter

Myers G.J. (1979). *The Art of Software Testing*. New York: John Wiley & Sons

Myers W. (1989). Allow plenty of time for large-scale software. *IEEE Software*, **6** (4), 92–9

Nissen J. and Wallis P.J.L. (eds.) (1985). *Portability and Style in Ada*, Cambridge: Cambridge University Press

Norman D.A. and Draper S.W. (eds.) (1986). *User-centered System Design*. Hillsdale NJ: Lawrence Erlbaum Associates

Oberndorf P.A. (1988). The common Ada programming support environment (APSE) interface set (CAIS). *IEEE Trans. Software Engineering*, **14** (6), 742–48

OSF (Open Software Foundation) (1990). *Motif Style Guide*. Englewood Cliffs NJ: Prentice-Hall

Osterweil L. (1987). Software processes are software too. In *Proc. 9th Int. Conf. on Software Engineering*, 2–12

Osterweil L.J. and Fosdick L.D. (1976). DAVE – a validation, error detection and documentation system for FORTRAN programs. *Software – Practice and Experience*, **6**, 473–86

Ould M. and Roberts C. (1988). Defining formal models of the software development process. In *Software Engineering Environments* (Brereton P., ed.). Chichester: Ellis Horwood

Oviedo E.I. (1980). Control flow, data flow and program complexity. In *Proc. 4th COMPSAC*, Los Alaminitos CA: IEEE Press

Parnas D. (1972). On the criteria to be used in decomposing systems into modules. *Comm. ACM*, **15** (2), 1053–58

Parnas D.L., van Schouwen J. and Shu P.K. (1990). Evaluation of safety-critical software. *Comm. ACM*, **33** (6), 636–51

Perrow C. (1984). *Normal Accidents: Living with High-Risk Technologies*. New York: Basic Books

Perry D.K. and Cannon W.M. (1966). A vocational interest scale for programmers. In *Proc. 4th Annual Computer Personnel Conf.*, ACM, New York

Peterson J. (1977). Petri nets. *ACM Computer Surveys*, **9** (3), 223–52

Peterson J.L. (1981). *Petri Net Theory and the Modeling of Systems*. New York: McGraw-Hill

Petschenik N.H. (1985). Practical priorities in system testing. *IEEE Computer*, **18** (5), 18–23

Potts C. (1988). The other interface: specifying and visualising computer systems. In *Working with Computers: Theory versus Outcome* (van der Veer G.C., Green T.R.G., Hoc J.-M. and Murray D.M., eds.). London: Academic Press

Preece J. and Keller L. (eds.) (1990). *Human–Computer Interaction*. Hemel Hempstead: Prentice-Hall

Pressman R.S. (1987). *Software Engineering – A Practitioners Approach* 2nd edn. New York: McGraw-Hill

Putnam L.H. (1978). A general empirical solution to the macro software sizing and estimating problem. *IEEE Trans. Software Engineering*, **4** (3), 345–61

Ramamoorthy C.V. and Ho S.F. (1975). Testing large software with automated software evaluation systems. *IEEE Trans. Software Engineering*, **1** (1), 46–58

Randell B. (1975). System structure for software fault tolerance. *IEEE Trans. Software Engineering*, **1** (2), 220–32

Reid P. and Welland R.C. (1986). Software development in view. In *Software Engineering Environments* (Sommerville I., ed.). Stevenage: Peter Perigrinus

Reps T. and Teitelbaum T. (1984). The synthesizer generator. In *Proc. ACM SIGSOFT/SIGPLAN Symp. on Practical Software Development Environments*, 42–8

Rittel H. and Webber M. (1973). Dilemmas in a general theory of planning. *Policy Sciences*, **4**, 155–69

Robertson G., McCracken D. and Newell A. (1981). The ZOG approach to man–machine communication. *Int. J. Man–Machine Studies*, **14**, 461–88

Rochkind M.J. (1975). The source code control system. *IEEE Trans. Software Engineering*, **1** (4), 255–65

Ross D.T. (1977). Structured analysis (SA). A language for communicating ideas. *IEEE Trans. Software Engineering*, **3** (1), 16–34

Rosson M.B., Maass S. and Kellog W.A. (1988). The designer as user: building requirements for design tools from design practice. *Comm. ACM*, **31** (11), 1288–99

Royce W.W. (1970). Managing the development of large software systems. In *Proc. WESTCON*, San Francisco CA

Rumbaugh J., Blaha M., Premerlani W., Eddy S. and Lorensen W. (1991). *Object-oriented Modeling and Design*. Englewood Cliffs NJ: Prentice-Hall

Sackman H., Erikson W.J. and Grant E.E. (1968). Exploratory experimentation studies comparing on-line and off-line programming performance. *Comm. ACM*, **11** (1), 3–11

Salter K.G. (1976). A methodology for decomposing system requirements into data processing requirements. *Proc. 2nd Int. Conf. on Software Engineering*, San Francisco

Satterthwaite E. (1972). Debugging tools for high level languages. *Software – Practice and Experience*, **2**, 197–217

Scheifler R.W. and Gettys J. (1986). The X window system. *ACM Trans. Graphics*, **5** (2), 79–109

Schoman K. and Ross D.T. (1977). Structured analysis for requirements definition. *IEEE Trans. Software Engineering*, **3** (1), 6–15

Selby R.W., Basili V.R. and Baker F.T. (1987). Cleanroom software development: an empirical evaluation. *IEEE Trans. Software Engineering*, **13** (9), 1027–37

Shaw M.E. (1964). Communication networks. In *Advances in Experimental Social Psychology*. New York: Academic Press

Shaw M.E. (1971). *Group Dynamics. The Psychology of Small Group Behaviour*. New York: McGraw-Hill

Shepherd M. (1990). Design metrics; an empirical analysis. *IEE/BCS Software Engineering J.*, **5** (1), 3–10

Shepherd S.B., Curtis B., Milliman P., Borst M. and Love T. (1979). First year results from a research program in human factors in software engineering. *AFIPS 79*, 1021–7

Shneiderman B. (1980). *Software Psychology*. Cambridge MA: Winthrop Publishers Inc

Shneiderman B. (1983). Designing computer system messages. *Comm. ACM*, **25** (9), 610–11

Shneiderman B. (1986). *Designing the User Interface*. Reading MA: Addison-Wesley

Silberschaltz A., Peterson J. and Galvin P. (1991). *Operating System Concepts* 3rd edn. Reading MA: Addison-Wesley

Simpson H. (1986). The MASCOT method. *IEE/BCS Software Engineering J.*, **1** (3), 103–20

Smith D.R., Kotik G.B. and Westfold S.J. (1985). Research on knowledge-based software environments at Kestrel Institute. *IEEE Trans. Software Engineering*, **11** (11), 1278–95

Soloway E., Ehrlich K., Bonar J. and Greenspan J. (1982). What do novices know about programming. In *Directions in Human-Computer Interaction* (Badre A. and Shneiderman B., eds.). Norwood NJ: Ablex Publishing Co.

Sommerville I. and Morrison R. (1987). *Software Development with Ada*. Wokingham: Addison-Wesley

Sommerville I. and Thomson R. (1989). An approach to system evolution. *Comp. J.*, **32** (5), 386–98

Sommerville I., Beer S.J. and Welland R.C. (1987). Describing software design methodologies. *Comp. J.*, **30** (2), 128–33

Sommerville I., Welland R.C., Potter S.J. and Smart J.D. (1989) The ECLIPSE user interface. *Software – Practice and Experience*, **19** (4), 371–92

Spivey J.M. (1989). *The Z Notation: A Reference Manual*. London: Prentice-Hall

Spivey J.M. (1990). Specifying a real-time kernel. *IEEE Software*, **7** (5), 21–8

Stefik M.J., Bobrow D.G. and Kahn K.M. (1986). Integrating access-oriented programming into a multiparadigm environment. *IEEE Software*, **3** (1), 10–18

Stroustrup B. (1986). *The C++ Programming Language*. Reading MA: Addison-Wesley

Symons C.R. (1988). Function-point analysis: difficulties and improvements. *IEEE Trans. Software Engineering*, **14** (1), 2–11

Tanenbaum A.S., Klint P. and Bohm W. (1978). Guidelines for software portability. *Software – Practice and Experience*, **8**, 681–98

Taylor R.N., Selby R.W., Young M., Belz F.C., Clarke L.A., Wileden J.C., Osterweil L. and Wolf A.L. (1988). Foundations for the Arcadia environment architecture. *SIGSOFT Software Engineering Notes*, **13** (5), 1–13

Tedd M. (1989). PCTE+: the evolution of PCTE. In *Software Engineering Environments: Research and Practice* (Bennett, K., ed.). Chichester: Ellis Horwood

Teichrow D. and Hershey E.A. (1977). PSL/PSA: a computer aided technique for structured documentation and analysis of information processing systems. *IEEE Trans. Software Engineering*, **3** (1), 41–8

Teitelbaum T. and Reps T. (1981). The Cornell program synthesiser: a syntax-directed programming environment. *Comm. ACM*, **24** (9), 563–73

Teitleman W. (1984). A tour through Cedar. *IEEE Software*, **1** (2), 44–53

Teitleman W. and Masinter L. (1984). The Interlisp programming environment. In *Interactive Programming Environments* (Barstow D.R., Shrobe H.E. and Sandewall E., eds.). New York: McGraw-Hill

Thomas I. (1989). PCTE interfaces: supporting tools in software engineering environments. *IEEE Software*, **6** (6), 15–23

Tichy W. (1982). Design, implementation and evaluation of a revision control system. In *Proc. 6th Int. Conf. on Software Engineering*, Tokyo

Took R. (1986). The presenter – a formal design for an autonomous display manager. In *Software Engineering Environments* (Sommerville I., ed.). Stevenage: Peter Perigrinus

Tracz W. (ed.) (1988). *Software Reuse: Emerging Technology*. Washington DC: IEEE Computer Society Press

Tully C.J. (ed.) (1988). *Proc. 4th Int. Software Process Workshop*, Devon, UK

Turner D.A. (1985). MIRANDA: a non-strict functional language with polymorphic types. *Lecture Notes in Computer Science* 201. Berlin: Springer-Verlag

Wallis P.J.L. (1982). *Portable Programming*. London: Macmillan

Walston C.E. and Felix C.P. (1977). A method of programming measurement and estimation. *IBM Systems J.*, **16** (1), 54–73

Warboys B. (1989). The IPSE 2.5 project: a process model based architecture. In *Software Engineering Environments: Research and Practice* (Bennett K., ed.). Chichester: Ellis Horwood

Ward P. and Mellor S. (1985). *Structured Development for Real–time Systems*. Englewood Cliffs NJ: Prentice-Hall

Warnier J.D. (1977). *Logical Construction of Programs*. New York: Van Nostrand Reinhold

Wasserman A.I. (1981). User software engineering and the design of interactive information systems. In *Proc. 5th Int. Conf. on Software Engineering*, IEEE Press, 387–93.

Wasserman A.I., Pircher P.A., Shewmake D.T. and Kersten M.L. (1986). Developing interactive information systems with the user software engineering methodology. *IEEE Trans. Software Engineering*, **12** (2), 326–45

Weinberg G. (1971). *The Psychology of Computer Programming*. New York: Van Nostrand Reinhold

Welland R.C., Beer S. and Sommerville I. (1987). Software design automation in an IPSE. *Proc. 1st European Conf. on Software Engineering*, Strasbourg

Welland R.C., Beer S. and Sommerville I. (1990). Method rule checking in a generic design editing system. *IEE/BCS Software Engineering J.*, **5** (2), 105–15

Wikstrom A. (1988). *Standard ML*. Englewood Cliffs NJ: Prentice-Hall

Wirth N. (1971). Program development by stepwise refinement. *Comm. ACM*, **14** (4), 221–7

Wirth N. (1976). *Systematic Programming, An Introduction*. Englewood Cliffs NJ: Prentice-Hall

Won K. (1990). Object-oriented data bases: definition and research directions. *IEEE Trans. Data and Knowledge Engineering*, **2** (3), 327–41

Young D.A. (1990). *X Window Systems programming and Applications with Motif*. Englewood Cliffs NJ: Prentice-Hall

Young M., Taylor R.N. and Troup D.B. (1988). Software environment architectures and user interface facilities. *IEEE Trans. Software Engineering*, **14** (6), 697–708

Yourdon E. (1979) *Managing the Structured Techniques*. Englewood Cliffs NJ: Prentice-Hall

Zave P. (1989). A compositional approach to multiparadigm programming. *IEEE Software*, **6** (5), 15–27

Zave P. and Schell W. (1986). Salient features of an executable specification language and its environment. *IEEE Trans. Software Engineering*, **12** (2), 312–25

Author Index

Subject Index